PRAISE FOR THE FIRST EDITIC

"Even longtime users of FreeBSD may be surprised at the power and features it can bring to bear as a server platform, and *Absolute BSD* is an excellent guide to harnessing that power."
—UNIXREVIEW.COM

" . . . provides beautifully written tutorials and reference material to help you make the most of the strengths of this OS."
—LINUXUSER & DEVELOPER MAGAZINE

" . . . a great resource for people new to BSD and those who have been using it for years. Michael Lucas has a writing style which is very easy to read and absorb."
—FRESHMEAT

"A very fine piece of work, it isn't about how to implement BSD solutions, but it is about managing systems in situ."
—;LOGIN:

" . . . packed with a lot of information."
—DAEMON NEWS

PRAISE FOR *ABSOLUTE OPENBSD* BY MICHAEL LUCAS

"*Absolute OpenBSD* by Michael Lucas is a broad and mostly gentle introduction into the world of the OpenBSD operating system. It is sufficiently complete and deep to give someone new to OpenBSD a solid footing for doing real work and the mental tools for further exploration. . . . The potentially boring topic of systems administration is made very readable and even fun by the light tone that Lucas uses."
—CHRIS PALMER, PRESIDENT, SAN FRANCISCO OPENBSD USERS GROUP

" . . . a well-written book that hits its market squarely on target. Those new to OpenBSD will appreciate the comprehensive approach that takes them from concept to functional execution. Existing and advanced users will benefit from the discussion of OpenBSD-specific topics such as the security features and pf administration."
—SLASHDOT

"I recommend *Absolute OpenBSD* to all programmers and administrators working with the OpenBSD operating system (OS), or considering it."
—UNIXREVIEW.COM

PRAISE FOR *PGP & GPG* BY MICHAEL LUCAS

"*PGP & GPG* is another excellent book by Michael Lucas. I thoroughly enjoyed his other books due to their content and style. *PGP & GPG* continues in this fine tradition. If you are trying to learn how to use PGP or GPG, or at least want to ensure you are using them properly, read *PGP & GPG*."
—TAOSECURITY

"The world's first user-friendly book on email privacy. Unless you're a cryptographer, or never use email, you should read this book."
—LEN SASSAMAN, CODECON FOUNDER

" Excellent tutorial, quick read, and enough humor to make it enjoyable."
—INFOWORLD

"An excellent book that shows the end-user in an easy to read and often entertaining style just about everything they need to know to effectively and properly use PGP and OpenPGP."
—SLASHDOT

PRAISE FOR *CISCO ROUTERS FOR THE DESPERATE* BY MICHAEL LUCAS

" . . . this book isn't a reference—it's a survival guide, a 'break glass in case of emergency' safety harness. . . . What I found remarkable was how it was obviously written for people like me—those of us who have little interest in router management but whose jobs depend on the consistent, trusted functioning of such infrastructure.
—ASP.NETPRO

"If only *Cisco Routers for the Desperate* had been on my bookshelf a few years ago! It would have definitely saved me many hours of searching for configuration help on my Cisco routers. . . . I would strongly recommend this book for both IT Professionals looking to get started with Cisco routers, as well as anyone who has to deal with a Cisco router from time to time but doesn't have the time or technological know-how to tackle a more in-depth book on the subject."
—BLOGCRITICS MAGAZINE

ABSOLUTE
FREEBSD
2ND EDITION

THE *COMPLETE* GUIDE TO *FREEBSD*

by Michael W. Lucas

NO STARCH
PRESS

San Francisco

Printed on recycled paper in the United States of America

11 10 09 08 07   1 2 3 4 5 6 7 8 9

ISBN-10: 1-59327-151-4
ISBN-13: 978-1-59327-151-0

Publisher: William Pollock
Production Editors: Christina Samuell and Megan Dunchak
Cover and Interior Design: Octopod Studios
Developmental Editor: William Pollock
Technical Reviewer: John Baldwin
Copyeditor: Dmitry Kirsanov
Compositor: Riley Hoffman
Proofreader: Alina Kirsanova
Indexer: Nancy Guenther

For information on book distributors or translations, please contact No Starch Press, Inc. directly:

No Starch Press, Inc.
555 De Haro Street, Suite 250, San Francisco, CA 94107
phone: 415.863.9900; fax: 415.863.9950; info@nostarch.com; www.nostarch.com

Library of Congress Cataloging-in-Publication Data

```
Lucas, Michael, 1967-
  Absolute FreeBSD : the complete guide to FreeBSD / Michael W. Lucas. -- 2nd ed.
      p. cm.
  Includes index.
  ISBN-13: 978-1-59327-145-9
  ISBN-10: 1-59327-145-X
 1. FreeBSD. 2. UNIX (Computer file) 3. Internet service providers--Computer programs. 4. Web
servers--Computer programs. 5. Client/server computing. I. Title.
QA76.76.063L83 2007
004'.36--dc22
                                        2007036190
```

For Liz. With luck, this one is the right size to plug that dang gopher hole.

BRIEF CONTENTS

CONTENTS IN DETAIL

3
START ME UP! THE BOOT PROCESS

61

4
READ THIS BEFORE YOU BREAK SOMETHING ELSE!
(BACKUP AND RECOVERY)

89

5
KERNEL GAMES
117

6
THE NETWORK
145

7
SECURING YOUR SYSTEM
177

8
DISKS AND FILESYSTEMS   209

9
ADVANCED SECURITY FEATURES   261

11
MAKING YOUR SYSTEM USEFUL   315

12
ADVANCED SOFTWARE MANAGEMENT   343

14
THE INTERNET ROAD MAP: DNS

411

17
WEB AND FTP SERVICES
499

18
DISK TRICKS WITH GEOM   529

19
SYSTEM PERFORMANCE AND MONITORING   569

20
THE FRINGE OF FREEBSD   603

21
SYSTEM (AND SYSADMIN) PANICS AND CRASHES   637

AFTERWORD   655

APPENDIX
SOME INTERESTING SYSCTL MIBS   661

INDEX   675

FOREWORD

It gives me great pleasure to write the foreword to
Michael Lucas's *Absolute FreeBSD*. For five years, Michael's
Absolute series has provided the definitive guide to BSD
software, not just as a reference, but also as a narrative for real human beings.
This is an important distinction, because while there is no lack of excellent
reference material on FreeBSD, this book provides a nuts-and-bolts tutorial
that readers will find an invaluable companion.

Michael is an active long-term contributor in the FreeBSD community.
Absolute FreeBSD draws on his experience with the many ways in which people
use FreeBSD in the real world—what they want to do, what works, and what
doesn't. Apart from covering the use of FreeBSD, Michael will tell you about
the thousands of software developers—from hobbyists to professional developers and university professors—who write FreeBSD and about the evolution
of this community and its software. What I would like to do is invite you to
become a part of that community.

FreeBSD is a powerful network operating system with state-of-the-art
features that make it not only one of the most widely used pieces of software
in the world, but also an easy and practical tool on which to build and
provision services. From the Yahoo! and Verio websites to NetApp storage

products, from Cisco anti-spam appliances and Juniper routers to the root nameservers—it's hard to throw a rock on the Internet without hitting FreeBSD. However, FreeBSD is not the product of any one company, but of a large open source community: the FreeBSD Project, made up of developers, users, and countless supporters and advocates. While you can, as many people do, use FreeBSD simply as a piece of software without ever interacting with that community, you can significantly enrich your FreeBSD experience by becoming a part of that community.

Whether you are a first-time user or a kernel hacker, the resources available via the *http://www.freebsd.org* website, countless mailing lists, regional user groups, and conferences can be invaluable. Have a question? Just email *questions@FreeBSD.org*, and one or more of the hundreds of volunteers will undoubtedly answer it. Want to learn more about the exciting new features coming in future FreeBSD versions? Read the Project's quarterly status reports, development mailing lists, or attend one of the many regional BSD conferences taking place around the world; at the time of writing, the most recent addition is the first BSDConTR in Istanbul, Turkey.

These resources are a product of the FreeBSD Project and its community, a large number of collaborating individuals and companies, as well as the FreeBSD Foundation, a nonprofit organization coordinating funding, legal resources, and support for development work and community activities. Michael's easy-to-use book provides a gateway for newbies to benefit from this community's expertise and to become active users of FreeBSD themselves.

FreeBSD is open source software, available for you to use and distribute at no charge. By helping to support, advocate, or even develop FreeBSD, you can give back to the FreeBSD Project and help this community grow.

Whether you are a new user of FreeBSD or an experienced one, I am confident you will find *Absolute FreeBSD* a book you want to keep close at hand.

Robert N.M. Watson
FreeBSD Core Team Member
President, FreeBSD Foundation
Cambridge, UK
September 2007

ACKNOWLEDGMENTS

I would like to thank all the members of the FreeBSD community for their hard work, dedication, and friendship. FreeBSD has saved my hide on numerous occasions, and I'm delighted to give something back. In that community, however, there are a few people who I want to specifically thank by name.

Doug Barton, Ceri Davies, Alex Dupre, Max Laier, Alexander Leidinger, Remko Lodder, Benno Rice, Tom Rhodes, Gleb Smirnoff, and Robert Watson all provided valuable feedback on this book. Some of them read individual chapters that they have special expertise in, while others read the whole manuscript, whether they knew about the topics or not. Wilko Bulte not only did a review of this book, he volunteered to do so *after* reviewing the entire first edition of this book back in 2001. He certainly deserves some sort of "iron man" award! John Baldwin did an excellent final technical review, catching an astonishing variety of errors ranging from subtle to blatant. Any errors in this book were introduced by myself despite these people's best efforts.

I'd like to thank David Boyd, David O'Brien, and Wilko Bulte for donating a variety of hardware that made it possible for me to write this book. I'd especially like to thank Matt Olander of iXSystems, who sent me a complete amd64 server when I really, *really* needed one. Speaking of hardware, as I was finishing this book, I was wondering where I would find a good kernel panic to write about in the last chapter. FreeBSD obliged me. Thanks to Scott Long for fixing that panic, so I could actually write Chapter 18.

As always, the folks at No Starch Press have worked their butts off to bring this to you. You all deserve a long vacation after putting up with me— tell Bill I said it's okay. Similarly, the fine staff at the School of Chinese Martial Arts deserve a vacation from me. Sadly, now that this book is done I'll be spending some quality time on the mats, so they don't get any time off. Sorry, folks.

And, as always, I'm grateful that my wife did not succumb to the temptation to bash me over the head with a shovel and bury me and my laptop behind the garage while I was finishing this book. She's been more than patient waiting for me to finish up so I could take out the trash. Last March's trash, that is . . .

Michael Lucas
St. Clair Shores, Michigan
September 2007

INTRODUCTION

Welcome to *Absolute FreeBSD*! This book is a one-stop shop for system administrators who want to build, configure, and manage FreeBSD servers. It will also be useful for those folks who want to run FreeBSD on their desktops, servers, diskless system farms, and so on. By the time you finish this book, you should be able to use FreeBSD to provide network services. You should also understand how to manage, patch, and maintain your FreeBSD systems and have a basic understanding of networking, system security, and software management. We'll discuss FreeBSD version 7, which is the version recommended for production use at the time this book is being released; however, most of this book applies to earlier and later versions as well.

What Is FreeBSD?

FreeBSD is a freely available Unix-like operating system, used widely by Internet service providers, in appliances and embedded systems, and anywhere that reliability on commodity hardware is paramount. One day last week, FreeBSD miraculously appeared on the Internet, fully formed, extruded directly from the mutant brain of its heroic creator's lofty intellect. Just kidding; the truth is far more impressive. FreeBSD is a result of almost three decades of continuous development, research, and refinement. The story of FreeBSD begins in 1979, with BSD.

BSD: FreeBSD's Granddaddy

Many years ago, AT&T needed a lot of specialized, custom-written computer software to run its business. It was not allowed to compete in the computer industry, however, so it could not sell its software. Instead, AT&T licensed various pieces of software and the source code for that software to universities at low, low prices. The universities could save money by using this software instead of commercial equivalents with pricey licenses, and university students with access to this nifty technology could read the source code to see how everything worked. In return, AT&T got exposure, some pocket change, and a generation of computer scientists who had cut their teeth on AT&T technology. Everyone got something out of the deal. The best-known software distributed under this licensing plan was Unix.

Compared with modern operating systems, the original Unix had a lot of problems. Thousands of students had access to its source code, however, and hundreds of teachers needed interesting projects for their students. If a program behaved oddly, or if the operating system itself had a problem, the people who lived with the system on a day-to-day basis had the tools and the motivation to fix it. Their efforts quickly improved Unix and created many features we now take for granted. Students added the ability to control running processes, also known as *job control*. The Unix S51K filesystem made system administrators cry like small children, so they replaced it with the Fast File System, whose features have spread into every modern filesystem. Many small, useful programs were written over the years, gradually replacing entire swaths of Unix.

The Computer Science Research Group (CSRG) at the University of California, Berkeley, participated in these improvements and also acted as a central clearinghouse for Unix code improvements. The CSRG collected changes from other universities, evaluated them, packaged them, and distributed the compilation for free to anyone with a valid AT&T UNIX license. The CSRG also contracted with the Defense Advanced Research Projects Agency (DARPA) to implement various features in Unix, such as TCP/IP. The resulting collection of software came to be known as the Berkeley Software Distribution, or BSD.

BSD users took the software and improved it further, then fed their enhancements back into BSD. Today, we consider this to be a fairly standard way for an open source project to run, but in 1979 it was revolutionary. BSD was also quite successful; if you check the copyright statement on an old BSD system, you'll see this:

```
Copyright 1979, 1980, 1983, 1986, 1988, 1989, 1991, 1992, 1993, 1994
         The Regents of the University of California. All rights reserved.
```

Yep, 15 years of work—a lifetime in software development. How many other pieces of software are not only still in use, but still in active development, 15 years after work began? In fact, so many enhancements and improvements went into BSD that the CSRG found that over the years, it had replaced almost all of the original Unix with code created by the CSRG and its contributors. You had to look hard to find any original AT&T code.

Eventually, the CSRG's funding ebbed, and it became clear that the BSD project would end. After some political wrangling within the University of California, in 1992 the BSD code was released to the general public under what became known as the BSD license.

The BSD License

BSD code is available for anyone to use under what is probably the most liberal license in the history of software development. The license can be summarized as follows:

- Don't claim you wrote this.
- Don't blame us if it breaks.
- Don't use our name to promote your product.

This means that you can do almost anything you want with BSD code. (The original BSD license did require that users be notified if a software product included BSD-licensed code, but that requirement was later dropped.) There's not even a requirement that you share your changes with the original authors! People were free to take BSD and include it in proprietary products, open source products, or free products—they could even print it out on punch cards and cover the lawn with it. You want to run off 10,000 BSD CDs and distribute them to your friends? Enjoy. Instead of *copyright*, the BSD license is sometimes referred to as *copycenter*, as in *Take this down to the copy center and run off a few for yourself.* Not surprisingly, companies such as Sun Microsystems jumped right on it: It was free, it worked, and plenty of new graduates had experience with the technology. One company, BSDi, was formed specifically to take advantage of BSD Unix.

The AT&T/CSRG/BSDi Iron Cage Match

At AT&T, UNIX work continued apace even as the CSRG went on its merry way. AT&T took parts of the BSD Unix distribution and integrated them with its UNIX, then relicensed the result back to the universities that provided those improvements. This worked well for AT&T until the company was broken up and the resulting companies were permitted to compete in the computer software business. AT&T had one particularly valuable property: a high-end operating system that had been extensively debugged by thousands of people. This operating system had many useful features, such as a variety of small but powerful commands, a modern filesystem, job control, and TCP/IP. AT&T started a subsidiary, Unix Systems Laboratories (USL), which happily started selling Unix to enterprises and charging very high fees for it, all the while maintaining the university relationship that had given it such an advanced operating system in the first place.

Berkeley's public release of the BSD code in 1992 was met with great displeasure from USL. Almost immediately, USL sued the university and the software companies that had taken advantage of the software, particularly BSDi. The University of California claimed that the CSRG had compiled BSD from thousands of third-party contributors unrelated to AT&T, and so it was the CSRG's intellectual property to dispose of as it saw fit.

This lawsuit motivated many people to grab a copy of BSD to see what all the fuss was about, while others started building products on top of it. One of these products was 386BSD, which would eventually be used as the core of FreeBSD 1.0.

In 1994, after two years of legal wrangling, the University of California lawyers proved that the majority of AT&T UNIX was actually taken in its entirety from BSD, rather than the other way around. To add insult to injury, AT&T had actually violated the BSD license by stripping the CSRG copyright from files it had assimilated. (Only a very special company can violate the world's most liberal software license!) A half-dozen files were the only sources of contention, and to resolve these outstanding issues, USL donated some of them to BSD while retaining some as proprietary information.

Once the dust settled, a new version of BSD Unix was released to the world as BSD 4.4-Lite. A subsequent update, BSD 4.4-Lite2, is the grandfather of the current FreeBSD, as well as ancestor to every other BSD variant in use today.

The Birth of FreeBSD

One early result of BSD was 386BSD, a version of BSD designed to run on the cheap 386 processor.[1] The 386BSD project successfully ported BSD to Intel's 386 processor, but it stalled. After a period of neglect, a group of 386BSD users decided to branch out on their own and create FreeBSD so that they

---

[1] At the time, several thousand dollars for a computer was dirt cheap. You young punks have no idea how good you have it.

could keep the operating system up to date. (Several other groups started their own branches off of 386BSD around the same time, of which only NetBSD remains.)

386BSD and FreeBSD 1 were derived from 1992's BSD release, the subject of AT&T's wrath. As a result of the lawsuit, all users of the original BSD were requested to base any further work on BSD 4.4-Lite2. BSD 4.4-Lite2 was not a complete operating system—in particular, those few files AT&T had retained as proprietary were vital to the system's function. (After all, if those files hadn't been vital, AT&T wouldn't have bothered!) The FreeBSD development team worked frantically to replace those missing files, and FreeBSD 2.0 was released shortly afterward. Development has continued ever since.

Today, FreeBSD is used across the Internet by some of the most vital and visible Internet-oriented companies. Yahoo! runs almost entirely on FreeBSD. IBM, Nokia, Juniper, NetApp, and many other hardware companies use FreeBSD in embedded systems where you'd never even know it unless someone told you. The fact is, if a company needs to pump serious Internet bandwidth, it's probably running FreeBSD or one of its BSD relatives. Like smog, spiders, and corn syrup, FreeBSD is all around you; you simply don't see it because FreeBSD just works. The key to FreeBSD's reliability is the development team and user community—which are really the same thing.

FreeBSD Development

There's an old saying that managing programmers is like herding cats. Despite the fact that the FreeBSD development team is scattered across the world and speaks dozens of languages, for the most part, the members work well together as parts of the FreeBSD team. They're more like a pride of lions than a collection of house cats. Unlike some other projects, all FreeBSD development happens in public. Three groups of people are responsible for FreeBSD's progress: committers, contributors, and users.

Committers

FreeBSD has about 500 developers, or committers. *Committers* have read-and-write access to the FreeBSD master source code repository and can develop, debug, or enhance any piece of the system. (The term *committer* comes from their ability to commit changes to the source code.) Because these commits can break the operating system in both subtle and obvious ways, committers carry a heavy responsibility. Committers are responsible for keeping FreeBSD working or, at worst, not breaking it as they add new features and evaluate patches from contributors. Most of these developers are volunteers; only a handful are actually paid to do this painstaking work, and most of those people are paid only as it relates to other work. For example, Intel employs a committer to ensure that FreeBSD properly supports its network cards. FreeBSD has a high profile in the Internet's heavy-lifting crowd, so Intel needs its cards to work on FreeBSD.

To plug yourself into the beehive of FreeBSD development, consider subscribing to the mailing list *FreeBSD-hackers@FreeBSD.org*, which contains most of the technical discussion. Some of the technical talk is broken out into more specific mailing lists—for example, fine details of the networking implementation are discussed in *FreeBSD-net@FreeBSD.org.*

Every few years, the committer team elects a small number of its members to serve as a core team, or Core. Core's work is simultaneously vital, underrated, and misunderstood. *Core* is theoretically responsible for the overall management of FreeBSD, but in practice, it manages little other than resolving personality disputes and procedural conflicts among committers. Core also approves new committers and delegates responsibility for large parts of FreeBSD to individuals or groups. For example, it delegates authority over the ports and packages system to the ports management team. Core does not set architectural direction for FreeBSD, nor does it dictate processes or procedures; that's up to the committers, who must agree en masse. Core does suggest, cajole, mediate, and inspire, however.

Core also experiences the worst part of management. Some of the key functions of management in a company are oversight, motivation, and handling problems between people. Oversight is provided by the millions of users who will complain loudly when anything breaks or behaves unexpectedly, and FreeBSD committers are self-motivated. The ugly part of management is settling a squabble between two people, and that's the part that Core has its hands full of. The status one gets from saying, "I'm in Core" is an insufficient reward for having to manage an argument between two talented developers who have gotten on each other's nerves.

Contributors

In addition to the committer team, FreeBSD has thousands of contributors. *Contributors* don't have to worry about breaking the main operating system source code repository; they just submit patches for consideration by committers. Committers evaluate contributor submissions and decide what to accept and what to reject. A contributor who submits many high-quality patches is often asked to become a committer himself.

For example, I spent several years contributing to FreeBSD whenever the urge struck me. Any time I feel that I've wasted my life, I can look at the FreeBSD website and see where my work was accepted by the committers and distributed to thousands of people. After I submitted the first edition of this book to the publisher, I spent my spare time submitting patches to the FreeBSD FAQ. Eventually, some members of the FreeBSD Documentation Project approached me and asked me to become a committer. As a reward, I got an email address and the opportunity to humiliate myself before thousands of people, once again demonstrating that no good deed goes unpunished.

If I had never contributed anything, I'd remain a user. Nothing's wrong with that, either.

Users

Users are the people who run FreeBSD systems. It's impossible to realistically estimate the number of FreeBSD users, although organizations such as the BSDstats Project (*http://www.bsdstats.org*) are making an effort. After all, you can download the whole of FreeBSD for free and never register, upgrade, or email a mailing list. Companies such as Netcraft estimate that between 5 and 15 percent of all computers attached to the Internet are BSD-based. If you remove all the Windows boxes on corporate desktops, the percentage rises considerably.

Since FreeBSD is by far the most popular open source BSD, that's not an inconsiderable number of machines. And since one FreeBSD server can handle hundreds of thousands of Internet domains, a disproportionate number of sites use FreeBSD as their supporting operating system. This means that there are hundreds of thousands, if not millions, of FreeBSD system administrators out in the world today.

Other BSDs

FreeBSD might be the most popular BSD, but it's not the only one. BSD 4.4-Lite2 spawned several different projects, each with its own focus and purpose. Those projects in turn had their own offspring, several of which thrive today.

NetBSD

NetBSD is similar to FreeBSD in many ways, and NetBSD and FreeBSD share developers and code. NetBSD's main goal is to provide a secure and reliable operating system that can be ported to any hardware platform with minimal effort. As such, NetBSD runs on VAXes, PocketPC devices, and high-end SPARC and Alpha servers. I run NetBSD on my HP Jornada handheld computer.[2]

OpenBSD

OpenBSD branched off from NetBSD in 1996 with the goal of becoming the most secure BSD. OpenBSD was the first to support hardware-accelerated cryptography, and its developers are rightfully proud of the fact that their default installation was largely immune to remote exploits for several years. The OpenBSD team has contributed several valuable pieces of software to the world, the most notable being the OpenSSH suite used by almost every operating system and hardware vendor today.

---

[2] If you're ever in a position where you need to prove that you are Alpha Geek amongst the pack, running Unix on your palmtop will almost certainly do it.

Mac OS X

Mac OS X? That's right. Apple incorporates large chunks of FreeBSD into its Mac OS X on an ongoing basis. If you're looking for a stable operating system with a friendly face and a powerful core, Mac OS X is unquestionably for you. While FreeBSD makes an excellent desktop for a computer professional, I wouldn't put it in front of Grandma. I would put Mac OS X in front of Grandma without a second thought, however, and I'd even feel that I was doing the right thing. But Mac OS X includes many things that aren't at all necessary for an Internet server, and it only runs on Apple hardware, so I don't recommend it as an inexpensive general-purpose server.

What's more, code goes both ways. FreeBSD has incorporated code originally developed for Mac OS X. And while you cannot view the user interface source code for Mac OS X, you can get the source code to its BSD core and Mach kernel. Apple has released both under the code name *Darwin*.

FreeBSD's Children

Several projects have taken FreeBSD and built other projects or products on top of it. The award-winning FreeNAS transforms an *x*86 system into a network fileserver with just a simple menu. FreeSBIE is a bootable CD that lets you run FreeBSD without installing it. The m0n0wall project is also a bootable CD, but it transforms your system into a firewall with a nice web management interface. PC-BSD puts a friendly face on FreeBSD, trying to make FreeBSD usable by Grandma. Other projects like this appear from time to time; while not all are successful, I'm sure by the time this book comes out, we'll have one or two more solid members of this group.

Other Unixes

Several other operating systems derive from or emulate primordial Unix in one way or another. This list is by no means exhaustive, but I'll touch on the high points.

Solaris/OpenSolaris

The best-known Unix is Sun Microsystems' Solaris and its new offspring, OpenSolaris. Solaris runs on high-end hardware that supports dozens of processors and gobs of disk. (Yes, *gobs* is a technical term, meaning *more than you could possibly ever need, and I know very well that you need more disk than I think you need.*) Solaris, especially early versions of Solaris, had strong BSD roots. Many enterprise-level applications run on Solaris. Solaris runs mainly on the SPARC hardware platform manufactured by Sun, which allows Sun to support interesting features such as hot-swappable memory and mainboards. OpenSolaris increasingly targets commodity hardware, however.

AIX

Another Unix contender is IBM's entry, AIX. AIX's main claim to fame is its journaling filesystem, which records all disk transactions as they happen and allows for fast recovery from a crash. It was also IBM's standard Unix for many years, and anything backed by Big Blue shows up all over the place. AIX is largely based on BSD.

Linux

Linux is a close cousin of Unix, written from the ground up. Linux is similar to FreeBSD in many ways, though FreeBSD has a much longer heritage and is more friendly to commercial use than Linux. Linux includes a requirement that any user who distributes Linux must make his or her changes available to the end user, while BSD has no such restriction. Of course, a Linux fan would say, "FreeBSD is more vulnerable to exploitation than Linux." Linux developers believe in share-and-share-alike, while BSD developers offer a no-strings-attached gift to everyone. It all depends on what's important to you.

Many new Unix users have a perception of conflict between the BSD and Linux camps. If you dig a little deeper, however, you'll find that most of the developers of these operating systems communicate and cooperate in a friendly and open manner. It's just a hard fringe of users and developers that generate friction, much like different soccer teams' hooligans or fans of different *Star Trek* series.

IRIX, HP/UX, and So On

Other Unixes include Silicon Graphics' IRIX, a solid Unix for graphics applications, and Hewlett-Packard's HP/UX, popular in large enterprises. A quick web search uncovers many smaller contenders, such as Tru64 Unix and the suicidal SCO Group's UnixWare. You'll also find old castoffs such as Apple's A/UX and Microsoft's Xenix. (Yes, Microsoft was a licensed Unix vendor, back in that age when dinosaurs watched the skies nervously and my dad hunted mammoth for tribal rituals.) Many high-end applications are designed to run best on one particular flavor of Unix. All modern Unixes have learned lessons from these older operating systems, and today's Unixes and Unix-like operating systems are remarkably similar.

FreeBSD's Strengths

After all this, what makes FreeBSD unique?

Portability

The FreeBSD Project's goal is to provide a freely redistributable, stable, and secure operating system that runs on the computer hardware that people are most likely to have access to. Today this means Intel x86-compatible systems such as the 486, the various Pentiums, AMD, and so on, as well as AMD's amd64 architecture (copied by Intel as EM64T). Older x86 systems no longer work out of the box with newer versions of FreeBSD, but most of those systems are either long dysfunctional or aren't about to change operating systems any time soon.

The ARM platform used in embedded devices is a new addition to FreeBSD and is well supported on specific embedded boards. FreeBSD also supports Sun's SPARC systems and Intel's Itanium (IA64), as well as the PowerPC processor recently used by Apple. While these other platforms are not afterthoughts, they don't receive the same level of attention that x86 and amd64 do.

Power

Since FreeBSD runs adequately on 386 hardware, it runs extremely well on modern computers. It's rather nice to have an operating system that doesn't demand a Pentium III and half a gig of RAM just to run the user interface. As a result, you can actually dedicate your hardware to accomplishing real work rather than tasks you don't care about. If you choose to run a pretty graphical interface with all sorts of spinning geegaws and fancy whistles, FreeBSD will support you; it just won't penalize you if you don't want that. FreeBSD will also support you on the latest n-CPU hardware.

Simplified Software Management

FreeBSD also simplifies software management through the Ports Collection. Traditionally, running software on a Unix-like system required a great deal of expertise. The Ports Collection simplifies this considerably by automating and documenting the install, uninstall, and configuration processes for thousands of software packages.

Optimized Upgrade Process

Unlike operating systems that require painful and risky upgrade procedures, FreeBSD's simple upgrade process builds an operating system optimized for your hardware and applications. This lets FreeBSD use every feature supported by your hardware, instead of just the lowest common denominator. If you change hardware, you can rebuild your operating system to best handle that particular hardware. Vendors such as Sun and Apple do exactly this, but they control both the hardware and the software; FreeBSD pulls off the same trick on commodity hardware.

Advanced Filesystem

A *filesystem* is how information is stored on the physical disk—it is what maps the file *My Resume* to a series of zeroes and ones on a hard drive. FreeBSD supports very sophisticated filesystems and can support files up to a petabyte (one thousand thousand gigabytes). Its default filesystem is highly damage resistant and reads and writes files extremely quickly. The BSD filesystem is advanced enough that many commercial Unix vendors have used it as a basis for their own filesystems.

Who Should Use FreeBSD?

While FreeBSD can be used as a powerful desktop or development machine, its history shows a strong bias towards web, mail, file, and support services. FreeBSD is most famous for its strengths as an Internet server, and it is an excellent choice as an underlying platform for any network service. If major firms such as Yahoo! count on FreeBSD to provide reliable service, it will work as well for you.

If you're thinking of running FreeBSD (or any Unix) on your desktop, you'll need to understand how your computer works. FreeBSD is not your best choice if you need point-and-click simplicity. If that's your goal, get a Mac so you can use the power of Unix when you need it and not worry about it the rest of the time. If you want to learn FreeBSD, though, running it on your desktop is the best way—as we'll discuss later.

Who Should Run Another BSD?

NetBSD and OpenBSD are FreeBSD's closest competitors. Unlike competitors in the commercial world, this competition is mostly friendly. FreeBSD, NetBSD, and OpenBSD freely share code and developers; some people even maintain the same subsystems in multiple operating systems.

If you want to use old or oddball hardware, NetBSD is a good choice for you. For several years I ran NetBSD on an ancient SGI workstation that I used as a Domain Name System (DNS) and fileserver. It did the job well until the hardware finally released a cloud of smoke and stopped working.

OpenBSD has implemented an impressive variety of security features. Many of the tools are eventually integrated into FreeBSD, but that takes months or years. If you have real security concerns but don't need sophisticated multiprocessor support, you might look at OpenBSD.

If you're just experimenting to see what's out there, any BSD is good!

Who Should Run a Proprietary Operating System?

Operating systems such as Solaris, Windows, AIX, and their ilk are still quite popular, despite the open source operating systems gnawing at their market share. High-end enterprises are pretty tightly shackled to these operating systems. While this is slowly changing, you're probably stuck with commercial operating systems in such environments. But slipping in an occasional FreeBSD machine to handle basic services such as monitoring and department file serving can make your life much easier at much lower cost. Yahoo! and NetApp have built entire businesses using FreeBSD instead of commercial operating systems.

Of course, if the software you need only runs on a proprietary operating system, your choice is pretty clear. Still, always ask a vendor if a FreeBSD version is available; you might be pleasantly surprised.

How to Read This Book

Many computer books are thick and heavy enough to stun an ox, if you have the strength to lift them high enough. Plus, they're either encyclopedic in scope or so painfully detailed that they're difficult to actually read. Do you really need to reference a screenshot when you're told click OK or accept the license agreement? And when was the last time you actually sat down to read the encyclopedia?

Absolute FreeBSD is a little different. It's designed to be read once, from front to back. You can skip around if you want to, but each chapter builds on what comes before it. While this isn't a small book, it's smaller than many popular computer books. After you've read it once, it makes a decent reference.

If you're a frequent buyer of computer books, please feel free to insert all that usual crud about "read a chapter at a time for best learning" and so on. I'm not going to coddle you—if you picked up this book, you either have two brain cells to rub together or you're visiting someone who does. (If it's the latter, hopefully your host is smart enough to take this book away from you before you learn enough to become dangerous.)

What Must You Know?

This book is aimed at the new Unix administrator. Two decades ago, the average Unix administrator had kernel programming experience and was working on his master's degree in computer science. Even a decade ago, he was already a skilled Unix user with real programming skills and most of a bachelor's degree in comp sci. Today, Unix-like operating systems are freely available, computers are cheaper than food, and even 12-year-old children can run Unix, read the source code, and learn enough to intimidate older folks. As such, I don't expect you to know a huge amount about Unix before firing it up.

To use this book to its full potential, you need to have familiarity with some basic tasks, such as how to change directories, list files in a directory, and log in with a username and password. If you're not familiar with basic commands and the Unix shell, I recommend you begin with a book like *UNIX System Administration Handbook* by Evi Nemeth and friends (Prentice Hall PTR, 2006). To make things easier on newer system administrators, I include the exact commands needed to produce the desired results. If you learn best by example, you should have everything you need right here.

You'll also need to know something about computer hardware—not a huge amount, mind you, but something. For example, it helps to know how to recognize an IDE, SCSI, or SATA cable. Your need for this knowledge depends on the hardware you're using, but if you're interested enough to pick up this book and read this far, you probably know enough.

For the New System Administrator

If you're new to Unix, the best way to learn is to eat your own dog food. No, I'm not suggesting that you dine with Rover. If you ran a dog food company, you'd want to make a product that your own dog eats happily. If your dog turns his nose up at your latest recipe, you have a problem. The point here is that if you work with a tool or create something, you should actually use it. The same thing applies to any Unix-like operating system, including FreeBSD.

Desktop FreeBSD

If you're serious about learning FreeBSD, I suggest wiping out the operating system on your main computer and running FreeBSD instead. Yes, I know, now that dog food doesn't sound so bad. But learning an operating system is like learning a language; total immersion is the quickest and most powerful way to learn. That's what I did, and today I can make a Unix-like system do anything I want. In fact, this book was composed entirely on a FreeBSD laptop, using the open source text editor XEmacs and the OpenOffice.org business suite. I also use FreeBSD to watch movies, rip and listen to MP3s, balance my bank accounts, process my email, and surf the Web. As I write this, I have a dozen animated BSD daemons running around on top of my desktop windows, and I occasionally take a break to zap them with my mouse. If this doesn't count as a Stupid Desktop Trick, I don't know what does.[3]

Many Unix system administrators these days come from a Windows background. They're beavering away in their little world when management swoops by and says, "You can handle one more system, can't you? Glad to

---

[3] In the first edition of this book, I neglected to mention exactly how to do a similar Stupid Desktop Trick, which generated more questioning email than any other topic in the whole book. That's a mistake I won't make again!

hear it! It's a Unix box, by the way," and then vanishes into the managerial ether. Once the new Unix administrator decides to not slit his wrists, the boss's wrists, or start a fresh and exciting career as a whale autopsy technician, he tentatively pokes at the system. He learns that ls is like dir and that cd is the same on both platforms. He can learn the commands by rote, reading, and experience. What he cannot learn, coming from this background, is how a Unix machine thinks. Unix will not adjust to you; you must adjust to it. Windows and OS X require similar adjustments, but they hide this behind a glittering facade. With that in mind, let's spend a little time learning how to think about Unix.

How to Think About Unix

These days, most Unix systems come with pretty GUIs out of the box, but they're just eye candy. The real work happens on the command line, no matter how many tools purport to hide it. The command line is actually one of Unix's strengths, and it is responsible for its unparalleled flexibility.

Unix's underlying philosophy is *many small tools, each of which does a single job well.* My laptop's local programs directory (*/usr/local/bin*) has 662 programs in it. I have installed every one of them, either directly or indirectly. Most are small, simple programs that only do one task, with occasional exceptions, such as the office suite. This array of small tools makes Unix extremely flexible and adaptable. Many commercial software packages try to do everything; they wind up with all sorts of capabilities but only mediocre performance in their core functions. Remember, at one time you needed to be a programmer to use a Unix system, let alone run one. Programmers don't mind building their own tools. The Unix concept of channels encouraged this.

Channels of Communication

People used to GUI environments such as Windows and Mac OS X are probably unfamiliar with how Unix handles output and input. They're used to clicking something and seeing either an OK message, an error, nothing, or (all too often) a pretty blue screen with nifty high-tech letters explaining in the language called Geek why the system crashed. Unix does things a little differently.

Unix programs have three channels of communication: standard input, standard output, and standard error. Once you understand how each of these channels works, you're a good way along to understanding the whole system.

Standard input is the source of information. When you're at the console typing a command, the standard input is the data coming from the keyboard. If a program is listening to the network, the standard input is the network. Many programs can rearrange standard input to accept data from the network, a file, another program, the keyboard, or any other source.

The *standard output* is where the program's output is displayed. This is frequently the console (screen). Network programs usually return their output to the network. Programs might send their output to a file, another program, over the network, or anywhere else available to the computer.

Finally, *standard error* is where the program sends its error messages. Frequently, console programs return their errors to the console; others log errors in a file. If you set up a program incorrectly, it just might discard all error information.

These three channels can be arbitrarily arranged, a concept that is perhaps the biggest hurdle for new Unix users and administrators. For example, if you don't like the error messages appearing on the terminal, you can redirect them to a file. If you don't want to repeatedly type a lot of information into a command, you can put the information into a file (so you can reuse it) and dump the file into the command's standard input. Or, better still, you can run a command to generate that information and put it in a file, or just pipe (send) the output of the first command directly to the second, without even bothering with a file.

Small Programs, Channels, and the Command Line

Taken to its logical extreme, these input/output channels and the variety of tools seem overwhelming. When I saw a sysadmin type something like the following during my initial Unix training session, I gave serious consideration to changing careers.

```
$ tail -f /var/log/messages | grep -v popper | grep -v named &
```

Lines of incomprehensible text began spilling across the screen, and they kept coming. And worse still, my mentor kept typing as gibberish poured out! If you're from a point-and-click computing environment, a long string of commands like this is definitely intimidating. What do all those funky words mean? And an ampersand? You want me to learn *what*?

Think of learning to use the command line as learning a language. When learning a language, we start with simple words. As we increase our vocabulary, we also learn how to string the words together. We learn that placing words in a certain order makes sense, and that a different order makes no sense at all. You didn't speak that well at three years old—give yourself some slack and you'll get there.

Smaller, simpler programs and channels of communication provide almost unlimited flexibility. Have you ever wished you could use a function from one program in another program? By using a variety of smaller programs and arranging the inputs and outputs as you like, you can make a Unix system behave in any manner that amuses you. Eventually, you'll feel positively crippled if you can't just run a command's output through `| sort -rnk 6 | less`.[4]

---

[4] This ugly thing takes the output of the last command, sorts it in reverse order by the contents of the sixth column, and presents it one screen at a time. If you have hundreds of lines of output, and you want to know which entries have the highest values in the sixth column, this is how you do it. Or, if you have lots of time, you can dump the output to a spreadsheet and fiddle with equally obscure commands for a much longer time.

Everything Is a File

You can't be around Unix for very long before hearing that everything is a file. Programs, account information, and system configuration are all stored in files. Unix has no Windows-style registry; if you back up the files, you have the whole system.

What's more, the system identifies system hardware as files! Your CD-ROM drive is a file, */dev/acd0*. Network cards appear as files in */dev/net*. Even virtual devices, such as packet sniffers and partitions on hard drives, are files.

When you have a problem, keep this fact in mind. Everything is a file or is in a file, somewhere on your system. All you have to do is find it!

Notes on the Second Edition

When I wrote my first technical book, the members of the BSD family had huge amounts in common. A system administrator familiar with one BSD could sit down at a different one and have the environment tuned nicely in an hour or two. Some tools were in a different place, the boot sequences were slightly different, and some features didn't quite match, but on the whole, each was just another derivative of BSD 4.4. That was five years ago, and in the meantime each BSD has marched down a different path. While they still have a lot in common, the differences are broad enough that I no longer feel comfortable saying that much of this book is largely applicable to all three BSDs. As such, this is *Absolute* FreeBSD, *2nd Edition*, instead of just *Absolute* BSD, *2nd Edition*.

You'll find other changes from the first edition, of course. The differences between FreeBSD 4 and FreeBSD 7 vary from the dramatic to the subtle, and either can trip you up if you're not careful. Many tools for making Sendmail manageable and friendly have been integrated into the system, so I cover Sendmail instead of Postfix. (I still like Postfix, but this is a FreeBSD book.) In 2000, it was unthinkable to have a computer without a floppy disk drive; now, some computers ship without any integrated removable-media drives whatsoever. This makes diskless work much more important, because for some hardware, it's the only way to get an operating system on the machine! Lastly, FreeBSD has evolved greatly in the last five years, and I've learned more in that time than I would have believed possible. Hopefully, this combination makes *Absolute FreeBSD, 2nd Edition* a quantum leap better than its predecessor.

Contents of This Book

Absolute FreeBSD, 2nd Edition contains the following chapters.

Chapter 1: Getting More Help

This chapter discusses the information resources the FreeBSD Project and its devotees provide for users. No one book can cover everything, but knowing how to use the many FreeBSD resources on the Internet helps fill any gaps you find here.

Chapter 2: Installing FreeBSD
This chapter gives you an overview of installing FreeBSD and offers advice on an optimal install.

Chapter 3: Start Me Up! The Boot Process
This chapter teaches you about the FreeBSD boot process and how to make your system start, stop, and reboot in different configurations.

Chapter 4: Read This Before You Break Something Else!
Here we discuss how to back up your data on both a system-wide and a file-by-file level, and how to make your changes so that they can be easily undone.

Chapter 5: Kernel Games
This chapter describes configuring the FreeBSD kernel. Unlike some other operating systems, you are expected to tune FreeBSD's kernel to best suit your purposes. This gives you tremendous flexibility and lets you optimize your hardware's potential.

Chapter 6: The Network
Here we discuss the network and how it works in FreeBSD.

Chapter 7: Securing Your System
This chapter teaches you how to make your computer resist attackers and intruders.

Chapter 8: Disks and Filesystems
This chapter covers some of the details of working with hard drives in FreeBSD, support for other filesystems, and a few network filesystems.

Chapter 9: Advanced Security Features
Here we discuss some of the more interesting security features found in FreeBSD.

Chapter 10: Exploring /etc
This chapter describes the many configuration files in FreeBSD and how they operate.

Chapter 11: Making Your System Useful
Here I describe the ports and packages system that FreeBSD uses to manage add-on software.

Chapter 12: Advanced Software Management
This chapter discusses some of the finer points of running software on FreeBSD systems.

Chapter 13: Upgrading FreeBSD
This chapter teaches you how to use FreeBSD's upgrade process. The upgrade system is among the most remarkable and smooth of any operating system.

Chapter 14: The Internet Road Map: DNS
This chapter describes DNS and teaches you how to install and troubleshoot it.

Chapter 15: Small System Services

Here we discuss some of the small programs you'll need to manage in order to use FreeBSD properly.

Chapter 16: Spam, Worms, and Viruses (Plus Email, If You Insist)

This chapter describes how to set up an email system on FreeBSD to reliably deliver mail and repel spam and viruses.

Chapter 17: Web and FTP Services

This chapter teaches you how to set up and secure these two vital Internet services.

Chapter 18: Disk Tricks with GEOM

This chapter goes over some of the fancy techniques FreeBSD supports for mirroring disks, exporting disk devices across the network, and generally having a good old time protecting and manipulating your data.

Chapter 19: System Performance and Monitoring

This chapter covers some of FreeBSD's performance-testing and troubleshooting tools and shows you how to interpret the results. We also discuss system logging and FreeBSD's SNMP implementation.

Chapter 20: The Fringe of FreeBSD

This chapter teaches you some of the more interesting tricks you can do with FreeBSD, such as running systems without disks and with tiny disks, as well as some live failover and redundancy setups.

Chapter 21: System (and Sysadmin) Panics and Crashes

This chapter teaches you how to deal with those rare occasions when a FreeBSD system fails, how to debug problems, and how to create a useful problem report.

Appendix: Some Interesting sysctl MIBs

This appendix provides basic information about some of the kernel-tuning options available for your use.

Okay, enough with the introductory stuff. Onward!

1

GETTING MORE HELP

As thick as this book is, it still can't possibly cover everything you must know about FreeBSD. After all, Unix has been kicking around for close to four decades, BSD is over a quarter-century old, and FreeBSD is already a teenager. Even if you memorize this book, it won't cover every situation you might encounter—especially when FreeBSD starts acting like a typical teenager and needs a good smack. The FreeBSD Project supports a huge variety of information resources, including numerous mailing lists and the FreeBSD website, not to mention the official manual and Handbook. Its users maintain even more documentation. The flood of information can be overwhelming in itself, and it can make you want to just email the world and beg for help. But before you send a question to a mailing list, confirm that the information you need isn't already available.

Why Not Just Email for Help?

The FreeBSD mailing lists are the best-known support resources. Many mailing list participants are very knowledgeable and can answer your questions very quickly. But remember, when you mail a question to a FreeBSD mailing list, you are asking tens of thousands of people all over the world to take a moment to read your email. You're also asking that one or more of them take the time to help you instead of watching a favorite movie, enjoying dinner with their families, or catching up on sleep. Problems arise when these experts answer the same question 10, 50, or even hundreds of times. They become grumpy. Some get downright tetchy.

What makes matters worse is that these same people have spent a great deal of time and effort making the answers to most of these questions available elsewhere. If you make it clear that you have already searched the resources and your answer really doesn't appear therein, you will probably receive a polite, helpful answer. If you ask a question that has already been asked several hundred times, however, the expert on that subject just might snap and go ballistic on you. Do your homework, and chances are you'll get an answer more quickly than a fresh call to the mailing list could provide.

The FreeBSD Attitude

"Homework? What do you mean? Am I back in school? What do you want, burnt offerings on bended knee?" Yes, you are in school. The information technology business is nothing but lifelong, self-guided learning. Get used to it or get out. Burnt offerings, on the other hand, are difficult to transmit via email and are not quite so useful today.

Most commercial operating systems conceal their inner workings. The only access you have to them is through the options presented by the vendor. Even if you want to learn how something works, you probably can't. When something breaks, you have no choice but to call the vendor and grovel for help. Worse, the people paid to help you frequently know little more than you do.

If you've never worked with open source software vendors, FreeBSD's support mechanism might surprise you. There is no toll-free number to call and no vendor to escalate within. No, you may not speak to a manager, for a good reason: You are the manager. Congratulations on your promotion!

Support Options

Having said that, you're not entirely on your own. The FreeBSD community includes numerous developers, contributors, and users who care very deeply about FreeBSD's quality, and they're happy to work with you. FreeBSD provides everything you need: complete access to the source code used to create the system, the tools needed to turn that source code into programs, and the same debuggers used by the developers. Nothing is hidden; you can see the innards, warts and all. You can view FreeBSD's development history since the beginning, including every change ever made and the reason for it. These tools might be beyond your abilities, but that's not the Project's problem. Various community members are even happy to provide guidance as you develop your own skills so you can use those tools yourself. You'll have lots of help fulfilling your responsibilities.

As a grossly overgeneralized rule, people help those like themselves. If you want to use FreeBSD, you must make the jump from eating what the vendor gives you to learning how to cook. Every member of the FreeBSD user community learned how to use it, and they welcome interested new users with open arms. If you just want to know what to type without really understanding what's going on behind the scenes, you'll be better off reading the documentation: The general FreeBSD support community simply isn't motivated to help those who won't help themselves or who can't follow instructions.

If you want to use FreeBSD but have neither the time nor the inclination to learn more, invest in a commercial support contract. It might not be able to put you in touch with FreeBSD's owner, but at least you'll have someone to yell at. You'll find several commercial support providers listed on the FreeBSD website.

It's also important to remember that the FreeBSD Project only maintains FreeBSD. If you're having trouble with some other piece of software, a FreeBSD mailing list is not the place to ask for help. FreeBSD developers are generally proficient in a variety of software, but that doesn't mean that they want to help you, say, configure KDE.

The first part of your homework, then, is to learn about the resources available beyond this book. These include the integrated manual, the FreeBSD website, the mailing list archives, and other websites.

Man Pages

Man pages (short for *manual pages*) are the primordial way of presenting Unix documentation. While man pages have a reputation for being obtuse, difficult, or even incomprehensible, they're actually quite friendly—for particular users. When man pages were first created, the average system administrator was a C programmer and, as a result, the pages were written by programmers, for programmers. If you can think like a programmer, man pages are perfect for you. I've tried thinking like a programmer, but I only achieved real success after remaining awake for two days straight. (Lots of caffeine and a high fever help.)

Over the last several years, the skill level required for system administration has dropped; no longer must you be a programmer. Similarly, man pages have become more and more readable. Man pages are not tutorials, however; they explain the behavior of one particular program, not how to achieve a desired effect. While they're neither friendly nor comforting, they should be your first line of defense. If you send a question to a mailing list without checking the manual, you're likely to get a terse *man whatever* in response.

Manual Sections

The FreeBSD manual is divided into nine sections. Roughly speaking, the sections are:

1. General user commands
2. System calls and error numbers
3. C programming libraries
4. Devices and device drivers
5. File formats
6. Game instructions
7. Miscellaneous information
8. System maintenance commands
9. Kernel interfaces

Each man page starts with the name of the command it documents followed by its section number in parenthesis, like this: reboot(8). When you see something in this format in other documents, it's telling you to read that man page in that section of the manual. Almost every topic has a man page. For example, to see the man page for the editor vi, type this command:

```
$ man vi
```

In response, you should see the following:

```
VI(1)                                                                    VI(1)

NAME
       ex, vi, view - text editors

SYNOPSIS
       ex [-eFGRrSsv] [-c cmd] [-t tag] [-w size] [file ...]
       vi [-eFGlRrSv] [-c cmd] [-t tag] [-w size] [file ...]
       view [-eFGRrSv] [-c cmd] [-t tag] [-w size] [file ...]

LICENSE
       The vi program is freely redistributable. You are welcome to copy,
       modify and share it with others under the conditions listed in the
       LICENSE file. If any company (not individual!) finds vi sufficiently
       useful that you would have purchased it, or if any company wishes to
       redistribute it, contributions to the authors would be appreciated.

DESCRIPTION
       Vi is a screen oriented text editor. Ex is a line-oriented text editor
       Ex and vi are different interfaces to the same program, and it is
       possible to switch back and forth during an edit session. View is the
:
```

The page starts with the title of the man page (vi) and the section number (1), and then it gives the name of the page. This particular page has three names: ex, vi, and view. Typing man ex or man view would take you to this same page.

Navigating Man Pages

Once you're in a man page, pressing the spacebar or the PGDN key takes you forward one full screen. If you don't want to go that far, pressing ENTER or the down arrow scrolls down one line. Typing B or pressing the PGUP key takes you back one screen. To search within a man page, type / followed by the word you're searching for. You'll jump down to the first appearance of the word, which will be highlighted. Typing N subsequently takes you to the next occurrence of the word.

This assumes that you're using the default BSD pager, more(1). If you're using a different pager, use that pager's syntax. Of course, if you know so much about Unix that you've already set your preferred default pager, you've probably skipped this part of the book entirely.

Finding Man Pages

New users often say that they'd be happy to read the man pages, if they could find the right one. You can perform basic keyword searches on the man pages with apropos(1) and whatis(1). apropos(1) searches for any man page name or description that includes the word you specify. whatis(1) does the same search, but only matches whole words. For example, if you're interested in the vi command, you might try the following:

```
$ apropos vi
BUS_ADD_CHILD(9)        - add a device node to the tree with a given priority
BUS_PRINT_CHILD(9)      - print information about a device
BUS_READ_IVAR(9), BUS_WRITE_IVAR(9) - manipulate bus-specific device instance
variables
DEVICE_ATTACH(9)        - attach a device
...
```

This continues for a total of 581 entries, which is probably far more than you want to look at. Most of these have nothing to do with vi(1), however; the letters *vi* just appear in the name or description. *Device driver* is a fairly common term in the manual, so that's not surprising. On the other hand, whatis(1) gives more useful results in this case.

```
$ whatis vi
ex(1), vi(1), view(1)   - text editors
etags(1), ctags(1)      - generate tag file for Emacs, vi
$
```

There are only two results, and both clearly have relevance to vi(1). On other searches, apropos(1) gives better results than whatis(1). Experiment with both and you'll quickly learn how they fit your style.

Section Numbers and Man

You might find cases where a single command appears in multiple parts of the manual. For example, every man section has an introductory man page that explains the contents of the section. To specify a section to search for a man page, give the number immediately after the man command.

```
$ man 3 intro
```

This pulls up the introduction to section 3 of the manual. I recommend you read the intro pages to each section of the manual, if only to help you understand the breadth and depth of information available.

Man Page Contents

Man pages are divided into sections. While the author can put just about any heading he likes into a man page, several are standard. See mdoc(7) for a partial list of these headings as well as other man page standards:

- NAME gives the name(s) of a program or utility. Some programs have multiple names—for example, the vi(1) text editor is also available as ex(1) and view(1).

- SYNOPSIS lists the possible command-line options and their arguments, or how a library call is accessed. If I'm already familiar with a program but just can't remember the option I'm looking for, I find that this header is sufficient to remind me of what I need.

- DESCRIPTION contains a brief description of the program, library, or feature. The contents of this section vary widely depending on the topic, as programs, files, and libraries all have very different documentation requirements.

- OPTIONS gives a program's command-line options and their effects.

- BUGS describes known problems with the code and can frequently save a lot of headaches. How many times have you wrestled with a computer problem only to learn that it doesn't work the way you would expect under those circumstances? The goal of the BUGS section is to save you time and describe known errors and other weirdness.[1]

- SEE ALSO is traditionally the last section of a man page. Remember that Unix is like a language, and the system is an interrelated whole. Like duct tape, the SEE ALSO links hold everything together.

If you don't have access to the manual pages at the moment, many websites offer them. Among them is the main FreeBSD website.

---

[1] It's called *honesty*. IT professionals may find this term unfamiliar, but a dictionary can help.

FreeBSD.org

The FreeBSD website (*http://www.freebsd.org*) contains a variety of information about general FreeBSD administration, installation, and management. The most useful portions are the Handbook, the FAQ, and the mailing list archives, but you'll also find a wide number of articles on dozens of topics. In addition to documents about FreeBSD, the website also contains a great deal of information about the FreeBSD Project's internal management and the status of various parts of the Project.

If you find that the main website works slowly for you, try using a mirror site. The main site offers a drop-down box with a choice of national mirrors, or you can just try *http://www.<countrycode>.freebsd.org*. Almost every country has a local site that provides a duplicate of the FreeBSD website. I frequently find that a mirror is more responsive than the main website.

Web Documents

The FreeBSD documentation is divided into articles and books. The difference between the two is highly arbitrary: As a rule, books are longer than articles and cover broader topics, while articles are short and focus on a single topic. The two books that should most interest new users are the Handbook and the Frequently Asked Questions (FAQ).

The Handbook is the FreeBSD Project's tutorial-style manual. It is continuously updated, describes how to perform basic system tasks, and is an excellent reference when you're first starting on a project. In fact, I have deliberately chosen not to include some topics in this book because they have adequate coverage in the Handbook.

The FAQ is designed to provide quick answers to the questions most frequently asked on the FreeBSD mailing lists. Some of the answers aren't suitable for inclusion in the Handbook, while others just point to the proper Handbook chapter or article.

Several other books cover a variety of topics, from kernel debugging to Project organization.

Of the 50 or so articles available, some are kept only for historical reasons (such as the road map to releasing FreeBSD version 5), while others discuss the subtleties of specific parts of the system such as serial ports or CVSup. A few are old enough that they're retained for only a handful of users who are still stuck with 20th-century systems.

These documents are very formal, and they require preparation. As such, they always lag a bit behind the real world. When a new feature is first rolled out, the appropriate Handbook entry might not appear for weeks or months. If the web documentation seems out of date, your best resource for up-to-the-minute answers is the mailing list archive.

The Mailing List Archives

Unless you're really on the bleeding edge, someone has probably struggled with your problem before and posted a question about it to the mailing lists. After all, the archives go back to 1994 and contain close to two million messages. The only problem is that there are two million pieces of email, any one of which might contain the answer you seek. (When the first edition of this book came out, the archives contained only one million messages; they have nearly doubled in size in the last few years!)

While FreeBSD provides a search facility for its web pages and the mailing list archive, it pales beside the one offered by Google. Google has a BSD-specific search site at *http://www.google.com/bsd*. Search for your error message on Google, both in the regular web search and the Groups search. Google Groups also indexes the FreeBSD mailing lists, and you can search the FreeBSD.org website on Google by including the search term *site:freebsd.org* in your query. Additionally, the Rambler search engine has a very good FreeBSD-specific search engine at *http://freebsd.rambler.ru*. Rambler runs on FreeBSD, and it employs at least one FreeBSD committer.

Other Websites

FreeBSD's users have built a plethora of websites that you might check for answers, help, education, products, and general hobnobbing. Here are some of my favorites:

Daemon News (*http://bsdnews.com*)
This site provides links to news postings on all BSD topics, not just FreeBSD.

FreeBSD Mall (*http://www.freebsdmall.com*)
The people who run FreeBSD Mall have been commercial supporters of FreeBSD since the beginning. They sell FreeBSD on CD and DVD and offer training and support contracts, as well as FreeBSD paraphernalia such as clothes and toys. FreeBSD Mall is owned by IX Systems.

O'Reilly Network BSD Developer Center (*http://www.onlamp.com/bsd*)
This site hosts a variety of BSD articles, as well as content of interest to BSD users. In my utterly unbiased opinion, the most fascinating thing on the site is the Big Scary Daemons column on BSD, but everything else there is also pretty good.

Using FreeBSD Problem-Solving Resources

Okay, let's pick a common problem and use the FreeBSD resources to solve it. I've seen this question more than once, on several different FreeBSD mailing lists, so we'll start with it.

I've just installed FreeBSD on my 486 and the network isn't working. When I try to ping anything, the console shows ed0: timeout. What's wrong?

We'll use several different methods to find an answer.

Checking the Handbook/FAQ

The Handbook doesn't have anything relevant to the problem. In the FAQ, however, this entry appears under Troubleshooting:

I keep seeing messages like "ed1: timeout". What's wrong?

That looks pretty darn close. Read the entry and try the solution presented.

Checking the Man Pages

As we go on, you'll see that the numbers after device names are simply instances of a particular device. If you see ed0, it just means device ed, unit number 0. Every device driver has a man page, so if you type man ed to bring up the manual entry for this device, you'll see the following:

```
ED(1)                    FreeBSD General Commands Manual                   ED(1)

NAME
     ed, red --  text editor

SYNOPSIS
     ed  [-] [-sx] [-p string] [file]
     red [-] [-sx] [-p string] [file]

DESCRIPTION
     The ed utility is a line-oriented text editor. It is used to create,
...
```

A text editor? What? My text editor is fine! Something obviously isn't right. Look closely at this man page; it's from section 1 of the manual, the General Commands section. You need to search the manual for other entries containing *ed*. As the letters *ed* appear in an awful lot of manual pages, use the more specific whatis(1) search.

```
$ whatis ed
ed(1), red(1)            - text editor
ed(4)                    - NE-2000 and WD-80x3 Ethernet driver
```

Bingo! The text editor ed(1) is a general-purpose command. We want the ed in section 4 of the manual. Type man 4 ed to bring up the manual page for the network device. It's pretty long, though, about 500 lines. Being lazy,

I'd rather not read the whole thing—I'd rather just search for the part that has the information I need. Looking at the error message, I guess that *timeout* might be a good keyword to look for. Type **/timeout** and press ENTER.

```
ed%d: device timeout  Indicates that an expected transmitter interrupt
did not occur. Usually caused by an interrupt conflict with another card
on the ISA bus.
```

Bingo again! Here we have a terse explanation of the problem and a probable cause (interrupt timeout). We have a good old-fashioned IRQ conflict, and if you're actually on a 486, you know more about this problem than you want to.

Checking the Mailing List Archives

You could use the FreeBSD website search engine to search the mailing list archives, but I prefer either Google or Rambler. A search for *ed0: timeout site:FreeBSD.org* spits out a whole bunch of results. Some of them date from 1994. When I did this right now, the first response answered the question. When I did this for the first edition, the first result was correct then, as well. Now, isn't that faster than composing an email to a mailing list?

Using Your Answer

Any answer you get for our ed0 timeout example assumes that you know what an IRQ is and how to adjust one on your hardware. This is fairly typical of the level of expertise required for basic problems. If you get an answer that is beyond your comprehension, you need to do the research to understand it. While an experienced developer or system administrator is probably not going to be interested in explaining IRQs to you, he or she might be willing to point you to a web page that explains them, if you ask nicely.

**ASKING AGAIN . . . AND AGAIN . . .
AND AGAIN . . .**

Some of the emails answering this problem date from 1994. Yes, that's right, over a dozen years ago! Remember when I mentioned people being sick of answering the same questions over and over again? Some of these questions have been asked many times over the years. Be sure you've checked all the resources where you might find assistance for your problem. If you truly can't find any other help, then perhaps your problem is unique enough to warrant broadcasting it to the world.

Emailing for Help

When you finally decide to ask for help, do so in a way that allows people to actually provide the assistance you need. You must include all the information you have at your disposal, as we will soon discuss. There's a lot of suggested information to include, and you can choose to skip some or all of it. If you slack off and fail to provide all the necessary information, one of the following things will happen:

- Your question will be ignored.
- You will receive a barrage of email asking you to gather this information.

On the other hand, if you actually want help solving your problem, include the following pieces of information in your message:

- A complete problem description. A message like *How do I make my modem work?* only generates a multitude of questions: What do you want your modem to do? What kind of modem is it? What are the symptoms? What happens when you try to use it? How are you trying to use it?
- The output of `uname -a`. This gives the operating system version and platform.
- If you have upgraded your system via csup, give the date and time of your last update. (This is the date of the newest files in */usr/src*.)
- Any error output. Be as complete as possible, and include any messages from the console or from your logs, especially */var/log/messages* and any application-specific logs. Messages about hardware problems should include a copy of */var/run/dmesg.boot*.

It's much better to start with a message like *My modem isn't dialing my ISP. The modem is a BastardCorp v.90 model BOFH667. My OS is version 7.2 on a dual-core Opteron. There are no error messages in /var/log/messages or /var/log/ppp.log.* You'll skip a whole round of email with a message like this, and you'll get better results more quickly.

Writing Your Email

First, *be polite*. People often say things in email that they wouldn't dream of saying to someone's face. These lists are staffed by volunteers who are answering your message out of sheer kindness. Before you click that Send button, ask yourself, *Would I be late for my date with the hot twins down the hall to answer this message?*[2] The fierce attitude that is occasionally necessary when working with corporate telephone-based support only makes these knowledge-able people delete your emails unread. Their world doesn't have to include

---

[2] Several developers have assured me that they absolutely would accept a date with said hot twins in lieu of politeness. Large sacks of money also suffice, preferably large, unmarked bills.

surly jerks. Screaming until someone helps you is a valuable skill when dealing with commercial software support, but it will actively hurt your ability to get FreeBSD support.

Send your email in plaintext, not HTML. Many FreeBSD developers read their email with a text-only email program such as mutt or elm. These are very powerful tools for handling large amounts of email, but they do not display HTML messages without contortions. To see for yourself what this is like, install */usr/ports/mail/mutt* and read some HTML email with it. If you are using a graphic mail client such as Microsoft Outlook, either send your email in plaintext or make sure that your messages include both a plaintext and an HTML version. All mail clients *can* do this; it's just a question of discovering where your GUI hides the buttons. What's more, be sure to wrap your text at 72 characters. Sending email in HTML, or without decent line-wrapping, is an invitation to have your email discarded unread.

Harsh? Not at all, once you understand whom you're writing to. Most email clients are poorly suited to handling thousands of messages a day, scattered across dozens of mailing lists, each containing a score of simultaneous conversations. The most popular email clients make reading email easy, but they do not make it efficient; when you get that much email, efficiency is far more important than ease. As most people on those mailing lists are in a similar situation, plaintext mail is very much the standard for them.

On a similar note, most attachments are unnecessary. You do not need to use OpenPGP on messages sent to a public mailing list, and those business-card attachments just demonstrate that you aren't a system administrator. Don't use a long email signature. The standard for email signatures is four lines. That's it; four lines, each no longer than 72 characters. Long ASCII art signatures are definitely out.

Second, stay on topic. If you are having a problem with X.org, check the X.org website. If your window manager isn't working, ask the people responsible for the window manager. Asking the FreeBSD folks to help you with your Java Application Server configuration is like complaining to hardware salespeople about your fast-food lunch. They might have an extra ketchup packet, but it's not really their problem. On the other hand, if you want your FreeBSD system to no longer start the mail system at boot time, that's a FreeBSD issue.

Sending Your Email

When you've composed your nicely detailed and polite question, send it to *FreeBSD-questions@FreeBSD.org*. Yes, there are other FreeBSD mailing lists, some of which are probably dedicated to what you're having trouble with. As a new user, however, your question is almost certainly best suited to the general questions mailing list. I've lurked on many of the other mailing lists for a decade now, and have yet to see a new user ask a question on any of them that wouldn't have been better served by *FreeBSD-questions*. Generally, the questioner is referred back to *FreeBSD-questions* anyway.

This goes back to the first point about politeness. Sending a message to the architectural mailing list asking about what architectures FreeBSD runs on is only going to annoy the people who are trying to work on architectural issues. You might get an answer, but you won't make any friends. Conversely, the people on *FreeBSD-questions* are there because they are volunteering to help people just like you. They want to hear your intelligent, well-researched, well-documented questions. Quite a few are FreeBSD developers, and some are even Core members. Others are slightly more experienced users who have transcended what you're going through now and are willing to give you a hand up, as well.

Responding to Email

Your answer might be a brief note with a URL, or even just two words: *man such-and-such*. If that's what you get, that's where you need to go. Don't ask for more details until you've actually checked that resource. If you have a question about the contents of the reference you're given, or if you're confused by the reference, treat it as another problem. Narrow down the source of your confusion, be specific, and ask about that. Man pages and tutorials are not perfect, and some parts appear contradictory or mutually exclusive until you understand them.

Finally, follow through. If someone asks you for more information, provide it. If you don't know how to provide it, learn how. If you develop a bad reputation, nobody will want to help you.

Email Is Forever

Those of us who were on the Internet back in the '80s remember when we treated it as a private playground. We could say whatever we wanted, to whomever we wanted. After all, it was purely ephemeral. Nobody was keeping this stuff; like CB radio, you could be a total jackass and get away with it.

That's no longer true. In fact, it's the exact opposite of true. Potential employers, potential dates, even family members might scan the Internet for your postings to mailing lists or message boards, trying to learn what sort of person you are. I have rejected hiring more than one person based on their postings to a mailing list. I want to work with a system administrator who sends polite, professional messages to support forums, not childish and incoherent rants without sufficient detail to offer any sort of guidance. And I'd think a lot less of my in-laws if I stumbled across a message from one of them on some message board where they acted like fools. The FreeBSD mailing lists are widely archived; choose your words well, because they will haunt you for decades.

Now that you know how to get more help when things go wrong, let's install FreeBSD.

2

INSTALLING FREEBSD

Just getting FreeBSD running on your computer isn't enough, no matter how satisfying it might be the first time. It's important that your install be successful. *Successful* means that your system must be configured appropriately for its purpose. A web server, an email server, a desktop system, or a database server all have different operational requirements, and meeting those requirements can be greatly eased by planning before you ever boot the hardware. Proper planning makes installing FreeBSD much less painful. On the downside, you'll get much less experience in reinstalling FreeBSD, because you'll only have to do it once. If mastering the installation program is your only goal, you can skip all this boring stuff about "thinking ahead" and go right to the middle of this chapter.

I'm assuming that you want to run FreeBSD in the real world, doing real work, in a real environment. This environment might even be your laptop—while you might argue that your laptop isn't a real production system, I challenge you to erase all the data on it without backing it up and tell me that again. If you're just using a test machine that you truly don't care about, then I still recommend following the best practices so that you develop good habits.

Consider what hardware you need or have. Then, decide how to best use that hardware, what parts of FreeBSD you need to install, and how to divide your hard disk. Only after all of that can you actually boot your computer and install FreeBSD. Finally, do some brief post-install setup, and your system is ready to go!

FreeBSD Hardware

FreeBSD supports a lot of different hardware, including both different architectures and devices for each architecture. One of the project's goals is to support the most widely available hardware, and the list of that hardware has broadened over the last few years to include far more than the "personal computer." Today, the supported hardware includes:

amd64   AMD's 64-bit extensions to the 32-bit i386, copied by Intel as EM64T, and sometimes called x64. This hardware can run both the 32-bit i386 and 64-bit amd64 versions of FreeBSD. (Linux calls this the *x*86-64 platform.)

i386   The good old-fashioned Intel-compatible personal computer.

powerpc   The PowerPC processor found in older Apple computers and many embedded devices.

pc98   Similar to i386, but popular in Japan.

sparc64   Used in high-end servers from Sun Microsystems.

xbox   Yes, FreeBSD can run on Microsoft's Xbox.

FreeBSD supports many network cards, hard drive controllers, and other add-ons for each architecture. Since many of these architectures use similar interfaces and hardware, this isn't as much of a challenge as you might think: SCSI is SCSI anywhere, and an Intel Ethernet card doesn't become magically different just by putting it in a sparc64 machine.

For the most part, FreeBSD doesn't care about the supporting hardware so long as it works. Most readers are primarily familiar with the i386 architecture, so that's where we'll spend a fair amount of time. The amd64 platform is quickly becoming popular, however, so we'll touch on that, as well as sparc64.

FreeBSD has been ported to a variety of other platforms, such as the ARM architecture and Intel's Itanium. These ports are either incomplete or of little utility to anyone except a developer. While it's nifty that many ARM boards run FreeBSD, you can't go to a computer shop and buy one to play with.

Although FreeBSD runs just fine on ancient hardware, that hardware must be in acceptable condition. If your old Pentium crashes because it has bad RAM, using FreeBSD won't stop the crashes.

Sample Hardware

This book was written using the following sample hardware:

- Dual-core amd64 SATA Sager 9750 laptop
- Dual-CPU Opteron rackmount
- Pentium 800 i386 system
- Soekris net4801 board and case
- Sun Ultra 1
- External SCSI array

BUY DRINKS FOR THESE PEOPLE

Much of this hardware was a gift from people who liked the first edition of this book. Their names all appear in the opening credits. If you find this book useful, I heartily encourage you to buy any of them a drink, a meal, or a Maserati. I would have had no crash boxes without them. Without crash boxes to test to destruction, I wouldn't have had the ability to learn FreeBSD's real limits, especially after my boss forcefully explained to me that paying customers do not appreciate being research subjects.

Proprietary Hardware

Some hardware vendors believe that keeping their hardware interfaces secret prevents competitors from copying their designs and breaking into their market. This has generally been proven to be a bad idea, especially as the flood of generic parts has largely trampled these secretive hardware manufacturers over the last few years. Yet a few vendors, especially video and sound card makers, still cling to this strategy.

Developing device drivers for a piece of hardware without its interface specifications is quite difficult. Some hardware can be well-supported without full documentation and is common enough to make struggling through this lack of documentation worthwhile. The FreeBSD sound driver team, in particular, has done an excellent job of reverse-engineering sound cards' interfaces and now provides generic sound card infrastructure that works well even for poorly documented cards. Other hardware, such as the chipset used on the PCI bus in Sun UltraSPARC III systems, cannot be supported without full and complete documentation.

If a FreeBSD developer has specifications for a piece of hardware and interest in that hardware, he'll probably implement support for it. If not, that hardware won't work with FreeBSD. In most cases, unsupported proprietary hardware can be replaced with less expensive and more open options.

Some hardware vendors provide closed-source binary drivers for their hardware. For example, Nvidia offers a binary-only driver for their video hardware. FreeBSD also employs some clever tricks to use Windows network drivers, notably those for the wireless Ethernet cards supported by "Project Evil."[1] For the most part, however, the best support comes from open-source FreeBSD drivers.

IS MY HARDWARE SUPPORTED?

The easiest way to tell if your particular hardware is supported is to check the release notes for the release of FreeBSD you plan to install. The release notes are available at *http://www.freebsd.org*.

What We Won't Cover

We won't cover ISA cards; PCI has been around for a decade now, and I strenuously doubt that anyone uses ISA cards in a production setting.[2] The FreeBSD Handbook has decent instructions for making your ISA cards work.

PowerPC and pc98 are all older systems, generally in decline, so we won't bother discussing them specifically. Like a dinosaur, older server-grade hardware tends to be difficult to kill with anything short of a meteor strike. And running FreeBSD on an Xbox, while fun, is more of a stunt than an idea worth implementing in production.

Hardware Requirements

While FreeBSD has minuscule hardware requirements, you'll get the best results out of it if you give it enough to work with. The following recommendations are for i386 systems, but other platforms have similar requirements.

Chapter 19 discusses how to measure your system's performance so that you can maximize your hardware utilization.

Processor

Your brand of CPU is irrelevant. FreeBSD doesn't care if you're running an Intel, AMD, IBM, or Cyrix/Via CPU. During the boot process, the FreeBSD kernel probes the CPU and uses whatever chip features it finds. I've run effective servers on 486 machines before—in fact, I've filled an Internet T1 with a 486. For you folks who are just learning, I recommend that you get a Pentium or faster system. Some of the techniques in this book take days on a 486, and I'm no longer that patient. Those same operations take less than an hour on my dual-core laptop.

---

[1] Yes, this really is called Project Evil. And implementing the Windows kernel interface in the FreeBSD kernel makes the project worthy of the name.

[2] And if you are, you either have been in this business long enough that you probably aren't even reading this book, or you are a total nut job. Mind you, the latter is not a disadvantage in this field.

Memory

Memory (as in RAM) is good. Adding more RAM accelerates a system better than anything else. I recommend at least 64MB of RAM, but if you have a system with 256MB or greater you'll find FreeBSD easier going. If you are really trying to shrink your system, you can run a carefully crafted kernel in 16MB—but you can't run the installer in that amount of memory.

Hard Drives

Hard drives can be a big performance bottleneck. While IDE drives are dirt cheap, they don't perform as well as SAS, SCSI, or even SATA drives. A SAS or old-fashioned SCSI system transfers data to and from each drive at the full controller speed, while IDE and SATA drives split their throughput between all of the drives on the channel. A SCSI controller can have up to 15 drives on a channel, while a standard IDE controller can have no more than 2. SATA controllers tend to put only one drive on a channel, taking the easy route to good throughput. While you can use splitters to attach more than one drive to a SATA channel, multiple SATA drives on a single channel have no greater throughput than a single drive. 15 drives, each running at full speed, versus 2 drives averaging half speed, make a huge difference in the amount of data throughput!

If you have IDE or SATA drives, put your hard disks on separate controllers if possible. Many systems now have a hard drive on one IDE controller and a CD drive on the other. When you add a second hard drive, put it on the same controller as the CD drive. Most likely, you won't be using the CD nearly as often as the hard drive, and this way each drive will have a dedicated controller.

The base FreeBSD system can fit into 500MB, and stripped-down versions can fit into 32MB. You'll be happiest with at least 5GB of disk space on your test system, although I'm assuming that you have at least 10GB. Some add-on software requires far more disk space—building the OpenOffice.org suite, for example, takes 10GB of /usr all on its own! Again, any hard drive new enough to be workable will probably be at least that large.

Preinstall Decisions

Before installing your server, decide what you'll use it for. Is this a web server? Database server? Network logging server? We'll discuss the requirements for each in the appropriate section.

Partitioning

Partitions are logical divisions of a hard drive. FreeBSD can handle different partitions in different ways, and can even allow different filesystems or different operating systems on different partitions. If you're doing your first FreeBSD install, and you really don't know how you want to partition your disk, you can just use the automated partitioning suggested by the installer. If you have more complicated needs, I suggest that you write down your desired partitioning on a piece of paper before you begin.

Partitioning might seem like a pain. If you're familiar with some other Unix-like operating systems, such as some distributions of Linux, you might want to create a single large root partition and put everything on it. If Windows or Linux let you dump everything on one big disk, why divide your FreeBSD disk into smaller, less flexible pieces? What are the advantages of partitioning?

On a physical level, different parts of the disk move at different speeds. By putting frequently accessed data on the fastest parts of the disk, you optimize system performance. The only way to arrange this is by using partitions. On a logical level, FreeBSD handles each partition separately. This means that you can set each partition to have different operating rules. Partitions that contain user data should not have *setuid programs* (programs that run as root), and you might not want them to have programs at all. You can enforce that easily with partitions.

If the disk is damaged, chances are the damage is limited to a single partition. You can boot the system from an intact partition and attempt to recover data from the damaged partition. With a single large partition, any damage to that partition becomes damage to your entire system, reducing or eliminating chances of recovery.

Partitions can limit problems caused by poor system administration. Unattended programs can completely fill a hard drive with logs. Larger hard drives don't mean that the problem takes longer to show up; they just mean that software writes more logs. While Chapter 19 discusses ways to contain logs, a full hard drive can even prevent you from connecting to the system to fix the problem! Partitioning confines such problems to a subset of the system.

Finally, many backup programs—i.e., dump(8)—work at the partition level. On a production system, you'll want to set different backup strategies for different types of data. FreeBSD's standard partitions are / (root), swap space, */var*, */tmp*, and */usr*.

/ (root)

The root partition holds the core system configuration files, the kernel, and the most essential Unix utilities. Every other partition lies "under" the root partition or is subordinate to it. With an intact root partition, you can boot the system to the bare-bones single-user mode and perform repairs on the rest of the system. Your system needs fast access to the root partition, so put it first on the disk. Because root holds only the basic utilities and configuration files, it doesn't need to be large; FreeBSD defaults to configuring 512MB for a root partition, which is more than sufficient.

Swap Space

The next partition on your drive should be the *swap space*—the disk space used by virtual memory. When FreeBSD uses up all the physical RAM, it moves information that has been sitting idle from memory into swap. If things go well, your system doesn't need swap space—but if you do need swap, it must be fast.

So, how much swap space do you need? This is a matter of long debates between system administrators. The short answer is, "it depends." Long-running wisdom says that you should have at least twice as much swap as you have physical memory. Long-running wisdom has become obsolete, however, and the capacity of modern systems has invalidated this rule of thumb. When a process runs out of control and starts allocating memory (say, in an infinite loop), the kernel will kill the process once the system runs out of virtual memory. If your system has 6GB RAM and 9GB swap, this process will need to consume 15GB of memory before the kernel kills it! i386 systems have about 3GB of virtual address space, and they must share that with the kernel, shared libraries, the stack, and so on. The i386 platform limits memory usage to 512MB per process, which means that the kernel will stop a runaway process fairly quickly. 64-bit systems, like amd64, have vast virtual memory space and a process could conceivably devour gigabytes of memory. If a system is thrashing gigabytes of memory between disk and RAM, it will be unresponsive, slow, and generally troubled. Today, you should have enough swap to do your work. I recommend provisioning as much swap space as you have RAM, perhaps even a few megabytes more.

The main use for swap on modern systems is for a dump in case of a system panic and crash. For maximum safety, you want enough swap space to dump the entire contents of your RAM to swap. This is a worst-case crash dump. FreeBSD 7.0 and later defaults to using a kernel minidump, however, which only dumps the kernel memory. A minidump is much smaller than a full dump—a system with 8GB RAM has an average minidump size of about 250MB. You can probably get away with only providing 1GB of swap, which leaves plenty of room for even a bloated kernel minidump.

/tmp

The /tmp directory is the system-wide temporary space, open to all system users. If you do not create a separate /tmp partition, it will be included on your root partition. This means that your system-wide temporary space will be subject to the same conditions as the rest of your root drive. This probably isn't what you want, especially if you plan to mount your root partition read-only.

Requirements for a /tmp directory are generally a matter of opinion—after all, you can always just use a chunk of space in your home directory as temporary space, and there's always the /var/tmp directory if you have large files that you need to work with temporarily. On a modern hard drive, I like to have at least 512MB in a /tmp directory. Automated software installers frequently want to extract files in /tmp, and having to work around these installers when /tmp fills up is possible but tedious.

On systems where you don't expect /tmp to use much space (for example, web servers and database servers), you might want to use a memory filesystem for /tmp. We'll discuss memory filesystems in Chapter 8. If you intend to use a memory filesystem, do not create a separate /tmp partition.

/var

The /var partition contains frequently changing logs, mail spools, temporary run files, upgrade files from tools such as portsnap and FreeBSD-update, and so on. If your server is a web server, your website logs go to this partition. You might need to make it 2GB or more. On a small "generic" mail server or web server I'd use a third of my remaining disk space for /var. If the server handles only email, databases, or logs, I'd kick this up to 70 percent or more, or just assign sufficient space to the other partitions and throw everything left on */var*. If you're really cramped for space, you might assign as little as 30MB to */var*.

Make */var* larger than physical memory. By default, FreeBSD writes crash dumps to */var/crash*. We'll discuss crash dumps in Chapter 21, but for now, take my word for it; if you have enough empty space in */var* to write the contents of your physical memory, that will help should you ever start having serious system trouble.

/usr

The */usr* partition holds the operating system programs, system source code, compilers and libraries, add-on software, and all the other little details that make the system actually do anything. Much of this changes only when you upgrade your system. It also holds users' home directories, which change regularly and rapidly. If you have many users, consider creating a separate */home* partition. While you can assign quotas to control disk space, a separate partition will protect your all-important OS files.

On a modern hard drive, I recommend using at least 6GB for */usr*. This provides enough room to run the operating system, store the main system source code, and build upgrades to the next version of FreeBSD. On a web server where users upload website files to their home directories, I suggest giving this partition the majority of your hard drive.

Other Partitions

Experienced system administrators always have their favorite partitions; also, some companies have standards on how systems should be partitioned. Different Unix vendors have attempted to impose their partitioning standards on the world. You'll see partitions like */opt* and */u1* on different Unix systems.

If you have a preferred partitioning scheme, use it. You can steer FreeBSD to install add-on software in a different partition if you like. Or, you can have users' home directories in */gerbil* if it makes you happy. The best advice I have to offer to readers whom I'll never meet and whose systems I will never log on to is this: You are the one who must live with your partitioning, so think first!

Multiple Hard Drives

If you have more than one hard drive of comparable quality, and you are not using them for RAID, you can still make excellent use of them: Put your data on one hard drive and the operating system on another. One of your partitions will contain the information that makes your server special. Database servers store their data in */var*, so put */var* on its own hard drive. If it's a web server, put */usr* on the second hard drive.

If you have a special function for this server, consider making a private partition just for that function. There's nothing wrong with creating a */home*, */www*, or */data* partition on the second hard drive and dedicating that entire drive to the system's primary purpose.

In general, segregating your operating system from your data increases system efficiency. Like all rules of thumb, this is debatable. But no system administrator will tell you that this is an actively bad idea.

With multiple hard drives, you can improve the efficiency of your swap space by splitting it amongst the drives. Put the first swap partition on the second slot of the drive with your root partition, and the other swap partitions on the first slots of the other drives. This splits reads and writes among multiple disk controllers and thus gives you some redundancy at the controller level. Remember, however, that a crash dump must fit entirely within a single swap partition.

For swap splitting to work best, however, the drives must be SAS or SCSI. If you have IDE or SATA drives, they must be on different IDE controllers for best results. Remember that each IDE controller splits its total data throughput among all the hard drives connected to it. If you have two hard drives on the same IDE controller and you're accessing both drives simultaneously, each disk works, on average, only half as fast as it would work alone on the same channel. The major bottleneck in using swap space is disk speed, and you won't gain anything by creating contention on your IDE bus.

Another option is to gain some resiliency by implementing a software-based RAID. This provides protection against a hard drive failure by sharing and mirroring the data amongst multiple hard drives. We discuss FreeBSD's RAID features in Chapter 18. Your slices on each drive must be of identical size to use software RAID. This is easiest to accomplish if all your drives are the same size, but that's not strictly necessary.

Partition Block Size

This section describes options that can really impair system performance. If you're new to FreeBSD, read this section *only* for your information—don't actually try it! This is for experienced Unix administrators who know *exactly* what they're doing, or at least know enough to be leery of the whole topic.

Block size refers to the size of the filesystem building blocks used to store files. Each block can be divided into fragments. FreeBSD defaults to 16KB block sizes (16,384 bytes) and 2KB (2,048 bytes) fragments. Files use a combination of fragments and blocks. For example, a 15KB file would be assigned to one block, while a 17KB file would be assigned to one block and one fragment. We'll discuss blocks and fragments in Chapter 18.

If you know exactly what you're doing, and you want to change the block size, you can do that in the installer. Be warned that FreeBSD behaves optimally if each block contains eight fragments; you can choose ratios other than 1:8 but only at a performance cost.

Choosing Your Distribution(s)

A *distribution* is a particular subset of FreeBSD. You'll choose one or more distributions during the installation process. While you can add pieces later, it's best and easiest just to make the right choice in the beginning. The installer offers nine distribution sets:

All   This contains absolutely everything that is considered part of FreeBSD, including the X Window System. (FreeBSD uses the X.org implentation of X.) If this is a test machine, definitely choose this option.

Developer   This includes everything except the games and X.

X-Developer   This includes everything except the games.

Kern-Developer   This includes the FreeBSD programs and documentation, but only the kernel source code.

X-Kern-Developer   This is the Kern-Developer distribution plus the X Window System.

User   This includes the FreeBSD operating system programs and documentation only—no source code, no X.

X-User   This is the User distribution plus X.

Minimal   This contains only the core FreeBSD programs, without documentation or source code of any sort. This is a good choice if your disk is really, really small.

Custom   Define your own distribution set.

If you're installing a test machine to learn FreeBSD on, definitely choose All. An Internet server is probably best served by the User distribution, or perhaps X-User if you're already familiar with the X Window System. Power users might want the Custom distribution.

Games?

Yes, FreeBSD includes very simple games. These are small, text-based games that were typical on systems of 20 years ago. New users will find the FreeBSD tips provided by fortune(6) useful, but if you want to play modern games look in */usr/ports/games* and read Chapter 11.

X WINDOW SYSTEM

The X Window System is the standard graphic interface for Unix-like operating systems. If you expect to sit at the console of your machine on a regular basis and do day-to-day work, you probably want the X Window System. If you don't expect to be using this system to browse the Web or perform other graphics-oriented tasks, you probably don't need the X Window System. You can always add the X Window System later.

The FreeBSD FTP Site

Just as the main source of information about FreeBSD is the FreeBSD website, the main source of FreeBSD itself is the FreeBSD FTP server. You can purchase CDs of FreeBSD, and while they're a decent investment, many people prefer to just use the Internet to grab what they need. Even if you have a CD, you'll interact with the FTP servers eventually.

The primary FreeBSD FTP server is *ftp.freebsd.org*, but many servers mirror it to reduce the load on the primary server and provide speedy, reliable access. You'll find a comprehensive list of FreeBSD FTP servers at *http://www.freebsd.org*, although you can also pick mirrors easily enough without the list. Every mirror server has a name following this pattern:

```
ftp<number>.<country>.freebsd.org
```

The country code is optional; if there's no country code, it's usually assumed to be in the continental United States. For example, we have *ftp14.freebsd.org*, *ftp2.uk.freebsd.org*, *ftp5.ru.freebsd.org*, and so on.

As a rule, the FTP mirrors with lower numbers are more heavily loaded than those with higher numbers. Try a site around *ftp12.freebsd.org*, or some high-numbered server under your country code, to see if you can get a speedy connection.

FTP Server Content

Many FreeBSD mirrors also mirror other software, but all FreeBSD content can be found under */pub/FreeBSD*. While the contents of the FTP server vary over time, let's take a look at the important files found there:

```
CERT
ERRATA
ISO-IMAGES-amd64
ISO-IMAGES-i386
ISO-IMAGES-ia64
ISO-IMAGES-pc98
ISO-IMAGES-ppc
ISO-IMAGES-sparc64
README.TXT
distfiles
doc
ports
releases
snapshots
tools
torrents
```

Lot of stuff, isn't it? Fortunately, you don't have to dig through all this to get everything you need to install, but a few directories merit particular attention:

CERT   This directory contains all FreeBSD security advisories since the project's inception. We'll discuss security advisories in Chapter 7.

ERRATA   This directory contains all errata for different releases of FreeBSD. We'll discuss errata in Chapter 13.

ISO-IMAGES   All of the directories that begin with *ISO-IMAGES* contain CD disc images for different architectures of FreeBSD. For example, ISO-IMAGES-i386 contains ISO images for installing FreeBSD on the i386 architecture. You can burn these images to CD to perform a CD install. (See your CD recorder documentation for help in doing so.)

README.TXT   These are the various subdirectories on the FTP site and their contents. You might want to consult this file for the changes since this book was written.

distfiles   This directory contains quite a few source code and binary files for the many third-party applications that run on FreeBSD. This is definitely the largest directory on the FreeBSD.org FTP server; don't just download everything here or your hard drive might burst.

doc   This directory contains the latest set of FreeBSD documentation, subdivided by language. If you're reading this book in English, you probably want the en (English) subdirectory. You'll find all the articles and books there in a variety of formats, compressed for easy downloading.

ports   Within this directory you'll find all the infrastructure and packages for the ports system. We'll discuss ports in Chapter 11.

releases   This directory contains the most recent versions of FreeBSD released along each development track. Older versions can be found on the server *ftp-archive.freebsd.org*. We'll discuss development tracks in Chapter 13.

snapshots   This directory contains recent versions of FreeBSD-current and FreeBSD-stable. This is where you'll find the latest testing release of the bleeding-edge and production versions of FreeBSD.

tools   Here you'll find various Windows programs that can be used to prepare a multiboot system to run FreeBSD.

torrents   BitTorrent users will find this directory useful; it contains torrent seeds for the most recent release(s) of FreeBSD. (If you don't use BitTorrent yet, you should check it out.)

Now that you know how to find everything you'll need, let's go on to the install process itself.

The Install Process

One of the more interesting[3] parts of a new operating system is figuring out how to get the OS running on your computer in the first place. On many modern systems it's pretty straightforward: throw the CD into the system and boot from it. However, FreeBSD can be used on systems so old that they don't support booting from CD. That's no problem; you can boot just as well from floppy disk. FreeBSD can also be used on systems so new that they don't have either floppy or CD drives. What then?

Any OS installation process has three parts: booting the installer program, accessing the installation media, and copying the software onto the hard drive. Even a Windows installer boots a "mini-Windows" to install Windows proper. FreeBSD provides options for each of these stages. Once your computer is booted and you have a usable installation media, running through the program to install the software to disk is straightforward.

Choosing Boot Media

If you have a system that boots from CD, this is probably the easiest way to go. You can get FreeBSD CDs from a variety of vendors or from the FTP site. Make sure that your computer's BIOS is set to boot from CD before the hard disk and reboot your computer with the FreeBSD disc in the CD drive. If you need help with configuring your computer's BIOS, check the manufacturer's documentation.

If your computer cannot boot from CD but can boot from floppy disk, download floppy disk images from the Internet and boot from those. Many older computers have CD drives that will not work as boot devices, but once the system is running you can use them for installation media.

Some modern computers have neither a floppy disk nor a CD drive. This is often the case with small rackmount servers, where space is expensive. With such a system, you can either install a CD drive or use PXE installation, as discussed in Chapter 20. (PXE installation requires bootstrapping from an existing FreeBSD machine, however.)

---

[3] The ancient Chinese curse "May you live in interesting times" certainly applies here.

NO REMOVABLE-MEDIA DRIVES?

If your soon-to-be-FreeBSD machine lacks both a CD drive and a floppy, doesn't have the power cables or physical space to install a CD drive, cannot boot off a USB device for whatever reason, and you don't yet have the knowledge to set up a PXE installer (this is a lot of "ifs," but a whole slew of older small rackmount servers fit this description), don't despair. You *can* get a CD drive on your computer for the install.

The safest thing to do is remove your hard drive and install it on a system with a removable-media drive. Unlike some other operating systems, FreeBSD will let you install on one machine and run on another.

If that's not an option, here's a trick I've used more than once. (It might electrocute the hardware or yourself, and will certainly invalidate your warranty. The author is not responsible for barbecued hardware or system administrators!)

Find an old computer running any operating system with an IDE CD drive. Put the old machine next to your FreeBSD box, unplug it, and open the case. Open the case of your FreeBSD machine. On the old computer, detach the CD drive's IDE cable at the controller end. Leave the power attached to the CD drive. Attach the dangling IDE cable from the old machine to an open port on your FreeBSD system's IDE controller. Turn on the old computer; the CD will power up even though it's not attached to the old computer's IDE controller. Now turn on the new computer, and it will pick up the CD as an attached device.

After the install, put everything back just the way you found it, and nobody will ever know.

Choosing Installation Media

The two most common sources of installation media are CD and FTP.

CDs are great when you have many machines to install and these machines have CD drives. They're fast and easy, and work even if the network is down. A variety of vendors produce FreeBSD CDs and DVDs. iX Systems, in particular, has supported FreeBSD for many years, and recently purchased FreeBSD Mall, the original producer of FreeBSD CDs. The DVD sets have far more content, including many files that can be downloaded separately from the Internet, but the CD sets have everything you truly need. From now on I'm going to only mention CDs, but everything that applies to a CD is also true of a DVD. If you don't want to purchase a CD, you can fetch an ISO image from the FreeBSD FTP server and burn it to CD yourself.

Several dozen FTP servers carry FreeBSD ISO images, installation media, and related materials. The FreeBSD installer can FTP the software directly from these servers. To use the FTP installation method, however, you must have a working Internet connection, and the installation speed will be largely dependent upon the network between you and your chosen FTP server. There is also a chance that an intruder has hacked into the FTP server and uploaded a bad version of FreeBSD for the unsuspecting public, but the

FreeBSD team watches carefully for such events and deals with them swiftly. The FreeBSD release team also provides cryptographic checksums for every release in the release announcement, which you can use to verify releases.

Preparing Boot Floppies

You will need several floppy disks (four as of this writing, but possibly more in the future). Find the release directory for the architecture and version you want to install. You'll find a floppies subdirectory there. For example, for an i386 system and FreeBSD release 7.0, look in *ftp://ftp.freebsd.org/pub/freebsd/ releases/i386/7.0-RELEASE/floppies.* (You'll also find this directory in the root directory of a FreeBSD CD.) You'll find several files with the *.flp* extension, one named *boot.flp* and several numbered *kernX.flp* files, such as *kern1.flp* and *kern2.flp.* These files are floppy disk images. Download them all.

You need to put these images onto floppy disks. The catch is, you cannot use basic file-level copying, such as drag-and-drop in Windows. An image file must be copied onto the disk in a particular way.

If you're already running a Unix-like system, the dd(1) command does everything you need. You'll need to know your floppy drive's device name, which is probably */dev/fd0, /dev/floppy,* or */dev/rfd0.* If the device name is */dev/fd0,* as it is on BSD systems, you'd enter

```
# dd if=kern1.flp of=/dev/fd0
```

to write the *kern1.flp* image to the floppy disk. Copy each disk image to a separate floppy disk.

If you're running Microsoft Windows, you'll need a special utility to copy disk images. Microsoft doesn't provide one, but FreeBSD does, and you'll find it in the tools subdirectory of the main site. It's called *fdimage.exe.*

This is a free Windows program to copy disk images, and it's quite easy to use. It takes only two arguments: the name of the image file and the name of the drive the disk is in. For example, to copy the image *boot.flp* to the floppy in your a: drive, open a DOS prompt and enter the following:

```
c:> fdimage boot.flp a:
```

Once the floppy drive finishes churning (which may take a while), repeat the process for all other disk images you have downloaded.

Preparing Boot CDs

If you've purchased an official FreeBSD CD, your install media is ready. If not, you need to choose an ISO image from the FTP site and burn it. The first step is to find your image directory. Go to the FTP site and choose the ISO image for your architecture. In that directory you'll find a directory for each current release. For example, ISO images for FreeBSD 7.0 for i386 can be found at *ftp://ftp.freebsd.org/pub/freebsd/ISO-IMAGES-i386/7.0*. You'll find multiple images there.

The name of an ISO image is composed of the release number, the label RELEASE, the architecture, and a comment, all separated by hyphens. For example, these are the names of the ISO images available for 7.0:

```
7.0-RELEASE-i386-bootonly.iso
7.0-RELEASE-i386-disc1.iso
7.0-RELEASE-i386-disc2.iso
```

The image labeled *disc1* contains the entire FreeBSD distribution, the X Window System, a few basic packages, and a *live filesystem* that can be used to perform repairs when your server goes bad.

The image labeled *disc2* contains the most popular pieces of software for FreeBSD precompiled and ready for use with this release.

The *bootonly* image boots the FreeBSD installer so that you can do an FTP install. Many people ask, "If you already have a CD drive, why would you want to do an FTP install?" The standard FreeBSD ISO image contains a lot of stuff. If you're not installing the full distribution, you won't need a lot of it. Not everyone has unlimited, unmetered bandwidth on tap.[4]

Once you've chosen your image, burn it to CD. CD burning methods vary widely among operating systems; even within the Unix-like world, different operating systems have chosen different ways to burn CDs. On Windows, many CD burning programs are available, such as Nero and Stomp. Here's how you would burn an image to disc on a FreeBSD system with a standard IDE CD burner:

```
# burncd -f /dev/acd0 data imagename fixate
```

Check your operating system's instructions on burning an image file to physical media. Be sure to burn this file as an image, not as a regular file. One clear hint that you're doing it wrong is if your burning software complains that the file won't fit on a single CD. The image file will overflow a single CD if you're burning it as a regular file, but not if you burn it as an image.

FTP Media Setup

If you're installing from CD, the install media is ready—it's the same disk you're booting from. But to do an FTP install, you must choose an FTP server and understand how to connect your machine to the local network.

Choosing an FTP server is half guesswork. Find the list of FTP mirror sites and start pinging them. You're looking for an FTP server with low ping times—that's a good sign that it's fairly accessible from your location. Once you have a couple of candidates, FTP to them from your desktop machine.

---

[4] And those of us who do have it must learn to refrain from taunting those of you who don't.

See how responsive they are. Pick one that feels snappy, and make sure that it has the release you want to install. Take note of the FTP server's name for use in the install process.

If your local network uses Dynamic Host Configuration Protocol (DHCP) to assign IP addresses and other network information, you're ready to go. Otherwise, if your network administrators assign IP addresses by hand, get the following information from them:

- IP address for your FreeBSD system
- Netmask for your FreeBSD system
- IP addresses of nameservers for your network
- IP address of your default gateway
- Proxy server information (if necessary)

Without this information—and without DHCP—you will be unable to connect to a network to perform an FTP install.

Actually Installing FreeBSD

Now that you've made all the decisions about how you're going to install FreeBSD, all that remains is the grunt work of walking through the installer. Put your boot media in the drive and power up the computer. You'll see a series of startup screens and system debugging information, which we cover in Chapter 3.

The first menu you see will offer you a chance to choose your keyboard layout. This includes a list of all the keyboard maps supported by FreeBSD. Note that this does not affect the language of the installer, merely the keyboard layout.

FreeBSD next presents you with the first installation screen (Figure 2-1).

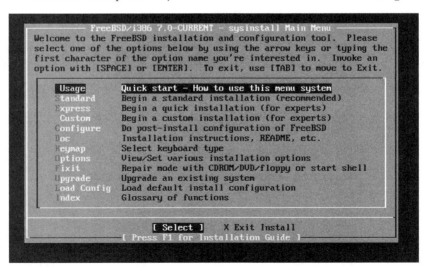

Figure 2-1: The main sysinstall screen

This is sysinstall(8), the notoriously ugly FreeBSD installer. While other operating systems have pretty graphical installers with mouse-driven menus and multicolor pie charts, FreeBSD's looks like an old DOS program. While replacements have been promised time and time again, as I write this it looks like sysinstall will be with us for the foreseeable future.

Use the spacebar to select options from sysinstall menus, not the ENTER key.

Use the arrow keys to go down to the **Standard** installation, and press ENTER. You'll see the fdisk warning with some simple instructions (Figure 2-2).

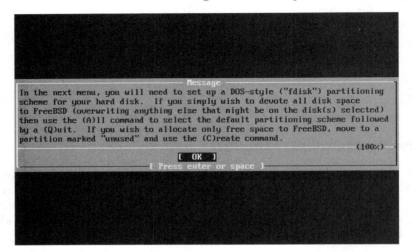

Figure 2-2: The fdisk instructions

Skim the instructions to be sure they haven't changed since this was printed, and then press ENTER.

If you have multiple hard drives, FreeBSD will let you choose which drive you want to install on. Press the spacebar to select a drive (Figure 2-3).

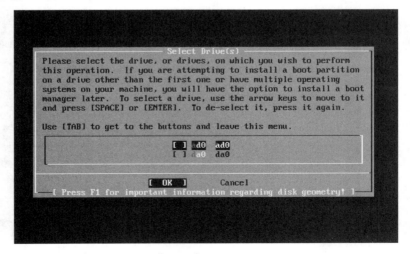

Figure 2-3: Selecting an installation drive

Some hard drives will flash up a scary-looking warning about disk geometry at this point. It is not a concern on most modern hardware. We will talk about disk geometry in Chapters 8 and 18; you can look there if you're interested. Just press ENTER to continue to the fdisk screen (Figure 2-4).

```
Disk name:      ad0                                     FDISK Partition Editor
DISK Geometry:  19457 cyls/255 heads/63 sectors = 312576705 sectors (152625MB)

Offset       Size(ST)        End     Name  PType       Desc  Subtype    Flags

        0   312581808   312581807       -     12      unused        0




The following commands are supported (in upper or lower case):

A = Use Entire Disk   G = set Drive Geometry   C = Create Slice   F = `DD' mode
D = Delete Slice      Z = Toggle Size Units    S = Set Bootable   | = Wizard m.
T = Change Type       U = Undo All Changes     W = Write Changes

Use F1 or ? to get more help, arrow keys to select.
```

Figure 2-4: The fdisk menu

Here you determine how much of your hard drive you want to use for FreeBSD. For a server, you want to use the entire hard drive. Press A to allocate the whole hard drive to FreeBSD, and then press Q to finish. The installer will drop you into the MBR selector, shown in Figure 2-5.

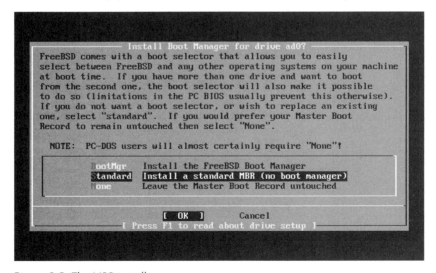

Figure 2-5: The MBR installer

Arrow down to **Standard**, then TAB to highlight **OK**. This installs a standard master boot record (MBR), which removes any existing boot manager that your computer could use if it booted any other operating system. (We're building Internet servers and won't be sharing the hard drive with, say, Windows Vista.) Press ENTER to proceed.

If you have multiple hard drives, the installer will return you to the hard drive selection screen. Choose your next hard drive, or use the TAB key to take you down to the **OK** button and proceed to the next step of the install; sysinstall then displays instructions for using the partitioning tool (Figure 2-6).

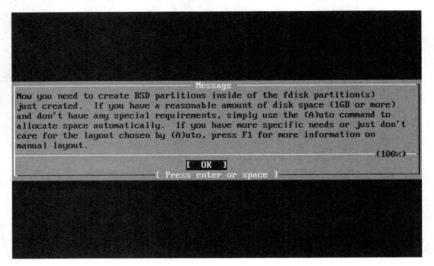

Figure 2-6: Partitioning instructions

Read the instructions to be sure they haven't changed since this was printed, then press ENTER to continue.

You should now have the partitioning menu. We talked about partitioning earlier in this chapter, and you should have already made your decisions on how to partition your drive. This is where you implement your choices (Figure 2-7).

To take FreeBSD's default, generic partition recommendations, press A. Otherwise, press C to create a partition. You'll get a box asking for the size of your partition. Enter the desired partition size, using *M* for megabytes and *G* for gigabytes. The installer will then ask you if this is a filesystem or a swap space. If you say it's a partition, it will ask you for the partition mount point (*/*, */usr*, */var*, and so on).

When you have created all your partitions, press Q to exit the partition editor.

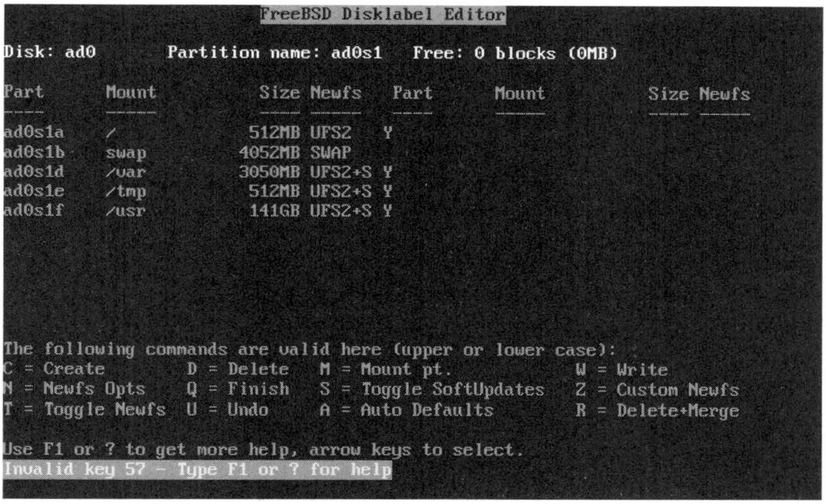

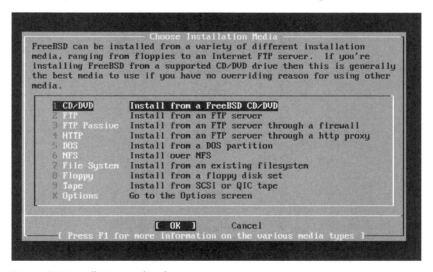

Figure 2-7: The partition editor

Now you'll be asked for an installation source (Figure 2-8).

Figure 2-8: Installation media choices

Arrow down to highlight your installation media, and press ENTER to select it. FreeBSD will either spin up your CD to confirm it's usable, ask you to select your FTP server, or ask you to configure whatever other installation media you've chosen. I recommend using either FTP or CD.

The next menu asks how much of FreeBSD you would like to install (Figure 2-9). While FreeBSD offers many stripped-down versions for limited hard drives, these days hard drives are much, much larger than FreeBSD. On a vaguely modern machine I recommend always installing everything, especially if you're just learning about FreeBSD. Arrow down to highlight **All** and use ENTER to select it.

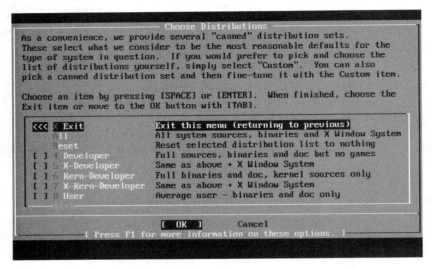

Figure 2-9: Choosing a distribution set

sysinstall then asks if you want to install the Ports Collection. You do, even though you don't know what it is yet. Select **Yes**.

You'll be brought back to the distribution selection menu. Arrow up to **Exit this menu** and press ENTER.

sysinstall offers you a last chance to change your mind before installing. Once you say **Yes, install**, sysinstall will format your hard drive, your CD drive will light up, and in a few minutes you'll have a FreeBSD install.

The installer will then ask several questions to set up basic system services for you.

Configuring the Network

The installer asks if you want to set up a network device. Say **Yes**.

You'll get a whole choice of network interfaces to configure (Figure 2-10). Yes, FreeBSD can run TCP/IP over FireWire! It can also run TCP/IP over a parallel port. Neither is terribly common, but it can be done. Look for an entry that looks like an Ethernet card and choose it. In Figure 2-10, we see an *Intel EtherExpress Pro/100B PCI Fast Ethernet* card that looks about right. Scroll down and press ENTER to configure it.

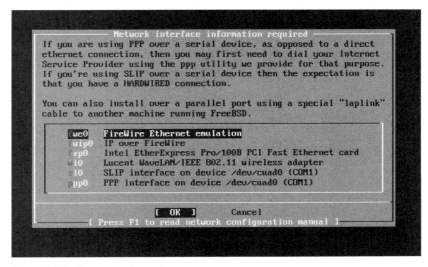

Figure 2-10: The network interfaces menu

You'll be asked if you want to try IPv6 configuration of this interface. You probably don't. You'll then be asked if you want to try DHCP configuration. As this is a server, you probably don't. This will take you to the Network Configuration screen shown in Figure 2-11.

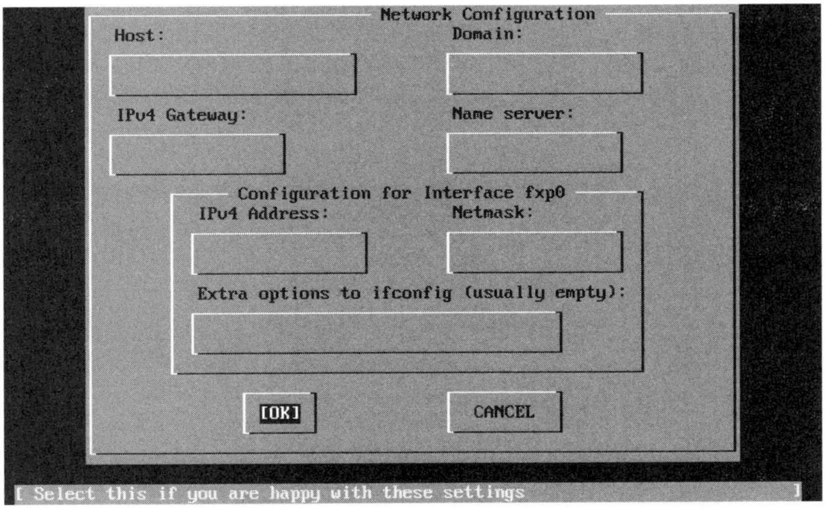

Figure 2-11: Network configuration

Here you fill in your hostname and domain name, as well as the network information you got from your network administrator.

Even if you use DHCP configuration, you must still set a host and a domain. Otherwise, your system will boot calling itself *Amnesiac*. (You can use a DHCP server to set a hostname, but that's an advanced topic most environments aren't equipped to provide.)

Miscellaneous Network Services

The installer then asks you several questions related to the system function. Unless you are an experienced system administrator, you don't want most of these functions to start. We will enable some of them as we proceed through the book. Once you understand the systems described, you can enable them for later installs.

For example, the installer asks if this is a network gateway, or if you want to configure inetd. Answer **No** to both. When asked if you want to enable SSH login, say **Yes**—that is a secure, safe service required on almost all systems. Do not enable the anonymous FTP server, the NFS server, the NFS client, or customize syscons at this time.

Time Zone

The installer prompts you to set your time zone. You'll be asked if the system clock is set to UTC: Answer **No** and walk through the screens presented. You'll be asked to choose a continent, a country, and then a time zone.

Linux Mode

Now the installer will ask you if you want to enable Linux mode. I suggest you answer **No** at this point. If you need Linux mode, we'll learn how to activate it in Chapter 12.

PS/2 Mouse

USB mice work automatically, but PS/2 and older mice need special setup. The installer will offer to set up a PS/2 mouse for you. If you have a standard two- or three-button PS/2 mouse plugged in, answer **Yes** and choose **Enable** from the menu. You should see a mouse pointer on your screen, and it should wiggle when you move it.

sysinstall will ask if your mouse is working. If the mouse pointer wiggles when you move the mouse, you can answer **Yes**. In all honesty, I haven't had a PS/2 mouse fail on me in the last 10 years. Older types of mice can be difficult, but are increasingly uncommon.

Adding Packages

The installer asks if you want to install any additional software packages. If you're an experienced system administrator, you probably know what software you want to install. You probably have a favorite shell, and it's probably not installed on FreeBSD by default.

FreeBSD divides software packages into categories. Find the category that you think should include your desired software, and select the category to bring up a list of all the software on your install media in that category. Find the software you want, and press the spacebar to select it. For example, to install the popular Bash shell, scroll down to the Shells category, press ENTER, scroll down to Bash, and press the spacebar. Then press ENTER to go back to the Package Selection menu.

When you have chosen all the packages you want to install, return to the main Package Selection menu. Press TAB to move the cursor from OK to **Install**, then press ENTER. Your system will install the selected packages.

Adding Users

Whenever possible, you should do everything while signed on as a regular user and only use the root account when you must change the system. That will happen frequently at first, but will grow less common as time passes. Before you can sign on as a regular user, however, you must create a regular user account. The installer gives you a chance to create users during the installation process. Say **Yes** when asked and you'll see Figure 2-12.

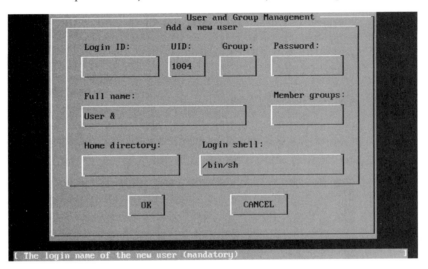

Figure 2-12: Adding a user

Your first selection in this screen should be the **Login ID**, or username. Your company might have a standard for usernames. I prefer the first and middle initial and full last name (not using the middle initial creates a surprising number of duplicates).

FreeBSD assigns the UID.

The FreeBSD default is to have the user in a group of the same name as the username; for example, the user mwlucas is automatically in the group mwlucas. Experienced system administrators can change this.

Full name is the user's full name. Other system users can see this name when they log in, so don't set it arbitrarily. I've seen new system administrators get in trouble when they give a customer a full name of, say, *Pain in the Tuckus.*

Member groups is just a list of other system groups this account is part of. If you want this user to be able to use the root password and become root, add the group wheel in the Member groups space. Only system administrators need to be in the wheel group.

The *Home directory* is where the users' files are kept. The default is generally fine.

Finally, choose a shell for your new user. Older admins and greybeards-in-training frequently prefer */bin/sh*. The examples in this book are written in the BSD standard shell */bin/tcsh*, which I find a very friendly shell. If you have a preferred choice, use it.

Select **OK** when you're done to create your user.

Root Password

Now the installer tells you to set your root password. If your machine doesn't have a root password, anyone can log in without using any password. As root has absolute control over your hardware and software, this would be bad. FreeBSD will ask you to enter your root password twice. Remember your root password, as recovering it is a bit of an annoyance. We talk about the root password and security in Chapter 7.

Post-Installation Setup

Finally, you're asked if you want to do any post-installation setup of your FreeBSD server. The FreeBSD Configuration Menu (Figure 2-13) provides an easy way to do basic initial setup on your computer.

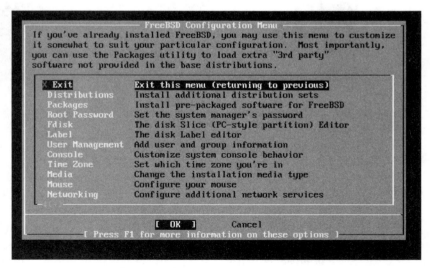

Figure 2-13: Post-installation configuration

In this menu you'll be able to enable or disable everything the installer asked during earlier parts of the install, as well as set all sorts of interesting network functions. If you have an NTP server on your network, for example, you can use the menus here to enable it on your FreeBSD machine. We will see how to enable all of these services later in this book, but if you already know what you're doing you can configure them here as well.

Restart!

Once you've finished your post-install configuration, go back to the main sysinstall menu and select **Exit**. Your computer will then reboot into a fully installed FreeBSD system, ready to perform all of the examples in this book.

If you want to use sysinstall(8) later to configure your system, you can run it at any time. By the end of this book, you'll learn how to do everything that sysinstall can do quicker and more flexibly at the command line.

Now let's see what actually happened at that reboot.

3

START ME UP!
THE BOOT PROCESS

While FreeBSD will boot easily and automatically when you turn on the power, understanding exactly what happens at each stage will make you a better system administrator. Intervention during the boot process is rarely necessary, but one day you'll be glad you know how to do it. And once you're comfortable with adjusting the boot process, you'll find you can solve problems you've previously accepted and endured.

We'll start by discussing how the system loader starts, then look at some interesting changes you can make and the information you can gather from the boot loader's command line, including booting alternate kernels and starting in single-user mode. We'll cover serial consoles, a standard system management tool. The FreeBSD multi-user startup process is responsible for starting all the various services that make your computer useful, and we'll give attention to that as well. In addition, we'll cover the information FreeBSD records about the boot process and how FreeBSD turns itself off without corrupting data.

The boot process itself can be divided into three main parts: the loader, single-user startup, and multi-user startup.

Power-On and the Loader

Every i386 computer has a Basic Input/Output System (BIOS) with just enough brains to look for an operating system somewhere on a disk. (Other hardware platforms have console firmware or bootroms that perform the same function.) If the BIOS finds an operating system on a disk, it hands control of the computer to that operating system. If the BIOS doesn't find an operating system, it complains and gives up. Most BIOSes are rather dumb and can only recognize operating systems by very simple indicators. The *boot blocks* are sections of the disk that are specifically designed to be recognized as an operating system by the BIOS. On those boot blocks, FreeBSD installs software that is only smart enough to load the main FreeBSD startup program, loader(8). The loader presents you with a FreeBSD logo on the right and a menu of seven options on the left. These are the options:

1. Boot FreeBSD [default]
2. Boot FreeBSD with ACPI disabled
3. Boot FreeBSD in safe mode
4. Boot FreeBSD in single-user mode
5. Boot FreeBSD with verbose logging
6. Escape to loader prompt
7. Reboot

If you wait 10 seconds, the loader will automatically boot FreeBSD by default. Several other options are only needed for debugging or trouble-shooting. While you don't have to memorize all these options, you should be comfortable with using the basic ones when required.

Boot FreeBSD with ACPI disabled

ACPI is the Advanced Configuration and Power Interface, an Intel/Toshiba/Microsoft standard for configuring hardware. It replaces the legacy standards APM (Advanced Power Management[1]), PnPBIOS, the MP table, the $PIR table, and a whole bunch of other standards even

---

[1] The lesson here is: Never name anything *advanced*. One day, it won't be.

more obscure. We discuss ACPI in Chapter 5. ACPI provides many benefits to modern hardware, but some hardware has troublesome ACPI implementations. On the other hand, much new SMP hardware absolutely requires ACPI.

If your newly installed system will not boot normally, try booting it with ACPI disabled. If your system has worked well for some time, but suddenly has trouble booting, disabling ACPI probably won't help.

Boot FreeBSD in safe mode

FreeBSD's *safe mode* turns on just about every conservative option in the operating system. ATA hard disks run without DMA or write caching, limiting their speed but increasing their reliability by working around cabling issues and other physical problems. EISA slots are not probed, and ACPI is disabled. On i386 systems, SMP is disabled. USB keyboards will no longer work in single-user mode. This option is useful for disaster recovery and debugging older or otherwise troublesome hardware.

Boot FreeBSD in single-user mode

Single-user mode is a minimal startup mode that is very useful on damaged systems, even when the damage was self-inflicted. It's the earliest point where FreeBSD can provide a command prompt, and is important enough to have its own section later in this chapter.

Boot FreeBSD with verbose logging

FreeBSD learns a lot about a computer as it boots. Much of this information is irrelevant to day-to-day use, but very helpful when debugging. When you boot in verbose mode, FreeBSD prints all the details it can about every system setting and attached device. (This information will be available afterwards in */var/run/dmesg.boot*, as discussed later in this chapter.) You might try verbose mode once on each of your machines, just to glimpse the complexity within your computers.

Escape to loader prompt

The loader includes a command-line interpreter, where you can issue commands to tweak your system to boot exactly the way you need. We'll cover this in detail in "The Loader Prompt" on page 66.

Reboot

Once more, this time with feeling! Of these options, the most important are single-user mode and the loader prompt.

Single-User Mode

FreeBSD can perform a minimal boot, called *single-user mode*, that loads the kernel and finds devices but doesn't automatically set up your filesystems, start the network, enable security, or run any standard Unix services. Single-user mode is the first point at which the system can possibly give you a command prompt, however, and you can perform any or all of those non-automated activities yourself.

When you choose a single-user mode boot, you'll see the regular system startup messages flow past. Before any programs start, however, the kernel offers you a chance to choose a shell. You can enter any shell on the root partition; I usually just take the default of */bin/sh*, but use */bin/tcsh* if you prefer.

Disks in Single-User Mode

In single-user mode, the root partition is mounted read-only and no other disks are mounted. (We'll discuss disks and filesystems in Chapter 8, but for now just follow along.)

Many of the programs that you'll want to use are on partitions other than the root, so you'll want them all mounted read-write and available. To make sure that your filesystems are in a usable state, run the following commands:

```
# fsck -p
# mount -a
```

The fsck(8) program "cleans" the filesystems, confirms that they are internally consistent and that all the files that a disk thinks it has are actually present and accounted for. Make the filesystems accessible with mount(8).

The -a flag mounts every filesystem listed in */etc/fstab* (see Chapter 8), but if one of these filesystems is causing your problems, you can mount the desired filesystems individually by specifying them on the command line (for example, mount /usr). If you're an advanced user with NFS filesystems configured (see Chapter 8), you'll see error messages for those filesystems at this point because the network isn't up yet.

If you have trouble mounting partitions by name, try using the device name instead. The device name for the root partition is probably either */dev/ad0s1a* (for IDE disks) or */dev/da0s1a* (for SCSI disks). You'll also need to specify a mount point for this partition. For example, to mount your first IDE disk partition as root, enter the command:

```
# mount /dev/ad0s1a /
```

If you have network filesystems on your server but your network is not yet up, you can mount all your local partitions by specifying the filesystem type. Here, we mount all of the local filesystems of type UFS, FreeBSD's default filesystem type:

```
# mount -a -t ufs
```

Programs Available in Single-User Mode

The commands available for your use depend on which partitions are mounted. Some basic commands are available in */bin* and */sbin*, on the root partition, and are available even if root is mounted read-only. Others live in

/usr and are inaccessible until you mount that partition. (Take a look at */bin* and */sbin* on your system to get an idea of what you'll have to work with when things go bad.)

NOTE   *If you've scrambled your shared library system (see Chapter 12), none of these programs will work. If you're that unlucky, FreeBSD provides statically-linked versions of many core utilities in the /rescue directory.*

The Network in Single-User Mode

If you want to have network connectivity in single-user mode, use the shell script */etc/netstart*. This script calls the appropriate scripts to start the network, gives IP addresses to interfaces, and enables packet filtering and routing. If you want some, but not all, of these services, you'll need to read that shell script and execute the appropriate commands manually.

Uses for Single-User Mode

In single-user mode, your access to the system is only limited by your knowledge of FreeBSD and Unix.

For example, if you've forgotten your root password you can reset it from single-user mode:

```
# passwd
Changing local password for root
New Password:
Retype New Password:
#
```

NOTE   *Note that you weren't asked for the old root password. In single-user mode, you're auto-matically root, and passwd(8) doesn't ask root for any password.*

Or, if you find that there's a typo in */etc/fstab* that confuses the system and makes it unbootable, you can mount the root partition with the device name, then edit */etc/fstab* to resolve the issue.

Or, if you have a program that panics the system on boot and you need to stop that program from starting again, you can either edit */etc/rc.conf* to disable the program, or just set the permissions on the startup script so that it cannot execute.

```
# chmod 444 /usr/local/etc/rc.d/program.sh
```

We'll discuss third-party programs (ports and packages) in Chapter 11.

NOTE   *There's a reason all of these examples involve recovering from human errors. Hardware failures are not common, and FreeBSD failures even less so. If it wasn't for human error, our computers would almost never let us down. As you learn more about FreeBSD, you'll be more and more capable in single-user mode.*

We'll refer to single-user mode throughout this book, but for now, let's look at the loader prompt.

The Loader Prompt

The loader prompt is a small computing environment that allows you to make basic changes to your computer's boot environment and the variables that must be configured early in the boot process. When you escape to a loader prompt (option 6 in the boot menu), you'll see the following:

```
OK
```

This is the loader prompt. While the word *OK* might be friendly and reassuring, it's one of the few friendly things about the loader environment. This is not a full-featured operating system; it's a tool for configuring a system boot which is not intended for the ignorant nor the faint of heart. Any changes you make at the loader prompt only affect the current boot. To undo changes, reboot again. (We'll see how to make loader changes permanent in the next section.)

To see all the commands available to the loader, enter a question mark.

```
OK ?
Available commands:
  heap             show heap usage
  reboot           reboot the system
  bcachestat       get disk block cache stats
...
```

The first three commands in the loader, listed above, are pretty much useless to anyone except a developer. Instead, we'll focus on the commands useful to a system administrator.

To view the disks that the loader knows about, use lsdev.

```
OK lsdev
❶ cd devices:
disk devices:
    disk0:    ❷BIOS drive C:
      ❸disk0s1a: FFS
       disk0s1b: swap
       disk0s1d: FFS
       disk0s1e: FFS
       disk0s1f: FFS
    disk1:    ❹BIOS drive D:
       disk1s1a: FFS
       disk1s1b: swap
pxe devices:
```

The loader checks for CD drives ❶ and doesn't find any. (The loader will only find CD drives if you boot from a CD, so don't be alarmed at this.) It finds two hard drives, known to the BIOS as drives C ❷ and D ❹. It then describes the partitions it finds on these hard drives. As we'll see in Chapter 8, the root partition generally ends in *a*. This means that the only root partition here is shown as disk0s1a ❸. On an unfamiliar system that's having trouble booting, you might find this knowledge useful.

The loader has variables set within the kernel and by a configuration file. View these variables and their settings with the show command.

```
OK show
LINES=24
acpi_load=YES
autoboot_delay=NO
...
```

The spacebar advances to the next page. These values include IRQ and memory addresses for old ISA cards, low-level kernel tunables, and information gleaned from the BIOS. We'll see a partial list of loader variables in "Loader Configuration" on page 69, and additional values will be brought up throughout the book in the appropriate sections.

You can change these values for a single boot with the set command. For example, to change the value console to comconsole, you would enter:

```
OK set console=comconsole
```

By the time the loader gives you a command prompt, it has already loaded the system kernel into memory. The kernel is the heart of FreeBSD and is detailed in Chapter 5. If you've never worked with a kernel before, just file these tidbits away until you get to that chapter. Use the lsmod command to view the kernel and kernel modules currently in memory.

```
OK lsmod
 0x400000: ❶/boot/kernel/kernel (elf kernel, 0x6a978c)
   ❷modules: ❸elink.1 io.1 splash.1 agp.1 nfsserver.1 nfslock.1 nfs.1 nfs4.1
wlan.1 if_gif.1 if_faith.1 ether.1 sysvshm.1 sysvsem.1 sysvmsg.1 cd9660.1
isa.1 pseudofs.1 procfs.1 msdosfs.1 usb.1 cdce.0 random.1 ppbus.1 pci.1
pccard.1 null.1 mpt_raid.1 mpt.1 mpt_cam.1 mpt_core.1 miibus.1 mem.1 isp.1
sbp.1 fwe.1 firewire.1 exca.1 cardbus.1 ast.1 afd.1 acd.1 ataraid.1 atapci.1
ad.1 ata.1 ahc.1 ahd.1 ahd_pci.1 ahc_pci.1 ahc_isa.1 ahc_eisa.1 scsi_low.1
❹cam.1
 0xaaa000: ❺/boot/kernel/snd_via8233.ko (elf module, 0x6228)
   modules: snd_via8233.1
 0xab1000: ❻/boot/kernel/sound.ko (elf module, 0x23898)
   modules: sound.1
 0xad5000: ❼/boot/kernel/atapicam.ko (elf module, 0x4bac)
   modules: atapicam.1
```

While some of this information is of value only to developers, a system administrator can still learn a lot. Perhaps the most obviously useful information is the path to the loaded kernel ❶. This should always be */boot/kernel/kernel* unless you configured the loader to look elsewhere.

You'll also get a list of the modules included in each loaded kernel file ➋. The example lists modules from the main kernel itself, ranging from elink ➌ to cam ➍. The loader has also pulled in the files *snd_via8233* ➎, *sound* ➏, and *atapicam* ➐, with their respective modules.

To completely erase the loaded kernel and all modules from memory, use the unload command.

```
OK unload
```

You won't get any confirmation, but a subsequent lsmod will show that the loader no longer remembers any kernel files.

To load a different kernel, use load.

```
OK load boot/kernel.good/kernel
boot/kernel.good/kernel text=0x4a6324 data=0x84020+0x9908c
syms=[0x4+0x67220+0x4+0x7e178]
```

The loader will respond with the name of the file and some low-level information about it.

While I touch on loading alternate kernels here, before doing this you really need to understand why you would want to and how to do it safely. Go read the discussion on "Booting an Alternate Kernel" on page 137.

Once your system boots just the way you need it to, you'll probably want to make those settings permanent. FreeBSD lets you do this through the loader configuration file, */boot/loader.conf*. Before you can make changes, however, you must understand FreeBSD's default configuration filesystem.

Default Files

FreeBSD separates configuration files into default files and customization files. The *default files* contain variable assignments and are not intended to be edited; instead, they're designed to be overridden by another file of the same name. Default configurations are kept in a directory called default.

For example, the boot loader configuration file is */boot/loader.conf*, and the default configuration file is */boot/defaults/loader.conf*. If you want to see a comprehensive list of loader variables, check the default configuration file.

During upgrades, the installer replaces the default configuration files but does not touch your local configuration files. This separation ensures that your local changes remain intact while still allowing new values to be added to the system. FreeBSD adds features with every release, and its developers go to great lengths to ensure that changes to these files are backward compatible. This means that you won't have to go through the upgraded configuration and manually merge in your changes; at most you'll have to check out the new defaults file for nifty configuration opportunities and new system features.

The loader configuration file is a good example of these files. The */boot/defaults/loader.conf* file contains dozens of entries much like this:

```
verbose_loading="NO"                     # Set to YES for verbose loader output
```

The variable verbose_loading defaults to NO. To change this setting, do not edit */boot/defaults/loader.conf*—instead, add the line to */boot/loader.conf* and change it there. Your */boot/loader.conf* entries override the default setting, and your local configuration contains only your local changes. A sysadmin can easily see what changes have been made and how this system differs from the out-of-the-box configuration.

> ### DON'T COPY THE DEFAULT CONFIG!
>
> One common mistake is to copy the default configuration to the override file and then make changes there directly. Such copying will cause major problems in certain parts of the system. You might get away with it in one or two places, but eventually it will bite you. Copying */etc/defaults/rc.conf* to */etc/rc.conf*, for example, will prevent your system from booting. You have been warned.

The default configuration mechanism appears throughout FreeBSD, especially in the core system configuration.

Loader Configuration

To make loader setting changes permanent, use the configuration file */boot/loader.conf*. Settings in this file are fed directly into the boot loader at system startup. (Of course, if you enjoy being at your console every time the system boots, then you don't have to bother with this!)

If you look at the default loader configuration, you'll see many options that resemble variables listed in the loader. For example, here we can set the name of the console device:

```
console="vidconsole"
```

Throughout the FreeBSD documentation, you'll see references to *boot-time tunables* and *loader settings*. All of these are set in *loader.conf*. This includes many sysctl values that are read-only once the system is up and kicking. (For more on this, see Chapter 5. I present a list of popular kernel sysctls in Appendix A.) Here, we set the kernel variable kern.maxusers to 32.

```
kern.maxusers="32"
```

Some of these variables do not have a specific value set in *loader.conf*; instead, they appear as empty quotes. This means that the loader normally lets the kernel set this value, but if you want to override the kernel you can.

```
kern.nbuf=""
```

The kernel has an idea of what the value of `kern.nbuf` should be, but you can have the loader dictate a different value if you must.

We'll discuss system tuning via the boot loader in the appropriate section—for example, kernel values will be discussed in Chapter 5, where they will make something resembling sense—but here are some commonly used loader values that affect the appearance and operation of the loader itself and basic boot functionality. As FreeBSD matures, the developers introduce new loader values and alter the functionality of old ones, so be sure to check */boot/defaults/loader.conf* on your installation for the current list.

boot_verbose="NO"

This toggles the verbose boot mode that you can reach through the boot menu. In a standard boot, the kernel prints out a few basic notes about each device as it identifies system hardware. When you boot in verbose mode, the kernel tells each device driver to print out any and all information it can about each device as well as display assorted kernel-related setup details. This is useful for debugging and development, but not generally for day-to-day use.

autoboot_delay="10"

This is the number of seconds between the display of the boot menu and the automatic boot. I frequently turn this down to 2 or 3 seconds, as I want my machines to come up as quickly as possible.

beastie_disable="NO"

This controls the appearance of the boot menu (originally, an ASCII art image of the BSD "Beastie" mascot decorated the boot menu). If set to YES, the boot menu will not appear.

loader_logo="fbsdbw"

You can choose which logo appears to the right of the boot menu. The default "FreeBSD" in ASCII art is the `fbsdbw` option. Other options include `beastiebw` (the original logo), `beastie` (the logo in color), and `none` (to have the menu appear without any logo).

Serial Consoles

All this console stuff is nice, but it can be a problem when your FreeBSD system is in a co-location facility on the other side of the country or on another continent. A keyboard and monitor are nice, too, but in many data centers you won't have room for them. And how do you reset the machine remotely when it won't respond to the network? A serial console solves all these problems and more.

A serial console simply redirects the computer's keyboard input and video to the serial port instead of the keyboard and monitor. Serial consoles appear on all sorts of network equipment, from Cisco routers and Ethernet switches to network-based KVM switches. Many physical security systems, such as keypad-based door locks, also have serial consoles. By hooking up a standard null modem cable to the serial port and attaching the other end to another computer's serial port, you can access the first system's boot messages from the second computer. This is especially useful if the machines are at a remote location. Your system must have a serial port to have a serial console. An increasing number of systems are arriving "legacy-free," meaning that they lack such basic features as serial ports or PS/2 keyboard and mouse ports.

Serial consoles can occur in both hardware and software.

Hardware Serial Consoles

Real Unix hardware (such as Sparc64 systems) has hardware serial console capability. On these boxes, you can attach a serial cable to the serial console port and have unfettered access to the hardware configuration, boot messages, and startup messages. Most x86 hardware does not allow this; you must be at the keyboard looking at the monitor to control the BIOS, and you must press the spacebar to interrupt the loader. A few x86 and amd64 motherboards do have this functionality, and more and more vendors such as Dell and HP are offering serial port consoles as a feature on their higher-end machines—but this is a special feature you must search for. (The HP RILOE serial console support even lets you control power over the serial console, which is very nice.)

If your machine doesn't have a serial console, nothing any operating system can do will give you access to the PC-style BIOS messages across the serial port. Boot messages all appear before the operating system starts and even before the hard drive is accessed. Fortunately, hardware exists to work around this. The best I've seen is the PC Weasel (*http://www.realweasel.com*). It's a video card with a serial port instead of a video port. The PC Weasel lets you access the BIOS, interrupt the boot to come up in single-user mode, and in general do whatever you like with the system as if you were at the console.

Hardware serial consoles do not require any operating system support.

Software Serial Consoles

If you don't need early access to the BIOS messages but only to the boot loader, FreeBSD's software serial console will suffice. As FreeBSD boots, the loader decides where to print console messages and from where to accept input. While this defaults to the monitor and keyboard, with a few tweaks you can redirect the console to a serial port. You cannot access the BIOS, but this serial console gives you the ability to tweak your boot in almost any way. FreeBSD lets you set the console in two different places. For production systems, it's best to set the console in the file */boot/config*. This gives you access to the first stage of the boot process. You have three choices: Use the standard keyboard/video/mouse as a console, use a serial port as a console, or use a dual console. The standard console is the default, so choosing this setup requires no action. To force FreeBSD to use a serial console, enter -h all by itself in */boot/config*.

Dual consoles let you use either the standard or the serial console as needed. You must pick one console to be the primary console, however. There are certain low-level tasks, such as booting from an alternate loader or breaking into the debugger, which you can only perform from the primary console, but otherwise the consoles are functionally identical. Enter -D in */boot/config* to enable a dual console with the standard console as primary. Enter -Dh in */boot/config* to enable a dual console with the serial console as primary. I recommend using a dual console.

You can also control consoles from */boot/loader.conf*. These entries take effect slightly later in the boot process, during the final stage of the kernel bootstrapping process. To use the serial console exclusively, add this entry to */boot/loader.conf*:

```
console="comconsole"
```

To switch back to the default video console, remove this line or comment it out. You can also set the keyboard and video console in */boot/loader.conf* explicitly with this line:

```
console="vidconsole"
```

You can specify a dual console configuration by listing both comconsole and vidconsole, with the preferred console first. Here, we prefer the serial console:

```
console="comconsole vidconsole"
```

If you're in a server-room situation, you might want to switch back and forth between a standard console and a serial console. I generally manage large arrays of FreeBSD systems via the serial console.

KEYBOARD AUTODETECTION

In some FreeBSD documentation found on the Web, you'll see references to using keyboard autodetection to choose a console. The idea is that you want to use the serial console unless you have a keyboard plugged in. This worked just fine in the days of AT and PS/2 keyboards, but autodetection of USB keyboards is prone to failure. You're better off choosing a dual-console configuration rather than relying on keyboard autodetection.

Serial Console Physical Setup

No matter what sort of serial console you have, you'll need to plug into it correctly to make it work. You'll need a null modem cable, available at any computer store or from online vendors. While the gold-plated serial cables are not worth the money, don't buy the cheapest model you can find either; if you have an emergency and need the serial console, you're probably not in the mood to deal with line noise!

Plug one end of the null modem cable into the serial console port on your FreeBSD server—by default the first serial port (COM1 or sio0, depending on what operating system you're used to). You can change this with a kernel recompile, but it's generally simplest to just use the default on a server.

Plug the other end of your null modem cable into an open serial port on another system. I recommend either another FreeBSD (or other Unix) system or a terminal server, but you can use a Windows box if that's all you have.

If you have two FreeBSD machines at a remote location, make sure that they each have two serial ports. Get two null modem cables and plug the first serial port on each box into the second serial port of the other machine. That way, you can use each machine as the console client for the other. If you have three machines, daisy-chain them into a loop. By combining twos and threes, you can get serial consoles on any number of systems. I've worked data centers with 30 or 40 FreeBSD machines, where installing monitors was simply not practical, and we used serial consoles to great effect. Once you have a rack or two of servers, however, investing in a terminal server is a really good idea. You can find them cheaply on eBay.

Another option is to use two DB9-to-RJ45 converters, one standard and one crossover. These allow you to run your console connections over a standard CAT5 cable. If you have a lights-out data center where human beings are not allowed, you can have your serial consoles come out near your desk, in your warm room, or anywhere else your standard Ethernet-style patch panels reach. Most modern data facilities are better equipped to handle Ethernet than serial cables.

Serial Console Use

Now that you're all set up, configure your client to access the serial console. The key to using a serial console is to remember the following settings:

- 9600 baud
- 8 bits
- no parity
- 1 stop bit

Enter these values into any terminal emulator on a client computer, and the serial console will "just work." You can find terminal emulators for Microsoft platforms (HyperTerm being the most famous), Macintosh, and almost any other operating system. A few years ago, I frequently used a Palm handheld with a serial cable to access serial consoles.

FreeBSD accesses serial lines with tip(1), a program that allows you to connect to remote systems in a manner similar to telnet. To run tip, do this as root:

```
# tip portname
```

A port name is shorthand for specifying the serial port number and speed to be used on a serial port. The file */etc/remote* contains a list of port names. Most of the entries in this file are relics of the eon when UUCP was the major data-transfer protocol and serial lines were the norm instead of the exception.[2] At the end of this file, you'll see a few entries like:

```
# Finger friendly shortcuts
sio0|com1:dv=/dev/cuad0:br#9600:pa=none:
sio1|com2:dv=/dev/cuad1:br#9600:pa=none:
sio2|com3:dv=/dev/cuad2:br#9600:pa=none:
sio3|com4:dv=/dev/cuad3:br#9600:pa=none:
sio4|com5:dv=/dev/cuad4:br#9600:pa=none:
sio5|com6:dv=/dev/cuad5:br#9600:pa=none:
sio6|com7:dv=/dev/cuad6:br#9600:pa=none:
sio7|com8:dv=/dev/cuad7:br#9600:pa=none:
```

The sio entries are the standard Unix-type device names, while the com names were added for the convenience of people who grew up on *x*86 hardware. Assume that you have two FreeBSD boxes wired back-to-back, with each one's serial port 1 null-modemed into serial port 2. Both machines are configured to use a serial console. You'll want to connect to your local serial port 2 to talk to the other system's serial console:

```
# tip sio1
connected
```

You won't see anything else, no matter what you type.

If you log into the other system and reboot it, you'll abruptly see action in your tip window:

```
Shutting down daemon processes:.
Stopping cron.
Shutting down local daemons:.
Writing entropy file:.
Terminated
.
Waiting (max 60 seconds) for system process 'vnlru' to stop...done
Waiting (max 60 seconds) for system process 'bufdaemon' to stop...done
```

---

[2] This might not predate dinosaurs, but it was before spam. Imagine that.

```
Waiting (max 60 seconds) for system process 'syncer' to stop...
Syncing disks, vnodes remaining...1 0 0 done
All buffers synced.
Uptime: 1m1s
Shutting down ACPI
Rebooting...
```

There will be a long pause while the system runs its BIOS routines and hands control over to the serial console. Eventually you'll see something like this:

```
/boot/kernel/kernel text=0x4a6324 data=0x84020+0x9908c
syms=[0x4+0x67220+0x4+0x7e178]
/boot/kernel/snd_via8233.ko text=0x3a14 data=0x328 syms=[0x4+0xa10+0x4+0xac5]
loading required module 'sound'
/boot/kernel/sound.ko text=0x17974 data=0x37a8+0x10d8
syms=[0x4+0x3290+0x4+0x3d7d]
/boot/kernel/atapicam.ko text=0x2a30 data=0x1d8+0x4 syms=[0x4+0x7b0+0x4+0x7d6]
```

This indicates that the loader initially found and read the kernel files before showing the loader menu. Congratulations! You're using a serial console. Press the spacebar to interrupt the boot just as if you were at the keyboard. It doesn't matter how far away the system is; you can change your booting kernel, get a verbose boot, bring it up in single-user mode, or manually fsck the hard drive—whatever. A software serial console might not show you the BIOS, but chances are that's set up correctly already. Once you've used a serial console for a while, it won't matter if the machine is on the other side of the world or the other side of the room; getting out of your chair just to access the console will feel like too much work.

If you allow the boot to continue, however, you'll get to a point where the boot messages stop and the serial console freezes. This is because it's a console; it's not a logon device. (Being able to log onto a machine via the serial console is quite useful on occasion; see Chapter 20 for details.)

If a system in a remote location entirely locks up, you can connect to your serial console and have the "remote hands" at the colocation facility power-cycle the system. It might not be good for your computer, but it's also not good for it to be locked up. With the serial console, you can boot into single-user mode and fix the problem by digging through the logs and whatever other troubleshooting you feel capable of. We'll discuss troubleshooting this sort of problems in Chapter 21.

Serial Console Disconnection

The tip(1) program uses the tilde (~) as a control character. To disconnect the serial console, press ENTER and then type the disconnect sequence "tilde-dot" at any time:

```
~.
```

You'll be gracefully disconnected.

Startup Messages

A booting FreeBSD system displays messages indicating the hardware attached to the system, the operating system version, and the status of various programs and services as they start. These messages are important when you first install your system or when you do troubleshooting. The boot messages always start off the same way, with a statement listing the copyrights for the FreeBSD Project and the Regents of the University of California:

```
Copyright (c) 1992-2007 The FreeBSD Project.
Copyright (c) 1979, 1980, 1983, 1986, 1988, 1989, 1991, 1992, 1993, 1994
    The Regents of the University of California. All rights reserved.
FreeBSD 7.0-CURRENT-SNAP010 #0: Tue Dec 13 11:25:44 UTC 2005
    root@harlow.cse.buffalo.edu:/usr/obj/usr/src/sys/GENERIC
```

We also get a notice of the version of FreeBSD that's booting, along with the date and time it was compiled. You can also see who compiled this kernel, what machine it was built on, and even where in the filesystem this kernel was built. If you build a lot of kernels, this information can be invaluable when trying to identify exactly what system features are available.

```
WARNING: WITNESS option enabled, expect reduced performance.
```

The kernel will print out diagnostic messages throughout the boot process. The message shown above means that I have debugging and fault-identifying code enabled in this particular kernel, and my performance will suffer as a result. In this case I don't care about the performance impact, for reasons which will become clear momentarily.

```
Timecounter "i8254" frequency 1193182 Hz quality 0
```

This message identifies a particular piece of hardware. The *timecounter*, or *hardware clock*, is a special piece of hardware, and while your computer needs one, it's such a low-level device that the end user really can't do much with it directly. Now and then, you'll see messages like this for hardware that isn't directly visible to the user but is vital to the system. FreeBSD errs on the side of printing too much information, rather than obscuring details that might be critical. For example, it'll also show all the information it can about the CPU in the system:

```
CPU: AMD Athlon(tm) 64 X2 ❶Dual Core Processor 4200+ (❷2200.10-MHz 686-class CPU)
    Origin = "AuthenticAMD"  Id = 0x20fb1  Stepping = 1
```

```
❸ Features=0x178bfbff<FPU,VME,DE,PSE,TSC,MSR,PAE,MCE,CX8,APIC,SEP,MTRR,PGE,MCA,C
MV,PAT,PSE36,CLFLUSH,MMX,FXSR,SSE,SSE2,HTT>
    Features2=0x1<SSE3>
❹  AMD Features=0xe2500800<SYSCALL,NX,MMX+,FFXSR,LM,3DNow+,3DNow>
    AMD Features2=0x3<LAHF,CMP>
    Cores per package: 2
```

You probably didn't know that a simple CPU could have so many details and features, did you? Here's why I'm not worried about the performance hit caused by the WITNESS option shown earlier: This box has a dual-core processor ❶, each core is pretty darn fast ❷ and supports a whole bunch of features important to modern CPUs ❸ as well as a few AMD-specific features ❹. I have CPU power to spare[3] and a fair amount of memory as well.

```
❶real memory  = 1072693248 (1023 MB)
❷avail memory = 1040453632 (❸992 MB)
```

The real memory ❶ is the amount of RAM physically installed in the computer, while the avail memory ❷ is the amount of memory left over after the kernel is loaded. I have 992 MB of RAM ❸ available for real work, which more than suffices for the load on this system.

```
FreeBSD/SMP: Multiprocessor System Detected: 2 CPUs
```

The kernel also prints messages about the hardware it finds and how it's going to handle that hardware. For example, in the snippet above, the kernel announces that it's found both cores of the CPU and is ready to manage them.

```
❶ioapic0 <Version 0.3> ❷irqs 0-23 on motherboard
❸ioapic1 <Version 0.3> irqs 24-47 on motherboard
```

Here's a fairly typical device driver entry. This device is known as ioapic, and the kernel has found that this hardware is version 0.3 and has extra information associated with it ❷. What's more, we've found two devices of that type, numbered 0 ❶ and 1 ❸. (All device drivers are numbered starting with zero.) You can find out more about the device handled by a given driver by reading the manual page for the driver. Almost all—but not all—device drivers have manual pages.

```
npx0: [FAST]
npx0: <math processor> on motherboard
npx0: INT 16 interface
```

Not all device drivers print all their information on a single line. Here we have a single device, npx0, that takes up three lines with just a single instance of the device. The only way to know that this is a single math processor rather than three separate ones is to check the number of the device. All of these are for device number zero, so it's a single device.

```
❶acpi0: <PTLTD    RSDT> on motherboard
❷pcib0: <ACPI Host-PCI bridge> port 0xcf8-0xcff ❸on acpi0
❹pci0: <ACPI PCI bus> on ❺pcib0
```

---

[3] I would say, "Eat your heart out," except that by the time this book hits the shelves, this laptop will be sadly out of date.

One interesting thing about the boot messages is that they display how your computer's components are attached to one another. Here, we have an ACPI system directly on the motherboard ❶ and a PCI bridge ❷ attached to acpi0 ❸. We also find a PCI bus ❹ attached to the PCI bridge ❺, and as you read on, you'll find individual devices attached to that bus. You might not be equipped to do much with this information now, but you'll find that having it available will be valuable when you have to troubleshoot a problem.

This is all good, but too esoteric to be of use at the moment. How about something usable right now?

```
❶ firewire0: <IEEE1394(FireWire) bus> on fwohci0
❷ fwe0: <Ethernet over FireWire> on firewire0
```

This system has FireWire ❶, and FreeBSD can identify and use it! Now that's useful, at least if you have FireWire equipment. And FreeBSD can do Ethernet over FireWire ❷? That's kind of cool.[4]

Even if you don't have FireWire, chances are you have a network connection of some sort.

```
❶ re0: <RealTek 8169SB Single-chip ❷ Gigabit Ethernet> port 0x1000-0x10ff mem
0xd2206800-0xd22068ff irq 19 at device 8.0 on pci0
```

This entry shows that a network card is assigned to the interface re0 ❶, and that the card speaks gigabit Ethernet ❷. We also see all sorts of information about its memory address, IRQ, and its PCI bus attachment.

Every device on your computer has one or more entries like the above. Taken as a whole, they describe your computer's hardware in reasonable detail. If you boot in verbose mode, you'll see even more detail—probably far more than you want.

DMESG.BOOT

While the boot information is handy, chances are it will disappear from the screen by the time you need it. For future reference, the boot messages are stored in the file */var/run/dmesg.boot*. This means that you can inspect your kernel's hardware messages even after your system has been up and running for months.

One key thing that the kernel displays in the boot messages is the device name for each piece of hardware. This is critical information for managing your system. Every piece of hardware has a device node name, and to configure it, you'll need to know that name. For example, earlier we saw an entry

---

[4] FreeBSD's default Ethernet-over-FireWire driver uses a method only supported by FreeBSD, mainly because we were here first. To use the Ethernet over FireWire compatible with Mac OS X and Windows XP, look at fwip(4).

for an Ethernet card called re0. The card uses the re(4) driver, and the first instance of this driver has number zero. Your second card of this type would be re1, then re2, and so on.

Most devices that can be configured or managed have a device node entry somewhere under */dev*. For example, our network card is represented by the file */dev/net/re0*. These files are called *device nodes*, and are a convenient way to address a particular piece of hardware. Most device nodes cannot be directly accessed as a regular file; you can't cat(1) a device node or copy another file to it. However, device nodes are used as arguments to specialized programs. For example, the hard drive that showed up at boot as ad4 is the same as the device node */dev/ad4*. When you want to mount that hard drive, you can use the device node name and be sure you're getting that exact piece of hardware.

Multi-User Startup

Beyond single-user mode you'll find multi-user mode. This is the standard operating mode for a Unix-like OS. If you're doing real work, your system is in multi-user mode.

When FreeBSD finishes inspecting the hardware and attaching all the device drivers appropriately, it runs the shell script */etc/rc*. This script mounts all filesystems, brings up the network interfaces, configures device nodes, identifies available shared libraries, and does all the other work necessary to make a system ready for normal work. Most systems have different startup requirements; while almost every server needs to mount a hard drive, a web server's operating requirements are very different from those of a database server even if it's running on absolutely identical hardware. This means that */etc/rc* must be extremely flexible. It achieves this flexibility by delegating everything to other shell scripts responsible for specific aspects of the system.

The */etc/rc* script is controlled by the files */etc/defaults/rc.conf* and */etc/rc.conf*.

/etc/rc.conf and /etc/defaults/rc.conf

Much like the loader configuration file, the configuration of */etc/rc* is split between two files: the default setting file */etc/defaults/rc.conf* and the local settings file */etc/rc.conf*. Settings in */etc/rc.conf* override any values given in */etc/defaults/rc.conf*, exactly as with the loader.

The */etc/defaults/rc.conf* file is huge and contains quite a few variables, frequently called *knobs* or *tunables*. We aren't going to discuss all of them, not only because knobs are added continually and such a list would be immediately obsolete, but because quite a few knobs aren't commonly used on servers. Almost everything in a standard FreeBSD system has one or more *rc.conf* knobs, from your keyboard map to TCP/IP behavior. For a complete, up-to-date list, read the rc.conf(5) manual page on your system.

In the next few sections, we'll examine some common entries from */etc/rc.conf*. Each of these appears in */etc/defaults/rc.conf* and can be edited by placing an override in */etc/rc.conf*. Each variable appears with its default setting.

Startup Options

The following *rc.conf* options control how FreeBSD configures itself and starts other programs. These far-reaching settings affect how all other system programs and services run.

If you're having a problem with the startup scripts themselves, you might enable debugging on */etc/rc* and its subordinate scripts. This can provide additional information about why a script is or isn't starting.

```
rc_debug="NO"
```

If you don't need the full debugging output, but would like some additional information about the */etc/rc process*, enable informational messages with rc_info:

```
rc_info="NO"
```

One common problem with systems that have little memory is a shortage of swap space. We'll go into the details of swap usage in Chapter 19, but you can configure a file for use as additional swap immediately at system boot:

```
swapfile="NO"
```

Filesystem Options

FreeBSD can use memory as a filesystem, as we will discuss in Chapter 8. One common use for this feature is to make */tmp* really fast by using memory rather than a hard drive as its back end. Once you've read Chapter 8, you might consider implementing this. *rc.conf* has variables to let you enable a memory-backed */tmp* and set its size transparently and painlessly. You can also choose the options FreeBSD will use to complete the filesystem. (The impatient among you are probably wondering what the flag -S means. It means *disable soft updates*. If you have no idea what this means, either, wait for Chapter 8.) If you want to use a memory filesystem */tmp*, set tmpmfs to YES and set tmpsize to the desired size of your */tmp*.

```
tmpmfs="AUTO"
tmpsize="20m"
tmpmfs_flags="-S"
```

Another popular FreeBSD filesystem feature is its integrated encrypted partitions. FreeBSD supports two different filesystem encryption systems out of the box: GBDE and GELI. *Geom Based Disk Encryption (GBDE)* was FreeBSD's first encrypted filesystem designed for military-grade use. GELI is a little more friendly and complies with different standards than GBDE. (You definitely want to read Chapter 18 before enabling either of these!)

```
gbde_autoattach_all="NO"
gbde_devices="NO"
gbde_attach_attempts="3"
gbde_lockdir="/etc"
geli_devices=""
geli_tries=""
geli_default_flags=""
geli_autodetach="YES"
geli_swap_flags="-a aes -l 256 -s 4096 -d"
```

By default, FreeBSD mounts the root partition read/write upon achieving multi-user mode. If you want to run in read-only mode instead, you can set the following variable to NO. Many people consider this more secure, but it might interfere with operation of certain software, and it will certainly prevent you from editing any files on the root partition!

```
root_rw_mount="YES"
```

When a booting FreeBSD attempts to mount its filesystems, it checks them for internal consistency. If the kernel finds major filesystem problems, it can try to fix them automatically with fsck -y. While this is necessary in certain situations, it's not entirely safe. (Be sure to read Chapter 8 very carefully before enabling this!)

```
fsck_y_enable="NO"
```

The kernel might also find minor filesystem problems which it resolves on-the-fly using a *background fsck* while the system is running in multi-user mode, as discussed in Chapter 8. There are legitimate concerns about the safety of using this feature in certain circumstances. You can control the use of background fsck and set how long the system will wait before beginning the background fsck.

```
background_fsck="YES"
background_fsck_delay="60"
```

Miscellaneous Network Daemons

FreeBSD includes many smaller programs (or daemons) that run in the background to provide specific services. We'll cover quite a few of these integrated services throughout the book, but here are a few specific ones that will be of interest to experienced system administrators. One popular daemon is syslogd(8). Logs are a Good Thing. Logs are so very, *very* good that large parts of Chapter 20 are devoted to the topic of logging with, for, by, and on FreeBSD.

```
syslogd_enable="YES"
```

Once you have decided to run the logging daemon, you can choose exactly how it will run by setting command-line flags for it. FreeBSD will use these flags when starting the daemon. For all the programs included in *rc.conf* that can take command-line flags, these flags are given in this format.

```
syslogd_flags="-s"
```

Another popular daemon is inetd(8), the server for small network services. (We cover inetd in Chapter 15.)

```
inetd_enable="NO"
```

One job commonly run with FreeBSD is Domain Name System, or DNS, with the industry-standard daemon named(8). DNS is the road map of the Internet and makes it possible for mere humans to use the network. Because DNS must be configured in order to be useful, FreeBSD ships with it disabled by default. We cover DNS in Chapter 14.

```
named_enable="NO"
```

Most facilities use the Secure Shell (SSH) daemon for remote logins. If you want to connect to your system remotely over the network, you'll almost certainly need SSH services.

```
sshd_enable="NO"
```

While the SSH daemon can be configured via the command line, you're generally be better off using the configuration files in */etc/ssh/*. See Chapter 15 for details.

```
sshd_flags=""
```

FreeBSD also incorporates extensive time-keeping software and functions to ensure that the system clock remains synchronized with the rest of the world. You'll need to configure this for it to be useful; we will cover that in Chapter 15.

```
ntpd_enable="NO"
ntpd_flags="-p /var/run/ntpd.pid -f /var/db/ntpd.drift"
```

FreeBSD also includes a small SNMP daemon for use in facilities with SNMP-based management tools. We'll cover configuring SNMP in Chapter 19.

```
bsnmpd_enable="NO"
```

Network Options

These knobs control how FreeBSD configures its network facilities during boot.

Every machine on the Internet needs a hostname. The hostname is the fully qualified domain name of the system, such as *www.absolutefreebsd.org*. Many programs will not run properly without this.

```
hostname=""
```

FreeBSD includes a few different integrated firewall packages. We're going to briefly cover PF, the Packet Filter, in Chapter 9. PF is enabled and disabled in *rc.conf*.

```
pf_enable="NO"
```

TCP/IP is an old networking protocol and has been extended and modified several times. Some of these modifications have been lumped together as *TCP extensions*, as covered in Chapter 6. Most operating systems can take advantage of TCP extensions, but many older ones can't. If you have trouble communicating with much older hosts, disable TCP extensions.

```
tcp_extensions="YES"
```

You might be interested in failed attempts to connect to your system over the network. This will help detect port scans and network intrusion attempts, but will also collect a lot of garbage. It's interesting to set this for a short period of time just to see what really happens on your network. (Then again, knowing what's *really* going on tends to cause heartburn.) Set this to 1 to log failed connection attempts.

```
log_in_vain="0"
```

Routers use ICMP redirects to inform client machines of the proper network gateways for particular routes. While this is completely legitimate, on some networks intruders can use this to capture data. If you don't need ICMP redirects on your network, you can set this option for an extremely tiny measure of added security. If you're not sure if you're using them, ask your network administrator.

```
icmp_drop_redirect="NO"
```

If you *are* the network administrator and you're not sure if your network uses ICMP redirects, there's an easy way to find out—just log all redirects received by your system to */var/log/messages*.[5] Note that if your server is under attack, this can fill your hard drive with redirect logs fairly quickly.

```
icmp_log_redirect="NO"
```

To get on the network, you'll need to assign each interface an IP address. We'll discuss this in some detail in Chapter 6. You can get a list of your network interfaces with the ifconfig(8) command. List each network interface on its own line, with its network configuration information in quotes. For example, to give your em0 network card an IP address of 172.18.11.3 and a netmask of 255.255.254.0, you would use:

```
ifconfig_em0="inet 172.18.11.3 netmask 255.255.254.0"
```

If your network uses DHCP, use the value dhcp as an IP address.

```
ifconfig_em0="dhcp"
```

Similarly, you can assign aliases to a network card. An alias is not the card's actual IP address, but the card answers for that IP address, as discussed in Chapter 6. FreeBSD supports hundreds of aliases on a single card, with *rc.conf* entries in the following form:

```
ifconfig_em0_aliasnumber="address netmask 255.255.255.255"
```

The alias numbers must be continuous, starting with 0. If there's a break in numbering, aliases above the break will not be installed at boot time. (This is a common problem, and when you see it, check your list of aliases.) For example, an alias of 192.168.3.4 would be listed as:

```
ifconfig_em0_alias0="192.168.3.4 netmask 255.255.255.255"
```

Network Routing Options

FreeBSD's network stack includes many features for routing Internet traffic. These start with the very basic, such as configuring an IP for your default gateway. While an IP address will get you on the network, a default router will give you access to everything beyond your LAN.

```
defaultrouter=""
```

---

[5] And if you've never heard of ICMP redirects, run, do not walk, to your nearest book pusher and get a copy of *The TCP/IP Guide* by Charles M. Kozierok (No Starch Press, 2005). Once you have it, *read* it.

Network control devices such as firewalls must pass traffic between different interfaces. While FreeBSD won't do this by default, it's simple to enable. Just tell the system that it's a gateway and it will connect multiple networks for you.

```
gateway_enable="NO"
```

If your system needs to speak Routing Information Protocol, use the router_enable knob to start it at boot. I would argue that this knob is misnamed—many routers use routing protocols other than RIP, but the knob has had this name for decades now. If you don't specifically need the RIP protocol, then leave this knob alone!

```
router_enable="NO"
```

Console Options

The console options control how the monitor and keyboard behave. You can change the language of your keyboard, the monitor's font size, or just about anything else you like. For example, the keyboard map defaults to the standard US keyboard, frequently called QWERTY. You'll find all sorts of keymaps in the directory */usr/share/syscons/keymaps*. I prefer the Dvorak keyboard layout, which has an entry there as *us.dvorak*. By changing the keymap knob to *us.dvorak*, my system will use a Dvorak keyboard once it boots to multi-user mode.

```
keymap="NO"
```

FreeBSD turns the monitor dark when the keyboard has been idle for a time specified in the blanktime knob. If you set this to NO, FreeBSD will not dim the screen. Mind you, new hardware will dim the monitor after some time as well, to conserve power. If your screen goes blank even if you've set the blanktime knob to NO, check your BIOS and your monitor manual.

```
blanktime="300"
```

FreeBSD can also use a variety of fonts on the console. While the default font is fine for servers, you might want a different font on your desktop or laptop. My laptop has one of those 17-inch screens proportioned for watching movies, and the default fonts look kind of silly at that size. You can choose a new font from the directory */usr/share/syscons/fonts*. Try a few to see how they look on your systems. The font's name includes the size, so you can set the appropriate variable. For example, the font *swiss-8x8.fnt* is the Swiss font, 8 pixels by 8 pixels. To use it, you would set the font8x8 knob.

```
font8x16="NO"
font8x14="NO"
font8x8="NO"
```

You can use a mouse on the console, even without a GUI. By default, FreeBSD will try to autodetect your mouse type. If you have a PS/2 or USB mouse, chances are that it will just work when you enable the mouse daemon, without any special configuration. Some older and more unusual types of mice require manual configuration, as documented in moused(8).

```
moused_enable="NO"
moused_type="AUTO"
```

You can also change the display on your monitor to fit your needs. If you have an odd-sized monitor, you can change the number of lines of text and their length to fit, change text colors, change your cursor and cursor behavior, and do all sorts of other little tweaks. You can get a full list of different options in man vidcontrol(8).

```
allscreens_flags=""
```

Similarly, you can adjust your keyboard behavior almost arbitrarily. Everything from key repeat speed to the effect of function keys can be configured, as documented in kbdcontrol(8).

```
allscreens_kbdflags=""
```

Other Options

This final potpourri of knobs might or might not be useful in any given environment, but they are needed frequently enough to deserve mention. For example, not all systems have access to a printer, but those that do will want to run the printing daemon lpd(8). We brush up against printer configuration in Chapter 15.

```
ldp_enable="NO"
```

The sendmail(8) daemon manages transmission and receipt of email between systems. While almost all systems need to transmit email, most FreeBSD machines don't need to receive email. The sendmail_enable knob specifically handles incoming mail, while sendmail_outbound_enable allows the machine to transmit mail. See Chapter 16 for more details.

```
sendmail_enable="NO"
sendmail_outbound_enable="YES"
```

One of FreeBSD's more interesting features is its ability to run software built for other operating systems. The most common compatibility mode is for Linux software, but FreeBSD also supports SCO Unix binaries and SVR4 software. We will discuss this feature in Chapter 12. Don't enable any of these compatibility modes without reading that chapter first!

```
linux_enable="NO"
```

A vital part of any Unix-like operating system is shared libraries. You can control where FreeBSD looks for shared libraries. Although the default setting is usually adequate, if you find yourself regularly setting the LD_LIBRARY_PATH environment variable for your users, you should consider adjusting the library path instead. See Chapter 12 for more advice on this.

```
ldconfig_paths="/usr/lib /usr/X11R6/lib /usr/local/lib"
```

FreeBSD has a security profile system that allows the administrator to control basic system features. You can globally disallow mounting hard disks, accessing particular TCP/IP ports, and even changing files. See Chapter 7 for details on how to use these.

```
kern_securelevel_enable="NO"
kern_securelevel="-1"
```

Now that you know a smattering of the configuration knobs FreeBSD supports out of the box, let's see how they're used.

The rc.d Startup System

FreeBSD bridges the gap between single-user mode and multi-user mode via the shell script */etc/rc*. This script reads in the configuration files */etc/defaults/rc.conf* and */etc/rc.conf* and runs a collection of other scripts based on what it finds there. For example, if you have enabled the USB daemon, */etc/rc* runs a script written specifically for starting that daemon. FreeBSD includes scripts for starting services, mounting disks, configuring the network, and setting security parameters. You can use these scripts to stop and restart services exactly as the system does at boot, ensuring system integrity and making your life generally easier. These scripts live in */etc/rc.d*.

WHAT IS rcNG?

Once upon a time, FreeBSD included a handful of monolithic /etc/rc scripts that configured the entire system. Each specific daemon or service was started by a few lines buried inside one of these scripts. While this worked well for the majority of systems, it wasn't very flexible and couldn't accommodate all users. NetBSD developed the current system of small shell scripts for specific services, and FreeBSD quickly adopted it. The current startup method is the *next generation RC scripts*, or *rcNG*. This system is currently the only one used in any production version of FreeBSD, and any references you may see to *rcNG* are leftovers from the transition era.

Once you have a feature enabled in *rc.conf*, you can control it via an *rc.d* script. For example, suppose you realized you had to run the SSH daemon on a system that previously hadn't run it. Set sshd_enable to YES, and go to the directory */etc/rc.d*. There you'll find a script called *sshd*.

```
#./sshd start
Starting sshd.
#
```

No *rc.d* script runs unless enabled in *rc.conf*, however. This ensures that everything that was running before will still be running after a reboot. You can also stop a service with the stop command, check its state with the status command, and reload it with restart. If you really do want to start a program just once with its *rc.d* script, and you don't want it to run after the next reboot, you can use the forcestart command.

We'll look at *rc.d* in more detail in Chapter 12, when we discuss customizing and writing your own *rc.d* scripts.

Shutdown

FreeBSD makes the *rc.d* startup system do double duty; not only must it handle system startup, it must shut all those programs down when it's time to power down. Something has to unmount all those hard drives, shut down the daemons, and clean up after doing all the work. Some programs don't care if they're unceremoniously killed when the system closes up for the night—after all, after the system goes down any clients connected over SSH will be knocked off and any web pages that are being requested aren't going to be delivered. Database software, however, cares very much about how it's turned off, and just killing the process will damage your data. Many other programs that manage actual data are just as particular, and if you don't let them clean up after themselves you will regret it.

When you shut down FreeBSD with either the shutdown(8) or reboot(8) commands, the system calls the shell script */etc/rc.shutdown*. This script calls each *rc.d* script in turn with the stop option, reversing the order they were called during startup, thereby allowing server programs to terminate gracefully and disks to tidy themselves up before the power dies.

Now that you understand how FreeBSD starts up and shuts down, let's look at some basic tools you can use to ensure that your system will continue to boot even after you've been experimenting with it.

4

READ THIS BEFORE YOU BREAK
SOMETHING ELSE!
(BACKUP AND RECOVERY)

The most common cause of system failure is those pesky humans, but hardware and operating systems also fail. Hackers learn new ways to disrupt networks and penetrate applications, and you'll inevitably need to upgrade and patch your system on a regular basis. (Whether or not you *will* upgrade and patch is an entirely separate question.) Any time you touch a system there's a chance you'll make a mistake, misconfigure a vital service, or otherwise totally ruin your system. Just think of how many times you've patched a computer running any OS and found something behaving oddly afterward! Even small system changes can damage data. You should therefore always assume that the worst is about to happen. In our case, this means that if either the hardware or a human being destroys the data on your hard drive, you must be able to restore that data.

Worse still, if you're reading this book, you're probably just learning how to configure your FreeBSD system and therefore aren't well prepared for a disaster. As a new user, you'll need to test a variety of configurations and review the history of what you've done. There's little more frustrating than saying, "But this worked last month, what did I change?" Will you really recall every change you've made over the last weeks, or months, or years? What about changes made by your co-workers? In fact, if you're experimenting hard enough you might even utterly destroy your system, so you'll need a way to recover your important data.

This chapter begins with the large-scale approach of backing up the entire computer. This approach won't work well if you only want to back up individual files, so we'll handle these separately. If a file can change three times a day, and you take weekly backups, you will lose valuable information when the file disappears. Finally, should you suffer a partial or near-total disaster, we'll consider recovering and rebuilding with single-user mode and the fixit disk.

System Backups

You only need a system backup if you care about your data. That isn't as inane as it sounds. The real question is, "How much would it cost to replace my data?" A low-end tape backup system can run several hundred dollars. How much is your time worth, and how long will it take to restore your system from the install media? If the most important data on your hard disk is your web browser's bookmarks file, a backup system probably isn't worth the investment. But if your server is your company's backbone, you'll want to take this investment very seriously.

A complete backup and restore operation requires a tape drive and media. You can also back up to files, across the network, or to removable media such as CDs or DVDs. Today's industry standard, however, is tape, so we'll focus on that. To use a tape drive you'll need a backup program, and we'll discuss the standard backup programs shipped with FreeBSD.

Backup Tapes

FreeBSD supports SCSI, USB, and IDE tape drives. SCSI drives are faster and more reliable than IDE drives, although IDE drives are cheaper. USB tape drives are not always standards-compliant and hence not always compatible with FreeBSD. Definitely check the release notes or the FreeBSD mailing list archives to confirm that your tape drive is compatible with FreeBSD.

Once you've physically installed your tape drive, you need to confirm that FreeBSD recognizes it. The simplest way is to check the */var/run/dmesg .boot* file, as discussed in Chapter 3. SCSI and USB tapes show up as sa devices while IDE tape drives show up as ast. For example, the following three lines from *dmesg.boot* describe the SCSI tape device in this machine:

```
❶sa0 at ❷ahc0 bus 0 target ❸9 lun 0
sa0: <SONY ❹SDT-10000 0110> Removable Sequential Access SCSI-2 device
sa0: ❺40.000MB/s transfers (20.000MHz, offset 8, 16bit)
```

Of all the information we have on this tape drive, the most important is that your FreeBSD system knows this device as sa0 ❶. We also see that it's attached to the SCSI card ahc0 ❷ at SCSI ID 9 ❸, what the drive's model number is ❹, and it can run at 40MB per second ❺.

Tape Drive Device Nodes, Rewinding, and Ejecting

Before you can use your tape drive for backups you have to know how to control it. As with many Unix devices with decades worth of history, the way you access a tape drive controls how it behaves. Tape drives have several different device nodes, and each one makes the tape drive behave differently. The most basic tape-control mechanism is the device node used to access it.

For your average SCSI tape drive, you only need worry about three nodes: */dev/esa0*, */dev/nsa0*, and */dev/sa0*. Similarly, IDE tapes mainly use */dev/east0*, */dev/nast0*, and */dev/ast0*.

Tapes are sequential access devices, meaning that data is stored on the tape linearly. A particular section of tape contains certain data, and to access that data you must roll the tape to expose that section. To rewind or not to rewind is an important question.

NOTE   *The behavior of different tape device nodes varies between operating systems. Different versions of Unix, with different tape management software, handle tapes differently. Do not make assumptions with your backup tapes!*

If you use the node name that matches the device name, the tape drive will automatically rewind when your command finishes. Our sample SCSI tape drive has a device name of sa0, so if you run a command using */dev/sa0* as the device node, the tape will rewind when the command finishes.

If you don't want the tape to automatically rewind when the command completes, stop it from rewinding by using the node name that starts with *n*. Perhaps you need to append a second backup from a different machine onto the tape, or you want to catalog the tape before rewinding and ejecting. In our example, use */dev/nsa0* to run your command without rewinding.

To automatically eject a tape when a command finishes, use the node that begins with *e*. For example, if you're running a full system backup, you probably want the tape to eject when the command finishes so the operator can put the tape in a case to ship off-site or place in storage. Our example uses the */dev/esa0* device name to eject the tape when the command finishes. Some older tape drives might not support automatic ejection; they'll require you to push the physical button to work the lever that winches the tape out of the drive. The easiest way to identify such a drive is to try to eject it via the device node and see what happens.

The $TAPE Variable

Many programs assume that your tape drive is */dev/sa0*, but that isn't always correct. Even if you have only one SCSI tape drive, you might want it to eject automatically (*/dev/esa0*) or to rewind it upon completion (*/dev/nsa0*). Or, you might have an IDE tape drive which goes by an entirely different name.

Many (but not all) backup-related programs use the environment variable $TAPE to control which device node they use by default. You can always override $TAPE on the command line, but setting it to your most commonly used choice can save you some annoyances later.

If you're using the default FreeBSD shell, set $TAPE with the following command:

```
# setenv TAPE /dev/sa0
```

Tape Status with mt(1)

Now that you know how to find your tape drive, you can perform basic actions on it—such as rewinding, retensioning, erasing, and so on—with mt(1). One basic thing mt does is checking a tape drive's status, as follows:

```
#mt status
Mode       Density          Blocksize      bpi       Compression
Current: ❶0x25:DDS-3        variable       97000     ❷DCLZ
---------available modes---------
0:         0x25:DDS-3       variable       97000     DCLZ
1:         0x25:DDS-3       variable       97000     DCLZ
2:         0x25:DDS-3       variable       97000     DCLZ
3:         0x25:DDS-3       variable       97000     DCLZ
---------------------------------
❸ Current Driver State: at rest.
---------------------------------
File Number: 0   Record Number: 0        Residual Count 0
```

You don't have to worry about most of the information here, but if you want to go through it line-by-line, the mt(1) man page contains a good description of all the features. At the very least, if the command returns anything useful, this means mt(1) can find your tape drive.

One of the first things we see is the drive density ❶. Older drives can have tapes of different densities for different purposes, but modern tape drives pack data as tightly as possible. This particular tape drive is a DDS-3 model; while you could choose to use another density, all the choices it offers are DDS-3. We also see that this tape drive offers hardware compression with the DCLZ algorithm ❷. Near the bottom, we see what the tape drive is doing right now ❸.

The status command might give you different sorts of messages. The most problematic is the one that tells you that your tape drive is not configured:

```
#mt status
mt: /dev/nsa0: Device not configured
```

This means that you don't actually have a tape at the device node that your $TAPE variable points at. You can experiment with device nodes and mt(1) by using the -f flag to specify a device node (for example, mt -f /dev/nsa1 status), although you should get this information from *dmesg.boot*.

If you're sure that your device node is correct, perhaps you don't have a tape inserted into the drive, or the tape drive needs cleaning.

Another response you might get from `mt status` is `mt: /dev/nsa0: Device busy`. You asked for the status of your tape, and it replied, "I can't talk now, I'm busy." Try again later, or check `ps -ax` to see what commands are using the tape drive. When you're working with actual tape, only one program instance can access it at a time. You cannot list the contents of a tape while you're extracting a file from that tape.

Other Tape Drive Commands

You can do more with a tape drive than just check to see if it's alive. The mt(1) subcommands I use most frequently are `retension`, `erase`, `rewind`, and `offline`.

Tapes tend to stretch, especially after they're used the first time. (I know perfectly well that modern tape vendors all claim that they prestretch their tapes, or that their tapes cannot be stretched, but that claim and two slices of bread will get you a bologna sandwich.) *Retensioning* a tape is simply running the tape completely through, both forwards and back, with the command `mt retension`. Retensioning takes all the slack out of the tape and makes backups more reliable.

Erasing removes all data from a tape. This isn't a solidly reliable erasure which you'd need to conceal data from a data recovery firm or the IRS; `mt erase` simply rolls through the tape and overwrites everything once. This can take a very long time. If you want to erase the tape quickly, you can use `mt erase 0` to simply mark the tape as blank.

The `mt rewind` command rolls a tape back to the beginning, same as accessing the device through its default device node.

When you *offline* a tape, you rewind and eject it so that you can put a new tape in. The command is, oddly enough, `mt offline`.

TAPE DRIVE TEMPERAMENT

Not all tape drives support all functions. Older tape drives in particular are quite touchy, even crotchety, requiring very specific settings to work acceptably. If you have a problem with a particular drive, check the *FreeBSD-questions* mailing list archive for messages from others with the same problem. You'll probably find your answer there.

To Rewind or Not?

One thing to remember about tape is that it's a linear storage medium. Each section of tape holds a particular piece of data. If you back up multiple chunks of data to tape, avoid rewinding after each backup operation. Imagine that you wrote a backup of one system to tape, rewound the tape, and backed up another system. The second backup would overwrite the first, because it used the same chunk of tape. When you run multiple backups on a single tape, use the appropriate device node to ensure you don't rewind the tape between tasks.

Backup Programs

Two popular packages for backing up systems are tar(1) and dump(8). You'll certainly encounter other backup tools too, such as pax and cpio. You'll also find network-based backup software for FreeBSD, such as Amanda and Bacula, that can back up an entire network. These tools are well suited for certain environments, but aren't as universal as dump and tar. Once you learn dump and tar, however, you will find it easy to master any other backup software.

tar(1) was designed for files, and you can restore tar backups on almost any operating system. dump(8) works on partitions and filesystems, and can only be restored on the same operating system that the dump was taken on. If you're backing up an entire computer, use dump. If you're backing up individual files, or might want to restore your backup to a foreign computer, use tar.

tar

The *tar* (short for *tape archiver*) utility can back up anything from a single file to your whole computer. Unlike dump, tar works on the files and directories only and has no knowledge of the underlying filesystem, which has its advantages and disadvantages. tar is a common standard recognized by almost every operating system vendor; you can find tar for Windows, Linux, Unix, BSD, Mac OS X, AS/400, VMS, Atari, Commodore 64, QNX, and just about everything else you might encounter.

tar(1) can back up files to tape or to a file. A backup file containing tarred files is known as a *tarball*. Since tar works on files, it's very easy to restore just one file from a tarball.

FreeBSD uses a version of tar written from scratch to replace the older GNU tar, called *bsdtar*. bsdtar can behave completely consistently with GNU tar, and can also behave in strict accordance with POSIX tar. If you're at all concerned about the differences between GNU tar, POSIX tar, and bsdtar, read man tar(1) for all the gory details. bsdtar is actually built on libarchive(3), a library that developers use to add support for backup archives into other programs. tar(1) can be dumb. If your filesystem is corrupt in any way, tar will back up what it thinks you asked for. It will then happily restore files that were damaged during the original backup, overwriting working-but-incorrect files with not-working-and-still-incorrect versions. These sorts of problems rarely happen, but tend to be unforgettable when they do.

tar Modes

tar(1) can perform several different actions, controlled by the command-line flags. These different actions are called modes. You'll need to read the manual page for a complete description of all tar modes, but the most commonly used ones are listed below.

Create an Archive

Use *create mode* (-c) to create a new archive. Unless you specify otherwise, this flag backs up everything to your tape drive ($TAPE, or */dev/sa0* if you haven't set $TAPE). To back up your entire system, you'd tell tar to archive everything from the root directory down:

```
# tar -c /
```

In response, your tape drive should light up and, if your tape is big enough, eventually present you with a complete system backup. Many modern hard drives are bigger than tape drives can hold, however, so it makes sense to only back up the vital portions of your system. For example, if the only files on your computer that you need are on the partitions */home* and */var*, you could specify those directories on the command line:

```
# tar -c /home /var
```

List Archive Contents

List mode (-t) lists all the files in an archive. Once you've created an archive, you can use this mode to list the tape's contents.

```
# tar -t
.
.snap
dev
tmp
...
```

This lists all the files in your backup and might take a while to run. Note that the initial slashes are missing from filenames; for example, */tmp* shows up as *tmp*. This becomes important during restores.

Extract Files from Backup

In *extract mode*, tar retrieves files from the archive and copies them to the disk. (This is also called *untarring*.) tar extracts files in your current location; if you want to overwrite the existing */etc* directory of your system with files from your backup, go to the root directory first. On the other hand, to restore a copy of */etc* in my home directory, I would go to my home directory first.

```
# cd /home/mwlucas
# tar -x etc
```

Remember when I said that the missing initial slash would be important? Here's why. If the backup included that initial slash, tar would always extract files relative to the root directory. The restored backup of */etc/rc.conf* would always be written to */etc/rc.conf*. Without the leading /, you can recover the file anywhere you want; the restored */etc/rc.conf* can be */home/mwlucas/etc/rc.conf*. If I'm restoring files from a machine that's been decommissioned, I don't want them to overwrite files on the current machine; I want them placed elsewhere so they won't interfere with my system.

Verify Backups

Once you have a backup, you probably want to confirm that it matches your system. *Diff mode* (-d) compares the files on tape to the files on disk. If everything on the tape matches the system, tar -d will run silently. A perfect match between tape and system is *not* normal, however. Log files usually grow during the backup process, so the log files on tape should not match the files on disk. Similarly, if you have a database server running, the database files might not match. If you truly want a perfect backup (also called a *cold backup*), you'll need to shut down to single-user mode before taking the backup. You must decide which errors you can live with and which need correction.

Other tar Features

tar has several other features that can make it more friendly or useful. These include verbose behavior, different types of compression, permissions restore, and the most popular option, using a file instead of a tape device.

Use a File Instead of Tape

The -f flag allows you to specify another device or file as the destination for your archive. In all of the preceding examples I'm either using the default tape drive */dev/sa0*, or I have set $TAPE. If I have neither of these, I'd need to specify a tape drive with -f:

```
# tar -c -f /dev/east0 /
```

Instead of using a tape at all, you can use a tar file, or tarball. Source code distributed via the Internet is frequently distributed as tarballs. Use the -f flag to specify a filename. For example, to back up the chapters of this book as they were written, I ran the following every so often to create the tarball *bookbackup.tar*:

```
#tar -cf bookbackup.tar /home/mwlucas/absolutefreebsd/
```

This file can easily be backed up on machines elsewhere—so even if my house burns down, the book would be safe. I could then run phone and power lines to the neighbor's house, borrow a laptop, find an open wireless access point, run tar -xf bookbackup.tar, and work amidst the charred timbers while waiting for the insurance company. (I couldn't do much else at the time, anyway.)

Verbose

The -v flag makes tar verbose. Normally, tar runs silently, except when it encounters an error. This is good most of the time (who wants to read the complete list of files on the server every time a backup runs?), but sometimes you like to have the warm fuzzy feeling of watching a program do its work. Adding the -v flag makes tar print the name of each file it processes. You can use the verbose flag to create a complete list of all the files that are being backed up or restored. In a routine backup or restore, this verbosity makes errors difficult to see.

gzip

The gzip flag (-z) runs the files through the gzip(1) compression program on their way to or from the archive. Compressed tarballs usually have the extension *.tar.gz* or *.tgz*, and on rare occasion *.taz*. Compression can greatly reduce the size of an archive; many backups shrink by 50 percent or more with compression. While all modern versions of tar support gzip, older versions don't, so if you want absolutely everybody to be able to read your backup, don't use -z.

Compression

In contrast, all Unix versions of tar can use the -Z flag to compress files with compress(1). The compress program isn't as efficient as gzip, but it does reduce file size. Tarballs compressed with -Z have the extension *.tar.Z*.

bzip Compression

FreeBSD's tar supports bzip compression, which shrinks files even more tightly than gzip, with the -y flag. bzip uses more CPU time than gzip, but these days CPU time is not nearly as limited as when gzip came out. Not all versions of tar support bzip compression, either. If you'll only be reading your files on a FreeBSD machine, or are comfortable installing bzip on other platforms, use the -y flag.

COMPRESSION AND FREEBSD TAR

FreeBSD's libarchive autodetects compression types used in backups. While you must specify your desired compression when creating an archive, when extracting an archive you can let tar(1) determine the compression type and let it Do The Right Thing automatically.

Permissions Restore

The -p flag restores the original permissions on extracted files. By default, tar sets the owner of an extracted file to the username that's extracting the file. This is fine for source code, but for system restores you really want to restore the file's original permissions. (Try to restore these permissions by hand some time; you'll learn quite a bit about why you should have done it right the first time.)

And More, More, More . . .

Tar has many, many more functions to accommodate decades of changes in backups, files, filesystems, and disks. For a complete list of functions, read man tar(1).

dump

dump(8) is a disk-block backup tool. In some ways, it looks similar to tar(1), but the significant difference is that dump is aware of the underlying file-system and takes advantage of the filesystem layout. We'll talk more about filesystems in Chapter 8, but for now, all you need to know is that a filesystem is the scheme by which zeroes and ones are arranged on the physical hard drive. dump is specifically integrated with FreeBSD's UFS2 filesystem. New sysadmins aren't as likely to be familiar with dump as with tar, but dump is more efficient and safer than tar. When you have a choice, use dump.[1]

One drawback of dump is that it works on filesystems, not on files. You can't dump /etc unless you want to dump all of the root partition. You can restore individual files, however.

On the positive side, dump uses separate programs for backup and recovery (dump(8) and restore(8), respectively). This means that you don't have to worry about confusing your flags and accidentally overwriting the file you're trying to recover from. dump is considerably faster than tar, too.

User Control

One significant advantage of dump(8) is that users can offer a certain amount of advice to the program. For example, they can mark a file as "do not dump," and it won't be backed up. Many users have stuff that they don't care about, and they will happily agree to not back those things up if it means that the data they do care about is backed up.

To set the nodump flag on a file, use chflags(1):

```
#chflags nodump filename
```

When you set the nodump flag on a directory, everything in or below that directory is not backed up. For example, I use chflags to avoid backing up my downloads directory to save time and space during backups, because I can always download those items again.

dump Levels

One of dump's more interesting features is its ability to do very specific incremental backups via *dump level*, a number from 0 to 9. The default dump level is 0, which tells dump to copy everything that isn't marked nodump. Higher levels of dump mean, "Back up any files that have been changed or created since a dump of any lower level." This level pattern means that you can do full backups, differential backups since a full backup, or incremental backups—just by changing the dump level.

---

[1] Some sysadmins will disagree and insist that tar(1) is better. This is an argument of epic proportions in the Unix community, and any recommendation I make will undoubtedly anger the people devoted to the other tool. I firmly believe that the only way to finally settle this is for all the people who are fanatic devotees of one tool or the other to meet on the field of honor at dawn and settle it with their weapon of choice. The rest of us will just get on with our lives.

For example, say you start each Monday with a level 0 dump. On Tuesday you could do a level 1 dump, and only files that changed since Monday will be backed up. If you perform a level 2 dump on Wednesday, everything that changed since Tuesday will be backed up. On the following Thursday, you run another level 1 dump. Any files that were changed since Monday will be backed up, including files that were backed up on Wednesday.

I recommend using only level 0 dumps because they are far, far easier to restore from than a series of incremental backups. Level 0 dumps take longer to run than incremental dumps, however, and take up more tape space, but in most cases reducing recovery time is more important than the cost of tape. With proper planning, you can run level 0 dumps overnight.

Specify the desired dump level as a command-line argument; for example, run a level 2 dump with dump -2.

dump, Tape Drives, and Files

Unfortunately, dump(8) and restore(8) don't recognize $TAPE and just send everything to */dev/sa0*. You can specify a particular tape drive with -f. Similar to tar, dump lets you point -f at a file. While dump files are not generally suitable for distribution in the same way tar files are, it's a great way to experiment and become familiar with dump.

Before dump runs a backup, it attempts to calculate how many tapes it will need for the backup. Unfortunately, dump's ability to automatically detect the size of a tape has weakened over time. When dump was new, a 1MB tape drive was serious business and every vendor had their own standards for tape formats. Today, tape drives are much more generic and standardized, and vendors must interoperate more freely. The size of tapes has also dramatically changed: For example, I'm writing this book using a 40GB tape drive discarded by a previous employer for the blameless but irremediable crime of being too small to bother keeping. Between enhanced standardization and dramatically expanded capacity, dump has a really hard time figuring out how large a tape is. The best way to deal with this problem is to tell dump to not bother calculating the size of the tape; instead, just run until the tape hits the end, and request another tape then. Use the -a flag for this.

dump and Live Filesystems

One problem with backups is that on a working machine, the filesystem tends to change while the backup is running. This isn't a problem with filesystems where the data is fairly static, or where changes in one part don't affect changes in another, but it is a serious issue when your data is highly dynamic, volatile, and/or interrelated. Many databases have this problem. You probably don't want to shut down your database server just to get a good backup, and you might not even be able to dump the database to a file so you can get a cold backup. Dump takes advantage of UFS2's snapshot facility to get around this and ensure that a backup is internally consistent. We'll cover snapshots in Chapter 8, but for now, just remember that a snapshot is an image of a disk at an exact moment in time. Even as the data on the disk changes, the snapshot remains unchanged and static, so you can back it up easily.

Specify -L to dump a snapshot. If you back up a live UFS2 filesystem without using this flag, dump will complain and tell you to use -L.

This will not eliminate the "live database" problem, of course; just because the filesystem is consistent doesn't mean that the database on the filesystem will be consistent as well. But you can shut down the database for a moment, start the dump, and start the database again, letting dump copy the snapshot taken while the database was shut down. This reduces the downtime window for backups to only a second or two.

Timestamps and dump

The file /etc/dumpdates records everything you've dumped on your system along with the dates when it was dumped. This is especially important if you do incremental backups. Use -u to update this record whenever you dump a filesystem.

Running dump

Putting all this together, we can back up a filesystem. Here I tell dump to not calculate the number of tapes required, use a snapshot to back up a live filesystem, and run a level 0 dump of my /usr partition.

```
# dump -auL /usr
❶   DUMP: Date of this level 0 dump: Sat Apr  5 08:26:03 2008
❷   DUMP: Date of last level 0 dump: the epoch
❸   DUMP: Dumping snapshot of /dev/ad0s1f (/usr) to /dev/sa0
❹   DUMP: mapping (Pass I) [regular files]
    DUMP: mapping (Pass II) [directories]
❺   DUMP: estimated 3944900 tape blocks.
    DUMP: dumping (Pass III) [directories]
    DUMP: dumping (Pass IV) [regular files]
❻   DUMP: 11.54% done, finished in 0:38 at Sat Apr  5 09:09:25 2008
    DUMP: 28.12% done, finished in 0:25 at Sat Apr  5 09:01:40 2008
    DUMP: 40.69% done, finished in 0:21 at Sat Apr  5 09:02:58 2008
    DUMP: 57.26% done, finished in 0:14 at Sat Apr  5 09:01:02 2008
    DUMP: 72.60% done, finished in 0:09 at Sat Apr  5 09:00:33 2008
    DUMP: 87.49% done, finished in 0:04 at Sat Apr  5 09:00:24 2008
    DUMP: 99.99% done, finished soon
    DUMP: DUMP: 4095026 tape blocks on 1 volume
❼   DUMP: finished in 2130 seconds, throughput 1922 KBytes/sec
❽   DUMP: level 0 dump on Sat Apr  5 08:26:03 2008
    DUMP: Closing /dev/sa0
❾   DUMP: DUMP IS DONE
```

There's a whole bunch of important stuff here. First, dump prints the current date ❶ and the date of the last backup ❷. The date shown here, the epoch, is just a fancy way of saying *from the beginning of time*. As far as Unix is concerned, time began in 1970, so this isn't as far back as you might think. What this really means is that /etc/dumpdates says that this partition has never been backed up, which isn't necessarily the same as *never*.

Before doing any work, dump reminds you which partition you're backing up and which tape drive it will use ❸.

dump then performs a preliminary analysis of the target partition, measuring the targeted files and directory structure so it can estimate how much tape it will need ❹. Once it has this number, dump tells you about it ❺ and proceeds to actually back up the files ❻. Every few minutes, dump prints out how far it's gotten and how much longer it expects to take, so you won't think that the machine has gone to sleep on you. Note that the percentages and estimated time of completion slide around a bit—the lesson here is that any software timers telling a user how much time remains on a job have never worked right and probably never will, no matter what operating system you're running.

Once the job finishes, dump will tell you how much data it archived and how fast it worked ❼, then print the date once again ❽. This isn't the time the job finished, but rather the date of the backup. Although this job finished around 9 AM, you're backing up a snapshot of the filesystem from 8:26 AM.

Finally, dump announces it's really done ❾. You can eject the tape now.

Throwing Data Overboard with nodump

The system administrator can use the -h flag to decide when to honor the nodump flag. This flag takes a dump level as an argument.

By default, a level 0 dump archives any files marked nodump. At dump level 1 or higher, the nodump flag is honored. The -h flag changes this behavior by specifying the minimum dump level to start obeying the nodump flag. Any dumps of levels below that given by -h will archive everything, regardless of the nodump flag.

This gives you an easy way to stretch your backup capacity, if you're doing level 0 dumps. When your backups suddenly overflow the tape, start honoring the nodump flag to shrink your backups. This will buy you a couple of days, giving you a little breathing room to order new tapes.

Restoring from a dump

Archives are useless unless you can recover from them. dump's recovery utility, restore(8), can recover either complete filesystems or individual files. As with tar and dump, the -f flag lets you choose the device or file you wish to restore from.

Checking the Contents of an Archive

To list the contents of your dump, use restore's -t flag:

```
#restore -t
❶ Dump    date: Sat Apr  5 08:26:03 2008
  Dumped from: the epoch
❷ Level 0 dump of /usr on test1.blackhelicopters.org:/dev/ad0s1f
  Label: none
```

```
  ❸2    ❹.
   3     ./.snap
94208    ./bin
97995   ❺./bin/bc
...
```

restore lets us know when this backup was taken ❶, what exactly was backed up ❷, and what dump level was used. It then starts to print the names of all files in the backup and their locations in the filesystem. Each file is listed with its inode number ❸. (We'll talk about inodes in Chapter 8).

One thing to note is that the files are listed relative to their point in the original filesystem. We've backed up the root directory, listed here as a single dot ❹. This directory is actually the root of the */usr* filesystem, or */usr.* The file *./bin/bc* ❺ was not actually in */bin/bc* on the original system; it belongs in */usr/bin/bc.*

This is important to remember when you're looking for a particular file in your backups. restore's -t flag will let you check a backup for the presence of a particular file. Suppose I want to recover the file */usr/home/mwlucas/.cshrc.* The first thing to do is check for this file in the archive:

```
#restore -t /usr/home/mwlucas/.cshrc
...
./usr/home/mwlucas/.cshrc is not on the tape
```

What do you mean, this file isn't on tape? Where's my data? It's time to *panic!* No, hang on a moment. Remember, this archive doesn't know anything about */usr*; paths are recorded relative to */usr*. I must search for *home/mwlucas/.cshrc.*

```
# restore -t home/mwlucas/.cshrc
...
   871426     ./home/mwlucas/.cshrc
```

My *.cshrc* is in the archive. Whew! Now to get it out.

Restoring dump Data

Once you know that a file is in an archive, you can recover it in two ways: on a file-by-file basis or as a complete filesystem.

Restoring a File

If you only want a few select pieces, use -x and the filename to extract only the named file. For example, to recover my *.cshrc* from tape, I'd run the following:

```
#restore -x home/mwlucas/.cshrc
You have not read any tapes yet.
If you are extracting just a few files, start with the last volume
and work towards the first; restore can quickly skip tapes that
have no further files to extract. Otherwise, begin with volume 1.
❶ Specify next volume #: 1
❷ set owner/mode for '.'? [yn] y
```

First, restore asks you for the volume number ❶. This is the number of the tape you're using from this backup. If an archive is split among multiple tapes, dump(8) told you the number of each tape as you shuffled them through the backup process. (You did label your tapes, right?) If you have only one tape, it's volume 1.

Once restore finds the file, it confirms that you want to restore the original permissions and owner of the file ❷. I want this file to be owned by me, just as it was originally, so I type y. My current directory now has a directory *home/mwlucas* containing my *.cshrc*.

Restoring a Filesystem

Restoring an entire filesystem is easy—perhaps too easy. It is best to restore a filesystem on an empty partition, rather than over the existing partition. If you need extensive restoration, it's best to erase the partition and start over. If you need to keep a few select files from the damaged filesystem, back up those few files individually, erase and reformat the partition, restore the backup, and copy those select files back.

In the following example, we will completely erase a partition on a second hard drive and recover from our backup tape. We won't go into details on the disk work being done here—you'll want to read Chapter 8 for that information—but it can be summarized like this:

1.   Build a new filesystem with newfs.

2.   Attach that filesystem to the system, under */mnt*.

3.   Go into that directory.

4.   Restore the filesystem from the default tape device */dev/sa0*.

This is how you accomplish all of that:

```
# newfs /dev/ad1s1g
# mount /dev/ad1s1g /mnt
# cd /mnt
# restore -r
```

That's simple enough that you probably want to destroy a disk just to restore it, don't you?

RESTORES AND FURTHER BACKUPS

Any time you perform a full disk restore, run another level 0 dump before taking another incremental dump. restore(8) rearranges data on the disk. If you take an incremental dump of your newly restored filesystem and attempt to use it with a pre-restore level 0 dump, you will get incoherent results, destroy data, and trigger a rain of toads. Always run a level 0 dump immediately upon restoring a filesystem, so further incremental backups will work. And have I mentioned how much easier life is when you always run full backups?

Interactive Restores

One of restore(8)'s more interesting features is interactive mode (-i) with which you can crack open a dump and access it with a command-line tool, marking files that you want to restore. Interactive mode is terribly useful when a user says, "I accidentally erased my resume. It's somewhere in my home directory. I'm not sure exactly what it's called, but the name has the word *resume* somewhere in it. Can you get it back?" Obviously the -t flag won't help us; we don't know the filename! Instead, we can wander around in restore's interactive mode until we find the file. It won't be that hard, and the user will owe us one.[2] Run restore with the -i flag, and you'll get an interactive dump session with a command prompt that behaves much like a regular Unix command prompt but only supports those commands necessary for restore. Depending on your tape drive, it might take a moment or two for the command prompt to appear.

```
#restore -i
restore > ls
.:
.snap/    bin/      games/    include/  libdata/  local/    ports/    share/
X11R6/    compat/   home/     lib/      libexec/  obj/      sbin/     src/
restore > cd home/mwlucas
```

This should look somewhat familiar; it's the top-level directory of our dump—in this case, everything under */usr*. You can maneuver around the filesystem with cd and list files with ls, just like in a regular shell. Once you find the file you want to restore, use the add command to add it to the list of files to extract. When you've found all the files, use the extract command to start the file recovery.

```
restore > add ssh.tar
restore > add .cshrc
restore > extract
You have not read any tapes yet.
...
```

The rest of the process looks just like a noninteractive restore; you're asked for a volume number and if you want to have restore to reset the permissions properly. When it's complete, backups of your selected files will appear in your current directory.

Once you have recovered the files, use the quit command to leave restore.

---

[2] Collecting that favor encourages the user to not repeat their daft mistake; it's not just a way to get your lawn mowed. The secret to being a successful sysadmin is a professional demeanor, a sense of humor, and a baseball bat.

Multiple Backups on One Tape

If your tape drive has sufficient capacity, you'll probably want to place multiple backups on a single tape. dump(8) only backs up one partition at a time, after all, and having separate tapes for different partitions of the same machine is inefficient. If you're using tar(1) for backups, you might still have several different backups on a single tape. The key to multiple backups on a single machine is mt(1) and controlling rewinds.

Remember, the default device node tells mt, tar, and dump to rewind after every command. This means that your second backup will overwrite your first. By changing the device node, you change this behavior. If you run a backup without rewinding, then run another backup, the second backup will appear as a second file on the tape. By controlling the tape position, you can choose where you are writing or restoring.

For example, the following commands dump three filesystems in succession—*root*, */var*, and */tmp*—on the same tape:

```
# dump -f /dev/nsa0 -auL /
# dump -f /dev/nsa0 -auL /var
# dump -f /dev/nsa0 -auL /tmp
```

The tape is now at the end of the third file. You can rewind and eject the tape, label the tape with the files it contains and the date of the backup, and store it safely.

If you want to see how many backups you have on the tape, just run mt status and look at the last line.

```
...
File Number: 3  Record Number: 0        Residual Count 0
```

Note that the file number has changed to 3. You have three files on this tape.

To access a file, position the tape drive at the file and use tar or restore to pull data from the tape. When the tape is rewound, it's in place to access the first file. Advance to later files with mt(1)'s fsf command. mt fsf takes one argument, the number of files to move forward. If you're at the beginning of the tape and want to move to the second file, just run this:

```
# mt -f /dev/nsa0 fsf 1
```

This moves the tape forward one file. Note that we've specified the -f /dev/nsa0 option, to use the "do not rewind" device node. It would do us no good to move forward a file and automatically rewind.

Now use the -t option of your archive extraction program to view the contents of that file. You can easily identify the backup by its contents. As you list the contents, restore(8) even prints the date and time the backup was taken and the partition in the backup. If you want to go backwards on the tape, use mt bsf and the number of files you wish to move.

Tapes require a slightly different mindset than disks, but they're really not hard and are still the most commonly used backup media. Now let's consider some other methods to protect you, your data, your system, and what we system administrators laughingly call our minds.

Revision Control

Generally speaking, revision control is the process of tracking changes. In the Unix world, this means recording changes to source code or configuration files. Revision control allows a developer to see how a piece of code looked on a specific date, and an administrator to see how the system was configured before a program stopped working. Even a lowly writer can use revision control to see how a manuscript has changed over time. If you're not using revision control, you're making your job more difficult than it has to be.

While you'll encounter many revision control systems, from primordial Unix's Source Code Control System (SCCS) to Microsoft's glitzy Visual SourceSafe, we'll discuss Revision Control System, or RCS, included with almost all Unix systems. Once you master RCS, you can apply its concepts to almost any other revision control system.

BEST PRACTICE IN REVISION CONTROL

I've seen a lot of revision control practices in system administration at many facilities over the years. Perhaps the most common method is saving copies of each file with the date appended (i.e., *rc.conf.20060510*). This makeshift revision control is not only not a good practice; it is actively bad practice. Nothing ensures that it records every change made, and there's no tracking system to record why a change was made. As one of my minions said at one point, "RCS is like medicine that tastes bad; you need to have it, or you'll never get better." Become comfortable with RCS, use it in a disciplined manner, and in a few months you'll wonder how you ever accomplished anything without it.

Revision control systems keep a record of all changes that happen to a file and why the changes were made. First, you mark the file as checked out, telling the system that you are reserving the right to change the file. You then edit the file as you need, record the changes in the system, and *check in* the file so others can edit it. RCS accomplishes this with three basic commands: ci(1), co(1), and rcs(1).

Think of revision control as a library—no, not the Web—an old-fashioned brick-and-mortar library with honest paper books. To use revision control on a file, you must first tell RCS to keep track of it, like giving it to the library. To use the file, you check it out, like taking a book home from the library. Once checked out, nobody else can save or edit that file, although any legitimate user can access, view, use, copy, or compile that file while you have it checked out. Once you finish with the file, you check it back in, thus releasing it for others to check out. This is the heart of any revision control system. Any file under revision control is said to be *in RCS*.

Every file in RCS has a version number. Every time you return a file to the system, RCS compares the returned file to the version you checked out. If there is any change at all, the version number is incremented and the changes are recorded, along with the date and the reason for the change. You can track specific versions of a file by the version number.

Initializing Revision Control

Begin the revision control process by checking in a file with ci(1), much like giving a book to the library. One good file to put under version control is */etc/rc.conf*, so you can track basic system changes. To start the RCS process, enter ci *filename* as shown here:

```
#ci rc.conf
❶ rc.conf,v  <--  rc.conf
enter description, terminated with single '.' or end of file:
NOTE: This is NOT the log message!
>> ❷system configuration file
>> ❸.
❹ initial revision: 1.1
done
```

When you initially check in a file, ci creates or edits a revision control file. This file has the same name as the original file, with a *,v* extension. In this example, *rc.conf* becomes *rc.conf,v* ❶. You're then prompted for a description of the file, which will be available to any RCS user later. The description doesn't have to be detailed, especially on a standard system file like *rc.conf*; the brief system configuration file given here ❷ is fine. The description is much more important with source code files or configuration files for custom, complex programs. Once you've finished the description, enter a single dot on a line by itself ❸ to exit ci. You'll be told the revision number of the file ❹, which is always 1.1 when you first check it in.

If you use ls immediately after checking something in, you'll notice that the file appears to have vanished. Instead, you'll see only the revision control file with the same name but a trailing *,v*. This is the RCS file, where the file and its revision information are stored. If you have lots of files in RCS, the *,v* files can quickly clutter a directory. You can neaten the directory by creating a directory called RCS, in all caps. The ci program will then put the *,v* files in that directory, keeping the working directory clean.

While it's fine for some files to disappear when checked in, configuration files, web pages, and the like shouldn't just vanish. To avoid this, when checking in a file you can leave a copy in the working directory with ci -u. If a file is checked in and has vanished, and you want to put a clean copy in the working directory without editing it, use co(1).

```
#co rc.conf
❶ rc.conf,v  -->  rc.conf
❷ revision 1.1
done
```

As the computer won't boot properly without rc.conf, it's important to have it available. RCS has extracted the file *rc.conf* from *rc.conf,v* ❶ so that version 1.1 ❷ of this file is available for use. But if you look closely at these files, you'll see something that might surprise you.

```
#ls -l rc.conf*
-r--r--r--  1 root   wheel   321 Apr 10 21:40 rc.conf
-r--r--r--  1 root   wheel   527 Apr 10 21:33 rc.conf,v
```

The user root owns these files, but the permissions have been set to read-only (-r--r--r--). Even though I have the root password, I no longer have permission to edit my own files! This is because the file isn't checked out to me. I've checked it in—handed it over to the Revision Control System Librarian. I can view the file, but if I want to edit it, I must ask the RCS system for it.

> ### WARNING TO VI(1) USERS!
>
> If you or your group owns the file, a w! will force a permission change and allow you to write to the file without ever checking it out. Everything will look fine, but the next person who checks out the file will overwrite your changes! Be careful with using w! at any time, under any circumstances—it's meant as an emergency measure, not standard practice. If vi complains that you don't have permission to save a file, there's a good reason. Ignore it at your peril.

Editing Files in RCS

To edit a file, I must check it out and lock it for my use. This prevents anyone else from editing the file while I'm making my changes. Use co -l to check out and lock a file:

```
#co -l rc.conf
rc.conf,v  -->  rc.conf
revision 1.1 ❶(locked)
done
```

This looks much like the check-out we did before, but notice the word locked ❶. This file is checked out and locked by me. I am the only one who can edit and save this file until I unlock it. Running ls -l at this point will show that the file's permissions are now set to read and write, allowing me to save my work (we'll discuss permissions in Chapter 7). Anyone else who tries to check this file out will get a warning that the file is in use, along with the username of the person who has locked the file.

Checking Back In

When finished with my changes, I check the file in and, since I want other people to be able to edit the file, use the -u flag to lease an unlocked copy in the current directory.

```
#ci -u rc.conf
rc.conf,v  <-- rc.conf
❶new revision: 1.2; previous revision: 1.1
enter log message, terminated with single '.' or end of file:
>> ❷clean up unneeded services
>> ❸.
done
```

When you check something in, ci gives you the new version number of
the file ❶ and requests a log message ❷. Enter a brief description of your
changes here. On a multi-user system, you might want to enter why you are
making this change. If you have a trouble ticket system, it's a good idea to list
your ticket number here; that way, people can reference the ticket and get
the whole story behind the change. As with the description message on the
first check-in, end your comments with a dot on a line by itself ❸.

These log messages allow others to know what changes you've made to a
file without digging through all the changes—or, alternatively, to see what
you were trying to do when your change broke something. Your own RCS
logs can also be useful to you, months later, when you stare at something
wondering just what was going on inside your head at the time.

Now that you understand the basics of checking files in and out, let's
examine some of the more useful functions of RCS. These include viewing
logs, getting old versions of files, breaking locks, finding differences between
file versions, and putting RCS identifiers in files.

Viewing RCS Logs

The quickest way to see the change history of a file is to view the RCS log with
rlog(1). This displays all the log messages entered for a particular file. Here
we check the RCS log for */etc/rc.conf* from a different machine:

```
#rlog rc.conf
```

```
❶ RCS file: RCS/rc.conf,v
   Working file: rc.conf
❷ head: 1.3
   branch:
   locks: strict
   access list:
   symbolic names:
   keyword substitution: kv
   total revisions: 3;    selected revisions: 3
   description:
❸ system boot config
   ----------------------------
❹ revision 1.3
❺ date: 2006/02/17 22:23:45;  ❻author: mwlucas;  state: Exp;  ❼lines: +2 -2
❽ rename new interfaces
   ----------------------------
   revision 1.2
```

```
        date: 2006/02/16 20:09:46;  author: mwlucas;  state: Exp;  lines: +4 -0
❾ *** empty log message ***
        ----------------------------
        revision 1.1
        ...
```

All sorts of useful information appears here. We see that the RCS file is in a subdirectory called RCS ❶, and that the file is at version 1.3 ❷. The file description that you entered when first checking in the file appears at the top of the log entries ❸.

Each revision then has its own entry. Revision 1.3 ❹ was checked in on February 17, 2006 ❺, at 10:23 PM. The file was checked in by the user mwlucas ❻—apparently I was working late that day. The change wasn't very large; I added two lines and removed two lines from this file ❼. Finally, the log message tells me that I renamed two interfaces ❽. I have absolutely no memory of doing any of this, which is not terribly surprising if I was working that late!

Interestingly, I didn't leave a message for revision 1.2. Apparently I was feeling sloppy that day. I wonder what I changed?

Reviewing a File's Revision History

To see what changed between two versions of a file, use rcsdiff(1). This program takes three arguments: two revision numbers and a filename, as shown below. I recommend adding the -u flag to make the changes more readable and show them in context.

```
#rcsdiff -u -rolderversionnumber -rnewerversionnumber filename
```

For example, if I ran rcsdiff -u -r1.1 -r1.2 rc.conf, I would see the following:

```
RCS file: RCS/rc.conf,v
retrieving revision 1.1
retrieving revision 1.2
❶ diff -u -r1.1 -r1.2
--- rc.conf     2006/02/10 18:09:54     1.1
+++ rc.conf     2006/02/16 20:09:46     1.2
@@ -10,12 +10,16 @@
 ifconfig_sk0="name internet inet 172.16.88.3 netmask 255.255.255.0"
 ifconfig_sk1="name dmz inet 192.168.3.1 netmask 255.255.255.0"
 ifconfig_sk2="name mwlprivate inet 192.168.0.1 netmask 255.255.255.252"
❷ +
 +
 usbd_enable="YES"
 sshd_enable="YES"
 ntpd_enable="YES"
❸ -syslogd_flags="-l /var/run/log -l /var/named/var/run/log"

 moused_enable="YES"
```

```
      named_enable="YES"

      apache21_enable="YES"
❹ +snmpd_enable="YES"
```

The `rcsdiff` command just checks out the two revisions of the file you
give it and runs diff(1) on them ❶. rcsdiff recognizes most diff(1) options, so
if you're comfortable with diff, you can tweak the output as you like. Lines
beginning with a plus sign ❷ have been added to the file, and lines that
begin with a minus sign ❸ have been removed. Here I added some white
space, removed my custom `syslogd_flags` (thus reverting to the behavior
shown in */etc/defaults/rc.conf*), and enabled snmpd ❹. Well, that's okay. I wish
I had left a message for myself to make digging through the diff unnecessary,
but at least now I know what I did. This is all useful knowledge, especially on
a production system, and especially on a production system administered by
multiple people.

You can also use rcsdiff between arbitrary revision numbers, allowing you
to view all the changes made between any two revisions. In the preceding
example, we chose to view the differences between two consecutive versions,
but I could have asked for the differences between revisions 1.1 and 1.3, or
even for all the changes made over the previous year.

Getting Older Versions

If the differences between two versions are extensive enough, reading a diff
can be difficult. In some cases, the diff doesn't provide sufficient context to
understand what's going on. The simplest thing to do in those cases is just
get the old version of the file and read it. You can use the -r flag to pull an
old version of a file out of RCS. Specify the version number immediately after
-r, without a space:

```
#co -r1.1 rc.conf
rc.conf,v  -->  rc.conf
revision 1.1
done
```

We've checked out version 1.1, overwriting the existing *rc.conf*.
Wait a minute! Overwriting the existing file is probably not correct,
especially for a vital system file. To put the file elsewhere, use the -p flag to
print the file to your screen and redirect that output to a file.

```
#co ❶-r1.1 ❷-p rc.conf ❸> /tmp/rc.conf.original
rc.conf,v  -->  standard output
revision 1.1
```

Here we've checked out revision 1.1 of *rc.conf* ❶, and used the -p flag ❷
to print the file directly to the terminal. The right angle bracket ❸ redirects
the output from the screen to a file, in this case */tmp/rc.conf.original*.

Breaking Locks

If you don't check a file back in when you're done, nobody else will be able to check out and lock that file. If you've gone home for the day, they'll be piqued—perhaps even outright miffed. If you've gone on vacation, expect your vacation to be interrupted. Fortunately, it isn't necessary to wait for your return to unlock the file; they can break the lock and claim it for themselves. This is like a librarian showing up at your house with a chainsaw to claim that overdue book.

As a potential lock breaker, you must exercise caution. If someone is really editing a file when you break the lock, they'll go past annoyed straight to angry. Do your best to find the person before you break a lock! Once you've decided to break the lock, however, run rcs -u on the file. RCS will ask you to enter a message explaining why you're breaking the lock, which it will email to the lock holder.[3]

When you break the lock, the file will be available for another user to edit. The changes made by the negligent unlocker will still be in the existing file, however. Checking out the file again will overwrite that file and eliminate any changes made. You might wish to copy that file to a temporary location before you check out and lock the file again, in case those changes are important.

AUTOMATED LOCK SEARCHES

A web search will show any number of methods for identifying all files that have been left locked on a system. If people consistently leave files locked on your system, you might consider running a script via cron to identify these files and the culprits who left them locked, and automatically mailing the list to the system administration team on a daily basis.

Multiple Check-ins

It's not uncommon to change several files simultaneously as part of a single change. For example, a DNS change might require changes to two or more zone files (see Chapter 14). These files all need the same log message, and you won't want to type it repeatedly. The -m flag lets you specify a log message on the command line. For example, here I'm checking in the files *blackhelicopters.org.db* and *absolutefreebsd.com.db* with the log message update for new mail server.

```
# ci -u -m"update for new mail server" blackhelicopters.org.db
absolutefreebsd.com.db
```

---

[3] Personally, I take this message as an opportunity to insult the person who left the file locked, but your site policy might differ.

Note the lack of a space between the -m and the quotes around your check-in message. RCS will check in each file consecutively and use your message in the log.

RCS and ident Strings

ident strings make it easy for someone viewing a file to see the RCS information about that file. For example, if I have a program that began behaving oddly a week ago, I just want to know what changed at that time. I could run rlog(1) on all the configuration files to see when things were changed, but that's a bit annoying. It's much nicer to look at the file and have the information presented to me. That's where ident strings come in. You can put ident strings in files stored in RCS, and when you check the file out, RCS will automatically update them.

ident strings have the form $string$. For example, the RCS ident string Id puts information about the last change in the file. I always put #Id in the first line of critical configuration files, such as */etc/rc.conf*. The leading hash mark tells */etc/rc* that this line is a comment and should be skipped; but once I've checked in this file, this line appears as:

#$Id: rc.conf,v ❶1.3 ❷2006/04/12 ❸17:12:49 ❹mwlucas ❺Exp $

The simple little ident string has expanded quite a bit! We can see at a glance the file's version number ❶, the date ❷ and time ❸ of the last change, and who last changed this file ❹. It's an easy way to answer the question, "Has this file changed lately, and who should I talk to about that change?" The last bit of the line is the RCS state ❺, an arbitrary string that you can assign with ci(1) or rcs(1). A few people use this to mark a file as *experimental* or *production* or *don't change for any reason whatsoever*. On the other hand, most people do nothing at all with RCS state, and that's generally the best idea in system administration.

While Id is the most commonly used ident string, you have several others to choose from, including $Header$ and Log. $Header$ is very similar to Id, except that it gives the full path for the RCS file instead of just the filename. Log adds the RCS log message to the file itself; when you view the file you will see all the RCS log messages. While the log messages can be overwhelming on files that change frequently, they can be useful in files that change less frequently. For example, the */etc/rc.conf* files on my servers don't change that often after about a month of production use. If I put this ident string in the file, I will see all the RCS log messages every time I view the file. This makes changes very obvious. Most other ident strings are just a subset of Id, $Header$, or Log. For a full list, see ident(1).

Now that you can back up your system and track the work you do, you're able to work more freely, knowing that you can always restore your past changes.

Recording What Happened

You can now back up your entire system, as well as track changes in a single file. All that remains is to track what's happening on the screen in front of you. script(1) is one of those rarely mentioned but quite useful tools every sysadmin should know. It logs everything you type and everything that appears on the screen. You can record errors and log output for later dissection and analysis. For example, if you're running a program that fails in the same spot every time, you can use script to copy your keystrokes and the program's response. This is notably useful when upgrading your system or building software from source code; the last 30 lines or so of the log file make a nice addition to a help request.

To start script(1), just type script. You'll get your command prompt back and can continue working normally. When you want the recording to stop, just type exit or press CTRL-D. Your activity will appear in a file named *typescript*. If you want the file to have a particular name or be in a particular location just give that name as an argument to script:

```
# script /home/mwlucas/debug.txt
```

This is extremely useful to record exactly what you typed, and exactly what the system responded with, for reporting problems to *FreeBSD-questions @FreeBSD.org*.

The Fixit Disk

The best way to learn an operating system is to play with it, and the harder you play the more you learn. If you play hard enough, you'll certainly break something, which is a good thing—having to fix a badly broken system is arguably the fastest way to learn. If you've just rendered your system unbootable, or plan to learn quickly enough to risk doing that, this section is for you. If your system is deeply hosed, you'll learn a lot, quickly.

Single-user mode (discussed in Chapter 3) gives you access to many different commands and tools. What if you've destroyed those tools, however? Perhaps you've even damaged the statically linked programs in */rescue*. That's where the fixit disk comes in.

A fixit disk is a "live filesystem" image of a FreeBSD system on CD. It includes all the programs that come by default with FreeBSD. The installation CD comes with a fixit disk image. When you boot of the install media, you can choose to enter fixit mode instead of installing.

You must have some familiarity with system administration to use the fixit system successfully. Essentially, the fixit disk gives you a command prompt and a variety of Unix utilities. You get to use the boot time error messages and that ballast you keep between your ears to fix the problem. It's you against the computer. Of the half-dozen times I've resorted to the fixit disk, the computer won the first three. The time was well spent, however, as I've developed the ability to restore a damaged system. Definitely finish reading this book before you even try.

It's impossible to outline a step-by-step fixit process for generic problem situations; the exact steps you must follow depend on the exact damage you've inflicted on your poor, innocent computer. If you're really desperate, however, fixit mode gives you a shot at recovery without reinstalling. I've had problems where I've accidentally destroyed my /etc directory, or fried the getty(1) program that displays a login prompt. Careful use of fixit mode can repair these problems in a fraction of the time a reinstall would take.

NOTE *It's important to use a fixit disk that's roughly equivalent to the FreeBSD version you're running. A point or two off won't make much difference, but you won't be happy trying to fix a 6.5 system with an 8-current fixit disk.*

Boot off the installation media. When you reach the first menu, you'll see a choice offering to enter fixit mode. Select it. You'll then get a choice of using a CD or a floppy disk. Use the CD option, as you booted off the disc. (A fixit floppy only contains a handful of programs; while you can make one, these days it's much easier to just use the CD.) While it might not include your favorite editor or shell, those are in the category of "nice to have" rather than "absolutely needed."

At times, all you can hope for is to get the hard drive mounted so that you can read remaining data from it. The fixit CD contains all the tools you need to get the system on the network so you can mount a hard drive in read-only mode and copy any surviving data to another machine. This lets you do a last backup before blowing away the system and reinstalling. If the fixit disk doesn't give you a needed tool to perform a recovery, you might also try a bootable CD version of FreeBSD, such as FreeSBIE. We'll touch on FreeSBIE in Chapter 20.

Now that you can recover from almost any mistake you might make, let's dive into the heart of FreeBSD: the kernel.

5

KERNEL GAMES

A common first step in optimizing FreeBSD is configuring the kernel. If you're new to Unix administration, the word *kernel* might be intimidating. After all, the kernel is one of those secret parts of a computer that mere mortals are not meant to dabble in. In some versions of Unix, kernel tampering is unthinkable. Microsoft doesn't advertise that its operating systems even have kernels, which is like glossing over the fact that human beings have brains.[1] While high-level users can access the kernel through a variety of methods, this isn't widely acknowledged or encouraged. In most parts of the open source Unix-like world, however, meddling with the kernel is a very viable and even expected way to enhance system performance. It would probably be an excellent way to tune other operating systems, if you were allowed to do so.

---

[1] Yes, I could make any number of editorial comments here, but they're all too easy. I do have *some* standards, you know.

The FreeBSD kernel can be dynamically tuned, or changed on the fly, and most aspects of system performance can be adjusted as needed. We'll discuss the kernel's sysctl interface and how you can use it to alter a running kernel.

At the same time, some parts of the kernel can only be altered while the system is booting, and some kernel features require extensive reconfiguration. For example, you might need to add support for new devices or remove support for devices you don't use. The best way to do this is to build your own kernel.

FreeBSD has a modular kernel, meaning that entire chunks of the kernel can be loaded or unloaded from the operating system, turning entire subsystems on or off as desired. This is highly useful in this age of removable hardware, such as PC cards and USB devices. Loadable kernel modules can impact performance, system behavior, and hardware support.

Finally, we'll cover basic debugging of your kernel, including some of the scary-looking messages it gives out as well as when and how to boot alternate kernels.

What Is the Kernel?

You'll hear many different definitions of a kernel. Many are just flat-out confusing, some are technically correct but confusing to the novice, while others are wrong. The following definition isn't complete, but it'll do for most people most of the time and it's comprehensible: *The kernel is the interface between the hardware and the software.*

The kernel lets the software write data to disk drives and to the network. When a program wants memory, the kernel handles all the low-level details of accessing the physical memory chip and allocating resources for the job. It translates an MP3 file to a stream of zeros and ones that your sound card understands. When a program requests CPU time, the kernel schedules a time slot for it. In short, the kernel provides all the software interfaces that programs need in order to access hardware resources.

While the kernel's job is easy to define (at least in this simplistic manner), it's actually a complicated task. Different programs expect the kernel to provide different interfaces to the hardware, and different types of hardware provide interfaces differently. For example, FreeBSD supports a few dozen families of Ethernet cards, each with its own requirements that the kernel must handle. If the kernel cannot talk to the network card, the system is not on the network. Different programs request memory to be arranged in different ways, and if you have a program that requests memory in a manner the kernel doesn't support, you're out of luck. The way your kernel investigates some hardware during the boot sequence defines how the hardware behaves, so you have to control that. Some devices identify themselves in a friendly manner, while others lock up if you dare to ask them what they're for.

The kernel and its modules are files in the directory */boot/kernel*. Files elsewhere in the system are not part of the kernel, and such files are collectively called the *userland*, meaning that they're intended for users even if they use kernel facilities.

Since a kernel is just a set of files, you can have alternative kernels on hand for special situations. On systems where you've built your own kernel, you will find */boot/kernel.old*, a directory containing the kernel that was installed before your current kernel. I like to copy the kernel installed with the system into */boot/kernel.install*. You can also create your own special kernels. The FreeBSD team makes configuring and installing kernels as simple as possible. The simplest way to alter a kernel is through the sysctl interface.

sysctl

The sysctl(8) program allows you to peek at the values used by the kernel and, in some cases, to set them. Just to make things more confusing, these values are also sometimes known as sysctls. sysctl is a powerful feature because, in many cases, it will let you solve performance issues without rebuilding the kernel or reconfiguring an application. Unfortunately, this power also gives you the ability to sweep the legs out from under a running program and make your users really, really unhappy.

The sysctl(8) program handles all sysctl operations. Throughout this book, I'll point out how particular sysctls change system behavior, but first, you need to understand sysctls in general. Start by grabbing all the human-visible sysctls on your system and saving them to a file so you can study them easily.

```
# sysctl -A > sysctl.out
```

The file *sysctl.out* now contains hundreds of sysctl variables and their values, most of which will look utterly meaningless. A few of them, however, you can interpret without knowing much:

```
kern.hostname: humvee.blackhelicopters.org
```

This particular sysctl, called `kern.hostname`, has the value `humvee .blackhelicopters.org`. Oddly enough, the system I ran this command on has a hostname of *humvee.blackhelicopters.org*, and the sysctl hints that this is the kernel's name for the system it's running on. If only they were all this easy . . .

```
kern.ipc.msqids: Format: Length:3520
Dump:0xe903e903e903e903c0010100168f7542...
```

I have no idea what the variable `kern.ipc.msqids` represents, and I know even less about what the value means. Still, if I'm having trouble, I can get this information by asking for help from a software vendor or on a mailing list.

sysctl MIBs

The sysctls are organized in a tree format called a Management Information Base, or MIB, with several broad categories such as net (network), kern (kernel), and vm (virtual memory). Table 5-1 lists the roots of the sysctl MIB tree on a system running the GENERIC kernel.

Table 5-1: Roots of the sysctl MIB Tree

sysctl	Function
kern	Core kernel functions and features
vm	Virtual memory system
vfs	Filesystem
net	Networking
debug	Debugging
hw	Hardware
user	Userland interface information
p1003_1b	POSIX behavior*
compat	Kernel compatibility with foreign software (see Chapter 12)
security	Security-specific kernel features
dev	Device driver information

* *POSIX* is an international standard for Unix-like operating system behavior. Unfortunately, much of POSIX has changed over the years, and occasionally in ways that make systems compliant with one version of POSIX not compliant with another version. If you're so deeply into POSIX that you know what these differences are, you can use these sysctls to see exactly how FreeBSD behaves and which version of the standard it matches.

Each of these categories is divided further. For example, the net category, covering all networking sysctls, is divided into categories such as IP, ICMP, TCP, and UDP. The concept of a Management Information Base is used in several other parts of system administration, as we'll see in Chapter 20 and you'll see throughout your career. The terms *sysctl MIB* and *sysctl* are frequently used interchangeably. Each category is named by stringing together the parent category and all of its children to create a unique variable name, such as:

```
...
kern.maxfilesperproc: 11095
kern.maxprocperuid: 5547
kern.ipc.maxsockbuf: 262144
kern.ipc.sockbuf_waste_factor: 8
kern.ipc.somaxconn: 128
...
```

Here we have five sysctls plucked from the middle of the kern category. The first two are directly beneath the kern label and have no sensible grouping with other values other than the fact that they're kernel-related. The remaining three all begin with kern.ipc; they're part of the IPC (inter-process communication) section of kernel sysctls. If you keep reading the sysctls you saved, you'll see that some sysctl variables are several categories deep.

sysctl Values

Each MIB has a value that represents some buffer, setting, or characteristic used by the kernel. By changing the value, you'll change how the kernel operates. For example, some sysctls control how much memory the kernel allocates for each network connection. On networks with specific problems, you might get better performance by changing these values.

Each sysctl value is either a string, or an integer, or a binary value, or an opaque. *Strings* are free-form texts of arbitrary length; *integers* are ordinary whole numbers; *binary* values are either 0 (off) or 1 (on); and *opaques* are pieces of machine code that only specialized programs can interpret. Many sysctl values are not well documented; there is no single document listing all available sysctl MIBs and their functions. A MIB's documentation generally appears in a man page for the corresponding function, or sometimes only in the source code. For example, the original documentation for the MIB kern.securelevel (discussed in Chapter 7) is in init(8). Although sysctl documentation has expanded in recent years, many MIBs still have no documentation. Appendix A lists some commonly tweaked sysctls and their uses.

Fortunately, some MIBs have obvious meanings. For example, as we discuss later in this chapter, this is an important MIB if you frequently boot different kernels:

```
kern.bootfile: /boot/kernel/kernel
```

If you're debugging a problem and have to reboot with several different kernels in succession, you can easily forget which kernel you've booted (not that this has ever happened to me, really). A reminder can therefore be helpful.

Viewing sysctls

To view all the MIBs available in a particular subtree of the MIB tree, use the sysctl command with the name of the part of the tree you want to see. For example, to see everything under kern, enter this command:

```
# sysctl kern
kern.ostype: FreeBSD
kern.osrelease: 7.0-CURRENT-SNAP010
kern.osrevision: 199506
...
```

This list goes on for quite some time. If you're just becoming familiar with sysctls, you might use this to see what's available. To get the exact value of a specific sysctl, give the full MIB name as an argument:

```
# sysctl kern.securelevel
kern.securelevel: -1
```

The MIB kern.securelevel has the integer value -1. We'll discuss the meaning of this sysctl and its value in Chapter 7.

An easy way to get some idea of what a sysctl does is to use the -d switch with the full MIB. This prints a brief description of the sysctl:

```
# sysctl -d kern.maxfilesperproc
kern.maxfilesperproc: Maximum files allowed open per process
```

This brief definition tells you that the sysctl controls exactly what you might think it does. While this example is fairly easy, other MIBs might be much more difficult to guess.

Changing sysctls

Some sysctls are read-only. For example, take a look at the hardware MIBs:

```
hw.model: AMD Athlon(tm) 64 X2 Dual Core Processor 4200+
```

The FreeBSD Project has yet to develop the technology to change AMD hardware into sparc64 hardware via a software setting, so this sysctl is read-only. If you were able to change it, all you'd do is crash your system. FreeBSD protects you by not allowing you to change this value. An attempt to change it won't hurt anything, but you'll get a warning. On the other hand, consider the following MIB:

```
vfs.usermount: 0
```

This MIB determines if users can mount removable media such as CD-ROM and floppy drives. Changing this MIB requires no extensive tweaks within the kernel or changes to hardware; it's only an in-kernel permissions setting. To change this value, use the sysctl(8) command, the sysctl MIB, an equal sign, and the desired value:

```
# sysctl vfs.usermount=1
vfs.usermount: 0 -> 1
```

sysctl(8) responds by showing the sysctl name, the old value, and the new value. This sysctl is now changed. A sysctl that can be tuned on the fly like this is called a *run-time tunable sysctl*.

Setting sysctls Automatically

Once you have tweaked your kernel's settings to your whim, you will want those settings to remain after a reboot. You'll use the file */etc/sysctl.conf* for this. List each sysctl you want to set and the desired value in this file. For example, to have the same vfs.usermount sysctl set at boot, add the following on a separate line in */etc/sysctl.conf*:

```
vfs.usermount=1
```

Boot-Time Tunable sysctls

Some values are so deeply embedded in the kernel that they can only be adjusted when initializing the kernel during boot. You'll find many examples of these *boot-time tunable sysctls* (or *tunables*), frequently related to low-level hardware settings. As an example, when the kernel first probes an IDE hard drive, the device driver must choose whether or not to use DMA, PIO, write caching, or any other hard drive–specific settings. This decision must be made immediately upon starting the hard drive, and you can't change your mind without rebooting the machine. You can set these variables in the system loader via */boot/loader.conf,* as discussed in Chapter 3.

Much like *sysctl.conf,* setting tunable values in *loader.conf* will let you really mess up a machine. The good news is that these values are easily unset.

> **TOO MANY TUNABLES?**
>
> Don't become confused between sysctl values that can only be set at boot, sysctl values that can be tuned on the fly, and sysctls that can be set on the fly but have been configured to automatically adjust at boot. Remember that boot-time tunable sysctls involve low-level kernel functions, while run-time tunables involve higher-level functions. Having sysctls adjust themselves at boot is merely an example of saving your work—it does not change the category that the sysctl belongs to.

Dropping Hints on Device Drivers

Many device drivers need to have sysctl flags set early during boot. You'll learn about these by reading their man pages, this book, and other documentation. While these have no entry in the default *loader.conf* file, you can still add them to your *loader.conf* to have them set automatically at boot. For example, to disable DMA on ATAPI devices (which we'll discuss in Chapter 8), just put the desired sysctl setting in *loader.conf:*

```
hw.ata.atapi_dma="0"
```

The kernel will set this flag at boot and the device driver will behave accordingly.

Additionally, much old hardware requires the kernel to address it at very specific IRQ and memory values. If you're old enough to remember plug-and-pray, "hardware configuration" floppy disks, and special slots for bus master cards, you know what I'm talking about and probably have one of these systems polluting your hardware closet even today. (If you're too young for that, buy one of us geezers a drink and listen to our horror stories.[2]) You can tell FreeBSD to probe for this hardware at any IRQ or memory address you specify, which is very useful when you have a card with a known

---

[2] Actually, listening is optional.

configuration but the floppy that can change that configuration biodegraded years ago. Look in */boot/device.hints* where you'll see lots of entries like this:

```
hint.❶ed.❷0.❸disabled="1"
❹ hint.ed.0.port="0x280"
❺ hint.ed.0.irq="10"
❻ hint.ed.0.maddr="0xd8000"
```

These entries are all hints for the ed device driver ❶. The entry is used for ed device number zero ❷. The disabled keyword ❸ means that FreeBSD won't check for this device automatically at boot; if another ed card is found, it can be assigned device number zero. If you enable this device, FreeBSD will probe for a card at port 0x280 ❹, IRQ 10 ❺, and memory address 0xd8000 ❻, and if a card exists there, it will be assigned the device name ed0. Of course, if that card isn't supported by the ed(4) Ethernet driver, you'll have other problems!

sysctl(8) gives you the power to do all this with your kernel, but tuning only takes you so far. Kernel modules will take you another leap forward.

TESTING BOOT-TIME TUNABLES

All of these hints and boot-time tunable sysctls are available in the boot loader and can be set interactively at the OK prompt, as discussed in Chapter 3. You can test settings without editing *loader.conf*, find the value that works for you, and only then make the change permanent in a file.

Kernel Modules

Kernel modules are parts of a kernel that can be started (or loaded) when needed and unloaded when unused. Kernel modules can be loaded when you plug in a piece of hardware and removed with that hardware. This can save a bit of system memory and greatly expands your flexibility.

Just as the default kernel is held in the file */boot/kernel/kernel*, kernel modules are the other files under */boot/kernel*. Take a look in that directory and you'll see hundreds of kernel module files. Each kernel module name ends in *.ko*. Generally speaking, the file is named after the functionality contained in the module. For example, the file */boot/kernel/joy.ko* handles the "joy" joystick driver documented in joy(4). This kernel module makes your joystick show up as device joy0.

Viewing Loaded Modules

In Chapter 3, we saw how to look at kernel modules loaded before boot, but that won't help when the system is up and running. The kldstat(8) command will show what kernel modules are in use at the moment.

```
# kldstat
  Id Refs Address    Size     Name
❶ 1    15 0xc0400000 6a978c   kernel
❷ 2     1 0xc0aaa000 6228     snd_via8233.ko
❸ 3     2 0xc0ab1000 23898    sound.ko
```

This laptop has three kernel modules loaded. The first is the kernel proper ❶; then, we have a sound card driver ❷ and the sound subsystem ❸. (As this computer is a laptop, that's not surprising.) Each module contains one or more submodules, which you can view using kldstat -v, but the kernel itself has a few hundred submodules—so be ready for a lot of output.

Loading and Unloading Modules

Loading and unloading kernel modules is done with kldload(8) and kldunload(8). For example, my laptop is usually hooked to the network via a wired Ethernet connection. When I attach to a wireless network, I need to load the *wlan_wep.ko* kernel module that handles WEP encryption. I use the kldload command and the file containing the kernel module for that feature:

```
# kldload /boot/kernel/wlan_wep.ko
```

Once I'm done with my wireless connection, I'll unload the module.[3] For this, I don't need to specify the filename, but just the name of the kernel module as it is shown in kldstat's output:

```
# kldunload wlan_wep.ko
```

If all possible functions were compiled into the kernel, it would be rather large. Using modules, you can have a smaller, more efficient kernel and only load rarely used functionality when it's required.

kldload(8) and kldunload(8) do not require the full path to the kernel module, nor do they require the *.ko* at the end of the file. If you remember the exact name of the kernel module, you could just use:

```
# kldload wlan_wep
# kldunload wlan_wep
```

Personally, my weak brain relies on tab completion in my shell to remind me of the module's full and proper name.

Loading Modules at Boot

Use */boot/loader.conf* to load modules at boot. The default *loader.conf* includes many examples of loading kernel modules, but the syntax is always the same. Take the name of the kernel module, chop off the trailing *.ko*, and add the

---

[3] Actually I probably won't bother, as I'll be shutting down the laptop. But you get the idea.

string _load="YES". For example, to load the module */boot/kernel/procfs.ko* automatically at boot, add this to *loader.conf*:

```
procfs_load="YES"
```

The hard part, of course, is knowing which module to load. The easy ones are device drivers; if you install a new network or SCSI card that your kernel doesn't support, you can load the driver module instead of reconfiguring the kernel. In this case, you'll need to find out which driver supports your card; the man pages and Google are your friends there. I'll be giving specific pointers to kernel modules to solve particular problems throughout this book.

Wait a minute, though; why would FreeBSD make you load a device driver to recognize hardware if it recognizes almost everything at boot? That's an excellent question! The answer is that you may have built your own custom kernel and removed support for hardware you're not using. You don't know how to build a kernel? Well, let's fix that right now.

Build Your Own Kernel

Eventually, you'll find that you cannot tweak your kernel as much as you like using only sysctl and modules, and your only solution will be to build a customized kernel. This sounds much harder than it is; we're not talking about writing code here—just editing a text file and running a couple of commands. If you follow the process, it's perfectly safe. If you *don't* follow the process, well, it's like driving on the wrong side of the road. (Downtown. During rush hour.) But the recovery from a bad kernel isn't that bad, either.

The kernel shipped in a default install is called GENERIC. GENERIC is configured to run on a wide variety of hardware, although not necessarily optimally. GENERIC boots nicely on most hardware from the last decade or so. Newer hardware, however, often has optimizations that GENERIC won't support, as it is aimed at the lowest common denominator. Even so, it's perfectly suitable for use in a production environment. When you customize your kernel, you can include these optimizations, add support for new hardware, remove support for hardware you don't need, or enable nifty new features.

Building a kernel is often considered a rite of passage, and the FreeBSD support community won't think twice about asking you to rebuild your kernel to include or exclude a certain feature. While you shouldn't think that rebuilding the kernel will solve every problem, it's a useful tool to have in your system administration toolbox.

Preparations

You must have the kernel source code before you can build a kernel. If you followed my advice back in Chapter 2, you're all set. If not, you can either go back into the installer and load the kernel sources, or download the source code from a FreeBSD FTP mirror, or jump ahead to Chapter 13 and use csup(8). If you don't remember if you installed the kernel source code, look into your */sys* directory. If it contains a bunch of files and directories, you have the kernel sources.

Before building a new kernel, you must know what hardware your system has. This can be difficult to determine; the brand name on a component doesn't necessarily describe the device's identity or abilities. Many companies use rebranded generic components—I remember one manufacturer that released four different network cards under the same model name and didn't even put a version number on the first three. The only way to tell the difference was to keep trying different device drivers until one of them works. Similarly, many different companies manufactured NE2000-compatible network cards. The outside of the box had a vendor's name on it, but the circuits on the card said *NE2000*. Fortunately, some vendors use a standard architecture for their drivers and hardware; you can be fairly sure that an Intel network card will be recognized by the Intel device driver.

The best place to see what hardware FreeBSD found on your system is the file */var/run/dmesg.boot*, discussed in Chapter 3. Each entry represents either a hardware or software feature in the kernel. As you work on a new kernel for a system, keep the *dmesg.boot* of that system handy.

Buses and Attachments

Every device in the computer is attached to some other device. If you read your *dmesg.boot* carefully, you can see these chains of attachments. Here's an edited set of boot messages to demonstrate:

```
❶ acpi0: <PTLTD    RSDT> on motherboard
❷ acpi_ec0: <Embedded Controller: GPE 0xb> port 0x62,0x66 on ❸acpi0
❹ cpu0: <ACPI CPU> on acpi0
  cpu1: <ACPI CPU> on acpi0
❺ pcib0: <ACPI Host-PCI bridge> port 0xcf8-0xcff on acpi0
❻ pci0: <ACPI PCI bus> on ❼pcib0
```

Our first device on this system is acpi0 ❶. You probably don't know what that is, but you could always use man acpi to learn. (Or, if you must, you could read the rest of this chapter.) There's an acpi_ec device ❷ on this system, and it's attached to acpi0 ❸. The CPUs ❹ are also attached to acpi0, as is a PCI bridge ❺. Finally, we have the first PCI bus, pci0 ❻, attached to the PCI bridge ❼ rather than acpi0. Common PCI devices are connected to a hierarchy of buses that are, in turn, attached to a PCI bridge to talk to the rest of the computer. You could read *dmesg.boot* and draw a tree of all the devices on the system; while that isn't necessary, understanding what's attached where makes configuring a kernel much more likely to succeed.

If you're in doubt, use pciconf(8) to see what's actually on your system. pciconf -lv will list every PCI device attached to the system, whether or not the current kernel found a driver for it.

Back Up Your Working Kernel

A bad kernel can render your system unbootable, so you absolutely must keep a good kernel around at all times. The kernel install process keeps your previous kernel around for backup purposes, in the directory */boot/kernel.old*. This is nice for being able to fall back, but I recommend that you go further.

If you don't keep a known good backup, here's what can happen. If you build a new kernel, find that you made a minor mistake, and have to rebuild it again, the system-generated backup kernel is actually the first kernel you made—the one with that minor mistake. Your working kernel has been deleted. When you discover that your new custom kernel has the same problem, or an even more serious error, you'll deeply regret the loss of that working kernel.

A common place to keep a known good kernel is */boot/kernel.good*. Back up your working, reliable kernel like this:

```
# cp -Rp /boot/kernel /boot/kernel.good
```

Don't be afraid to keep a variety of kernels on hand. Disk space is cheaper than time. I know people who keep kernels in directories named by date, so that they can fall back to earlier versions if necessary. Many people also keep a current copy of the GENERIC kernel in */boot/kernel.GENERIC* for testing and debugging purposes. The only way to have too many kernels is to fill up your hard drive.

Configuration File Format

FreeBSD's kernel is configured via text files. There's no graphical utility or menu-driven system for kernel configuration; it's still much the same as in 4.4 BSD. If you're not comfortable with text configuration files, building a kernel is just not for you.

Each kernel configuration entry is on a single line. You'll see a label to indicate what sort of entry this is, and then a term for the entry. Many entries also have comments, set off with a hash mark—much like this entry for the FreeBSD filesystem FFS:

```
options         FFS                 # Berkeley Fast Filesystem
```

Every kernel configuration file is made up of five types of entries: cpu, ident, makeoptions, options, and devices. The presence or absence of these entries dictates how the kernel supports the associated feature or hardware:

cpu   This label indicates what kind of processor this kernel supports. The kernel configuration file for the boring old PC hardware includes several CPU entries to cover processors such as the 486 (I486_CPU), Pentium (I586_CPU), and Pentium Pro through modern Pentium 4 CPUs (I686_CPU). The kernel configuration for amd64/EM64T hardware includes only one CPU type, as that architecture has only one CPU family. While a kernel configuration can include multiple CPU types, they must be of similar architectures; a kernel can run on 486 and Pentium CPUs, but you can't have a single kernel that will run on both Intel-compatible and Sparc processors.

`ident`   Every kernel has a single `ident` line, giving a name for the kernel. That's how the GENERIC kernel gets its name; it's an arbitrary text string.

`makeoptions`   This string gives instructions to the kernel-building software. The most common option is `DEBUG=-g`, which tells the compiler to build a debugging kernel. Debugging kernels help developers troubleshoot system problems.

`options`   These are kernel functions that don't require particular hardware. This includes filesystems, networking protocols, and in-kernel debuggers.

`devices`   Also known as *device drivers*, these provide the kernel with instructions on how to speak to certain devices. If you want your system to support a piece of hardware, the kernel must include the device driver for that hardware. Some device entries, called pseudodevices, are not tied to particular hardware, but instead support whole categories of hardware—such as Ethernet, random number generators, or memory disks. You might wonder what differentiates a pseudodevice from an option. The answer is that pseudodevices appear to the system as devices in at least some ways, while options have no device-like features. For example, the loopback pseudodevice is a network interface that only connects to the local machine. While no hardware exists for it, software can connect to the loopback interface and send network traffic to other software on the same machine.

Configuration Files

Fortunately, you don't normally create a kernel configuration file from scratch; instead, you copy an existing one and edit it. Start with the GENERIC kernel for your hardware architecture. It can be found in */sys/<arch>/conf*—for example, the i386 kernel configuration files are in */sys/i386/conf*, the amd64 kernel configuration files are in */sys/amd64/conf*, and so on. This directory contains several files, of which the most important are *DEFAULTS*, *GENERIC*, *GENERIC.hints*, *MAC*, and *NOTES*:

DEFAULTS   This is a list of options and devices that are enabled by default for a given architecture. That doesn't mean that you can compile and run *DEFAULTS*, but it is a starting point should you want to build a truly minimal kernel.

GENERIC   This is the configuration for the standard kernel. It contains all the settings needed to get standard hardware of that architecture up and running; this is the kernel configuration used by the installer.

GENERIC.hints   This is the hints file that is later installed as */boot/device .hints*. This file provides configuration information for older hardware.

MAC   This is a kernel configuration file that supports Mandatory Access Controls—a system for fine-grained access control used in high-security environments. You only need this configuration file if you're using MAC.

NOTES   This is an all-inclusive kernel configuration for that hardware platform. Every platform-specific feature is included in *NOTES*. You can find platform-independent kernel features in */usr/src/sys/conf/NOTES*.

Do not edit any of the files in the configuration directory directly. Instead, copy GENERIC to a file named after your machine and edit the copy. For example, my laptop is called *humvee.blackhelicopters.org*: I would copy the file *GENERIC* to a file called *HUMVEE* and open *HUMVEE* in my preferred text editor. Here's a snippet of a configuration file—the part that covers ATA devices:

```
# ATA and ATAPI devices
device          ata
device          atadisk         # ATA disk drives
device          ataraid         # ATA RAID drives
device          atapicd         # ATAPI CDROM drives
device          atapifd         # ATAPI floppy drives
device          atapist         # ATAPI tape drives
options         ATA_STATIC_ID   # Static device numbering
```

Hash marks (#) delimit comments; everything after a hash mark to the end of line is ignored. They're there to separate machine-friendly stuff from human-friendly stuff. For example, the first line of this snippet tells you that the following entries are all for ATA and ATAPI devices. Other lines have comments that start in the middle of the line, telling you what the entries are for.

Compare these entries to a couple of our ATA entries in */var/run/ dmesg.boot*:

```
ata1: <ATA channel 1> on atapci1
acd0: DVDR <PIONEER DVD-RW DVR-K16/1.33> at ata1-master UDMA33
```

The kernel configuration has an ATA bus, device ata, and the dmesg shows an ATA channel ata1. The DVD-RW drive is attached to ata1. Without the device ata in the kernel config, the kernel would not recognize the ATA bus. Even if the system figured out that a DVD drive is in the system, it wouldn't know how to get information to and from it. Your kernel configuration must include all the intermediary devices for the drivers that rely on them. On the other hand, if your system doesn't have ATA RAID drives, floppy drives, or tape drives, you can remove those device drivers from your kernel.

Trimming a Kernel

Once upon a time, memory was far more expensive than today and was only available in smaller quantities. When a system has 128MB of RAM, you want every bit of that to be available for work. It was important to have a kernel as small as possible. Today, when even a laptop has 2GB RAM, kernel size is almost irrelevant. Stripping unnecessary drivers out of a kernel to make it smaller might not be vital—but it isn't an actively dumb thing to do; it will teach you how to build a kernel, so that when the need appears you won't have to learn something new. So, we're going to use kernel trimming as a learning exercise, but don't consider it vital or even necessary.

Remove an entry from the kernel configuration by commenting it out.

CPU Types

On most architectures, FreeBSD supports only one or two types of CPU. The i386 platform supports three. Removing unnecessary CPU types from your kernel configuration will produce a kernel that takes full advantage of the features offered by your CPU—for example, consider the Pentium versus the Pentium II with MMX instructions. If those instructions are available on your CPU, you want to take advantage of them. On the other hand, stripping out unused CPU types from the kernel will produce a kernel that can only run on one type of CPU.

You only need to include the CPU you have. If you're not sure of the CPU in your hardware, check *dmesg.boot*. My laptop's *dmesg.boot* includes the following lines:

```
CPU: AMD Athlon(tm) 64 X2 Dual Core Processor 4200+ (2200.10-MHz 686-class CPU)
  Origin = "AuthenticAMD"  Id = 0x20fb1  Stepping = 1

Features=0x178bfbff<FPU,VME,DE,PSE,TSC,MSR,PAE,MCE,CX8,APIC,SEP,MTRR,PGE,MCA,C
MOV,PAT,PSE36,CLFLUSH,MMX,FXSR,SSE,SSE2,HTT>
...
```

As shown in bold, this is a 686-class CPU, which means that I can remove the I486_CPU cpu statements to make my kernel smaller and faster. As a result, the kernel will use 686-class CPU-specific optimizations instead of slower generic code. (Also, as it's a 64-bit i386-style chip, I could run either i386 or amd64 versions of FreeBSD, as discussed in Chapter 1. We're choosing to use i386 examples, however, as that's probably what most readers have.)

Basic Options

Following the CPU type configuration entries, we have a whole list of options for basic FreeBSD services such as TCP/IP and filesystems. An average system won't require all of these, but having them present provides a great deal of flexibility. You'll also encounter options rarely used in your environment as well as those you can remove from your custom kernel configuration. We won't discuss all possible kernel options, but will cover specific examples of different option types. I'll specifically mention those that can be trimmed from an Internet server. Consider the following:

#options	SCHED_ULE	# ULE scheduler
options	SCHED_4BSD	# 4BSD scheduler
options	PREEMPTION	# Enable kernel thread preemption

These options control how FreeBSD performs its internal scheduling. We'll discuss scheduling in Chapter 12. Preemption makes FreeBSD more efficient at multitasking.

options	INET	# InterNETworking
options	INET6	# IPv6 communications protocols

These options support networking. INET is the standard old-fashioned TCP/IP, while INET6 supports IPv6. Much Unix-like software depends on TCP/IP, so you certainly require INET. IPv6 has much more limited deployment, however; while eventually you'll have to understand it, that day hasn't come yet, so you can trim INET6 if you like.

options	FFS	# Berkeley Fast Filesystem
options	SOFTUPDATES	# Enable FFS soft updates support
options	UFS_ACL	# Support for access control lists
options	UFS_DIRHASH	# Improve performance on big
directories		

FFS is the standard FreeBSD filesystem, and the other options are all related to FFS. Soft updates is a method for ensuring disk integrity even when your system is shut down incorrectly. UFS access control lists allow you to grant very detailed permissions on files, and UFS_DIRHASH enables directory hashing to make directories with thousands of files more efficient. We discuss FFS and its options in more detail than you care for in Chapter 8.

options	MD_ROOT	# MD is a potential root device

This option (and all the other _ROOT options) lets the system use something other than a standard FFS filesystem as a disk device for the root partition. The installer uses a memory device (MD) as a root partition. If you're using a diskless system (Chapter 20), you'll need an NFS root partition. If you're running FreeBSD on a standard computer system, with a hard drive and a keyboard and whatnot, your kernel doesn't need any of these features.

options	NFSCLIENT	# Network Filesystem Client
options	NFSSERVER	# Network Filesystem Server

These two options support the Network File System (see Chapter 8). NFSCLIENT lets you mount partitions served by another machine across the network, while NFSSERVER allows you to offer partitions for other machines to mount.

```
options     MSDOSFS              # MSDOS filesystem
options     CD9660               # ISO 9660 filesystem
options     PROCFS               # Process filesystem (requires PSEUDOFS)
options     PSEUDOFS             # Pseudo-filesystem framework
```

These options support rarely used filesystems such as FAT, CDs, the process filesystem, and the pseudo-filesystem framework. We discuss these filesystems in Chapter 8, but all the functionality they require is available via kernel modules on those rare occasions they're used.

```
options     COMPAT_43TTY         # BSD 4.3 TTY compat [KEEP THIS!]
options     COMPAT_FREEBSD4      # Compatible with FreeBSD4
options     COMPAT_FREEBSD5      # Compatible with FreeBSD5
options     COMPAT_FREEBSD6      # Compatible with FreeBSD6
```

These compatibility options let your system run software built for older versions of FreeBSD, or software that makes assumptions about the kernel that were valid for older versions of FreeBSD but are no longer true. If you're installing a system from scratch, you probably won't need compatibility with FreeBSD 4, 5, or 6, but a surprising amount of software requires compatibility with 4.3 BSD. Keep the COMPAT_43TTY option, or your system *will* break.

```
options     SCSI_DELAY=5000      # Delay (in ms) before probing SCSI
```

The SCSI_DELAY option specifies the number of milliseconds FreeBSD waits after finding your SCSI controllers before probing them, giving them a chance to spin up and identify themselves to the SCSI bus. If you have no SCSI hardware, you can remove this line. If you have ancient SCSI hardware that starts up like an arthritic elephant, you might want to increase this to as much as 15000 (15 seconds).

```
options     SYSVSHM              # SYSV-style shared memory
options     SYSVMSG              # SYSV-style message queues
options     SYSVSEM              # SYSV-style semaphores
```

These options enable System-V-style shared memory and interprocess communication. Many database programs use this feature.

```
options     AHC_REG_PRETTY_PRINT # Print register bitfields in debug
                                 # output.  Adds ~128k to driver.
options     AHD_REG_PRETTY_PRINT # Print register bitfields in debug
                                 # output.  Adds ~215k to driver.
```

Options like these are only effective if you're using the hardware they reference. Otherwise, they're useless and can be removed.

Multiple Processors

The following two entries enable symmetric multiprocessing (SMP) in i386 kernels:

```
options      SMP                    # Symmetric MultiProcessor Kernel
device       apic                   # I/O APIC
```

The SMP option tells the kernel to schedule processes on multiple CPUs, while the apic handles input/output for SMP kernels. FreeBSD's i386 SMP implementation only supports SMP systems that fit the Intel SMP specification, which does not include 386 or 486 SMP systems. (Other platforms, such as sparc64, fully comply with their own standards, so SMP works just fine on them.) FreeBSD only supports multiple processors on Pentium and newer processors. In older versions of FreeBSD, SMP kernels performed poorly or wouldn't boot at all on single-CPU systems; the overhead of managing data for multiple processors created additional drag on the system. This is no longer the case, and FreeBSD now ships with SMP enabled by default.

Device Drivers

After all the options you'll find device driver entries, which are grouped in fairly sensible ways.

The first device entries are buses, such as device pci and device eisa. Keep these, unless you truly don't have that sort of bus in your system. A surprising number of "legacy-free" systems have an ISA bus buried somewhere inside them.

Next, we reach what most people consider *device drivers* proper—entries for floppy drives, SCSI controllers, RAID controllers, and so on. If your goal is to reduce the size of your kernel, this is a good place to trim heavily; remove all device drivers for hardware your computer doesn't have. You'll also find a section of device drivers for such mundane things as keyboards, video cards, PS/2 ports, and so on. You almost certainly don't want to delete these.

The network card device driver section is quite long and looks much like the SCSI and IDE sections. If you're not going to replace your network card any time soon, you can eliminate drivers for any network cards you aren't using.

We won't list all the device drivers here, as there's very little to be learned from such a list other than the hardware FreeBSD supported at the time I wrote this section. Check the release notes for the version of FreeBSD you're running to see what hardware it supports.

Pseudodevices

You'll find a selection of pseudodevices near the bottom of the GENERIC kernel configuration. As the name suggests, these are created entirely out of software. Here are some of the more commonly used pseudodevices.

```
device          loop          # Network loopback
```

The loopback device allows the system to communicate with itself via network sockets and network protocols. We'll discuss network connections in some detail in the next chapter. You might be surprised at just how many programs use the loopback device, so don't remove it.

```
device          random        # Entropy device
```

This device provides pseudorandom numbers, required for cryptography operations and such mission-critical applications as games. FreeBSD supports a variety of randomness sources, and they are all aggregated transparently into the random devices */dev/random* and */dev/urandom*.

```
device          ether         # Ethernet support
```

Ethernet has many device-like characteristics, and it's simplest for FreeBSD to treat it as a device. Leave this, unless you're looking for a learning opportunity.

```
device          sl            # Kernel SLIP
device          ppp           # Kernel PPP
```

The sl device supports SLIP (Serial Line Internet Protocol), and the ppp device supports kernel PPP (Point to Point Protocol). Both of these are old and obsoleted by userland PPP, unless you have specific requirements for them.

```
device          tun           # Packet tunnel.
```

The tun device is a *logical packet tunnel.* Software can use a tunnel interface to sneak packets in and out of the kernel. Such software includes userland PPP, the most popular choice for dial-up connections.

```
device          pty           # Pseudo-ttys (telnet etc)
```

A pty is a pseudoterminal. When you telnet or SSH (see Chapter 15) into the system, FreeBSD must keep track of your terminal session, send characters to your screen, and read what you type. The system wants to treat your remote connection just as it treats the physical monitor and keyboard attached to the system. The pseudoterminal is a terminal-like pseudodevice assigned to your connection.

```
device          md              # Memory "disks"
```

Memory disks allow you to store files in memory. This is useful for very fast, temporary data storage, as we'll learn in Chapter 8. For most (but not all) Internet servers, memory disks are a waste of RAM. You can also use memory disks to mount and access disk images. If you're not using memory disks, you can remove them from your kernel.

Removable Hardware

At the end of the GENERIC kernel, you will find support for FireWire and USB removable hardware. These features are all available in modules, as befits hardware that might or might not be present.

Building a Kernel

After reading through the previous section, you should be able to design a minimal kernel configuration. Before trying to add anything, I recommend trying to build and boot this minimal kernel to learn what your computer really needs. Now that you have a kernel configuration file that you like, build it.

You'll need to specify the name of the file containing your custom kernel configuration either on the command line, in */etc/make.conf*, or in */etc/src.conf*, with the KERNCONF variable.

```
# cd /usr/src
# make KERNCONF=MYKERNEL kernel
```

The build process first runs config(8) to find syntactical configuration errors. If config(8) detects a problem, it will report an error and stop. Some errors are blatantly obvious—for example, you might have accidentally deleted support for the Unix File System (UFS), but included support for booting off of UFS. One requires the other, and config will tell you exactly what's wrong. Other messages are strange and obscure; those that may take the longest to figure out are like this:

```
HUMVEE: unknown option "NET6"
```

NET6 is the IPv6 option, isn't it? No, that's *I*NET6. The error is perfectly self-explanatory—once you're familiar with all the supported kernel options. Read these errors carefully!

Once config(8) validates your kernel, you just wait. The kernel build process takes hours on a 486 but less than an hour on a new fast system. The compiler sends all sorts of cryptic messages scrolling down your screen. Once the build finishes, the system will move your current kernel to */boot/kernel.old* and install the new kernel in */boot/kernel*. Once this finishes, reboot your server and watch the boot messages.

```
Copyright (c) 1992-2006 The FreeBSD Project.
Copyright (c) 1979, 1980, 1983, 1986, 1988, 1989, 1991, 1992, 1993, 1994
        The Regents of the University of California. All rights reserved.
❶ FreeBSD 7.0-CURRENT #0: Thu May 11 01:16:19 EDT 2006
❷     mwlucas@humvee.blackhelicopters.org:/usr/src/sys/compile/HUMVEE
...
```

At boot time, FreeBSD shows you exactly what kernel it's running ❷ and when that kernel was built ❶. Congratulations, you've just built a kernel!

Troubleshooting Kernel Builds

If your kernel build fails, the first troubleshooting step is to look at the last lines of the output. Some of these errors are quite cryptic, but others will be self-explanatory. The important thing to remember is that errors that say, "Stop in *some directory*" aren't useful; the useful error will be before these. We talked about how to solve these problems in Chapter 1: Take the error message and toddle off to the search engine. Compile errors are usually the result of a configuration error.

Fortunately, FreeBSD insists upon compiling a complete kernel before installing anything. You haven't damaged your system by failing to build a kernel; your aborted compile is still sitting in the compile directory.

Booting an Alternate Kernel

So, what to do if your new kernel doesn't work, or if it works badly? Perhaps you forgot a device driver, or accidentally cut out the ppp pseudodevice and cannot dial out to the Internet. Don't panic! You did keep your old kernel, right? Here's what to do.

Back in Chapter 3, we discussed the mechanics of booting an alternate kernel. We'll go through the process of what to type here, but to see some of the in-depth details of loader management you'll want to go back to the earlier section. For now, we'll focus on the reasons to boot an alternate kernel and on how to do it correctly.

Start by deciding which kernel you want to boot. Your old kernel should be in a directory under */boot*; in this section, we'll assume that you want to boot the kernel in */boot/kernel.good*. Reboot and interrupt the boot to get a loader prompt. Remember that by the time you get the loader prompt, FreeBSD has already copied the kernel into memory, so the first thing you have to do is throw the bad kernel overboard:

```
ok unload
```

Now load the kernel you want, as well as ACPI (unless you don't use it) and any other kernel modules you normally load at boot:

```
ok load /boot/kernel.good/kernel
ok load /boot/kernel.good/acpi.ko
ok boot
```

Your system will now boot off the old kernel.

Inclusions, Exclusions, and Expanding the Kernel

Now that you can build a kernel, let's get a little fancy and see how to use inclusions, the various *no* configurations, and the *NOTES* file.

NOTES

FreeBSD's kernel includes all sorts of features that aren't included in GENERIC. Many of these special features are intended for very specific systems, or for weird corner cases of a special network. You can find a complete list of hardware-specific features in the file *NOTES* under each platform's kernel configuration directory—for example, */sys/amd64/conf/NOTES*. Hardware-independent kernel features—those that work on every platform FreeBSD supports—can be found in */sys/conf/NOTES*. If you have hardware that doesn't appear to be completely supported in the GENERIC kernel, take a look at *NOTES*. Some of these features are obscure, but if you have the hardware, you'll appreciate them. Let's take a look at a typical entry from *NOTES*:

```
# CPU_SOEKRIS enables support www.soekris.com hardware.
#
...
options         CPU_SOEKRIS
```

Soekris is a manufacturer of small systems perfect for homebrew embedding. We'll talk about those systems in Chapter 21; they aren't common enough for this entry to go into GENERIC, but if you have one of these devices, you can use the CPU_SOEKRIS option to enable the special features of that CPU.

If the *NOTES* file lists all the features for every possible device, why not just use it as the basis for your kernel? First, such a kernel would use up far more memory than the GENERIC kernel. While even small modern machines have enough memory to run GENERIC without trouble, if the kernel becomes ten times larger without the corresponding increase in functionality, people would get annoyed. Also, many of the options are mutually exclusive. You'll find features for Athlon CPUs, Cyrix CPUs, IBM CPUs, options to work around bugs in particular revisions of particular cards, and so on.

Inclusions and Exclusions

FreeBSD's kernel configuration has two interesting abilities that can make maintaining a kernel easier: the *no* options and inclusions.

The include feature lets you pull a separate file into the kernel configuration. For example, if you have a kernel configuration that can be described as "GENERIC with a couple extra tidbits," you could include the GENERIC kernel configuration with an `include` statement:

```
include GENERIC
```

So, if you want to build a kernel that has all the functionality of GENERIC but also supports the Soekris CPU, you could create a valid kernel configuration composed entirely of the following:

```
ident      MYKERNEL
include    GENERIC
options    CPU_SOEKRIS
```

You might think that this is actually more work than copying GENERIC to a new file and editing it, and you'd be correct. Why would you bother with this, then? The biggest reason is that as you upgrade FreeBSD, the GENERIC configuration can change. The GENERIC in FreeBSD 7.1 is slightly different from that in 7.0. Your new configuration is valid for both releases, and in both cases can be legitimately described as "GENERIC plus my options."

This works well for including items, but isn't very good for removing things from the kernel. For example, all of the Soekris CPUs are in small systems without SCSI or RAID cards. You could expand your configuration to exclude all of those device drivers with the `nodevice` keyword. A nodevice entry removes a previously included device entry. Similarly, the `nooption` keyword disables included options.

For an excellent example of this, take a look at the PAE kernel configuration. PAE is a configuration used for i386 systems with more than 4GB RAM, as discussed later in this chapter. Many older devices cannot run on a machine with this much memory, so they cannot be included in this configuration. No matter how much you upgrade your FreeBSD system, you know that the default PAE kernel is "GENERIC, plus the PAE feature, minus all the drivers that don't work with PAE."

How Kernel Options Fix Problems

Some kernel options are only used when a problem appears. For example, a few years ago a friend of mine had several web servers running on low-end i386 hardware. When one machine was serving several hundred pages per second, he started getting errors on the console:

```
Jun  9 16:23:17 ralph/kernel: pmap_collect: collecting pv entries --
suggest increasing PMAP_SHPGPERPROC
```

A couple hours after this message began appearing, the system crashed. Apparently we were supposed to take that suggestion seriously, so I did a little research on the Internet and read through *NOTES*, where I found the following entry:

```
# Set the number of PV entries per process. Increasing this can
# stop panics related to heavy use of shared memory. However, that can
# (combined with large amounts of physical memory) cause panics at
# boot time due the kernel running out of VM space.
#
# If you're tweaking this, you might also want to increase the sysctls
# "vm.v_free_min", "vm.v_free_reserved", and "vm.v_free_target".
#
# The value below is the one more than the default.
#
options          PMAP_SHPGPERPROC=201
```

This seemed simple enough. First, I backed up the old kernel to */boot/kernel.pmap-crash*. It wasn't exactly a good kernel, but it did keep the system running for several hours. We then increased PMAP_SHPGPERPROC to 400 and increased the system's RAM to 192MB. (This system was serving several hundred web pages per second on 64MB RAM, with one IDE disk and a Celeron 433 processor!) After installing our new kernel, the crashes stopped and the system ran for months at a time. In FreeBSD 7, this particular kernel option happens to be a run-time tunable sysctl, but many other options in the kernel can be changed this way.

Without this ability to tweak the kernel, we would have had no choice but to buy more hardware. Even though this hardware is pretty low-end, it handled the load with only a software tweak and a minor hardware addition. FreeBSD has quite a few options like this one for special situations—and it will tell you what it wants if you pay attention. (Mind you, if you're merely desperate to spend money, I happen to run a charity for homeless cash and can honestly assure you that I will find it a new home where it will be deeply appreciated.)

Sharing Kernels

If you have several identical servers, you don't need to build a kernel on each; you can share your custom-built kernel across them. The kernel and its modules are just files on disk, after all.

To share a kernel, build and install one kernel and test it every way you can. Then, tar up */boot/kernel* and copy the tarball to each of the other servers. Back up the original kernel on each server, then extract your tarball to install the new */boot/kernel*. Reboot, and you're done!

Testing Kernels Remotely

It's not uncommon to have a FreeBSD system in a remote facility, such as a co-location. You might not have a serial console, and talking a co-location technician through the boot loader is not something you would normally enjoy. The best you can hope for from these co-location facilities is that you'll get a pair of "remote hands" that can walk up to the machine and hit the power button for you. How can you possibly test a new kernel under those circumstances? The key here is that you want to confirm that a kernel boots the system properly—and if it doesn't boot properly, you want the boot to fall back to a known working kernel. It's a one-time test boot. That's where nextboot(8) comes in handy.

nextboot(8) is a way of saying, "Boot this kernel the next time you boot, but only once." nextboot takes at least one argument, -k, which is the directory under */boot* where the test kernel can be found. For example, I've built and installed a new kernel; I want this new kernel to be booted once, and if it doesn't work I want the following boot to go back to the previous kernel. First, I must put my test kernel some place other than */boot/kernel*, and have a good kernel in */boot/kernel*.

```
# mv /boot/kernel /boot/kernel.test
# mkdir /boot/kernel
# cp /boot/kernel.good/* /boot/kernel/
```

If you plan ahead, you can actually install your custom kernel in this location in the first place by setting the variable INSTKERNAME when you build the kernel. Give the name of the kernel when you do your kernel install, and make(1) will install it appropriately:

```
# cd /usr/src
# make KERNCONF=TESTKERNEL INSTKERNAME=test kernel
```

This will install your test kernel as */boot/kernel.test*.

Now that I have a known-good kernel as my default kernel, and my test kernel as */boot/kernel.test*, I tell nextboot(8) to try the test kernel with the -k flag, giving the name of the directory under */boot* where this kernel can be found:

```
# nextboot -k kernel.test
```

The next time the system is rebooted, the loader will run */boot/kernel.test* instead of */boot/kernel* and also erase the configuration that told it to load this kernel. When the system reboots once more, it will boot the standard kernel. The trick here is to make sure that the known good kernel is in the directory */boot/kernel*. If your new kernel works correctly, you can just do:

```
# mv /boot/kernel /boot/kernel.previous
# mv /boot/kernel.test /boot/kernel
```

Voilà! Your test kernel is now in production.

Kernel Stuff You Should Know About

A better title for this section would be "Tidbits That You'll Trip Over Unless You Know What They Are." If someone says you have a problem with ACPI, you should know what that is. When the system spews a scary message about "lock order reversals," you should know if freaking out and running away screaming is warranted. The four key areas here are ACPI, PAE, SMP, and lock order reversals.

ACPI

The Advanced Configuration and Power management Interface handles low-level hardware configuration, power configuration, and so on. It's the successor to several old protocols such as Plug-and-Play, the PCI BIOS hardware configuration system, and APM (Advanced Power Management). Like most other Unix-like operating system vendors, FreeBSD uses the reference implementation of ACPI provided by Intel.

This is just a hardware configuration protocol, what could possibly go wrong? Well, not all hardware vendors implement ACPI in exact accordance with the specification—rather, they implement just enough so that their hardware works with Microsoft operating systems and call it done. This means that people who use non-Microsoft operating systems need to work around this. FreeBSD includes various workarounds for these broken ACPI implementations, but these often take a little bit of time to reach a release.

Also, the first hardware that used ACPI often uncovered issues with ACPI itself. As with any complicated protocol, the first implementors learned a lot about how that protocol worked in the real world. If you have hardware built during this time, you might need to permanently disable ACPI by putting hint.acpi.0.disabled=1 in */boot/loader.conf.* If you think your hardware is having ACPI problems, you can disable it for a single boot with the boot menu discussed in Chapter 3.

PAE

For years, i386 computer hardware had a built-in limit where it could handle only up to 4GB of RAM. At that time, a system with 128MB of RAM was considered a high-end machine, but by now technology has hit the point where breaking the limit is not only conceivable but affordable. We've seen this sort of limit before, from the 640KB memory limit on the IBM PC to the 8GB limit on hard drives. System architects must pick limits somewhere, and they just try to aim high enough so they won't have to worry about those limits for another ten years or so. Physical Address Extensions (PAE) expands the memory limit to 64GB, which should satisfy us for another few years at least. By the time that sort of memory becomes common, most new systems will be running in 64-bit mode which has much higher limits.

Not all devices are compatible with PAE, so PAE cannot be in the GENERIC kernel. You'll find a PAE kernel configuration in */sys/i386/conf/PAE*. Only i386 hardware requires PAE; amd64, sparc64, and other high-end hardware has different memory limits that have not yet been reached.

PAE cannot be disabled at boot time or run time; it's either in the kernel or it isn't.

Symmetric Multiprocessing

Symmetric Multiprocessing (SMP) is having multiple general-purpose CPUs in a system. In theory, the operating system divides its workload evenly between the various CPUs. This is harder than it sounds, for reasons we'll discuss in Chapter 12. For SMP to work on your system, your kernel must include `options SMP` and `device apic`.

On occasion, some part of the system will have problems with SMP. It can be useful to disable SMP temporarily to troubleshoot a problem. If a problem exists when SMP is enabled, but disappears when SMP is disabled, that can help identify the problem. Disable SMP at boot by setting the boot-time tunable `kern.smp.disabled` to 1. Similarly, you might be asked to disable the APIC, which disables SMP as a side effect. Disable the APIC with the kernel hint `hint.apic.0.disabled="1"`.

Lock Order Reversals

A key part of implementing SMP is kernel locking. While you don't have to worry about kernel locking as a user, if you're running certain versions of FreeBSD (particularly, -current), on occasion your system console will print out a message about lock order reversals. These messages, produced by the kernel debugging feature WITNESS (see Chapter 13), mean that the in-kernel locking isn't as correct as the developers would hope. For the most part, these messages are harmless, but they do look scary and do indicate potential problems.

When you see a lock order reversal, the best thing to do is see if this particular LOR has been reported previously. A web search for the message will show if it's been previously reported. You can also search for the FreeBSD Lock Order Reversal page (maintained by Bjoern Zeeb as of this writing) and see if your LOR is listed there. If you can't find mention of your LOR anywhere on the Internet, you should let the FreeBSD developers know by writing to *FreeBSD-hackers@FreeBSD.org*.

You should now have a decent grip on managing the FreeBSD kernel. Let's go on and see some of the things you can do with the network.

6

THE NETWORK

FreeBSD is famous for its network performance. The TCP/IP network protocol suite was first developed on BSD, and BSD, in turn, included the first major implementation of TCP/IP. While competing network protocols were considered more exciting in the 1980s, the wide availability, flexibility, and liberal licensing of the BSD TCP/IP stack made it the de facto standard.

Many system administrators today have a vague familiarity with the basics of networking, but don't really understand how it all hangs together. Good sysadmins understand the network, however. Knowing what an IP address really is, how a netmask works, and how a port number differs from a protocol number is a necessary step towards mastering your profession. We'll cover some of these issues in this chapter. For a start, you must understand the network layers.

While this chapter gives a decent overview of TCP/IP, it won't cover many of the numerous details, gotchas, and caveats. If you need to learn more about TCP/IP, pick up one of the big thick books on the subject. *The TCP/IP Guide* by Charles M. Kozierok (No Starch Press, 2005) is an excellent place to start.

This book specifically covers TCP/IP version 4. Its successor, TCP/IP version 6, is not widely deployed as of this writing.

Network Layers

Each layer of the network handles a specific task within the network process and interacts only with the layers above and below it. People learning TCP/IP often laugh when they hear that all these layers simplify the network process, but this is really true. The important thing to remember right now is that each layer communicates only with the layer directly above it and the layer directly beneath it.

The classic OSI network protocol stack has seven layers, is exhaustively complete, and covers almost any situation with any network protocol and any application. The Internet, however, is just one such situation, and this isn't a book about networking or networked applications in general. We're limiting our discussion to TCP/IP networks such as the Internet and almost all corporate networks, so we only need to consider four layers of the network stack.

The Physical Layer

At the very bottom we have the physical layer: the network card and the wire, fiber, or radio waves leaving it. This layer includes the physical switch, hub, or base station, cables attaching that device to the router, and the fiber that runs from your office to the telephone company. The telephone company switch is part of the physical layer, as are transcontinental fiber optic cables. If it can be tripped over, dropped, or chainsawed, it's part of the physical layer. From this point on we'll refer to the physical layer as the *wire*, although it can be just about any sort of medium.

This is the easiest layer to understand—it's as simple as having intact hardware. If your wire meets the requirements of the physical protocol, you're in business. If not, you're bankrupt. Without a physical layer, the rest of the network can't work, period, end of story. One of the functions of Internet routers is to connect one sort of physical layer to another—for example, converting local Ethernet into T1/E1. The physical layer has no decision-making abilities and no intelligence; everything that runs over it is dictated by the datalink layer.

Datalink: The Physical Protocol

The datalink layer is where things get interesting. The datalink layer, or the physical protocol, transforms information into the actual ones and zeros that are sent over the physical layer in the appropriate encoding for that physical protocol. For example, Ethernet uses Media Access Control (MAC) addresses and the Address Resolution Protocol (ARP); dial-up and wide area networks use the Point to Point Protocol (PPP). In addition to the popular Ethernet and PPP datalink layers, FreeBSD supports others, including Asynchronous Transfer Mode (ATM), High Level Data Link Control (HDLC), and Internetwork Packet Exchange (IPX), as well as combinations such as the PPP over Ethernet (PPPoE) used by some home broadband vendors. While FreeBSD supports all of these datalink protocols, it doesn't support *every* datalink protocol ever used. If you have unusual network requirements, check the documentation for your version of FreeBSD to see if it's supported.

Some physical protocols have been implemented over many different physical layers. Ethernet, for instance, has been transmitted over twinax, coax, CAT3, CAT5, CAT6, CAT7, optical fiber, radio waves, and carrier pigeon. With minor changes in the device drivers, the datalink layer can address any sort of physical layer. This is one of the ways in which layers simplify the network. We'll discuss Ethernet in detail, as it's the most common network type FreeBSD systems use. By understanding Ethernet on FreeBSD, you'll be able to manage other protocols on FreeBSD as well—once you understand those protocols, of course!

The datalink layer exchanges information with the physical layer and the network layer.

The Network Layer

"The network layer? Isn't the whole thing a network?"

Yes, but the network layer is more specific. It maps connectivity between network nodes, answering questions like "Where are other hosts?" and "Can you reach this particular host?" This logical protocol provides a consistent interface to programs that run over the network, no matter what sort of physical layer you're using. The network layer used on the Internet is Internet Protocol, or IP. *IP* provides each host with a unique[1] address, known as an *IP address*, so that any other host on the network can find it.

The network layer talks to the datalink layer below it and the transport layer above it.

Heavy Lifting: The Transport Layer

The transport layer deals with real data for real applications and perhaps even real human beings. The three common transport layer protocols are ICMP, TCP, and UDP.

Internet Control Message Protocol (ICMP) manages basic connectivity messages between hosts with IP addresses. If IP provides a road and addresses, ICMP provides traffic lights and highway exit signs. Most of the time, ICMP just runs in the background and you never have to think about it.

The other well-known transport protocols are User Datagram Protocol (UDP) and Transmission Control Protocol (TCP). How common are these?

---

[1] Yes, I know about Network Address Translation, where not all IP addresses are unique. NAT is a lie, and lying to your network is a good route to trouble—ask anyone who uses NAT on a really large scale. But even with NAT, if you're on the Internet you have one or more unique IP addresses.

Well, the Internet Protocol suite is generally called *TCP*/IP. These protocols provide services such as multiplexing via port numbers and transmission of user data. *UDP* is a bare-bones transport protocol, offering the minimum services needed to transfer data over the network. TCP provides more sophisticated features such as congestion control and integrity checking.

In addition to these three, many other protocols run above IP. The file */etc/protocols* contains a fairly comprehensive list of transport protocols that use IP as an underlying mechanism. You won't find non-IP protocols here, such as Digital's LAT, but it contains many more protocols than you'll ever see in the real world. For example, here are the entries for IP and ICMP, the network-layer protocols commonly used on the Internet:

```
❶ip   ❷0   ❸IP     ❹# Internet protocol, pseudo protocol number
  icmp   1    ICMP    # Internet control message protocol
```

Each entry in */etc/protocols* has three key fields: an unofficial name ❶, a protocol number ❷, and any aliases ❸. The protocol number is used within network requests to identify traffic. You'll see it if you ever fire up a packet sniffer or start digging deeper into your network for any reason. As you can see, IP is protocol 0 and ICMP is protocol 1—if that's not the groundwork for everything else, it's hard to see what could be! TCP is protocol 6, and UDP is protocol 17. You'll also see comments ❹ giving slightly more detail about each protocol.

The transport layer speaks to the network layer below and to the applications above it.

Applications

Applications are definitely a part of the network. Applications open requests for network connectivity, send data over the network, receive data from the network, and process that data. Web browsers, email clients, JSP servers, and so on are all network-aware applications. Applications only have to communicate with the network protocol and the user. Problems with the user layer are beyond the scope of this book.[2]

The Network in Practice

So, you understand how everything hooks together and are ready to move on, right? Don't think so. Let's see how this works in the real world. Some of this explanation touches on stuff that we'll cover later in this chapter, but if you're reading this book you're probably conversant enough with networks to be able to follow it. If you're having trouble, reread this section after reading the remainder of this chapter. (Just buy a second copy of this book, cut these pages out of the second copy, and glue them in at the end of this chapter.)

Suppose a user connected to the Internet via your network wants to look at Yahoo! The user accesses his web browser and enters the URL.

---

[2] If my current research on reformatting and reinstalling users bears fruit, however, I will be certain to publish my results.

The browser application knows how to talk to the next layer down in the network, the transport layer. After kneading the user's request into an appropriate form, the browser asks the transport layer for a TCP connection to a particular IP address on port 80. (Purists might note that we're skipping the DNS request part of the process, but it is quite similar to what is being described and would only confuse our example.)

The transport layer examines the browser's request. Since the application has requested a TCP connection, the transport layer allocates the appropriate system resources for that sort of connection. The request is broken up into digestible chunks and handed down to the network layer.

The network layer doesn't care about the actual request. It's been handed a lump of data to be carried over the Internet. Much like your postman delivers letters without caring about the contents, the network layer just bundles the TCP data with the proper addressing information. The resulting mass of data is called a *packet*. The network layer hands these packets down to the datalink layer.

The datalink layer doesn't care about the contents of the packet. It certainly doesn't care about IP addressing or routing. It's been given a lump of zeroes and ones, and it has the job of transmitting those zeros and ones across the network. All it knows about is how to perform that transmission. The datalink layer may add the appropriate header and/or footer information to the packet for the physical medium used, creating a *frame*. Finally, it hands the frame off to the physical layer for transmission on the local wire, wave, or other media.

EACH INSIDE THE OTHER?

Yes, your original web request has been encapsulated by the TCP protocol. That request has been encapsulated again at the transport layer by the IP protocol, and once more by the datalink protocol. All these headers are piled on at the front and back of your original request. Have you ever seen that picture of a small fish being swallowed by a slightly larger fish, which is in turn being eaten by a larger fish, and so on? It's exactly like that. Or, if you prefer, a frame is like the outermost box in one of those gifts that arrive wrapped in a series of successively larger gift boxes. Unwrap one protocol and you'll find another.

The physical layer has no intelligence at all. The datalink layer hands it a bunch of zeroes and ones, and it transmits them to another physical device. It has no idea of what protocol is being spoken or how those digits might be echoed through a switch, hub, or repeater, but one of the hosts on this network is presumably the router of the network.

When the router receives the zeroes and ones, it hands them up to the datalink layer. The datalink layer strips its framing information and hands the resulting packet up to the network layer within the router. The router's network layer examines the packet and decides what to do with it based on its routing tables. It then hands the packet down to the appropriate datalink layer. This might be another Ethernet interface, or perhaps a PPP interface out of a T1.

Your wire can go through many physical changes as the data travels. Your copper T1 line could be aggregated into an optical fiber DS3, which is then transformed into an OC192 cross-country link. Thanks to the wonders of layering and abstraction, neither your computer nor your user need to know anything about any of these.

When the request reaches its destination, the computer at the other end of the transaction accepts the frame and sends it all the way back up the protocol stack. The physical wire accepts the zeroes and ones and sends them up to the datalink layer. The datalink layer strips the Ethernet headers off the frame and hands the resulting packet up to the transport layer. The transport layer reassembles the packets into a stream of data, which it then hands to an application—in this case, a web server. The application processes the request and returns an answer, which descends the protocol stack and travels across the network, bouncing up and down through various datalink layers on the way as necessary. This is an awful lot of work to make the machine go through just so you can get your "404 Page Not Found" error.

This example shows why layering is so important. Each layer only knows what it absolutely must about the layers above and below it, making it possible to swap out the innards of layers if desired. When a new datalink protocol is created, the other layers don't have to change; the network protocol just hands a properly formatted request to the datalink layer and lets that layer do its thing. When you have a new network card, you only need a driver that interfaces with the datalink layer and the physical layer; you don't have to change anything higher in the network stack, including your application. Imagine a device driver that had to be installed in your web browser, and your email client, and every other application you had on your computer, including the custom-built ones. You would quickly give up on computing and take up something sane and sensible, like skydiving with anvils.

Getting Bits and Hexes

As a system administrator you'll frequently come across terms like *48-bit address* and *18-bit netmask*. I've seen a surprising number of sysadmins who just nod and smile when they hear this, all the while thinking, "Yeah, whatever, just tell me what I need to do in my job." Unfortunately, math is a real part of the job, and you *must* understand bits. While it's not immediately intuitive, this understanding is one of the things that separate amateurs from professionals. You don't read a book like this if you want to stay an amateur.

Maybe you're muttering, "But I already know this!" Then skip it. But don't cheat yourself if you don't know it.

You probably already know that a computer treats all data as zeroes and ones, and that a single zero or one is a bit. When a protocol specifies a number of bits, it's talking about the number as seen by the computer. A 32-bit number has 32 digits, each being either zero or one. You were probably introduced to binary math, or *base 2*, back in elementary school and remembered it just long enough to pass the test. It's time to dust off those memories. Binary math is simply a different way to work with the numbers we see every day.

We use decimal math, or base 10, every day to pay the pizza guy and balance the checkbook. Digits run from 0 to 9. When you want to go above the highest digit you have, you add a digit on the left and set your current digit to zero. This is the whole "carry the one" thing you learned many years ago, and now probably do without conscious thought. In binary math the digits run from 0 to 1, and when you want to go above the highest digit you have, you add a digit on the left and set your current digit to 0. It's exactly the same as decimal math with eight fingers missing. As an example, Table 6-1 shows the first few decimal numbers converted to binary.

Table 6-1: Decimal and Binary Numbers

Decimal	Binary
0	0
1	1
2	10
3	11
4	100
5	101
6	110
7	111
8	1000

When you have a 32-bit number, such as an IP address, you have a string of 32 ones and zeros. Ethernet MAC addresses are 48-bit numbers and have 48 ones and zeros.

Just for fun, Unix also uses hexadecimal numbers in some cases (such as MAC addresses and netmasks). Hexadecimal numbers are 4 bits long. The binary number 1111, the full four bits, is equivalent to 15; this means that the digits in hexadecimal math run from 0 to 15. At this point, a few of you are looking at the two-digit number 15 that's supposed to be a single digit and wondering what I'm smoking and where you can get your own supply. Hexadecimal math uses the letters A through F as digits for the numbers 10 through 15. When you count up to the last digit and want to add one, you set the current digit to zero and add a digit to the left of the number. For example, to count to seventeen in hexadecimal, you say, "1, 2, 3, 4, 5, 6, 7, 8, 9, A, B, C, D, E, F, 10, 11." Take off a shoe and count along once or twice until you get the idea.

Hexadecimal numbers are usually marked with a *0x* in front. The number 0x12 is the hexadecimal equivalent of decimal 18, while the number 18 is plain old 18. If a hex number is not marked by a leading 0x, it's in a place where the output is always in hexadecimal, such as MAC addresses. The letters A to F are also a dead giveaway, but not entirely reliable; many hex numbers have no letters at all, just as many decimal numbers have no odd digits.

When you're working with hexadecimal, decimal, and binary numbers, the simplest thing to do is break out a scientific calculator. Today's medium-end or better calculators have functions to convert between the three systems, as do most software calculators.

BIT BY BYTES

Computer systems tend to work in bytes, where an 8-bit number is represented by a single character. The one exception is in the network stack, where everything is in bits. Thus, we have a 5 mega*byte* file on a machine with a 10 mega*bit* network connection. Do not confuse the two!

Remedial TCP/IP

Now that you know how all this is supposed to work, let's look at a real network protocol in depth. The dominant Internet protocol is TCP/IP, or Transmission Control Protocol over Internet Protocol. TCP is a transport protocol, while IP is a network protocol, but they're so tightly intertwined that they're generally referred to as a single entity. We'll start with IP and proceed to TCP and UDP.

IP Addresses and Netmasks

An IP address is a unique 32-bit number assigned to a particular node on a network. Some IP addresses are more or less permanent, such as those assigned to vital servers. Others change as required by the network, such as those used by dial-up clients. Individual machines on a shared network get adjoining IP addresses.

Rather than expressing that 32-bit number as a single number, an IP address is broken up into four 8-bit numbers usually shown as decimal numbers. While 192.168.1.1 is the same as 11000000.10101000.00000001.00000001 or the single number 11000000101010000000000100000001, the four decimal numbers are easiest for our weak minds to deal with.

IP addresses are issued in chunks by Internet service providers. Frequently these chunks are very small—say, 16 or 32 IP addresses. If your system is co-located on a server farm, you might only get a few IP addresses out of a block.

A *netmask* is a label indicating the size of the block of IP addresses assigned to your local network. The size of your IP block determines your netmask—or, your netmask determines how many IP addresses you have. If you've done networking for any length of time, you've seen the netmask 255.255.255.0 and know that it's associated with a block of 256 IP addresses. You might even know that the wrong netmask prevents your system from working. In today's world, however, that simple netmask is becoming less and less common. To understand why, you need to understand something about the history of IP addressing. Many years ago, IP addresses were issued in blocks of three sizes: class A, class B, and class C. This terminology has been obsolete for over a decade now, but we'll use it as a starting point.

Class A was very simple: The first of the four numbers in your IP address were fixed. The issuing agency (the InterNIC, back in the day) might give you a class A block, for example 10.0.0.0. You could assign any of the last three numbers in any manner you liked, but all your IP addresses began with 10. For example, you could delegate 10.1.0.0 through 10.1.1.255 to your data center, 10.1.2.0 through 10.1.7.255 to your Detroit office, and so on. Only very large companies such as Ford and Xerox, as well as influential academic computing institutions such as MIT, received class A blocks. Browsing the list of original class A owners is quite an education in who had influence in the 1980s.

In a class B block, the first two of the four numbers in the IP address were fixed. Your class B block looked something like 172.16.0.0. Every IP address you used internally began with the first two numbers 172.16, but you could assign the last two numbers as you wanted. Many mid-sized companies went after class B blocks.

Similarly, a class C block had the first three numbers fixed. This was the standard for small companies. The ISP would issue you a block such as 198.22.63.0 and let you assign the last number as you wanted.

This scheme wasted a lot of IP numbers. Many small companies don't need 256 addresses. Many medium-sized firms need more than 256, but fewer than the 65,000 in a class B block. And almost nobody needs the full 16 million addresses in a class A block. Before the Internet boomed, these choices were good enough. Back in the 1980s kids got beat up for messing around with computers and whatnot, but today's kids get beat up for not having their own e-commerce site. This has exerted upward pressure on demand for IP addresses.

Today's providers issue IP addresses by prefix length, commonly called a *slash*. You'll see IP blocks such as 192.168.1.128/25. While this looks confusing, it's merely a way of using classes with much greater granularity. You know that each decimal number in an IP address is 8 bits long. By using a class, you're saying that a certain number of bits are fixed—you cannot change them on your network. A class A block has 8 fixed bits, a class B has 16, and a class C has 24.

This isn't a class in binary math, so I won't make you draw it out and do the conversion, but think of an IP address as a string of binary numbers. On your network, you can change the bits on the far right, but not the ones on the far left. The only question is, "Where is the line that separates right from left?" There's no reason for that boundary to be on one of those convenient 8-bit lines that separate the decimal versions of the address. A prefix length is simply the number of fixed bits on your network. A /25 means that you have 25 fixed bits, or one more fixed bit than what used to be called a class C. You can play with 7 bits. You get a decimal netmask by setting the fixed bits to 1 and your network bits to 0, as in the following example of a /25 netmask:

```
11111111.11111111.11111111.10000000
```

11111111 is 255, while 1000000 is 128. Your netmask is 255.255.255.128. It's very simple, if you think in binary. You won't have to work with this every day, but if you don't understand the underlying binary concepts, the decimal conversion looks like total gibberish. With practice, you'll learn to recognize certain strings of decimals as legitimate binary conversions.

What does all this mean in practice? First off, blocks of IP addresses are issued in multiples of 2. If you have 4 bits to play with, you have 16 IP addresses ($2 \times 2 \times 2 \times 2 = 16$). If you have 8 bits to play with, you have 256 addresses ($2^8 = 256$). If someone says that you have exactly 19 IP addresses, you're either sharing an Ethernet with other people or they're wrong.

It's not uncommon to see a host's IP address with its netmask attached— e.g., 192.168.3.4/26. This gives you everything you need to get the host on the local network. (Finding the default gateway is another problem, but it's usually the top or bottom address in the block.)

Computing Netmasks in Decimal

You probably don't want to repeatedly convert between decimal and binary. Not only is it uncomfortable, it increases your chances of making an error. Here's a trick to calculate your netmask while remaining in decimal land.

You need to find how many IP addresses you have on your network. This will be a multiple of 2 almost certainly smaller than 256. Subtract the number of IP addresses you have from 256. This is the last number of your netmask. You'll still need to recognize legitimate network sizes. If your IP address is 192.168.1.100/26, you'll need to know that a /26 is 26 fixed bits, or 64 IP addresses. Look at the last number of your IP address, 100. It certainly isn't between 0 and 63, but it is between 64 and 127. The other hosts on your IP block have IP addresses ranging from 192.168.1.64 to 192.168.1.127, and your netmask is 255.255.255.192 (256 − 64 = 192).

At this point, I should mention that netmasks frequently appear as hex numbers. You might feel like giving up the whole thing as a bad job, but to simplify your life, Table 6-2 shows netmasks, IP information, and related goodness for /24 and smaller networks.

Table 6-2: Netmasks and IP Address Conversions

Prefix	Binary Mask	Decimal Mask	Hex Mask	Available IPs
/24	00000000	255.255.255.0	0xffffff00	256
/25	10000000	255.255.255.128	0xffffff80	128
/26	11000000	255.255.255.192	0xffffffc0	64
/27	11100000	255.255.255.224	0xffffffe0	32
/28	11110000	255.255.255.240	0xfffffff0	16
/29	11111000	255.255.255.248	0xfffffff8	8
/30	11111100	255.255.255.252	0xfffffffc	4
/31	11111110	255.255.255.254	0xfffffffe	2
/32	11111111	255.255.255.255	0xffffffff	1

Unusable IP Addresses

You now understand how slashes, netmasks, and IP address assignments work together and how, for example, a /28 has 16 IP addresses. Unfortunately, you cannot use all the IP addresses in a block. The first IP address in a block is the *network number* which is used for internal bookkeeping.

Similarly, the last number in any block of IP addresses is the broadcast address. According to the IP specifications, every machine on a network is supposed to respond to a request for this address. This allows you to ping the broadcast address and quickly determine which IP addresses are in use. For example, on a typical /24 network, the broadcast address is *x.y.z*.255. In the late 1990s, however, this feature was transformed into an attack technique. It's now disabled by default on almost every operating system and most network appliances.[3] If you need this feature, set the sysctl net.inet.icmp.bmcastecho to 1.

In any case, you cannot assign the first or the last IP address in a network to a device without causing network problems. Some systems fail gracefully, others fail gracelessly. Go ahead, try it sometime—preferably after hours, unless you want a good story to tell at your next job.

Assigning IP Addresses

You might think that each computer on a network has an IP address, but this isn't strictly true. Every network *interface* has an IP address. Most computers have only one network interface, so for them the difference is nonexistent. If you have multiple network cards, however, each card has a separate IP address. You can also have multiple IP addresses on a single card through aliasing. On the other hand, with special configuration you can bond multiple cards into a single network interface, giving the computer one virtual interface despite the many cards. While these distinctions are small, remember them when troubleshooting.

ICMP

The *Internet Control Message Protocol (ICMP)* is the standard for transmitting routing and availability messages across the network. Tools such as ping(8) and traceroute(8) use ICMP to gather their results. Proper network performance requires ICMP, but an intruder can use some types of ICMP traffic for reconnaissance. If you must block ICMP for security reasons, be sure to do so selectively.

UDP

The *User Datagram Protocol (UDP)* is the most bare-bones data transfer protocol that runs over IP. It has no error handling, minimal integrity verification, and no defense whatsoever against data loss. Despite these drawbacks, UDP can be a good choice for particular sorts of data transfer, and many vital Internet services rely on it.

---

[3] Except, for some reason, many printers. Put your printers behind a firewall!

When a host transmits data via UDP, the sender has no way of knowing if the data ever reached its destination. Programs that receive UDP data simply listen to the network and accept what happens to arrive. When a program receives data via UDP, it cannot verify the source of that data—while a UDP packet includes a source address, this address is easily faked. This is why UDP is called *connectionless*, or *stateless*.

With all of these drawbacks, why use UDP at all? Applications that use UDP most often have their own error-correction handling methods that don't mesh well with the defaults provided by protocols such as TCP. For example, simple client DNS queries must time out within just a few seconds or the user will call the helpdesk and whine. TCP times connections out only after two minutes. Since the computer wants to handle its failed DNS requests much more quickly, simple DNS queries use UDP. In cases where DNS must transfer larger amounts of data (for example, for zone transfers), it intelligently switches to TCP. Real-time streaming data, such as video conferencing, also uses UDP. If you miss a few pixels of the picture in a real-time video conference, retransmitting that data would simply add congestion. You can't go back in time to fill in those missing chunks of the picture, after all! You'll find similar reasoning behind almost all other network applications that use UDP.

UDP is also a *datagram* protocol, meaning that each network transmission is complete and self contained, and received as a single integral unit. While the application might not consider a single UDP packet a complete request, the network does. TCP is entirely different.

TCP

The *Transmission Control Protocol (TCP)* includes such nifty features as error correction and recovery. The receiver must acknowledge every packet it gets, otherwise the sender will retransmit any unacknowledged packets. Applications that use TCP can expect reliable data transmission. This makes TCP a *connected*, or *stateful*, protocol, unlike UDP.

TCP is also a *streaming* protocol, meaning that a single request can be split amongst several network packets. While the sender might transmit several chunks of data one after the other, the recipient could receive them out-of-order or fragmented. The recipient must keep track of these chunks and assemble them properly to complete the network transaction.

For two hosts to exchange TCP data, they must set up a channel for that data to flow across. One host requests a connection, the other host responds to the request, and then the first host starts transmitting. This setup process is known as the *three-way handshake*. The specifics are not important right now, but you should know that this process happens. Similarly, once transmission is complete the systems must do a certain amount of work to tear down the connections.

TCP is commonly used by applications—such as email programs, FTP clients, and web browsers—for its fairly generic set of timeouts and transmission features.

How Protocols Fit Together

You can compare the network stack to sitting with your family at a holiday dinner. The datalink layer (ARP, in the case of Ethernet) lets you see everyone else at the table. IP gives every person at the table a unique chair, except for the three young nephews using piano bench NAT. ICMP provides basic routing information, such as, "The quickest way to the peas is to ask Uncle Chris to hand them to you." TCP is where you hand someone a dish and the other person must say "Thanks" before you will let go. Finally, UDP is like tossing a roll at Aunt Betty; she might catch it, it might bounce off her forehead, or it could be snatched out of midair by the dog who has watched for his opportunity since the meal began. (Yes, my family holidays are more entertaining than most.)

Transport Protocol Ports

Have you ever noticed that computers have too many ports? We're going to add TCP and UDP ports into the stew. *Transport protocol ports* permit one server to serve many different services over a single transport protocol, multiplexing connections between machines.

When a network server programs starts, it attaches, or *binds*, to one or more logical ports. A logical port is just an arbitrary number ranging from 1 to 65536. For example, Internet mail servers bind to TCP port 25. Each TCP or UDP packet arriving at a system has a field indicating its desired destination port. Each incoming request is flagged with a desired destination port number. If an incoming requests asks for port 25, it is connected to the mail server listening on that port. This means that other programs can run on different ports, clients can talk to those different ports, and nobody except the sysadmin gets confused.

The */etc/services* file contains a list of port numbers and the services that they're commonly associated with. It's possible to run almost any service on any port, but by doing so you'll confuse other Internet hosts that try to connect to your system. If someone tries to send you email, their mail program automatically connects to port 25 on your system. If you run email on port 77 and you have a web server on port 25, you'll never get your email but your web server will start receiving spam. The */etc/services* file has a very simple five-column format.

❶qotd	❷17/❸tcp	❹quote	❺#Quote of the Day

This is the entry for the qotd service ❶, which runs on port 17 ❷ in the TCP protocol ❸. It's also known as the quote service ❹. Finally we have a comment ❺ that provides more detail; apparently *qotd* stands for Quote of the Day. Services are assigned the same port number in both TCP and UDP, even though they usually only run on one and not the other—for example, qotd has ports 17/tcp and 17/udp.

Many server programs read */etc/services* to learn which port to bind to on startup, while client programs read */etc/services* to learn which port they should try to connect to. If you run servers on unusual ports, you might have to edit this file to tell the server where to attach to.

As in all standards, there are often good reasons for breaking the rules. The SSH daemon, sshd, normally listens on port 22/tcp, but I've run it on ports 23 (telnet), 80 (HTTP), and 443 (HTTPS) for various reasons. Configuring this depends on the server program you're using. We'll see an example of this in Chapter 15.

Reserved Ports

Ports below 1024 in both TCP and UDP are called *reserved ports*. These ports are assigned only to core Internet infrastructure and important services such as DNS, SSH, HTTP, LDAP, and so on—services that should legitimately only be offered by a system or network administrator. Only programs with root-level privileges can bind to low-numbered ports. A user can provide, say, a game server on a high-numbered port, if the system policy allows—but that's a little different from setting up an official-looking web page visible to everyone stating that the main purpose of the machine is to be a game server! The port assignment for these core protocols is generally carved in stone.

You can view and change the reserved ports with the sysctls net.inet.ip.portrange.reservedhigh and net.inet.ip.portrange.reservedlow.

Every so often, someone thinks that they can disable this "bind-only-by-root" feature and increase their system's security—after all, if your application can be run as a regular user instead of root, wouldn't that increase system security? Most programs that run on reserved ports actually start as root, bind to the port, and then drop privileges to a special restricted user that has even less privilege than a regular user. These programs are designed to start as root and frequently behave differently when run as a regular user. A few programs, such as the Apache web server, are written so they can be started safely by a non-root user, but others are not.

Understanding Ethernet

Ethernet is extremely popular in corporate and home networks, and is the most common connection media for FreeBSD systems. Ethernet is a shared network; many different machines can connect to the same Ethernet and can communicate directly with each other. This gives Ethernet a great advantage over other network protocols, but Ethernet has physical distance limitations that make it practical only for offices, co-location facilities, and other comparatively small networks.

Many different physical media have supported Ethernet over the years. Once upon a time, most Ethernet cables were thick chunks of coaxial cable. Today, most are comparatively thin CAT5 cables with eight strands of very thin wire inside them. You might also encounter Ethernet over optical fiber or radio. For purposes of our discussion we'll assume that you're working with CAT5 or better cable, today's most popular choice. No matter what physical media you use, the theory of Ethernet doesn't change—remember, the physical layer is abstracted away.

Protocol and Hardware

Ethernet is a broadcast protocol, which means that every packet you send on the network can be sent to every workstation on the network. (Note that *can be*; some Ethernet hardware limits recipients of these broadcasts.) Either your network card or its device driver separates the data intended for your computer from the data meant for other computers. One side effect of Ethernet's broadcast nature is that you can eavesdrop on other computers' network traffic. While this can be very useful when diagnosing problems, it's also a security issue. Capturing clear-text passwords is trivial on an old-fashioned Ethernet. A section of Ethernet where all hosts can communicate directly with all other hosts without involving a router is called a *collision domain*, or *segment*.

Ethernet segments are connected via hubs or switches. An Ethernet *hub* is a central piece of hardware to physically connect many other Ethernet devices. Hubs simply forward all received Ethernet frames to every other device attached to the network. Hubs broadcast all Ethernet traffic that they receive to every attached host and other attached hubs. Each host is responsible for filtering out the traffic it doesn't want. This is old-school Ethernet.

Switches have largely supplanted hubs. A switch is like a hub, but filters which traffic it sends to each host by identifying the MAC and IP addresses of attached devices and, for the most part, by only forwarding packets to the devices they are meant for. Since each Ethernet host has a finite amount of bandwidth, switching reduces the load on individual systems by decreasing the amount of traffic each host must sort through.

Switch Failure

Switches fail, despite what Cisco would have you believe. Some failures are obvious, such as those where the magic black smoke is leaking out of the back of the box. When a switch loses its magic smoke, it stops working. Others are more subtle, and make it appear that the switch is still working.

Every switch manufacturer must decide how to handle subtle errors. Either the switch can shut down until it is attended to, or it can attempt to alert its manager and continue forwarding packets to the best of its ability. If you're a vendor, the choice is obvious—you stumble along as best you can, so that your customers don't think that your switches are crap. This means that your switch can start to act like a hub, and you might not know about it. The bad news is that if you were relying on the switch to prevent leakage of secure information, you are fated for disappointment. More than one switch has failed on me in this way, so don't be too surprised when it happens to you.

Installing and using a syslog server (see Chapter 19) can mitigate this risk. While it won't prevent switch failure, it will make it easier to listen to your switches when they try to complain.

Ethernet Speed and Duplex

Ethernet originally supported only a couple of megabits per second, but has expanded to handle tens-of-gigabits speeds. Most people use 10/100 megabits per second (Mbps) speeds. If a card is labeled *10/100Mbps*, it doesn't mean it can actually push that much traffic—I've seen 100Mbps cards that max out at less than 10Mbps, and gigabit cards choke on 100Mbps. Card quality is important when you want to push bandwidth, and the quality of the entire computer is important when pushing serious bandwidth.

The *duplex* setting determines if the card can both transmit and receive data at the same time. A *half-duplex* connection means that the Ethernet card is either transmitting or receiving at any given moment; it cannot do both. A *full-duplex* connection can both send and receive simultaneously.

MAC Addresses

Every Ethernet card has a unique identifier, a *Media Access Control (MAC) address*. This 48-bit number is sometimes called an *Ethernet address*. When a system transmits data to another host on the Ethernet, it first broadcasts an Ethernet request asking, "Which MAC address is responsible for this IP address?" If a host responds with its MAC address, further data for that IP is transmitted to that MAC address. This process is known as the *Address Resolution Protocol*, or *ARP*.

Use arp(8) to view your FreeBSD system's knowledge of the ARP table. The most common usage is the arp -a command, which shows all of the MAC addresses and hostnames that your computer knows of.

```
# arp -a
gw.blackhelicopters.org (192.168.3.1) at 00:00:93:34:4e:78 on fxp0 [ethernet]
sipura.blackhelicopters.org (192.168.3.5) at 00:00:93:c2:0f:8c on fxp0 [ethernet]
```

This full listing of ARP information is known as the *ARP table*, or *MAC table*. (The terms MAC and ARP are frequently used interchangeably, so don't worry about it too much.) Here we see that the host *gw.blockhelicopters.org* has an IP address of 192.168.3.1 and a MAC address of 00:00:93:34:4e:78, and that you can reach these hosts on the local system's interface fxp0.

If a MAC address shows up as incomplete, the host cannot be contacted on the local Ethernet. In this case, check your physical layer (the wire), the remote system, and the configuration of both systems.

Configuring Your Ethernet Connection

Before you try to configure your system to access a network via Ethernet, you must have basic IP address information. If your network offers Dynamic Host Configuration Protocol (DHCP) and your machine is a client, you can just use that and connect to the network as another client. If this machine will be a server, a static IP address is more sensible. Each server requires:

- An IP address
- The netmask for that IP address
- The IP address of the default gateway

Armed with this information, attach your system to the network with ifconfig(8) and route(8).

ifconfig(8)

The ifconfig(8) program displays the interfaces on your computer and lets you configure them. Start by listing the existing interfaces on your system by running ifconfig(8) without any arguments:

```
# ifconfig
❶fxp0: flags=8843<❷UP,BROADCAST,RUNNING,SIMPLEX,MULTICAST> mtu 1500
        options=3<RXCSUM,TXCSUM>
        inet ❸198.22.63.43 netmask ❹0xfffffff0 broadcast 198.22.63.47
        ether ❺00:02:b3:be:df:f5
        media: ❻Ethernet autoselect (10baseT/UTP)
        status: ❼active
rl0: flags=8802<BROADCAST,SIMPLEX,MULTICAST> mtu 1500
        options=8<VLAN_MTU>
        ether 00:20:ed:72:3b:5f
        media: Ethernet autoselect (10baseT/UTP)
        status: ❽no carrier
❾lo0: flags=8049<UP,LOOPBACK,RUNNING,MULTICAST> mtu 16384
        inet 127.0.0.1 netmask 0xff000000
```

Our first network interface is fxp0 ❶, or the first network card that uses the fxp(4) driver. The fxp(4) man page reveals that this is an Intel EtherExpress PRO card. You'll then see basic information about this card ❷, including that it is in the UP state, meaning it is either working or trying to work. It's assigned the IP address 198.22.63.43 ❸, the netmask 0xfffffff0 ❹ (or 255.255.255.240, per Table 6-2). You'll also see the MAC address ❺ and the connection speed ❻. Finally, the status entry shows that this card is active ❼: A cable is plugged in and we have a link light.

The second card, rl0, has almost none of this information associated with it. One key fact is the no carrier signal ❽: It's not plugged in and there is no link light. This card is not in use.

Finally we have the interface lo0 ❾, the loopback. This interface has the IP address 127.0.0.1 on every machine. This loopback address is used when the machine talks to itself. This is a standard software interface, which does not have any associated physical hardware. Do not attempt to delete the loopback interface and do not change its IP address—things will break in an amusing way if you do so. FreeBSD supports other software interfaces such as disc(4), faith(4), gif(4), and many more.

Adding an IP to an Interface

The install process will configure any network cards you have working at install time. If you didn't configure the network for all of your cards during the setup process, or if you add or remove network cards after finishing the install, you can assign an IP address to your network card with ifconfig(8). You need the card's assigned IP address and netmask.

```
# ifconfig interface-name IP-address netmask
```

For example, if your network card is fxp0, your IP address is 192.168.1.250, and your netmask is 255.255.255.0, you would type:

```
# ifconfig fxp0 192.168.1.250 255.255.255.0
```

Specify the netmask in dotted-quad notation as above, or in hex format (0xffffff00). Perhaps simplest of all is to use slash notation, like this:

```
# ifconfig fxp0 192.168.1.250/24
```

Ifconfig(8) can also perform any other configuration your network cards require, such as setting media type and duplex mode. The manual page for that card's driver lists supported media and duplex settings. Set the media type with the media keyword and duplex with the mediaopt keyword. Some combinations of cards and switches cannot successfully auto-negotiate a connection, so you'll need to manually set the speed and duplex on one side or the other. Some cards will speak either half-duplex or full-duplex at 100Mbps, but only full-duplex at 10Mbps speeds. (The gigabit Ethernet standard requires auto-negotiation, so hardcoding the duplex on such cards is not the best practice.) Some cards have multiple media connectors, or multiple media types on a single connector. You can combine all of this into a single command, of course.

```
# ifconfig fxp0 192.168.1.250/24 media 1000baseTX mediaopt full-duplex
```

To make this persist across reboots, add an entry to /etc/rc.conf telling the system to configure the card at boot. The entry has the form ifconfig_interfacename="ifconfig arguments". For example, configuring the re0 card would require an entry like this:

```
ifconfig_re0="192.168.1.250 255.255.255.0 media 1000baseTX mediaopt full-duplex"
```

Once you have a working configuration for your interface, just copy your ifconfig(8) arguments into a */etc/rc.conf* entry.

Testing Your Interface

Now that your interface has an IP address, try to ping the IP address of your default gateway. If you get a response, as shown in the following example, you're on the network. Interrupt the ping with CTRL-C.

```
# ping 192.168.1.1
PING 192.168.1.1 (192.168.1.1): 56 data bytes
64 bytes from 192.168.1.1: icmp_seq=0 ttl=64 time=1.701 ms
64 bytes from 192.168.1.1: icmp_seq=1 ttl=64 time=1.436 ms
^C
--- 192.168.1.1 ping statistics ---
2 packets transmitted, 2 packets received, 0% packet loss
round-trip min/avg/max/stddev = 1.436/1.569/1.701/0.133 ms
```

If you don't get any answers, your network connection isn't working. Either you have a bad connection (check your cables and link lights) or you have misconfigured your card.

Set Default Route

The default route is the address where your system sends all traffic that's not on the local network. If you can ping the default route's IP address, set it via route(8).

```
# route add default 192.168.1.1
```

That's it! You should now be able to ping any IP address on the Internet.

If you didn't choose nameservers during the system install, you will have to use the IP address rather than the hostname. We'll get DNS working the hard way in Chapter 14. In the meantime, an excellent source of real IP addresses are the root nameservers listed in */etc/namedb/named.root*.

Once you have a working default router, make it persist across reboots by adding the proper defaultrouter entry in */etc/rc.conf*:

```
defaultrouter="192.168.1.1"
```

Multiple IP Addresses on One Interface

A FreeBSD system can respond to multiple IP addresses on one interface. This is a popular server configuration, especially those running SSL websites. One server might support hundreds or thousands of domains and needs an IP address for each. Specify additional IP addresses for an interface with ifconfig(8) and the alias keyword. The netmask on an alias is always /32, regardless of the size of the network address block the main address uses.

```
# ifconfig fxp0 alias 192.168.1.225/32
```

Once you add an alias to the interface, the additional IP address appears in ifconfig(8) output. The main IP always appears first, and aliases follow.

```
# ifconfig fxp0
fxp0: flags=8843<UP,BROADCAST,RUNNING,SIMPLEX,MULTICAST> mtu 1500
        options=b<RXCSUM,TXCSUM,VLAN_MTU>
        inet6 fe80::202:b3ff:fe63:e41d%fxp0 prefixlen 64 scopeid 0x1
        inet 192.168.1.250 netmask 0xffffff00 broadcast 192.168.1.255
        inet 192.168.1.225 netmask 0xffffffff broadcast 192.168.1.255
        ether 00:02:b3:63:e4:1d
...
```

Other hosts that ping your aliased IP will get a response from this server.

Once you have the aliases working as you like, make them persist across reboots by adding another ifconfig statement in */etc/rc.conf*:

```
ifconfig_fxp0_alias0="192.168.1.225/32"
```

The only real difference between this entry and the standard *rc.conf*'s "here's my IP address" entry is the alias0 chunk. The alias keyword tells FreeBSD that this is an aliased IP, and the 0 is a unique number assigned to this alias. Every alias set in */etc/rc.conf* must have a unique number, and this number must be sequential. If you skip a number, aliases after the gap will not be installed at boot. This is the most common interface misconfiguration I've seen; FreeBSD needs rebooting so rarely that these errors in */etc/rc.conf* can go unnoticed for months!

Many daemons can be bound to a single address, so you can run multiple instances of the same program on the same server using multiple addresses. For example, named(8) (see Chapter 14) can be attached to a single IP address, but you can run multiple instances of named(8) on a single machine by using a separate IP address for each.

ALIASES AND OUTGOING CONNECTIONS

All connections from your FreeBSD system use the system's real IP address. You might have 2,000 addresses bound to one network card, but when you ssh from that machine, the connection comes from the primary IP address. Keep this in mind when writing firewall rules and other access-control filters. Jails initiate all connections from the jail IP address, but we won't cover jails until Chapter 9.

Renaming Interfaces

FreeBSD names its network interfaces after the device driver used by the network card. This is a fine old tradition in the Unix world and common behavior among most industrial operating systems. Some operating systems name their network interfaces by the type of interface—for example, Linux calls its Ethernet interfaces eth0, eth1, and so on. At times, it makes sense to rename an interface, either to comply with an internal standard or to make its function more apparent. For example, I have one device with twelve network interfaces, each plugged into a different network. Each network has a name such as *test*, *QA*, and so on. Renaming these network interfaces to match the attached networks makes sense.

While FreeBSD is flexible on interface names, some software isn't—it assumes that a network interface name is a short word followed by a number. This isn't likely to change any time in the near future, so it's best practice to use a short interface name ending in a digit. Use ifconfig(8)'s name keyword to rename an interface. For example, to rename fxp1 to test1, you would run:

```
# ifconfig fxp1 name test1
```

Running ifconfig(8) without arguments shows that you have renamed that interface.

```
...
test1: flags=8843<UP,BROADCAST,RUNNING,SIMPLEX,MULTICAST> mtu 1500
        options=b<RXCSUM,TXCSUM,VLAN_MTU>
...
```

Make this change permanent with the ifconfig_*interface*_name option in */etc/rc.conf.*

```
ifconfig_fxp1_name="test1"
```

FreeBSD renames interfaces early in the boot process, before setting IP addresses or other values. This means that any further interface configuration must reference the new interface name rather than the old. Full configuration of a renamed interface with IP addresses and aliases would look something like this:

```
ifconfig_fxp1_name="dmz2"
ifconfig_dmz2="192.168.1.2 netmask 255.255.255.0"
ifconfig_dmz2_alias0="192.168.1.3"
```

DHCP

Very few networks use DHCP for everything, including servers. A DHCP server will set the server's IP address, netmask, nameservers, and default gateway for you. If your network administrator configures servers via DHCP, you can tell the network card to take its configuration via DHCP with the following:

```
ifconfig_fxp0="DHCP"
```

Reboot!

Now that you have your network interfaces fully configured, be sure to reboot to test any changes you made to */etc/rc.conf*. If FreeBSD finds an error in */etc/rc.conf*, especially in network configuration, you'll have problems accessing the system remotely. It's much better to learn that you made a typo under controlled conditions as opposed to the middle of your sleeping hours.

Network Activity

Now that you're on the network, how can you see what's going on? There are several ways to look at the network, and we'll consider each in turn. Unlike many commercial operating systems, FreeBSD commands such as netstat(8) and sockstat(1) give you more information about the network than can possibly be healthy.

Current Network Activity

netstat(8) is a general-purpose network management program that displays different information depending on the flags it's given. One common question people have is, "How much traffic is my system pushing right now?" netstat(8)'s -w option displays how many packets and bytes your system is processing. The -w flag takes one argument, the number of seconds between updates. Adding the -d flag tells netstat(8) to include information about packets that never made it to the system. Here we ask netstat(8) to update its display every five seconds:

```
# netstat -w 5 -d
           input        (Total)           output
    packets errs       bytes  packets errs      bytes colls drops
      ❶34   ❷0     ❸44068     ❹23   ❺0     ❻1518   ❼0    ❽0
        33    0      42610       23    0       1518     0     0
...
```

Nothing appears to happen when you enter this command, but in a few seconds the display prints a single line of information. The first three columns describe inbound traffic, while the next three describe outbound traffic. We see the number of packets received since the last update ❶, the number of interface errors for inbound traffic since the last update ❷, and the number of bytes received since the last update ❸. The next three columns show the number of packets the machine transmitted since the last update ❹, the number of errors in transmission since the last update ❺, and how many bytes we sent ❻. We then see the number of network collisions that have occurred since the last update ❼, and the number of packets that have been dropped ❽. For example, in this display the system received 34 packets ❶ since netstat -w 5 -d started running.

Five seconds later, netstat(8) prints a second line describing the activity since the first line was printed.

You can make the output as detailed as you want, and run it as long as you like. If you'd like to get updates every second, just run netstat -w 1 -d. If once a minute is good enough for you, netstat -w 60 -d will do the trick. I find a five-second interval most suitable when I'm actively watching the network, but you'll quickly learn what best fits your network and your problems.

Hit CTRL-C to stop the report once you've had enough.

What's Listening on What Port?

Another popular question is, "Which ports are open and what programs are listening on them?" FreeBSD includes sockstat(1), a friendly tool to answer this question. It shows both active connections and ports available for client use.

The sockstat(1) program not only lists ports listening to the network, but lists any other listening ports (or *sockets*) on the system. We care most strongly about open network ports for TCP/IP version 4, so use the -4 flag[4] for sockstat(1). Here's trimmed sockstat(1) output from a *very* small server:

```
# sockstat -4
  USER      COMMAND     PID   FD PROTO  LOCAL ADDRESS          FOREIGN ADDRESS

  mwlucas   ❶sshd       11872  4 tcp4   ❷198.22.63.43:22       ❸24.192.127.92:62937
❹ root      sendmail    11433  4 tcp4   *:25                  *:*
❺ www       httpd       9048  16 tcp4   *:80                  *:*
❻ root      sshd        573    3 tcp4   *:23                  *:*
❼ root      sshd        426    3 tcp4   *:22                  *:*
❽ bind      named       275   20 udp4   198.22.63.8:53        *:*
```

The first column gives us the username that's running the program attached to the port in question. The second column is the name of the command. We then have the process ID of the program and the file descriptor number attached to the socket. The next column shows what transport protocol the socket uses—either tcp4 for TCP on TCP/IP version 4, or udp4 for UDP on TCP/IP version 4. We then list the local IP address and port number, and finally the remote IP address and port number for each existing connection.

Take a look at our very first entry. I'm running the program sshd ❶. A man page search takes you to sshd(8), the SSH daemon. The main sshd(8) daemon forked a child process on my behalf to handle my connection, so we see multiple instances of sshd(8) with different process IDs. I'm connected to the local IP address 198.22.63.43 ❷, on TCP port 22. The remote end of this connection is at the IP address 24.192.127.92 ❸, on port 62937. This is an SSH connection from a remote system to the local computer.

Other available connections include Sendmail ❹, the mail server, running on port 25. Note that this entry does not have any IP address listed as the

---

[4] -4 is for TCP/IP version 4. Remember, we're not looking at anything other than the network right now, and we're specifically ignoring IPv6.

foreign address. This socket is listening for incoming connections. Our httpd process ❺ is listening for incoming connections on port 80.

The astute among you might notice that this server has two SSH daemons available for incoming connections, one on port 23 ❻ and one on port 22 ❼. As /etc/services shows, SSH normally runs on port 22 while port 23 is reserved for telnet. Anyone who telnets to this machine will be connected to an SSH daemon, which won't work as they expect. The suspicious among you might suspect that this SSH server was set up to waltz around firewalls that only filter traffic based on source and destination ports and not the actual protocol. (I have no comment on such allegations.)

The last entry is for a nameserver, named ❽, awaiting incoming connections on port 53. This entry is notable for listening for UDP (and not TCP) connections and for attaching to the single IP address 198.22.63.8.

Port Listeners in Detail

sockstat(1) provides a nice high-level view of network service availability, but you can get a little more detailed information about individual connections with netstat(8). To view open network connections use netstat(8)'s -a flag. The -n flag tells netstat(8) to not bother translating IP addresses to hostnames; not only can this translation slow down the output, it can cause ambiguous output. Finally, the -f inet option tells netstat(8) to only worry about network connections. Here's matching netstat output from the same machine we just ran sockstat(1) on:

```
# netstat -na -f inet
Active Internet connections (including servers)
Proto Recv-Q Send-Q  Local Address           Foreign Address         (state)
tcp4       0     48   198.22.63.43.22         24.192.127.92.62937     ESTABLISHED
tcp4       0      0   *.25                    *.*                     LISTEN
tcp4       0      0   *.23                    *.*                     LISTEN
tcp4       0      0   *.80                    *.*                     LISTEN
tcp4       0      0   *.22                    *.*                     LISTEN
udp4       0      0   198.22.63.43.53         *.*
```

Here, we get no idea what program is attached to any port. The first entry in each column is the transport protocol used by the socket—mostly TCP, but the last line shows UDP.

The Recv-Q and Send-Q columns show the number of bytes waiting to be handled by this connection. If you see non-zero Recv-Q numbers for some connection most of the time, you know that the program listening on that port cannot process incoming data quickly enough to keep up with the network stack. Similarly, if the Send-Q column keeps having non-zero entries, you know that either the network or the remote system cannot accept data as quickly as you're sending it. Occasional queued packets are normal, but if they don't go away you might want to investigate why things are slow. You must watch your own system to learn what's normal.

The Local Address is, as you might guess, the IP address and network port number on the local system that the network connection is listening on. The network port appears at the end of the entry and is separated from the IP address by a dot. For example, 198.22.63.43.22 is the IP address 198.22.63.43, port 22. If the entry is an asterisk followed by a period and a port number, that means that the system is listening on that port on all available IP addresses. The system is ready to accept a connection on that port.

The Foreign Address column shows the remote address and port number of any connection.

Finally, the (state) column shows the status of the TCP handshake. You don't need to know all of the possible TCP connection states, so long as you learn what's normal. ESTABLISHED means that a connection exists and that data is probably flowing. LAST_ACK, FIN_WAIT_1, and FIN_WAIT_2 mean that the connection is being closed. SYN_RCVD, ACK, and SYN+ACK are all parts of connection creation. LISTEN indicates that the port is ready for incoming connections. In the preceding example, one TCP connection is running and four are ready to accept clients. As UDP is stateless, those connections list no state information.

By reading this output and combining it with information provided by sockstat(1), you can learn exactly which programs are behaving well and which are suffering bottlenecks.

If you're not interested in listening sockets but only those with active connections, use netstat(8)'s -b option instead of -a. Running netstat -nb -f inet will display only connections with foreign systems.

Network Capacity in the Kernel

The FreeBSD kernel handles network memory by using mbufs. An *mbuf* is a chunk of kernel memory used for networking. You'll keep tripping across mentions of mbufs throughout the FreeBSD network stack documentation, so it's important to have at least a vague idea of them.

FreeBSD automatically allocates network capacity at boot time based on the amount of physical RAM in the system. We assume that if you have a system with 4GB RAM, you want to use more memory for networking than on a little box with 128MB RAM. View how FreeBSD uses its resources with netstat -s and netstat -m. Let's look at the shortest one first.

netstat -m provides a generic view of kernel memory used for networking. The output can be divided into two general categories: how much is used and how many requests failed. The output below is trimmed to only include a few examples of these, but they all follow the same general format:

```
# netstat -m
...
❶32/372/404/❷25600 mbuf clusters in use (current/cache/total/max)
...
0/0/0 requests for mbufs ❸denied (mbufs/clusters/mbuf+clusters)
...
```

Here we see how many mbuf clusters are used ❶. You'd probably guess that these are related to mbufs, and you'd be right. You don't have to know exactly what mbuf clusters are; the important thing is that you know how many you can allocate ❷ and can see that you're under that limit.

Similarly, we can see how many different requests for mbufs the kernel has denied ❸. This system hasn't rejected any requests for mbufs, which means that we aren't having performance problems due to memory shortages. If your system starts rejecting mbuf requests because it's out of memory, you're in trouble. See "Optimizing Network Performance" below.

While `netstat -m` produces a dozen lines of output, `netstat -s` runs for pages and pages. It provides per-protocol performance statistics. Much like `netstat -m`, you can break up these statistics into categories of how much was done and how many problems did you have. Run both of these commands occasionally on your systems and review the results, so you know what passes for normal on your servers and can recognize abnormal numbers when you have problems.

Optimizing Network Performance

Now that you can see what's going on, how could you improve FreeBSD's network performance? There's a simple rule of thumb when considering optimizing: *don't*. Network performance is generally only limited by your hardware. On the other hand, many applications cannot process data as quickly as your network can. If you think that you need to optimize your performance, you're probably looking in the wrong spot. Check Chapter 19 for hints on investigating performance bottlenecks.

Generally speaking, network performance should be adjusted only when you experience network problems. This means that you should have output from `netstat -m` or `netstat -s` indicating that the kernel is having resource problems. If the kernel starts denying requests for resources or dropping connection requests, look at the hints in this section. If you have issues, or you think you should be getting better performance, look at the hardware first.

Optimizing Network Hardware

Not all network hardware is created equal. While anyone in IT hears this frequently, FreeBSD's open nature makes this obvious. For example, here's a comment from the source code of the rl network card driver:

```
The RealTek 8139 PCI NIC redefines the meaning of 'low end.' This is
probably the worst PCI ethernet controller ever made, with the possible
exception of the FEAST chip made by SMC. The 8139 supports bus-master
DMA, but it has a terrible interface that nullifies any performance
gains that bus-master DMA usually offers.
```

This can be summarized as, "This card sucks and blows at the same time. Buy another card." While this is the most vitriolic comment that I've seen in the FreeBSD source code, and this particular hardware is very hard to find today, the drivers for certain other cards say the same thing in a more polite manner. Optimizing network performance with low-end hardware is like putting a high-performance racing transmission in your 1982 Chevette. Replacing your cheap network card will probably fix your problems. Generally speaking, Intel makes decent network cards; they maintain a FreeBSD driver for their wired network cards and provide support so that the FreeBSD community can help maintain the drivers. (Wireless cards are another story.) Similarly, many companies that build server-grade machines make a point of using server-grade network cards. Some companies provide a FreeBSD driver, but do not provide documentation for their hardware. This means that the driver probably works, but you're entirely dependent upon the vendor's future fondness of FreeBSD for your updates. Companies that specialize in inexpensive consumer network equipment are not your best choice for high-performance cards—after all, the average home user has no idea how to pick a network card, so they go by price alone. If in doubt, check the FreeBSD-questions mailing list archives for recent network card recommendations.

Similarly, switch quality varies wildly. The claim that a switch speaks the protocol used in 10/100Mb connections doesn't mean that you can actually push 100Mbps through it! I have a 10Mb hub that only handles 0.5Mbps, and a 100Mb switch that bottlenecks at 15Mbps. Think of a switch speed as a protocol or a language: I could claim that I speak Russian, but twenty years after my studies ceased, my speech bottlenecks at about three words a minute. Again, switches designed for home use are not your best choice in a production environment.

If getting decent hardware doesn't solve your problems, read on.

Memory Usage

FreeBSD uses the amount of memory installed in a system to decide how much memory space to reserve for mbufs. Memory allocated for mbufs cannot be used for any other purpose, so preallocating gigs of RAM for mbufs will actually hurt system performance. Don't adjust the number of mbufs you create unless `netstat -m` tells you that you're short on mbuf space. If you have a mbuf problem, the real fix is to add memory to your machine. This will make FreeBSD recompute the number of mbufs created at boot and solve your problem. Otherwise, you'll just shift the problem to a different part of the system or a different application. You might configure gobs of memory for network connections and find that you've smothered your database server. If you're sure you want to proceed, though, here's how you do it.

Two sysctl values control mbuf allocation, `kern.maxusers` and `kern.ipc.nmbclusters`. The first, `kern.maxusers`, is a boot-time tunable. Your system automatically determines an appropriate `kern.maxusers` value from the system hardware at boot time. Adjusting this value is probably the best way to scale your system as a whole. In older versions of FreeBSD, `kern.maxusers` preallocated memory for networking and refused to release it for other tasks, so increasing `kern.maxusers` could badly impact other parts of the system. Modern FreeBSD does not preallocate network memory, however, so this is just an upper limit on networking memory. If `kern.maxusers` is too small, you'll get warnings in */var/log/messages* (see Chapter 19).

The sysctl `kern.ipc.nmbclusters` specifically controls the number of mbufs allocated by the system. Although this is run-time tunable, it's best to set it early at boot by defining it in */etc/sysctl.conf* (see Chapter 5). This allows you to shift kernel memory from other tasks specifically to (or from) networking. If you set this too high, however, you can actually starve the kernel of memory for other tasks and panic the machine.

```
# sysctl kern.ipc.nmbclusters
kern.ipc.nmbclusters: 25600
```

Mbufs are allocated in units called *nmbclusters* (sometimes called *mbuf clusters*). While the size of a mbuf varies, one cluster is about 2KB. You can use simple math to figure out how much RAM your current nmbcluster setting requires, and then calculate sensible values for your system and applications. This example machine has 25,600 nmbclusters, which means the kernel has reserved about 50MB RAM for networking purposes. This isn't much against my test laptop's gig of RAM, but it's clearly unsuitable on an antique Pentium.

To calculate an appropriate number of mbuf clusters, run `netstat -m` when the server is really busy. The second line of the output will give you the number of mbufs in use and the total number available. If your server at its busiest doesn't use nearly as many nmbclusters as it has available, you're barking up the wrong tree—stop messing with mbufs and replace your hardware already.[5] For example:

```
❶32/❷372/❸404/❹25600 mbuf clusters in use (current/cache/total/max)
```

This system is currently using 32 nmbclusters ❶ on this machine and has cached 372 previously used nmbclusters ❷. With this total of 404 clusters ❸ in memory at this time, our capacity of 25,600 clusters ❹ is 1.5 percent utilized. If this is your real system load, actually reducing the number of nmbclusters might make sense. Chances are, however, that your machine is so slightly loaded that any optimizations are pointless.

My personal rule of thumb is that a server should have enough mbufs to handle twice its standard high load. If your server uses 25,000 nmbclusters during peak hours, it should have at least 50,000 available to handle those brief irregular peaks.

---

[5] Some readers have already replaced their cruddy hardware before considering software optimizations. These readers may perceive this comment as unwarranted. I sincerely, wholeheartedly, and without reservation apologize to all three of you.

Network Capacity Planning

One day your boss will come to you and say, "What sort of server will you need to handle a hundred thousand simultaneous users?" I can't help you estimate your application's memory requirements (well, okay, I could, but that's a different book), but calculating the system's network memory requirements is very straightforward. Each TCP connection requires a send buffer and a receive buffer, while incoming UDP connections require only a receive buffer. FreeBSD tunes these buffers for each session, but they do have default values used to get the sessions started. You can get the default size in bytes from the sysctls *net.inet.tcp.sendspace*, *net.inet.tcp.recvspace*, and *net.inet.udp.recvspace*.

```
# sysctl net.inet.tcp.sendspace
net.inet.tcp.sendspace: 32768
# sysctl net.inet.tcp.recvspace
net.inet.tcp.recvspace: 65536
# sysctl net.inet.udp.recvspace
net.inet.udp.recvspace: 41600
```

Assume you have a web server that must handle a hundred thousand simultaneous connections. HTTP runs on TCP, so each connection will require both a send buffer and a receive buffer. Each connection needs 96KB of memory (32,768 bytes + 65,536 bytes = 98,304 bytes, or 96KB). To handle one hundred thousand simultaneous users we will need 9GB RAM (100,000 × 96KB = 9GB)! Presumably, you'd like to also run an application on this machine. Consider load balancing or caching solutions, or be prepared to write one heck of a check for a single machine.

Ask pointed questions any time someone suggests that you will have one hundred thousand *simultaneous* users. Unless you work at Yahoo! or one of its competitors, you're unlikely to ever see that kind of load. Even if your web app has 100,000 registered users, they will almost certainly never hit it simultaneously. How much money do you want to spend to accommodate that once-in-a-blue-moon spike?

ONCE-IN-A-LIFETIME VS. STANDARD LOAD

When the US Government's "do-not-call" telemarketing blacklist registration site went live, millions of users immediately tried to sign up. The first day, the site was fiendishly slow. After a week, the hardware handled the load without trouble. This was certainly correct capacity planning. Be sure you distinguish planning for once-in-a-lifetime events from planning for normal load.

Maximum Incoming Connections

The FreeBSD kernel provides capacity to handle a certain number of incoming new TCP connections. This doesn't refer to connections that the server previously received and is handling, but rather to people who are attempting to initiate connections simultaneously. For example, the web pages currently being delivered to client's don't count, but the incoming requests that haven't even reached the web server do.

The sysctl `kern.ipc.somaxconn` dictates how many simultaneous connection attempts the system will try to handle. This defaults to 128, which might not be enough for a highly loaded web server. If you're running a high-capacity server where you expect more than 128 new requests to be arriving simultaneously, you probably need to increase this sysctl. If users start complaining that they can't connect, this might be your culprit. Of course, very few applications will accept that many simultaneous new connections; you'll probably have to tune your app well before you hit this point.

Polling

Polling takes the time-honored idea of interrupts and IRQs and boots it out the window, replacing it with regular checks for network activity. In the classic interrupt-driven model, whenever a packet arrives at the network card, the card demands attention from the CPU by generating an interrupt. The CPU stops whatever it's doing and handles that data. This is grand, and even desirable, when the card doesn't process a huge amount of traffic. Once a system starts handling large amounts of data, however, the card generates interrupts continuously. Instead of constantly interrupting, the system is more efficient if the kernel grabs network data from the card at regular intervals. This regular checking is called *polling*. Generally speaking, polling is useful only if you push large amounts of traffic.

Polling is not available as a kernel module as of this writing, since it requires modifications to device drivers. This also means that not all network cards support polling, so be sure to check polling(4) for the complete list. Enable polling by adding `DEVICE_POLLING` to your kernel configuration. After your reboot, enable polling,on a per-interface basis with ifconfig(8).

```
# ifconfig re0 polling
```

Similarly, disable polling with the argument `-polling`. The ifconfig(8) command also displays if polling is enabled on an interface.

As you can enable and disable polling on the fly, enable polling when your system is under heavy load and see if performance improves.

Changing Window Size

FreeBSD uses three buffers for incoming connections: *net.inet.tcp.sendspace*, *net.inet.tcp.recvspace*, and *net.inet.udp.recvspace*. TCP/IP gurus know these settings as *window size*. By changing the size of these buffers, you change network performance. The default settings were chosen for a very specific reason, however: *They work*. Increasing the size of the buffers increases the amount of kernel memory required for every connection. Unless you increase your nmbclusters accordingly, you'll find yourself running out of memory for network services.

As of FreeBSD 7.0, these buffers automatically adjust themselves with network load. While you'll see references to tuning these sysctls in various places on the Internet, these are leftovers from many years of tweaking FreeBSD. You really don't want to adjust these values manually.

Other Optimizations

FreeBSD has about 150 networking-related sysctls. You have all the tools you need to optimize your system so greatly that it no longer passes any traffic at all. Be very careful when playing with network optimizations. Many settings that seem to fix problems actually only fix one set of problems while introducing another whole spectrum of issues. Some software vendors (i.e., Samba) recommend particular network sysctl changes. Try them cautiously and watch for unexpected side effects on other programs before accepting them as your new default. TCP/IP is a terribly, terribly complicated protocol, and FreeBSD's defaults reflect years of experience, testing, and sysadmin suffering.

Network Adapter Teaming

As network servers become more and more vital to business, redundancy becomes more important. We have redundant hard drives in a server and redundant bandwidth into a data center, but what about redundant bandwidth into a server? FreeBSD can treat two network cards as a single entity, allowing you to have multiple connections with a single switch. This is commonly called *network adapter teaming*. FreeBSD implements adapter teaming through lagg(4), the link aggregation interface.

lagg(4) is a kernel module that provides a lagg0 virtual interface. You assign physical interfaces to the lagg0 interface, making them part of the aggregated link. While you could use lagg(4) with only one physical interface, aggregating links only makes sense when you have two or more physical interfaces to assign to the aggregated link. lagg(4) allows you to implement seamless roaming between wired and wireless networks, failover, and several different aggregation protocols.

Aggregation Protocols

Not all network switches support all link aggregation protocols. FreeBSD has basic implementation of some complicated high-end protocols and also includes very basic failover setups. The three I recommend are Fast EtherChannel, LACP, and failover. (There are more schemes, which you can read about in lagg(4).)

Cisco's *Fast EtherChannel (FEC)* is a reliable link aggregation protocol, but only works on high- to medium-end Cisco switches running particular versions of Cisco's operating system. If you have an unmanaged switch, Fast EtherChannel is not a viable choice. Fast EtherChannel is complicated to configure (on the switch), so I recommend FEC only when it is already your corporate standard for link aggregation.

The *Link Aggregation Control Protocol (LACP)* is an industry standard for link aggregation. The physical interfaces are bonded into a single virtual interface with approximately the same bandwidth as all of the individual links combined. LACP provides excellent fault tolerance, and almost all switches support it. I recommend LACP unless you have a specific requirement for Fast EtherChannel or a switch that chokes when you use LACP.

If you do have a switch that chokes on LACP, use *failover*. The failover method sends traffic through one physical interface at a time. If that interface goes down, the connection fails over to the next connection in the pool. While you don't get aggregated bandwidth, you do get the ability to attach your server to multiple switches for fault tolerance.

As LACP is usually the best choice, we'll use it in our examples.

Configuring lagg(4)

The lagg interface is virtual, meaning there is no physical part of the machine that you could point to and say, "That is interface lagg0." Before you can configure the interface, you must create it. FreeBSD lets you create interfaces with ifconfig *interfacename* create, but you can also do this in */etc/rc.conf* with the cloned_interfaces statement.

Configuring a lagg(4) interface in *rc.conf* has three steps: creating the interface, bringing up the physical interfaces, and aggregating them. Here we create a single lagg0 interface out of two Intel gigabit Ethernet cards, em0 and em1.

```
cloned_interfaces="lagg0"
ifconfig_em0="up"
ifconfig_em1="up"
ifconfig_lagg0="laggproto lacp laggport em0 laggport em1 192.168.1.1 netmask
255.255.255.0"
```

First, you list lagg0 as a cloned interface, so FreeBSD will create this interface at boot. Then, bring interfaces em0 and em1 up, but don't configure them. Finally, tell the lagg0 interface what aggregation protocol to use, what physical interfaces belong to it, and its network information. These few lines of configuration give you a high-availability Ethernet connection.

This chapter has been a long march through networking, and your head is probably swimming with more than you ever thought you'd need to know. Let's stay a little more local for a while and look at basic system security.

7

SECURING YOUR SYSTEM

Securing your system means ensuring that your computer's resources are used only by authorized people for authorized purposes. Even if you have no important data on your system, you still have valuable CPU time, memory, and bandwidth. Many folks who thought that their systems were too unimportant for anyone to bother breaking into found themselves an unwitting relay for an attack that disabled a major corporation. You don't want to wake up one morning to the delightful sound of law enforcement agents kicking in your door because your insecure computer broke into a bank.

Sure, there are things worse than having some punk kid take over your servers—say, having the neighborhood loan shark break both your legs. Discovering that the company web page now says, "Ha ha, you've been r00ted!" is a decent competitor for second place. Even more comprehensible intrusions cause huge headaches. Most of the actual intrusions I've been involved with (not as attacker, but as a consultant to the victim) have originated from countries with government censorship, and traffic analysis showed that the intruders were actually just looking for unrestricted access to news sites. While I fully sympathize with these people, when I'm depending upon the stable operation of my servers to run my business, their intrusion is simply unacceptable.

Over the last few years, taking over remote computers has become much easier. Point-and-click programs for subverting computers can be found through search engines. When one bright attacker writes an exploit, several thousand bored teenagers with nothing better to do can download it and make life difficult for the rest of us. Even if the data on your system is worthless, you must secure the system's resources.

Generally speaking, operating systems are not broken into; the programs running on operating systems are. Even the most paranoiac, secure-by-default operating system in the world cannot protect badly written programs from themselves. Occasionally, one of those programs can interact with the operating system in such a way as to actually compromise the operating system. The most well-known of these are *buffer overflows*, where an intruder's program is dumped straight into the CPU's execution space and the operating system runs it. FreeBSD has undergone extensive auditing to eliminate buffer overflows as well as myriad other well-understood security issues, but that's no guarantee that they have been eradicated. New functions and programs appear continuously, and they can interact with older functions and each other in unexpected ways.

FreeBSD provides many tools to help you secure your system against attackers, both internal and external. While no one of these tools is sufficient, all are desirable. Treat everything you learn about system security as a tool in a kit, not as the answer to all your problems. For example, while simply raising a system's securelevel will not make your system secure, it can help when combined with reasonable permissions, file flags, regular patching, password control, and all the other things that make up a good security policy. We'll cover more advanced security tools in Chapter 9, but without the basic protections we discuss here, those tools won't secure your system.

Who Is the Enemy?

We'll arbitrarily lump potential attackers into four groups: script kiddies, botnets, disaffected users, and skilled attackers. You'll find a more detailed classification in books dedicated to security, but that's not what you're here for. These categories are easily explained, easily understood, and include 99 percent of all the attackers you're likely to encounter.

Script Kiddies

The most numerous attackers, *script kiddies*, are not sysadmins. They are not skilled. They download attack programs that work on a point-and-click basis and go looking for vulnerable systems. They're the equivalent of purse snatchers, preying upon old ladies holding their bags just a little bit too loosely. Fortunately, script kiddies are easy to defend against: Just keep your software up to date and follow good computing practices. Like locusts, they're easy to squash but there are just so darned *many* of them!

Botnets

Botnets are composed of machines that have been compromised by worms or viruses. The virus authors control the botnets and use them for anything from searching for more vulnerable hosts to sending spam or breaking into secure sites. Most botnets are composed of Windows machines, but there is no reason why Unix-like operating systems can't be assimilated into botnets. Solaris 10, for example, had a telnet daemon (in.telnetd) vulnerability that a worm subsequently exploited, causing havoc for Solaris users.

Fortunately, botnet defense is much like script kiddie defense; keeping your software patched and following good computing practices goes a long way.

Disaffected Users

The third group, your own users, causes the majority of security problems. Disaffected and rogue employees cause most security breaches. They're the people most likely to know where the security gaps are, to feel that the rules don't apply to them, and to have the time to spend breaking your security. If you tell an employee that company policy forbids him access to a computer resource, and if the employee feels that he should have access to it, he's likely to search for a way around the restriction. Anyone who feels that he is so fabulously special that the rules don't apply to him is a security risk. You might have all your servers patched and a downright misanthropic firewall installed, but if anyone who knows the password is *Current93* can dial the back room modem, you're in trouble.

The best way to stop people like these is simply to not be sloppy. Don't leave projects insecurely half-finished or half-documented. When someone leaves the company, disable his account, change all administrative passwords, inform all employees of that person's departure, and remind them not to share confidential knowledge with that person. Have a computer security policy with real violation penalties and have HR enforce it. And get rid of the unsecured modem, the undocumented telnet server running on an odd port, or whatever hurried hack you put into place thinking that nobody would ever find it.

Motivated Skilled Attackers

The most dangerous group—skilled attackers—are competent system administrators, security researchers, penetration specialists, and criminals who want access to your specific resources. Computer penetration is a lucrative criminal field these days, especially if the victim has resources that can be used for Distributed Denial of Service (DDoS) attacks or mass spam transmission. Compromising a web farm and turning it to evil is profitable. If you have valuable company secrets, you might be targeted by one of these intruders. If one of these people *really* wants to break into your network, he'll probably get there.

Still, security measures that stop the first three groups of people change the tactics of the skilled attacker. Instead of breaking into your computers over the network, he'll have to show up at your door dressed as a telco repairman lugging a packet sniffer, or dumpster-dive searching for old sticky notes with scribbled passwords. This dramatically increases his risk, possibly making an intrusion more trouble than it's worth. If you can make the intruder's break-in plan resemble a Hollywood script *no matter how much he knows about your network*, your security is probably pretty good.

HACKERS, INTRUDERS, AND RELATED SCUM

You'll frequently hear the word *hacker* used to describe people who break into computers. This word has different meanings depending on the speaker. In the technical world, a hacker is someone who is interested in the inner workings of technology. Some hackers are interested in everything; others have a narrow area of specialization. In the FreeBSD community, *hacker* is a title of respect. The main FreeBSD technical list is *FreeBSD-hackers@FreeBSD.org*. In the popular media, however, a hacker is someone who breaks into computer systems, end of story. If you're really interested in the term *hacker*, check out its entry in the Jargon File, which is available at *http://www.catb.org/jargon/html/H/hacker.html*.

To reduce confusion, I recommend completely avoiding the word *hacker*. In this book, I call people who break into computers *intruders*.* Technical wizards can be called by a variety of names, but they rarely object to "Oh Great and Powerful One."

---

* My editor *still* won't let me print what I call them in person.

FreeBSD Security Announcements

The best defense against any attackers is to keep your system up to date. This means you must know when to patch your system, what to patch, and how. An outdated system is a script kiddie's best friend.

The FreeBSD Project includes volunteers who specialize in auditing source code and watching for security issues with both the base operating system and add-on software. These developers maintain a very low-volume mailing list, *FreeBSD-security-notifications@FreeBSD.org*, and subscribing is a good idea. While you can monitor other mailing lists (such as BugTraq and CERT) for general announcements, the security notifications list is a single source for FreeBSD-specific information. To subscribe to the security notifications mailing list, see the instructions on *http://lists.freebsd.org/mailman/listinfo*. The FreeBSD security team releases advisories on that mailing list as soon as they are available.

Read advisories carefully and quickly act on those that affect you, as you can be certain that script kiddies are searching for vulnerable machines. The best thing you can do is address these problems as quickly as possible.

User Security

Remember when I said that your own users are your greatest security risk? Here's where you learn to keep the little buggers in line. FreeBSD has a variety of ways to allow users to do their work without giving them free reign on the system. We'll look at the most important tools here, starting with adding users in the first place.

Creating User Accounts

FreeBSD uses the standard Unix user management programs such as passwd(1), pw(8), and vipw(8). FreeBSD also includes a friendly interactive user-adding program, adduser(8). Only root may add users, of course. Just type adduser on the command line to enter an interactive shell.

The first time you run adduser(8), it prompts you to set appropriate defaults for all new user settings. Follow through the example session below so you can determine appropriate defaults for your system.

```
# adduser
❶ Username: gedonner
❷ Full name: Gregory E Donner
❸ Uid (Leave empty for default):
```

The username ❶ is the name of the account. Users on my systems get a username of their first initial, middle initial, and last name. You can assign usernames by whatever scheme you dream up. The full name ❷ is the user's real name. FreeBSD then lets you choose a numerical user ID (UID) ❸. FreeBSD starts numbering UIDs at 1,000; while you can change this, all UIDs below 1,000 are reserved for system use. I recommend just pressing ENTER to take the next available UID.

```
❶ Login group [gedonner]:
❷ Login group is gedonner. Invite gedonner into other groups? []: webmasters
❸ Login class [default]:
❹ Shell (sh csh tcsh nologin) [sh]: tcsh
❺ Home directory [/home/gedonner]:
```

The user's default group ❶ is important—remember, Unix permissions are set by owner and group. The FreeBSD default of having each user in their own group is usually the most sensible way for most setups. Any of the big thick books on system administration offers several grouping schemes—feel free to use one of those if it matches your needs more closely. In addition to the primary group, at this time you can add this user to other groups ❷, if appropriate.

A login class ❸ specifies what level of resources the user has access to. We'll talk about login classes later in this section.

The shell ❹ is the command-line environment. While the system default is */bin/sh*, I use tcsh[1] for people new to Unix. If you're deeply attached to another shell, feel free to use it instead. Knowledgeable users can change their own shells.

The home directory ❺ is where the user's files reside on disk. The user and that user's primary group own this directory.

```
❶ Use password-based authentication? [yes]:
❷ Use an empty password? (yes/no) [no]:
❸ Use a random password? (yes/no) [no]: y
❹ Lock out the account after creation? [no]: n
```

The password options give you a certain degree of flexibility. If all of your users are comfortable with SSH and public key cryptography, perhaps you can get away without using passwords. In the meantime, the rest of us are stuck with passwords ❶.

Use an empty password ❷ if you want the user to set his or her own password via telnet or the console. Whoever connects to that account first gets to set the password. This makes an empty password a good idea right up there with the idea of filling a dirigible with hydrogen and then lighting matches inside it.

A random password ❸, on the other hand, is a good idea for a new account. The random password generator FreeBSD provides is good enough for day-to-day use. Random passwords are usually hard to remember, which encourages the user to change his password as soon as possible.

When an account is locked ❹, nobody can use it to log in. This is generally counterproductive.

After entering all this information, adduser spits everything back at you for review and confirmation or rejection. Once you confirm, adduser verifies the account setup and provides you with the randomly generated password. It then asks you if you want to set up another user.

Configuring Adduser: /etc/adduser.conf

Creating new users on some Unix systems requires you to manually edit */etc/passwd*, rebuild the password database, edit */etc/group*, create a home directory, set permissions on that home directory, install dotfiles, and so on. This makes handling your local customizations routine—if you set everything by hand, you can manage your local account setup easily. adduser(8) hides a lot of the tedium, but uses a set of sensible defaults. For sites with different requirements, */etc/adduser.conf* lets you meet those requirements while retaining the high degree of automation.

To create your first initial *adduser.conf file*, run `adduser -C` and answer the questions.

---

[1] For interactive use, that is. Never, never, *never* program in *any* C shell. Read Tom Christiansen's classic paper "Csh Programming Considered Harmful" for a full explanation. (It's available at *http://www.faqs.org/faqs/unix-faq/shell/csh-whynot.*)

```
❶ Login group []:
❷ Enter additional groups []: cvsup
❸ Login class [default]:
❹ Shell (sh csh tcsh nologin) [sh]: tcsh
❺ Home directory [/home/]: /nfs/u1/home
❻ Use password-based authentication? [yes]:
  Use an empty password? (yes/no) [no]:
  Use a random password? (yes/no) [no]: yes
  Lock out the account after creation? [no]: no
```

The login group ❶ is the default user group. An empty login group means that the user account defaults to having its own unique user group (the FreeBSD default).

You can specify any additional user groups ❷ that new accounts belong to by default, as well as the login class ❸.

Choose a default shell ❹ for your users.

Your home directory location ❺ might vary from the standalone FreeBSD standard. In this example, I've specified a typical style of NFS-mounted home directories used when many users have accounts on many machines.

Finally, choose the default password behavior for new users ❻.

These default settings can save you a lot of typing at the command line, but once you have a basic configuration file you can add more obscure functions. Table 7-1 shows the *adduser.conf* entries I find most useful.

Table 7-1: Useful adduser Settings

Setting	Effect
defaultLgroup	The default group users will be added to (if empty, each user will be in his own group)
defaultclass	The login class assigned by default
passwdtype	Either no (account is disabled until password is set by root), none (no password is set), yes (set password when creating account), or random (assign a random password)
homeprefix	Directory for user home directories (e.g., */home*)
defaultshell	Shell selected by default (can be any shell in */etc/shells*)
udotdir	Directory containing user dotfiles, such as *.login* and *.cshrc*
msgfile	File containing email message sent to each user upon creation

Using these values, you can adjust adduser's default behavior to most closely match your requirements.

Editing Users: passwd(1), chpass(1), and Friends

Managing users isn't just about creating and deleting accounts. You'll need to change those accounts from time to time. While FreeBSD includes several tools for editing accounts, the simplest are passwd(1), chpass(1), vipw(8), and pw(8). These work on the tightly interrelated files */etc/master.passwd*,

/etc/passwd, */etc/spwd.db*, and */etc/pwd.db*. We'll start with the files and then review the common tools for editing those files.

The files */etc/master.passwd*, */etc/passwd*, */etc/spwd.db*, and */etc/pwd.db* hold user account information. Each file has a slightly different format and purpose. */etc/master.passwd* is the authoritative source of user account information and includes user passwords in encrypted form. Normal users do not have permission to view the contents of */etc/master.passwd*. Regular users need access to basic account information, however; how else can unprivileged system programs identify users? The file */etc/passwd* lists user accounts with all privileged information (such as the encrypted password) removed. Anyone can view the contents of */etc/passwd* to get basic account information.

Many programs need account information, and parsing a text file is notoriously slow. In this day of laptop supercomputers, the word *slow* isn't very meaningful, but this was a very real problem back when disco freely roamed the earth. For that reason, BSD-derived systems build a database file out of */etc/master.passwd* and */etc/passwd*. (Other Unix-like systems have similar functionality in different files.) The file */etc/spwd.db* is taken directly from */etc/master.passwd* and contains sensitive user information, but can only be read by root. The file */etc/pwd.db* can be read by anyone, but contains the limited subset of information contained in */etc/passwd*.

Any time any standard user management program changes the account information in */etc/master.passwd*, FreeBSD runs pwd_mkdb(8) to update the other three files. For example, the three programs passwd(1), chpass(1), and vipw(8) all allow you to make changes to the master password file, and all three programs trigger pwd_mkdb to update the related files.

Changing a Password

Use passwd(1) to change a password. A user can change his own password, and root can change anyone's password. To change your own password, just enter passwd at the command prompt.

```
# passwd
Changing local password for mwlucas
Old Password:
New Password:
Retype New Password:
```

When changing your own password, passwd(1) first asks for your current password. This is to ensure that nobody else can change your password without your knowledge. It's always good to log out when you walk away from your terminal, but when you don't, this simple check in passwd(1) prevents a lot of practical jokers from really annoying you. Then enter your new password twice, and it's done. When you're the superuser and want to change another user's password, just give the username as an argument to passwd.

```
# passwd mwlucas
Changing local password for mwlucas
New Password:
Retype New Password:
```

Note that root doesn't need to know the user's old password; the root user can change any user account on the system in any manner desired.

Changing Accounts with chpass(1)

The account has more information associated with it than just the password. The chpass(1) utility lets users edit everything they can reach in their account. For example, if I run chpass at the command prompt, I get an editor with the following text:

```
#Changing user information for mwlucas.
Shell: /bin/tcsh
Full Name: Michael W Lucas
Office Location:
Office Phone:
Home Phone:
Other information:
```

I'm allowed to edit six informational fields in my account. The first, my shell, can be set to any shell listed in */etc/shells* (see "Shells and /etc/shells" on page 188). I can change my full name; perhaps I want my full middle name listed, or perhaps I wish to be known to other system users as *Mr. Scabies*—this is where I set that. I can update my office location and office phone, so my co-workers can find me easily. This is another feature that was very useful on the university campuses where BSD grew up and where system users rarely had an idea of anyone's physical location. Now that we have extensive online directories and many more computers, it's less useful. I generally set my home phone number to 911 (999 in the UK), and I can put a little bit of personal information in the Other space. Also note what I *cannot* change as a regular user. The sysadmin sets my home directory, and I may not change it even if the system has a new hard drive with lots of empty space for my MP3 collection. My UID and GID numbers, similarly, are assigned by the system or the sysadmin.

On the other hand, if root runs chpass mwlucas, its heightened privileges give it a very different view.

```
#Changing user information for mwlucas.
Login: mwlucas
```
❶ `Password: $1$4d.nOPmc$uuBQy6ZL6hPQNTQef1jty.`
```
Uid [#]: 1001
Gid [# or name]: 1001
Change [month day year]:
Expire [month day year]:
Class:
Home directory: /home/mwlucas
Shell: /bin/tcsh
Full Name: Michael W Lucas
Office Location:
Office Phone:
Home Phone:
Other information:
```

As root, you can do anything you like to the poor user. Changing his login to *megaloser* is only the start of the havoc you can wreak. You even get access to the user's hashed password ❶. Don't alter this, unless you're comfortable computing password hashes in your head. Use passwd(1) to more safely and reliably change the user's password. You can also change the user's home directory, although chpass(1) doesn't move the user's files; you must copy them by hand.

You can also set a date for password changes and account expiration. Password expiration is useful if you've just changed a user's password and you want him to change it upon his first login. Account expiration is useful when someone asks for an account but insists it's only needed for a limited time. You can forget to go back and delete that account, but FreeBSD never forgets. Both of these fields take a date in the form *month day year*, but you only need the first three letters of the month. For example, to make a user's password expire on June 8, 2008, I would enter Jun 8 2008 in the Change space. Once the user changes his password the password expiration field is blanked out again but only the system administrator can extend an account expiration date.

The Big Hammer: vipw(8)

chpass is fine for editing individual accounts, but what happens when you must edit many accounts? Suppose your system has hundreds of users and a brand new hard disk for the home partition; do you really want to run chpass(1) hundreds of times? That's where vipw(8) comes in.

vipw lets you directly edit */etc/master.passwd*. When you finish your edits, vipw checks the password file's syntax to be sure you haven't ruined anything, then saves the new password file and runs pwd_mkdb(8). vipw can protect your password file from many basic mistakes, but if you're clever, you can still muck things up. You must understand the format of the password file to use vipw(8) properly.

If the information in */etc/master.passwd* conflicts with information in other files, programs assume that */etc/master.passwd* is correct. For example, */etc/group* doesn't list the user as a member of the user's primary group. The primary group that appears in */etc/master.passwd* is correct, even if the user doesn't show up as a member in */etc/group*.

Each line in */etc/master.passwd* is a single account record, containing 10 colon-separated fields. These fields are the following:

Username

This is either an account name created by the sysadmin, or a user created at install time to provide some system service. FreeBSD includes users for system administration, such as root, daemon, games, and so on. Each of these users owns a part of the base system. It also provides accounts for common services, such as the www user reserved for use by web servers. Add-on software might add its own system accounts as well.

Encrypted Password

The second field is the encrypted password. System users don't have a password, so you can't log in as one of them. User accounts have a string of random-looking characters here.

User ID

The third field is the user ID number, or UID. Every user has a unique UID.

Group ID

Similarly, the fourth field is the *group ID number*, or *GID*. This is the user's primary group. Usually this is identical to the UID, and the group has the same name as the username.

User's Class

The next field is the user's class as defined in */etc/login.conf* (see "Restricting System Usage" on page 197).

Password Expiration

This is the same as the password expiration date set via chpass(1), but here you'll see the time stored as seconds from the epoch. You can use date -j and the +%s output format to generate epochal seconds from a real date. To convert midnight, June 1, 2008 to epochal seconds, run date -j 200806010000 '+%s'.

Account Expiration

To have the account shut itself off on a certain day, set the account expiration date just as you would for password expiration.

Personal Data

This field is also known as the *gecos* field for very obscure historical reasons. This field contains the user's real name, office number, work phone number, and home phone number, all separated by commas. Do not use colons in this field; colons are reserved specifically for separating fields in */etc/master.passwd* itself.

User's Home Directory

The ninth field is the user's home directory. While this defaults to */home/<username>*, you can move this anywhere appropriate. You'll also need to move the actual home directory and its files when you change this field. Users with a nonexistent home directory cannot log in by default, although the requirehome setting in *login.conf* can change this.

User's Shell

The final field is the user's shell. If this field is empty, the system assigns the user the boring old */bin/sh*.

While chpass(1) lets you muck up individual user accounts, vipw(8) unleashes you on the entire userbase. Be careful with it!

Removing a User

The rmuser(8) program deletes user accounts. You'll be prompted for the username you want to delete and asked if you want to remove that user's home directory. That's really all you have to do; destruction is much easier than creation, after all.

Scripting with pw(8)

The pw(8) command provides a powerful command-line interface to user accounts. While useradd(8) walks you through setting up an account in a friendly manner, pw(8) lets you specify everything on a single command line. I find pw(8) cumbersome for day-to-day use, but if you manage many user accounts it is invaluable.

One thing I do use pw(8) for is locking accounts. While a locked account is active, nobody can log in to it. I've used this to great effect when a client was behind on a bill; users call quite quickly when they can't log in, and yet their websites continue to come up and their email continues to accumulate.

```
# pw lock mwlucas
```

Unlock the account with pw unlock *username*.
If you need scripts to manage your users, definitely read man pw(8).

Shells and /etc/shells

The *shell* is the program that provides the user's command prompt. Different shells behave differently and offer different shortcuts and features. Many people are very attached to particular shells and complain bitterly if their shell is not available on a system. You can install many shells from ports (see Chapter 11).

The file */etc/shells* contains a list of all legitimate user shells. When you install a shell from a port or a package, it adds an appropriate entry in */etc/shells*. If you compile your own shell from source, without using a FreeBSD port, you must list the shell by its complete path in */etc/shells*.

The FTP daemon won't allow a user to log in via FTP if his shell is not listed in */etc/shells*. If you use */sbin/nologin* as an FTP-only user shell, you must add it to this file, although a better way to handle such users is with login classes as discussed later in this chapter.

root, Groups, and Management

Unix security has been considered somewhat coarse because one superuser, *root*, can do anything. Other users are lowly peons who endure the shackles root places upon them. The problem is, root doesn't have a wide variety of shackles on hand and can't individualize them very well. While there is some truth to this, a decent administrator can combine groups and permissions to handle almost any problem securely.

The root Password

Certain actions require absolute control of the system, including manipulating core system files such as the kernel, device drivers, and authentication systems. Such activities are designed to be performed by root.

To use the root password, you can either log in as root at a console login prompt or, if you are a member of the group wheel, log in as yourself and use the switch user command su(1). (We'll discuss groups later in this section.) I recommend su; it logs who uses it, and can be used on a remote system. The command is very simple to use:

```
# su
Password:
#
```

Next, check your current user ID with the id(1) command:

```
# id
uid=0(root) gid=0(wheel) groups=0(wheel), 5(operator)
#
```

You now own the system—and I do mean *own* it. Consider every keystroke; carelessness can return your hard drive to the primordial state of unformatted empty wasteland. And share the root password sparingly if at all, because anyone who has the root password can inflict unlimited damage on the system.

Remember, only the users in the group wheel can use the root password to become root through su(1). Anyone can use the root password at the system console, which is why physical protection of your system is vital. If you give the root password to a regular user who does not have physical access to the console, they can type su and enter the root password as many times as they want, and it still won't work.

This naturally leads to the question, "Who needs root access?" Much of the configuration discussed in this book requires use of the root password. Once you have the system running properly, you can greatly decrease or discontinue use of the root password. For those remaining tasks that absolutely require root privileges, I recommend sudo (*/usr/ports/security/sudo*). One of the simplest ways to reduce the need for root access is through the proper use of groups.

Groups of Users

Unix-like operating systems classify users into *groups*, each group consisting of people who perform similar administrative functions. A sysadmin can define a group called *webmasters*, add the accounts of the people editing web pages to that group, and set the privileges on the web-related files so that the members of that group can edit those files. He can also create a group called *email*, add the email administrators to that group, and set the permissions of mail-related files accordingly. Using groups in this manner is a powerful and oft-neglected tool for system management.

Any user can identify the groups he belongs to with id(1). The preceding example showed that the user root is in the groups wheel and operator. Root is a special user, however, and can do anything he pleases. Here's my account, which is a little more realistic for an average user:

```
# id
uid=1001(mwlucas) gid=1001(mwlucas) groups=1001(mwlucas), 0(wheel),
68(dialer), 1006(cvsup)
```

My UID is 1001, and my username is mwlucas. My GID, primary group ID, is 1001, and my primary group is named mwlucas as well. This is all pretty standard for the first user on a system, and even in later users, the only thing that changes is the numbers assigned to the account and primary group. More interesting is what other groups I'm assigned to: In addition to my primary group I'm in the groups wheel, dialer, and cvsup. wheel members may use the root password to become root, dialer members may use tip(1) without becoming root, and cvsup members can use the CVS repository on the local system. Each of these groups has special privileges on my system, and as a member of those groups I inherit those privileges.

Group information is defined in */etc/group*.

/etc/group

The file */etc/group* contains all group information except for the user's primary group (which is defined with the user account in */etc/master.passwd*). Each line in */etc/group* contains four colon-delimited fields: the group name, the group password, the group ID number, and a list of members. Here's a sample entry:

```
wheel:*:0:root,mwlucas,gedonner
```

The group name is a human-friendly name for the group. This group is named wheel. Group names are arbitrary; you could call a group of users minions if you wished. Choose group names that give you an idea of what they're for; while you might remember that your minions may edit the company web page, will your co-workers understand that?

The second field, the group password, was a great idea that turned out to be a security nightmare. Modern Unix-like systems don't do anything with the group password, but the field remains because old programs expect to find something in this space. The asterisk is just a placeholder to placate such software.

The third field gives the group's unique numeric group ID (GID). Many programs use the GID rather than name to identify a group. The wheel group has a GID of 0, and the maximum GID is 65535.

Last is a comma-delimited list of all users in the group. The users root, mwlucas, and gedonner are members of the group wheel.

Changing Group Memberships

If you want to add a user to a group, add his username to the end of the line for that group. For example, the wheel group is the list of users that may use the root password. Here I add rwatson to the wheel group:

```
wheel:*:0:root,mwlucas,gedonner,rwatson
```

Mind you, the odds of me convincing rwatson (the president of the FreeBSD Foundation) to assume sysadmin duties on any of my systems range from negligible to nonexistent, but it's worth a try.

Creating Groups

To create a new group, you only need a name for the group and a group ID number. Technically, you don't even need a member for the group; some programs run as members of a group, and FreeBSD uses the group permissions to control those programs just as the users are controlled.

Traditionally, GIDs are assigned the next number up the list. GID is an arbitrary number between 0 and 65535. Generally speaking, GIDs below 1000 are reserved for operating system usage. Programs that need a dedicated group ID usually use one in this range. User accounts start numbering their GIDs at 1001 and go up. Some special groups might start numbering at 65535 and go down.

Using Groups to Avoid Root

In addition to being a security concern, the root password distribution policy can cause dissension in any organization. Many sysadmins refuse to share the root password with people who are responsible for maintaining part of the system, but do not offer an alternative and thereby prevent people from doing their job. Other sysadmins hand out root to dang near anyone who wants it and then complain when the system becomes unstable.

Both attitudes are untenable in the long run. When I'm a user, I insist that the sysadmin not give me the root password but instead set up a group that can do this task. While having root privileges can be convenient, not having responsibility when the system breaks is more convenient still.

One common situation is where a junior sysadmin is responsible for a particular portion of the system. I've had many DNS administrators work under me;[2] these people don't ever install software, recompile the kernel, or perform other sysadmin tasks. They only answer emails, update zone files, and reload the named daemon. New sysadmins often believe that they need root access to do this sort of work. By establishing your own groups, consisting of people who perform similar administrative functions, you avoid distributing the root password and still allow people to do their work. In this section, we'll implement group-level access control over nameserver files. The same principles apply to any files you choose to protect. Mail and web configuration files are other popular choices for group-based management.

System Accounts

FreeBSD reserves some user account names for integrated programs. For example, the nameserver runs under the user account bind and the group bind. Do not log in as the program user for this sort of work! If an intruder compromises the nameserver, he can only access the system with the privileges of the user bind.

What's more, do not allow the group of the system account user to own the files created for that function. Create a separate user and group to own program files. That way, our hypothetical nameserver intruder cannot even edit the files used by the DNS server, further minimizing potential damage. If the program regularly updates the files (e.g., a database's backend storage), you must give the program access rights, but chances are that a human being doesn't ever need to edit that file. Similarly, there's no reason a database should be able to edit its own configuration file.

Administrative Group Creation

The simplest way to create a group that owns files is to employ adduser(8) to make a user that owns them, and utilize that user's primary group as the group for the files. Because we already have a user called bind, we'll create an administrative user dns. The username isn't important, but you should choose a name that you'll remember easily.

Give your administrative user a shell of *nologin*, which sets a shell of */sbin/nologin*. This prevents anyone from actually logging in as the administrative user.

If you want, you could specify a particular UID and GID for these sorts of users. I've been known to choose UID and GID numbers that resemble those used by their related service accounts. For example, the user bind has a UID and GID of 53. I could give the user dns a UID of 10053 to make it easily

---

[2] Some even survived the experience.

recognizable. At other times, I start numbering my administrative groups at 65535 and work my way down. It doesn't matter so long as I'm completely consistent within an organization.

Do not add this administrative user to any other groups. Under no circumstances add this user to a privileged group such as wheel! Every user needs a home directory. For an administrative user, a home directory of */nonexistent* works well. This user's files are elsewhere in the system, after all. Lastly, let adduser(8) disable the account. While the shell prevents logins, an extra layer of defense won't hurt.

Now that you have an administrative user and a group, you can assign ownership of files to that user. A user and a group own every file. You can see existing file ownership and permissions with ls -l. (If you've forgotten how Unix permissions work, read ls(1) and chmod(1).) Many sysadmins pay close attention to file owners, somewhat less attention to worldwide permissions, and only glance at the group permissions.

```
# ls -l
total 3166
-rw-r-----  1 mwlucas  mwlucas     79552 Nov 11 17:58 rndc.key
-rw-rw-r--  1 mwlucas  mwlucas   3131606 Nov 11 17:58 absolutefreebsd.com.db
```

Here, I've created two files. The first file, *rndc.key*, can be read and written by the user mwlucas, it can be read by anyone in the group mwlucas, but no one else can do anything with it. The file *absolutefreebsd.com.db* can be read or written by the user mwlucas or anyone in the group mwlucas, but others can only read the file. If you're in the group mwlucas, you can edit the file *absolutefreebsd.com.db* without becoming root.

Change a file's owner and group with chown(1). You must know the name of the user and group whose ownership you want to change. In this case, we want to change both files to be owned by the user dns and the group dns.

```
# chown dns:dns rndc.key
# chown dns:dns absolutefreebsd.com.db
# ls -l
total 3166
-rw-r-----  1 dns  dns     79552 Nov 11 17:58 rndc.key
-rw-rw-r--  1 dns  dns   3131606 Nov 11 17:58 absolutefreebsd.com.db
```

These files are now owned by the user dns and the group dns. Anyone who is in the group dns can edit *absolutefreebsd.com.db* without using the root password. Finally, this file can be read by the user bind, who runs the name-server. Add your DNS administrators to the dns group in */etc/group*, and abruptly they can do their jobs.

The DNS administrators might think that they need the root password for restarting the nameserver program itself. However, this is easily managed with rndc(8). Other tasks can be managed with cron jobs, or with the add-on program sudo(8).

Interesting Default Groups

FreeBSD ships with several default groups. Most are used by the system and aren't of huge concern to a sysadmin—you should know that they're there, but that's different than working with them on a day-to-day basis. Here, I present for your amusement and edification the most useful, interesting, and curious of the default groups (Table 7-2). Adding your own groups simplifies system administration, but the groups listed here are available on every FreeBSD system.

Table 7-2: Interesting FreeBSD Groups

Group Name	Purpose
audit	Group for users who can access audit(8) information
authpf	Group for authenticating the PF packet filter
bin	Group to own general system binaries and programs
bind	Group for the built-in DNS server (see Chapter 14)
daemon	Used by various system services, such as the printing system
_dhcp	Group for DHCP client operations
dialer	Group which may access serial ports; useful for modems and tip(1)
games	Group to own the games
guest	Group for system guests (almost never used)
kmem	Group used by programs that can access kernel memory, such as fstat(1), netstat(1), and so on
mail	Group for the mail system (see Chapter 16)
mailnull	Default group for Sendmail (see Chapter 16)
man	Group to own the system man pages
network	Group to own network programs such as ppp(8)
news	Group to own the Usenet News subsystem (if installed)
nobody	Primary group for user nobody who has no privileges
nogroup	Group with no privileges
operator	Group that can access drives, generally for backup purposes
_pflogd	Group for PF logger
proxy	Group for FTP proxy in PF packet filter
smmsp	Group for the Sendmail Submission User (see Chapter 16)
sshd	Owner of the SSH server (see Chapter 15)
staff	The system administrators
sys	Another system group
tty	Group for programs that can write to terminals, such as wall(1)
uucp	Group for Unix-to-Unix Copy Protocol programs
wheel	Users who may use the root password
www	Group for web server programs (not web files)

Tweaking User Security

You can limit user activity, preventing any single user from utilizing too much memory or processor time. This is not as important today, now that even small computers have very fast processors and lots of memory, but it is still very useful in systems with dozens or hundreds of users. You can also control where users may log in from.

Restricting Login Ability

FreeBSD checks */etc/login.access* every time a user tries to log in. If *login.access* contains rules that forbid logins from that user, the login attempt fails immediately. This file has no rules by default, meaning that there are no login restrictions on anyone with a valid username and password.

/etc/login.access has three colon-delimited fields. The first either grants (+) or denies (-) the right to log in; the second is a list of users or groups; and the third is a list of connection sources. You can use an ALL or ALL EXCEPT syntax, which allow you to make simple but expressive rules. Rules are checked on a first-fit basis. When login(1) finds a rule where the user and the connection source match, the connection is immediately accepted or rejected. This makes rule order vital. The default is to allow logins. For example, to allow only members of the wheel group to log in from the system console, you might try this rule:

```
+:wheel: console
```

The problem with this rule, however, is that it doesn't actually deny users login privileges. Since the default is to accept logins, and since all this rule does is explicitly grant login privileges to the users in the wheel group, this won't stop anyone from logging in. If I'm not in the wheel group, and I try to log in, this doesn't deny me access.

You could try two rules like this:

```
+:wheel: console
-:ALL:console
```

This would achieve the desired effect, but is longer than you need. Use ALL EXCEPT instead.

```
-:ALL EXCEPT wheel: console
```

This rejects unwanted logins most quickly and runs less risk of administrator error. As a rule, it's best to build *login.access* lists by rejecting logins, rather than permitting them. FreeBSD immediately rejects non-wheel users at the console upon hitting this rule.

The last field in *login.access*, the connection source, can use hostnames, host addresses, network numbers, domain names, or the special values LOCAL and ALL. Let's see how they work.

Hostnames

Hostnames rely upon DNS or the hosts file. If you suspect that your name-server might suffer problems, you probably don't want to use this system; intruders can give a hostname any IP address that they like and fool your system into accepting the connection, and a nameserver failure could lock you out completely. Still, it's possible to use a rule like this:

```
-:ALL EXCEPT wheel:fileserver.mycompany.com
```

Users in the wheel group can log in from the fileserver, but nobody else can.

Host Addresses and Networks

Host addresses work like hostnames, but they're immune to DNS failures or spoofing.

```
-:ALL EXCEPT wheel:192.168.1.5
```

A network number is a truncated IP address, like this:

```
-:ALL EXCEPT wheel:192.168.1.
```

This allows anyone in the wheel group to log in from a machine whose IP address begins with 192.168.1, and denies everyone else access from those IP addresses.

LOCAL

The most complicated location is LOCAL, which matches any hostname without a dot in it (generally, only hosts in the local domain). For example, *www .absolutefreebsd.com* thinks that any machine in the domain *absolutefreebsd.com* matches LOCAL. This works via reverse DNS (see Chapter 14), which is very vulnerable to spoofing. Although my laptop claims that it has a hostname of *humvee.blackhelicopters.org*, its IP address has reverse DNS that claims it is somewhere in my cable modem provider's network. A machine in *absolutefreebsd.com* thinks that my laptop is not in the same domain and hence is not local. As such, I cannot use the LOCAL verification method.

Similarly, anyone who owns a block of IP addresses can give their addresses any desired reverse DNS. The LOCAL restriction is therefore not terribly useful.

ALL and ALL EXCEPT

ALL matches everything, and ALL EXCEPT matches everything but what you specify. These are the most useful connection sources, in my opinion. For example, if you had a highly secure machine only accessible from a couple of management workstations, you could have a rule like this:

```
-:ALL EXCEPT wheel:ALL EXCEPT 192.168.89.128 192.168.170.44
```

Tie It All Together

The point of these rules is to build a login policy that matches your real-world policies. If you provide generic services, but only allow your system administrators to log on remotely, a one-line *login.access* prevents any other users from logging in:

```
-:ALL EXCEPT wheel:ALL
```

This is great, if you can live with a restriction this tight. On the other hand, I've worked at several Internet service providers that used FreeBSD to provide client services. Lowly customers were not allowed to log onto the servers unless they had a shell account. System administrators could log in remotely, as could the DNS and web teams (members of the groups dns and webmasters). Only sysadmins could log onto the console, however.

```
-:ALL EXCEPT wheel:console
-:ALL EXCEPT wheel dns webmasters:ALL
```

Set this up in *login.access* once, and let group membership control all of your remote logins forever after.

Restricting System Usage

You can provide more specific controls with login classes. Login classes, managed through */etc/login.conf*, define the resources and information provided for users. Each user is assigned a class, and each class has limits on the system resources available. When you change the limits on a class, all users get the new limits when they next log in. Set a user's class when creating the user account, or change it later with chpass(1).

Class Definitions

The default *login.conf* starts with the default class, the class used by accounts without any other class. This class gives the user basically unlimited access to system resources and is suitable for application servers with a limited number of users. If this meets your needs, don't adjust the file at all.

Each class definition consists of a series of variable assignments that define the user's resource limits, accounting, and environment. Each variable assignment in the class definition begins and ends with a colon. The backslash character is a continuation character to indicate that the class continues on the next line, which makes the file more readable. Here's a sample of the beginning of one class:

```
❶default:\
        ❷:passwd_format=❸md5:\
        :copyright=/etc/COPYRIGHT:\
        :welcome=/etc/motd:\
...
```

This class is called default ❶. I've shown three of the dozens of variables in this class. The variable passwd_format ❷, for example, is set to md5 ❸. These variable assignments and the class name describe the class, and you can change the user's experience on the system by assigning the user to another class.

Some of *login.conf*'s variables don't have a value, but instead change account behavior just by being present. For example, the requirehome variable takes effect just by being included in the class. If this value is present, the user must have a valid home directory.

```
        :requirehome:\
```

After editing *login.conf*, you must update the login database to make the changes take effect.

```
# cap_mkdb /etc/login.conf
```

This rebuilds the database file */etc/login.conf.db* that is used for fast lookups, much like */etc/spwd.db*.

The default */etc/login.conf* includes several example classes of users. If you want an idea of what sort of restrictions to put on users for various situations, check those examples. The following section offers ideas about what can be set in a login class. For a complete listing of supported settings in your version of FreeBSD, read man login.conf(5).

Resource Limits

Resource limits allow you to control how much of the system any one user can monopolize at any one time. If you have several hundred users logged in to one machine and one of those users decides to compile OpenOffice.org, that person will consume far more than his fair share of processor time, memory, and I/O. By limiting the resources one user can monopolize, you can make the system more responsive for all users.

Table 7-3 defines the resource-limiting *login.conf* variables.

Table 7-3: Some *login.conf* Variables for Limiting Resource Use

Variable	Description
cputime	The maximum CPU time any one process may use
filesize	The maximum size of any one file
datasize	The maximum memory size of data that can be consumed by one process
stacksize	The maximum amount of stack memory usable by a process
coredumpsize	The maximum size of a core dump
memoryuse	The maximum amount of memory a process can lock
maxproc	The maximum number of processes the user can have running
openfiles	The maximum number of open files per process
sbsize	The maximum socket buffer size a user's application can set

Note that resource limits are frequently set per process. If you give each process 20MB of RAM and allow 40 processes per user, you've just allowed each user 800MB of memory. Perhaps your system has a lot of memory, but does it really have that much?

Current and Maximum Resource Limits

In addition to the limits listed above, you can specify current and maximum resource limits. *Current* limits are advisory, and the user can override them at will. This works well on a cooperative system, where multiple users willingly share resources but you want to notify those users who exceed the standard resource allocation. Users cannot exceed *maximum* limits.

If you do not specify a limit as current or maximum, FreeBSD treats it as a maximum limit.

To specify a current limit, add -cur to the variable name. To make a maximum limit, add -max. For example, to set a current and a maximum limit on the number of processes the user can have, use this input:

```
...
:maxproc-cur: 30:\
:maxproc-max: 60:\
...
```

One counterpart to resource limits is resource accounting. These days, accounting isn't as important as it was when today's inexpensive computers would cost tens of thousands of dollars, so we won't discuss it in this book. It's more important to restrict a single user from consuming your system than to bill for every CPU cycle someone uses. You should know that the capability exists, however.

Class Environment

You can also define environment settings in */etc/login.conf.* This can work better than setting them in the default *.cshrc* or *.profile*, because *login.conf* settings affect all user accounts immediately upon their next login. Some shells, such as zsh(1), do not read either of these configuration files, so using a class environment sets the proper environment variables for those users.

All of the environment fields recognize two special characters. A tilde (~) represents the user's home directory, while a cash symbol ($) represents the username. Here are a few examples from the default class that illustrate this:

```
:setenv=MAIL=❶/var/mail/$,BLOCKSIZE=K,FTP_PASSIVE_MODE=YES:\
:path=/sbin /bin /usr/sbin /usr/bin /usr/games /usr/local/sbin /usr/
local/bin /usr/X11R6/bin ❷~/bin:\
```

By using the $ character, the environment variable MAIL is set to */var/mail/<username>* ❶. Similarly, the last directory in the PATH variable is the *bin* subdirectory in the user's home directory ❷.

Table 7-4 lists some common *login.conf* environment settings.

Table 7-4: Common *login.conf* Environment Settings

Variable	Description
hushlogin	If present, no system information is given out during login.
ignorenologin	If present, these users can log in even when */var/run/nologin* exists.
ftp-chroot	If present, these users are chrooted when using FTP (see Chapter 15).
manpath	A list of directories for the $MANPATH environment variable.
nologin	If present, the user cannot log in.
path	A list of directories for the $PATH environment variable.
priority	Priority (nice) for the user's processes (see Chapter 19).
setenv	A comma-separated list of environment variables and their values.
umask	Initial umask setting; should always start with 0, see builtin(1).
welcome	Path to the login welcome message.
shell	The full path of a shell to be executed upon login. This overrides the shell in */etc/master.passwd*. The user's $SHELL, however, contains the shell from the password file, resulting in an inconsistent environment. Playing games with this is an excellent way to annoy your users.
term	The default terminal type. Just about anything that tries to set a terminal type overrides this.
timezone	The default value of the $TZ environment variable.

Password and Login Control

Unlike the environment settings, many of which can be set in places other than the login class, most login and authentication options can only be controlled from the login class. Here are some common authentication options:

minpasswordlength

This specifies the minimum length of a password. It only takes effect the next time the user changes his password; it does not go through and check that all current passwords are of this length. Here, we set the minimum password length to 28 characters. (This is a great way to encourage use of SSH keys.)

```
\:minpasswordlen=28:\
```

passwd_format

This sets the cryptographic hash used to store passwords in */etc/master .passwd*. The default is md5, for MD5 hashing. Other permissible options are des (DES), blf (Blowfish), and nthash (Windows NT). DES is most useful when you want to share passwords between different Unix-like operating systems. Blowfish might be overkill, but on modern systems CPU time is cheaper than dirt so it can't hurt. The nthash algorithm is most useful when you actively and passionately *want* someone to break into your system, but I can't recommend it for any other purpose.

mixpasswordcase

If present, FreeBSD complains if the user changes his password to an all-lowercase word.

host.allow

This value lets users in this class use rlogin and rsh. Do not do this.

host.deny

This value is used for rlogin and rsh. Avoid it like fuzzy green meat.

times.allow

You can schedule when users may log in. This requires a comma-delimited list of days and times. Days are given as the first two letters of the day's name (Su, Mo, Tu, We, Th, Fr, and Sa). Time is in standard 24-hour format. For example, if a user can only log in on Wednesdays, between 8 AM and 5 PM, you would use this entry:

```
:times.allow=We8-17:\
```

times.deny

The user cannot log in during this time window. Note that this does not kick off a user if he's already logged in. The format is the same as for times.allow. If times.allow and times.deny overlap, times.deny takes precedence.

File Flags

All Unix-like operating systems have the same filesystem permissions, assigning read, write, and execute privileges for a file to the file's owner, its group, and all others. FreeBSD extends the permissions scheme with *file flags* which work with permissions to enhance your system's security. Some flags are used for non-security-related functions, but we'll pay special attention to the security flags. You can find a complete list of file flags in man chflags(1).

Many of these flags have different effects depending on the system secure-level, which we will cover in the next section. Understanding securelevels requires an understanding of file flags, while file flags rely on securelevels. For the moment, just nod and smile when you encounter a mention of securelevels; all becomes clear in the next few pages.

Here are the common file flags:

sappnd

The system-level append-only flag can only be set by root. Files with this flag can be added to, but cannot be removed or otherwise edited. This is particularly useful for log files. Setting sappnd on a user's *.history* file can be interesting if the account is compromised. Since a common intruder tactic is to remove *.history* or symlink it to */dev/null* so that the admin cannot see what happened, sappnd ensures that script kiddies cannot cover their tracks in this manner. It's almost funny to review the record of someone trying to remove a sappnd file; you can almost see the attacker's frustration grow as he tries various methods.[3] This flag cannot be removed when the system is running at securelevel 1 or higher.

schg

Only root can set the system-level immutable flag. Files with this flag set cannot be changed in any way. They cannot be edited, moved, replaced, or overwritten. Basically, the filesystem itself prevents all attempts to alter this file. The flag cannot be removed when the system is running at securelevel 1 or greater.

sunlnk

Only root can set the system-level undeletable flag on a file. The file can be edited or altered, but it cannot be deleted. This is not as secure as the previous two flags because if a file can be edited, it can be emptied. It's still useful for certain circumstances, however. I've used it to solve problems when a program insisted on deleting its own log files upon a crash. It's not generally useful to set on any standard system files, however. This flag cannot be removed when the system is running at securelevel 1 or higher.

uappnd

The user-level append-only flag can only be set by the file owner or root. Like the system-level append-only flag sappnd, a file with this flag set can be added to but not otherwise edited or removed. This is most useful for logs from personal programs and the like; it is primarily a means to let users prevent accidental removal of their own files. The owner or root can remove this flag.

uchg

The user-level immutable flag can only be set by the owner or root. Like the schg flag, this immutable flag prevents anyone from changing the file. Again, root can override this, and it can be disabled by the user at any securelevel. This flag helps prevent mistakes, but it's not a way to secure your system.

---

[3] It's not funny enough to balance out letting intruders penetrate your system, of course, but it can provide a brief moment of light in an otherwise ghastly day.

`uunlnk`

The user-level undeletable flag can only be set by the owner or root. A file with this flag set cannot be deleted by the owner. Root can override that, and the user can turn this flag off at any time, making this mostly useless.

Setting and Viewing File Flags

Set flags with chflags(1). For example, to be sure that your kernel isn't replaced you could do this:

```
# chflags schg /boot/kernel/kernel
```

This would keep anyone, including you, from changing your kernel.

You can also recursively change the flags on an entire directory tree with the -R flag. For example, to make your entire */bin* directory immutable, run this command:

```
# chflags -R schg /bin
```

And boom! Your basic system binaries cannot be changed.

To see what flags are set on a file, use ls -lo.

```
# ls -lo log
-rw-r--r--  1 mwlucas  mwlucas  sappnd 0 Nov 12 12:37 log
```

The sappnd entry tells us that the system append-only flag is set on this log. For comparison, if a file has no flags set, it looks like this:

```
# ls -lo log
-rw-r--r--  1 mwlucas  mwlucas  - 0 Nov 12 12:37 log
```

The dash in place of the flag name tells us that no flag has been set.

An out-of-the-box FreeBSD install doesn't have many files marked with flags, but you can flag anything you want. On one system that I fully expected to be hacked I went berserk with chflags -R schg in various system directories to prevent anyone from replacing system binaries with trojaned versions. It might not stop an attacker from getting in, but it made me feel better to imagine how frustrated he would be once he gets to a command prompt.

To remove a file flag, use chflags and a no in front of the flag name. For example, to unset the schg flag on your kernel, enter this command:

```
# chflags noschg /boot/kernel/kernel
```

That said, you must be running at securelevel −1 to unset this flag. So, without further ado, let's discuss securelevels and what they mean to you.

Securelevels

Securelevels are kernel settings that change basic system behavior to disallow certain actions. The kernel behaves slightly differently as you raise the securelevel. For example, at low securelevels file flags can be removed. A file might be flagged immutable—but you can remove the flag, edit the file, and reflag it. When you increase the securelevel, the file flag cannot be removed. Similar changes take place in other parts of the system. Taken as a whole, the behavior changes that result from increased securelevels either frustrate or stop an intruder. Enable securelevels at boot with the *rc.conf* option `kern_securelevel_enable="YES"`.

Securelevels complicate system maintenance by imposing restrictions on your behavior. After all, many system administration tasks are also things intruders might do to cover their tracks. For example, at certain securelevels you cannot format or mount new hard drives while the system is running. On the other hand, securelevels hamper intruders even more than they hamper you.

Securelevel Definitions

Securelevels come in 5 degrees: −1, 0, 1, 2, and 3, with −1 being the lowest and 3 the highest. Once you enable securelevels with the `kern_securelevel_enable` *rc.conf* option, you can set the securelevel at boot with the `kern_securelevel` *rc.conf* variable. You can raise the securelevel at any time, not just at boot, but you cannot lower it without rebooting into single-user mode. After all, if you could lower the securelevel at any time so could your intruder!

Securelevel −1

The default provides no additional kernel security whatsoever. If you're learning FreeBSD and are frequently changing your configuration, remain at securelevel −1 and use the built-in file permissions and other Unix safeguards for security.

Securelevel 0

The only time securelevel 0 is used is during booting, and it offers no special features. When the system reaches multi-user mode, however, the securelevel is automatically raised to 1. Setting `kern_securelevel=0` in */etc/rc.conf* is effectively the same as setting `kern_securelevel=1`. This might be helpful, however, if you have startup scripts that perform actions prohibited by a higher securelevel.

Securelevel 1

At securelevel 1, the basic secure mode, things become interesting:

- System-level file flags may not be turned off.
- You cannot load or unload kernel modules (see Chapter 5).
- Programs cannot write directly to system memory via either */dev/mem* or */dev/kmem*.

- Nothing can access */dev/io*.
- Mounted disks cannot be written to directly. (You can write files to disk, you just cannot address the raw disk devices.)

The most obvious effect of securelevel 1 for ordinary users is that the BSD-specific filesystem flags cannot be altered. If a file is marked system-level immutable, and you want to replace it, too bad.

Securelevel 2

Securelevel 2 has all the behaviors of securelevel 1, with two additions:

- Disks cannot be opened for writing, whether mounted or not.
- You cannot alter system time by more than one second.

Both of these seem irrelevant to new sysadmins, but they provide important security protections. Although Unix provides handy tools like text editors to write files, it is also possible to bypass those tools and even bypass the actual filesystem to access the underlying ones and zeroes on the hard drive. If you do this, you can change any file regardless of the file permissions. The only time this commonly happens is when you install a new hard drive and must create a filesystem on it. Normally, only the root user can write directly to the disk in this manner. At securelevel 2, even root cannot do this.

Similarly, another old hacker trick is to change the system time, edit a file, and change the time back. That way, when the administrator looks for files that might be causing trouble, the tampered file appears to have been untouched for months or years, and hence not seem an obvious source of concern.

Securelevel 3

Securelevel 3 is the *network secure mode*. In addition to the settings of securelevels 1 and 2, you cannot adjust packet filter rules. The firewall on your host is immutable. If you have a system with packet filtering or bandwidth management enabled, and those rules are well tuned and unlikely to change, you can use securelevel 3.

Which Securelevel Do You Need?

The securelevel appropriate for your environment depends entirely upon your situation. For example, if you've just put a FreeBSD machine into production and are still fine-tuning it, leave the securelevel at −1. Once your system is tuned, however, you can raise the securelevel. Most production systems run just fine at securelevel 2.

If you use one of FreeBSD's packet filtering or firewall packages, securelevel 3 might look tempting. Be very sure of your firewall rules before you enable this, however! Securelevel 3 makes it impossible to change your firewall without disrupting your connection. Are you 100 percent certain that none of your customers will ever call in to say, "Here's a check, double my bandwidth"?

What Won't Securelevels and File Flags Accomplish?

Consider a case where someone compromises a CGI script on your Apache web server, uses that to bootstrap into a shell, and then uses the shell to bootstrap himself into root access.

If you've set the securelevel accordingly, perhaps this attacker will become frustrated because he can't replace your kernel with his specially compiled one. No problem; he can still replace assorted system programs with trojaned versions—so that the next time you log in, your new version of login(1) sends your password to an anonymous web-based mailbox or to an Internet newsgroup.

So, to protect your key files, you run around doing chflags schg -R /bin/*, chflags schg -R /usr/lib, and so on. Fine. If you forget one file—say, something obscure like */etc/rc.bsdextended*—your intruder can edit that file to include chflags -R noschg /. He can then reboot your system late at night when you might not notice. How often do you sit down and exhaustively audit your */etc/rc* files?

You think that your system is safe, with every file completely protected. But what about */usr/local/etc/rc.d*, the local program startup directory? The system boot process tries to execute any file with a name ending in *.sh* in this directory. Your intruder could therefore do a lot of damage by placing a simple shell script there. After all, */etc/rc* raises the securelevel at the end of the boot process. What if he were to create a shell script that kills the running */etc/rc* before it could raise the securelevel, then turns around and runs his own */var/.hidden/rc.rootkit* to finish bringing the system up?

Of course, these are only a couple of possibilities. There are others, limited only by your intruder's creativity. Just remember that system security is a thorny problem with no easy solution. Once intruders have a command prompt, it's you against them. And if they're any good, you won't even notice the penetration until it's too late. By following good computing practices and keeping your system up to date, you can stop them from intruding in the first place. Do not allow securelevels to make you lazy!

Living with Securelevels

If you've been liberal with the schg flag, you will soon find that you can't upgrade or patch your system conveniently. The fact is, the same conditions that make intruders' lives difficult can make yours a living hell if you don't know how to work with them.

If you've frozen your */etc/rc.conf* with schg, you must lower the securelevel to change the programs running on your system. Of course, the securelevel setting is in that file, so in order to edit it, you must take control of the system before */etc/rc* runs. That means you must boot into single-user mode (as discussed in Chapter 3), mount your filesystems, run chflags noschg on the files in question, and continue booting. You can even entirely disable securelevels in */etc/rc.conf* and work normally while the system runs. You'll restore service more quickly that way, but lose the protections of the file flags.

After you've finished maintenance, you can raise (but not lower) the securelevel by changing the kern.securelevel sysctl to your desired securelevel.

```
# sysctl kern.securelevel=3
```

Now that you can control file changes, let's consider controlling access to your system from the network.

Network Targets

Intruders normally break into applications that listen to the network, not the operating system itself. An operating system may or may not help defend a piece of software against network attacks, but the intrusion itself starts with the application. One way to reduce the number of attacks that can be carried out against your server is to identify all of the programs that are listening to the network and disable any that are not strictly necessary. FreeBSD provides sockstat(1) as an easy way to identify programs that are listening to the network.

We cover sockstat in detail in Chapter 6; running sockstat -4 shows all open IPv4 TCP/IP ports. Every network port you have open is a potential weakness and a potential target. Shut down unnecessary network services and secure those you must offer.

It's a good idea to regularly review which ports are open on your systems, because you might learn something that surprises you. You might find that some piece of software you've installed has a network component that you were not aware of, and it's been quietly listening to the network.

Once you know what's running, how do you turn off what you don't need? The best way to close these ports is to not start the programs that run them. Network daemons generally start in one of two places: */etc/rc.conf* or a startup script in */usr/local/etc/rc.d*. Programs that are integrated with the main FreeBSD system, such as sendmail(8), sshd(8), and rpcbind(8), have flags in *rc.conf* to enable or disable them, as do many add-on programs. A few add-on programs such as web servers start via scripts in */usr/local/etc/rc.d*. See Chapter 3 for details on enabling and disabling programs at startup.

WORKSTATION VS. SERVER SECURITY

Many companies I've seen have tightly secured servers, but pay little attention to workstation security. A prospective intruder doesn't care if a system is a server or a workstation, however. Many servers and firewalls have special rules for the sysadmin's workstation. An intruder will happily penetrate a workstation and try to leverage that into server access. While server security is key, don't neglect workstations—especially *your* workstation!

Putting It All Together

Once you have only the necessary network ports open, and you know which programs are using those ports, you know which programs you must be most concerned about securing. If the FreeBSD security team sends out an announcement of a problem with a service you don't run, you can safely delay implementing a fix until your next maintenance window. If, however, the security team announces a hole in programs you are using, you know you have to implement a fix as soon as possible. If they announce a serious security problem with a piece of network software you're using, you know you must act quickly. Simply being able to respond intelligently and quickly to real risks helps protect you against most intruders. Tools such as file flags and securelevels minimize the damage successful intruders can do. Finally, using groups to restrict your own system administrators to particular sections of the system can protect your computers from both accidental and deliberate damage.

8

DISKS AND FILESYSTEMS

The importance of managing filesystems and disks cannot be overemphasized. (Go ahead, try to emphasize it too much. I'll wait.) Your disks contain your data, making reliability and flexibility paramount to the operating system. FreeBSD supports a variety of filesystems and has many different ways to handle them. In this chapter we'll consider the most common disk tasks every system administrator performs.

Disk Drives 101

Most people treat disk drives as fragile magic boxes. If you treat a drive badly, you can make the drive screech and grind, and with enough abuse, you can let the magic smoke escape so it will never work again. To really understand filesystems, you must know a little bit about what's going on inside the drive. If you have a dusty old disk drive that you no longer have any respect for, feel free to crack the case and follow along.

Inside the hard drive case you'll find a stack of round aluminum or plastic disks, commonly called *platters*. When the drive is active, the platters spin at thousands of revolutions per minute. The RPM count on hard drives measures platter rotation speed.

A thin layer of magnetic media covers the platters. This magnetic material is arranged in thousands of circular rings, called *tracks*, that extend from the platter's inner core to its outer edge, much like the growth rings in a tree. These tracks hold data as strings of zeros and ones. Each track is subdivided into *sectors*. Each sector on the outer tracks holds more data than a corresponding sector on an inner track, and reading a constant amount of data takes less time on an outer track than on an inner track because any point on the outer track is moving faster.

Heads, mounted over each platter, write and read data as the platters pass by, much like a phonograph needle. These heads can read and write data quickly, but they must wait for the disk to move into the proper position under them. Drive performance basically boils down to how quickly those platters can move under the drive heads, which is what makes RPM important.

ATA, SATA, SCSI, AND SAS

I assume that you're familiar with the basics of the standard disk storage technologies. If you're not, please spend a few moments online with any of the excellent tutorials on these subjects, or even the brief articles available on Wikipedia. I'll make suggestions here and there about how these technologies can be used, but SCSI IDs and LUNs are a subject for another book.

Device Nodes

We touched briefly on device nodes in Chapter 3, but let's consider them in more detail. Device nodes are special files that represent hardware on the system. They're used as logical interfaces between user programs and either a device driver or a physical device. By using a command on a device node, sending information to a device node, or reading data from a device node, you're telling the kernel to perform an action upon a physical device. These actions can be very different for different devices—writing data to a disk is very different than writing data to a sound card. All device nodes exist in */dev*.

Before you can work with a disk or disk partition, you must know its device name. FreeBSD disk device nodes come from the names of the device drivers for that type of hardware. Device driver names, in turn, come from the chipset used in the device and not from what the device appears to be.

Table 8-1 shows the most common disk device nodes. See the man page for each if you want the full details.

Table 8-1: Storage Devices and Types

Device Node	Man Page	Description
/dev/fd*	fdc(4)	Floppy disks
/dev/acd*	acd(4)	IDE CD drives
/dev/ad*	ad(4)	ATA and SATA hard disks and partitions
/dev/cd*	cd(4)	SCSI CD drives
/dev/da*	da(4)	SCSI and SAS hard disks, USB and flash storage, etc.

Disks attached to most hardware RAID controllers don't use device names for each disk. Instead, these RAID controllers present a virtual disk for each RAID container, using a device node named after the RAID driver. For example, the amr(4) driver presents its virtual disks as */dev/amrd**. A few RAID cards use the cam(4) abstraction layer, so their hard drives do show up as */dev/da** devices.

Hard Disks and Partitions

While we discussed partitioning in Chapter 2, let's consider partitions from a disk device perspective. The first possible ATA disk on our first ATA controller is called */dev/ad0*. Subsequent disks are */dev/ad1*, */dev/ad2*, and so on. Subdivisions of each disk start with this name and add something at the end, like */dev/ad0s1b*. While you might expect a disk to be a monolithic whole, you'll see lots of subdivisions if you look in */dev* for everything that begins with */dev/ad0*.

```
# ls /dev/ad*
/dev/ad0        /dev/ad0s1a     /dev/ad0s1c     /dev/ad0s1e
/dev/ad0s1      /dev/ad0s1b     /dev/ad0s1d     /dev/ad0s1f
```

So, what are all these subdivisions? Think back to when you allocated disk space. If you followed the recommendations in this book, you used the whole disk for FreeBSD. You could have created a second chunk of disk for a second operating system, or even cut the disk into two FreeBSD sections. These sections are called partitions in the Microsoft and Linux worlds, and *slices* in FreeBSD land. The s1 in the preceding list represents these large partitions, or slices. The drive ad0 has one slice, ad0s1, with further subdivisions marked by letters.

In FreeBSD, a *partition* is a further subdivision within a slice. You created partitions inside the slice during the install. Each partition has a unique device node name created by adding a letter to the slice device node. For example, partitions inside the slice */dev/ad0s1* show up as */dev/ad0s1a*, */dev/ad0s1b*, */dev/ad0s1c*, and so on. Each partition you created—*/usr*, */var*, and so on—is assigned one of these device nodes.

You can assign partition device names almost arbitrarily, with some exceptions. Tradition says that the node ending in *a* (in our example, */dev/ad0s1a*) is the root partition, and the node ending in *b* (*/dev/ad0s1b*) is the swap space. The *c* label indicates the entire slice, from beginning to end. You can assign *d* through *h* to any partition you like. You can have only eight partitions in one slice, and up to four slices per drive. For example, the device node */dev/ad0s1a* is disk number 0, slice 1, partition 1, and is probably the root filesystem. The device node */dev/ad1s2b* is on disk number 2, and is probably swap space.

If you have non-ATA disks, substitute the appropriate device for */dev/ad.*

ATA DISK NUMBERING

Just because the first possible ATA disk on the system would be */dev/ad0* doesn't mean that you have to have a hard drive */dev/ad0* installed. My laptop's hard drive is */dev/ad4* because it's on a RAID controller, not on the built-in ATA controller. SCSI and SAS hard drives are smarter about this and generally number the first disk with */dev/da0* no matter where they're attached. Removing the kernel option ATA_STATIC_ID makes ATA disks start numbering at 0, if you desire.

The Filesystem Table: /etc/fstab

So, how does your system map these device names to partitions? With the filesystem table, */etc/fstab.* In that file, each filesystem appears on a separate line, along with any special options used by mount(8). Here's a sample entry from a filesystem table:

```
/dev/ad4s2a    /    ufs    rw    1    1
```

The first field in each entry gives the device name.

The second field lists the mount point, or the directory where the filesystem is attached. Every partition you can write files to is attached to a mount point such as */usr*, */var*, and so on. A few special partitions, such as swap space, have a mount point of none. You can't write files to swap space—at least, not if you want to use either the file or the swap space!

Next, we have the type of filesystem on this partition. The standard FreeBSD partition is of type ufs, or Unix Fast File System. The example below includes swap (swap space), cd9660 (CD), and nfs (Network File System). Before you can attach a partition to your directory tree, you must know what sort of filesystem it has. As you might guess, trying to mount a DOS floppy as an FFS filesystem will fail.

The fourth field shows the mount options used on this filesystem. The mount options tell FreeBSD to treat the filesystem in a certain matter. We'll discuss mount options in more detail later in this chapter, but here are a few special ones used only by */etc/fstab*:

ro   The filesystem is mounted as read-only. Not even root can write to it.

rw   The filesystem is mounted read-write.

noauto   FreeBSD won't automatically mount the filesystem, neither at boot nor when using mount -a. This option is useful for removable media drives which might not have media in them at boot.

The fifth field tells the dump(8) whether or not this filesystem needs dumping. If set to 0, dump won't back up the filesystem at all. Otherwise, the number gives the minimum dump level needed to trigger a backup of this filesystem. See Chapter 4 for details.

The last field, Pass#, tells the system when to check the filesystem's integrity during the boot process. All of the partitions in the same Pass# are checked in parallel with fsck(8). Only the root filesystem has a Pass# of 1, and it is checked first. All other filesystems are set to 2, which means that FreeBSD mounts them after the root filesystem. Swap and read-only media don't require integrity checking, so are set to 0.

With this knowledge, let's look at a complete /etc/fstab.

# Device	Mountpoint	FStype	Options	Dump	Pass#
❶ /dev/ad4s1b	none	swap	sw	0	0
❷ /dev/ad4s2a	/	ufs	rw	1	1
❸ /dev/ad4s1a	/amd64	ufs	rw	2	2
/dev/ad4s1f	/amd64/usr	ufs	rw	2	2
/dev/ad4s1d	/amd64/var	ufs	rw	2	2
❹ /dev/ad4s1e	/tmp	ufs	rw	2	2
❺ /dev/ad4s2e	/usr	ufs	rw	2	2
❻ /dev/ad4s2d	/var	ufs	rw	2	2
❼ /dev/ad4s3d	/home	ufs	rw	2	2
❽ /dev/acd0	/cdrom	cd9660	ro,noauto	0	0
❾ data:/mp3	/mp3	nfs	rw,noauto,soft	0	0

Our first entry, /dev/ad4s1b ❶, is swap space. It isn't mounted anywhere; FreeBSD uses swap as secondary memory.

The second entry ❷ is the root partition. Note the device name—while swap is partition b on slice 1, the root filesystem is partition a on slice 2. The root directory is on a different slice than the swap space!

The third partition is /dev/ad4s1a ❸. We'd normally expect the root partition to be here, but instead it's mounted as /amd64. The next two partitions are also on slice 1, but mounted under /amd64.

Our /tmp ❹ filesystem is a partition on slice 1, which contains the /amd64 filesystem.

The next entries, /usr ❺ and /var ❻, are normal-looking partitions on slice 2.

The next partition, /home ❼, is on the same disk, slice 3, partition d. Where the heck did slice 3 come from?

Our CD drive is mounted on /cdrom ❽ and is not automatically mounted at boot.

The final entry doesn't start with a device node. This is a Network File System (NFS) entry, and it tells us to mount the partition mp3 on the machine data as /mp3 on the local machine when we specifically request it. We'll talk about NFS later in this chapter.

This filesystem table comes from a dual-boot machine, running FreeBSD/i386 and FreeBSD/amd64. That's why the table doesn't look quite normal. I can access the amd64 filesystem and use the amd64 swap space while running the i386 slice.

What's Mounted Now?

If not all filesystems are mounted automatically at boot, and if the sysadmin can request additional mounts, how can you determine what's mounted right now on the system? Run mount(8) without any options to see a list of all mounted filesystems.

```
# mount
/dev/ad4s2a on / (ufs, local)
devfs on /dev (devfs, local)
/dev/ad4s1e on /tmp (ufs, local, soft-updates)
/dev/ad4s2e on /usr (ufs, local, soft-updates)
/dev/ad4s2d on /var (ufs, local, soft-updates)
/dev/ad4s3d on /usr/home (ufs, local, soft-updates)
```

Here we see that our filesystems are almost all standard UFS partitions. The word local means that the partition is on a hard drive attached to this machine. We also see soft-updates, a feature of the FreeBSD filesystem we'll discuss later in this chapter. If you're using features such as NFS or SMB to mount partitions, they'll appear here.

mount(8) is a quick way to get the device names for each of your partitions, but it also provides other functions.

Mounting and Unmounting Disks

mount(8)'s main purpose is to mount partitions onto your filesystem. If you've never played with mounting before, boot your FreeBSD machine into the single-user mode (see Chapter 3) and follow along.

In single-user mode FreeBSD has mounted the root partition read-only. The root partition contains just enough of the system to perform basic setup, get core services running, and find the rest of the filesystems. Those other filesystems are not mounted, so their content is inaccessible. Go ahead and look in */usr* on a system in single-user mode; it's empty. FreeBSD hasn't lost the files, it just hasn't mounted the partition with those files on it yet. To do anything interesting in single-user mode, you must mount other filesystems.

Mounting Standard Filesystems

To manually mount a filesystem listed in */etc/fstab*, such as */var* or */usr*, give mount(8) the name of the filesystem you want to mount.

```
# mount /usr
```

This mounts the partition exactly as listed in */etc/fstab*, with all the options specified in that file. If you want to mount all the partitions listed in */etc/fstab*, use mount's -a flag.

```
# mount -a
```

Mounting at Nonstandard Locations

Perhaps you need to mount a filesystem at an unusual point. I do this most commonly when installing a new disk. Use the device name and the desired mount point. If my */usr* partition is */dev/ad0s1e*, and I want to mount it on */mnt*, I would run:

```
# mount /dev/ad0s1e /mnt
```

Unmounting a Partition

When you want to disconnect a filesystem from the system, use umount(8) to tell the system to unmount the partition. (Note that the command is umount, not *un*mount.)

```
# umount /usr
```

You cannot unmount filesystems that are in use by any program. If you cannot unmount a partition, you're probably accessing it somehow. Even a command prompt in the mounted directory prevents you from unmounting the underlying partition.

How Full Is a Partition?

To get an overview of how much space each partition has left, use df(1). This provides a list of partitions on your system, the amount of space used by each one, and where it's mounted. The annoying thing about df is that it defaults to providing information in 1KB blocks. This was fine when disks were much much smaller, but counting out blocks can make you go cross-eyed today. Fortunately, the -h and -H flags provide human-readable output. The small -h uses base 2 to create a 1,024-byte megabyte, while the large -H uses base 10 for a 1,000-byte megabyte. Typically, network administrators and disk manufacturers use base 10, while system administrators use base 2.[1] Either works so long as you know which you've chosen. I'm a network administrator, so you get to suffer through my prejudices in these examples, despite what my tech editor thinks.

```
# df -H
Filesystem    Size    Used    Avail Capacity  Mounted on
/dev/ad4s2a   520M    301M    177M    63%     /
devfs         1.0k    1.0k    0B     100%     /dev
/dev/ad4s1e   520M    2.4M    476M    0%      /tmp
/dev/ad4s2e   11G     4.1G    5.9G    41%     /usr
/dev/ad4s2d   1.0G    322M    632M    34%     /var
/dev/ad4s3d   49G     43G     2.0G    96%     /usr/home
```

---

[1] This discussion is even less productive than the "Emacs versus vi" argument. And I bet you thought no such argument could exist!

Here we see the partition name, the size of the partition, the amount of space used, the amount of space available, the percent of space used, and the mount point. For example, the home directory on this machine is 96 percent full, but it still has 2GB of disk free. The root partition is only 63 percent full, but it has only 177MB free.

FFS holds back 8 percent of the disk space for on-the-fly optimization. This is used for moving files and reducing fragmentation. You can overfill your disks and see negative disk space remaining. When this happens, disk performance drops dramatically. It is best to keep a little free space on your partitions, so that FFS can continually defragment itself. While you can adjust the filesystem to reduce the amount of reserved space, this negatively impacts performance and is basically unwise. See tunefs(8) if you really want to try it.

The obvious question is, "What is taking up all that space?" If your systems are like mine, disk usage somehow keeps growing for no apparent reason. You can identify individual large files with ls -l, but recursively doing this on every directory in the system is impractical.

$BLOCKSIZE

Many disk tools show sizes in blocks of 512 bytes, or one-half KB. If you set the environment variable $BLOCKSIZE to k, df(1) and many other programs display file sizes in blocks of 1KB, which is much more useful. Others like a setting of 1M, for sizes in megabytes.

du(1) displays disk usage in a single directory. Its initial output is intimidating and can scare off inexperienced users. Here, we use du(1) to find out what's taking up all the space in my home directory:

```
# cd $HOME
# du
1         ./bin/RCS
21459     ./bin/wp/shbin10
53202     ./bin/wp
53336     ./bin
5         ./.kde/share/applnk/staroffice_52
6         ./.kde/share/applnk
...
```

This goes on and on, displaying every subdirectory and giving its size in blocks. The total of each subdirectory is given—for example, the contents of *$HOME/bin* totals 53,336 blocks, or roughly 53MB. I could sit and let du(1) list every directory and subdirectory, but then I'd have to dig through much more information than I really want to. And blocks aren't that convenient a measurement, especially not when they're printed left-justified.

Let's clean this up. First, du(1) supports an -h flag much like df. Also, I don't need to see the recursive contents of each subdirectory. We can control the number of directories we display with du's -d flag. This flag takes one argument, the number of directories you want to explicitly list. For example, -d0 goes one directory deep and gives a simple subtotal of the files in a directory.

```
# du -h -d0 $HOME
37G    /home/mwlucas
```

I have 37 gigs of data in my home directory? Let's look a layer deeper and identify the biggest subdirectory.

```
# du -h -d1
 38K    ./bin
 56M    ./mibs
...
 34G    ./mp3
...
```

Apparently I must look elsewhere for storage space, as the data in my home directory is too important to delete.

If you're not too attached to the -h flag, you can use sort(1) to find the largest directory with a command like du -kxd 1 | sort -n.

The Fast File System

FreeBSD's filesystem, the Fast File System (FFS), is a direct descendant of the filesystem shipped with BSD 4.4. One of the original FFS authors still develops the FreeBSD filesystem and has added many nifty features in recent years. FFS is sometimes called UFS (for Unix File System), and many system utilities still call FFS partitions UFS. FreeBSD is not the only operating system to still use the 4.4 BSD filesystem or a descendant thereof. If a Unix vendor doesn't specifically tout its "improved and advanced" filesystem, it is almost certainly running a derivative of FFS.

FFS is designed to be fast and reliable, and to handle the most common situations as effectively as possible while still supporting unusual situations reliably. FreeBSD ships with FFS configured to be as widely useful as possible on relatively modern hardware, but you can choose to optimize a particular filesystem for trillions of small files or a half-dozen 30GB files if you must. You don't have to know much about FFS's internals, but you do need to understand blocks, fragments, and inodes, if nothing else.

Blocks are segments of disk that contain data. FreeBSD defaults to 16KB blocks. Not all files are even multiples of 16KB, so FFS uses *fragments* to store leftovers. The standard is one-eighth of the block size, or 2KB. For example, a 20KB file would fill one block and two fragments. *Inodes* are index nodes, special blocks that contain basic data such as a file's size, permissions, and the list of blocks that this file uses. Collectively, the data in an inode is known as *metadata*, or data about data. This arrangement isn't unique to FFS; other filesystems such as NTFS use data blocks and index nodes as well. The indexing system used by each filesystem is largely unique, however.

Each filesystem has a certain number of inodes, proportional to the filesystem size. A modern disk probably has hundreds of thousands of inodes on each partition, which is sufficient to support hundreds of thousands of files. If you have a truly large number of very tiny files, however, you might need to rebuild your filesystem to support additional inodes. Use df -i to see how many inodes remain free on your filesystem. If you must rebuild your filesystem to increase the number of inodes, see Chapter 18.

Vnodes

Inodes and blocks worked wonderfully in Unix's early days, when hard drives were permanently attached to machines. As time passed, however, swapping disks between different machines and even different operating systems became common. CDs, with their unique read-only filesystem, became popular, floppy disks slowly converged on the FAT32 filesystem as a standard, and other Unix-like systems developed their own variant filesystems. Since BSD needed to speak to all those different systems, another layer of abstraction was needed.

That abstraction was the virtual node, or vnode. Users never manipulate vnodes directly, but you'll see references to them throughout the system documentation. The *vnode* is a translator between the kernel and whatever specific filesystem type you've mounted. Every tool that reads and writes to disks actually does so through vnodes, which map the data to the appropriate filesystem for the underlying media. When you write a file to an FFS filesystem, the kernel addresses data to a vnode which, in turn, is mapped to an inode. When you write a file to a FAT32 filesystem, the kernel addresses data to a vnode mapped to a point in the FAT32 filesystem. You use inodes only when dealing with FFS filesystems, but you'll use vnodes when dealing with any filesystem.

FFS Mount Types

Unlike Windows filesystems, FreeBSD treats FFS partitions differently depending on how they're mounted. The manner in which a partition is mounted is called the *mount type*. If you're mounting a partition manually, you can specify mount options on the command line, but if you're using */etc/fstab* to mount it, you must specify any choice in the Options column.

Use -o *mounttype* to specify a mount type on the command line, or specify the option in */etc/fstab* in the Options column.

Read-Only Mounts

If you want to look at the contents of a disk but not write to it, mount the partition read-only. In most cases, this is the safest and the most useless way to mount a disk, because you cannot alter the data on the disk or write any new data.

Many system administrators mount the root partition, and perhaps even */usr*, as read-only to minimize potential system damage from a loss of power or software problems. Even if you lose the physical hard drive due to a power surge or other hardware failure, the data on the platters remains intact. That's the advantage of read-only mounts. The disadvantage is that system maintenance becomes much more difficult because you cannot write to read-only disks!

Read-only mounts are especially valuable when your computer is damaged. While FreeBSD won't let you perform a standard read-write mount on a damaged or dirty filesystem, it can perform a read-only mount most of the time. This gives you a chance to recover data from a dying system.

To mount a filesystem read-only, use one of the options rdonly or ro. Both work identically.

Synchronous Mounts

Synchronous (or *sync*) *mounts* are the old-fashioned way of mounting filesystems. When you write to a synchronously mounted disk, the kernel waits to see whether the write is actually completed before informing the program. If the write did not complete successfully, the program can choose to act accordingly.

Synchronous mounts provide the greatest data integrity in the case of a crash, but they are also slow. Admittedly, "slow" is relative today, when even a cheap disk outperforms what was the high end several years ago. Consider using synchronous mounting when you wish to be truly pedantic on data integrity, but in almost all cases it's an overkill.

To mount a partition synchronously, use the option sync.

Asynchronous Mounts

While *asynchronous mounts* are pretty much supplanted by soft updates, you'll still hear about them. For faster data access at higher risk, mount your partitions asynchronously. When a disk is asynchronously mounted, the kernel writes data to the disk and tells the writing program that the write succeeded without waiting for the disk to confirm that the data was actually written. Asynchronous mounting is fine on disposable machines, but don't use it with important data. The performance difference between asynchronous mounts and noasync with soft updates is very small.

To mount a partition asynchronously, use the option async.

Noasync Mounts

Finally, we have a method that combines sync and async mounts, called *noasync*. This is FreeBSD's default. When using noasync mounts, data that affects inodes is written to the disk synchronously, while actual data is handled asynchronously. Combined with soft updates (see later in this chapter), a noasync mount creates a very robust filesystem.

Noasync mounts are the default, and you don't need to specify anything.

FFS Mount Options

FreeBSD supports several mount options in addition to the mount types. These options change the behavior of mounted filesystems.

noatime

Every file in FFS includes an access-time stamp, called the *atime*, which records when the file was last accessed. If you have a large number of files and don't need this data, you can mount the disk noatime so that FFS does not update this timestamp. This is most useful for flash media or disks that suffer from heavy load, such as Usenet news spool drives.

noexec

The noexec mount option prevents any binaries from being executed on this partition. Mounting */home* noexec can help prevent users from running their own programs, but for it to be effective, be sure to also mount */tmp*, */var/tmp*, and anywhere else users can write their own files noexec as well. Also note that a noexec mount doesn't prevent a user from running a shell script, which is just a set of instructions for a program elsewhere in the system. Another common use for a noexec mount is when you have on your server binaries for a different operating system or a different hardware architecture and you don't want anyone to execute them.

nosuid

The nosuid option prevents setuid programs from running on your system. Setuid programs allow users to run programs as if they're another user. For example, programs such as login(1) must perform actions as root but must be run by regular users. Setuid programs obviously must be written carefully so that intruders cannot exploit them to get unauthorized access to your system. Many system administrators habitually disable all unneeded setuid programs. You can use nosuid to disable setuid programs on a partition, but script wrappers like suidperl get around this.

nosymfollow

The nosymfollow option disables symlinks, or aliases to files. *Symlinks* are mainly used to create aliases to files that reside on other partitions. To create an alias to another file on the same partition, use a regular link instead. See ln(1) for a discussion of links.

Aliases to directories are always symlinks; you cannot use a hard link for that.

Soft Updates and Journaling with FFS

Soft updates is a technology to organize and arrange disk writes so that filesystem metadata remains consistent at all times, giving nearly the performance of an async mount with the reliability of a sync mount. While that doesn't mean that all data will be safely written to disk—a power failure at the wrong moment can still lose data—soft updates prevent many problems. If the system has a failure, soft updates can run its filesystem checks in the background while the system runs. In my opinion, soft updates are suitable for partitions of less than 80GB or so.

As of FreeBSD 7.0, FFS also supports *journaling*. A journaling filesystem records all changes made to the filesystem on a separate part of the disk, so that if the system shuts down unexpectedly, data changes can be recovered from the journal automatically upon restart. This eliminates the need to run fsck(8). Each journaled filesystem uses about 1GB for the journal, which means that journaling is wasteful on small filesystems. However, FreeBSD's journaling differs from most journaled filesystems in that the journal is maintained in a disk layer beneath the filesystem rather than in the filesystem itself. This journaling is brand new in FreeBSD and is still considered somewhat experimental.

For example, as of this writing, I have a logging host. Most of the partitions are less than 10GB, but */var* is almost two terabytes. I journal */var*, but use soft updates on the other partitions. Between background fsck and journaling, system recovery after an unexpected power outage is fast and painless.

We'll talk more about journaling and gjournal in Chapter 18.

Write Caching

FFS works best with SCSI and SAS drives due to the robustness of the SCSI architecture. FFS also works as well as the ATA architecture allows, with one critical exception: Many modern IDE drives support *write caching*.

Write caching IDE drives have a small onboard chip. This chip records data that needs to be written to the drive. This can be tricky for soft updates and for journaling, because these technologies expect honest hard drives—when the hard drive reports the data is written to disk, the soft updates mechanism expects the data to actually be on that platter. But IDE write caching reports success as soon as the data is stored in the drive's cache, not when it has been written to disk. It might be a second or more until that data is actually safely stored.

While this doesn't pose a big risk if it happens occasionally, write caching occurs continuously on a server. Therefore, if you care about your data, disable write caching by adding the following to */boot/loader.conf*:

```
hw.ata.wc=0
```

Disabling write caching slows the IDE drive, but eliminates the risk. I use write caching on desktop and laptop systems, where data is not being continuously written to the disk, but on servers it's a bad idea to leave caching on. You can either tell your management that the ATA-based server is throttled and you need more hardware, or you can tell them that you're missing data because you overstressed the hardware. Personally, I prefer the former.

Snapshots

FFS with soft updates can take an image of a disk at a moment in time, or a *snapshot*. You'll find these snapshots in the *.snapshot* directory in the root of each partition.

While you don't perform system administration on snapshots, various tools take advantage of snapshots. For example, dump(8) backs up a snapshot of each filesystem rather than the live filesystem so that you have an internally consistent backup. Background fsck (explained later in this chapter) uses snapshots to do its work. You can mount a snapshot and get a picture of your filesystem at a particular instant. While this is interesting, most system administrators don't find it terribly useful. Still, you'll see references to snapshots throughout working with FreeBSD.

Dirty Disks

No, disks don't get muddy with use (although dust on a platter will quickly damage it, and adding water won't help). A dirty FFS partition is one that's in a kind of limbo; the operating system has asked for information to be written to the disk, but the data is not yet completely written out. Part of the data block might have been written, the inode might have been edited but the data not written out, or any combination of the two. If the power goes out while your disk is dirty, the system reboots with *unclean disks*.

FreeBSD refuses to mount unclean disks read-write; you can write them read-only, but that's not suitable for normal operation. You must clean your disk.

fsck(8)

FreeBSD includes a filesystem integrity checking tool, fsck(8). When a rebooting system finds a dirty disk, it automatically checks the filesystem and tries to clean everything. You have already lost any data not written to disk, but fsck(8) verifies that every file is attached to the proper inodes and in the correct directory. If successful, everything is right where you left it—except for that unwritten data, of course!

Failed Automatic fscks Runs

Occasionally this automated fsck-on-reboot fails to work. When you check the console, you'll be looking at a single-user mode prompt and a request to run fsck(8) manually. At this point, you have a simple choice: run fsck or not. If you enter fsck at the command prompt, fsck(8) verifies every block and inode on the disk. It finds any blocks that have become disassociated from their inodes and guesses how they fit together and how they should be attached. fsck(8) might not be able to identify which directory these files belong in, however.

fsck asks if you want to perform these reattachments. If you answer n, it deletes the damaged files. If you answer y, it adds the lost file to a *lost+found* directory in the root of the partition, with a number as a filename. For example, the *lost+found* directory on your */usr* partition is */usr/lost+found*. If there are only a few files, you can identify them manually; if you have many files and are looking for particular ones, tools such as file(1) and grep(1) can help you identify them by content.

Turning Off the fsck Prompt

If your server was in the middle of a very busy operation when it became dirty, you could end up with many disassociated files. Instead of spending an hour at the console typing y over and over again to tell fsck to reassemble these files, type fsck -y at the single-user prompt. This makes fsck(8) believe that you're answering yes to every question.

> **DANGER!**
>
> Running fsck -y is not guaranteed safe. At times, when running experimental file-systems on -current or when doing other daft things, I've had the entire contents of a partition migrate to /usr/lost+found and /var/lost+found thanks to fsck -y. Recovery becomes difficult at that point. Having said that, in a production system running FreeBSD-stable with a standard UFS filesystem, I've never had a problem.

You can set your system to automatically try fsck -y on boot. I don't recommend this, however, because if there's the faintest chance my file-system will wind up in digital nirvana I want to know about it. I want to type the offending command myself and feel the trepidation of watching fsck(8) churn my hard drives. Besides, it's always unpleasant to discover that your system is trashed without having the faintest clue of how it got that way. If you're braver than I, you can set fsck_y_enable="YES" in *rc.conf*.

Avoiding fsck -y

What options do you have if you don't want to use fsck -y? Well, fsdb(8) and clri(8) allow you to debug the filesystem and redirect files to their proper locations. You can restore files to their correct directories and names. This is difficult,[2] however, and is recommended only for Secret Ninja Filesystem Masters.

Background fsck

Background fsck gives FFS some of the benefits of a journaled filesystem without using all the disk required by journaling. When FreeBSD sees that a background fsck is in process after a reboot, it mounts the dirty disk read-write. fsck(8) runs in the background while the server is running, identifying loose bits of files and tidying them up behind the scenes.

A background fsck actually has two major stages. When FreeBSD finds dirty disks during the initial boot process, it runs a preliminary fsck(8) assessment of the disks. fsck(8) decides if the damage can be repaired while the

---

[2] In the first edition of this book, I said using fsdb(8) and clri(8) was like climbing Mount Everest in sandals and shorts. Since writing that, I've tried them more than once and discovered that I was wrong. You don't get the shorts.

system is running, or if a full single-user mode fsck run is required. Most frequently, fsck thinks it can proceed and lets the system boot. After the system reaches single-user mode the background fsck runs at a low priority, checking the partitions one by one. The results of the fsck process appear in */var/log/messages*.

You can expect performance of any applications requiring disk activity to be lousy during a background fsck. fsck(8) occupies a large portion of the disk's possible activity. While your system might be slow, it will at least be up.

You *must* check */var/log/messages* for errors after a background fsck. The preliminary fsck assessment can make an error, and perhaps a full single-user mode's fsck on a partition really is required. If you find such a message, schedule downtime within a few hours to correct the problem. While inconvenient, having the system down for a scheduled period is better than the unscheduled downtime caused by a power outage and the resulting single-user mode's fsck -y.

Forcing Read-Write Mounts on Dirty Disks

If you really want to force FreeBSD to mount a dirty disk read-write without using a background fsck, you can. You will not like the results. At all. But, as it's described in mount(8), some reader will think it's a good idea unless they know why. Use the -w (read-write) and -f (force) flags to mount(8).

Mounting a dirty partition read-write corrupts data. Note the absence of words like *might* and *could* from that sentence. Also note the absence of words like *recoverable*. Mounting a dirty filesystem may panic your computer. It might destroy all remaining data on the partition or even shred the underlying filesystem. Forcing a read-write mount of a dirty filesystem is bad juju. Don't do it.

FFS Syncer at Shutdown

When you shut down your FreeBSD system the kernel synchronizes all its data to the hard drive, marks the disks clean, and shuts down. This is done by a kernel process called the *syncer*. During a system shutdown, the syncer reports on its progress in synchronizing the hard drive.

You'll see odd things from the syncer during shutdown. The syncer doesn't actually go down the list of inodes and blocks that need updating on the hard drive; it walks the list of vnodes that need synchronizing. Thanks to soft updates, writing one vnode to disk can generate another dirty vnode that needs updating. You can see the number of buffers being written to disk rapidly drop from a high value to a low value, and perhaps bounce between zero and a low number once or twice as the system really synchronizes the hard drive.

THE REAL DETAILS ON FFS

If you really want to know more about FFS, you can download a large diagram of the kernel internals of FFS at *http://phk.freebsd.dk/misc/ufs.pdf*. You'll need a large engineering or architectural printer, or 18 sheets of regular paper and a lot of clear tape.

Background fsck, fsck -y, Foreground fsck, Oy Vey!

All these different fsck(8) problems and situations can occur, but when does FreeBSD use each command? FreeBSD uses the following conditions to decide when and how to fsck(8) on a filesystem:

- If the filesystem is clean, it is mounted without fsck(8).
- If a filesystem without soft updates is dirty at boot, FreeBSD runs fsck on it. If the filesystem damage is severe, FreeBSD stops the fsck and requests your intervention. You can either run `fsck -y` or manually check each reconnection.
- If a filesystem with soft updates is dirty at boot, FreeBSD performs a very basic fsck(8) check. If the damage is mild, FreeBSD uses a background fsck(8) in multi-user mode. If the damage is severe, FreeBSD interrupts the boot and requests your intervention with either `fsck -y` or approval or rejection of each filesystem problem.
- If a journaled filesystem is dirty at boot, FreeBSD recovers the data from the journal and continues the boot. A journaled filesystem rarely needs fsck(8).

Using Foreign Filesystems

For our purposes, any partition or disk that isn't FFS is a *foreign filesystem*. FreeBSD includes extensive support for foreign filesystems, with the caveat that only those functions supported by the filesystem work. Microsoft's FAT32 doesn't support filesystem permissions, for example, and Linux filesystems don't support BSD-style file flags.

Each foreign filesystem needs support in the FreeBSD kernel. To make your life a little easier, mount(8) automatically loads the proper kernel modules on demand.

To mount any foreign filesystem, you need the same information needed to mount an FFS filesystem: a device name and a mount point. You'll also need the type of filesystem, although you might figure that out by trial and error. For example, FreeBSD provides a */cdrom* mount point for CDs. The first IDE CD on your system is */dev/acd0*. CDs use the ISO 9660 filesystem, and FreeBSD mounts them with `mount -t cd9660`(8). Here we mount our CD on */cdrom*:

```
# mount -t cd9660 /dev/acd0 /cdrom
```

You can now go to the */cdrom* directory and view the contents. Simple enough, eh?

If you try to mount a disk using the wrong mount command for its filesystem, you'll get an error. For example, any floppy disk in my house has either a FAT32 or an FFS filesystem on it; */dev/fd0* is the proper device node for floppy disks, and */media* is their standard mount point.

```
# mount /dev/fd0 /media
mount: /dev/fd0 on /media: incorrect super block
```

This floppy has a FAT32 filesystem. Had I tried `mount -t msdosfs` first, it would have worked.

You can unmount any filesystem with umount(8):

```
# umount /cdrom
```

umount(8) doesn't care about the filesystem type. It just disconnects the disk partition.

Supported Foreign Filesystems

Here are some of the most commonly used foreign filesystems, along with a brief description of each and the appropriate mount command.

FAT (MS-DOS)

FreeBSD includes extensive support for FAT, the DOS/Windows 9x File Allocation Table filesystem, commonly used on removable media and some dual-boot systems. This support covers the FAT12, FAT16, and FAT32 varieties. You *can* format a floppy disk with an FFS filesystem, however, so do not blindly assume that all floppy disks are FAT-formatted. As the most common use for a floppy these days is transferring files between machines, however, most are FAT32. The mount type is `msdosfs` (mount -t msdosfs).

If you handle a lot of FAT32 disks, investigate */usr/ports/tools/mtools*, a collection of programs for working with FAT filesystems that offer greater flexibility than the default FreeBSD tools.

ISO 9660

ISO 9660 is the standard CD filesystem. FreeBSD supports reading CDs and writing them as well if you have a CD burner. Just about every CD you encounter is formatted with ISO 9660. The mount command is `mount -t cd9660`.

cdrtools, in */usr/ports/sysutils/cdrtools*, contains many helpful tools for working with CD images, including tools that build an ISO image from files on disk.

UDF

UDF, or Universal Data Format, is a replacement for ISO 9660. You'll find UDF on some DVDs and on flash/USB devices larger than the 32GB supported under FAT32. As the capacity of removable media increases, you'll see more and more UDF filesystems. The mount command is `mount -t udf`.

NTFS

The Windows NT/2000/XP filesystem, NTFS, is tightly integrated with Microsoft's proprietary kernel. To write to an NTFS partition, you must have extensive knowledge of how the filesystem works. Since Microsoft does not make that information available, FreeBSD can safely mount NTFS partitions read-only but has limited read-write functionality. The mount command is `mount -t ntfs`.

I find NTFS mounts most useful when migrating from Windows systems to FreeBSD systems; just remove the hard drive from the old Windows machine, mount it in the FreeBSD machine, and copy your data from one to the other. NTFS support is also useful for dual-boot laptops.

As the NTFS filesystem has a closed specification and contains data encoded in a proprietary manner, FreeBSD's NTFS read support is not guaranteed to work.

ext2fs and ext3fs

The standard Linux filesystems, ext2fs and ext3fs, support many of the same features as the FreeBSD filesystem and can be safely written to and read from without any problems. Like the NTFS mounts, mounting Linux filesystems is most useful for disaster recovery or dual-boot systems. Despite the name, `mount -t ext2fs` supports mounting both ext2fs and ext3fs.

Linux filesystem users might find the tools in */usr/ports/sysutils/e2fsprogs* useful. They let you fsck(8) and assess Linux filesystems, among other things.

ReiserFS

ReiserFS is a filesystem with a small percentage of devotees amidst Linux users. FreeBSD supports read-only ReiserFS partitions. Support for mounting ReiserFS is implemented directly in mount(8); just run `mount -t reiserfs` *partition mountpoint*.

XFS

FreeBSD supports reading from SGI's XFS partitions, but writing to XFS is available on an experimental basis as of this writing. XFS is the oldest journaling filesystem in existence and has a well-debugged codebase. XFS is licensed under the GPL, however, which makes it a poor candidate for inclusion in the FreeBSD base system. If you're interested in journaling, please check out gjournal in Chapter 18.

Programs for formatting, mounting, and managing XFS partitions can be found in */usr/ports/sysutils/xfsprogs*.

ZFS

As of 7.0, FreeBSD includes experimental support for ZFS, ported from OpenSolaris. While the installer doesn't support ZFS, if you need the advanced ZFS features you can use them. ZFS's license is not suitable for making it the primary FreeBSD filesystem, but its high-end features can be very useful for certain applications on multiterabyte filesystems and on 64-bit systems. ZFS on 32-bit systems suffers from memory problems, but ZFS has a good reputation on 64-bit systems.

Permissions and Foreign Filesystems

The method used to mount a filesystem, and the person who mounts it, control the permissions of the mounted filesystem. For example, ext3fs and XFS store permissions in the filesystem and map them to UIDs. Since their permissions behave much like FFS, and all the permissions information needed is available within the filesystem and the kernel, FreeBSD respects the permissions on these filesystem.

NTFS has its own permission system. Since that system bears only a coincidental resemblance to that used by Unix-like systems, permissions are discarded when a NTFS partition is mounted on a FreeBSD system, and it's treated much like a CD or a floppy disk.

By default, only root can mount filesystems, and root owns all non-Unix filesystems. If that's not your preference, you can use the -u and -g flags to set the user ID and group ID of the owner when you're mounting a FAT32, NTFS, or ISO 9660 filesystem. For example, if you're mounting a FAT32 USB device for the user cstrzelc and want her to be able to edit the contents, use this command:

```
# mount -t msdosfs -u cstrzelc -g cstrzelc /dev/da0 /mnt
```

The user cstrzelc now owns the files on the device.

You might get sick of mounting media for your users, especially in a facility with dozens of machines. To let a user mount a filesystem, set the sysctl vfs.usermount to 1. The user can then mount any filesystem she wants on any mount point she owns. While cstrzelc couldn't mount the removable device on /mnt, she could mount it on /home/cstrzelc/mnt.

Removable Media Filesystems

Removable media has boomed in the last few years. While once we only had to worry about floppy disks, we now have CDs and USB devices. You must be able to manage any removable media that might wander in through the door of your data center. We'll discuss dealing with filesystems on floppy disks, USB devices, and CDs.

I recommend not plugging removable media willy-nilly into your production servers, for security reasons if nothing else. Who knows what's actually on that vendor's USB device? I prefer to mount those devices on my workstation, examine the contents, and then copy the desired data over to the FreeBSD machine. Removable media is just too easy for certain applications, however, and of course the rules change when it's my personal USB device.

Formatting FAT32 Media

Both floppy disks and USB media use the FAT32 filesystem. USB media uses the FAT32 filesystem, but usually comes preformatted. As USB media has a limited number of reads and writes, do not reformat it capriciously. That leaves floppies, which frequently need reformatting if used heavily. What most Windows users think of as "formatting a floppy" is actually a multistage process that includes formatting the disk, giving it a disk label, and creating a filesystem. You must perform all of these operations to use a floppy in FreeBSD.

NONSTANDARD FLOPPIES

We'll assume that you have a standard 1.44MB floppy disk, which has been the standard on x86 hardware for almost two decades. If you have a disk drive of 800KB or another uncommon size, you'll have to modify this process somewhat, but the general steps are the same.

Low-Level Formatting

First, perform a low-level format with fdformat(1). This program only requires two arguments: the floppy's size and the device name.

```
# fdformat -f 1440 /dev/fd0
Format 1440K floppy '/dev/fd0.1440'? (y/n): y
```

When you type y, fdformat(1) runs a low-level format to prepare the disk to receive a filesystem. Low-level formatting is the slowest part of making a floppy usable. Windows performs this sort of formatting when you request a complete format.

Creating an FFS Filesystem

After the low-level format, if you want to use FFS on your floppy, label the disk with disklabel(8). This writes basic identification information to the floppy, sets partition information, and can even mark a disk as bootable. Marking a disk as bootable doesn't actually put any programs on the disk; it simply puts a marker on the disk so the hardware BIOS identifies this disk as bootable. If you need an actual FreeBSD boot floppy, just copy the provided disk image from the installation media. Here, we'll install a plain disklabel without any special characteristics:

```
# disklabel -r -w /dev/fd0 fd1440
```

The -r option in this example tells disklabel to access the raw disk, because there is no filesystem on it yet. The -w option says to write to the disk. We're writing to */dev/fd0* and installing a standard 1.44MB floppy disk label. You can find a full list of floppy disk labels in */etc/disktab*, as well as labels for many other types of drives, as discussed in Chapter 10.

Finally, newfs(8) the disk to create a filesystem.

```
# newfs /dev/fd0
```

You'll see a few lines of newfs output and then get a command prompt back.

Note that using FFS on a floppy wastes space and does not provide the protection many people expect it would. While permission information is stored on the floppy, the system owner can override those privileges easily. Also, remember that FFS reserves 8 percent of disk space for its own overhead and bookkeeping. Do you really need a 1.32MB floppy? FFS is nifty, but FAT32 is a better choice for floppy disks.

Creating a FAT32 Filesystem

To swap data between a wide range of hardware, use the FAT32 filesystem on your floppy. While you still need to low-level format the floppy as discussed earlier, you don't need to disklabel it. Just use newfs_msdos(8):

```
# newfs_msdos /dev/fd0
```

You'll get a couple lines of output, and your floppy is done.

Using Removable Media

Handling removable media is just like working with fixed media such as hard drives. You must know the filesystem on the device, the device node where the device appears, and assign a mount point.

CDs use the ISO 9660 filesystem, while DVDs use either a UDF or a combination of ISO 9660 and UDF. USB devices and floppy disks are usually FAT32. Very new USB devices might be UDF. I expect UDF to become more common, especially as flash devices become larger.

The device node varies with the device type. IDE CDs are */dev/acd0*, while SCSI CDs appear at */dev/cd0*. Floppy disks are at */dev/fd0*. USB devices appear as the next available unit of */dev/da*. When you insert a USB device, a message giving the device node and type appears on the console and in */var/log/messages*.

Finally, you need a mount point. By default, FreeBSD includes a */cdrom* mount point for CD and DVD media. You'll also find a */media* mount point for general *removable media* mounts. You can create additional mount points as you like—they're just directories. For miscellaneous short-term mounts, FreeBSD offers */mnt*.

So, to mount your FAT32 USB device */dev/da0* on */media*, run:

```
# mount -t msdosfs /dev/da0 /media
```

Occasionally you'll find a USB device that has an actual slice table on it, and those devices will insist you mount */dev/da0s1* rather than */dev/da0*. This depends on how the device is formatted, not on anything in FreeBSD.

One annoyance with CD drives is that SCSI CD and ATA CD drives offer different interfaces to software. Much software is written to only use the SCSI interface, as SCSI is generally considered more reliable. If you encounter such a piece of software, check out atapicam(4) kernel module which provides a SCSI emulation layer to your ATA CD devices.

Ejecting Removable Media

To disconnect removable media from your FreeBSD system, you must unmount the filesystem. Your CD tray won't open until you unmount the CD, and the floppy drive won't eject your disk. You can probably forcibly remove a USB dongle, but doing so while the filesystem is mounted panics the server and might damage data on the device. Use umount(8) just as you would for any other filesystem:

```
# umount /cdrom
```

Removable Media and /etc/fstab

You can update */etc/fstab* with entries for removable media to make system maintenance a little easier. If a removable filesystem has an entry in */etc/fstab*, you can drop both the filesystem and the device name when mounting it. This means that you don't have to remember the exact device name or filesystem to mount the device. You probably already have an */etc/fstab*'s entry for your CD device.

```
/dev/acd0               /cdrom          cd9660   ro,noauto       0       0
```

While I'm sure you've already memorized the meaning of every column in */etc/fstab*, we'll remind you that entry means "mount */dev/acd0* on */cdrom*, using the ISO 9660 filesystem, read-only, and do not mount it automatically at boot." Using this as a template, make similar entries for USB devices and floppy disks.

```
/dev/fd0        /mnt          msdosfs  rw,noauto     0       0
❶/dev/da0       /medi         msdosfs  rw,❷noauto    0       0
```

FreeBSD doesn't provide these by default, but I find having them to be much easier on systems where I use removable media regularly. Confirm that your next available da device is */dev/da0* ❶, as trying to mount a hard drive that's already mounted won't work.

When listing removable media in */etc/fstab*, be sure to include the noauto ❷ flag. Otherwise, whenever you don't have the removable media in place, your boot will stop in single-user mode because a filesystem is missing.

Other FreeBSD Filesystems

In addition to FFS and non-FreeBSD filesystems, FreeBSD supports several special-purpose filesystems. Some of these are interesting but not generally useful, such as mount_umapfs(8), while others are very useful or even required in certain circumstances. We'll talk about memory filesystems, a popular optimization for certain environments; building filesystems on files; as well as the procfs and fdescfs filesystems occasionally required by software packages.

Memory Filesystems

In addition to using disks for partitions, FreeBSD lets you create partitions from files, from pure RAM, and from a combination of the two. One of the most popular uses of this is for *memory filesystems*, or *memory disks*. Reading and writing files to and from memory is much faster than accessing files on disk, which makes a memory-backed filesystem a huge optimization for certain applications. As with everything else in memory, however, you lose the contents of your memory disk at system shutdown.

Memory Disk /tmp

The most common place a memory filesystem is used is for */tmp*. This is so common that FreeBSD includes specific *rc.conf* support for it. Look for the following *rc.conf* variables:

```
❶ tmpmfs="YES"
❷ tmpsize="20m"
❸ tmpmfs_flags="-S"
```

By setting `tmpmfs` ❶ to YES, you're telling FreeBSD to automatically create a memory-based */tmp* filesystem at boot. Specify the size of your new */tmp* with the `tmpsize` ❷ variable. We'll discuss the flags ❸ a little later in this section.

If this is all you want to use a memory filesystem for, you're done. To create and use special memory devices with mdmfs(8), read on.

Memory Disk Types

Memory disks come in three types: malloc-backed, swap-backed, and vnode-backed.

Malloc-backed disks are pure memory. Even if your system runs short on memory, FreeBSD won't swap out the malloc-backed disk. Using a large malloc-backed disk is a great way to make your system run out of free memory and panic. This is most useful for embedded devices with no swap, as we'll see in Chapter 20.

Swap-backed disks are mostly memory, but they also access the system swap partition. If the system runs out of memory, it moves the least recently used parts of memory to swap as discussed in Chapter 19. Swap-backed disks are the safest way to use a memory filesystem.

Vnode-backed disks are files on disk. While you can use a file as backing for your memory disk, this is really only useful for filesystem developers who want to perform tests or for mounting a disk image.

Your application dictates the type of memory disk you need. If your system has no swap space and a read-only filesystem, a malloc-backed disk is your only choice. If you're running a workstation or a server and want a piece of fast filesystem for scratch space, you want a swap-backed disk. You only need a vnode-backed memory disk to mount a disk image.

Once you know what you want to do, use mdmfs(8) to perform the action.

Creating and Mounting Memory Disks

The mdmfs(8) utility is a handy front end for several programs such as mdconfig(8) and newfs(8). It handles the drudgery of configuring devices and creating filesystems on those devices, and makes creating memory disks as easy as possible. You only need to know the size of the disk you want to use, the type of the memory disk, and the mount point.

Swap-backed memory disks are the default. Just tell mdmfs(8) the size of the disk and the mount point. Here, we create an 8MB swap-backed memory disk on */home/mwlucas/test*:

```
# mdmfs -s 8m md /home/mwlucas/test
```

The -s flag gives the size of the disk. If you run mount(8) without any arguments, you'll see that you now have the memory disk device */dev/md0* mounted on that directory.

To create and mount a malloc-backed disk, add the -M flag.

To mount a vnode-backed memory disk, use the -F flag and the path to the image file.

```
# mdmfs -F diskimage.file md /mnt
```

The md entry we've been using all along here means, "I don't care what device name I get, just give me the next free one." You can also specify a particular device name if you like. Here, I used */dev/md9* as the memory disk device:

```
# mdmfs -F diskimage.file md9 /mnt
```

Memory Disk Headaches

Memory disks sound too good to be true for high-performance environments. They do have constraints that you must understand before you scurry around and implement them everywhere.

The big issue is that system shutdown erases memory disks. While this might not seem like a problem, I've been surprised more than once by losing a file on a filesystem I had forgotten was a memory disk.

Also, malloc-backed memory disks *never* release memory. When you write a file to a memory disk and then erase the file, the file still takes up memory. With a swap-backed memory disk FreeBSD eventually writes that file to swap as memory pressure rises. A memory disk on a long-running system will eventually exhaust your system's RAM.

The one way you can free this used memory is to unmount the memory disk, destroy the disk device, and re-create the memory disk. I find that performing this task on a monthly basis is more than sufficient, even on a busy server.

A couple months before release, FreeBSD 7.0 added a tmpfs(5) memory filesystem that is supposed to release memory back to the system. It's brand new to FreeBSD, however, and considered an experimental feature. If you're reading this a few releases into the future I'd recommend you check out tmpfs(5), but if you're installing 7.0 or 7.1, I'd let someone else discover the bugs for you.

Memory Disk Shutdown

To remove a memory disk you must unmount the partition and destroy the disk device. Destroying the disk device frees the memory used by the device, which is useful when your system is heavily loaded. To find the disk device, run mount(8) and find your memory disk partition. Somewhere in the output, you'll find a line like this:

```
/dev/md41 on /mnt (ufs, local, soft-updates)
```

Here, we see memory disk */dev/md41* mounted on */mnt*. Let's unmount it and destroy it.

```
# ❶umount /mnt
# mdconfig ❷-d ❸-u 41
```

Unmounting with umount ❶ is done exactly as with other filesystems. The mdconfig(8) call is a new one, however. Use mdconfig(8) to directly manage memory devices. The -d ❷ flag means *destroy*, and the -u ❸ gives a device number. The above destroys the device */dev/md41*, or the md device number 41. The memory used by this device is now freed for other uses.

Memory Disks and /etc/fstab

If you list memory disks in */etc/fstab*, FreeBSD automatically creates them at boot time. These entries look more complicated than the other entries, but aren't too bad if you understand the mdmfs(8) commands we've been using so far. To refresh your memory, here's the top of */etc/fstab* and a single standard filesystem:

# Device	Mountpoint	FStype	Options	Dump	Pass#
/dev/ad4s2a	/	ufs	rw	1	1

We're allowed to use the word *md* as a device name to indicate a memory disk. We can choose the mountpoint just as we would for any other device, and the filesystem type is mfs. Under Options, list *rw* (for read-write) and the command-line options used to create this device. To create our 8MB filesystem mounted at */home/mwlucas/test*, use the following */etc/fstab* entry:

md	/home/mwlucas/test	mfs	rw,-s 8m	0	0

Looks easy, doesn't it? The only problem is that the long line messes up your nice and even */etc/fstab*'s appearance. Well, they're not the only things that make this file ugly, as we'll soon see.

Mounting Disk Images

Memory disks can also be used to mount and access disk images. This is most useful for viewing the contents of CD images without burning them to disk. Just attach a memory disk to a file with the mdconfig(8) command's -a flag. Here, I attach a FreeBSD ISO to a memory device:

```
# mdconfig ❶-a -t ❷vnode -f ❸/home/mwlucas/7.0-CURRENT-snap.iso
❹md0
```

We tell mdconfig(8) to attach ❶ a vnode-backed ❷ memory device to the file specified ❸. mdconfig(8) responds by telling us the device ❹ it's attached to. Now we just mount the device with the proper mount command for the filesystem:

```
# mount -t cd9660 /dev/md0 /mnt
```

One common mistake people make at this point is mounting the image without specifying the filesystem type. You might get an error, or you might get a successful mount that contains no data—by default, mount(8) assumes that the filesystem is FFS!

When you're done accessing the data, be sure to unmount the image and destroy the memory disk device just as you would for any other memory device. While vnode-backed memory disks do not consume system memory, leaving unused memory devices around will confuse you months later when you wonder why they appear in /dev. If you're not sure what memory devices a system has, use mdconfig -l to view all configured md(5) devices.

```
# mdconfig -l
md0 md1
```

I have two memory devices? Add the -u flag and the device number to see what type of memory device it is. Let's see what memory device 1 (/dev/md1) is:

```
# mdconfig -l -u 1
md1     vnode     456M  /slice1/usr/home/mwlucas/iso/omsa-51-live.iso
```

I have an ISO image mounted on this system? Wow. I should probably reboot some month. Nah, thats too much work, I'll just unmount the filesystem.

Filesystems in Files

One trick used for jails (see Chapter 9) and homebrew embedded systems (see Chapter 20) is building complete filesystem images on a local filesystem. In the previous section, we saw how we could use memory disks to mount and access CD disk images. You can use the same techniques to create, update, and access FFS disk images. The downside of this is that each image takes up an amount of disk space equal to the size of the disk image. If you create a 500MB disk image, it takes up a full 500MB of space.

To use a filesystem in a file, you must create a file of the proper size, attach the file to a memory device, place a filesystem on the device, and mount the device.

Creating an Empty Filesystem File

The filesystem file doesn't initially contain any data; rather, it's just a file of the correct size for the desired filesystem. You could sit down and type a whole bunch of zeroes to create the file, but FreeBSD provides a unlimited source of nothing to save you the trouble. The */dev/zero* device is chock full of emptiness you can use to fill the file.

Use the same dd(1) command you used to copy the installation floppy images to your filesystem file. Here we copy data from */dev/zero* and to the file *filesystem.file*:

```
# dd ❶if=/dev/zero ❷of=filesystem.file ❸bs=1m ❹count=1k
1048576+0 records in
1048576+0 records out
1073741824 bytes transferred in ❺24.013405 secs (❻44714268 bytes/sec)
```

We take our data from the input file */dev/zero* ❶ and dump it to the output file *filesystem.file* ❷. Each transfer occurs in blocks of 1K ❹, and we do this one million times ❸. This takes a few seconds ❺ to complete, but as */dev/zero* doesn't have to generate the next character, the file fills quickly ❻. If you look in your current directory, you now have a 1GB file called *filesystem.file*.

One common source of confusion with dd(1) is the block size and count. Calculating the final size of a file with dd(1) is like moving a pile of sand; you break the job into loads and move a number of those loads. You can use several loads with a wheelbarrow, many loads with a bucket, or lots and lots of loads with a spoon. The size of each load is the block size, and the number of trips is the count. Perhaps you're using your bare hands, which would correspond to a small block size and a high count. Maybe you have a wheelbarrow, for a medium block size and a moderate count. Perhaps you have a steam shovel and can do the whole job in one scoop. The larger the block size, the more load you put on the system with each block. dd(1) recognizes a variety of abbreviations for increasing block size and count, as shown in Table 8-2.

Suppose you want a 1GB file. Remember that 1k is actually one kilobyte. One megabyte is a thousand kilobytes, and one gigabyte is one thousand megabytes. If you use a block size of 1 byte, and a count of one gig, you're asking your system to make 1,073,741,824 trips to the sand pile. Each trip is very easy, but there's an awful lot of them! On the other hand, if you select a block size of one gig and a count of 1, you're asking the system to pick up the whole pile at once. It will not be pleased. Neither will you. Generally speaking, a block size of 1m and a lower count produces reasonably quick results without overburdening your system. When you use a 1m block, the count equals the number of megabytes in the file. A count of 1k creates a 1GB filesystem, a count of 2k creates a 2GB filesystem, a count of 32 creates a 32MB filesystem, and so on.

Table 8-2: dd Abbreviations

Letter	Meaning	Multiplier
b	Disk blocks	512
k	Kilo	1024
m	Mega	1048576
g	Giga	1073741824
w	Integer	However many bytes per integer on your platform

Creating the Filesystem on the File

To get a filesystem on the file, you must first associate the file with a device with a vnode-backed memory disks. We did exactly this in the last section:

```
# mdconfig -a -t vnode -f filesystem.file
md0
```

Now, let's make a filesystem on this device. This is much like creating an FFS filesystem on a floppy disk with the newfs(8) command. We specify the -U flag to enable soft updates on this filesystem, as soft updates are useful on file-backed filesystems.

```
# newfs -U /dev/md0
/dev/md0: 1024.0MB (2097152 sectors) block size 16384, fragment size 2048
        using 6 cylinder groups of 183.77MB, 11761 blks, 23552 inodes.
        with soft updates
super-block backups (for fsck -b #) at:
 160, 376512, 752864, 1129216, 1505568, 1881920
```

newfs(8) prints out basic information about the disk such as its size, block and fragment sizes, and the inode count.

Now that you have a filesystem, mount it:

```
# mount /dev/md0 /mnt
```

Congratulations! You now have a 1GB file-backed filesystem. Copy files to it, dump it to tape, or use it in any way you would use any other filesystem. But in addition to that, you can move it just like any other file. We'll make use of this when we talk about jails in the next chapter, and it's a vital technique for building your own embedded systems.

File-Backed Filesystems and /etc/fstab

You can mount a file-backed filesystem automatically at boot with the proper entry in */etc/fstab*, much like you can automatically mount any other memory disk. You simply have to specify the name of the file with -F, and use -P to tell the system to not create a new filesystem on this file but just to use the one already there. Here we mount the file-backed filesystem we created on */mnt* automatically at boot time. (I told you we'd see */etc/fstab* entries uglier than the one we created for generic memory disks, didn't I?)

```
md     /mnt     mfs     rw,-P,-F/home/mwlucas/filesystem.file     0     0
```

Miscellaneous Filesystems

FreeBSD supports several lesser-known filesystems. Most of them are useful only in bizarre circumstances, but bizarre circumstances arise daily in system administration.

devfs(5) is the device filesystem used for */dev*. You cannot store normal files on a devfs filesystem; it only supports device nodes. The kernel and the device filesystem daemon devd(8) directly manage the contents of a device filesystem.

procfs(5) is the process filesystem; it contains lots of information about processes. It's considered a security risk and is officially deprecated on modern FreeBSD releases. You can learn a lot about processes from a mounted process filesystem, however. A few older applications still require a process filesystem mounted on */proc*; if a server application requires procfs, try to find a similar application that does the job without requiring it.

If you're using Linux mode (see Chapter 12), you might need the Linux process filesystem linprocfs(5). Much Linux software requires a process filesystem, and FreeBSD suggests installing linprocfs at */compat/linux/proc* when you install Linux mode. I'd recommend only installing linprocfs if a piece of software complains it's not there.

fdescfs(5), the file descriptor filesystem, offers a filesystem view of file descriptors for each process. Some software is written to require fdescfs(5). It's less of a security risk than procfs, but still undesirable.

Wiring Down Devices

SCSI disks don't always power up in the same order, but FreeBSD numbers SCSI drives in the order that they appear on the SCSI bus. As such, if you change the devices on your SCSI bus, you change the order in which they're probed. What was disk 0 when you installed FreeBSD could become disk 1 after you add a new disk drive. This change would cause partitions to be mounted on the wrong mount points, possibly resulting in data damage. You can have similar problems with SCSI buses—if you add another SCSI interface, your buses can be renumbered! What was */dev/da0* when you installed FreeBSD could become */dev/da1* or even */dev/da17* after you add a new tape drive. This causes FreeBSD to mount partitions on the wrong mount points.

To prevent this problem, you can hard-code disk numbering into the kernel, a process called *wiring down* the SCSI devices. To wire down the device you need the SCSI ID, SCSI bus number, and LUN (if used) of each device on your SCSI chain, available in */var/run/dmesg.boot*. For example, on a test system I have the following dmesg entries for my SCSI adapter:

```
ahc0: <Adaptec 2940B Ultra2 SCSI adapter> port 0xe000-0xe0ff mem 0xe8042000-
0xe8042fff irq 11 at device 20.0 on pci0
aic7890/91: Ultra2 Wide Channel A, SCSI Id=7, 32/253 SCBs
```

The first line shows that the main SCSI card is an Adaptec 2940B Ultra2 adapter. The second line gives us more information about the chipset on this card. This is really only one physical card. The host adapter is using SCSI ID 7, and no LUN.

A little later in *dmesg.boot* I have entries for all SCSI disks. While these entries include things such as disk capacity, model, speed, and features, the first line for each disk looks much like these:

```
❶da0 at ❷ahc0 ❸bus 0 ❹target 8 ❺lun 0
da1 at ahc0 bus 0 ❻target 9 lun 0
da2 at ahc0 bus 0 target 10 lun 0
...
```

This tells us that the disk da0 ❶ is on SCSI card ahc0 ❷, on SCSI bus 0 ❸, at SCSI ID 8 ❹, at LUN 0 ❺. Disk da1 is on the same card and bus, at SCSI ID 9 ❻.

To wire down a drive, tell the kernel exactly what SCSI bus number to attach to which SCSI card, and then the SCSI ID and LUN of each disk. Do this with kernel hints in */boot/device.hints*:

```
hint.❶scbus.❷0.at="❸ahc0"
hint.❹da.0.at="❺scbus0"
hint.da.0.target="❻8"
hint.da.1.at="scbus0"
hint.da.1.target="❼9"
```

Here, we've told FreeBSD to attach SCSI bus ❶ number 0 ❷ to card ahc0 ❸. Disk da0 ❹ is attached to SCSI bus 0 ❺ at SCSI ID 8 ❻, and disk da1 is attached to the same bus at SCSI ID 9 ❼. On your next reboot the drives will be numbered as you configured. If you add another SCSI card, or more SCSI hard drives, FreeBSD configures the new drives and buses with unit numbers other than those you've reserved for these devices. You can also use lun hints if you have targets with multiple LUNs.

Adding New Hard Disks

Before you can use a new hard drive, you must slice it, create filesystems, mount those filesystems, and move data to them. While FreeBSD has command-line tools that can handle all this for you, the simplest and fastest way is with sysinstall(8). We'll assume that you are adding disks to an existing system, and that your eventual goal is to move a part of your data to this disk.

> ## BACK UP, BACK UP, BACK UP!
>
> Before doing anything with disks, be sure that you have a complete backup. A single dumb fat-finger mistake in this process can destroy your system! While you rarely plan to reformat your root filesystem, if it happens you want to recover really, really quickly.

Creating Slices

Your first task in preparing your new hard disk is to create a slice and partition it. Follow these steps:

1. Become root and start sysinstall(8). Choose **Configure**, and then **Disk**.

2. This menu should look somewhat familiar; you used it when you installed FreeBSD. (You can see screenshots in Figure 2-4 in Chapter 2.) You'll see your existing FreeBSD disks and your new disk. Choose the new disk.

3. If this disk is recycled from another server, you might find that it has a filesystem on it. It's usually simplest to remove the existing partitions and start over. Use the arrow keys to move to any existing partitions, and press **D** to delete them.

4. Either create a slice by pressing **C**, or just use the whole disk by pressing **A**. In a server, you almost certainly want to use the entire disk. When you've chosen your slices, make the changes effective immediately by pressing **W**. You'll see a warning like this:

```
WARNING: This should only be used when modifying an EXISTING installation.
If you are installing FreeBSD for the first time then you should simply
type Q when you're finished here and your changes will be committed in one
batch automatically at the end of these questions. If you're adding a
disk, you should NOT write from this screen, you should do it from the
label editor.
```

---

5. Are you absolutely sure you want to do this now?

6. Yes, you're absolutely sure. Tab over to **Yes** and hit ENTER.

7. You'll then be asked if you want to install a boot manager on this disk. Additional disks don't need boot managers, so arrow down to **Standard** and press the spacebar. The sysinstall program tells you that it has written out the fdisk information successfully. You now have a FreeBSD slice on the disk. Hit **Q** to leave the fdisk part of sysinstall.

Creating Partitions

To create partitions on your disk, follow these steps:

1. Choose the **Label** option of sysinstall(8), on the same submenu as FDISK. Select your new disk to reach the disklabel editor. Here you can create a new partition with the **C** command, specifying its size in either megabytes, gigabytes, disk blocks, or disk cylinders. You can also decide if each new partition will be a filesystem or swap space. When you're asked for a mount point, use */mnt* for the moment. Sysinstall temporarily mounts the new partition at that location.

2. When the disk is partitioned as you need, press **W** to commit the changes. You'll get the same warning you saw in the fdisk menu, and then messages from newfs(8).

   Once newfs(8) finishes, exit sysinstall.

Configuring /etc/fstab

Now tell */etc/fstab* about your new disks. The configuration differs depending on whether the new partition is a filesystem or swap space. Every swap space entry in */etc/fstab* looks like this:

devicename	none	swap	sw	0	0

If your new swap partition is */dev/da10s1b*, you would add this line to */etc/fstab*:

/dev/da10s1b	none	swap	sw	0	0

Upon your next reboot, FreeBSD will recognize this swap space. You can also use swapon -a *devicename* to activate new swap without rebooting.

If you created a data partition, add a new entry as described earlier in this chapter, much like this:

/dev/da10s1d	/usr/obj	ufs	rw	2	2

Now you can just unmount the new partition from its temporary location, run mount /usr/obj, and your new disk is ready for files.

Installing Existing Files onto New Disks

Chances are that you intend your new disk to replace or subdivide an existing partition. You'll need to mount your new partition on a temporary mount point, move files to the new disk, then remount the partition at the desired location.

In our example above, we've mounted our new partition on */mnt*. Now you just need to move the files from their current location to the new disk without changing their permissions. This is fairly simple with tar(1). You can simply tar up your existing data to a tape or a file and untar it in the new location, but that's kind of clumsy. You can concatenate tar commands to avoid that middle step, however.

```
# tar cfC - /old/directory . | tar xpfC - /tempmount
```

If you don't speak Unix at parties, this looks fairly stunning. Let's dismantle it. First, we go to the old directory and tar up everything. Then pipe the output to a second command, which extracts the backup in the new directory. When this command finishes, your files are installed on their new disk. For example, to move */usr/src* onto a new partition temporarily mounted at */mnt*, you would do this:

```
# tar cfC - /usr/src . | tar xpfC - /mnt
```

Check the temporary mount point to be sure that your files are actually there. Once you're confident that the files are properly moved, remove the files from the old directory and mount the disk in the new location. For example, after duplicating your files from */usr/src*, you would run:

```
# rm -rf /usr/src/*
# umount /mnt
# mount /usr/src
```

MOVING LIVE FILES

You cannot safely move files that are changing as you copy. For example, if you're moving your email spool to a new partition, you must shut down your mail server first. Otherwise, files change as you're trying to copy them. Tools such as rsync (*/usr/ports/net/rsync*) can help reduce outage duration, but an interruption is still necessary.

Stackable Mounts

Suppose you don't care about your old data; you simply want to split an existing disk to get more space and you plan to recover your data from backup. Fair enough. All FreeBSD filesystems are *stackable*. This is an advanced idea that's not terribly useful in day-to-day system administration, but it can bite you when you try to split one partition into two.

Suppose, for example, that you have data in */usr/src*. See how much space is used on your disk, and then mount a new empty partition on */usr/src*. If you look in the directory afterwards, you'll see that it's empty.

Here's the problem: The new partition is mounted "above" the old disk, and the old disk still has all that data on it. The old partition has no more free space than before you moved the data. If you unmount the new partition and check the directory again, you'll see the data miraculously restored! The new mount obscured the lower partition.

Although you cannot see the data, data on the old disk still takes up space. If you're splitting a disk to gain space, and you just mount a new disk over part of the old, you won't free any space on your original disk. The moral is: Even if you are restoring your data from backup, make sure that you remove that data from your original disk to recover disk space.

Network Filesystems

A network filesystem allows accessing files on another machine over the network. The two most commonly used network filesystems are the original Network File System (NFS) implemented in Unix, and the CIFS (aka SMB) filesystem popularized by Microsoft Windows. We'll touch on both of these, but start with the old Unix standard of NFS.

Sharing directories and partitions between Unix-like systems is perhaps the simplest Network File System you'll find. FreeBSD supports the Unix standard Network File System out of the box. Configuring NFS intimidates many junior system administrators, but after setting up a file share or two you'll find it not so terribly difficult.

Each NFS connection uses a client-server model. One computer is the server; it offers filesystems to other computers. This is called *NFS exporting*, and the filesystems offered are called *exports*. The clients can mount server exports in a manner almost identical to that used to mount local filesystems.

One interesting thing about NFS is its statelessness. NFS does not keep track of the condition of a connection. You can reboot an NFS server and the client won't crash. It won't be able to access files on the server's export while the server is down, but once it returns, you'll pick up right where things left off. Other network file sharing systems are not always so resilient. Of course, statelessness also causes problems as well; for example, clients cannot know when a file they currently have open is modified by another client.

NFS INTEROPERABILITY

Every NFS implementation is slightly different. You'll find minor NFS variations between Solaris, Linux, BSD, and other Unix-like systems. NFS should work between them all, but might require the occasional tweak. If you're having problems with another Unix-like operating system, check the *FreeBSD-net* mailing list archive; the issue has almost certainly been discussed there.

Both NFS servers and clients require kernel options, but the various NFS commands dynamically load the appropriate kernel modules. FreeBSD's GENERIC kernel supports NFS, so this isn't a concern for anyone who doesn't customize their kernel.

NFS is one of those topics that have entire books written about them. We're not going to go into the intimate details about NFS, but rather focus on getting basic NFS operations working. If you're deploying complicated NFS setups, you'll want to do further research. Even this basic setup lets you accomplish many complicated tasks.

Enabling the NFS Server

Turn on NFS server support with the following *rc.conf* options. While not all of these options are strictly necessary for all environments, turning them all on provides the broadest range of NFS compatibility and decent out-of-the-box performance.

```
❶ nfs_server_enable="YES"
❷ rpcbind_enable="YES"
❸ mountd_enable="YES"
❹ rpc_lockd_enable="YES"
❺ rpc_statd_enable="YES"
```

First, tell FreeBSD to load the *nfsserver.ko* ❶ kernel module, if it's not already in the kernel. rpcbind(8) ❷ maps remote procedure calls (RPC) into local network addresses. Each NFS client asks the server's rpcbind(8) daemon where it can find a mountd(8) daemon to connect to. mountd(8) ❸ listens to high-numbered ports for mount requests from clients. Enabling the NFS server also starts nfsd(8), which handles the actual file request. rpc.lockd(8) ❹ ensures smooth file locking operations over NFS, and rpc.statd(8) ❺ monitors NFS clients so that the NFS server can free up resources when the host disappears.

While you can start all of these services at the command line, if you're just learning NFS it's best to reboot your system after enabling NFS server. Afterwards, you'll see rpc.lockd, rpc.statd, nfsd, mountd, and rpcbind listed in the output of sockstat(1). If you don't see all of these daemons listening to the network, check */var/log/messages* for errors.

Configuring NFS Exports

Now tell your server what it can share, or *export*. We could just export all directories and filesystems on the entire server, but any competent security administrator would have a (justified) fit. As with all server configurations, permit as little access as possible while still letting the server fulfill its role. For example, in most environments clients have no need to remotely mount the NFS server's root filesystem.

Define which clients may mount which filesystems and directories in */etc/exports*. This file takes a separate line for each disk device on the server and each client or group of clients that access that device. Each line has up to three parts:

- Directories or partitions to be exported (mandatory)
- Options on that export
- Clients that can connect

Each combination of clients and a disk device can only have one line in the exports file. This means that if */usr/ports* and */usr/home* are on the same partition, and you want to export both of them to a particular client, they must both appear in the same line. You cannot export *usr/ports* and */usr/home* to one client with different permissions. You don't have to export the entire disk device, mind you; you can export a single directory within a partition. This directory cannot contain either symlinks or double or single dots.

Of the three parts of the */etc/exports* entry, only the directory is mandatory. If I wanted to export my home directory to every host on the Internet, I could use an */etc/exports* line consisting entirely of this:

```
/home/mwlucas
```

We show no options and no host restrictions. This would be foolish, of course, but I could do it.[3]

After editing the *exports* file, tell mountd to reread it:

```
# /etc/rc.d/mountd restart
```

mountd(8) logs any problems in */var/log/messages*. The log messages are generally enigmatic: While mountd(8) informs you that a line is bad, it generally doesn't say why. The most common errors I experience involve symlinks.

Enabling the NFS Client

Configuring the client is much simpler. In */etc/rc.conf*, put:

```
nfsclient="YES"
```

Then, reboot or run /etc/rc.d/nfsclient start. Either will enable NFS client functions.

Now we can mount directories or filesystems exported by NFS servers. Instead of using a device name, use the NFS server's host name and the directory you want to mount. For example, to mount the directory */home/mwlucas* from my server *sardines* onto the directory */mnt*, I would run:

```
# mount sardines:/home/mwlucas /mnt
```

Afterwards, test your mount with df(1).

```
# df
Filesystem                1K-blocks       Used     Avail Capacity  Mounted on
/dev/ad4s1a                 1012974     387450    544488     42%    /
devfs                             1          1         0    100%    /dev
/dev/ad4s1f               109009798   12959014  87330002     13%    /usr
/dev/ad4s1e                 1012974      42072    889866      5%    /var
sardines:/home/mwlucas    235492762  150537138  66116204     69%    /mnt
```

---

[3] Why is there no safeguard against shooting yourself in the foot like this? Well, Unix feels that anyone dumb enough to do this doesn't deserve to be its friend. Various people keep trying to put Unix in therapy for this type of antisocial behavior, but it just isn't interested.

The NFS-mounted directory shows up as a normal partition, and I can read and write files on it as I please. Well, maybe not *entirely* as I please . . .

NFS and Users

File ownership and permissions are tied to UID numbers. NFS uses UID to identify the owner. For example, on my laptop the user mwlucas has the UID of 1001. On the NFS server, mwlucas also has the UID 1001. This makes my life easy, as I don't have to worry too much about file ownership; I have the same privileges on the server as on my laptop. This can be a problem on a large network, where users have root on their own machines. The best way around this is to create a central repository of authorized users via Kerberos. On a small network or on a network with a limited number of NFS users, this usually isn't a problem; you can synchronize */etc/master.passwd* on your systems or just assign the same UID to each user on each system.

The root user is handled slightly differently, however. An NFS server doesn't trust root on other machines to execute commands as root on the server. After all, if an intruder breaks into an NFS client you don't want the server to automatically go down with it. You can map requests from root to any other username. For example, you might say that all requests from root on a client will run as the user nfsroot on the server. With careful use of groups, you could allow this nfsroot user to have limited file access. Use the -maproot option to map root to another user. Here, we map UID 0 (root) on the client to UID 5000 on the server:

/usr/home/mwlucas -maproot=5000

If you really want the root user on the client to have root privileges on the server, you can use -maproot to map root to UID 0. This might be suitable on your home network or on a test system.

If you do not use a maproot statement, the NFS maps a remote root account to nobody:nobody by default.

Don't forget to restart mountd(8) after editing the exports file.

Exporting Multiple Directories

Many directories under */usr* would make sensible exports. Good candidates include */usr/src*, */usr/obj*, and */usr/ports/distfiles*. List all directories of the same partition on the same line in */etc/exports*, right after the first exported directory, separated by spaces. My */etc/exports* now looks like this:

/usr/home/mwlucas /usr/src /usr/obj /usr/ports/distfiles -maproot=5000

There are no identifiers, separators, or delimiters between the parts of the line. Yes, it would be easier to read if we could put each shared directory on its own line, but we can't; they're all on the same partition. The FreeBSD team could rewrite this so that it had more structure, but then FreeBSD's */etc/exports* would be incompatible with that from any other Unix.

As with many other configuration files, you can use a backslash to break a single line of configuration into multiple lines. You might find the above configuration more readable as:

```
/usr/home/mwlucas \
    /usr/src \
    /usr/obj \
    /usr/ports/distfiles \
    -maproot = 5000
```

Restricting Clients

To allow only particular clients to access an NFS export, list them at the end of the */etc/exports* entry. Here, we restrict our share above to one IP address:

```
/usr/home/mwlucas /usr/src /usr/obj /usr/ports/distfiles \
    -maproot=5000 192.168.1.200
```

You can also restrict file shares to clients on a particular network by using the -network and -mask qualifiers:

```
/usr/home/mwlucas /usr/src /usr/obj /usr/ports/distfiles \
    -maproot=5000 -network 192.168.0 -mask 255.255.255.0
```

This lets any client with an IP address beginning in 192.168.0 access your NFS server. I use a setup much like this to upgrade clients quickly. I build a new world and kernel on the NFS server, then let the clients mount those partitions and install the binaries over NFS.

Combinations of Clients and Exports

Each line in */etc/exports* specifies exports from one partition to one host or set of hosts. Different hosts can have entirely different export statements.

```
/usr/home/mwlucas /usr/src /usr/obj /usr/ports/distfiles \
    -maproot=5000 192.168.1.200
/usr -maproot=0 192.168.1.201
```

Here, I've exported several subdirectories of */usr* to the NFS client at 192.168.1.200. The NFS client at 192.168.1.201 gets to mount the whole of */usr*, and may even do so as root.

NFS Performance and Options

FreeBSD uses conservative NFS defaults, so that it can work well with any other Unix-like operating system. If you're working in a pure FreeBSD environment or if your environment only contains higher-end Unix systems, you can improve NFS performance with mount options.

First of all, NFS defaults to running over UDP. The tcp or -T option tells the client to request a mount over TCP.

Programs expect the filesystem to not disappear, but when you're using NFS it's possible that the server will vanish from the network. This makes programs on the client trying to access the NFS filesystem hang forever. By making your NFS mount *interruptible*, you will be able to interrupt processes hung on unavailable NFS mount with CTRL-C. Set interruptibility with intr.

FreeBSD can tell clients if and when a filesystem is no longer accessible. Programs will fail when trying to access the filesystem, instead of hanging forever.

Finally, you can set the size of read and write requests. The defaults are well-suited to networks of the early 1990s, but you can set the read and write size to more modern values with the -r and -w options. I find that 32768 is a good value for both. So, putting this all together, I could have my client mount an NFS file system like this:

```
# mount -o tcp,intr,soft,-w=32768,-r=32768 server:/usr/home/mwlucas /mnt
```

The same entry in */etc/fstab* looks like this:

```
server:/usr/home/mwlucas /mnt nfs rw,-w=32768,-r=32768,tcp,soft,intr 0 0
```

This general NFS configuration gives me good throughput speed on a local network, limited only by hardware quality.

While NFS is pretty straightforward for simple uses, you can spend many hours adjusting, tuning, and enhancing it. If you wish to build a complicated NFS environment, don't rely entirely on this brief introduction but spend time with a good book on the subject.

FreeBSD and CIFS

If you're on a typical office network, the standard network file sharing protocol is Microsoft's Common Internet File Sharing, or CIFS. (CIFS was once known as Server Message Block, or SMB.) This is the "Network Neighborhood" that Windows users can access. While originally provided only by Microsoft Windows systems, this protocol has become something of a standard. Thankfully, today there's an open source CIFS file sharing server called Samba. Many commercial products provide services via this protocol. FreeBSD includes kernel modules to support the filesystem and programs to find, mount, and use CIFS shares.

Prerequisites

Before you begin working with Microsoft file shares, gather the following information about your Windows network:

- Workgroup or Windows domain name
- Valid Windows username and password
- IP address of the Windows DNS server

Kernel Support

FreeBSD uses several kernel modules to support CIFS. The *smbfs.ko* module supports basic CIFS operations. The *libmchain.ko* and *libiconv.ko* modules provide supporting functions and load automatically when you load *smbfs.ko*. You can compile these statically in your kernel as:

```
options    NETSMB
options    LIBMCHAIN
options    LIBICONV
options    SMBFS
```

Of course, you can load these at boot time with the appropriate entries in */boot/loader.conf*.

Configuring CIFS

CIFS relies on a configuration file, either *$HOME/.nsmbrc* or */etc/nsmb.conf*. All settings in */etc/nsmb.conf* override the settings in user home directories. The configuration file is divided into sections by labels in square brackets. For example, settings that apply to every CIFS connection are in the [default] section. Create your own sections to specify servers, users, and shares, in one of the following formats:

```
[servername]
[servername:username]
[servername:username:sharename]
```

Information that applies to an entire server goes into a section named after the server. Information that applies to a specific user is kept in a username section, and information that applies to only a single share is kept in a section that includes the share name. You can lump the information for all the shares under a plain [servername] entry if you don't have more specific per-user or per-share information.

Configuration entries use the values from the CIFS system—for example, my Windows username is lucas_m, but my FreeBSD username is mwlucas, so I use lucas_m in *nsmb.conf*.

nsmb.conf Keywords

Specify a *nsmb.conf* configuration with keywords and values under the appropriate section. For example, servers have IP addresses and users don't, so you would only use an IP address assignment in the server section. To use a keyword, assign a value with an equal sign, as in *keyword=value*. Here are the common keywords; for a full list, see nsmb.conf(5).

workgroup=string

The workgroup keyword specifies the name of the Windows domain or workgroup you want to access. This is commonly a default setting used for all servers.

addr=a.b.c.d

The addr keyword sets the IP address of a CIFS server. This keyword can only appear under a plain [servername] label.

nbns=a.b.c.d

The nbns keyword sets the IP address of a NetBIOS (WINS) nameserver. You can put this line in the default section or under a particular server. If you have Active Directory (which is based on DNS), you can use DNS host names. Adding a WINS server won't hurt your configuration, however, and helps in testing basic CIFS setup.

password=string

The password keyword sets a clear-text password for a user or a share. If you must store passwords in */etc/nsmb.conf*, be absolutely certain that only root can read the file. Storing a password in *$HOME/.nsmbrc* is a bad idea on a multi-user system.

You can scramble your Windows password with smbutil crypt, generating a string that you can use for this keyword. The scrambled string has double dollar signs ($$) in front of it. While this helps prevent someone accidentally discovering the password, a malicious user can unscramble it easily.

CIFS Name Resolution

Let's build a basic *nsmb.conf* file. As an absolute minimum, we first need to find hosts, which means we need a workgroup name. We'll set the domain controller as the WINS server. I also have a user set up on the Windows-based servers to share files, so I'm going to use that as a default in *nsmb.conf*.

```
[default]
workgroup=BIGLOSER
nbns=192.168.1.66
username=unix
```

Armed with this information, we can perform basic SMB name queries.

```
# smbutil lookup ntserv1
Got response from 192.168.1.66
IP address of ntserv1: 192.168.1.4
```

If this works, you have basic CIFS functionality.

Other smbutil(1) Functions

Before you can mount a filesystem from a Windows host, you must log into the host. Only root can perform this operation.

```
# smbutil login //unix@ntserv1
Password:
```

So, our configuration is correct. Let's see what resources this server offers with smbutil's `view` command.

```
# smbutil view //unix@ntserv1
Password:
Share        Type        Comment
-------------------------------
IPC$         pipe        Remote IPC
ADMIN$       disk        Remote Admin
C$           disk        Default share
unix       disk
4 shares listed from 4 available
```

You'll get a list of every shared resource on the CIFS server. Now, assuming you're finished, log out of the server.

```
# smbutil logout //unix@ntserv1
```

Mounting a Share

Now that you've finished investigating, let's actually mount a share with mount_smbfs(8). The syntax is as follows:

```
# mount_smbfs //username@servername/share /mount/point
```

I have a share on this Windows box called *MP3* that I want to access from my FreeBSD system. To mount this as */home/mwlucas/smbmount*, I would do this:

```
# mount_smbfs //unix@ntserv1/MP3 /home/mwlucas/smbmount
```

mount(8) and df(1) show this share attached to your system, and you can access documents on this server just as you could any other filesystem.

Other mount_smbfs Options

mount_smbfs includes several options to tweak the behavior of mounted CIFS filesystems. Use the `-f` option to choose a different file permission mode and the `-d` option to choose a different directory permission mode. For example, to set a mount so that only I could access the contents of the directory, I would use `mount_smbfs -d 700`. This would make the FreeBSD permissions far more stringent than the Windows privileges, but that's perfectly all right with me. I can change the owner of the files with the `-u` option, and the group with the `-g` option.

Microsoft filesystems are case-insensitive, but Unix-like operating systems are case sensitive. CIFS defaults to leaving the case as it finds it, but that may not be desirable. The `-c` flag makes mount_smbfs(8) change the case on the filesystem: `-c l` changes everything to lowercase and `-c u` changes everything to uppercase.

Sample nsmb.conf Entries

Here are samples of *nsmb.conf* entries for different situations. They all assume they're part of a configuration where you've already defined a workgroup, NetBIOS nameserver, and a username with privileges to access the CIFS shares.

Unique Password on a Standalone System

You would use something like the following if you have a machine named desktop with a password-protected share. Many Windows 9*x* systems have this sort of password-protection feature.

```
[desktop:shareusername]
password=$$1789324874ea87
```

Accessing a Second Domain

In this example, we're accessing a second domain, named development. This domain has a username and password different from those at our default domain.

```
[development]
workgroup=development
username=support
```

CIFS File Ownership

Ownership of files between Unix-like and Windows systems can be problematic. For one thing, your FreeBSD usernames probably won't map to Windows usernames, and Unix has a very different permissions scheme compared to Windows.

Since you're using a single Windows username to access the share, you have whatever access that account has to the Windows resources, but you must assign the proper FreeBSD permissions for that mounted share. By default, mount_smbfs(8) assigns the new share the same permissions as the mount point. In our earlier example, the directory */home/mwlucas/smbmount* is owned by the user mwlucas and has permissions of 755. These permissions say that mwlucas can edit what's in this directory, but nobody else can. Even though FreeBSD says that this user can edit those files, Windows might still not let that particular user edit the files it's sharing out.

Serving CIFS Shares

Just as FreeBSD can access CIFS shares, it can also serve them to CIFS clients with Samba. You can find Samba in */usr/ports/net/samba3*. You'll find the Samba website at *http://www.samba.org*, along with many useful tutorials. Serving CIFS shares from FreeBSD is much more complicated than accessing them, so we'll end our discussion here before this book grows even thicker.

devfs

devfs(5) is a dynamic filesystem for managing device nodes. Remember, in a Unix-like operating system *everything* is a file. This includes physical hardware. Every device on the system has a device node under */dev*.

Once upon a time, the system administrator was responsible for making these device node files. Lucky sysadmins managed an operating system that came with a shell script to handle device node creation and permissions. If the OS authors had not provided such a shell script, or if the server had unusual hardware not included in that shell script, the sysadmin had to create the node with black magic and mknod(8). If any little thing went wrong, the device would not work. The other option was to ship the operating system with device nodes for every piece of hardware imaginable. System administrators could be confident—well, *mostly* confident—that the desired device nodes were available, somewhere, buried within the thousands of files under */dev*.

Of course, the kernel knows exactly what characteristics each device node should have. With devfs(5), FreeBSD simply asks the kernel what device nodes the kernel thinks the system should have and provides exactly those—and no more. This works well for most people. You and I are not "most people," however. We expect odd things from our computers. Perhaps we need to make device nodes available under different names, or change device node ownership, or configure our hardware uniquely. FreeBSD breaks the problem of device node management into three pieces: configuring devices present at boot, global availability and permissions, and configuring devices that appear dynamically after boot with devd(8).

DEVICE MANAGEMENT AND SERVERS

For the most part, device node management on servers works without any adjustment or intervention. The place I most often need to muck with device nodes is on laptops and the occasional workstation. FreeBSD's device node management tools are very powerful and flexible, and include support for things I wouldn't expect to use in a century. We'll only touch upon the basics. Don't think that you must master devfs(5) to get your server running well!

---

devfs at Boot: devfs.conf

The big problem sysadmins have with a dynamic devfs is that any changes made to it disappear on reboot. When device nodes were permanent files on disk, the sysadmin could symlink to those nodes or change their permissions without worrying that his changes would vanish. With an automated, dynamic device filesystem, this assurance disappears. (Of course, you no longer have to worry about occult mknod(8) commands either, so you're better off in the long run.) The device node changes could include, for example:

- Making device nodes available under different names
- Changing ownership of device nodes
- Concealing device nodes from users

At boot time, devfs(8) creates device nodes in accordance with the rules in */etc/devfs.conf*.

devfs.conf

The */etc/devfs.conf* file lets you create links, change ownership, and set permissions for devices available at boot. Each rule has the following format:

action	realdevice	desiredvalue

The valid actions are link (create a link), perm (set permissions), and own (set owner). The realdevice entry is a preexisting device node, while the last setting is your desired value. For example, here we create a new name for a device node:

❶link	❷acd0	❸cdrom

We want a symbolic link ❶ to the device node */dev/acd0* ❷ (an ATAPI CD drive), and we want this link to be named */dev/cdrom* ❸. If we reboot with this entry in */etc/devfs.conf*, our CD device at */dev/acd0* also appears as */dev/cdrom*, as many desktop multimedia programs expect.

To change the permissions of a device node, give the desired permissions in octal form as the desired value:

perm	acd0	666

Here, we set the permissions on */dev/acd0* (our CD device, again) so that any system user can read or write to the device. Remember, changing the permissions on the */dev/cdrom* link won't change the permissions on the device node, just the symlink.

Finally, we can also change the ownership of a device. Changing a device node's owner usually indicates that you're solving a problem the wrong way and that you may need to stop and think. FreeBSD happily lets you mess up your system if you insist, however. Here, we let a particular user have absolute control of the disk device */dev/da20*:

own	da20	mwlucas:mwlucas

This might not have the desired effect, however, as some programs still think that you must be root to carry out operations on devices. I've seen more than one piece of software shut itself down if it's not run by root, without even trying to access its device nodes. Changing the device node permissions won't stop those programs' complaints when they are run by a regular user.

Configuration with devfs.conf(5) solves many problems, but not all. If you want a device node to simply be invisible and inaccessible, you must use devfs rules.

Global devfs Rules

Every devfs(5) instance behaves according to the rules defined in *devfs.rules*. The devfs rules apply to both devices present at boot and devices that appear and disappear dynamically. Rules allow you to set ownership and permissions on device nodes and make device nodes visible or invisible. You cannot create symlinks to device nodes with devfs rules.

Similar to */etc/rc.conf* and */etc/defaults/rc.conf*, FreeBSD uses */etc/devfs.rules* and */etc/defaults/devfs.rules*. Create an */etc/defvs.rules* for your custom rules and leave the entries in the defaults file alone.

devfs Ruleset Format

Each set of devfs rules starts with a name and a ruleset number between square brackets. For example, here are a few basic devfs rules from the default configuration:

```
[❶devfsrules_hide_all=❷1]
❸add hide
```

The first set of rules is called devf s_hide_all ❶ and is ruleset number 1 ❷. This ruleset contains only one rule ❸.

Ruleset Content

All devfs rules (in files) begin with the word add, to add a rule to the ruleset. You then have either a path keyword and a regex of device names, or a type keyword and a device type. At the end of the rule, you have an *action*, or a command to perform. Here's an example of a devfs rule:

```
add path da* user mwlucas
```

This rule assigns all device nodes with a node name beginning with da to the ownership of mwlucas. On a multi-user system, or a system with SCSI hard drives, this would be a bad idea. On a laptop, where the only device nodes beginning with da are USB storage devices, it's not such a bad idea.

Devices specified by path use standard shell regular expressions. If you want to match a variety of devices, use an asterisk as a wildcard. For example, path ad1s1 matches exactly the device */dev/ad1s1*, but path ad*s* matches every device node with a name beginning with ad, a character, the letter s, and possibly more characters. You could tell exactly what devices are matched by a wildcard by using it at the command line.

```
# ls /dev/ad*s*
```

This lists all slices and partitions on your ATA hard drives, but not the devices for the entire drive.

The type keyword indicates that you want the rule to apply to all devices of a given type. Valid keywords are disk (disk devices), mem (memory devices), tape (tape devices), and tty (terminal devices, including pseudoterminals). The type keyword is rarely used exactly because it's so sweeping.

If you include neither a path nor a type, devfs applies the action at the end of the rule to all device nodes. In almost all cases, this is undesirable.

The ruleset action can be any one of group, user, mode, hide, and unhide. The group action lets you set the group owner of the device, given as an additional argument. Similarly, the user action assigns the device owner. Here, we set the ownership of da disks to the username desktop and the group usb:

```
add path da* user desktop
add path da* group usb
```

The mode action lets you assign permissions to the device in standard octal form:

```
add path da* mode 664
```

The hide keyword lets you make device nodes disappear, and unhide makes them reappear. Since no program can use a device node if the device is invisible, this is of limited utility except when the system uses jail(8). We'll look at that specific use of hide and unhide in the next chapter.

Once you have a set of devfs rules you like, enable them at boot in */etc/rc.conf*. Here, we activate the devfs ruleset named laptoprules:

```
devfs_system_rulesets="laptoprules"
```

Remember, devfs rules apply to the devices in the system at boot and the devices configured dynamically after startup. To finish up, let's look at dynamic devices.

Dynamic Device Management with devd(8)

Hot-swappable hardware is much more common now than it was even ten years ago. In the last century, laptop network cards were considered cutting-edge. While you might drop a new CD into the workstation's cup holder, you wouldn't hot-plug a whole CD drive into your desktop. Today, that's entirely different. Flash drives are essentially USB-based hard drives that you can attach and detach at will, and other USB hardware lets you add keyboards, mice, and even network cards on a whim.

FreeBSD's devfs dynamically creates new device nodes when this hardware is plugged in and erases the nodes when the hardware is removed, making using these dynamic devices much simpler. devd(8) takes this a step further by letting you run userland programs when hardware appears and disappears.

devd Configuration

devd(8) reads its configuration from */etc/devd.conf* and any file under */usr/local/etc/devd/*. I recommend placing your local rules in */usr/local/etc/ devd/devd.conf* to simplify upgrades. You could also add different rules files for different types of devices, if you find your devd(8) configuration becoming very complicated. You'll find four types of devd(8) rules: attach, detach, nomatch, and notify.

attach rules are triggered when matching hardware is attached to the system. When you plug in a network card, an attach rule configures the card with an IP address and brings up the network.

detach rules trigger when matching hardware is removed from the system. detach rules are uncommon, as the kernel automatically marks resources unavailable when the underlying hardware disappears, but you might find uses for them.

The nomatch rules triggers when new hardware is installed but not attached to a device driver. These devices do not have device drivers in the current kernel.

devd(8) applies notify rules when the kernel sends a matching event notice to userland. For example, the console message that a network interface has come up is a notify event. Notifications generally appear on the console or in */var/log/messages*.

devd(8) rules also have priority, with 0 being the lowest. Only the highest matching rule is processed, while lower-priority matching rules are skipped. Here's a sample devd(8) rule:

```
❶notify ❷0 {
        match "system"          ❸"IFNET";
        match "type"            ❹"ATTACH";
        action ❺"/etc/pccard_ether $subsystem start";
};
```

This is a notify ❶ rule, which means it activates when the kernel sends a message to userland. As a priority 0 ❷ rule, this rule can only be triggered if no rule of higher-priority matches the criteria we specify. This rule only triggers if the notification is on the network system IFNET ❸ (network), and only if the notification type is ATTACH ❹—in other words, when a network interface comes up. Under those circumstances, devd(8) takes action and runs a command to configure the network interface ❺.

devd(8) supports many options to handle all sorts of different situations. If you want to automatically mount a particular USB flash disk on a certain mount point, you can do that by checking the serial number of every USB device you put in. If you want to configure Intel network cards differently than 3Com network cards, you can do that too. We'll do enough with devd(8) to introduce you to its abilities, mainly through examples, but we won't delve deeply into it.

devd(8) Example: Laptops

I use my laptop both at work and at home. At work I use a wired connection, while at home I use wireless. Both require very particular setups, different DNS servers, and different configurations all around. I could cheat by renumbering my home network to match my work network, but experience tells me that my home network will last much longer than my attachment to any one job. (Maybe I'm wrong.[4]) I want the laptop to configure itself for home when I plug in my wireless card. I want the laptop to configure itself for work when I plug in the CAT5 cable to the integrated network interface.

If a wired interface is configured to use DHCP, plugging in the cable tells FreeBSD to start dhclient(8) and configure the network. When I plug in a wireless card, FreeBSD checks for a configuration and tries to start the network. Here's my wireless configuration from */etc/rc.conf* (this is all one line in the configuration, but it is broken to fit in this book):

```
ifconfig_wi0="inet dhcp ssid WriteFaster wepkey
0xdeadbeefbadc0decafe1234567 weptxkey 1 wepmode on channel 1"
```

When I insert my wireless card, the kernel attaches the card to the driver wi0. This is an attach event, and devd(8) searches its configuration for a corresponding rule. The following entry in */etc/devd.conf* matches:

```
❶attach ❷0 {
        ❸media-type "802.11";
        ❹action "/etc/pccard_ether $device-name start";
};
```

We inserted a card into the laptop, and FreeBSD attached the wi(4) driver to it. This is an attach ❶ event. This rule has a priority of 0 ❷, so any other matching rule will run before this default rule. Anything with a media type of 802.11 ❸ (wireless) matches this rule. When an attach event matches this rule, FreeBSD runs a command ❹ to configure the network. I could run a custom script instead of using the built-in FreeBSD support, but why bother when the default configuration does everything I need?

Unlike the wireless I use at home, the Ethernet interface I use at work is always attached to my system. The interface might not be plugged into a network, but the card itself is always attached. I don't want to configure this interface every time the system boots, because if the interface isn't plugged in I'll have a long delay while my laptop's SSH daemon and other services time out on DNS queries. At work I have a variety of NFS mounts, as well as custom client/server settings not available from the DHCP server.

---

[4] It would be nice, some day, to have employment that didn't end with four corporate security gorillas dragging me to the door in chains, with my new ex-boss screeching in the background about federal regulators, crème brûlée, and caffeinated lemurs. I'm certain this is just coincidence, mind you, as nobody's ever pressed charges.

This means that I need to run a custom shell script to configure my network for work, but only when the network cable is plugged in. I want devd to watch for a notification that the interface has come up and then run my custom shell script. I've written the custom entry below and placed it in */usr/local/etc/devd/devd.conf*:

```
❶notify ❷10 {
          match "system"          ❸"IFNET";
          match "type"            ❹"LINK_UP";
          media-type              ❺"ethernet";
❻#        action "/etc/rc.d/dhclient start $subsystem";
        ❼action "/home/mwlucas/bin/jobnetwork.sh";
};
```

This is a notification ❶ rule, which means it triggers when the kernel sends a matching notification message to the system. It also has a priority of 10 ❷, so it runs before any of FreeBSD's default rules. This rule triggers on the network ❸ system, when a link comes up ❹ (i.e., when we plug in a network cable), if the link is Ethernet ❺. When all of these conditions are met, FreeBSD runs a shell script ❼ in my home directory.

Note that this rule has a commented-out line ❻. When I said I wrote this rule, I lied. I actually copied the default entry from */etc/devd.conf* and modified it slightly. FreeBSD already has rules for handling network interfaces coming up, but I wanted to do something a little different. Instead of coming up with all these conditions myself, I found a entry that was almost right and modified it. I suggest you do the same. Just be sure to give your customized rule a higher priority than the default rule, so FreeBSD uses your rule instead of its own.

Another devd Example: Flash Drives

Copying an entry is cheating, I hear you cry. Well, let's try an example where FreeBSD doesn't have any infrastructure in place. On my laptop, I want any USB storage mounted on */media* automatically. The first USB storage device plugged into a laptop shows up in FreeBSD as */dev/da0*, but the device name is umass0. (If you already have other USB or SCSI devices, these numbers will differ for you.) Generally speaking, all flash media is formatted with the FAT32 fileystem, so you would use mount -t msdosfs to mount it.

When the device is plugged in, FreeBSD attaches it to the kernel, so we use an attach rule:

```
attach 10 {
      match "device-name"    ❶"umass0";
      action "/home/mwlucas/bin/mountusb.sh";
};
```

I assign this rule a priority of 10, so it overrides any new priority 0 functions FreeBSD might install during an upgrade. (If FreeBSD grows the ability to do this automatically, I'll probably use that instead, but I don't want an upgrade to change my system behavior unless I know about it.) Here, we match on the device name ❶. When the device appears, a shell script in my directory runs.

Why not just run the mount(8) command? USB devices need a moment or two to warm up and stabilize before they can be accessed. Also, some USB flash drives need to be poked before they really start to work. The shell script I use here is terribly simpleminded, but it suffices:

```
#!/bin/sh
sleep 2
/usr/bin/true > /dev/da0
/sbin/mount -t msdosfs /dev/da0s1 /media
```

While this handles mounting the device for me, devd(8) won't unmount the device. FreeBSD expects the sysadmin to unmount filesystems before removing the underlying devices. It's no different from unmounting a CD or floppy disk before ejecting it.

While devd(8) has many more advanced features, these two examples cover all the features I've needed or wanted to use in several years. Please read the manual page if you seek further enlightenment. Now that you have a little bit too much understanding of FreeBSD filesystems, let's look at its more advanced security features.

9

ADVANCED SECURITY FEATURES

FreeBSD includes a variety of tools for securing network traffic and users. You can allow and disallow connections to or from certain parts of the Internet. You can cage users in a virtual machine, or *jail*, where they can access everything that's important to them but nothing that's important to you. Packet filtering lets you control who can access your system. In this chapter, we'll examine these tools and techniques, look at monitoring your system's security, and discuss how to react if you suffer an intrusion.

Let's start with a very basic security topic: unprivileged users.

Unprivileged Users

An *unprivileged user* is a specific user for a specific task. He has only the rights necessary to perform that limited task. Many programs run as unprivileged users or use unprivileged users to perform specific duties.

"Only the rights needed to perform its duties" sounds like every user account, doesn't it? That's true, but the account used by the least privileged human being still has more rights than many programs need. Anyone with shell access has a home directory. The normal user may create files in that home directory, run text editors, or process email. Your average shell user needs these minimal privileges, but programs do not. By having a program, particularly a network daemon, run as a very restricted user you control the amount of damage an intruder can do to either the program or the user.

FreeBSD includes several unprivileged users. Take a look at /etc/passwd and you'll see accounts like audit, bind, uucp, and www. These are all unprivileged accounts for use by specific server daemons. See what they have in common.

Unprivileged users do not have normal home directories. Many have a home directory of /nonexistent, while others such as sshd have a special home directory such as /var/empty. Having a home directory where you may not write or read files makes the account less flexible, but good enough for a server daemon. These users do own files on the system, but they usually cannot write to those files.

Similarly, nobody should ever log into these accounts. If the account bind is reserved for the DNS system, nobody should actually log into the system as that user! Such an account must have a user shell that specifically denies logging in, like /usr/sbin/nologin. How does all this enhance system security? Let's look at an example.

The web server is generally run under the unprivileged account www. Suppose that an intruder discovered a security flaw in the version of the web server program you're using and can make the web server execute arbitrary code. This is among the worst types of security holes, where an intruder can make the server program do absolutely anything within its power. What *is* within this program's power?

The intruder probably wants a command prompt on the system. A command prompt on a Unix-like system is the door to so much more access, after all. The unprivileged user has an assigned shell that specifically disallows logins. This really annoys intruders and requires them to work much harder to reach that command prompt.

If he's really clever, though, the nologin shell won't stop the intruder. Let's assume that through clever trickery he makes the web server execute a simple shell such as /bin/sh and offer him the prompt. He's in and can wreak untold damage . . . or can he?

He has no home directory and does not have permissions to create one. That means that any files he wants to store must go in a globally accessible directory such as /tmp or /var/tmp, increasing his visibility. The Apache configuration file is owned by root or by your web server administration group, and the www user is not part of that group. The intruder might have a path into the web server, but he can't reconfigure it. He can't change the website files, as the www user doesn't own them. The www user doesn't have access to anything at all on the system, actually. Having broken into the web server program, he now has to break into FreeBSD or the web application.

An unprivileged user doesn't solve all security problems, mind you. Our compromised www user can view web application source files. If your application is badly written or has database passwords hard-coded into hidden files, you're still in a lot of trouble. Still, if you've kept your system updated and patched, he'll have a very hard time penetrating FreeBSD itself.

The nobody Account

For years, system administrators used the account *nobody* as a generic unprivileged user. They'd run web servers, proxy servers, and whatever else as nobody. This was better than running those programs as root, but not as good as having separate users for each daemon. If an intruder successfully penetrated one of these programs, he had access to them all. Our hypothetical web server intruder would abruptly have access not only to the web server, but to whatever other programs run as that same user! If you're using NFS, remember that NFS defaults to mapping remote root accounts to nobody. The whole point of using unprivileged users is to minimize the possible damage from a successful intrusion.

While you might test with the nobody account, don't deploy production services with it. Use separate unprivileged accounts liberally.

A Sample Unprivileged User

Here are parameters useful for a generic unprivileged user:

username   Assign a username related to the user's function. For example, the default user for web servers is www.

home directory   */nonexistent*

shell   */usr/sbin/nologin*

UID/GID   Choose to use a special range of user and group IDs for unprivileged users.

full name   Assign a name describing the user's function.

password   Use chpass(1) to assign the user a single asterisk as their encrypted password. This disables the account password.

These settings make your unprivileged user very unprivileged indeed. You can set all of this easily with adduser(8), giving the account no password, the correct home directory, and an appropriate shell.

Network Traffic Control

System administrators must have the ability to control traffic to and from their systems. Unwanted visitors must be stopped while legitimate users get access. FreeBSD provides a variety of tools that allow you to control outside access to your systems. We'll focus on TCP wrappers and packet filtering, two popular access-control methods.

The TCP wrappers, or simply *wrappers*, control access to network daemons. While the program must be written to support TCP wrappers, most modern software has supported wrappers for many years. Wrappers are fairly simple to configure and don't require much networking knowledge.

Packet filtering controls which traffic the system allows to pass through it and which traffic it rejects. Most firewalls are packet filters with a pretty GUI on top, but you can use FreeBSD packet filtering and proxy software to build a solid firewall in and of itself. A rejected connection request never reaches any userland program; it is blocked in the network stack. Packet filtering can control access to any program, service, or network port, but does require more networking knowledge.

If you want to use either wrappers or packet filtering, you must decide whether you want a default accept or default deny traffic control policy.

Default Accept vs. Default Deny

One of the essential decisions in any security policy is between default accept and default deny. A *default accept* security stance means that you allow any type of connection except what you specifically disallow. A *default deny* stance means that you only allow connections from specified parts of the Internet and/or to specified services, and you refuse all other connections. The default is used unless you make a specific rule dictating otherwise. Once you have chosen your default security stance, you create exceptions one way or another to either provide or block services as necessary. The choice is really between whether you offer services to the world (default accept) or only to a select few (default deny).

For example, company policy might dictate that the Intranet web server must only be accessible from within the company. If so, adopt a default deny stance and explicitly list who may access the server. Alternatively, if you have a public website but want to block certain parts of the Internet from accessing it for whatever reason, adopt a default accept stance. I always recommend a default deny stance. If you do not make a choice, you've chosen default accept.

Choosing a default does not mean that the default must be implemented without exceptions. My public web servers have a default deny security stance, but I specifically allow the world to access the websites. The machine rejects attempts to connect to other programs unless they come from one of a few specified IP addresses. This is a perfectly acceptable default deny stance.

Different security tools implement these stances in different ways. For example, with TCP wrappers, the *first* matching rule is applied. If your last rule denies everything, you've established a policy that says, "Unless I've specifically created a rule earlier to permit this traffic, block it." On the other hand, with the PF packet filter, the *last* matching rule applies. If your first rule says, "Block all traffic," you've implemented a policy that says, "Unless I specifically create a later rule to permit this traffic, block it."

Both policies annoy the system administrator. If you have a default accept policy, you'll spend your time continually plugging holes. If you choose a default deny policy, you'll spend your time opening access for people. You will repeatedly apologize for either choice. With default deny, you will say things like, "I've just activated service for you. I apologize for the inconvenience." With default accept, you will say things like, ". . . and that is why the intruders were able to access our internal accounting database and why we lost millions of dollars." In the latter case, "I apologize for the inconvenience" *really* doesn't suffice.

TCP Wrappers

Remember from Chapter 6 that network connections are made to various programs that listen for connection requests. When a program is built with TCP wrappers support, the program checks the incoming request against the wrappers configuration. If the wrappers configuration says to reject the connection, the program immediately drops the request. Despite the name, TCP wrappers work with both TCP and UDP connections. Wrappers are a long-running Unix standard that have been incorporated into FreeBSD. Individual programs might or might not work with wrappers; while just about everything in the base FreeBSD system does, some third-party software doesn't.

TCP wrappers are implemented as a shared library, called *libwrap*. As we'll see in Chapter 12, shared libraries are small chunks of code that can be shared between programs. Any program that links with libwrap may use the TCP wrappers functions.

Wrappers most commonly protect inetd(8), the super server that handles network requests for smaller programs. We'll discuss inetd in Chapter 15. While our examples cover inetd(8), you can protect any other program that supports wrappers in exactly the same way. While wrappers help protect inetd(8), make sure inetd(8) doesn't offer any unnecessary services, just as you do for the main system.

Configuring Wrappers

Wrappers check each incoming connection request against the rules in */etc/hosts.allow*, in order. The first matching rule is applied, and processing stops immediately. This makes rule order very important. Each rule is on a separate line and is made up of three parts separated by colons: a daemon name, a client list, and a list of options. Here's a sample rule:

```
ftpd : all : deny
```

The daemon name is ftpd; the client list is all, meaning all hosts; and the option is deny, telling wrappers to reject all connections. Nobody can connect to the FTP server on this host unless an earlier rule explicitly grants access.

In the early examples I refer to only two options: accept and deny. They allow and reject connections, respectively. We'll discuss the additional options later.

Daemon Name

The daemon name is the program's name as it appears on the command line. For example, inetd(8) starts the ftpd(8) program when it receives an incoming FTP request. The Apache web server starts a program called httpd, so if your version of Apache supports wrappers, give the daemon name as httpd. (Note that Apache doesn't run out of inetd, but it can support wrappers anyway.) One special daemon name, ALL, matches all daemons that support wrappers.

If your system has multiple IP addresses, you can specify, as part of the daemon name, different wrapper rules for each IP address that a daemon listens on:

```
ftpd@192.168.1.1 : ALL : deny
ftpd@192.168.1.2 : ALL : accept
```

In this example, we have two daemon names, ftpd@192.168.1.1 and ftpd@192.168.1.2. Each has a separate TCP wrapper rule.

The Client List

The client list is a list of specific IP addresses, network address blocks, hostnames, domain names, and keywords, separated by spaces. Hostnames and IP addresses are simple: Just list them.

```
ALL : netmanager.absolutefreebsd.com 192.168.1.5 : allow
```

With this rule at the top of */etc/hosts.allow*, wrappers allow my netmanager machine and any host with an IP address of 192.168.1.5 to connect to any service on this host. (I could block this access by other means, mind you.)

Specify network numbers in the client list with a slash between the IP address and the netmask, as discussed in Chapter 6. For example, if script kiddies attack your server from a bunch of addresses that begin with 216.132.204, you could block them like this:

```
ALL : 216.136.204.0/255.255.255.0 : deny
```

You can also use domain names in client lists, by prefacing them with a dot. This works through reverse DNS, which means that anyone who controls the DNS server for a block of addresses can work around this restriction.

```
ALL : .mycompany.com : allow
```

If you have a long list of clients, you can even list them in a file and put the full path to the file in the client space in */etc/hosts.allow*. I've been on networks with large numbers of widely scattered hosts, such as an ISP or corporate network environment with network management workstations scattered across the world. Each workstation shared the same wrapper rules as every other workstation and appeared on half a dozen lines in *hosts.allow*. By maintaining a single file with a workstation list, I could centralize all changes.

In addition to specifically listing client addresses and names, wrappers provide several special client keywords to add groups of clients to your list. Table 9-1 shows the keywords and their usage.

Table 9-1: TCP Wrappers Keywords

Keyword	Usage
ALL	This matches every possible host.
LOCAL	This matches every machine whose hostname does not include a dot. Generally, this means machines in the local domain. Machines on the other side of the world who happen to share your domain name are considered "local" under this rule.
UNKNOWN	This matches machines with unidentifiable hostnames or usernames. As a general rule, any host making an IP connection has a known IP address. Tracing hostnames, however, requires DNS, and tracking usernames requires identd(8). Be very careful using this option, because transitory DNS issues can make even local hostnames unresolvable and most hosts don't run identd(8) by default. You don't want a service to become unusable just because your nameserver was misconfigured—especially if that machine *is* your nameserver!
KNOWN	This matches any host with a determinable hostname and IP address.
PARANOID	This matches any host whose name does not match its IP address. You might receive a connection from a host with an IP address of 192.168.84.3 that claims to be called *mail.absolutefreebsd.com*. Wrappers turn around and check the IP address of *mail.absolutefreebsd.com*. If wrappers get a different IP address, the host matches this rule. System administrators who do not have time to maintain their DNS are the most likely to have unpatched, insecure systems.

Most of the client keywords listed in Table 9-1 require a working DNS server. If you use these keywords, you must have a very reliable DNS service and you must remember the vital link between DNS and the rest of your programs. If your DNS server fails, daemons that use wrappers and those keywords cannot identify any hosts. This means that everything matches your UNKNOWN rule, which probably denies the connection. Also, broken DNS on the client end can deny remote users access to your servers, as your DNS servers won't be able to get proper information from the client's servers. Finally, if you use DNS-based wrapping extensively, an intruder only needs to overload your nameserver to create a very effective Denial of Service attack against your network.

TCP wrappers provide additional keywords, but they're not as useful or secure as these. For example, it's possible to allow connections based on the username on the remote machine. You don't want to rely on a client user-name on a remote machine, however. For example, if I set up wrappers to only allow someone with a username of mwlucas to connect to my home system, someone could easily add an account of that name to his FreeBSD system and get right in. Also, this relies on the same rarely used identd protocol that was mentioned earlier. You can find a few other obscure keywords of similar usefulness in hosts_access(5).

The ALL and ALL EXCEPT Keywords

Both daemon names and client lists can use the ALL and ALL EXCEPT keywords. The ALL keyword matches absolutely everything. For example, the default *hosts.allow* starts with a rule that permits all connections, from all locations, to any daemon:

```
ALL : ALL : accept
```

This matches all programs and all clients. You can limit this by giving a specific name to either the client list or the daemon list.

```
ALL : 192.168.1.87 : deny
```

In this example, we reject all connections from the host 192.168.1.87.

Categorically blocking access to all hosts isn't that great an idea, but remember that TCP wrappers follow rules in order and quit when they reach the first matching rule. The ALL keyword lets you set a default stance quite easily. Consider the following ruleset:

```
ALL : 192.168.8.3 192.168.8.4 : accept
ftpd : ALL : accept
ALL : ALL : deny
```

Our workstations 192.168.8.3 and 192.168.8.4 (probably the sysadmin's workstations) may access anything they want. Anyone in the world may access the FTP server. Finally, we drop all other connections. This is a useful default deny stance.

Use the ALL EXCEPT keyword to compress rules. ALL EXCEPT allows you to list hosts by exclusion; what isn't listed matches. Here we write the same rules with ALL EXCEPT:

```
ALL : 192.168.8.3 192.168.8.4 : accept
ALL EXCEPT ftpd : ALL : deny
```

Of course, this rule relies on having a default accept policy that permits the FTP connection later.

Some people find rules more clear when written with ALL, others prefer ALL EXCEPT. The important thing to remember is that the first matching rule ends the check, so be careful slinging ALL around.

If you're just learning about wrappers, it's a good idea to allow any connections from the local host; you're likely to discover a number of programs that break when they can't talk to the local machine. Put a rule like this early in your *hosts.allow*:

```
ALL : localhost : allow
```

Options

We've already seen two options, `allow` and `deny`. `allow` permits the connection, `deny` blocks it. The first rule in the default *hosts.allow* applies to all daemons and clients, and it matches and allows all possible connections. This rule can't be first in your *hosts.allow* if you want to wrap your services, but it's a good final rule in a default accept security stance. Similarly, an `ALL:ALL:deny` rule is a good final rule in a default deny security stance. TCP wrappers support other options besides the simple `allow` and `deny`, however, giving you a great deal of flexibility.

> **LONG RULES**
>
> If you're using a lot of options, wrapper rules can get very long. The *hosts.allow* file can use the backslash (\) followed by a return as a line-continuation character, to help keep rules readable.

Logging

Once you have decided to accept or reject the connection attempt, you can also log the connection. Suppose you want to permit but specifically log all incoming requests from a competitor. Similarly, you might want to know how many connections your server rejects because of DNS problems when using the `PARANOID` client keyword. Logging is good. More logging is better. Disk space is cheaper than your time.

The severity option sends a message to the system log, syslogd(8). You can configure syslogd to direct these messages to an arbitrary file based on the syslogd facility and level you choose (see Chapter 20).

```
telnetd : ALL : severity auth.info : allow
```

This example permits but logs all telnet connections.

Twisting

The `twist` option allows you to run arbitrary shell commands and scripts when someone attempts to connect to a wrapped TCP daemon and returns the output to the remote user. `twist` only works properly with TCP connections. (Remember, UDP is connectionless; there is no connection to return the response over, so you must jump through very sophisticated and annoying hoops to make `twist` work with UDP. Also, protocols that transmit over UDP frequently don't expect such a response and are not usually equipped to receive or interpret it. Using `twist` with UDP is not worth the trouble.) `twist` takes a shell command as an argument and acts as a deny-plus-do-this rule. You must know basic shell scripting to use `twist`; very complicated uses of `twist` are possible, but we'll stick with the simple ones.

`twist` is useful for a final rule in a default deny stance. Use `twist` to return an answer to the person attempting to connect as follows:

```
ALL : ALL : twist /bin/echo "You cannot use this service."
```

If you want to deny just a particular service to a particular host, you can use more specific daemon and client lists with `twist`:

```
sendmail : .spammer.com : twist /bin/echo \
    "You cannot use this service, spam-boy."
```

Actually, this is not effective against spam, but it's a good example. Also, putting a rude message in `twist` output might annoy legitimate users who get caught by it, and it just might motivate the illegitimate user to try harder.

If you're feeling friendly you can tell people why you're rejecting their connection. The following `twist` rejects all connections from people whose hostname does not match their IP address and tells them why:

```
ALL : PARANOID : twist /bin/echo \
    "Your DNS is broken. When you fix it, come back and try again."
```

Using `twist` holds the network connection open until the shell command finishes. If your command takes a long time to finish, you could find that you're holding open more connections than you like. This can impact system performance. A script kiddie can use `twist` to overload your system, creating a very simple DoS attack. Make `twist` simple and quick-finishing.

Spawning

Like `twist`, the `spawn` option denies the connection and runs a specified shell command. Unlike `twist`, `spawn` does not return the results to the client. Use `spawn` when you want your FreeBSD system to take an action upon a connection request, but you don't want the client to know about it. Spawned commands run in the background. The following example allows the connection but logs the client's IP address to a file:

```
ALL : PARANOID : spawn (/bin/echo %a >> /var/log/misconfigured ) \
    : allow
```

Wait a minute, where did the %a come from? TCP wrappers support several variables for use in `twist` and `spawn` commands, so you can easily customize your responses. This particular variable, %a, stands for *client address*. It expands into the client's IP address in the shell command before the command is run. Table 9-2 lists other variables.

Table 9-2: Variables for twist and spawn Scripts

Variable	Description
%a	Client address.
%A	Server IP address.
%c	All available client information.
%d	Name of the daemon connected to.
%h	Client hostname, or IP address if hostname not available.
%H	Server hostname, or IP address if hostname not available.
%n	Client hostname, or UNKNOWN if no hostname is found. If the hostname and the IP address don't match, this returns PARANOID.
%N	Server hostname, but if no hostname is found, this returns either UNKNOWN or PARANOID.
%p	Daemon's process ID.
%s	All available server information.
%u	Client's username.
%%	A single % character.

Use these variables anywhere you would use the information they represent in a shell script. For example, to log all available client information to a file whenever anyone connects to a wrapped program, you could use this:

```
ALL : ALL : spawn (/bin/echo %c >> /var/log/clients) : allow
```

Spaces and backslashes are illegal characters in shell commands and might cause problems. While neither appears in hostnames under normal circumstances, the Internet is almost by definition not normal. TCP wrappers replace any character that might confuse the command shell with an underscore (_). Check for underscores in your logs; they might indicate possible intrusion attempts, or just someone who doesn't know what they're doing.

Wrapping Up Wrappers

Let's take all the examples given so far in this section and build a complete */etc/hosts.allow* to protect a hypothetical network system. We must first inventory the network resources this system offers, the IP addresses we have on the network, and the remote systems we wish to allow to connect.

- Our IP range is 192.168.0.0/16. Our server provides POP3, ftpd(8), SSH, and portmap(8).

- We have a competitor who we do not want to access our system, with an IP address range of 10.5.4.0/23. (Specifically blocking a competitor from using services you provide to the rest of the world is not generally effective, as they'll just go to the local coffee shop and use the free wireless. Still, you might have other reasons for blocking particular addresses.)

- We make the somewhat paranoid decision that hosts with incorrect DNS information might be attackers, and reject connections from them.
- Anyone on the Internet may attempt to access our FTP, SSH, and POP3 servers.
- Hosts on our network may use the portmap daemon, but hosts on other networks cannot.
- The local host can communicate with itself.
- Everything that's not permitted is denied.

While these requirements are fairly complicated, they boil down to a very simple ruleset:

```
#reject all connections from hosts with invalid DNS and from our competitor
ALL : PARANOID 10.5.4.0/23 : deny
#localhost can talk to itself
ALL : localhost : allow
#our local network may access portmap, but no others
portmap : ALL EXCEPT 192.168.0.0/16 : deny
#allow SSH, pop3, and ftp, deny everything else
sshd, POP3, ftpd : ALL : allow
ALL : ALL : deny
```

You can find many more commented-out examples in */etc/hosts.allow* or in hosts_allow(5) and hosts_access(5).

Packet Filtering

To control access to networked programs that do not support TCP wrappers, or whenever your needs exceed what wrappers provide, use one of FreeBSD's kernel-level packet filtering tools. If you need a packet filter, it is best to entirely replace your TCP wrappers implementation with packet filtering. Using both tools at once on the same machine will simply confuse you.

A packet filter compares every network packet that enters the system to a list of rules. When a rule matches the packet, the kernel acts based upon that rule. Rules can tell the system to allow, drop, or alter the packet. You can't use the nifty options provided by TCP wrappers, however; instead of spitting a comparatively friendly rejection message back at the client, the connection is severed at the network level before the client even reaches the application.

While the idea of packet filtering is straightforward enough, your first implementation will be a complete nightmare—er, I mean, "valuable learning experience." Be prepared to spend hours experimenting and don't be discouraged by failures. In my experience, it is ignorance of basic TCP/IP that causes grief with packet filtering, rather than the packet filter itself. Trying to filter network traffic without understanding the network is frustrating and pointless. The only way to really understand TCP/IP is to do real work with it, however. If Chapter 6 isn't enough, grab a copy of *The TCP/IP Guide* by Charles M. Kozierok (No Starch Press, 2005).

FreeBSD suffers from a wealth of packet filters: IPFW, IP Filter, and PF.

IPFW is the primordial FreeBSD packet filtering software. It's tightly integrated with FreeBSD; in fact, the generically named files */etc/rc.firewall* and */etc/rc.firewall6* are purely for IPFW. While quite powerful and very popular with more experienced FreeBSD administrators, it's a little difficult for a beginner.

The second packet filter, IP Filter, is not a FreeBSD-specific firewall program but is supported on several Unix-like operating systems. It is primarily the work of one individual, Darren Reed, who has by heroic effort developed the overwhelming majority of the code and ported it to all those operating systems. IP Filter is not the most popular FreeBSD firewall software, however.

We'll focus on the imaginatively named PF, or *packet filter*. PF originated in OpenBSD and was designed to be very powerful, flexible, and easy to use. The average FreeBSD administrator can use PF to achieve any effect possible with the other two packet filters.

NOTE   *For in-depth discussion of PF you might check out Peter N.M. Hansteen's* The Book of PF *(No Starch Press, 2007) or my book* Absolute OpenBSD *(No Starch Press, 2003), which contains several chapters about PF. You might also look at the PF FAQ online, but that doesn't include haiku.*

Enabling PF

PF includes the packet filtering kernel module, *pf.ko*, and the userland program pfctl(8). Before using PF, you must load the kernel module. The simplest way is to enable PF in *rc.conf*:

```
pf_enable="YES"
```

PF defaults to the accept all stance, which means that you won't lock yourself out of your server merely by enabling the firewall.

Default Accept and Default Deny in Packet Filtering

The security stances (default accept and default deny) are critical in packet filtering. If you use the default accept stance and want to protect your system or network, you need numerous rules to block every possible attack. If you use the default deny stance, you must explicitly open holes for every little service you offer. In almost all cases, default deny is preferable; while it can be more difficult to manage, its increased security more than makes up for that difficulty.

When using a default deny stance, it's very easy to lock yourself out of remotely accessing your machine. When you have an SSH connection to a remote machine and accidentally break the rule that allows SSH access, you're in trouble. Everybody does this at least once, so don't be too embarrassed when it happens to you. The point is, it's best to not learn about packet filtering on a remote machine; start with a machine that you can console into, so you can recover easily. I've cut my own access many times, generally because I'm not thinking straight when solving an unrelated packet filtering problem. The only fix is to kick myself as I climb into the car, drive to the remote location, and apologize profusely to the people I've inconvenienced as I fix the problem. Fortunately, as I grow older, this happens less and less.[1]

Still, in almost all circumstances, a default deny stance is correct. As a new administrator, the only way you can reasonably learn packet filtering is if you have convenient access to the system console. If you're not entirely confident in your configuration, do not set up a packet filtering system across the country unless you have either a competent local administrator or a serial console.

Basic Packet Filtering and Stateful Inspection

Recall from Chapter 6 that a TCP connection can be in a variety of states, such as opening, open, closing, and so on. For example, every connection opens when the client sends a SYN packet to the server to request connection synchronization. If the server is listening on the requested port, it responds with a SYN-ACK, meaning, "I have received your request, and here is basic information for our connection." The client acknowledges receipt of the information with an ACK packet, meaning, "I acknowledge receipt of the connection information." Each part of this three-way handshake must complete for a connection to occur. Your packet filtering ruleset must permit all parts of the handshake, as well as the actual data transmission, to occur. Allowing your server to receive incoming connection requests is useless if your packet filter rules do not permit transmitting that SYN-ACK.

In the early 1990s, packet filters checked each packet individually. If a packet matched a rule, it was allowed to pass. The system did not record what it had previously passed and had no idea if a packet was part of a legitimate transaction or not. For example, if a packet arrived marked SYN-ACK with a destination address inside the packet filter, the packet filter generally decided that the packet had to be the response to a packet it had previously approved. Such a packet *had* to be approved to complete the three-way handshake. As a result, intruders forged SYN-ACK packets and used them to circumvent seemingly secure devices. Since the packet filter didn't know who had previously sent a SYN packet, it couldn't reject illegitimate SYN-ACK packets. Once an intruder gets packets inside a network, he can usually trigger a response from a random device and start to worm his way in.

Modern packet filters use stateful inspection to counteract this problem. *Stateful inspection* means keeping track of every connection and its current condition. If an incoming SYN-ACK packet appears to be part of an ongoing connection, but nobody sent a corresponding SYN request, the packet is rejected. While this complicates the kernel, writing stateful inspection packet filter rules is easier than writing old-fashioned rules. The packet filter must

---

[1] I've learned to make one of my minions drive in and apologize.

track many, many possible states, so this is harder to program than it might seem—especially when you add in problems such as packet fragmentation, antispoofing, and so on.

If you've started to think, "Hey, packet filtering sounds like a firewall," you're right, to a point. The word *firewall* is applied to a variety of network protection devices. Some of these devices are very sophisticated; some lose intelligence contests to cinderblocks. These days, the term *firewall* is nothing more than marketing buzzword with very little concrete meeting. The word *firewall* is like the word *car*. Do you mean a rusty 1972 Gremlin with a six-horsepower engine and an exhaust system that emits enough fumes to breach the Kyoto Accords, or a shiny 2005 Chevy SSR hardtop convertible with a five-hundred-horsepower engine, a fancy tricolor paintjob, and the Stereo System of The Apocalypse? Both have their uses, but one is obviously designed for performance. While the Gremlins of firewalls might have their place, it's preferable to get the best you can afford.

Having said that, FreeBSD can be made as solid a firewall as you desire. Packet filtering is only the beginning: If you wander through */usr/ports/net* and */usr/ports/security*, you'll find a variety of application proxies that can let your FreeBSD system go up against Checkpoint or a PIX and come out on top, for tens of thousands of dollars less.

Configuring PF

Configure PF in */etc/pf.conf*. This file contains statements and rules whose formats vary with the features they configure. Not only is the rule order extremely important, but also the order in which features are configured. If you try to do stateful inspection before you reassemble fragmented packets, for example, connections will not work properly.

The default */etc/pf.conf* has the sample rules in the proper order, but if you're in the slightest danger of becoming confused, I suggest that you put large comment markers between the sections, in capital letters if necessary. (Use hash marks to comment *pf.conf*.) The features must be entered in this exact order:

1. Macros
2. Tables
3. Options
4. Packet normalization
5. Bandwidth management
6. Translation
7. Redirection
8. Packet filtering

Yes, PF does more than just filter packets. It's a general-purpose TCP/IP manipulation tool. We won't cover all of its features here; that's a topic for another book.

Macros

A macro lets you define variables to make writing and reading rules easier. For example, here are macros to define your network interface and your IP address:

```
interface="fxp0"
serveraddr="192.168.1.2"
```

Later in your rules, you may describe your network interface as $interface and your server's IP address as $serveraddr. This means that if you renumber your server or change your network card, making one change in your *pf.conf* fully updates your rules.

Tables and Options

PF can store long lists of addresses through tables. That's a more sophisticated use of PF than we're going to use, but you should know the capability exists.

Similarly, PF has a variety of options that control network connection timing, table sizes, and other internal settings. The default settings are generally adequate for normal (and most abnormal) use.

Packet Normalization

TCP/IP packets can be broken up in transit, and processing these shards of data increases system load and the amount of work your server must do to both serve the request and filter the packets. A system must reassemble these fragments before handing them on to your client software, while deciding what to do with any other random crud that arrives. PF refers to this reassembly as *scrubbing*. For example, to reassemble all fragments coming in your network interface, drop all fragments too small to possibly be legitimate, and otherwise sensibly sanitize your incoming data stream, use the following rule:

```
scrub in all on $interface
```

This affects all packets entering the computer.

While scrubbing seems like just a nice thing to have, it's actually quite important, since PF filters are based on whole packets. Fragments are much more difficult to filter and require special handling unless reassembled. Not scrubbing your traffic causes connectivity problems.

Bandwidth, Translation, and Redirection

We'll discuss bandwidth management a little later, but for now just recognize that PF can control how much traffic is allowed to go to a particular port or IP address.

Two critical parts of a firewall are Network Address Translation (NAT) and port redirection. PF has many functions to support NAT and port redirection, which we aren't going to cover because we aren't building firewalls.

Traffic Filtering Rules

Now for what we're really looking for. Traffic filtering rules have this general format:

```
❶pass ❷out ❸on $interface proto ❹{ tcp, udp } all ❺keep state
```

The first word is a keyword ❶ labeling what sort of rule this is. Each rule type has its own keywords. This particular rule is a packet filtering rule. We then learn which direction ❷ matching packets are traveling. This rule matches packets going out, or leaving the system. PF rules also label the interface ❸ matching packets apply to. The remainder of the rule line varies with the sort of rule. In this case, packets match only if they are leaving the system on the interface in the macro $interface and only if they match the rest of the rule.

Now define the traffic that matches the rule. Define traffic by network protocol, port, or TCP/IP flags ❹. This simple example matches all TCP and UDP traffic.

Finally, we tag this rule with keep state ❺. This tells PF to apply stateful inspection to this rule, allowing further traffic that is part of this connection.

Taken as a whole, this sample rule passes all TCP and UDP traffic leaving the system. This server can make any desired outbound connections. This is very typical for an Internet server.

Connections allowed into the system are only slightly more complicated. Here, we allow outsiders access to our web server:

```
pass in on $interface proto ❶tcp from ❷any to ❸($interface) ❹port 80
❺flags S/SA keep state
```

You can understand much of this from our earlier example. We're passing traffic in on our network interface, so long as it's TCP ❶. We accept traffic from any source ❷ so long as it's going to our server interface ❸. (The parentheses around the interface mean, "whatever IP address is on this interface," which is useful for DHCP hosts.) We're specifically allowing port 80 traffic ❹.

The only complicated part is the flags keyword ❺. This checks for specific TCP/IP flags. The letters in front of the following slash indicate the TCP flags that must be set in the packet, while the letters behind the slash indicate the flags you're checking. The S stands for SYN, and the A stands for ACK. This means, "Out of the SYN and ACK flags, only the SYN flag may be set." While this sounds scary, it really just means, "This rule only matches new incoming connections."

Adding the keep state to the end of this rule tells PF to keep track of this connection and allow the rest of the TCP/IP transaction to occur.

This whole rule means, "Allow new incoming connections to TCP port 80." Web servers normally run on port 80.

Complete PF Rule Sample

Here's a sample set of PF rules for protecting a small Internet server. Start from here and edit this to match your server's requirements.

```
   interface="em0"
   scrub in all
❶ block in on $interface
❷ #allow SSH and POP3 traffic from our network
   pass in on $interface proto tcp from 192.168.1.0/24 to $interface port 22
   pass in on $interface proto tcp from 192.168.1.0/24 to $interface port 110
❸ #allow SMTP (25), HTTP (80), and HTTPS (443) to the world
   pass in on $interface proto tcp from any to $interface port 25
   pass in on $interface proto tcp from any to $interface port 80
   pass in on $interface proto tcp from any to $interface port 443
❹ #allow the world to query our DNS server
   pass in on $interface proto tcp from any to $interface port 53
   pass in on $interface proto udp from any to $interface port 53
❺ #allow outgoing traffic
   pass out on $interface proto { tcp, udp } all
```

We start by defining a macro for our interface name, so that if we change network cards we won't need to rewrite all our rules. Then we scrub our incoming traffic. Both of these come straight from the examples earlier.

The first interesting thing we do is set a default deny policy with a block statement ❶. Everything not explicitly permitted is forbidden.

Our next two rules allow two particular protocols only from certain IP addresses ❷. We may use POP3 and SSH from 192.168.1.0/24, which is probably our office or management network.

We offer email, web, and HTTPS services ❸ to the world at large, using rules taken right from our earlier example but changing the port numbers. We also offer DNS services ❹ to the world, but have slightly different rules for it. DNS runs over both TCP and UDP. This is exactly the sort of thing you can learn only by reading big thick books on TCP/IP, or by scouring mailing list archives and pulling out your hair[2] trying to make it work. PF purists will certainly notice that these rules could be compressed and optimized, but for a small server this style is adequate. Finally, our server may initiate outgoing TCP and UDP connections on any port ❺.

---

[2] I recommend keeping your hair trimmed too short to pull for exactly this reason.

This simple policy defines basic rules for communicating with our server. While it's not perfect, it can cause an intruder a lot of headaches. Suppose someone breaks into your web server and starts a command prompt with root privileges listening on port 10000. Their hard work will be wasted, as your firewall rules don't allow incoming connections on that port.

Activating PF Rules

Manage PF with pfctl(8). If your rules have no errors, pfctl(8) runs silently; it only produces output when you have errors. As a firewall error can cause you much grief, it's best to check your rules before activating them. While a rule check only parses the file, checking for grammatical errors in the rules themselves, activating rules with grammatical errors either leaves your system unprotected, or locks you out, or both. Use the -n flag to check a file for problems, and -f to specify the PF rules file.

```
# pfctl -nf /etc/pf.conf
```

If you get errors, fix them and try again. If this runs silently, activate your new rules by removing the -n flag.

```
# pfctl -f /etc/pf.conf
```

Changing PF configuration is very quick. This means you can have several PF configurations for different times or situations. Perhaps you want to only allow access to certain services at certain parts of the day; you could schedule a pfctl run to install appropriate rules for those times. Or maybe you have separate rules for disaster situations and want to install a special ruleset when you lose your Internet connection. Using pfctl(8) makes all these simple.

If you want to see the rules currently running on your firewall, use pfctl -sr.

```
# pfctl -sr
❶ No ALTQ support in kernel
  ALTQ related functions disabled
  scrub in all ❷fragment reassemble
  block drop in on ❸em0 all
  pass in on wi0 inet proto tcp from 192.168.1.0/24 to 192.168.1.201 port = ssh
  flags S/SA keep state
  ...
```

PF starts off complaining that something called ALTQ isn't available ❶. We'll get to that in the next section. It then shows the rules you wrote, with additional defaults explicitly stated ❷. pfctl(8) expands the macros ❸ defined in the configuration. This lets you confirm that those rules remain in play weeks or months after you loaded them.

Finally, remove all rules from your running configuration with the `-Fa` (flush all) flags.

```
#  pfctl -Fa
```

You'll see PF systematically erase all rules, NAT configurations, and anything else in your configuration. Do not manually clear the configuration before loading a new configuration; just load the new rules file to erase the old rules.

PF is terribly powerful, very flexible, and can abuse TCP/IP in almost any way you like (and some ways you won't like). We've barely scratched the surface. Check out some of the resources listed on page 273 to explore PF in depth.

Public Key Encryption

Many server daemons rely upon public key encryption to ensure confidentiality, integrity, and authenticity of communications. Many different Internet services also use public key encryption. You need a basic grasp of public key encryption to run services like secure websites (https) and secure POP3 mail (pop3ssl). If you're already familiar with public key encryption, you can probably skip this section. If not, prepare for a highly compressed introduction to the topic.

Encryption systems use a key to transform messages between readable (cleartext) and encoded (ciphertext) versions. Although the words *cleartext* and *ciphertext* include the word *text*, they aren't restricted to text; they can also include graphics files, binaries, and any other data you might want to send.

All cryptosystems have three main purposes: integrity, confidentiality, and nonrepudiation. *Integrity* means that the message has not been tampered with. *Confidentiality* means that the message can only be read by the intended audience. And *nonrepudiation* means that the author cannot later claim that he or she didn't write that message.

Older ciphers relied on a single key, and anyone with the key could both encrypt and decrypt messages. You might have had to do a lot of work to transform the message, as with the Enigma engine that drove the Allies nuts during World War II, but the key made it possible. A typical example is any code that requires a key or password. The one-time message pads popular in spy novels are the ultimate single-key ciphers, impossible to break unless you have that exact key.

Unlike single-key ciphers, public key (or asymmetric) encryption systems use two keys: a private key and a public key. Messages are encrypted with one key and decrypted with the other, and digital signatures ensure the message is not tampered with en route. The math to explain this is really quite horrendous, but it does work—just accept that really, really large numbers behave really, really oddly. Generally. the key owner keeps the private key secret but hands the public key out to the world at large, for anyone's use.

The key owner uses the private key while everyone else uses the public key. The key owner can encrypt messages that anyone can read, while anyone in the public can send a message that only the key owner can read.

Public key cryptography fills our need for integrity, confidentiality, and nonrepudiation. If an author wants anyone to be able to read his message, while ensuring that it isn't tampered with, he can encrypt the message with his private key. Anyone with the public key (i.e., the world) can read the message, but tampering with the message renders it illegible.

Encrypting messages this way also ensures that the author of the message has the private key. If someone wants to send a message that can only be read by a particular person, he can encrypt the message with the desired audience's public key. Only the person with the matching private key can read the message.

This works well so long as the private key is kept private. Once the private key is stolen, lost, or made public, the security is lost. A careless person who has his private key stolen could even find others signing documents for him. Be careful with your keys, unless you want to learn that someone used your private key to order half a million dollars' worth of high-end graphics work-stations and have them overnighted to an abandoned-house maildrop in inner-city Detroit.[3]

Configuring OpenSSL

FreeBSD includes the OpenSSL toolkit for handling public key cryptography. While many programs use OpenSSL functionality, the system administrator doesn't need OpenSSL directly very often. While OpenSSL works fine out of the box, I find it worthwhile to set a few defaults to make my life easier down the road. Configure OpenSSL with the file */etc/ssl/openssl.cnf.* Almost all of the settings in this file are correct as they are, and you should not change them unless you are a cryptographer. The few things useful to change are the defaults for generating cryptographic signatures. Each default value is marked by the string _default. You'd be most interested in the following settings for common OpenSSL operations, shown with the default settings:

```
❶ countryName_default            = AU
❷ stateOrProvinceName_default    = Some-State
❸ O.organizationName_default     = Internet Widgits Pty Ltd
```

The countryName_default ❶ is the two-letter code for your nation—in my case, US. The stateOrProvinceName_default ❷ is the name of your local state and can be of any length. I would set this to Michigan. O.organizationName_default ❸ is your company name. If I'm buying a signed certificate, I would put the same thing here that I want to appear on the certificate. If I'm just testing how programs work with SSL and don't have a real company name, I might use the name of the company I work for or something that I make up.

---

[3] This really happened. And before you ask, no, I wasn't the recipient! A friend gave me my high-end graphics workstations. Really.

The following values do not show up in *openssl.cnf*, but if you set them, they appear as defaults in the OpenSSL command prompts. I find these useful, even though they change more frequently than the previous defaults—they remind me of the correct format of these answers, if nothing else.

❶	localityName_default	= Detroit
❷	organizationalUnitName_default	= Authorial Division
❸	commonName_default	= www.absolutefreebsd.com
❹	emailAddress_default	= mwlucas@absolutefreebsd.com

The localityName_default ❶ is the name of your city. The organizationalUnitName_default ❷ is the part of your company this certificate is for. One of the most commonly misunderstood values in OpenSSL, commonName_default ❸ is the hostname of the machine this certificate is for, as it appears in reverse DNS (see Chapter 14). Finally, emailAddress_default ❹ is the email address of the site administrator.

These values all show up in prompts in the OpenSSL command as default choices and might save you annoyance later.

Certificates

One interesting thing about public key encryption is that the author and the audience don't have to be people. They can be programs. Secure Shell (SSH) and the Secure Sockets Layer (SSL) are two different ways programs can communicate without fear of intruders listening in. Public key cryptography is a major component of the *digital certificates* used by secure websites and secure mail services. When you open Firefox to buy something online, you might not realize that the browser is frantically encrypting and decrypting web pages. This is why your computer might complain about "invalid certificates"; someone's public key has either expired or the certificate is self-signed.

Many companies, such as VeriSign, provide a public key signing service. These companies are called *Certificate Authorities (CAs)*. Other companies that need a certificate signed provide proof of their identity, such as corporate papers and business records, and those public key signing companies sign the applicant's certificate with their CA certificate. By signing the certificate, the Certificate Authority says, "I have inspected this person's credentials and he, she, or it has proven their identity to my satisfaction." They're not guaranteeing anything else, however. A SSL certificate owner can use the certificate to run a website that sells fraudulent or dangerous products, or use it to encrypt a ransom note. Signed SSL certificates guarantee certain types of technical security, not personal integrity or even unilateral technical security. Certificates do not magically apply security patches for you.

Web browsers and other certificate-using software include certificates for the major CAs. When the browser receives a certificate signed by a Certificate Authority, it recognizes the certificate as legitimate. Essentially the web browser says, "I trust the Certificate Authority, and the Certificate Authority trusts this company, so I will trust the company." So long as you trust the CA, everything works.

Most CAs are big companies, but CACert is a grassroots effort to provide free SSL certificates for everyone who can verify their identity. CACert is becoming more and more accepted, and while its root certificate is not in Internet Explorer, I expect to see it in Mozilla Firefox before long.

Using a certificate that is not signed by a Certificate Authority is perfectly fine for testing. It might also suffice for applications within a company, where you can install the certificate in the client web browser or tell your users to trust the certificate. We'll look at both ways.

Both uses of the certificate require a host key.

SSL Host Key

Both signed and self-signed certificates require a private key for the host. The host key is just a carefully crafted random number. The following command creates a 1,024-bit host key and places it in the file *host.key*:

```
# openssl genrsa 1024 > host.key
```

You'll see a statement that OpenSSL is creating a host key, and dots crossing the screen as key generation proceeds. In only a few seconds, you'll have a file containing a key. The key is a plaintext file that contains the words BEGIN RSA PRIVATE KEY and a bunch of random characters.

Protect your host key! Make it owned by root and readable only by root. Once you place your certificate in production, anyone who has that key can use it to eavesdrop on your private communications.

```
# chown root host.key
# chmod 400 host.key
```

Place this host key in a directory with the same permissions that we placed on the key file itself.

Create a Certificate Request

You need a certificate request for either a signed or self-signed certificate. We don't do much with OpenSSL so we won't dissect this command. Go to the directory with your host key and enter this verbatim:

```
# openssl req -new -key host.key -out csr.pem
```

In response you'll see instructions and then a series of questions. By hitting ENTER you'll take the default answers. If you've configured OpenSSL, the default answers are correct.

```
❶ Country Name (2 letter code) [US]:
❷ State or Province Name (full name) [Michigan]:
❸ Locality Name (eg, city) [Detroit]:
❹ Organization Name (eg, company) [Absolute FreeBSD]:
❺ Organizational Unit Name (eg, section) [Authorial Division]:
❻ Common Name (eg, YOUR name) [www.absolutefreebsd.com]:
❼ Email Address [mwlucas@absolutefreebsd.com]:
```

The two-letter code for the country ❶ is defined in the ISO 3166 standard, so a quick web search will find this for you. If you don't know the state ❷ and city ❸ you live in, ask someone who occasionally leaves the server room. The organization name ❹ is probably your company, and you list the department or division name ❺ as well. If you don't have a company, list your family name or some other way to uniquely identify yourself, and for a self-signed certificate you can list anything you want. Different CAs have different standards for noncorporate entities, so check the CA's instructions.

The common name ❻ is frequently misunderstood. It is not your name, it is the name of the server as shown in reverse DNS. You must have a server name here, or the request will be useless.

I suggest using a generic email address ❼ rather than an individual's email address. In this case I *am* Absolute FreeBSD, whatever that is. You don't want your certificates tied to an individual who might leave the company for whatever reason.

```
Please enter the following 'extra' attributes
to be sent with your certificate request
❶ A challenge password []:
❷ An optional company name []:
```

The challenge password ❶ is also known as a *passphrase*. Again, keep this secret because anyone with the passphrase can use your certificate. Use of a certificate passphrase is optional, however. If you use one, you must type it when your server starts. That means that if your web server crashes, the website will not work until someone enters the passphrase. While passphrase use is highly desirable, this might be unacceptable. Hit ENTER to use a blank passphrase.

You've already entered quite a few company names, so a third ❷ is probably unnecessary.

Once you return to a command prompt, you'll see a file *csr.pem* in the current directory. It looks much like your host key, except that the top line says BEGIN CERTIFICATE REQUEST instead of BEGIN RSA PRIVATE KEY.

Get a Signed Certificate

Submit *csr.pem* to your Certificate Authority, who will return a file that looks much like one of the preceding files. Save that to a file called *signature.pem* and run the following commands:

```
# cp csr.pem cert.pem
# cat signature.pem >> cert.pem
```

This copies the host key to a certificate file and then attaches the signature to the certificate. This is a complete signed certificate. This signed certificate is good for any SSL service, including web pages, pop3ssl, or any other SSL-capable daemon.

Sign a Certificate Yourself

A self-signed certificate is technically identical to a signed certificate, but it is not submitted to a Certificate Authority. Instead, you provide the signature yourself. Most customers won't accept a self-signed certificate on a production service, but it's perfectly suitable for testing. To sign your own CSR, run the following:

```
# openssl x509 -req -days ❶365 -in csr.pem -signkey host.key  -out
❷selfsigned.crt
Signature ok
subject=/C=US/ST=Michigan/L=Detroit/O=Absolute FreeBSD/OU=Authorial Division/
CN=www.absolutefreebsd.com/emailAddress=mwlucas@absolutefreebsd.com
Getting Private key
#
```

That's it! You now have a self-signed certificate good for 365 days ❶ in the file *selfsigned.crt* ❷. You can use this key exactly like a signed certificate, so long as you're willing to ignore the warnings your application displays.

If you sign your own certificates, client software generates warnings that the "certificate signer is unknown." This is expected—after all, people outside my office have no idea who Michael W. Lucas is, or why he's signing web certificates. VeriSign and other CAs are trusted. I'm trusted by the people who know me,[4] but not trusted by the world at large. For this reason, don't use self-signed certificates anywhere the public will see it because the warnings will confuse, annoy, or even scare them away. Spend a hundred dollars or so and have a real CA sign your production certificates.

SSL Trick: Connecting to SSL-Protected Ports

I said we wouldn't do much with OpenSSL, and that's correct. There's one facility the software offers that's too useful to pass up, however, and once you know it you'll use this one trick at least once a month and be glad you have it.

Throughout this book we test network services by using telnet(1) to connect to the daemon running on that port and issuing commands. This works well for plaintext services such as SMTP, POP3, and HTTP. It doesn't work for encrypted services such as HTTPS. You need a program to manage the encryption for you when you connect to these services. OpenSSL includes the `openssl s_client` command, which is intended for exactly this sort of client debugging. While you'll see a lot of cryptographic information, you'll also get the ability to issue plaintext commands to the daemon and

---

[4] Well, most of them, anyway. Quite a few. A few, at least. Oh, never mind.

view its responses. Use the command openssl s_client -connect with a hostname and port number, separated by a colon. Here, we connect to the secure web server at *www.absolutefreebsd.com*:

```
# openssl s_client -connect www.absolutefreebsd.com:443
CONNECTED(00000003) depth=1 /O=VeriSign Trust Network/OU=VeriSign, Inc./
OU=VeriSign International Server CA - Class 3/OU=www.verisign.com/CPS
Incorp.by Ref.
...
```

You'll see lots of stuff about chains of trust and limitations of liability, as well as lines and lines of the random-looking digital certificate. After all that, however, you'll see a blank line with no command prompt. You're speaking directly to the server daemon. As this is a web server, let's try a HTTP command:

```
GET /
```

The system responds with:

```
Object Moved
This document may be found <a href="https://www.nostarch.com/">here</
a>read:errno=0
```

This lets you test encrypted network services just as easily as you can test unencrypted services.

Some of you are probably wondering why we encrypt the service if it's so easy to talk to the encrypted service. The encryption does not protect the daemon; it protects the data stream between the client and the server. SSL encryption prevents someone from eavesdropping your network conversation in transit—it does not protect either the server or the client. SSL cannot save you if someone breaks into your desktop.

From this point on, I'll assume that you understand this OpenSSL command and what happens when we use it.

Jails

One of Unix's oldest security mechanisms is the idea of a changed root, or *chroot*, which confines a user or program to a subsection of the filesystem to protect other users and the rest of the filesystem. chroot is useful for services such as named(8), but isn't so helpful for complicated programs that expect to have wide access to the system. chrooting your web or email server requires a great deal of work and often involves adding many programs to the chroot. If you're a web hosting company, your clients certainly won't like being chrooted!

What's worse, clients who understand the power of Unix-like systems frequently make requests to complicate things further. They want to install software or reconfigure the web server to enable the latest nifty Apache module. In short, they want root access, and under most Unix systems you can't hand your root access willy-nilly to clients on a multi-user server.

Unless, of course, you're on FreeBSD. FreeBSD developers faced this problem long ago and solved it by dramatically improving the chroot facility. They solved it so well that you can build a lightweight virtual server on FreeBSD and isolate that server from the rest of your system. This is called a *jail*.

Think of a jail as something like a client-server environment. The main server is the host system, and each jailed system is a client. Changes made to the host can be reflected across all systems, but changes to the jail can't affect the main system (unless you allow your jails to fill up the disk drive or some such thing).

To the user, the jail looks like a nearly complete FreeBSD system, missing only a few device nodes. The user can have root access and install whatever software he likes without interfering with other clients. All processes running in the jail are restricted to the jail environment, and the kernel does not give them access to any information outside their jail. The jail filesystem does not know about files or filesystems outside the jail. Since no program or process in the jail knows anything about anything outside the jail, and cannot read or write anything outside the jail, the user is locked in. Moreover, if the jail is hacked, the intruder can't break out of the jail either. This helps secure your system while meeting the client's needs.

On modern hardware with inexpensive (but not cheap!) disks and gigabytes of RAM, a single FreeBSD system can host dozens of jailed web servers. From a sales perspective, a jailed machine is a good compromise between a virtual domain on a shared server and a private dedicated server.

Jail Host Server Setup

First, set up your host server to properly support jails. Jails do impose a number of special requirements on a server, the most annoying of which is that daemons cannot bind to all available IP addresses.

Each jail is tied to a particular IP address and is defined by that IP address. You must add an IP alias to your network card for your jail, as discussed in Chapter 6.

The jail must have exclusive access to that IP address; nothing on the host system can use it. That IP is the only network address the jail can have.[5] If your host server has a daemon that binds to all available IP addresses on the system, that daemon will prevent a jail from starting. Look at your server's sockstat(1) output; any entries where the local address includes an asterisk indicates a daemon listening on all available IP addresses.

---

[5] As of this writing, the FreeBSD Foundation is supporting work to fully virtualize the IP stack for use in jails. This will allow a jail to access more than a single IP, as well as enjoy a much more complete access to the TCP/IP stack, but might or might not be available by the time you read this.

```
# sockstat -4
...
root      inetd     895    5    tcp4   ❶*:21                *:*
root      sshd      822    4    tcp4   ❷*:22                *:*
root      syslogd   601    7    udp4   ❸*:514               *:*
...
```

In this sample, we see that inetd has bound to all IP addresses on port 21 ❶, sshd has bound to all addresses on port 22 ❷, and syslogd has bound to all addresses on port 514 ❸. We must configure all of these services to only attach to the main server IP.

The easiest way to configure your jail server properly is to decide that your main server is only a jail host and provides no other services. You need sendmail, named, and other services? No problem! Set up a services jail that contains these daemons. Not only is it easier than properly reconfiguring all those programs, but it also provides an additional layer of security for your other jails. An intrusion on your host system automatically grants the intruder access to all of your jails, while an intrusion on a single jail confines the intruder to that single jail.

You don't have to configure jailed programs to attach to only a single IP address. The jailed process only has access to a single IP, so telling a daemon to attach to all available IP addresses works just as expected.

Here are some common problematic daemons on host servers. In all of these examples, we'll assume that the jail host has an IP address of 192.168.1.1.

syslogd

The system logger opens a socket so that it can send log messages, even if it's not receiving any logs. Use the -b option to bind syslogd(8) to a particular IP address with a *rc.conf* entry:

```
syslogd_flags="-b 192.168.1.1"
```

To keep syslogd from opening even that sending socket, use -ss. You cannot log remotely if you do that, however. We'll discuss syslogd(8) in detail in Chapter 19.

inetd

Generally speaking, it's best to run inetd from within a jail rather than on the host server. inetd(8) can be restricted to a single address with the -a flag, much like the following in *rc.conf*:

```
inetd_flags="-wW -C 60 -a 192.168.1.1"
```

Note that inetd usually runs with default flags specified in */etc/defaults/rc.conf*. My release of FreeBSD defaults to running inetd with the flags -wW -C 60. Instead of just binding inetd to a single address, I added my flags to the default flags.

sshd

The option ListenAddress in */etc/sshd/sshd_config* tells sshd(8) which address to attach to.

```
ListenAddress 192.168.1.1
```

Providing SSH on a jail host is actually very sensible; if the only service your jail host offers is sshd(8), you've done well.

NFS

NFS programs such as rpcbind(8) and nfsd(8) bind to all IP addresses on a system, and changing this behavior is difficult. Don't run an NFS server on your jail host. You can use NFS in your jails, however. If you must combine NFS and jail, don't use the main host but configure a jail to export your NFS mounts.

Jail and the Kernel

Now that our network is ready to host a jail, let's look at the kernel. The jail's default settings are adequate for jails, but the sysadmin has the ability to tweak certain settings. In most cases, changing these settings causes nothing but grief.

The jail system has its own sysctl tree, security.jail. You can only change this tree from the host system, not from within a jail, and changes to these sysctls affect all jails running on the host.

security.jail.set_hostname_allowed

By default, the root user in a jail can set the jail's local hostname. Since programs running a jail use the hostname to communicate, changing the jailed hostname can confuse the host administrator. Change this sysctl from 1 to 0 to disable changing the hostname.

security.jail.socket_unixiproute_only

A jail defaults to communicating via IP and local Unix sockets. While it isn't likely that a jailed user might want to use, say, IPX, it is theoretically possible. The jail system only supports IP, however, so allowing the use of other protocols might let jailed programs "leak" out of the jail somehow. The jail system only virtualizes IP, not IPX or other network protocols, so any non-IP protocols you use are accessible in all jails. This access is probably harmless, but it's unwise to assume that you're smarter than every malicious intruder out there. The default of 1 restricts the system to IP only; set this to 0 to allow use of any network protocol other than IP.

security.jail.sysvipc_allowed

System V IPC is a Unix standard for allowing interprocess communication via shared memory. Basically, related programs can use one chunk of memory to store information. Many database programs require IPC. The jail system does not build separate areas of memory for each jail. Enabling IPC allows information to leak between jails. Compromising a system through this requires a moderately skilled attacker. The default value of 0 disallows IPC, setting this to 1 enables it.

security.jail.enforce_statfs

This controls jailed users' ability to see information on filesystems. By default (security.jail.enforce_statfs=2), jailed programs can only see mount points within the jail and the path to the root directory is trimmed so that the jailed user doesn't even see where on the disk his jail is. If you set this to 1, the user can only see the mount points within the jail but he can see where his jail is on the host disk. If you set this to 0, the jailed user can see all mounts points on the system. There's very rarely a good reason to change this.

security.jail.allow_raw_sockets

Raw sockets allow direct access to the network subsystem. If you do not completely trust your jailed users or programs, do not allow them access to raw sockets. Programs such as ping and traceroute use TCP/IP raw sockets, so some customers like this feature. From a security standpoint, however, there's very little reason to allow this and many reasons not to. The default of 0 prevents raw socket access, but set this to 1 to allow it.

security.jail.chflags_allowed

By default, jailed users cannot use filesystem flags and chflags(1) (see Chapter 7). Remember, many of these flags cannot be cleared without rebooting the jail into single-user mode. Your customers can get themselves into trouble with chflags(1), but only you can get them out of trouble. This is a recipe for customer support headaches. Change this from 0 to 1 to allow chflags.

security.jail.jailed

This read-only value tells you if you're running sysctl(8) from the host server (0) or from within a jail (1).

security.jail.list

On the host system, this displays a list of all active jails.

Client Setup

Decide where you want to put your jails. I recommend using a separate partition, so that if your customers use up all their disk space they don't affect your host system. Some admins just keep an eye on their users and raise the cost for disk hogs. File-backed partitions (see Chapter 8) are an easy way to create partitions for jails without slicing up your disks beyond recognition. In this example, we'll install our first jail in */var/jail/jail1*.

The basic process for installing a jail is the same as used for upgrading FreeBSD: Build system binaries from source, then install them. With a jail, you just install those binaries in a different location. If you've upgraded your system, you've already built the programs, but if not go to */usr/src* and run:

```
# make buildworld
```

Once you have built the system, you just install it. Use the DESTDIR option to choose a different installation directory. We need to use an extra step to install our */etc* and */var* directories, however. (These steps are not needed in an upgrade, as your host system already has those directory trees.)

```
# make installworld DESTDIR=/var/jail/jail1
# make distribution DESTDIR=/var/jail/jail1
# mount -t devfs devfs /var/jail/jail1/dev
```

The last entry installs device nodes in your jail. While not strictly necessary, many programs expect to have basic devices such as terminals, random number generators, and so on. You'll want devfs in your jail at least in your basic setup stage.

REDUCING JAIL SPACE

If you search the Internet you'll find many different ways to reduce the amount of disk space a jail takes. Union mounts and NFS can considerably reduce your disk space requirements, but the more you use clever tricks, the less support you'll get from the FreeBSD user community.

Decorating Your Cell: In-Jail Setup

At this point your jail is ready to boot for the first time. You shouldn't confuse *boot for the first time* with *ready for use*, however, because you still have a few tasks to complete from within the jail itself. Use the jail(8) command to start a jail, like this:

```
# jail <path to jail> <jail hostname> <jail IP> <command>
```

For example, our first jail is in the directory */var/jails/jail1*. I'm assigning it a hostname of *jail.absolutefreebsd.com* and an IP address of 192.168.1.4. I'd like to jail a command prompt:

```
# jail /var/jails/jail1 jail.absolutefreebsd.com 192.168.1.4 /bin/sh
```

The earliest point where a system can give you a command prompt is single-user mode. While this isn't exactly a single-user mode jail, no programs other than */bin/sh* are running within the jail.

If you look around you'll see that you're in a minimal FreeBSD install. You'll find all the user programs you'd expect from a basic FreeBSD system, but nothing else: You have no user accounts, no root password, no network daemons, and absolutely nothing optional. Before you use your jail, it's best to install all of these.

Create /etc/fstab

Many programs expect to find *ature/fstab* and complain if it's not there. This is perfectly sensible in a real server, but */etc/fstab* is useless on a jailed machine. It's best to create an empty file just to shut up complaining programs, however.

```
# touch /etc/fstab
```

Configure DNS Resolution

You'll probably want to configure a DNS server in */etc/resolv.conf*. You can probably copy */etc/resolv.conf* from your host system into the jail. Note that you must do this from the host system, as your jail can't access the host's */etc*.

sendmail

You don't have to configure sendmail(8) in the jail, at least not yet, but you'll get warnings about an out-of-date aliases database. Run newaliases(8) to silence those warnings.

/etc/rc.conf

Add the following to the jail's */etc/rc.conf*:

```
network_interfaces=""
sshd_enable="YES"
```

You cannot configure your interface from within a jail, but the startup scripts generally expect that you'll try. Tell FreeBSD not to bother, as you cannot configure the interface anyway.

You can only access the jail over the network, so you need SSH.

Root Password and User Account

Your jail does not yet have a root password. Set one with passwd(1). You'll also need a user account. Run adduser(8) to add at least one user.

Other Setup

If you like, you can set the time zone with tzsetup(8), install add-on packages, copy your personal files to your home directory, and so on, but none of that is necessary at this point. Exit the shell, and your jail shuts down.

Jail and /etc/rc.conf

Now that the jail is ready to run, tell the host system about it. The simplest way to manage a jail is with */etc/rc.conf* settings. Here are some example settings for use with jails:

```
❶ jail_enable="YES"
❷ jail_list="jail1 jail2 jail3"
```

These two options control generic jail settings. By setting `jail_enable` to YES ❶, you tell the system startup scripts to look for and process additional jail settings. The `jail_list` ❷ contains a list of all the jails on your system, separated by spaces. By setting both of these, you can use the FreeBSD startup system to manage your jails. Each jail also has its own set of rc variables, which tell the system where each jail lies and how to configure it.

```
❶ jail_jail1_rootdir="/var/jails/jail1"
❷ jail_jail1_hostname="jail.absolutefreebsd.com"
❸ jail_jail1_ip="192.168.1.4"
❹ jail_jail1_devfs_enable="YES"
❺ jail_jail1_devfs_ruleset="devfsrules_jail"
```

These entries configure one individual jail. Add similar lines for each additional jail you build, substituting the name of that jail for `jail1` in each variable. Each jail must have a root directory ❶, a hostname ❷, and an IP address ❸.

Many programs complain or fail if they cannot find expected device nodes in */dev*. Some device nodes make sense for a jail, such as virtual terminals and the random number generator. Some do not, such as the disk devices and network interfaces. You can provide device nodes via devfs ❹, but then apply rules ❺ so that users in the jail can only access the appropriate device nodes. We talked about devfs in Chapter 8. FreeBSD includes a jail-appropriate set of rules for jailed devfs as `devfsrules_jail` in */etc/defaults/devfs.rules*.

You can find options for other jail features in */etc/defaults/rc.conf*, but these cover basic jail operations.

Jail Startup and Shutdown

With the above *rc.conf* settings, you can use */etc/rc.d/jail* to manage your jails, both en masse and on a jail-by-jail basis. To start all of your jails, just run:

```
# /etc/rc.d/jail start
```

You can start a single jail by giving its name as an argument:

```
# /etc/rc.d/jail start jail1
```

Once you start your jail, use SSH and log in. Now you can add packages, configure the local system, and in general play with your "new" FreeBSD box. Play around a little, try to break out of the jail. Try to go to a directory you know exists on the system, but is outside the jail directory. Even as root, from within a jail you cannot view or access processes running on the host system. Even with powerful tools like Perl and cc(1) fully available, letting you build any tools you like, you cannot disrupt the host system. You could even csup in the jail and rebuild world, although this is *not* a good idea. Remember, your kernel and userland must be in sync; a jailed userland whose versions don't match those of the running kernel will not crash the host, but it certainly won't behave as expected!

Managing Jails

Jails do complicate process management. If you're logged in to a jail host server, you can see all the processes in all your jails. Which processes are running in your server, and which belong in a jail?

Running ps -ax on the host system shows all processes on the system, including all the jailed processes. A STAT of J means that the process is running in a jail. If you have only a few jails, each with a dedicated purpose, you might successfully guess whose process this is. For example, if you see a jailed named(8) process, and you have only one jailed nameserver, it's a good bet that it's where that process is running. Most of the time, however, we're not that lucky. That's where two special tools come in, jls(8) and jexec(8).

jls

The jls(8) program lists all jails running on the system.

```
# jls
  JID  IP Address      Hostname                    Path
 ❶1 ❷192.168.1.4   ❸jail.absolutefreebsd.com   ❹/var/jails/jail1
   2  192.168.1.5     jail2.blackhelicopters.org   /var/jails/jail2
...
```

Each jail has a unique Jail ID, or JID ❶. The *JID* is much like a process ID; while we know that each jail has one, the exact JID issued to a jail varies. If you stop a jail and start it again, it will have a different JID. jls(8) also lists the IP address ❷, hostname ❸, and root directory ❹ of the jail.

jexec

jexec(8) allows the jail host administrator to execute commands within any of the jails running on the system without going to all the trouble of logging into the jail. This helps give the jail owner a sense of privacy—after all, you don't know their root password and don't even need a logon to their system. You must know the jail's JID to use jexec on a jail. To discover which processes run on a jailed system, just run `ps -ax` from within the jail. For example, suppose our first jail, *jail.absolutefreebsd.com*, has a jail ID of 1. To execute `ps -ax` within the jail, run:

```
# jexec 1 ps -ax
```

You'll see a list of processes running on the jailed system just as if you logged in.

jexec(8) lets you run any command on the client jails from the main host. You can install software, restart daemons, stop runaway processes, or change user passwords.

Processes and procfs

Remember back in Chapter 8, when I said not to use procfs? A jail host is the only exception I know to that rule. While procfs has a spotty security history, your jail server should have no services on it and no untrusted users. The only use I know of for the process filesystem is identifying a jail from a process ID. If you see a database program that has somehow started using too much memory or CPU, and you must identify it in a hurry, check its PID under */proc* to identify its jail.

/proc contains a directory for each running process. To determine which jail a process is held in, find the directory for its process ID and check therein for a file named *status*. The last word in the *status* file is the hostname of the jail the process is confined in. If the process is not jailed, the last word is a hyphen.

Jail Shutdown

When you shut down the host server, the various client jails shut down as well. Shutting down a jail without shutting down the host is pretty simple. Stop all the jails or a single jail with the `/etc/rc.d/jail stop` command. Here, we stop jail1:

```
# /etc/rc.d/jail stop jail1
```

This runs the standard shutdown process within the jail and exits. The jail disappears from jls(8).

Programs such as shutdown(8) and reboot(8) are useless for shutting down a jail. Their main tasks are to sync and unmount disks, disconnect the network, and so on. A virtual machine does not have these responsibilities.

What's Wrong with Jails

Jails give you huge amounts of flexibility on very little hardware. A small 80GB disk can support a dozen or more jails easily when using textbook methods, and if you look around for the Secret Ninja Jail Techniques, you can triple that. Why not run all of your services on jailed servers and only use the "real" machine as a jail host?

Maintenance, that's why.

With all those jails, you have a greatly increased maintenance load for that one machine. If you have two dozen jailed web servers on one machine, and an Apache security problem appears, you must patch two dozen jailed web servers. With planning, scripting, and practice this isn't an insurmountable problem, but many sysadmins are weak at planning and practice.[6] You can do it, but you must understand the commitment you're making when deploying flocks of jails.

On the other hand, many companies have successfully deployed hundreds of jails and manage them all automatically. Jails solve many problems even as they create others and give you the luxury of choosing your headaches.

Preparing for Intrusions with mtree(1)

One of the worst things to happen to a sysadmin is something that makes him think that his system could have been penetrated. If you find mysterious files in */tmp*, or extra commands in */usr/local/sbin*, or if things "just don't feel right," you'll be left wondering if someone has compromised your system. The worst thing about this feeling is that there's no way to prove it hasn't happened. A skilled attacker can replace system binaries with his own customized versions, so that his actions are never logged and your attempts to find him will fail. Having Sherlock Holmes examine your server with a magnifying glass is useless when the magnifying glass has been provided by the criminal and includes the special criminal-cloaking feature! People have even hijacked the system compiler so that freshly built binaries include the hijacker's backdoor.[7] What makes matters worse is that computers do weird things all the time. Operating systems are terribly complicated, and applications are worse. Maybe that weird file in */tmp* is something your text editor barfed up when you hit the keys too fast, or perhaps it's a leftover from a sloppy intruder.

The *only* way to recover a penetrated system is to reinstall it from scratch, restore the data from backup, and hope that the security hole that led to the penetration is fixed. That's a thin hope, and doubt is so easy to acquire that many system administrators eventually stop caring or lie to themselves rather than live with the constant worry.

Most intruders change files that already exist on the system. FreeBSD's mtree(1) can record the permissions, size, dates, and cryptographic checksums of files on your system. If you record these characteristics when your system is freshly installed, you have a record of what those files look like intact. When an intruder changes those files, a comparison will point out the difference. When you have the feeling you've been hacked, you can check that same information on the existing files and see if any have changed.

---

[6] We often script well enough to work around the planning and practice weaknesses.

[7] I would say *intruder* here except that the person in question was Ken Thompson, one of the creators of Unix and C. He had a miraculous ability to log into any Unix system, anywhere in the world, including systems developed years after he stopped working on Unix. See *http://www.acm.org/classics/sep95*.

Running mtree(1)

The following command runs mtree(1) across your root partition and stores md5 and sha1 cryptographic checksums, placing them in a file for later analysis:

```
# mtree ❶-x ❷-ic ❸-K cksum ❹-K md5digest ❺-K sha256digest ❻-p / ❼-X /
home/mwlucas/mtree-exclude > ❽/tmp/mtree.out
```

While you can use mtree(1) across the entire server, most people use -x ❶ to run it once per partition. You don't want to record checksums on filesystems that change frequently, such as the database partition on your database server. The -ic flag ❷ tells mtree to print its results to the screen, with each subsequent layer in the filesystem indented. This format matches the system mtree files in */etc/mtree*. The -K flag accepts several optional keywords; in this case we want to generate standard checksums ❸, md5 checksums ❹, and sha1 checksums ❺. The -p flag ❻ tells mtree which partition to check. Almost every partition has files or directories that change on a regular basis and that you therefore don't want to record checksums for. Use -X ❼ to specify a file containing a list of paths not to match. Finally, redirect the output of this command to the file */tmp/mtree.out* ❽.

The exclusion file can be tricky. Normally, I don't want to audit the contents of */tmp* or */var/tmp*. I can use the same file to exclude both directories. Having an exclusion file with this single line excludes the *tmp* directory in the root of the filesystem being checked:

```
./tmp
```

Generally speaking, an intruder will want to replace files on the root or */usr* partition. Record checksums for both partitions. If your server is a web server, the intruder might also target any CGI or PHP applications on your system.

mtree(1) Output: The Spec File

mtree(1)'s output is known as a specification, or *spec*. While this specification was originally intended for use in installing software, we're using it to verify a software install. Your spec starts with comments showing the user who ran the command, the machine the command ran on, the filesystem analyzed, and the date. The first real entry in the spec sets the defaults for the install we're not running, and begins with /set.

```
/set type=file uid=0 gid=0 mode=0755 nlink=1 flags=none
```

mtree(1) has picked these settings as defaults based on its analysis of the files in the partition. The default filesystem object is a file, owned by UID 0 and GID 0, with permissions of 0755, with one hard link and no filesystem flags. After that, every file and directory on the system has a separate entry. Here's the entry for the root directory:

---

❶.   ❷type=dir ❸nlink=24 ❹size=512 ❺time=1171639839.0

This file is the dot (.) ❶, or *the directory we're in right now*. It is a directory ❷, and has 24 hard links ❸ to it. The size of the directory is 512 bytes ❹, and it was modified 1,171,639,839.0 seconds into Unix epochal time ❺. The Unix epoch began January 1, 1970.

> ## EPOCHAL SECONDS AND REAL DATES
>
> Don't feel like counting seconds since the epoch began? To convert epochal seconds into normal dates, run date -r seconds. Cut off the .0 at the end of mtree's time, however; date(1) only likes whole seconds.

In some ways the entry for the directory is rather boring. An intruder can't realistically replace the directory itself, after all! Here's an entry for an actual file in the root directory.

.cshrc   mode=0644 nlink=2 size=801 time=1141972532.0 \
       ❶cksum=3359466860 ❷md5digest=67b0d2664a9c2fcccb517e3069ca8125 \
       ❸sha256digest=6624a34d5e068cca1f64142e077b8c64869dc2207bf7ff4f292a7f1f3e237b4

We see the filename and the same mode, link, size, and time information, but we have a few new entries: the checksum ❶, the md5 checksum ❷, and the sha256 checksum ❸. These cryptographic checksums are computed from the contents of the file. While it is theoretically possible for an intruder to craft a file that matches a particular checksum, and while cryptographers are constantly trying to find practical ways to create files that match arbitrary md5 and sha256 checksums, it's extremely unlikely that an intruder can create a fake file that matches all three different checksums, contains his backdoor, and still functions well enough that the system owner won't immediately notice a problem. By the time this happens, we will have additional checksum algorithms resistant to those methods and will switch to them.

Saving the Spec File

The spec file contains the information needed to verify the integrity of your system after a suspected intrusion. Leaving the spec file on the server you want to verify means that an intruder can edit the file and conceal his wrongdoing. You must not save the file on the system itself! Now and then someone will suggest that you checksum the mtree spec file but keep it on the server. That's not useful; if someone tampers with the mtree file and the checksum, how would you know? Or worse—if someone tampered with the spec file and you caught it, you couldn't tell what change had been made!

Copy your spec file to a safe location, preferably on an offline media such as a floppy disk or CD.

Reacting to an Intrusion

When something raises your suspicions and you begin to think that you might have suffered an intrusion, create a new mtree spec file and compare it with the one you previously created. mtree(1) can specifically check for differences between spec files if you specify two files on the command line. This generates thousands of lines of output, so be sure to redirect it to a file for easier analysis.

```
# mtree -f savedspec -f newspec > mtree.differences
```

Files that have not changed appear on a single line, like this:

```
sbin/conscontrol file
```

The file *sbin/conscontrol* hasn't changed between the two files. On the other hand, here we have two lines for the file *sbin/devd*:

```
❶sbin/devd file cksum=3950957068 size=328396 md5digest=14d0cc1dbe
a86c69ebd4af1dec2312d0 sha1digest=7acd1bdf46581b1d6a3231ca62b2c47e6e1dcf07
❷sbin/devd file cksum=4141842183 size=328428 md5digest=5ab5ec4213
03ca770ac2cccd546bcf11 sha1digest=51f5fbc24d47f11115474714040b8cce0eb9b6c9
```

Compare the old ❶ and new ❷ checksums for the file *sbin/devd*, as well as the sizes. None of them match. Something changed the devd(8) binary. Don't hit the panic button yet, but start asking your fellow system administrators pointed, hard questions. If you can't get a good answer as to why this binary changed, you might look for your backup tapes.

Monitoring System Security

So, you think your server is secure. Maybe it is, for now.

Unfortunately, there's a class of intruders with nothing better to do than to keep up on the latest security holes and try them out on systems they think might be vulnerable. Even if you read *FreeBSD-security* religiously and apply every single patch, you still might get hacked one day. While there's no way to be absolutely sure you haven't been hacked, the following hints will help you find out when something does happen:

- Be familiar with your servers. Run ps -axx on them regularly, and learn what processes normally run on them. If you see a process you don't recognize, investigate.

- Examine your open network ports with netstat -na and sockstat. What TCP and UDP ports should your server be listening on? If you don't recognize an open port, investigate. Perhaps it's innocent, but it might be an intruder's backdoor.

- Unexplained system problems are hints. Many intruders are ham-fisted klutzes with poor sysadmin skills, who use click-and-drool attacks. They'll crash your system and think that they're tough.

- Truly skilled intruders not only clean up after themselves, but also ensure that the system has no problems that might alert you. Therefore, systems that are unusually stable are also suspicious.

- Unexplained reboots might indicate someone illicitly installing a new kernel. They might also be a sign of failing hardware or bad configuration, so investigate them anyway.

- FreeBSD sends you emails every day giving basic system status information. Read them. Save them. If something looks suspicious, investigate.

I particularly recommend two tools to increase your familiarity with your system. The first, */usr/ports/sysutils/lsof*, lists all open files on your system. Reading lsof(8) output is an education in and of itself; you probably had no idea that your web server opened so much crud. Seeing strange files open indicates either that you're not sufficiently familiar with your system or that someone's doing something improper.

The second tool is */usr/ports/security/nessus*, an automated vulnerability scanner. Running Nessus security audits on your own machines is an excellent way to see your system as an attacker would.

If You're Hacked

After all this, what do you do if your system is hacked? There is no easy answer. Huge books are written on the subject. Here are a few general suggestions, however.

First and foremost: A hacked system cannot be trusted. If someone has gained root access on your Internet server, he could have replaced any program on the system. Even if you close the hole he broke in through, he could have installed a hacked version of login(8) that sends your username and password to an IRC channel somewhere every time you log in. Do not trust this system. An upgrade cannot cleanse it, as even sysinstall(8) and the compiler are suspect.

While tools such as rkhunter (*/usr/ports/security/rkhunter*) might help you verify the presence of intruders, nothing can verify that the intruder *isn't* there. Feel free to write *FreeBSD-security@FreeBSD.org* for advice. Describe what you're seeing and why you think you're hacked. Be prepared for the ugly answer, though: Completely reinstall your computer from known secure media (FTP or CD) and restore your data from backup. You did read Chapter 4, right?

Good security practices reduce your chances of being hacked, just as safe driving reduces your chances of being in a car wreck. Good luck!

10

EXPLORING /ETC

The */etc* directory contains the basic configuration information needed to boot a Unix-like system. Every time I get saddled with an unfamiliar system, one of the first things I do is scope out */etc*. The fastest way to go from a junior sysadmin to a midgrade one is to read */etc* and the associated man pages. Yes, all of it. Yes, this is a lot of reading. Understanding */etc* means that you understand how the system hangs together. As you progress as a sysadmin, you're going to pick up this information piecemeal anyway, so you might as well take the easier route and master this part of your toolkit at the beginning.

I discuss many */etc* files in a chapter where they're most important, such as */etc/services* in Chapter 6 and */etc/fstab* in Chapter 8. Also, some files are of only historical interest or are gradually being removed. This chapter covers important */etc* files that don't quite fit anywhere else.

/etc Across Unix Species

Different Unix-like systems use different */etc* files. In many cases, these files are simply renamed or restructured files from primordial BSD. The first time I encountered an IBM AIX system, for example, I went looking for a BSD-style */etc/fstab*. It wasn't there. A little hunting led me to */etc/filesystems*, which is an IBM-specific */etc/fstab*. Apparently IBM felt that a file named for an abbreviation of *filesystem table* was confusing, so they renamed the file. Knowing this information existed somewhere in */etc*, and knowing which files it obviously wasn't in, greatly shortened my search.

Even radically different FreeBSD systems have almost identical */etc* directories. While some add-on programs insert their own files here, you can expect certain files to be on every FreeBSD system you encounter.

Remember that */etc* is the heart of FreeBSD, and that changes to these files can damage or destroy your system. Before you change any files, review the information on RCS in Chapter 4. Create an */etc/RCS* directory and use ci(1) and co(1) religiously when experimenting. While having to manually recover a scrambled filesystem can turn an adequate sysadmin into a pretty good one, it's one of the least pleasant ways to get there.

/etc/adduser.conf

This file lets you configure the defaults for new users. See Chapter 7 for details.

/etc/amd.map

FreeBSD has the ability to automatically mount and unmount NFS filesystems upon demand through the automounter daemon, amd(8). See its man page for details.

/etc/bluetooth, /etc/bluetooth.device.conf, and /etc/defaults/bluetooth.device.conf

FreeBSD supports Bluetooth, a standard for short-range wireless communication. Unlike 802.11, Bluetooth is designed for short-range but high-level services such as voice communications. This book is about servers, so we won't cover Bluetooth, but you should know that your FreeBSD laptop can attach to your Bluetooth-equipped cellphone and connect to the Internet if you desire.

/etc/crontab

The cron(8) daemon lets users schedule tasks. See Chapter 15 for examples and details.

/etc/csh.*

The *etc/csh.** files contain system-wide defaults for csh and tcsh. When a user logs in with either of these shells, the shell executes any commands it finds in */etc/csh.login*. Similarly, when the user logs out, */etc/csh.logout* is executed. You can place general shell configuration information in */etc/csh.cshrc*.

/etc/devd.conf

devd(8) manages detachable hardware such as USB, PCCard, and Cardbus devices. When you insert a wireless card into your laptop, devd(8) notices the arrival and fires up the appropriate system processes to configure the card as per */etc/rc.conf*. We discuss devd(8) briefly in Chapter 8, but if you think you need to edit */etc/devd.conf* on a server, you're probably doing something wrong.

/etc/devfs.conf, /etc/devfs.rules, and /etc/defaults/devfs.rules

FreeBSD manages device nodes through devfs(5), a virtual filesystem that dynamically provides device nodes as hardware boots, appears, and disappears. See Chapter 8 for more information.

/etc/dhclient.conf

Many operating systems give you very basic DHCP client configuration with no way to fine-tune or customize it; you either use it or you don't. In most cases, an empty */etc/dhclient.conf* file gives you full DHCP client functionality, but it won't work correctly in all situations. Perhaps your network is having trouble, or you're at a conference where some script kiddie thinks it's fun to set up a second DHCP server and route everyone's traffic through his machine so he can capture passwords.

Your server better not be configured via DHCP (unless it's diskless), so we won't go into any depth on this. You should be aware that you can configure FreeBSD's DHCP client functionality, however.

/etc/disktab

Once upon a time, hard disks were rare and exotic creatures that came in only a few varieties. In */etc/disktab* you'll find low-level descriptions of many different kinds of disks, from the 360KB floppy disk to a Panasonic 60MB laptop hard drive. (Yes, laptops came with 60MB hard drives, and we were durned happy to have them.)

Today, this file is mostly used for removable media such as 1.44MB floppy disks and zip disks. While we provided a description of formatting standard floppy disks in Chapter 8, this file contains the descriptions needed to format other removable media. If you want to put a filesystem on your LS 120 disk or zip drive, you'll find the necessary label here at the beginning of an entry.

Editing */etc/disktab* is only useful if you have multiple identical hard drives that you want to partition and format in exactly the same way. If you need to make your own entries, read disktab(5).

/etc/freebsd-update.conf

This file is used by freebsd-update(8) when getting binary updates for your server. See Chapter 13 for details.

/etc/fstab

See Chapter 8 for a discussion on the filesystem table, */etc/fstab*.

/etc/ftp.*

The FTP daemon ftpd(8) uses these files to determine who may access the system via FTP and what access they have upon a successful connection. They're discussed in detail in Chapter 17.

/etc/group

Assigning users to groups is covered in painful detail in Chapter 7.

/etc/hosts

This is a hard-coded list of hostname to IP address mappings, as discussed in Chapter 14.

/etc/hosts.allow

The */etc/hosts.allow* file controls who can access the daemons compiled with TCP Wrappers support. Learn about it in Chapter 9.

/etc/hosts.equiv

The */etc/hosts.equiv* file is used by the r-services (rlogin, rsh, etc.) to let trusted remote systems log in or run commands on the local system without providing a password or even logging in. Hosts listed in this file are assumed to have performed user authentication on a trusted system, so the local system doesn't have to bother reauthenticating the user.

Such blatant trust is very convenient on friendly networks, much as leaving the doors of your Manhattan townhouse unlocked saves you the trouble of digging out your door keys every time you get home. There is no such thing as a friendly network these days. A single disgruntled employee can largely destroy a corporate network with this service, and a machine using the r-services is pretty much dog meat for the first script kiddie who wanders by. In fact, */etc/hosts.equiv* and its related services have bitten even top-notch security experts who thought they could use it safely. I suggest leaving this file empty and perhaps even making it immutable (Chapter 9).

/etc/hosts.lpd

The */etc/hosts.lpd* file is one of the simplest files in */etc*. Hosts listed here, each on its own line, may print to the printer(s) controlled by this machine. While you can use hostnames, that would allow DNS issues to choke printing, so use IP addresses instead.

Unlike most other configuration files, */etc/hosts.lpd* does not accept network numbers or netmasks; you must list individual hostnames or IP addresses.

/etc/inetd.conf

inetd(8) handles incoming network connections for smaller daemons that don't run frequently. See the section on inetd in Chapter 15.

/etc/localtime

This file contains local time zone data, as configured by tzsetup(8). It is a binary file, and you cannot edit it with normal tools. tzsetup(8) actually copies this file from a subdirectory of */usr/share/zoneinfo*. If your time zone changes, you'll need to upgrade FreeBSD to get the new time zone files and then rerun tzsetup(8) to configure time correctly.

/etc/locate.rc

locate(1) finds all files of a given name. For example, to find *locate.rc*, enter the following:

```
# locate locate.rc
/etc/locate.rc
/usr/share/examples/etc/locate.rc
/usr/src/usr.bin/locate/locate/locate.rc
```

You'll see that a file called *locate.rc* can be found in three places: in the main */etc* directory, in the system examples directory, and in the system source code.

Once a week your FreeBSD system scans its disks, builds a list of everything it finds, and stores that list in a database. The list-building program, locate.updatedb(8), takes its settings from *etc/locate.rc*. The following variables in this file all change how your locate.updatedb builds your locate database:

- TMPDIR contains the temporary directory used by locate.updatedb(8), and defaults to */tmp*. If you're short on space in */tmp*, change this path to a place where you have more room.

- While you can change the location of the database itself with the FCODES variable, this affects other parts of FreeBSD that expect to find that database in its default location. Be prepared for odd results, especially if you leave an old locate database in the default location of */var/db/locate.database*.

- The SEARCHPATHS variable gives the directory where you want to start building your database. This defaults to /, the whole disk. To index only a portion of your disk, set that value here.

- PRUNEPATHS lists directories you don't want to index. This defaults to excluding temporary directories that traditionally contain only short-lived files.

- The FILESYSTEMS variable lists the types of filesystems you want to index. By default, locate.updatedb(8) only indexes UFS (FreeBSD) and ext2fs (Linux) filesystems. Listing NFS (Chapter 8) filesystems is a bad idea; all of your servers simultaneously indexing the fileserver will bottleneck either the network or the fileserver.

/etc/login.*

You can control who may log into your system, and what resources those users may access, by using */etc/login.access* and */etc/login.conf*. See Chapter 7 for instructions.

/etc/mail/mailer.conf

FreeBSD allows you to choose any mail server program you like via */etc/mail/mailer.conf*, as covered in Chapter 16.

/etc/make.conf

To make, or compile, a program is to build it from source code into machine language. We'll discuss building software in detail in Chapter 11. */etc/make.conf* controls how that building process works, letting you set options that directly affect software builds. Remember, anything you add to *make.conf* affects all software built on the system, including system upgrades. This may cause upgrade failures.[1] Many of the options from *make.conf* are only useful for developers.

If you're interested in setting options that affect only system upgrades, use */etc/src.conf* instead.

Here are some common features set in *make.conf.* Any values set here require the same syntax used by make(1). For the most part, following the examples is best.

CFLAGS

This option specifies optimization settings for building nonkernel programs. Many other Unix-like operating systems suggest compiling software with particular *compiler flags,* or CFLAGS. This practice is actively discouraged on FreeBSD. System components that require compiler flags already have that specified in the software configuration, and add-on software has that configuration set for it separately. While people might recommend other settings for CFLAGS, custom options are not supported by the FreeBSD Project.

In general, FreeBSD code is expected to compile most correctly out of the box. The only thing that adding compiler options can do is impair your performance. If you build FreeBSD with nonstandard flags and have problems, remove those flags and build it again.

COPTFLAGS

The COPTFLAGS optimizations are used only for building the kernel. Again, settings other than the defaults can build a non-working kernel.

CXXFLAGS

CXXFLAGS tells the compiler what optimizations to use when building C++ code. Be sure to use the += syntax when using CXXFLAGS, so that you add your instructions to those specified in the software. Everything that I said above about CFLAGS applies equally well to CXXFLAGS.

CPUTYPE=i686

Certain software can be optimized for different CPU types. By identifying your CPU type in */etc/make.conf* you tell the compiler to optimize for your CPU.

This is most effective if you upgrade your system from source (see Chapter 13). FreeBSD will not only optimize everything in the base system for your processor, but any third-party software you build afterwards will also have the same optimizations.

On a standalone machine, always set CPUTYPE to match your CPU. If you build FreeBSD on one machine and then NFS export */usr/obj* and */usr/src* to other machines so they can upgrade without building, set CPUTYPE to the lowest common denominator of CPUs on your systems.

---

[1] Having weird crap in *make.conf* during a system upgrade will make people laugh at you when you ask for help. But commercial software support techs do that, too, so that's OK.

As of this writing, FreeBSD recognizes the CPU types shown in Table 10-1.

Table 10-1: CPU Types

Architecture	Valid Types
i386 architecture, Intel	core2, core, nocona, pentium4m, pentium4, prescott, pentium3m, pentium3, pentium-m, pentium2, pentiumpro, pentium-mmx, pentium, i486, i386
i386 architecture, VIA	c3, c3-2
i386 architecture, AMD	opteron, athlon64, athlon-mp, athlon-xp, athlon-4, athlon-tbird, athlon, k8, k7, k6-2, k6, k5
amd64 architecture, Intel	nocona, prescott, core, core2
amd64 architecture, AMD	opteron, athlon64

INSTALL=install -C

When FreeBSD installs a program, it blindly copies the new binary on top of the old one. By using install -C instead of a naked install, install(1) compares the new program to the existing one and does not install the new binary if it is identical to the old one. This prevents pointless timestamp changes in */usr/include*, so make(1) won't assume software is out of date just because a header file has been replaced with a newer, but identical, version. This can also accelerate upgrades and save disk writes. Disk writes are not usually much of an issue, but it's an option if you want it.

NOTE   *We'll look at the* make.conf *options useful for the Ports Collection in Chapter 11 and some unusual options for stripping down FreeBSD in Chapter 20.*

/etc/master.passwd

This file contains the core information for all user accounts, as discussed in Chapter 7.

/etc/motd

The *message of the day (motd)* file is displayed to users when they log in. You can place system notices in this file, or other information you want shell users to see. The welcome option in */etc/login.conf* can point different users to different motd files, so you can have separate messages for each login class.

/etc/mtree

mtree(1) builds directory hierarchies with permissions set according to a predefined standard. The */etc/mtree* directory stores that standard for the FreeBSD base system. The FreeBSD upgrade process uses mtree records to install the system correctly. If you damage file or directory permissions in your base system, you can use mtree(1) to restore them to the defaults. While you don't generally need to edit these files, they can be useful if you muck too much with your system.

/etc/namedb

The *etc/namedb* files control the system nameserver. See Chapter 14 for details on how name service works.

/etc/netstart

This shell script is designed specifically for bringing up the network while in single-user mode. Having a network in single-user mode is terribly useful for any number of reasons, from mounting NFS shares to connecting to remote machines in order to verify configurations. Just run */etc/netstart*. This script has no effect when in full multi-user mode.

/etc/network.subr

This shell script isn't intended for human use; rather, other network configuration scripts use the subroutines defined herein to support common functions.

/etc/newsyslog.conf

This file configures the rotation and deletion of log files. See Chapter 19 for more information.

/etc/nscd.conf

nscd(8) caches the results of name service lookups to optimize system performance. See Chapter 15 for details.

/etc/nsmb.conf

FreeBSD's Windows file-share mounting system uses */etc/nsmb.conf* to define access to Windows systems, as described in Chapter 8.

/etc/nsswitch.conf

Name Service Switching is covered in Chapter 14.

/etc/opie*

OPIE, or *One-time Passwords In Everything*, is a one-time password system derived from S/Key. While still used in a few places, it's no longer very popular. You can read opie(4) if you're interested. For the most part, OPIE has been largely replaced by systems like Kerberos.

/etc/pam.d/*

Pluggable Authentication Modules (PAM) allow the system administrator to use different authentication, authorization, and access control systems. If you're using Kerberos or some other centralized authentication system, you'll need to work with PAM.

/etc/pccard_ether

This script starts and stops removable network cards, such as Cardbus cards and USB Ethernet. Its name is just a leftover of history, when the only cards available were PC Cards. For the most part, devd(8) runs this script as needed, as discussed in Chapter 8.

/etc/periodic.conf and /etc/defaults/periodic.conf

periodic(8) runs every day to handle basic maintenance and emails the results to root as status messages. periodic(8) just runs shell scripts stored in */etc/periodic* and */usr/local/etc/periodic*. Every one of these scripts is enabled or disabled in */etc/periodic.conf*.

periodic(8) runs programs either daily, weekly, or monthly. Each set of programs has its own settings—for example, daily programs are configured separately from monthly programs. These settings are controlled by entries in */etc/periodic.conf*. While we only show examples from the daily scripts, you'll find very similar settings for the weekly and monthly scripts as well.

daily_output="root"

If you want the status email to go to a user other than root, list that user's name here. Unless you have a user whose job it is to specifically read periodic email, it's best to leave this at the default and forward root's email to an account you read. You could also give a full path to a file if you prefer, and even have newsyslog(8) (see Chapter 19) rotate the periodic log.

daily_show_success="YES"

With this set to YES, the daily message includes information on all successful checks.

daily_show_info="YES"

When set to YES, the daily message includes general information from the commands it runs.

daily_show_badconfig="NO"

When set to YES, the daily message includes information on periodic commands it tried to run but couldn't. These messages are generally harmless and involve subsystems that your system just doesn't support or include.

daily_local="/etc/daily.local"

You can define your own scripts to be run as part of the daily, weekly, and monthly periodic(8) jobs. These default to */etc/daily.local*, */etc/weekly.local*, and */etc/monthly.local*, but you can place them anywhere you like.

Each script in the daily, weekly, and monthly subdirectories of */etc/periodic* has a brief description at the top of the file, and most have configuration options in */etc/defaults/periodic.conf*. Skim through these quickly, looking for things that are of interest to you. The defaults enabled are sensible for most circumstances, but there's extra functionality you can enable with a simple setting in */etc/periodic.conf*. For example, if you use GEOM-based disk features, you'll find the daily GEOM status messages useful. Since anything I could list here would be obsolete before I could deliver this manuscript, let alone before the book reaches you, I won't go into detail about the various scripts.

/etc/pf.conf

We cover the basics of the PF packet filter in Chapter 9.

/etc/pf.os

PF can identify operating systems by the packets they send, allowing you to write firewall rules such as "Show FreeBSD users my real home page, but show Windows users a page suggesting that they get a real operating system." See pf.os(5) for more information.

/etc/phones

Modem users can store phone numbers for remote modems in */etc/phones*, aliasing them so that they can just type home instead of the full phone number. Only tip(1) and cu(1) use this file, however, so it's not as useful as you might think.

/etc/portsnap.conf

portsnap provides updates for the ports tree, as discussed in Chapter 11.

/etc/ppp

FreeBSD supports modems with ppp(8). Read the manual page for more information.

/etc/printcap

This file contains printer configuration information. Printing on Unix-like systems can be very complicated, especially with the vast variety of printers you can use. Making your FreeBSD machine send print jobs to a print server isn't hard at all, however. We cover the topic in Chapter 15.

/etc/profile

/etc/profile contains the default account configuration information for the */bin/sh* shell, much like */etc/csh.** for csh and tcsh users. Whenever a */bin/sh* user logs in, he inherits what's in this file. Users can override */etc/profile* with their own *.profile*. Bash and other sh derivatives also use this file.

While tcsh is the standard FreeBSD shell, sh and derivatives (particularly bash) are quite popular. Consider keeping settings in */etc/profile* and */etc/csh.login* synchronized to ease troubleshooting in the future.

/etc/protocols

In Chapter 6 we discussed network protocols. */etc/protocols* lists the various network protocols you might encounter, as explained in that chapter.

/etc/rc*

Whenever your system boots to the point where it can execute userland commands, it runs the shell script */etc/rc*. This script mounts all filesystems, brings up the network interfaces, configures devfs(5), finds and catalogs shared libraries, and performs all the other tasks required to set up a system.

Different systems have radically different startup tasks. A terminal server with three 48-port serial cards works completely differently from a web server. Instead of a single monolithic */etc/rc script* that handles every task, FreeBSD segregates each startup process into a separate shell script that addresses a specific need.

Additionally, you'll find a few scripts directly under */etc*, such as */etc/rc.firewall* and */etc/rc.initdiskless*. These scripts were split out on their own years before the rcNG startup system came along, and remain in their historical locations so as to not break legacy software.

We discussed the FreeBSD startup system in Chapter 3.

/etc/remote

This file contains machine-readable configurations for connecting to remote systems over serial lines. Today, this is only of interest if you use your system as a serial client—for example, if you want to connect to a serial console. We discuss serial consoles in Chapter 20.

/etc/rpc

Remote Procedure Calls (RPC) is a method for executing commands on a remote computer. Much like TCP/IP, RPC has service and port numbers. */etc/rpc* contains a list of these services and their port numbers. The most common RPC consumer is NFS, discussed in Chapter 8.

/etc/security/

This directory contains configuration information for the audit(8) security utility.

/etc/services

This file contains a list of network services and their associated TCP/IP ports. We discussed */etc/services* in detail in Chapter 6.

/etc/shells

This file contains the list of all legitimate user shells, as discussed in Chapter 7.

/etc/snmpd.config

FreeBSD includes a basic SNMP implementation, which we discuss in Chapter 19.

/etc/src.conf

This file contains machine instructions for building FreeBSD from source. It's a parallel of *make.conf* for the source tree alone. Values set in */etc/make.conf* affect building FreeBSD from source as well, though; the difference is that */etc/src.conf* only affects building FreeBSD but not ports and packages.

/etc/sysctl.conf

This file contains information on which kernel sysctls are set during the boot process. See Chapter 5.

/etc/syslog.conf

This file controls which data goes into your system logs and where those logs are stored. See Chapter 19.

/etc/termcap

This file contains the settings and capabilities of different terminal types. In the age when terminals came in dozens of different types and vendors released new terminals on an almost daily basis, understanding this file was vital. Now that the world has largely converged on vt100 as a standard, however, the default configuration is suitable for almost everyone.

/etc/ttys

This file contains all of the system terminal devices (the windows containing a command prompt). The name is a relic of the time when terminals were physical monitors, but today most users use the virtual terminals generated by telnet or SSH.

We'll use this file to set up serial logins in Chapter 20.

11

MAKING YOUR SYSTEM USEFUL

Unlike operating systems such as Microsoft Windows and Red Hat Linux, which tend to throw absolutely everything you might ever need into the base install, FreeBSD systems are minimal—and that's a good thing. Windows systems in particular have thousands of objects in the main system directory and just about every shared library you can imagine. Whenever you boot the system, Windows loads many of those libraries and objects into main system memory. I don't know what each object is for, but I guarantee that I will never use many of them—when I use Windows, it's only for SSH and Firefox. All these objects do for me is consume RAM. This is, of course, Microsoft's approach to operating systems—give 'em everything you've got, and add whipped cream and a cherry on top. Red Hat Linux includes a similar amount of stuff, but at least it isn't automatically loaded into the system at boot and you can choose to remove it easily.

A basic FreeBSD install includes *exactly* enough to make the system run, plus a few extra bits that have been traditionally included with Unix systems. You can choose whether to install additional programs or source code. Even a complete, running FreeBSD install takes up much less disk space than either a Windows or a Red Hat Linux install. A Windows install only supporting SSH and Firefox would be much smaller and simpler—in fact, it would look a lot more like FreeBSD.

The advantage to this sparseness is that it includes only necessary system components. Debugging becomes much simpler, and you know that no shared library you've never even heard of, and would never use, can be responsible for your problems. The downside is that you must decide what you do need and install programs to support those functions. FreeBSD makes software installation as simple as possible.

Making Software

Building software is complicated because source code must be processed very specifically to create a workable, running program—let alone one that works well! While programmers could include installation instructions with each program, full of lines like Now type `ar cru .libs/lib20_zlib_plugin.a istream-zlib.o zlib-plugin.o`, this would be downright sadistic. While Unix admins might seem to approve of sadism, they categorically disapprove of cruelty when it is directed at themselves; if something can be automated, it will be.

The main tool for building software is make(1). When run, make looks in the current directory for a file called *Makefile*, which is full of instructions much like that horrid example in the previous paragraph. make(1) reads the instructions and carries them out, automating the installation process no matter how complicated it might be. You don't really have to know the internals of a *Makefile*, so we're not going to dissect one here.

Each *Makefile* includes one or more *targets*, or sets of instructions to carry out. For example, typing make install tells make(1) to check the *Makefile* for a procedure called *install* and, if found, execute it. A target's name usually relates to the process to be carried out, so you can safely assume that make install installs the software. You'll find targets to install, configure, and uninstall most software. make(1) handles a huge variety of functions, some of which far outstrip the creators' original intents. But that's part of the fun of Unix!

Source Code and Software

Source code is the human-readable instructions for building the actual machine code that makes up a program. You might have already been exposed to source code in some form. If you've never seen it, take a look at a few files under */usr/src*. While you don't have to read source code, you should be able to recognize it two out of three times.

Once you have source code for a program, you build (or *compile*) the program on the type of system you want to run it on. (Building software for a foreign platform via cross-compiling demands that you know much more about building software, and is not always possible.) If the program was written for an operating system that is sufficiently similar to the platform you're building it on, it works. If your platform is too different from the original, it fails. Once you've built the software successfully on your system, you can copy the resulting program (or *binary*) to other identical systems, and it should run.

Some programs are sufficiently well written that they can be compiled on many different platforms. A few programs specifically include support for widely divergent platforms; for example, the Apache web server can be compiled on both Windows and Unix just by typing make install. This is quite uncommon, however, and represents heroic effort by the software authors.

Generally speaking, if you can build a program from source, it runs. A sufficiently experienced sysadmin can use the source code and error messages to learn why a program won't build or run. In many cases, the problem is simple and can be fixed with minimal effort. This is one reason why access to source code is important.

Back in the age when every sysadmin was a programmer, this debugging absorbed a major portion of the admin's time. Every Unix-like system was slightly different, so every sysadmin had to understand his platform, the platform the software was designed for, and the differences between the two before he could hope to make a piece of code run. The duplication of effort was truly horrendous.

Over the years, tools such as autoconf were created to help address these cross-platform issues. Not every program used these tools, and when they broke, the sysadmin was returned to square one. System administrators had to edit the source code and *Makefiles* just to have a chance of making the programs work. And *working* is not nearly the same as *working well*, let alone *working correctly*.

The FreeBSD Ports Collection was designed to simplify this process for FreeBSD users.

The Ports and Packages System

Ports are instructions for compiling software on FreeBSD, and *packages* are precompiled ports.

Packages install quickly and easily, while ports take more time but can be customized for your environment. The whole system is called the *Ports Collection*, the *ports tree*, or simply *ports*. All these terms refer to the ports themselves, the system for building ports, and packages.

The basic idea behind the ports and packages system is that if source code must be modified to run on FreeBSD, the modifications should be automated. If you need other software to build this program from source code or to run the software, those dependencies should be documented and tracked. If you're going to automate the changes, you might as well record what the program includes so you can easily install and uninstall it. And since you have a software-building process that produces exactly the same result each time, and you've recorded everything that the process creates, you can copy the binaries and install them on any similar FreeBSD system.

Ports

A port is a set of instructions on how to apply fixes to, or *patch*, a set of source code files. By combining patches with the software's original installation process, the FreeBSD Project maintains a complete record of everything necessary to install the software. This frees you from struggling to install the program and lets you concentrate on configuring it.

Ports Tree Installation

If you followed the installation instructions in Chapter 2, you installed the ports tree in */usr/ports*. In that directory you should find several files and a couple dozen directories. If you don't have anything in */usr/ports*, you apparently can't follow instructions. That's okay—I can't either—but you must install the ports tree to continue. We'll discuss portsnap(8) in Chapter 13, but you can use it now to install the ports tree:

```
# portsnap fetch
Looking up portsnap.FreeBSD.org mirrors... 3 mirrors found.
Fetching public key from portsnap3.FreeBSD.org... done.
Fetching snapshot tag from portsnap3.FreeBSD.org... done.
Fetching snapshot metadata... done.
Fetching snapshot generated at Thu May 15 20:09:15 EDT 2008:
a2b71859b1a44878d19f879e2d1c801d785761670cc745  5% of   47 MB   29 kBps 26m32s
```

portsnap searches for a mirror of the portsnap files, cryptographically verifies the integrity of the files on the portsnap server, downloads the files, and verifies the integrity of the download itself. After downloading, install the ports tree:

```
# portsnap extract
```

This gives you a current tree with all the latest FreeBSD ports.

Ports Tree Contents

Most of the directories you see here are software categories. Each category contains a further layer of directories, and each of those directories is a piece of software. FreeBSD has almost 17,000 ports as I write this, so using the directory tree and categorizing software properly is vital. Of the files and directories in this category that aren't software categories, the major ones are described below.

The *CHANGES* file lists changes made to the FreeBSD ports infrastructure. It is primarily of use to the FreeBSD ports developers and people interested in the internals of the Ports Collection.

COPYRIGHT contains the licensing information for the Ports Collection as a whole. While each individual piece of software supported by the Ports Collection has its own copyright and licensing information, the Ports Collection is licensed under the BSD license.

The *GIDs* file contains a list of all the group IDs used by software in the Ports Collection. Many pieces of software use an unprivileged user, and the Ports Collection needs a GID for these users. This file helps prevent software conflicts, as each port has its own assigned *GIDs*.

KNOBS contains a list of all tunable settings available in the Ports Collection. You can set any of these on the command line or in */etc/make.conf* to enable the corresponding feature in software that supports it. We'll talk more about tunable settings later in this chapter.

In *LEGAL*, you'll see a list of all legal restrictions on software in the Ports Collection. Some pieces of software have specific limitations on them—such as no commercial use, no redistribution, no monetary gain, and so on. Individual ports also list these restrictions, this is just a master list built from all the ports.

MOVED lists all of the ports that have moved from one category to another. As the FreeBSD ports team creates new categories, they move ports from one place to another. Automated management tools such as portmaster(8) need to find moved ports.

The *Makefile* contains high-level instructions for the whole Ports Collection.

The *Mk* subdirectory contains detailed, low-level instructions for the whole Ports Collection. Many types of programs expect to integrate together, and these files ensure that different parts of the same tool are built and installed in a compatible manner. For example, the KDE and GNOME desktop suites include dozens or hundreds of smaller programs, and each must be built correctly to interoperate. If you look in this directory, you'll see the files *bsd.gnome.mk* and *bsd.kde.mk* dedicated to configuration of these programs, as well as files for Apache, Emacs, GCC, Perl, and many other software families. If you really want to learn how the Ports Collection works, read this directory.

The *README* file contains a high-level introduction to the Ports Collection.

The *Templates* directory contains skeleton files used by other portions of the Ports Collection.

The *Tools* directory contains programs, scripts, and other automation, mostly used by ports developers.

The *UIDs* file contains unprivileged user IDs used by ports in the system. Much like the *GIDs* file, this helps the ports developers avoid conflicts between unprivileged users required by ported software.

UPDATING contains notes for use when upgrading your software. Updates that require special intervention appear here in the reverse date order. We'll discuss this file in Chapter 13.

The *distfiles* directory contains the original source code for ported software. When a port downloads a chunk of source code, that source code is kept under */usr/ports/distfiles*.

All of the other directories are categories of ports. The following shows the contents of the arabic ports directory, where software specific to the Arabic language is kept. Much software elsewhere in the Ports Collection supports Arabic, but this category is for software focused on Arabic—such as fonts, translations of certain types of documents, and so on. This category isn't useful for most people, but it has the serious advantage of being small enough to fit in this book. Some ports categories have hundreds of entries.[1]

Makefile	ae_fonts_ttf	kacst_fonts	khotot	php_doc
Makefile.inc	arabtex	katoob	koffice-i18n	
ae_fonts_mono	aspell	kde3-i18n	libitl	

The Makefile contains instructions for all of the ports in the directory. The file *Makefile.inc* contains metainstructions for the ports in this directory. All of the other directories are individual software packages. We'll dissect one of those directories in "Using Ports" on page 331.

Finding Software

Some of these categories have hundreds of ports in them, so how can you ever hope to find *anything*? The file */usr/ports/INDEX-7* contains a list of all ports in alphabetical order. Each port is described on a single line, with fields separated by pipe symbols (|). While this is convenient for system tools, it's not particularly human-readable. Run make print-index in */usr/ports* to get a longer, much more intelligible index. This index is filled with entries like this:

```
Port:    p5-Compress-Bzip2-2.09
Path:    /usr/ports/archivers/p5-Compress-Bzip2
Info:    Perl5 interface to bzip2 compression library
Maint:   demon@FreeBSD.org
Index:   archivers perl5
B-deps:  perl-5.8.8
R-deps:  perl-5.8.8
E-deps:  perl-5.8.8
P-deps:  perl-5.8.8
F-deps:
WWW:     http://search.cpan.org/dist/Compress-Bzip2/
```

The index starts with the name of the port and the full path to the port directory. Info gives a very brief description of the port. The Maint heading lists the port's maintainer, a person or team who has assumed responsibility for this software's integration into the Ports Collection. The Index space lists every category where this port can be filed. B-deps lists the build dependencies—that is, other software that must be installed to build this port. Some software must be extracted or decompressed by particular tools, specified in E-deps. The P-deps field lists any dependencies for patching the software—rare pieces of software must be patched with a certain tool. The F-deps field is similar, specifying *fetch dependencies*—that is, any special software that must be used to download the software. Finally, the WWW space gives the home page of the software.

---

[1] 17,000 ports. 60-odd categories. Some categories have 11 members. You do the math.

Finding by Name

Knowing how to read the index is nice, but how can it help you find a piece of software? If you know the name of the software, search *INDEX* for it with make search. Here, I look for net-snmp:

```
# cd /usr/ports
# make search name=net-snmp
❶ Port:   net-snmp-5.3.1_3
  Path:   /usr/ports/net-mgmt/net-snmp
  Info:   An extendable SNMP implementation
  Maint:  kuriyama@FreeBSD.org
  B-deps: autoconf-2.59_2 libtool-1.5.22_4 m4-1.4.8_1 openssl-0.9.8e perl-5.8.8
  R-deps: openssl-0.9.8e perl-5.8.8
  WWW:    http://net-snmp.sourceforge.net/

  Port:   p5-Net-SNMP-5.2.0
  ...
  Port:   p5-Net-SNMP-365-3.65
  ...
```

As of this writing, FreeBSD has three ports with net-snmp in their name. One is the original net-snmp ❶ software collection; the two others are Perl libraries that use SNMP over the network but otherwise have nothing to do with net-snmp. The fields in the description are taken straight from the *INDEX* we saw earlier.

If you don't need this much detail in your search results, you can use make quicksearch to find software.

This doesn't work for all software, however. For example, if you're looking for the popular Midnight Commander file manager, you might try this command:

```
# make search name=midnight
#
```

Well, that was less than helpful. Let's try a more general search.

Finding by Keyword

If you don't know the software's exact name, try a keyword search. This scans more fields and returns more hits. If you're searching for a common word, however, the key search can provide far too much information.

```
# make search key=midnight
```

This returns every port with the string midnight in its description, name, or dependencies. We'll quickly learn that Midnight Commander can be found under */usr/ports/misc/mc*.

Other Ways to Browse the Ports Collection

If you prefer using a web browser, build an HTML index. Just go to */usr/ports* and, as root, type make readmes to generate a *README.html* file with the index of your ports tree. You can click through various categories and even view detailed descriptions of every port.

If none of these options work, try the FreeBSD Ports Tree search at *http://www.freebsd.org/cgi/ports.cgi*. Also, the FreshPorts search engine at *http://www.freshports.com* provides a separate but very nice search function.

Between the web browser and the search engine, you should be able to find a piece of software to meet your needs.

Legal Restrictions

While most of the software in the Ports Collection is free for any use, some of it has a more restrictive license. The */usr/ports/LEGAL* file lists legal restrictions on the contents of the Ports Collection. The most common restriction is a prohibition on redistribution; the FreeBSD Project does not include such software on its FTP sites or on a CD image, but provides instructions on how to build it. For example, for a long time FreeBSD did not have a Java license. You couldn't download a compiled, ready-to-go FreeBSD Java package, and the Project could not redistribute the Java source code. FreeBSD could, however, distribute instructions on how to build the Sun-provided Java source code on FreeBSD. A FreeBSD user who wanted Java had to download the source code from a Sun Microsystems web page, download the patchset from a FreeBSD site, and build his own version of Java on FreeBSD. Today, the FreeBSD Foundation supplies a complete, licensed Java package that can be quickly installed.

Similarly, some pieces of software prohibit commercial use or embedding in commercial products. A few cannot be exported from the United States, thanks to Department of Commerce rules restricting the export of cryptography.[2] If you're building FreeBSD systems for redistribution, export, or commercial use, you need to check this file.

Fortunately, most of the software in the Ports Collection is free for either commercial or noncommercial use. These restricted packages are the exception, not the norm.

Using Packages

Packages are precompiled software from the Ports Collection, bundled up for a particular version of FreeBSD. We're going to discuss using packages first, as they're generally easier and faster than ports. Once you have a grip on packages, we'll proceed to ports.

---

[2] Most of this nonexportable software is available from non-US sources and can be downloaded anywhere in the world. Meanwhile, ex-KGB cryptographers without these regulations will happily provide strong crypto to anyone at low, low rates.

Installing software as a package can save you a great deal of time because you don't have to compile it from source. Unless a piece of software has legal restrictions prohibiting distribution in compiled form, it's probably available as a package. Other software, such as Adobe Acrobat, is only available in precompiled form. Packages are available on CD and via FTP, and have the same name as the port they come from.

CD Packages

If you have a FreeBSD CD set, you already have a fairly extensive collection of compiled packages. To use them, mount the CD and read the package file. If you have downloaded a CD, but not burned it to a physical disk, you can mount that image and install packages from it instead. (See Chapter 8 for details on using removable media and mounting disk images.)

Once you have the CD mounted, look at the *packages* directory. Here's that directory from a recent FreeBSD installation CD:

```
# cd /cdrom/packages/
# ls
❶ All          emulators     linux       textproc      x11-servers
  INDEX        graphics      perl5       x11
  devel        lang          print       x11-fonts
```

This looks like a stripped-down */usr/ports* directory, and it is. Packages are just precompiled ports, so they're stored in the same directory categories as the ports they're built from. A single CD doesn't have nearly enough room to store all 17,000 FreeBSD packages, however. The installation CDs have only the very basic packages that almost everyone wants, such as the X Window System and Perl. The second FreeBSD CD image contains a more complete selection of packages. For example, here's the *x11* directory from a FreeBSD 6.2 installation CD.

```
# ls x11
libdrm-2.0.2.tbz          xorg-documents-6.9.0.tbz      xterm-220.tbz
xorg-6.9.0.tbz            xorg-libraries-6.9.0.tbz
xorg-clients-6.9.0_3.tbz  xorg-manpages-6.9.0.tbz
```

In the ports tree, the x11 category contains 342 ports. The installation CD contains only 7, but they're the X Window System core components. The ports tree contains, for example, the tools for configuring a Synaptics touchpad in GNOME—important for those who happen to own that touchpad and use GNOME, but not worth the precious space on the installation CD.

One interesting difference between the ports tree and the package tree is the directory *All* ❶. This directory contains all of the packages in the CD. The entries in each directory are just links to the actual file in the *All* directory.

To see what a package does, you can search in */usr/ports* just as we searched for a port by name earlier in this chapter. Note, however, that the *packages* directory has an *INDEX* file containing only the packages on this disk. While you can't use the fancy make search name= functions that work in */usr/ports*, you can search the *INDEX* file directly with grep(1). Here, we identify the package libdrm:

```
# cd /cdrom/packages
# grep ^libdrm INDEX
libdrm-2.0.2|/usr/ports/graphics/libdrm|/usr/local|❶Userspace interface to
kernel Direct Rendering Module services|/usr/ports/graphics/libdrm/pkg-descr|
x11@FreeBSD.org|graphics x11|||http://dri.freedesktop.org|||1
#
```

For those of you not comfortable with grep(1), we're searching for the string libdrm in the file *INDEX*. The caret character (^) indicates that the string libdrm must appear at the beginning of a line. The *INDEX* file contains all the information provided in make search, just in a less friendly format. A pipe symbol (|) delimits the fields, and the fourth field ❶ contains a description of the package.

FTP Packages

Frequently, a package doesn't exist on CD because the FreeBSD Project has limited space on the CD sets and can't possibly fit 17,000+ packages onto them. Also, software on CD is built for a particular release of FreeBSD. If you install FreeBSD 7.1 from CD, upgrade your system to 7.3, and want to install packages for 7.3, the FreeBSD 7.1 CDs won't help you. If you're tracking -stable or -current (see Chapter 13), you'll have the same problem.

If a package doesn't exist on CD, you can only get it via FTP. The FreeBSD Project provides packages for almost all of the 17,000+ items in the Ports Collection via FTP. Every FreeBSD FTP mirror carries packages for recent FreeBSD releases, and some carry packages for older (or very old!) releases. We talked about finding a good mirror for your own use in Chapter 2. Each official FreeBSD FTP mirror carries packages at the URL:

```
ftp://mirror.freebsd.org/pub/freebsd/ports/architecture/packages-version/
```

For example, the i386 packages for FreeBSD 6.2 can be found at *ftp://ftp.freebsd.org/pub/freebsd/ports/i386/packages-6.2-release* and all the other mirror servers in the same directory. If you go look at the FTP site you'll see all of the categories in */usr/ports*—and many more. While the Ports Collection places each port in a category, some ports could fit into multiple categories easily. For example, the Perl SNMP ports we saw earlier could easily be classified as either network management tools or Perl programs, depending on your personal bias. The FTP servers have enough room to provide a port under all of its possible classifications, which makes it easier for users to find and actually uses less bandwidth. The quicker you find what you're looking for and go away, the happier the mirror maintainers are.

Just as the CDs, each FTP site has an *All* directory where the actual packages are kept. Unlike the CDs, however, on the FTP site you'll find thousands and thousands of packages!

Installing Packages

If you have the file on a local disk, install it with pkg_add(1).

```
# pkg_add xorg-6.9.0.tbz
```

pkg_add(1) extracts and verifies the compressed package file, and installs the package as specified in the packing instructions. Under most circumstances, pkg_add(1) runs silently and just returns you to a command prompt. On occasion, the package installation routine prints a message when the package is installed. Pay attention to those messages and do as they recommend if you want the software to work correctly.

If pkg_add(1) finds that the package has dependencies—other programs required for this package to work correctly—it tries to install those packages from the same source. The FreeBSD CD sets are designed to accommodate this. For example, the xorg package above has several dependencies, but they're included on the installation CD. If a required package is missing, however, pkg_add complains about the missing package by name and fails. In that case, find the required package on another disk and install it first, or just install it over FTP.

pkg_add(1) also supports installing automatically over FTP. The -r flag makes the system go out onto the Internet and fetch the packages automatically from the FreeBSD FTP server.

```
# pkg_add -r xorg
```

The advantage of this is that the system automatically finds the proper FTP server and directory, downloads the proper version of the package and all of its dependencies, and installs everything. The downside is that if a package install fails, FreeBSD discards the downloaded package(s)! Use the -K flag to make FreeBSD keep the downloaded package in the current directory.

You can also download the package individually from the FTP site and install it at the command line. This won't handle dependencies for you, but when you try to install the package, pkg_add(1) will print out all of the missing dependencies. You can download them or install them remotely. This method is most useful when you're stuck behind a firewall and must jump through hoops to download files.

With large packages, I often use a hybrid approach. For example, OpenOffice.org is over 100MB and requires several smaller packages as dependencies. I'll download OOo from an FTP server, and then try to install it. pkg_add(1) fails, complaining about required but missing programs. I then install those smaller packages with pkg_add -r, then try again to install OOo from the downloaded package.

pkg_add(1) Environment Settings

Shell environment variables can modify how pkg_add(1) behaves. You can control where the system unpacks packages, where it downloads packages from, other places the system can check for packages, and so on. It's best to set any needed environment variables in your login script, so that you use them consistently.

Here are the most useful pkg_add(1) environment settings.

PKG_TMPDIR

The PKG_TMPDIR environment variable controls where pkg_add unpacks its temporary files. A package is a compressed tarball of software files, with some added installation instructions. To install the package, you must decompress and untar it. If you're short on space in the standard directories used by pkg_add, the untar cannot complete and the install fails. By default, pkg_add(1) tries to use the directory in the environment variable TMPDIR. If that variable doesn't exist, pkg_add(1) tries to use */tmp*, */var/tmp*, and */usr/tmp*, in that order. Set PKG_TMPDIR to a directory where you have enough free space:

```
# setenv PKG_TMPDIR /home/mwlucas/garbage
```

PACKAGEROOT

By default, pkg_add -r attempts to download every requested package from *ftp://ftp.freebsd.org*. This probably isn't the best choice for you. The primary FreeBSD mirror is very heavily used and can suffer from congestion. It might also be further away from your computer. You can frequently get better performance by choosing a less heavily used mirror. The PACKAGEROOT environment variable tells pkg_add(1) to use a different FTP server. Set PACKAGEROOT to a protocol and server name, not a full path. For example, to use *ftp5.us.freebsd.org* as your source for packages, set:

```
# setenv PACKAGEROOT ftp://ftp5.us.freebsd.org
```

PACKAGESITE

This lists an exact path to check for a package repository. You might use this if you wish to install only packages from a particular release, or if you have a local package repository. (We'll discuss a local package repository later in this chapter.) Set PACKAGESITE as an absolute URL, as in this example for a legacy, unsupported FreeBSD release:

```
# setenv PACKAGESITE ftp://ftp-archive.freebsd.org/pub/FreeBSD-Archive/old-
releases/i386/5.4-RELEASE/packages/All
```

PKGDIR

This directory specifies a location to place copies of packages downloaded through `pkg_add -Kr`. This lets you keep downloaded packages organized.

```
# setenv PKGDIR /usr/ports/packages/All
```

What Does a Package Install?

Now that your software is installed, how do you find it on your system? There's no Start menu, after all! Not to worry. For a complete list of the contents of every package installed on your system, see */var/db/pkg*. This directory contains a subdirectory for every port or package installed on the system, and those subdirectories contain a list of everything each piece of software contains. For example, now that we've installed xorg 6.9, we have a directory */var/db/pkg/xorg-6.9.0*. If you look in that directory, you'll see the following:

```
# ls /var/db/pkg/xorg-6.9.0/
+COMMENT        +CONTENTS        +DESC        +MTREE_DIRS
```

The *+COMMENT* file contains a brief description of the package, and *+DESC* contains a longer description. The file *+MTREE_DIRS* contains a mtree(1) description of this package. The interesting file is *+CONTENTS*, which lists every file installed by the package, all of the package's dependencies, and any uninstallation instructions. (The package doesn't need installation instructions now that it's installed, but uninstallation instructions could be important when you want to remove the package.)

```
# more /var/db/pkg/xorg-6.9.0/+CONTENTS
❶ @comment PKG_FORMAT_REVISION:1.1
❷ @name xorg-6.9.0
❸ @comment ORIGIN:x11/xorg
❹ @cwd /usr/local
❺ @pkgdep expat-2.0.0_1
❻ @comment DEPORIGIN:textproc/expat2
  @pkgdep libdrm-2.0.2
  @comment DEPORIGIN:graphics/libdrm
  ...
```

The first line is the version number ❶ of the format the package record is stored in. When FreeBSD changes package storage formats, the package management tools can read this to determine how to handle this package. Then we have the name of the package ❷, followed by the `ORIGIN` ❸ that indicates which category and directory this package's originating port can be found. The `cwd` label ❹ indicates where the files belonging to this package are installed. All paths to files in this package listing are relative to this directory. The `pkgdep` comment ❺ indicates a dependency on another piece of software, in this case expat-2. We also have the directory ❻ in the ports tree where this dependency can be found.

The xorg package is a bit of a cheat, however; it installs no files! FreeBSD's xorg package only exists to provide all of the dependencies required by the X Window System. The only entries you'll find in the +*CONTENTS* file are references to other packages. Let's look at the +*CONTENTS* of another package, one that actually includes files of its own. Here, we look at the contents of */usr/ports/archivers/zip*:

```
# cd /var/db/pkg/zip-2.32
# more +CONTENTS
...
```
❶ @cwd /usr/local
❷ man/man1/zip.1.gz
❸ @comment MD5:1c3dc2c955ff2e3d9a6b38b1f6150ca9
❹ @unexec rm -f %D/man/cat1/zip.1 %D/man/cat1/zip.1.gz
❺ bin/zip
```
@comment MD5:af81366669c5e1cd1fca37ea5fd70d62
bin/zipcloak
...
```

Once again, we have the working directory ❶, but then we have an actual file ❷. The combination of directory and file tells us that the zip package installed a file */usr/local/man/man1/zip.1.gz*. This is a manual page, which is good to know. We also have a comment giving the md5 checksum❸ of this file, and instructions ❹ for removing this file when the package is deleted. The package isn't just a man page, however; it also includes an actual binary file ❺. You know that zip(1) was installed as */usr/local/bin/zip*. Reading this file gives you the name and location of every file installed by the package.

Much of this information on files and directories is also available through pkg_info(1), but it's often easier to just look for yourself.

Uninstalling Packages

Use pkg_delete(1) to uninstall packages:

```
# pkg_delete xorg-6.9.0
```

You can specify a package name by the path to the package database directory—for example, the following works just fine:

```
# pkg_delete /var/db/pkg/xorg-6.9.0
```

Uninstalling a package does not uninstall any of its dependencies. As the xorg package only exists as a collection of dependencies required for the X Window System, uninstalling it really doesn't do much of anything. You must uninstall each dependency separately.

Problems can happen when you uninstall a package required by other packages. For example, the xorg package requires expat, libdrm, xorg-libraries, and many other packages. Uninstalling one of these without uninstalling the xorg package would break the xorg package and, almost certainly, related software. Any software that depends on a piece of software you've uninstalled will probably fail to work properly. You can use pkg_delete -f to force an uninstall of a package. pkg_delete(1) will warn you about dependent packages, but will obey.

Package Information

At the time you install your software, you probably know what it does and what dependencies it installed. A lot of that knowledge, however, will probably leak out of your brain once you've got the software working, and weeks or months later you won't remember it at all. Personally, I'm lucky to remember that I have a piece of software installed at all, let alone what version it was.

FreeBSD includes pkg_info(1), a tool to examine installed packages in a more friendly manner than by manually searching /var/db/pkg. pkg_info(1) uses the contents of /var/db/pkg to provide answers, but handles automatically a lot of boring manual searching and sorting for you. When run without any options, pkg_info lists each installed package with a brief description:

```
# pkg_info
915resolution-0.5.2_1,1 Resolution tool for Intel i915 video cards
ORBit-0.5.17_3     High-performance CORBA ORB with support for the C language
ORBit2-2.14.7      High-performance CORBA ORB with support for the C language
OpenSSH-askpass-1.2.2.2001.02.24 Graphical password applet for entering SSH
passphrase
Xaw3d-1.5E_1       A 3-D Athena Widget set that looks like Motif
...
```

Wow. My laptop has an awful lot of crud on it. This is useful when I decide to clean up my system and want a brief list so I can decide what to keep and what to delete.

Other pkg_info(1) Options

pkg_info(1) can provide all sorts of information about installed packages, from the detailed description to the script used to uninstall the package. All pkg_info arguments require either a package or filename for analysis, or the -a flag which means *for all packages*. For example, to learn which packages on your system require other packages, use pkg_info -aR:

```
# pkg_info -aR
Information for 915resolution-0.5.2_1,1:

Information for ORBit-0.5.17_3:

Required by:
gnome-libs-1.4.2_6
gnomecanvas-0.22.0_5
gnome-print-0.37_3
...
```

So the package 915resolution stands aloof and alone, needing nothing and not needed by any other package. If I don't need it, I can delete it. On the other hand, ORBit is required by many other packages, and I cannot arbitrarily delete it.

To find out the space needed by the files within a package, use the -s option. Note that this only includes the files installed by the package itself; files created by the package are another matter entirely. Do you count your MP3 files as part of your MP3 player's space requirements?

Another common question is, "Which package installed this file?" More than once I've been browsing through *usr/local/bin* on a Saturday night[3] and come across a file that I don't recognize, haven't used, and suspect I don't need. Use the -W flag with pkg_info to perform a sort of "reverse lookup" on files to see which packages they came from.

```
# pkg_info -W /usr/local/bin/gtail
/usr/local/bin/gtail was installed by package coreutils-6.7
```

Package Problems

FreeBSD packages seem like a great system, don't they? Well, almost. The package system has a few problems, notably the lags in the software porting process and the software synchronization requirements.

The overwhelming majority of packages contain software produced by third parties—folks who release their software on a schedule completely independent of FreeBSD. When these third parties release an updated version of their software, the maintainer or the FreeBSD ports team updates the FreeBSD port. This takes time. A small but popular port might be updated in hours, while large and less frequently used software might take days or weeks. A huge program with many dependencies and high visibility, such as GNOME or KDE, might not be updated for several weeks while all of the testing occurs. Many users feel that a new release of their favorite tool rates an immediate update of the FreeBSD package for that software, but that's logistically impossible. The FreeBSD folks refuse to rush or release software they know is buggy, not only from a concern for the quality of their work but because they get blamed for any problems with the software. If taking extra time reduces user complaints in the long term, that's what happens.

Also, many packages rely upon others to function properly. When the FreeBSD ports team changes a package, that change cascades through all the dependent packages. That's why you'll see packages with names like sudo-1.6.8.12_1. The software is named sudo, it's at version 1.6.8.12, and its FreeBSD port version number is 1. This is the second version of the FreeBSD port for sudo 1.6.8.12 (the first didn't get a number). The port changed slightly in some way, perhaps because a dependency changed, or perhaps the build method changed. Often these changes are purely internal and don't affect the software's behavior or performance.

---

[3] No, reading *usr/local/bin* is not my idea of a fun Saturday night. But my wife gets upset when I spend the evening putting random household objects in the microwave just to see what happens to them, so I make do.

If you're running a FreeBSD release and only installing software from the CD or the version shipped with your release, this interdependency isn't much of a concern. After all, the packages built for a release do not change. On the other hand, you might be running an older version of FreeBSD, but want a program that was just released. Or perhaps you're continually upgrading your system and have older versions of some software.

For example, the package OpenOffice-2.2 requires the package libiconv-1.9.2_2. If you have libiconv-1.9.1 installed, pkg_add notices that you do not have the proper dependencies installed. It will probably install anyway, but the installed software might not run correctly, depending on changes in the software itself. The smart thing to do is upgrade your libiconv install before installing the package.

One way around this problem is to always use packages from the same date or time. If you set the PACKAGESITE environment variable to the packages directory for a certain FreeBSD release, all of your packages will always match. In many cases this works just fine, as you probably don't need the absolutely latest version of many pieces of software. I think Emacs 19 worked just as well as Emacs 21, so the differences between Emacs 21.3 and Emacs 21.1 don't bother me.

Of course, this means that you won't get any security updates for packages. While this might be all right for a laptop, it's completely unacceptable for a server. I recommend that in this case you use ports rather than packages. Instead of checking for installed programs by the name of the package, ports check for the existence of the program itself. To continue our earlier example, installing OpenOffice.org from a port means that OOo builds against the version of libiconv you have installed, if that version supports all the features OOo needs. This makes the port much more flexible.

Using Ports

Installing software from ports takes longer than using packages, and the Ports Collection requires a live Internet connection. In exchange, the Ports Collection can produce more optimal results than packages. Let's take a look at a port, and not just any port. Perhaps the biggest single piece of software that runs on FreeBSD is OpenOffice.org, in */usr/ports/editors/openoffice.org-2*. This software contains a word processor, spreadsheet, presentation tool, and other assorted pieces that make it a pretty serious contender against Microsoft Office. The directory contains:

Makefile	distinfo	files	pkg-descr	pkg-plist

The *Makefile* contains the basic instructions for building the port. If you read this file, you'll quickly find that it's only a few hundred lines long. That's not a huge amount of instructions for such a complicated piece of software. Most of that file is dedicated to customizations that are only rarely used. There's almost no information about OOo itself in here, and not much about how to build software on FreeBSD. (Most of the FreeBSD ports system's *Makefiles* are in */usr/ports/Mk*; editing those files is difficult, and you really don't want to go there until you're very comfortable with make(1).)

The *distinfo* file contains checksums for the various files the port downloads, so that your system can be sure that the file transferred without error and that nobody tampered with the file before you got it.

The files directory contains all the add-on files and patches required to build this port on FreeBSD. This massive office suite, with over a hundred megabytes of source code, builds on FreeBSD with only 18 patches. Most of these patches just provide integration into the FreeBSD package system and aren't actually required to build OpenOffice.org on FreeBSD.

The file *pkg-descr* contains a lengthy description of the software.

Finally, the *pkg-plist* file is a list of all the files installed (the "packing list"). The port only installs the files listed in the packing list.

Combined, these files comprise the tools and instructions needed to build the software.

Installing a Port

If you're familiar with source code, you've probably already noticed that a port contains no actual source code. Sure, there are patches to apply to the source code, and scripts to run on the source code, but no actual source code! You might rightly ask, just how building software from source is supposed to work without source code?

When you activate a port, FreeBSD automatically downloads the appropriate source code from an approved Internet site. The port then checks the downloaded code for integrity errors, extracts the code to a temporary working directory, patches it, builds it, installs everything, and records the installation under */var/db/pkg*. If the port has dependencies, and those depedencies are not installed, it interrupts the build of the current port to build the dependencies from source. To trigger all this, you just go into the port directory and type:

```
# make install
```

You'll see lots of text scroll down your terminal as the port carries out its work, and you'll get your command prompt back when it finishes.

This all-in-one installation process handles any changes in dependencies. If a port requires another program, the port simply glosses over any minor changes in that program. If a required program's API or ABI changes, the port will handle this for you whereas a package would fail to work correctly.

As you grow more experienced in building from source, however, you'll find that this all-in-one approach isn't appropriate for every occasion. Not to worry; the Ports Collection provides the ability to take the port-building process exactly as far as you like, because make install actually runs a whole series of subcommands. If you specify one of these subcommands, make(1) runs all previous commands as well as the one you specify. For example, make extract runs `make config`, `make fetch`, `make checksum`, `make depends`, and `make extract`. These subcommands are listed below, in order:

make config

Many ports have optional components. Running `make config` lets you select which of those options you wish to support in this port. The options you select are saved for future builds of the port. These options affect how the port is built—for example, if you choose to build a program with SNMP support, you'll probably be adding a dependency on SNMP software elsewhere in the ports tree.

make fetch

Once you have configured the port, the system searches a preconfigured list of Internet sites for the program source code. The port's *Makefile* lists the authoritative download site for the file. If the source code is not at that location, the port checks a list of backup sites provided by the Ports Collection. When the port finds the source code, it downloads it. The original, downloaded source code is called a *distfile* and is stored in */usr/ports/distfiles*.

If the port requires a particular program to fetch a distfile, the port will install that program as part of this step.

make checksum

Next, as a security measure, `make checksum` confirms that the distfile's cryptographic checksum matches the one given in the port's *distinfo* file. If the distfile's master FTP server was broken into by a malicious hacker who had the source code replaced with a Trojan horse, or if the download was corrupted, this step detects it and stops the build with a warning about a checksum mismatch. It doesn't matter if the source code was corrupted during download, or if some malicious intruder put his backdoor code into the distfile before you downloaded it—you don't want to waste your time building it, and you certainly don't want to install it!

**FOOT-SHOOTING METHOD #839:
IGNORING THE CHECKSUM**

Software authors, especially free software authors, sometimes make minor changes to their code, but don't change the software version or the filename of the distfile. The FreeBSD port rightfully notices this problem and doesn't work after such a change. If you're absolutely certain that the distfile has not been compromised or corrupted, you can override this check with `make NO_CHECKSUM=YES install`. I highly recommend that you do not do this without checking with the software author. Checking with the author ensures that you're not installing compromised software, and you'll also help the software author learn about the importance of version numbers and release engineering.

---

make extract

Once FreeBSD has the port distfiles, it must uncompress and extract them. Most source code is compressed with either gzip(1) or bzip(1), and collated with tar(1), but some is distributed by other means (Zip files, compress(1), etc.). This command creates a *work* subdirectory in the port and extracts the tarball there. If the port requires a particular program to extract the distfile, it will install it now.

make patch

This command applies any patches in the port to the extracted source code in the *work* subdirectory. If the port requires a special patch program instead of the base system's patch(1), the port installs it now.

make depends

The make depends stage checks to see if the necessary dependencies are installed. For example, a window manager requires X.org. If the dependencies are not installed, this stage recurses through the various dependencies and installs them.

make configure

Next, FreeBSD checks to see if the software has a configure script. This is not the same as the make config step performed by the port. If the software came with its own configure script, the port runs it. Some ports interrupt the build at this stage to prompt you for information, but most run silently.

make build

This step complies the checked, extracted, patched, and configured software.

make install

Finally, make install installs the software and records it under */var/db/pkg*.

Integrated Port Customizations

Many software packages have extensive custom-build features. While enabling these features isn't hard for any individual piece of software, there is no universal method for defining them. With one piece of software you might have to edit the *Makefile*; with another, you may have to offer flags to the configure script. Learning how to make these changes takes time and can be an annoyance. The FreeBSD Ports Collection offers two ways to consistently configure these options on your system.

The newer, prettier method is supported by make config. This brings up a dialog box much like those you saw when you first installed FreeBSD. For example, the popular Snort intrusion detection software includes support for logging to different types of databases, integration with dynamic firewall rules, and so on. If you go to */usr/ports/security/snort* and type make config, you'll see a menu much like the one shown on Figure 11-1.

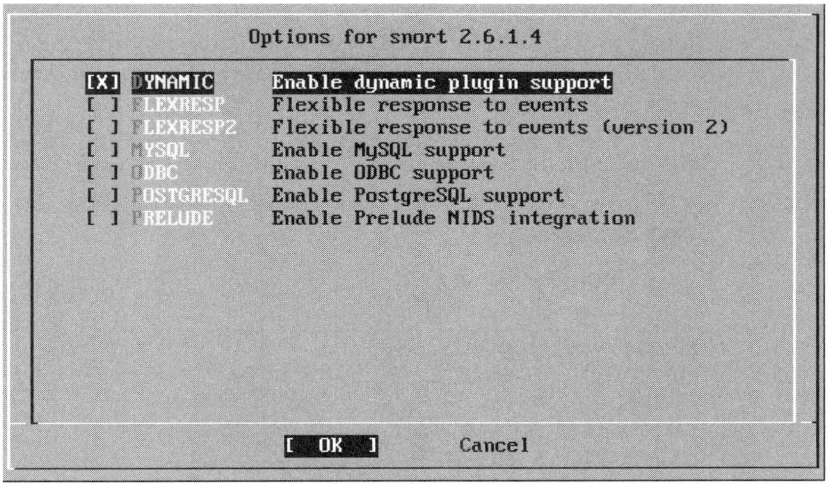

```
                    Options for snort 2.6.1.4

        [X] DYNAMIC         Enable dynamic plugin support
        [ ] FLEXRESP        Flexible response to events
        [ ] FLEXRESP2       Flexible response to events (version 2)
        [ ] MYSQL           Enable MySQL support
        [ ] ODBC            Enable ODBC support
        [ ] POSTGRESQL      Enable PostgreSQL support
        [ ] PRELUDE         Enable Prelude NIDS integration




                   [  OK  ]          Cancel
```

Figure 11-1: Port configuration

Use the spacebar to select options you like and the arrows and TAB key to move around. Hit ENTER over either OK or Cancel to finish. The port records your desired options in */var/db/ports/<portname>/options*, so that when you upgrade or rebuild the software it can simply reuse the same options. Snort is a good example of this because it has many popular options. Many people use different sorts of databases to log Snort events.

This pretty, graphical choice of options is fairly new in FreeBSD, however, and isn't used in every port. Many ports still announce additional features when you first type make install. For example, when you start to build OpenOffice.org, you'll get this message:

```
OPTIONS:

You can compile OOo with debug symbols with WITH_DEBUG=1

If you set WITH_DEBUG=2, you add internal
OOo debug support.

You can compile OOo without Mozilla connectivity with
make -DWITHOUT_MOZILLA
...
```

OOo actually lists several more options, but you get the idea. If you see this sort of announcement and you want to use one of the options provided, press CRTL-C to abort the port build. You can then set these options on the command line:

```
# make WITH_DEBUG=1 install
```

This changes the way the port is built, enabling debugging support and improving the quality of any bug reports you file with the OOo team. Here's one area where ports shine over packages. You cannot do this customization with a package.

Not all ports announce all options, however. If you're really curious about the available options, read the port's *Makefile*. Let's check out a *Makefile* next.

Port Makefiles

At the top of a *Makefile* you'll see a lot of stuff that describes the port:

```
PORTNAME=       ❶apache
PORTVERSION=    ❷2.2.4
PORTREVISION=   ❸2
CATEGORIES=     ❹www
MASTER_SITES=   ❺${MASTER_SITE_APACHE_HTTPD} \
                ${MASTER_SITE_LOCAL:S/%SUBDIR%\//clement\/:aprmysql/}
DISTNAME=       ❻httpd-${PORTVERSION}
DISTFILES=      ❼${DISTNAME}.tar.bz2 \
                apr_dbd_mysql.rev-57.c:aprmysql
```

This port is named apache ❶ and handles version 2.2.4 ❷ of that software. It's the second revision ❸ of this port for this version, so it's going to show up in */var/db/pkg* as apache-2.2.4_2. FreeBSD puts this port under */usr/ports/www* ❹. The MASTER_SITES variable generally lists the Internet sites where the software can be downloaded. Apache has many mirror sites, however, and many ports use that list of mirrors. Instead of updating dozens or hundreds of ports every time Apache adds or removes a mirror site, the Ports Collection defines an internal variable ❺ that contains a list of the mirror sites, so updates can be made in only one place. DISTNAME contains the basic name of the software's distribution file as it is released by the vendor, and DISTFILES shows the full name of that software. For example, the Apache source files are all named *httpd-<something>* ❻, and the actual file for a release is named *httpd-<version>.tar.bz2* ❼.

Further down the *Makefile* you'll find variables giving the maintainer's email address, a brief description of the port, and so on. Then you'll find entries like these:

```
❶ .if defined(WITH_EXCEPTION_HOOK)
   CONFIGURE_ARGS+=        --enable-exception-hook
   .endif
   ...
❷ .if defined (WITH_LDAP) || defined (WITH_LDAP_MODULES)
   USE_OPENLDAP=           YES
   CONFIGURE_ARGS+=        --with-ldap \
                           --with-ldap-lib="${LOCALBASE}/lib" \
                           --with-ldap-include="${LOCALBASE}/include"
   .endif
   ...
```

The `.if defined` statements are build options for the port. The first line in this example is a variable you need to set to get this functionality. I don't know what the exception hook ❶ is, and in all honesty I don't really care. If you're intimate with Apache, however, you might care about this a great deal. FreeBSD offers you a simple means to add this feature to your build. Similarly, if you want LDAP support, define `WITH_LDAP=YES` ❷ on the command line when you build Apache and, when you build the port, it will demand OpenLDAP as a dependency.

Is this an annoyance? Yes. But the alternative is to muck through the original software distribution and learn how that particular software's author wants these settings configured. True, experienced system administrators probably know how to do this for their favorite software. But they don't know how to do it for all 17,000+ packages in the Ports Collection.

If you use subcommands of `make install` to build the port (for example, `make patch` and then `make install`), you must include any options you want with every `make` command. Otherwise, the port might not build correctly. For example, if you wanted to build Apache with LDAP support, but wanted to apply a custom patch before installing, run:

```
# make patch WITH_LDAP=YES
```

After applying your patch, run:

```
# make install WITH_LDAP=YES
```

Otherwise you would patch the software with the customization option requiring LDAP, but you wouldn't actually build it with LDAP support. Your software would be internally inconsistent.

The hardest part of customizing the way your software builds is deciding which options you'd like. Unfortunately, there's no easy answer to this question, so it's best to check the software manual or website to help you decide. More than once I've installed a piece of software, read the documentation, uninstalled the software, and reinstalled it again with the correct options.

Uninstalling and Reinstalling

One nice thing about installing ports is that an installed port is treated just like a package. You can uninstall a port with pkg_delete(1) and learn about it with pkg_info(1). Since the port's installation is recorded under */var/db/pkg*, you can also go through the contents file and investigate every file the port includes.

You can also uninstall a port from the port directory. For example, FreeBSD includes several different versions of the Apache web server. You might need to evaluate several different versions and have to install and uninstall each repeatedly. Running `make deinstall` in the port directory erases the program from the main system.

After uninstalling a port, the compiled program and source files still live under the *work* subdirectory in the port. Running `make reinstall` will reinstall the uninstalled program. You can uninstall and reinstall as many times as you like.

Tracking Port Build Status

How does the Ports Collection keep track of what's already been done? If you can run `make extract` and then `make install`, how does FreeBSD know what it has already finished? The Ports Collection uses hidden files to keep note of what's been done. You can see these by doing a "long list" of the port's *work* directory:

```
# cd /usr/ports/games/oneko/work
# ls -la
total 502
...
-rw-r--r--  1 root  wheel         0 Apr 22 14:59 .build_done.oneko._usr_X11R6
-rw-r--r--  1 root  wheel         0 Apr 22 14:59
.configure_done.oneko._usr_X11R6
-rw-r--r--  1 root  wheel         0 Apr 22 14:59 .extract_done.oneko._usr_X11R6
-rw-r--r--  1 root  wheel         0 Apr 22 14:59 .install_done.oneko._usr_X11R6
-rw-r--r--  1 root  wheel         0 Apr 22 14:59 .patch_done.oneko._usr_X11R6
...
```

The files whose names begin with a dot are *hidden* files that don't show up in a normal directory listing. The Ports Collection uses these files to keep track of what stage the build process is in. Every port uses these files. See the file *.install_done.oneko._usr_X11R6*? This means that the install process has finished.

On more than one occasion, after multiple `make install/deinstall` cycles, I've had a port refuse to reinstall itself. That's generally caused by the hidden file indicating that the install has finished. Remove that file, and the reinstall can proceed.

Cleaning Up Ports

Ports can take up a lot of room. A software suite such as X.org can take up a few hundred megabytes, while OpenOffice.org needs almost nine gigabytes to build! The Ports Collection includes a method to remove preinstallation files you're no longer using.

Once you have your programs installed and configured as desired, you really don't need the copy of the source code or the intermediate files used to build the software any longer. You can remove it with `make clean`. This erases the *work* directory of the current port and all dependencies, so be sure you're happy with your new program before doing this. You can also clean a port immediately upon install by running `make install clean` when you install it.

You might also want to remove the original distfiles, stored in */usr/ports/distfiles*. The make `distclean` command removes the distfiles for the current port and all dependencies.

To clean the entire ports tree, run make `clean -DNOCLEANDEPENDS` directly under */usr/ports*. This takes some time, however, and while there are faster ways to remove every *work* directory in the ports tree, this one is directly supported by the FreeBSD Project.

Building Packages

If you're using ports, you can build your own packages to install on other FreeBSD machines, which saves a lot of time and ensures that you have identical software running on every machine. If you have several machines running OOo, for example, and you want them to all have identical features, you can build OOo once and then make a package out of it to install on all the other machines.

The command to create a package is make `package`. This installs the program on the local machine and creates a package in the port's directory. Simply copy this package to other systems and run pkg_add(1) to install it.

If you create the directory */usr/ports/packages*, the Ports Collection will create a packages tree in that location. Instead of placing the new package in the port's directory, the port will place the package in the appropriate category under */usr/ports/packages*.

LOCAL PACKAGE REPOSITORIES

Remember the PACKAGESITE environment variable? Set that to a path on your local anonymous FTP server (Chapter 17) or an NFS share (Chapter 8) and put your custom packages there. You can then use pkg_add -r on your other machines, and they will automatically grab packages from your local repository.

Changing the Install Path

If you have dozens, or even hundreds, of FreeBSD systems, all with mostly identical configurations, you might find the default port or package installation path of */usr/local* problematic. In many large server farms, */usr/local* is reserved for programs that are unique to the individual machine, and other software packages that are used by every system in the server farm are expected to be installed elsewhere, such as */opt* or */usr/pkg*. Set this during the port build with the PREFIX variable:

```
# make PREFIX=/usr/pkg install clean
```

The port installs all of its files under this directory. For example, programs that normally go into */usr/local/bin* end up in */usr/pkg/bin*.

Setting make Options Permanently

If you get sick and tired of typing the same options repeatedly when building ports, you can list them in */etc/make.conf*, as make(1) applies any options in this file to your ports. If a variable doesn't mean anything to the software, having it set won't hurt.

For example, suppose your standard database program is MySQL. You want any software that can support MySQL to be built to work with it. Define the variable WITH_MYSQL in */etc/make.conf*:

```
WITH_MYSQL=YES
```

Now, any port you install that has optional MySQL support will automatically configure itself appropriately.

LOCAL DISTFILE REPOSITORIES

If you have several machines that you maintain with ports, it's best to create a local distfile repository. You can download the distfiles from the Internet once on one machine, and then other machines can access those files over the local LAN, making builds faster and reducing external bandwidth use. Set the environment variable MASTER_SITE_OVERRIDE to the location of your central distfile repository; now, when you build a port, the system will check that location first. This could be a local anonymous FTP server, or even a path to an NFS share.

Ports and Package Security

It's hard to keep track of security for ports. Each software vendor has its own process for handling security problems. An update to a port might mean that there's a security problem, or it might mean that there's a newer version available. How do you know which ports can be insecure?

FreeBSD provides portaudit(1), a tool for comparing your installed ports against a database of security vulnerabilities. If a security problem is discovered in a port, the FreeBSD team updates the portaudit security database to describe the problem. The next time you run portaudit(1), you'll be notified of the problem. Start by installing portaudit:

```
# cd /usr/ports/ports-mgmt/portaudit
# make all install clean
```

By default, portaudit(1) integrates itself with periodic(1) so that it runs every day. During this run, it automatically downloads the latest vulnerability database from *http://www.freebsd.org* and compares it with the list of ports on your system. The results appear in the daily periodic report mailed to root, along with a link to a URL describing the problem and suggested fixes. Here's a sample message you might see:

```
Affected package: mozilla-1.7.13_2,2
Type of problem: mozilla -- multiple vulnerabilities.
Reference: <http://www.FreeBSD.org/ports/portaudit/e6296105-449b-11db-ba89-
000c6ec775d9.html>
```

Additionally, the Ports Collection runs portaudit(1) every time you try to install a port. If the port has known security problems, it stops you. If you really and truly want to install insecure software, override this with `make install DISABLE_VULNERABILITIES=YES` to install the port.

Running portaudit(1) every night does not make your system secure. A perfectly secure version of a server program configured incorrectly will be just as insecure as the world's best bank vault when you forget to close the door and hang out a sign that says *FREE MONEY*. I encourage you to use a program such as Nessus to check for security problems.

This chapter gets you up and running with FreeBSD software, but the next chapter kicks software management up a notch.

12

ADVANCED SOFTWARE MANAGEMENT

While the last chapter covered the simple cases of installing and running software on FreeBSD, FreeBSD also makes some difficult things possible and offers opportunities for system administrators to better meet the needs of the users. Knowing how the system really works helps you make better decisions. For example, while multiple processors, multicore processors, and HyperThreading can all increase system performance, they don't always help as much as you might think. Knowing how different types of multiprocessing affect different types of workloads tells you where you can improve performance and where you cannot. Multiprocessing impacts threading libraries and schedulers, so we'll cover them as well.

For your programs to start at boot and stop cleanly at shutdown, you must be able to create and edit proper startup and shutdown scripts. While some programs stop nicely when you just kill the operating system under them, others (for example, databases) demand a gentler shutdown. Starting and stopping system services cleanly is an excellent habit to develop, so we'll learn more about the FreeBSD startup and shutdown scripts.

Under normal circumstances, you'll never need to know how FreeBSD's linking and shared library support works, but we'll discuss them anyway. Why? Because normal circumstances are, oddly, quite rare in the computer business.

Finally, FreeBSD can run software designed for other operating systems. We'll learn how to do this, focusing on the popular Linux compatibility package that allows FreeBSD to use unmodified Linux software, as well as on running software written for other hardware architectures.

Using Multiple Processors: SMP

Computers with multiple CPUs have been around for decades, but now they are exploding in popularity. FreeBSD has supported the use of multiple CPUs since version 3, but multiprocessor and multicore hardware is just becoming common. Modern operating systems use *symmetric multiprocessing (SMP)*, or multiple identical processors. (Yes, some multiple processor systems don't require identical CPUs. You probably have one in your computer right now, as many video cards have a small processor specifically for graphics tasks.)

SMP systems have many advantages over single processors, and it's not just the obvious "more power!" If you think about it at the microscopic level, in very small timeframes, a CPU can only do one thing at a time. Every process on the computer competes for processor time. If the CPU is performing a database query, it isn't accepting the packet that the Ethernet card is trying to deliver. Every fraction of a second the CPU does a *context switch* and works on some other request, as directed by the kernel. This happens so often and so quickly that the computer appears to be doing many things at once—much as a television picture appears to be moving when it's really just showing individual pictures one after the other very quickly.

I have WindowMaker providing a desktop, Firefox displaying ancient submissions to a mailing list, and OpenOffice.org accepting my typing. Network interrupts are arriving; the screen is displaying text; the MP3 player is streaming Blue Oyster Cult to my earphones—all apparently seamlessly multitasking. Actually, this only appears simultaneous to my feeble brain. In reality, the computer merely switches from one task to another very quickly. One millisecond, it's sending another sliver of sound to my headphones, and the next, it's updating text on the screen.

With multiple processors, your computer really *can* perform multiple operations simultaneously. This is very useful—but system complexity skyrockets.

Kernel Assumptions

To understand SMP and the problems associated with it, we must delve into the kernel. All operating systems face the same challenges when supporting SMP, and the theory here is applicable across a wide variety of platforms. FreeBSD is somewhat different from many other operating systems, however, because it has 30 years of Unix heritage to deal with, and its development model doesn't allow the work to stop for months at a time. What follows is a gross simplification. Kernel design is a tricky subject, and it's almost impossible for any description to do it justice. Nevertheless, here's a rough stab at it.

FreeBSD divides CPU utilization into time slices. A *time slice* is the length of time one CPU spends doing one task. One process can use the CPU either for a full time slice or until there is no more work for it to do, at which point the next task may run. The kernel uses a priority-based system to allocate time slices and to determine which programs may run in which time slices. If a process is running, but a higher-priority process presents itself, the kernel allows the first process to be interrupted, or *preempted*. This is commonly referred to as *preemptive multitasking*.

Although the kernel is running, it isn't a process. Any process has certain data structures set up by the kernel, and the kernel manipulates those data structures as it sees fit. You can consider the kernel a special sort of process, one that behaves very differently from all other processes. It cannot be interrupted by other programs—you cannot type `pkill kernel` and reboot the system.

The kernel has special problems, not faced by other parts of the system. Imagine that you have a program sending data over the network. The kernel accepts data from the program and places it in a chunk of memory to be handed to the network card. If the computer can only do one thing at a time, nothing happens to that piece of memory or that network card until the kernel gets back to that task. If you have multiple processors, however, the computer can perform multiple tasks simultaneously. What if two different CPUs, both working on kernel tasks, direct your network card to perform different actions at the same time? The network card behaves much as you do when you have your boss screaming in one ear and your mom in the other; nothing you do can satisfy them. What if one CPU allocates memory for a network task, while the other CPU allocates that same memory for a filesystem task? The kernel becomes confused, and the results will not please you.

Older FreeBSD and Unix kernels declare that the kernel is nonpreemptive and cannot be interrupted. This simplifies kernel management because everything becomes completely deterministic: When a part of the kernel allocates memory, it can count on that memory being unchanged when it executes the next instruction. No other part of the kernel will alter that chunk of memory. When the computer could only do one thing at a time, this was a safe assumption. Start doing many things at once, however, and this assumption blows apart.

SMP: The First Try

The first implementation of SMP support in FreeBSD was very simple minded. Processes were scattered between the CPUs, achieving a rough balance, and there was a lock on the kernel. Before a CPU would try to run the kernel, it would check to see if the lock was available. If the lock was free, the CPU held the lock and ran the kernel. If the lock was not free, the CPU knew that the kernel was being run elsewhere and went on to handle something else. This lock was called the *Big Giant Lock (BGL)*, or later just *Giant*. Under this system, the kernel could know that data would not change from under it. Essentially, Giant guaranteed that the kernel would only run on one CPU, just as it always had.

This strategy worked kind of adequately for two CPUs. You could run a medium-level database and a web server on a twin-CPU machine and feel confident that the CPU wouldn't be your bottleneck. If one CPU was busy serving web pages, the other would be free to answer database queries. But if you had an eight-CPU machine, you were in trouble; the system would spend a lot of time just waiting for Giant to become available!

This simplistic SMP technique is neither efficient nor scalable. The standard textbooks on SMP rarely mention this method because it's so clunky. Some other SMP-handling methods are worse, however. For example, the default setup of a twin-processor Windows 2000 system dedicates one processor to the user interface and the other to everything else. This technique also rarely appears in the textbooks, although it does help your mouse appear more responsive.

Today's SMP

A new SMP method was implemented in FreeBSD 5.0 and is being continually refined even today. FreeBSD has fragmented Giant into many smaller locks, and now every part of the kernel uses the smallest possible lock to perform its tasks.

Initially, the locks were implemented on core kernel infrastructure, such as the scheduler (the part of the kernel that says which tasks may have which time slices), the network stack, the disk I/O stack, and so on. This immediately improved performance, because while one CPU was scheduling tasks the other could be processing network traffic. Then, locks were pushed lower into the various kernel components. Each part of the network stack developed its own lock, then each part of the I/O subsystem, and so on—allowing the kernel to do multiple things simultaneously. These separate kernel subprocesses are called *threads*. Each type of locking has its own requirements. You'll see references to many different locks such as mutexes, sx locks, rw locks, spinlocks, and semaphores. Each has its own benefits and drawbacks, and each must be carefully applied within the kernel.

Fine-grained locking is *a lot* harder than it sounds. Lock too finely, and the kernel spends more time processing locks than pushing data. Lock too coarsely, and the system wastes time waiting for locks to become available. Locking sufficient for a 2-processor system stalls and chokes a 32-processor system. Lock adjustment and tuning has taken years, is still ongoing, and will continue throughout the life of FreeBSD.

SMP Problems: Deadlocks, Deadly Embraces, and Lock Order Reversals

All of these kernel locks have complicated rules for their use, and they interact with each other in myriad ways. The rules protect against unexpected lock interactions. Suppose that kernel thread A needs resources Y and Z, kernel thread B also needs Y and Z, but B needs Z before it needs Y. If A locks Y while B locks Z, then A winds up waiting for Z while B waits for Y. Neither thread can proceed until the missing resource is freed. This *deadly embrace* will destabilize the system, probably bringing it down. Proper locking avoids this problem, among others.

You might see a console message warning of a *lock order reversal*, meaning that locks have been applied out of order. While this kernel notice is not always an omen of impending doom, it's important to pay attention.

The WITNESS kernel option specifically watches for locking order and lock ordering violations. WITNESS is enabled by default on FreeBSD-current (see Chapter 13), and if you report a problem with your system, the development team might ask you to enable it. WITNESS makes the kernel inspect every action it takes for locking order violations, which reduces system performance. Running WITNESS, reading the messages, and acting on them is an excellent way to help improve FreeBSD, however.

Handling Lock Order Reversals

When you get one of these Lock Order Reversal messages, copy the LOR message in its entirety. In addition to appearing on the console, such messages are logged to */var/log/messages* for your convenience. Once you have the lock order message, check the Lock Order Reversal status page, currently at *http://sources.zabbadoz.net/freebsd/lor.html*. This site contains a list of all previously reported lock order reversals. Compare the first few lines of your LOR message to the LOR messages on the site. If your LOR appears on this page, the associated comment will give you some insight as to how to proceed. Many of the LORs on this page are known to be harmless, while some are patched in a later version of FreeBSD.

If your LOR does not appear on the Lock Order Reversal site, check the FreeBSD mailing list archives for the first couple of lines of your LOR. If you find your Lock Order Reversal on the mailing lists, read the message and take the recommended action. There's no need to post a "me too" message on the mailing list unless a developer specifically asked for notification of further LORs of that type.

If you have a new Lock Order Reversal, congratulations! Discovering a new LOR is not as satisfying as discovering a new insect species—you don't get to name your LOR, for one thing—but it does help the FreeBSD Project. File a problem report for your new Lock Order Reversal, as discussed in Chapter 21. Provide full details on your system, especially the work being performed at the time the Lock Order Reversal appeared.

Processors and SMP

You'll see three different types of multiprocessor systems: multiple processors, multiple cores, and HyperThreading. You need to understand the differences among them, as the different processor types have a direct impact on system and application behavior.

Multiple processors are physically separate chips on the mainboard. They are what we traditionally think of as processors, with the ability to cooperate with one another. The processors are all independent, with their own processor features (such as cache, registers, and so on), each controlling its own hardware.

Multicore processors have multiple computing units inside a single chip. They are growing in popularity, as multicore systems use less power and generate less heat than comparable multiple-processor systems. The cores might share onboard features, such as cache and registers. Each core might be slower than a single standalone processor, but the multiple cores provide additional parallelism. Multicore CPUs have better performance on threaded applications or on systems with many processes running, but an application that runs as a single monolithic process would do better on a faster single-core CPU. A machine, especially a server, can have multiple multicore processors.

HyperThreading is a proprietary Intel technology that allows a single-core processor to split itself into multiple virtual processors. The virtual processor is not a full-fledged CPU, however; for example, it's only available when the first CPU is waiting for something. Under a strict definition of SMP, this qualifies as *symmetric multiprocessing*, as all of the CPUs are treated equally. This virtual processor isn't as powerful as the real processor, so it's not really equal. While someone could write a time slice scheduler that would take advantage of this, it's not very useful for the vast majority of workloads. No Unix-like operating system has a HyperThreading-smart scheduler. Also, HyperThreading presents a variety of security problems. A task running on one virtual processor can capture data—such as cryptographic keys—from a task running on another virtual processor. For this reason, FreeBSD disables HyperThreading by default. If you want to try HyperThreading on an Intel CPU, set the sysctl machdep.hyperthreading_allowed to 1 and evaluate your application performance. If you have a system where users do not actually log in, then the security issues are probably not important in your case. (If you provide jailed virtual machines, then you *do* have users logging in.)

Using SMP

Remember that multiple processors don't necessarily make the system faster. One processor can handle a certain number of operations per second. A second processor just means that the computer can handle twice as many operations per second, but those operations are not necessarily any faster.

Think of the number of CPUs as the lanes on a road. If you have one lane, you can move one car at a time past any one spot. If you have four lanes, you can move four cars past that spot. Although the four-lane road won't allow those cars to reach their destination more quickly, there'll be a lot more of them arriving at any one time. If you think this doesn't make a difference, contemplate what would happen if someone replaced your local freeway with a one-lane road. CPU bandwidth is important.

While one CPU can only do one thing at a time, one process can only run on one CPU at a time. Most processes cannot perform work on multiple processors simultaneously. Threaded programs are an exception, as we'll see later in this chapter. Some programs work around this limitation by running multiple processes simultaneously and letting the operating system scatter them as needed between processors. Apache did this for many years. Threaded programs are specifically designed to work with multiple processors and don't have to take such actions. Many threaded programs simply create a whole bunch of threads to process data and scatter those threads across CPUs, which is a simple and effective way to handle parallelism. Other programs do not handle multiple CPUs at all. If you find that one of your CPUs is 100 percent busy while the other is mostly idle, you're running a program that does not handle multiple CPUs in any way. We will dive into performance issues in Chapter 19.

SMP and make(1)

The make(1) program, which is used to build software, can start multiple processes. If your program is cleanly written, you can use multiple processes to build it. This doesn't help for small programs, but when you're building a large program such as FreeBSD itself (see Chapter 13) or OpenOffice.org, using multiple processors can really accelerate the work. Use make(1)'s -j flag to tell the system how many processes to start simultaneously. A good choice is the number of processors or cores in the system plus one. For example, on a dual-processor system with two cores on each processor, I would run five processes to build a program.

```
# make -j5 all install clean
```

Not all programs can handle being built with the -j flag. If you have problems with a build, stop using -j and try again.

Chapter 19 presents various ways to evaluate and measure performance.

Schedulers

The *scheduler* is the portion of the kernel that decides which tasks and processes may run on the CPUs, and in which order. This is a critical system component that largely determines system performance. A scheduler that chooses well makes the system perform smoothly; a scheduler that chooses badly creates slowness despite idle CPUs. The scheduler cannot arbitrarily assign priorities: Telling the database server that it can have every available time slot at the expense of disk I/O will not make the database run faster when it is waiting for a disk write to complete. Schedulers must account for different types of processors, memory, workloads, and other variables. While it might seem simple to write a scheduler for a particular type of work, creating a scheduler that works equally well on a database server, web server, desktop, and laptop is *hard*.

FreeBSD has two main schedulers, 4BSD and ULE. The 4BSD scheduler is the historical scheduler inherited from 4.4 BSD. Over the last few decades it has been well tested under a vast array of workloads. The scheduler is showing its age, however, and doesn't work all that well on four-CPU and larger systems. The 4BSD scheduler is the default in FreeBSD 7.0 and appears in kernel configuration as the option SCHED_4BSD.

The ULE scheduler was written specifically for multiprocessor systems, but it also runs perfectly fine on systems with only a single processor. ULE has demonstrated impressive performance improvements on multiprocessor systems, but doesn't have 4BSD's long history of testing and debugging. While ULE will probably become the default scheduler at some point in the future, it isn't as of this writing. Activate ULE with the SCHED_ULE kernel option.

Generally speaking, the ULE scheduler provides better performance on SMP systems with complicated applications, such as database servers. The FreeBSD team uses MySQL and PostgreSQL benchmarks in particular as test loads, and expects the results to equal or exceed the same test loads on the same hardware running current versions of Linux.[1]

WHICH SCHEDULER SHOULD YOU USE?

I recommend trying ULE on all systems. Should you discover that your system behaves badly with ULE, report the problem and, if necessary, fall back to the 4BSD scheduler. A kernel can only use one scheduler at a time.

Startup and Shutdown Scripts

The startup and shutdown scripts are known as *rc scripts* after */etc/rc*, the script that manages the multiuser boot and shutdown process. While the main rc scripts are in */etc/rc.d*, scripts in other locations manage add-on software. Ports and packages install startup scripts, but if you install your own software, you'll need to create your own rc script. If you've never used shell scripts before, read carefully. Shell scripting is not hard, and the best way to learn is by reading examples and making your own variations on those examples. Additionally, to change an existing package's startup or shutdown process, you must understand how the startup scripts function.

During boot and shutdown, FreeBSD checks */usr/local/etc/rc.d* for additional shell scripts to be integrated into the startup/shutdown process. (You can define additional directories with the local_startup *rc.conf* variable, but for now we'll assume that you have only the default directory.) The startup process specifically looks for executable shell scripts and assumes that any script it finds is a startup script. It executes that script with an argument of start. During shutdown, FreeBSD runs those same commands with an argument of stop. The scripts are expected to read those arguments and take appropriate actions.

rc Script Ordering

The most interesting thing about rc scripts is that they are self-ordering. Instead of encoding the startup order in the filenames, as many other Unix-like operating systems do, each script identifies what resources it needs before it can start. The rc system uses that information to sort the scripts into

---

[1] The FreeBSD and Linux kernel teams compete politely in this space, each trying to outdo the other. The end result is that both operating systems improve. At times, FreeBSD is faster; at other times Linux is faster. Both systems become better as a result. The FreeBSD performance team just makes sure that we spend more time in the lead.

order. This is performed by rcorder(8) at boot and at shutdown, but you can do this by hand at any time to see how it works. Just give rcorder the paths to your startup scripts as arguments.

```
# rcorder /etc/rc.d/* /usr/local/etc/rc.d/*
rcorder: Circular dependency on provision `mountcritremote' in file `archdep'.
rcorder: requirement `usbd' in file `/usr/local/etc/rc.d/hald' has no
providers.
dumpon
initrandom
geli
gbde
encswap
...
```

rcorder(8) has sorted all the scripts in */etc/rc.d* and */usr/local/etc/rc.d* into the order used at system boot. First, we see warnings: Some scripts have circular dependencies. These conflicts are not necessarily bad, because not all scripts run on every system. In this example, the script mountcritremote wants to run after the script archdep but the archdep script in turn must run after mountcritremote. The conflict can't be too bad, because my system still boots. This system has no critical remote filesystems, so the mountcritremote script doesn't actually do anything, making the error meaningless. Similarly, the hald script must run after the nonexistent usbd script. FreeBSD 7.0 doesn't have a usbd(8) daemon, but older versions of FreeBSD supported by the ports tree do. The rc system is intelligent enough to skip over these annoyances.

The rc scripts sort themselves into order based upon markers within the scripts themselves.

A Typical rc Script

The rc system undergoes constant slow evolution. Before writing your own script, take a look at one of the simpler scripts in */etc/rc.d* to confirm that what I describe is still the standard. While you might see minor changes, the script should be very similar to this example:

```
#!/bin/sh

❶ # PROVIDE: rpcbind
❷ # REQUIRE: NETWORKING ntpdate syslogd named

❸ . /etc/rc.subr

❹ name="rpcbind"
❺ rcvar='set_rcvar'
❻ command="/usr/sbin/${name}"

❼ load_rc_config $name
❽ run_rc_command "$1"
```

The PROVIDE label ❶ tells rcorder(8) the official name of this script. If another rc script needs rpcbind(8) to be running before it runs, it lists this as a dependency. Similarly, the REQUIRE label ❷ lists other scripts that must run before this script runs. This script must run after the scripts NETWORKING, ntpdate, syslogd, and named.

To use the self-ordering startup, we must include the rc script infrastructure from */etc/rc.subr* ❸. Your rc script must define the name of the command ❹ as it's listed in */etc/rc.conf.*

The rcvar statement ❺ is a leftover from the days when FreeBSD and NetBSD shared rc scripts, but the rc system expects to find it. You also need to identify exactly which command you want to run ❻—after all, it's quite possible to have multiple commands of the same name on your system, just in different directories. Next, load the configuration for this command from */etc/rc.conf* ❼. Finally, you can actually run your command ❽.

While this might look intimidating, it's not really that hard in practice. Start your customized rc script by copying an existing one. Set the command name to that of your command and change the path appropriately. Decide what the script must have run before it: Do you need the network to be running? Do you need particular daemons to be started already, or do you need to run your program before certain daemons? If you really don't know, have your script run at the very end by using a REQUIRE statement with the name of the last script run on your system. By looking through other rc scripts that provide similar functions, you'll learn how to do almost anything in a startup script.

With this simple script, you can enable, disable, and configure your program by adding information to */etc/rc.conf.* For example, if your custom daemon is named tracker, the startup script will look for variables tracker_enable and tracker_flags in */etc/rc.conf* and use them each and every time you run the startup script.

Special rc Script Providers

The rc system has a few special providers that define major points in the boot process. Use these to make writing rc scripts easier.

The FILESYSTEMS provider guarantees you that all local filesystems are mounted as defined in */etc/fstab.*

The NETWORKING provider appears after all network functions are configured. This includes setting IP addresses on network interfaces, PF configuration, and so on.

The SERVERS provider means that the system has enough basic functionality to support basic servers such as named(8) and the NFS support programs. Remote filesystems are not mounted yet.

The DAEMON provider ensures all local and remote filesystems are mounted, including NFS and CIFS, and that more advanced network functions such as DNS are operational.

At LOGIN, all network system services are running and FreeBSD is beginning to start up services to support logins via the console, FTP daemons, SSH, and suchforth.

By using one of these providers in a REQUIRE statement in your custom rc script, you can specify when, generally, you want your custom program to run without going too far into nitty-gritty details.

Using Scripts to Manage Running Programs

People who have done shell scripting probably realize that the script above doesn't actually include any cases for starting, stopping, querying, or restarting the program. rcNG provides all of that for you. You want to restart your custom daemon? Just run:

```
# /usr/local/etc/rc.d/customscript restart
```

and rcNG handles all of the tedious details.

Readers with some Unix experience probably think, "Hey, why bother using the script when I can just use the command line?" If you're familiar with a program, you probably know the exact command line needed to start and stop it. This is true, but it's not best practice. On a production server, the system administrator must start and stop each program exactly the same way every single time. By using the rcNG infrastructure, you know that the way the program starts at any random time is exactly how the program starts at system boot. Similarly, you want the program to stop exactly the same way every time, including system shutdown. While there's a certain macho pride in learning all the command-line arguments to every server daemon on your system, accepting the necessity of a consistent startup and shutdown and using the system tools to provide it each and every time is part of the difference between Unix *experience* and Unix *expertise*.

Vendor Startup/Shutdown Scripts

Perhaps you're installing a complicated piece of software, and the vendor doesn't support FreeBSD's rc system. This isn't a problem. Most vendor-supplied scripts expect to get a single argument, such as start or stop. Remember that at boot time FreeBSD runs each rc script with an argument of start, and at system shutdown it runs the scripts with an argument of stop. By adding PROVIDE and REQUIRE statements as comments to this vendor script and confirming that it accepts those arguments, you can make the script run at the proper time in the startup and shutdown process. Use of the rc system features in management scripts is not mandatory.

Debugging Custom rc Scripts

Local scripts, such as those installed by the Ports Collection, are run by */etc/rc.d/localpkg*. If your custom script is causing problems, you might try running the localpkg script with debugging to see how your script is interacting with the rc system. The best way to do this is to use debugging.

```
# /bin/sh -x /etc/rc.d/localpkg start
```

This attempts to start every local daemon on your server again, which might not be desirable on a production system. Try it on a test system first. Also, remember that the -x debugging flag is not passed on to the child scripts; you're debugging the system startup script */etc/rc.d/localpkg* itself, not the local scripts.

Managing Shared Libraries

A shared library is a chunk of compiled code that provides common functions to other compiled code. Shared libraries are designed to be reused by as many different programs as possible. For example, many programs must generate *hashes*, or cryptographic checksums, on pieces of data. If every program had to include its own hashing code, programs would be harder to write and more unpleasant to maintain. What's more, programs would have interoperability problems if they implemented hashes slightly differently, and program authors would have to learn an awful lot about hashes to use them. By using a shared library (in this example, libcrypt), the program can access hash generation functions without any compatibility and maintenance problems. This reduces the average program size, both on disk and in memory, at a cost in complexity.

Shared Library Versions and Files

Shared libraries have a human-friendly name, a version number, and an associated file. The human-friendly name is usually (but not always) similar to the associated file. For example, version 2 of the shared library called libpthread is in the file */lib/libpthread.so.2*. On the other hand, version 10 of the lightweight resolver library lwres is in the file */usr/lib/liblwres.so.10*.

Historically, when changes to the library made it incompatible with earlier versions of the library, the version number was incremented. For example, libpthread.so.2 became libpthread.so.3. The FreeBSD team does not bump these versions except at the beginning of a release cycle (see Chapter 13). Each library also has a symlink for the library name without a version, pointing to the latest version of the library. For example, you'll find that */usr/lib/libwres.so* is actually a symlink pointing to */usr/lib/libwres.so.10*. This makes compiling software much easier, as the software only has to look for the general library file rather than a specific version of that library.

FreeBSD 7 adds *symbol versioning*, which lets shared libraries support multiple programming interfaces. With symbol versioning, a shared library provides every program with the version of the library the program requires. If you have a program that requires version 2 of a library, version 3 will support the functions just as well.

Just because FreeBSD supports symbol versioning does not mean that all the software in the Ports Collection supports it. You must be alert for library version problems.

Attaching Shared Libraries to Programs

So, how does a program get the shared libraries it needs? FreeBSD uses ldconfig(8) and rtld(1) to provide shared libraries as needed; there are also a few human-friendly tools for you to adjust and manage shared library handling.

rtld(1) is perhaps the simplest program to understand. Whenever a program starts, rtld(8) checks to see what shared libraries the program needs. rtld(8) searches the library directories to see if those libraries are available, and then links the libraries with the program so everything works. You can't do very much at all with rtld(1), but it provides the vital glue that holds shared libraries together. Every modern program uses the shared library ld-elf.so that provides this for ELF binaries. (ELF is the binary format used on modern FreeBSD systems, as we'll see later in this chapter.) This functionality is so vital to system function that when you upgrade FreeBSD, the upgrade process retains the previous version of this shared library just in case it goes bad.

The Library Directory List: ldconfig(8)

Instead of searching the entire hard drive for anything that looks like a shared library every time any dynamically linked program is run, the system maintains a list of shared library directories with ldconfig(8). (Older versions of FreeBSD built a cache of actual libraries on a system, but modern versions just keep a list of directories to check for shared libraries.) If a program cannot find shared libraries that you know are on your system, this means ldconfig(8) doesn't know about the directory where those shared libraries live.[2] To see the libraries currently found by ldconfig(8), run `ldconfig -r`.

```
# ldconfig -r
/var/run/ld-elf.so.hints:
        search directories: /lib:/usr/lib:/usr/lib/compat:/usr/local/lib:/usr/
local/lib/nss
        0:-lcrypt.3 => /lib/libcrypt.so.3
        1:-lkvm.3 => /lib/libkvm.so.3
        2:-lm.4 => /lib/libm.so.4
        3:-lmd.3 => /lib/libmd.so.3
...
```

With the -r flag, ldconfig(8) lists every shared library in the shared library directories. We first see the list of directories searched, then the individual libraries in those directories. On my laptop, this list includes 433 shared libraries.

If a program dies at startup with a complaint that it cannot find a shared library, that library won't be in this list. Your problem then amounts to installing the desired library into a shared library directory, or adding the

---

[2] Or, perhaps, the libraries you *believe* are on your system are not the same as the libraries that actually *are* on your system. Never rule out your own failure until you conclusively identify the problem!

library directory to the list of directories searched. You could just copy every shared library you need to *usr/lib*, but this makes system management very difficult—much like with a filing cabinet where everything is filed under *P* for *paper*. Adding directories to the shared library list is a better idea in the medium to long term.

Adding Library Directories to the Search List

If you've added a new directory of shared libraries, you must add it to the list ldconfig(8) searches. Check these ldconfig(8) entries in *etc/defaults/rc.conf*:

```
ldconfig_paths="/usr/lib/compat /usr/local/lib /usr/local/lib/compat/pkg"
ldconfig_local_dirs="/usr/local/libdata/ldconfig"
```

The ldconfig_paths variable lists common locations for libraries. While out-of-the-box FreeBSD doesn't have the directory */usr/local/lib*, most systems grow one shortly after install. Similarly, libraries for compatibility with older versions of FreeBSD go in */usr/lib/compat*. */usr/local/lib/compat/pkg* is the location for storing old versions of libraries installed by packages. ldconfig(8) looks in */lib* and */usr/lib* by default, but the paths in this variable are common locations for shared libraries.

Ports and packages use the ldconfig_local_dirs variable to get their shared libraries into the search list without just dumping everything into */usr/local/lib*. Each package can install a file in one of these directories. The file is named after the package and contains just a list of directories with the libraries installed by the package. ldconfig checks these directories for files, reads the paths in the files, and treats those as additional library paths. For example, the port nss (*/usr/ports/security/nss*) installs shared libraries in */usr/local/lib/nss*. The port also installs a file */usr/local/libdata/ldconfig/nss*, containing only a single line with this path in it. The ldconfig startup script adds the directories in these files to its list of places to check for shared libraries.

/USR/LOCAL/LIB VS. PER-PORT LIBRARY DIRECTORIES

Isn't */usr/local/lib* specifically for libraries installed by ports and packages? Why not just put all your shared libraries into that directory? Most ports do exactly that, but sometimes having a separate directory makes maintenance simpler. For example, I have Python 2.4 installed on my laptop, and */usr/local/lib/python24* includes 587 files! Dumping all those into */usr/local/lib* would overwhelm my non-Python libraries and make it harder to find the files installed by ports with only one or two shared libraries.

To get your directory of shared libraries into the search list, either add it to the ldconfig_paths in */etc/rc.conf*, or create a file listing your directory in */usr/local/libdata/ldconfig*. Either works. Once you add the directory, the libraries in that directory are immediately available.

---

ldconfig(8) and Weird Libraries

Shared libraries have a couple of edge cases that you should understand, and many more that you really don't have to worry about. These include libraries for different binary types and libraries for other architectures.

FreeBSD supports two different formats of binaries, *a.out* and *ELF*. System administrators don't need to know the details of these binary types, but you should know that ELF binaries are the modern standard and became FreeBSD's standard in version 3.0, back in 1998. Older versions of FreeBSD used a.out. Programs compiled as one type cannot use shared libraries of the other type. While a.out binaries have largely vanished, the cost of supporting them is so low that this support has never been removed. ldconfig(8) maintains separate directory lists for a.out and ELF binaries, as you can see from the output of */etc/rc.d/ldconfig*. You'll find separate configuration options for ldconfig(8) with a.out libraries in *rc.conf*.

Another odd case is when you're running 32-bit binaries on a 64-bit FreeBSD install. This is most common when you're running the amd64 install and want to use a program from an older version of FreeBSD. 64-bit binaries cannot use 32-bit libraries, so ldconfig(8) keeps a separate directory list for them. You'll find options to configure those directories in *rc.conf* as well. Don't mix your 32-bit and 64-bit libraries!

LD_LIBRARY_PATH

While FreeBSD's built-in shared library configuration system works well if you're the system administrator, it won't work if you're just a lowly user without root access.[3] Also, if you have your own personal shared libraries, you probably don't want them to be globally available. Sysadmins certainly won't want to take the risk of production programs linking against random user-owned libraries! Here's where LD_LIBRARY_PATH comes in.

Every time rtld(1) runs, it checks the environment variable LD_LIBRARY_PATH. If this variable has directories in it, it checks these directories for shared libraries. Any libraries in these directories are included as options for the program. You can specify any number of directories in LD_LIBRARY_PATH. For example, if I want to do some testing and use libraries in */home/mwlucas/lib* and */tmp/testlibs* for my next run of a program, I would just set the variable like this:

```
# setenv LD_LIBRARY_PATH /home/mwlucas/lib:/tmp/testlibs
```

You can set this automatically at login by entering the proper command in *.cshrc* or *.login*.

---

[3] While most readers of this book will be sysadmins, you can tell your users to buy this book and read this section. They won't, but maybe they'll shut up and leave you alone.

Advanced Software Management   **357**

What a Program Wants

Lastly, there's the question of what libraries a program requires to run correctly. Get this information with ldd(1). For example, to discover what libraries Emacs needs, enter this command:

```
# ldd /usr/local/bin/emacs
/usr/local/bin/emacs:
        libXaw3d.so.8 => /usr/local/lib/libXaw3d.so.8 (0x281bb000)
        libXmu.so.6 => /usr/local/lib/libXmu.so.6 (0x2820e000)
        libXt.so.6 => /usr/local/lib/libXt.so.6 (0x28222000)
        libSM.so.6 => /usr/local/lib/libSM.so.6 (0x2826d000)
...
```

This output tells us the names of the shared libraries Emacs requires and the locations of the files that contain those libraries. If your program cannot find a necessary library, ldd(1) tells you so. The program itself announces the name of the first missing shared library when you try to run it, but ldd(1) gives you the complete list so that you can use a search engine to find all missing libraries.

Between ldconfig(8) and ldd(1), you should be fully prepared to manage shared libraries on your FreeBSD system.

Threads, Threads, and More Threads

One word you'll hear in various contexts is *thread*. Some CPUs support HyperThreading. Some processes have threads. FreeBSD has three different threading libraries. Some parts of the kernel run as threads. My pants have many many threads (although some have fewer than my wife thinks necessary for those pants to be worn in public). What are all these threads, and what do they mean?

In most contexts, a thread is a lightweight process. Remember, a *process* is a task on the system, a running program. Processes have their own process ID in the system and can be started, stopped, and generally managed by the user. Threads are pieces of a process, but they are managed by the process and cannot be directly addressed by the user. A process can only do one thing at a time, but individual threads can act independently. If you have a multi-processor system, one process can have threads running on multiple processors simultaneously.

Any threaded program needs to use a *threading library* that tells the application how to use threads on that operating system by interacting with the kernel. Threading libraries implement threading in different ways, so using particular libraries can impact application performance.

Similarly, a kernel thread is a subprocess within the kernel. FreeBSD has kernel threads that handle I/O, network, and so on. Each thread has its own functions, tasks, and locking. The threading within the kernel does not use any userland libraries.

HyperThreading is a marketing term and is not related to system threads. While you need to understand what HyperThreading is and how it impacts your system (as we discussed in the last section), it's not really part of threading.

Userland Threading Libraries

FreeBSD supports three different threading libraries: libc_r, libkse, and libthr.

The historical threading library, libc_r, implements threads entirely in userland. A process's threads are emulated within a single process. There's no scalability, nor any advantage from multiple processors. libc_r is largely unsupported, performs poorly, and is also the oldest FreeBSD threading library. FreeBSD keeps libc_r in the source tree, but no longer installs it by default. Using libc_r is not recommended, but if under some bizarre circumstances you must, you can install it from the sources:

```
# cd /usr/src/lib/libc_r
# make obj all install clean
```

The default threading library in FreeBSD 6.0 was libkse, an ambitious attempt to provide M:N threads. *M:N* threads mean that the system has *M* processors and a pool of *N* userland threads at any one time. This is theoretically the most powerful threading model, but it is very complicated and extremely difficult to implement correctly. Very few operating systems support M:N threads, and while FreeBSD's implementation worked, it did not perform optimally. libkse still ships with FreeBSD, but is no longer the default.

The libthr library is FreeBSD's new default threading library. libthr uses a simpler threading model than libkse, but provides much higher performance, in part due to its simplicity.

You'll also see references to the threading library libpthread(3). The *pthread* part is shorthand for *POSIX threads*, so this can be any threading library that complies with the POSIX specification. On FreeBSD, libpthread is just an alias for the system's default threading library.

Most of the time, the default library works perfectly. It's possible that running a particular program will expose a bug in either the program or in the threading library. Changing threading libraries can help narrow down the bug. Also, a program may perform better with a nonstandard thread library. You can make a particular program use a threading library different from what the rest of the system uses by remapping shared libraries.

Remapping Shared Libraries

Occasionally, you'll find a piece of software that you want to run with particular shared libraries not used by the rest of the system. For example, FreeBSD's standard C library is libc. You could have a second copy of libc with special functions provided just for a particular program, and you can make only that program use the special libc while using the standard libc for everything else. FreeBSD allows you to change any shared library any application gets. This sounds weird, but it is terribly useful in all sorts of edge cases. rtld(1) can lie to client programs, when */etc/libmap.conf* tells it to.

For example, suppose that your database server has better performance with a particular threading library that's not your default. ldd(1) might tell you that the program expects to use the standard shared library libpthread (aka libthr), but you might decide to try the M:N libkse threading library instead. You don't want to change the threading library used by the rest of the system, only the threading library used by that one program. When the program says, "I need libpthread," you want rtld(1) to say, "Here you go," and attach it to libkse instead. You can configure this for the whole system, for individual program names, or for the program at a specific full path.

/etc/libmap.conf has two columns. The first column is the name of the shared library the program is requesting, the second is the shared library to be provided instead. All changes take place the next time the program is executed; no reboot or daemon restart is required. For example, here we tell the system, whenever any program requests libpthread, to offer it libkse instead. These global overrides must appear first in *libmap.conf*:

```
libpthread.so.2        libkse.so.2
libpthread.so          libkse.so
```

"May I have libpthread.so.2?" "Certainly, here's libkse.so.2."

Globally remapping libraries is a rather bold step that might get you talked about by other sysadmins, but remapping libraries on a program-by-program basis is much less ambitious and more likely to solve more problems than it creates. Simply specify the desired program in brackets before the remapping statements. If you specify the program by its full path, the remap will only work if you call the program by its full path. If you give only the name, the remap will work whenever you run any program of that name. For example, here we remap csup(8) so that it uses libkse instead of libpthread when called by its full path:

```
[/usr/bin/csup]
libpthread.so.2        libkse.so.2
libpthread.so          libkse.so
```

How can you prove this worked? Well, check ldd(1):

```
# ldd /usr/bin/csup
/usr/bin/csup:
        libcrypto.so.5 => /lib/libcrypto.so.5 (0x2808f000)
        libz.so.3 => /lib/libz.so.3 (0x281b8000)
```

```
❶libpthread.so.2 => ❷/usr/lib/libkse.so.2 (0x281c9000)
    libc.so.7 => /lib/libc.so.7 (0x281db000)
```

You can see that when */usr/bin/csup* requests libpthread.so.2 ❶, rtld(1) attaches it to libkse.so.2 ❷ instead. We specified the full path to the csup binary, however, so we need to call the program by its full path. Try to use ldd on csup without calling it by its full path:

```
# cd /usr/bin
# ldd csup
csup:
        libcrypto.so.5 => /lib/libcrypto.so.5 (0x2808f000)
        libz.so.3 => /lib/libz.so.3 (0x281b8000)
        libpthread.so.2 => /lib/libpthread.so.2 (0x281c9000)
        libc.so.7 => /lib/libc.so.7 (0x281ef000)
```

By going to */usr/bin* and running ldd directly on csup without having to specify the full path, rtld doesn't see the full path to the csup(1) binary. */etc/libmap.conf* says to only use libthr for the full path of */usr/bin/csup*, so when plain naked csup requests libpthread.so.2, it is offered libpthread.so.2.

If you want to have a program use the alternate library no matter if it's called by full path or base name, just give the program name in brackets rather than the full name:

```
[csup]
libpthread.so.2          libkse.so.2
libpthread.so            libkse.so
```

Similarly, you can choose an alternate library for all of the programs in a directory by listing the directory name followed by a trailing slash. In this example, we force all programs in a directory to use an alternate library:

```
[/home/oracle/bin/]
libpthread.so.2          libkse.so.2
libpthread.so            libkse.so
```

Using *libmap.conf* lets you arbitrarily remap shared libraries. While it's most commonly used for threading libraries (and occasionally for Linux mode programs), you can inflict whatever libraries you like on your programs. You can also use LD_LIBRARY_PATH to adjust libraries, of course, but that only affects users who have that variable set.

Running Software from the Wrong OS

Traditional software is written for a particular OS and only runs on that OS. Many people built healthy businesses changing software so that it would run on another system, a process called *porting*. As an administrator, you have a few different ways to use software written for a platform other than FreeBSD. The most effective is to recompile the source code to run natively on FreeBSD.

If this isn't possible, you can run nonnative software under an emulator such as Wine, or by reimplementing the application binary interface (ABI) of the software's native platform.

Recompilation

Many pieces of software in the Ports Collection are actually ports of software originally designed for other platforms. (That's why it's called the *Ports* Collection.) Software written for Linux, Solaris, or other Unix-like operating systems can frequently be recompiled from source code with little or no modification and run flawlessly on FreeBSD. By simply taking the source code and building it on a FreeBSD machine, you can run foreign software natively on FreeBSD.

Recompiling works best when the platforms are similar. For example, FreeBSD and Linux provide many similar system functions; both are built on the standard C functions, both use similar tools, both use the GCC compiler, and so on. Over the years, the various Unix-like operating systems have diverged. Each version of Unix has implemented new features, new libraries, and new functions, and if a piece of software requires those functions it won't build on other platforms. The POSIX standard was introduced, in part, to alleviate this problem. POSIX defines the minimal acceptable Unix and Unix-like operating systems. Software written using only POSIX-compliant system calls and libraries should be immediately portable to any other POSIX-compliant operating system, and most Unix vendors comply with POSIX. The problem is ensuring that developers comply with POSIX. Many open source developers care only about having their software run on their preferred platform. For example, much Linux-specific software out there is not POSIX-compliant. And POSIX-only code does not take advantage of any special features offered by the operating system.

For example, FreeBSD has the hyper-efficient data-reading system call kqueue(2). Other Unix-like operating systems use select(2) and poll(2) instead. The question application developers ask themselves is whether they should use kqueue(2), which would make their software blindingly fast on FreeBSD but useless everywhere else, or if they should use select(2) and poll(2) to allow their software to work everywhere, albeit more slowly. The developer can invest more time and support kqueue(2), select(2), and poll(2) equally, but while this makes users happy it rather sucks from the developer's point of view.

FreeBSD takes a middle road. If a piece of software can be recompiled to run properly on FreeBSD, the ports team generally makes it happen. If the software needs minor patches, the ports team includes the patches with the port and sends them to the software developer as well. Most software developers gladly accept patches that would allow them to support another operating system. Even though they might not have that OS available to test, or they might not be familiar with the OS, a decent-looking patch from a reputable source is usually accepted.

Emulation

If software would require extensive redesign to work on FreeBSD, or if the source code is simply unavailable, we can try emulation. An *emulator* translates system and library calls for one operating system into the equivalent calls provided by the local operating system, so programs running under the emulator think that they're running on their native system. Translating all these calls creates additional system overhead, however, which impacts the program's speed and performance.

FreeBSD supports a wide variety of emulators, most of which are in the Ports Collection under */usr/ports/emulators*. In most cases, emulators are useful for education or entertainment. If you have an old Commodore 64 game that you've had an itch to play again, install */usr/ports/emulators/frodo*. (Be warned: Mounting that C64 floppy on a modern FreeBSD system will teach you more about disks than man was meant to know.) There's a Nintendo GameCube emulator in */usr/ports/emulators/gcube*, a PDP-11 emulator in */usr/ports/emulators/sim*, and so on. Emulators, though way cool, are not really useful for servers, so we won't cover them in any depth.

ABI Reimplementation

In addition to recompiling and emulating, the final option for running foreign programs is the one FreeBSD is best known for: *ABI (application binary interface) reimplementation*. The ABI is the part of the kernel that provides services to programs, including everything from managing sound cards to reading files to printing on the screen to starting other programs. As far as programs are concerned, the ABI is the operating system. By completely implementing the ABI of a different operating system on your native operating system and providing the userland libraries used by that operating system, you can run nonnative programs as if they were on the native platform.

While ABI reimplementation is frequently referred to as emulation, it isn't. When implementing ABIs, FreeBSD is not emulating the system calls but providing them for the application. No program runs to translate the system calls to their FreeBSD equivalents, and there's no effort to translate userland libraries into FreeBSD ones. By the same token, it would be incorrect to say, "FreeBSD implements Linux" or "FreeBSD implements Solaris." When this technique was created, there was no one word to describe it, and even today there isn't really a good description. You can say that FreeBSD implements the Linux system call interface and includes support for directing a binary to the appropriate system call interface, but that's quite a mouthful. You'll most often hear it referred to as a *mode*, as in "Linux mode" or "System V mode." By far, the best-supported mode is Linux mode.

The problem with ABI reimplementation is overlap. Many operating systems include system calls with generic names, such as read, write, and so on. FreeBSD's read(2) system call behaves very different from Microsoft's read() system call. When a program uses the read call, how can FreeBSD know which version it wants? You can give your system calls different names, but then you're violating POSIX and confusing the program. FreeBSD works around this by providing multiple ABIs and controlling which ABI a program uses through *branding*.

Binary Branding

Operating systems generally have a system function that executes programs. When the kernel sends a program to this execution engine, it runs the program.

Decades ago, the BSD (Unix at the time) program execution system call was changed to include a special check for programs that began with #!/bin/sh, and to run them with the system shell instead of the execution engine. BSD took this idea to its logical extreme: Its execution engine includes a list of different binary types. Each program's binary type directs it to the correct ABI. Thus, a FreeBSD system has multiple ABIs, can keep them separate, and can support programs from a variety of different operating systems.

The nifty thing about this system is that there's minuscule overhead. As FreeBSD must decide how to run the program anyway, why not have it decide what ABI to use? After all, binaries for different operating systems all have slightly different characteristics, which FreeBSD can use to identify them. FreeBSD just makes this process transparent to the end user. A binary's identification is called its *branding*. FreeBSD binaries are branded *FreeBSD*, while binaries from other operating systems are branded appropriately.

Supported ABIs

As a result of this ABI redirection, FreeBSD can run Linux and SVR4 binaries as if they were compiled natively. Older versions of FreeBSD could also run OSF/1 and SCO binaries, but the demand for these platforms has dramatically decreased.[4]

SVR4, or System V Release 4, was the last major release of AT&T UNIX. It appears as early versions of Solaris and SCO Unix. (Some SCO software is reported to perform more quickly and reliably under FreeBSD's SVR4 mode than on actual SCO Unix.) Not much SVR4 software is still in use, but should you need this capability it's there.

Linux mode, also known as the *Linuxulator*, allows FreeBSD to run Linux software. This ABI has been the most thoroughly tested because Linux's source code is available and its ABI is well documented. In fact, Linux mode works so well that many programs in the Ports Collection rely on it. I use the Linux versions of Macromedia Flash and Adobe Acrobat without trouble and have even made commercial software, such as PGP Command Line, run in Linux mode. We'll focus on Linux mode, as it's the most valuable for the average user.

---

[4] OSF/1 is tied to defunct hardware (the awesome Alpha processor), while SCO Unix appears to have died of shame.

Foreign Software Libraries

While ABI reimplementation solves one major issue, programs require more than just the ABI. Without shared libraries, supporting programs, and the rest of the userland, most programs will not run properly. No matter which ABI you use, you must have access to the userland for that platform.

To use SVR4 mode, you need a Sun Solaris 2.5.1 CD. Older versions of Solaris are not freely available, so the FreeBSD Project can't just provide these for you. This isn't insurmountable, but it makes using SVR4 mode slightly more difficult and much more expensive. If you have the CD, look at */usr/ports/emulators/svr4_base*.

The Linux userland is freely available. Since the barrier to entry is so low, we'll discuss Linux mode in some detail. Once you have a thorough understanding of how it works, you can apply this knowledge to any other ABI compatibility mode you wish to use.

Using Linux Mode

To install the Linuxulator, pick a piece of software that needs Linux mode and install that instead. The Ports Collection is smart enough to realize that a piece of software needs Linux mode and chooses the appropriate pieces of Linux to install. For example, I use Adobe Acrobat Reader (*/usr/ports/print/acroread7*) to view PDFs. Installing this port triggers installation of Linux mode.

The port downloads a large number of Linux system files and installs them under */usr/compat/linux*. A Linux program uses this userland rather than the FreeBSD userland.

The port also loads the Linux mode kernel module. To make FreeBSD load that module automatically at boot, use this *rc.conf* entry:

```
linux_enable="YES"
```

That's it! You should now be able to run Linux programs without any further configuration. All that's left are the minor annoyances and peccadilloes of Linux mode. Sadly, there's a few of those. . . .

WHAT IS LINUX_BASE?

You'll see many references to something called *linux_base*. Historically, you installed a Linux userland from a port called linux_base, and then you installed software on top of those files. Modern FreeBSD makes this transparent to the user, allowing you to install the software you need and not worry about the requirements. The various linux_base ports you'll see in */usr/ports/emulators* are designed for developer use and compatibility testing, not for you to install!

The Linuxulator Userland

Just as the *linux.ko* kernel module provides the Linux ABI, the Linuxulator requires a very minimal Linux userland. Take a look under */usr/compat/linux* and you'll see something much like the following:

```
# ls
bin     etc     lib     media   mnt     opt     proc    sbin    selinux srv
sys     usr     var
```

Looks a lot like the contents of FreeBSD's */* directory, doesn't it? If you poke around a bit you'll find that, generally speaking, the contents of */usr/compat/linux* are comparable to your core FreeBSD installation. You'll find many of the same programs in both.

One thing Linux devotees immediately notice about any linux_base port is that its contents are minimal compared to a typical Linux install. That's because each Linux-based port installs only what it requires to run. The Ports Collection expands the Linux userland as necessary when you install a new port.

Whenever possible, programs in Linux mode try to stay under */usr/compat/linux*, which is somewhat like a weak jail (see Chapter 9). When you execute a Linux binary that calls other programs, the Linux ABI first checks for the program under */usr/compat/linux*. If the program doesn't exist there, Linux mode looks in the main system. For example, suppose you have a Linux binary that calls ping(8). The ABI first searches under */usr/compat/linux/* for a ping program; as of this writing, it will find none. The ABI then checks the main FreeBSD system, finds */sbin/ping*, and uses it. The Linuxulator makes heavy use of this fallback behavior to reduce the size of the Linux mode's userland.

Alternatively, suppose a Linux binary wants to call sh(1). The Linux ABI checks under */usr/compat/linux*, finds */usr/compat/linux/bin/sh*, and executes that program instead of the FreeBSD native */bin/sh*.

Testing Linux Mode

Now that you have some idea what's installed in Linux mode, testing Linux functionality is easy. Run the Linux shell and ask it what operating system it is running on:

```
# /usr/compat/linux/bin/sh
sh-3.00$ ❶uname -a
❷Linux stretchlimo.blackhelicopters.org ❸2.4.2 ❹FreeBSD 7.0-CURRENT #7: Wed
Apr 23 21:00:47 EDT 2008 i686 i686 i386 GNU/Linux
sh-3.00$
```

When we ask what type of system ❶ this command prompt is running on, this shell responds that it's a Linux system ❷ running on top of a Linux 2.4.2 ❸ kernel called FreeBSD ❹. Pretty cool, eh?

Remember, however, that Linux mode is not a complete Linux userland. You cannot cross-compile software in the default Linuxulator install. You can only perform very basic tasks.

Identifying and Setting Brands

Branding software binaries is easier than branding cattle, but not nearly as adventurous. Most modern Unix-like binaries are in ELF format, which includes space for a comment. That's where the brand lives. FreeBSD assigns each program an ABI by the brand on that binary. If a binary has no brand, it is assumed to be a FreeBSD binary. FreeBSD recognizes three brands: FreeBSD, Linux, and SVR4.

View and change brands with brandelf(1):

```
# brandelf /bin/sh
File '/bin/sh' is of brand 'FreeBSD' (9).
```

No surprise there. This is a FreeBSD binary, so it will be executed under the FreeBSD ABI. Let's try a Linux binary:

```
# brandelf /usr/compat/linux/bin/sh
File '/usr/compat/linux/bin/sh' is of brand 'Linux' (3).
```

If you have a foreign program that won't run, check its branding. If it isn't branded or is branded incorrectly, you've probably discovered your problem: FreeBSD is trying to run the program under the native FreeBSD ABI. Change this by setting the brand manually with `brandelf -t`. For example, to brand a program Linux, do this:

```
# brandelf -t Linux /usr/local/bin/program
```

The next time you try to run the program, FreeBSD will run it under the Linux ABI and the Linux userland, and the program should work as expected.

linprocfs

Linux uses a process filesystem, or *procfs*. FreeBSD eliminated procfs some time ago as a security risk, but if you're running Linux mode, some Linux programs will require it. Using Linux software that requires procfs means accepting that risk. FreeBSD makes a Linux procfs available as linprocfs(5).

To enable linprocfs(5), add the following to */etc/fstab* after installing the Linuxulator:

```
linproc          /compat/linux/proc          linprocfs rw          0          0
```

FreeBSD loads filesystem kernel modules on demand, so just type `mount /compat/linux/proc` to activate linprocfs(5) without rebooting.

Debugging Linux Mode with truss(1)

Linux mode isn't Linux, and nowhere is this more clear than when a program breaks. Many programs have cryptic error messages, and Linux mode can obscure them further. The best tool I've ever found for debugging Linux mode is truss(1), the FreeBSD system call tracer. Some people have told me that using truss(1) for this is like putting the 12-cylinder engine from a Mack truck into a Volkswagen Beetle, but after much thought and careful consideration I've decided that I don't care. It works. Once you learn about truss(1), you'll wonder how you ever lived without it.

truss(1) identifies exactly which system calls a program makes and the results of each call. Remember, system calls are a program's interface to the kernel. When a program tries to talk to the network, or open a file, or even allocate memory, it makes a system call. This makes truss(1) an excellent way to see why a program is failing. Programs make a lot of system calls, which means that truss(1) generates a huge amount of data, making debugging with truss(1) a good candidate for script(1).

For example, I once had to install a Linux version of PGP Command Line on a FreeBSD system.[5] According to the manual, the -h flag describes how to use the program. While I have the full manual, this tells me if the program runs at all in Linux mode:

```
# pgp -h
/home/mwlucas:unknown (3078: could not create directory, Permission denied)
```

Here's the good news: The program runs! The bad news is, it chokes on something. What directory does it want to create? truss(1) can tell me that. Start a script(1) session, run the program again, and exit script(1).

Your script file will be hundreds or thousands of lines long; how can you possibly find the problem? Search for a relevant part of your error message, or for the string ERR. In this case, I searched for the string directory and found this near the end of the output:

```
...
linux_open("/home/mwlucas/.pgp/randseed.rnd",0x8002,00) ERR#2 'No such file or directory'
linux_open("/home/mwlucas/.pgp/randseed.rnd",0x80c1,0600) ERR#2 'No such file or directory'
linux_open("/home/mwlucas/.pgp/randseed.rnd",0x8002,00) ERR#2 'No such file or directory'
...
```

Aha! The program can't open a file in */home/mwlucas/.pgp*, as the directory doesn't exist. Once I create a *.pgp* directory, not only does the -h test succeed but my more complicated tests all perform flawlessly.

In addition to truss(1), you could use ktrace(1) and linux_kdump (*/usr/ports/devel/linux_kdump*) to parse the output. I suggest you try both tools and use whichever feels most comfortable to you.

---

[5] See *PGP & GPG* (No Starch Press, 2006) by yours truly. I could have either gotten PGP to run in the Linuxulator, or installed a Linux box just for a couple chapters in a book; the choice was clear.

Remember, commercial software vendors do not support their Linux
software in FreeBSD's Linux mode. If you are in an industrial environment
with service-level agreements and run the risk of paying penalties, think very
carefully before using Linux mode. The main benefit of commercial software
is having someone to blame when it breaks, but FreeBSD's Linux mode
eliminates that benefit.

Running Software from the Wrong Architecture

64-bit computing is becoming more popular, especially with AMD's creation
of the 64-bit i386-compatible architecture. Being able to run both 32-bit and
64-bit operating systems is a nearly irresistible selling point for hardware.
Software must be written for 64-bit platforms, however. While the open source
world has dealt with 64-bit computing for years thanks to Sun Solaris, many
programs were written for 32-bit operating systems. When you run FreeBSD's
amd64 platform, you will eventually find some piece of software that is only
available for i386 hardware. What to do?

Here's the good news: If your kernel has the COMPAT_IA32 option (already
in GENERIC), FreeBSD/amd64 can run all FreeBSD/i386 software. What
you cannot do is use FreeBSD/amd64 shared libraries for FreeBSD/i386
software. This means that if you want to run a complicated 32-bit program on
a 64-bit computer, you must provide 32-bit versions of the necessary libraries.
This is well supported; if you check *rc.conf* you'll find the ldconfig(8)'s options
ldconfig32_paths and ldconfig_local32_dirs. These options are specifically for
telling your amd64 system where to find 32-bit libraries.

Even more surprising, however, is that FreeBSD/amd64 can run Linux's
32-bit binaries! As 32-bit Linux software is far more common than 64-bit,
FreeBSD's Linux mode works with 32-bit software. Just include the option
COMPAT_LINUX32 in your kernel. No additional or unusual configuration is
required; Linux mode on amd64 works exactly like Linux mode on i386.
FreeBSD does not currently support running 64-bit Linux software, but just
about everything available specifically for 64-bit Linux is also available for
64-bit FreeBSD.

While there's always more to learn about software management, you now
know enough to get by. Let's go on and learn about upgrading FreeBSD.

13

UPGRADING FREEBSD

Upgrading network servers is perhaps the most annoying task in the system administrator's routine. I can manage unexplained behavior on my desktop after an upgrade, but when a whole company or hundreds of customers depend on one system, even thinking of touching that system makes my bowels churn. Any operating system upgrade can expand your burgeoning gray hair collection. Even very experienced system administrators, faced with a choice between upgrading a system in-place and jabbing red-hot needles into their own eyes, frequently have to sit down and consider their choices. While a few Unix-like systems have straightforward upgrade procedures, they require several hours to complete and a certain amount of luck.

On the other hand, one of FreeBSD's greatest strengths is its upgrade procedure. I've had machines running through three different major releases of FreeBSD and innumerable patch levels in between without reinstalling the system. Very few Windows admins routinely upgrade servers from Windows 2000 to Windows 2003, which is only one major upgrade. (Those people deserve every penny they make, by the way.) I decommission FreeBSD systems only when they are so old that the risk of hardware failure keeps me awake at night. One system started off as a FreeBSD 2.2.5 system, was upgraded to FreeBSD 3, and finally to FreeBSD 4. When FreeBSD 4.8 came out, the hard drive began making funny noises, so I elected to install the new version on a new system. The successor system ran FreeBSD 5 and 6 until it finally died.[1] The only time I suffered major inconvenience was when jumping major version numbers—that is, from FreeBSD 5 to 6. I spent a couple of hours of my time making those jumps. Just try that with other operating systems.

FreeBSD Versions

Why is upgrading FreeBSD a relatively simple matter? The key is FreeBSD's development method. FreeBSD is a continually evolving operating system. If you download the current version of FreeBSD in the afternoon, it will be slightly different from the morning version. Developers from around the world continually add changes and improvements, which makes the traditional strict release numbering used by less open software impractical. At any given moment, you can get several different versions of FreeBSD: releases, errata branches, -stable, -current, and snapshots.

Releases

If you're in a production environment, you should probably install a release version of FreeBSD and then patch your system to the proper errata branch.

A FreeBSD release has a conventional version number, like those you'd see on any other software: 5.5, 6.3, 7.0, and so on. A *release* is simply a copy of the most stable version of FreeBSD at a particular moment in time. Three or four times a year, the Release Engineering team asks the developers to focus on resolving outstanding problems rather than making major changes. The Release Engineering team cuts several release candidates from this code and offers each for public testing. When the FreeBSD team is satisfied with the results of their own and the community's testing, the result is given a release number. The development team then returns their attention to their regular projects.[2]

Errata Branches

An *errata branch* is a particular FreeBSD release plus any security and stability patches issued for that release. While the FreeBSD team works very hard to assure that each and every release is bug free, that goal just isn't realistic. It sometimes happens that a security junkie with nothing better to do discovers a new way to breach deployed servers a week after FreeBSD's latest release. The security team provides the errata branches

---

[1] "In the data center, nobody can hear your power supply scream."

[2] Despite what you might think, "annoying the users" is not a regular project for FreeBSD developers. It's a fringe benefit.

to support users who want their systems to remain as stable as humanly possible without sacrificing security.

Each release has its own errata branch. For example, FreeBSD 7.0-errata is different than FreeBSD 7.1-errata, and upgrading between the two is just as error-prone as upgrading from FreeBSD 7.0 to FreeBSD 7.1. API and ABI changes are completely, absolutely, entirely forbidden in an errata branch; applications that work on a release will perform in exactly the same manner on any version of the errata branch. For maximum stability, stay with the errata branch of the version you installed.

As of this writing, the FreeBSD Project supports errata branches for two years after release, but this can change. Watch *http://www.freebsd.org/security* or the *FreeBSD-announce@FreeBSD.org* mailing list for updates on support scheduling and end-of-life notices. Of course, with the source code available, it's possible for you to continue to support an old release for as long as you use it. You just can't expect the FreeBSD team to keep doing all the work for you forever!

FreeBSD-current

FreeBSD-current, or just *-current*, is the bleeding-edge, latest version of FreeBSD which contains code that is making its first public appearance. While the developers have test servers and post patches for review before applying, that's still much less exposure than the wide userbase of FreeBSD-current. FreeBSD-current is where much initial peer review takes place; at times, -current undergoes radical changes that give experienced system administrators migraines.

FreeBSD-current is made available for developers, testers, and interested parties, but it is not intended for general use. Support for user questions about -current is very slim because the developers simply don't have time to help a user fix his web browser while thousands more critical problems demand attention. Users are expected to help fix these problems or to patiently endure them until someone else fixes them.

To make matters worse, -current's default settings include assorted debugging code, special warnings, and related developer features. These make -current run slower than any other version of FreeBSD. You can disable all this debugging, but if you do so, you won't be able to file a proper trouble report when you have a problem. This means that you're even more out on your own. Check out the file */usr/src/UPDATING* on your -current system for debugging details.

If you can't read C and shell code, or don't feel like debugging your OS, or don't like computer functions failing arbitrarily, or just don't like being left hanging until your problem annoys someone who can fix it, -current is not for you. The brave are certainly welcome to try -current, as is anyone willing to devote a large amount of time to learning and debugging FreeBSD or anyone who needs a lesson in humility. You are not forbidden to use -current; you're just on your own. -current isn't always the bleeding edge, but sometimes it might be the why-are-my-fingers-suddenly-little-wiggling-stumps? edge. You have been warned.

To run -current you *must* read the *FreeBSD-current@FreeBSD.org* and *cvs-src@FreeBSD.org* mailing lists. These are high-traffic lists with hundreds of warnings, alerts, and comments a day. If you're reading this book, you probably shouldn't post on these lists; just read and learn. If someone discovers that the newest filesystem patches transform hard drives into zombie minions of Cthulhu, this is where the information will be made available.

-current Code Freezes

Every 12 to 18 months, FreeBSD-current goes through a month of *code freeze,* during which no non-critical changes are permitted and all known critical problems are being fixed. The goal is to stabilize FreeBSD's latest and greatest and to polish off the rough corners. At the end of the code freeze (or shortly after), -current becomes the *.0* release of a new version of FreeBSD. For example, FreeBSD 6.0 was -current at one point, as was FreeBSD 7.0.

Once the .0 release is out the door, current work branches into two lines: FreeBSD-current and FreeBSD-stable.

FreeBSD-stable

FreeBSD-stable (or just *-stable*) is the "bleeding edge for the average user," containing some of the most recent peer-reviewed code. FreeBSD-stable is expected to be calm and reliable, requiring little user attention. Once a piece of code is thoroughly tested in -current, it might be merged back into -stable. The -stable version is the one that is mostly safe to upgrade to at almost any time; you might think of it as FreeBSD-beta.

As -stable ages, the differences between -stable and -current become greater and greater, to the point where it becomes necessary to branch a new -stable off of -current. The older -stable is actively maintained for several months while the new -stable is beaten into shape. Some users upgrade to the new version of -stable immediately, others are more cautious. After a release or two of the new -stable, the older -stable is obsoleted and the developers encourage users to migrate to the new version. After some time, the older -stable will be receiving only critical bug fixes, and finally it will be abandoned entirely. You can see how this works in Figure 13-1.

Every so often -stable is polished and tested. Developers stop backporting features from -current and focus on testing. When everyone's happy with -stable's quality, it's issued a number and released. For example, the fourth release of FreeBSD 7 is FreeBSD 7.3. FreeBSD 7.3-release is just a point on the continuum of FreeBSD-stable 7.

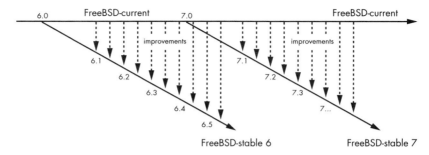

Figure 13-1: FreeBSD development branches

Users of FreeBSD-stable must read the *FreeBSD-stable@FreeBSD.org* mailing list. While this mailing list has a moderate level of traffic and a fair amount of question-and-answer exchanges that really should be on *-questions@,* important messages from developers generally have a subject beginning with HEADS UP. Look for those messages; they generally mean that a change in the system can ruin your day if you don't know about it.

THE STABILITY OF -STABLE

The word *stable* describes the code base, not FreeBSD itself. Running code from a random point along a stable branch doesn't guarantee that your system will be stable, only that the underlying code won't change radically. The API and ABI are expected to remain unchanged. While the developers take pains to ensure that -stable remains, well, stable, mistakes can and do happen. If this risk worries you, run an errata branch.

Merging from -current

The phrase *merged from -current (MFC)* means that a function or subsystem has been backported from FreeBSD-current into FreeBSD-stable (or, rarely, into an errata branch). Not all features are MFC'd, however. The point of FreeBSD-current is that it's where major changes take place, and many of those changes require months of testing and debugging. Those large changes cannot be backported, as they would badly impact the -stable users who expect a stable codebase. New drivers, bug fixes, and minor enhancements can be MFC'd—but that's about it. The FreeBSD Project makes it a point to not MFC large changes that could break user applications.

Snapshots

Every month or so, the FreeBSD Release Engineering team releases snapshots of -current and -stable and makes them available on an FTP site. Snapshots are just points along the development branch; they undergo no special packaging or testing. Snapshots do not receive the same attention to quality that releases do, but are intended as a good starting point for people interested in running -current or -stable. There is only modest quality control, and many developers have no idea that a snapshot has come out until it appears on the FTP servers. You will find bugs. You will find errors. You will experience issues that will turn your mother's hair white, assuming you haven't done that to the poor woman already.

FreeBSD and Testing

Each version and release of FreeBSD is tested in a variety of ways. Individual developers check their work on their own hardware and ask each other to double-check their work. If the work is sufficiently complicated, they might use a private Perforce source code repository to offer their work to a broader community before committing it to -current. Coverity has donated analysis software to the FreeBSD team so that the source code can be automatically audited, tested, and debugged on an ongoing basis, catching many errors before they have a chance to affect real-world users. Corporations such as Yahoo!, Sentex, and iX Systems have donated high-quality test facilities to the FreeBSD Project, providing a build/test server farm for the security team and a network performance test cluster for the kernel team. Several highly regarded FreeBSD developers have made testing a major issue within the Project.

Ultimately, however, a volunteer project with a few hundred developers cannot purchase all computer hardware ever made, nor can they run that hardware under all possible loads. The FreeBSD Project as a whole relies on donations from hardware vendors who want their equipment to run FreeBSD, companies who want to use FreeBSD on the equipment they already own, and on the user base.

The most useful testing comes from users who have real-world equipment and real-world testbeds with real-world workloads. Sadly, most of these users perform testing when they put a release CD into the computer, run an install, and fire up the system. At that point, it's too late to benefit the release. Any bugs you find might help the next release, but in the meantime an upgrade to the errata branch for that release might fix your problem. The solution here is obvious—test FreeBSD on your real-world workloads before the release is cut. Requests for testing of new -stable releases appear on *FreeBSD-stable@FreeBSD.org*. By testing a -stable or -current, you will get even better value from FreeBSD.

Which Version Should You Use?

-current, -stable, -errata, snapshots—the head spins. Yes, this seems complicated, but it all works to ensure levels of quality. Users can rest assured that an errata branch is as stable as possible and has been through extensive testing and peer review. The same user knows that the nifty new features in -stable and -current are available, if he's willing to assume the risk inherent in each version. So, which version should you use? Here are my suggestions:

Production

> If you're using FreeBSD in a production setting, track an errata branch of a -stable release.

Test

> If you're interested in how FreeBSD changes will affect your environment, track -stable on a test system.

Development

> Operating system developers, people with too much spare time and too little excitement, and blind idiots should run -current. When -current destroys your MP3 collection, debug the problem and submit a patch to fix it.

Hobby

> If you're a hobbyist, run any version! Just keep in mind the limitations of the branch you choose. If you're just learning Unix, I'd recommend -release. Once you have your feet under you, upgrade to -stable. If you have nothing but utter contempt for your data, the masochists on -current welcome like-minded company.

Upgrade Methods

FreeBSD provides three main ways to upgrade: sysinstall, binary, and source.

FreeBSD supports binary updates through FreeBSD Update. This is very similar to the binary update services offered for Windows, Firefox, and other commercial software. You can use FreeBSD Update to upgrade on an errata branch.

sysinstall is the FreeBSD installer; it can be used to upgrade to whatever release that installer ships with. For example, the installer for FreeBSD 7.5 can be used to upgrade to FreeBSD 7.5. Use sysinstall when upgrading from one release or snapshot to another.

Using source code allows you to build the programs that make up FreeBSD and install them to your hard drive. For example, if you have the source code for FreeBSD 7.5, you can upgrade to that version. This requires more effort to set up and use, but gives you much more flexibility. Upgrade from source when tracking -stable or -current.

PROTECT YOUR DATA!

Chapter 4 is called "Read This Before You Break Something Else!" for good reason. Upgrades can destroy your data. Back up your system before attempting any sort of upgrade! I upgrade my laptop every week or so, just for fun (see my earlier comment about blind idiots and -current). But before I upgrade, I make sure that all my important data is on a tarball safely cached on another machine. Copy your data to tape, file, or whatever, but don't run an upgrade without a fresh backup. You have been warned.

Binary Updates

Many operating systems offer binary updates, where users can download new binaries for their operating system. FreeBSD provides a similar program with FreeBSD Update, allowing you to easily upgrade your system along an errata branch. FreeBSD Update does not let you track -stable or -current, only an errata branch. For example, if you installed FreeBSD 7.0, FreeBSD Update will help you upgrade to 7.0-errata but not 7.0-stable or 7.1-release.

FreeBSD Update is designed to be used with standard systems running the GENERIC kernel. If you have upgraded from source, FreeBSD Update is not suitable for your system. Similarly, FreeBSD Update only provides patches to the GENERIC kernel. If you have a custom kernel, you must build updates to your kernel by hand instead of relying upon the update service.

Perform binary updates with freebsd-update(8), as configured in */etc/freebsd-update.conf*.

/etc/freebsd-update.conf

freebsd-update(8) is designed to be seamless for the average user, and updating its configuration is rarely advisable. You might have unusual circumstances, however, so here are the most useful options you'll find in this file:

KeyPrint 800...

KeyPrint lists a cryptographic signature for the update service. If the FreeBSD Update service suffered a security breach and an intruder replaced the patches with Trojan horse versions, the FreeBSD Project would need to repair the breach and issue new cryptographic keys. In this case, the breach would be announced on the security announcements mailing list (and would also be big news in the IT world). In other words, there's no reason to change this in normal use and very little reason to change it in abnormal use.

ServerName update.freebsd.org

The ServerName tells freebsd-update(8) where to fetch its updates from. While the FreeBSD Project does provide the tools to build your own updates, those tools are poorly documented. Configuring your own update server is for the brave.

Components src world kernel

By default, FreeBSD Update provides the latest patches for the source code in */usr/src*, the userland (world), and the GENERIC kernel. You might not need all of these components, however. While the kernel and userland are mandatory, you might not have the source code installed on your machine. In that case you could eliminate the src entry and only fetch the userland and kernel updates. You could also choose to receive only portions of the source code update, as described in freebsd-update.conf(5).

UpdateIfUnmodified /etc/ /var/

> FreeBSD Update provides updates to configuration files in */etc*. If you have modified these files, however, you probably don't want freebsd-update(8) to overwrite them. Similarly, */var* is very fluid, designed for customization by the system administrator; you don't want FreeBSD Update to muck with your settings. FreeBSD Update only applies patches to files in the directories listed in UpdateIfUnmodified if they are unchanged from the default.

MailTo root

> If you schedule a run of FreeBSD Update (as described later in this chapter), freebsd-update(8) sends an email of the results to the account listed in MailTo.

KeepModifiedMetadata yes

> Perhaps you've modified the permissions or owner of a system file or command. You probably don't want freebsd-update(8) to change those permissions back. With KeepModifiedMetadata set to yes, freebsd-update(8) leaves your custom permissions and ownership unchanged.

Running freebsd-update(8)

Updating your system with binary updates has two stages: downloading the updates and applying them.

To download the latest updates to your errata branch, run freebsd-update fetch.

```
# freebsd-update fetch
```

You'll see the program finding the download sources for the patches, comparing cryptographic keys for those download sources, and eventually downloading patches. Finally you'll see a message similar to this:

```
The following files will be updated as part of updating to 7.0-RELEASE-p2:
/boot/kernel/kernel
/etc/rc.d/jail
/usr/bin/dig
...
```

freebsd-update(8) stores these files in */var/db/freebsd-update*. To install the downloaded files, run freebsd-update install:

```
# freebsd-update install
Installing updates... done.
```

That's really everything. Reboot your system, and you'll see that you're running the newest errata branch!

Scheduling Binary Updates

Best practice would say to download and apply updates at a consistent time on a regular schedule, such as on your monthly maintenance day. FreeBSD Update includes specific support for this, to avoid flooding the download servers with requests every hour, on the hour. The `freebsd-update cron` command tells the system to download the updates at a random point in the next hour. Put this command in */etc/crontab* to download updates during that one-hour window. This helps reduce the load on the download servers. You'll get an email when the system has updates, so you can schedule a reboot at your convenience.

Optimizing and Customizing FreeBSD Update

Two common questions about FreeBSD Update concern the custom builds of FreeBSD and distributing updates locally.

Many people build their own versions of FreeBSD for internal use. Frequently, this is just a version of FreeBSD with various sections cut out, as we'll do with NanoBSD in Chapter 20, but some companies use extensive modifications. If you have deleted files from your FreeBSD install, freebsd-update(8) will not attempt to patch them.

Similarly, many companies like to have internal update servers for patch management. The FreeBSD Update system is specifically designed to work with caching web proxies. While all the files are cryptographically signed and verified, they are transmitted over vanilla HTTP so that your proxy can cache them. This reduces bandwidth usage.

If you really want to build your own FreeBSD Update server, the code for the update server is available in the FreeBSD CVS repository under the *projects* directory. If you don't understand what this means, you really should not be building your own update server.

Upgrading via sysinstall

The FreeBSD installer, sysinstall(8), can also upgrade a system from one release of FreeBSD to another or from the errata branch of one release to another release. The sysinstall upgrade path simply overwrites the old binaries on disk with the binaries from the next release. For example, if you're running 7.1-errata, you can use sysinstall to upgrade to 7.2. Note that this sort of upgrade is most successful when making comparatively small jumps. Updating from 7.1 to 7.2 with sysinstall(8) is very likely to be successful, updating from 7.1 to 7.5 might give you headaches, and updating from 7.1 to 9.0 will probably cause problems.

The installation CD includes upgrade instructions in the *Install* document. Before you consider upgrading, read those instructions. Also check *http://www.freebsd.org* for any last-minute errata that may affect your upgrade. Finally, confirm the integrity of your backups.

You should also know that very few developers actually use sysinstall for upgrades. It's provided only for the end users who really don't want to build their own binaries. This means that the sysinstall upgrade method has a few more rough corners compared to other methods, such as updating from source code.

The easiest way to upgrade via sysinstall is to boot off the installation CD for the release you want to upgrade to. Then follow these steps:

1. When you reach the graphic install menu, choose the **Upgrade an Existing System** option.

2. sysinstall reminds you to read the upgrade instructions. If you haven't yet read them, do so now.

3. You must now choose the distribution components. Here, it's best to update exactly the same software you installed originally. For example, if you installed the Developer distribution set, upgrade the Developer distribution set. Choosing a different distribution set causes headaches. For example, if you installed a complete FreeBSD 7.0 system but only upgrade to a minimal FreeBSD 7.1 install, you'll have programs from 7.1 but documentation from 7.0.

4. sysinstall asks if you wish to install the Ports Collection. If you are using portsnap(8) or csup(1) (see the discussions of those tools later in this chapter) to update your Ports Collection, you do not want to install the Ports Collection. If you are not updating your Ports Collection separately, install the new Ports Collection.

5. Back at the Distribution Sets menu, arrow up to **Exit** and leave the menu.

6. If you selected the system sources as an upgrade target, sysinstall(8) tells you that it cannot update the sources. That's fine, proceed anyway.

7. Now you're asked for a backup directory to store your original */etc* in. Remember, */etc* holds your vital system configuration information. The default */usr/tmp/etc* might be fine, but I usually back up */etc* somewhere on the root partition, such as */oldetc*.

8. Finally, sysinstall asks for your installation source. Use the CD you booted from.

9. After offering you one last chance to change your mind, sysinstall overwrites all the system binaries you chose to install. It replaces your kernel with a GENERIC kernel of the new version and replaces many files in */etc*.

10. Reboot.

11. After booting again, go through */etc* and verify that your vital system files are in the condition you want. While your password and group files and */etc/fstab* should be intact, you'll want to check */etc/rc.conf* and any other files you've edited.

12. Reboot again. Your base system is now safely upgraded. You must upgrade any third-party software separately.

Upgrading via Source

Another way to update your system is to build it from source code. FreeBSD is self-hosting, meaning that it includes all the tools needed to build FreeBSD. If you want to build the latest version of FreeBSD from source code, your first step is to get the latest source.

When a developer releases improvements to FreeBSD, the changes are made available worldwide within about an hour (66 minutes, to be pedantic). The FreeBSD master source code server tracks the source code, all changes made to that code, and the author of those changes. Developers can check in new code, and users can check out the latest versions through *Concurrent Versions System (CVS)*. CVS is a decent system for source code management, but an awful tool for source code distribution. CVS requires large amounts of system resources and bandwidth, and heavy usage eats hard drives. FreeBSD's resources are all donated, and it's only polite to not waste them. Thus, instead of using CVS, the Project uses a custom-written CVS repository mirroring protocol. This is much faster, more efficient, easier on the servers, and generally nicer when supporting millions of users all over the world. The master CVS source code repository is replicated to the worldwide CVSup servers, and users download the source code from those mirrors with a tool called *csup*.

csup connects to a FreeBSD CVSup mirror, compares the source code on your machine to the source code on the server, and copies any changes to your local hard drive. As complex as this might sound, it's actually fairly simple to use.

CSUP, CVSUP, CVS, AND SUP?

A lot of FreeBSD documentation and websites mention using a tool called CVSup for source code updates. csup replaced CVSup for average end users, so you can ignore any references you see to CVSup or cvsup(1) as a program. A lot of related documentation still mentions CVSup, however; for example, the mirror servers are called *cvsup servers*, the sample configurations are in */usr/share/example/cvsup*, and so on. Similarly, CVSup is a combination of CVS and sup (Software Update Protocol). You'll see occasional mentions of these tools, but you don't need to know them.

Begin by confirming that your system has the FreeBSD source code installed under */usr/src*. The source code looks like this:

```
# ls /usr/src
COPYRIGHT            UPDATING       include        sbin
LOCKS               bin            kerberos5      secure
MAINTAINERS         contrib        lib            share
Makefile            crypto         libexec        sys
Makefile.inc1       etc            ports-supfile  tools
ObsoleteFiles.inc   games          release        usr.bin
README              gnu            rescue         usr.sbin
```

This is the top directory of the FreeBSD source tree, which contains all the code needed to build all of FreeBSD. We discussed source code at length in Chapter 11. Go ahead and look through these directories to get an idea of what source code looks like.

If you find that this directory is empty, you haven't installed the source. But don't worry, you can install the source code from the installation CD by doing the following as root:

```
# mount /dev/acd0c /cdrom
# cd /cdrom/src
# ./install.sh all
```

If you don't have an install CD, you can grab the source tarball from a FreeBSD FTP mirror.

However you install the source, you start with the source code for the version of FreeBSD you installed. For example, the CDs for FreeBSD 7.0 contain the source code for FreeBSD 7.0. This source code is useful for managing the system as it is installed, but it isn't what you want for an upgrade; if you build and install the source code for FreeBSD 7.0, you'll end up reinstalling FreeBSD 7.0. csup compares the source code on your disk to the source code available on the Internet, and downloads the changes between the two versions. csup then applies these *diffs* to the source code you have on disk, changing it to the source code of the version you want. This is far more efficient than redownloading the entire 450MB source tree every time you want to upgrade! Even if you skip a release or two between upgrades, csup will only have to download a megabyte or two of new source code to complete the changes.

To update your source tree, tell csup what to update, where to update it from, and how to perform the updates.

Selecting Your Supfile

csup uses a configuration file, or *supfile*, to update your source repository. See */usr/share/examples/cvsup* for sample supfiles for updating to different versions. Once you've chosen or written a supfile that meets your needs, you can use that supfile forever. A recent */usr/share/examples/cvsup* contains the following samples:

cvs-supfile   This supfile maintains the entire FreeBSD source repository. While most users have no need for this, FreeBSD developers need it. Only use this if you roll your own releases, including floppy disk images, CD images, and so on. To get the entire CVS repository, you must use CVSup instead of csup.

doc-supfile   This supfile tells csup to update the system's local documentation (the FAQ, Handbook, and associated articles).

gnats-supfile   Use this to make a local copy of the FreeBSD Problem Report (PR) database. Again, most users won't want this.

ports-supfile This supfile updates your ports tree to the latest version (see Chapter 11).

stable-supfile Use this supfile to upgrade your source code to the latest -stable version.

standard-supfile This brings your source code up to the latest for the version of FreeBSD you are running. If you've installed a snapshot of FreeBSD 7-stable, it upgrades the source code to the latest FreeBSD 7-stable. If you're running -current, it upgrades the source code to the most recent -current. If you're tracking the FreeBSD 7.1 errata branch, it will bring your system up to the latest errata release of that version. (Historically, the *standard-supfile* only tracked -current.)

www-supfile This supfile downloads the latest version of the FreeBSD website.

The various components that can be updated with csup are called collections. For example, there is the source code collection, the documentation collection (*doc-supfile*), the Ports Collection (*ports-supfile*), and so on. Many collections are also broken up into subcollections. The source tree has subcollections for components such as userland programs, compilers, the kernel, and so on. Our main concern when upgrading FreeBSD is the source collection.

Modifying Your Supfile

Once you've chose the supfile you want, you must modify it to fit your environment. First, copy your chosen sample supfile under */etc* and open it in your preferred editor. Any line beginning with a hash mark (#) is a comment, and the sample supfiles have more comments than actual configuration entries. Most supfiles have seven entries, much like this:

```
❶ *default host=CHANGE_THIS.freebsd.org
❷ *default base=/var/db
❸ *default prefix=/usr
❹ *default release=cvs ❺tag=RELENG_6
❻ *default delete use-rel-suffix
❼ *default compress
❽ src-all
```

Your first step is to choose a source code mirror, or *CVSup server*. You'll find a complete list of mirrors at the FreeBSD website, but they generally have a name in the format *cvsup<number>.<countrycode>.freebsd.org*. For example you'll find *cvsup15.us.FreeBSD.org* (the fifteenth US CVS mirror), *cvsup2.si.freebsd.org* (the second Slovenian mirror), and so on. Ping each server to determine which has the shortest response time from your part of the Internet, or use */usr/ports/sysutils/fastest_cvsup* to automatically determine which CVSup server has the fastest response time. Put your choice in the default host space marked by `CHANGE_THIS.freebsd.org` ❶.

The `default base` ❷ tells csup where to store status files, including a list of uploaded files. This accelerates future updates. The default means that you'll find these files in */var/db/sup*.

The `default prefix` ❸ is where csup looks for the collection you've chosen. The default path is an *src* subdirectory under the prefix or, in this case, */usr/src*. Don't change this unless you want to store the system source code in a nonstandard location. csup(1) expects to control everything in this directory and can erase anything that doesn't seem to belong.

The `default release` ❹ indicates the data repository you're synchronizing—in this case, the CVS repository. The `tag` ❺ is a branch of the repository; this is where you select the desired FreeBSD version. Table 13-1 shows common sample tags.

Table 13-1: Common FreeBSD Version Tags

Tag	Version
RELENG_7	FreeBSD 7-stable
RELENG_6	FreeBSD 6-stable
RELENG_7_0	FreeBSD 7.0-release with errata
.	FreeBSD-current

When a developer removes some source files from the main FreeBSD repository, csup must remove those files from your system to maintain an identical copy. The `delete` keyword ❻ gives csup permission to do so. Similarly, the `use-rel-suffix` option allows csup to share a common base directory among several versions of the source without confusing them.

Compression ❼ saves bandwidth and costs nothing but CPU time. Use it.

Finally, tell csup which collection to update. The `src-all` ❽ flag tells csup to update the entire source tree. The sample stable-supfile contains a commented-out list of subcollections, such as `usr.bin` (the contents of */usr/bin*), `contrib` (the */usr/src/contrib directory*), `sys` (the kernel), and so on. You could theoretically update just one part of the source tree, but this is a spectacularly bad idea. Installing the */usr/bin* programs from FreeBSD-current on your FreeBSD-stable system causes all sorts of unpredictable problems and is completely unsupported.

You can specify multiple collections in a single supfile. For example, I need access to the source code collection for FreeBSD 7-stable. As a documentation committer, I need the latest documentation collection. Finally, I want the latest ports tree so I can install the most recent software on my computer. You'll find sample supfiles for each of these collections in */usr/share/examples/cvsup*, but I don't want to run csup once for each collection. I list each of these collections in my supfile.

A Complete Supfile

Here's my complete supfile, including all the changes needed to update my source code:

```
❶ *default host=cvsup15.us.freebsd.org
  *default base=/var/db
  *default prefix=/usr
❷ *default release=cvs tag=RELENG_7
  *default delete use-rel-suffix
  *default compress
  src-all
❸ ports-all tag=.
❹ doc-all tag=.
```

Note how few changes I've made to the sample. I chose a nearby CVSup server ❶ and set my desired version of FreeBSD ❷. The last two lines are the interesting bit, where I add the ports-all ❸ and doc-all ❹ collections. Only the source code collection has releases or branches; if I ask for the RELENG_7 version of the ports tree, the CVSup server would have no idea what I'm talking about and I wouldn't get any updates. By adding tag=. to the end of the collection name, I tell csup to get the latest version of this collection.

Blocking Updates: The Refuse File

While I want the whole source tree and the whole documentation tree, I only use certain parts of the ports tree. If you look under */usr/ports* you'll see subdirectories for software in Arabic, French, German, Hebrew, Hungarian, Japanese, Korean, Polish, Portuguese, Russian, Ukrainian, and Vietnamese. While I'm glad that this software is available for people who speak those languages, the chances that I will need any of these programs range from negligible to nonexistent. To tell csup to not update these directories, make a file */var/db/sup/refuse* that contains the directories you don't want updated, much like this:

```
ports/arabic
ports/french
ports/german
...
ports/vietnamese
```

The refuse file cannot contain comments.

While you can refuse anything you like, it's best to not refuse anything under */usr/src*. If you refuse updates to a critical system program, that program will eventually become incompatible with the rest of the system.

Refuse files work by pattern matching, so a refuse file entry saying sys would block everything that contains the word sys, which happens to include the entire kernel source code under */usr/src/sys*. Make your refuse entries specific enough to block only what you really want to block.

If you use a refuse file, it's best to delete the corresponding files from your hard drive. It's better to have something fail because the software doesn't exist than to have it fail in creative and difficult to diagnose ways because it exists but hasn't been updated in three years.

Also, refuse files create risk. Updating only a part of the source tree will almost certainly cause build failures. The Ports Collection is designed to work as an integrated whole, and refusing parts of it can be problematic. While the documentation tree is nicely segmented, you might have trouble even there. A refuse file might cause more trouble than it's worth, but only you can decide that.

Updating System Source Code

Once you've created a supfile, run csup by becoming root and running this command:

```
# csup supfile
❶ Cannot connect to 2001:468:902:201:209:3dff:fe11:442c: Protocol not supported
Connected to 128.205.32.21
Updating collection src-all/cvs
 Edit src/Makefile
 Edit src/Makefile.inc1
...
```

The first thing we see is a scary-looking warning ❶ that csup cannot connect to a really long string of hexadecimal numbers. That long string is an IPv6 address, which FreeBSD supports but most Internet service providers do not yet provide. csup then prints out each file it edits, and eventually prints Finished successfully when complete.

Congratulations! You now have the latest source code.

Using csup to Get the Whole Source Tree

You can run csup without a local source tree installed. csup compares what you have (nothing) with what you need (everything) and installs what you're missing (the whole tree). Mirror maintainers prefer that you install the source from CD if you have it, however; they're donating servers and bandwidth for this service and would like as many people as possible to benefit from it. A full uncompressed source tree fills about 450MB of disk space, while downloading updates to an existing tree only needs a few megabytes. Even with compression, you're using a lot of donated bandwidth. The technical term for this type of activity is *rude*.

Building FreeBSD from Source

Once you have the latest source code, look at */usr/src/UPDATING*. This file lists, in reverse chronological order, any warnings and special notices about changes to FreeBSD that are of special interest to people who build from source. This file tells you if you must take any special actions before rebuilding your system or if any major system functionality has changed. If you want your system to work after the upgrade, follow those instructions exactly. Also examine the new GENERIC or NOTES kernel configuration files for any new options or interesting kernel changes.

> ## CUSTOMIZING YOUR FREEBSD BUILD
>
> Remember back in Chapter 11 when we discussed */etc/make.conf*? FreeBSD uses a separate file to handle customizations for building FreeBSD itself. While settings in */etc/make.conf* affect all software built on the system, anything in */etc/src.conf* affects only building FreeBSD from source.

If you hang around the FreeBSD community for a while, you'll hear all sorts of stories about special methods people use for building FreeBSD. You'll hear anecdotal evidence that one method is better, faster, or stronger than the standard. While you are certainly free to use any method you like to update your system, the only method supported by the FreeBSD Project is that documented at the end of */usr/src/UPDATING*. If you follow some other procedure and have trouble, you will be referred to the documented procedure. The procedure described in this book has been used since FreeBSD 6-current and has changed only slightly from 5-current, but I still recommend double-checking these instructions against those in */usr/src/UPDATING*.

Build the World

First, build the new userland:

```
# cd /usr/src
# make buildworld
```

The make buildworld command builds from source the basic tools needed to build the system compiler, then builds the compiler and associated libraries. Finally, it uses the new tools, compiler, and libraries to build all the software included in a core FreeBSD install. (This is much like building a car starting with the instruction, "Dig iron ore out of the mine.") The buildworld places its output under */usr/obj*. It can take anywhere from one to several hours, depending on your hardware. You can continue working normally as the buildworld runs, if your hardware is robust enough; while the build consumes system resources, it won't take any of your attention.

When the `buildworld` finishes, confirm that it completed without errors. If the build ends with a bunch of messages like those you see during a failed kernel compile, do not proceed with the upgrade. If you can't figure out why the build failed, go to Chapter 1 and see how you can get help. Never attempt to install a damaged or incomplete upgrade.

Build, Install, and Test a Kernel

The best way to test your upgrade is to build a new GENERIC kernel. This separates problems in your custom kernel from general FreeBSD issues. The impetuous are certainly welcome to upgrade straight to their custom kernel configuration, but if your kernel fails, you'll need to try a GENERIC kernel. Be sure to compare your custom kernel to the new GENERIC configuration, however, to catch any changes you must make to your custom setup.

By default, the kernel upgrade process builds a GENERIC kernel. If you want to upgrade straight to a custom kernel, use the variable `KERNCONF` to tell make(1) the kernel name. You can set `KERNCONF` on the command line, in */etc/make.conf*, or in */etc/src.conf*.

You can build a new kernel in one of two ways. The `make buildkernel` command builds a new kernel, but does not install it. Follow a `make buildkernel` with a `make installkernel` to install the kernel. The `make kernel` command runs these two commands right after each other. Use the one that best matches your schedule. For example, if I'm doing a system upgrade at work during my Sunday maintenance window, I might run `make buildworld` and `make buildkernel` during the preceding week to save a few hours of my precious weekend. I don't want to install that kernel before the maintenance day, however—if the machine has a problem on Friday and needs a reboot, I want to boot the old production kernel and not the new, upgraded kernel. On Sunday morning, when I'm ready to actually upgrade, I run `make installkernel`. On the other hand, using `make kernel` makes sense when upgrading my laptop. So, to upgrade with my custom kernel I would run:

```
# make KERNCONF=HUMVEE kernel
```

Again, do not attempt to install a kernel that did not successfully compile. If your `make buildkernel` errors out and dies, fix that problem before proceeding.

Once you have a new kernel installed, reboot your computer into single-user mode. The system should restart normally. Userland programs might not work as you expect, however; many of them depend on certain kernel interfaces, which can change during an upgrade. Those are generally mentioned in */usr/src/UPDATING*. If your system runs correctly with the new kernel, proceed. Otherwise, fully document the issue and boot the old kernel to restore service while you solve the problem.

Optimization with Parallel Builds

Experienced system administrators have probably used the -j flag of the make utility to increase build speed. This starts multiple make processes and allows the system to take advantage of multiple CPUs. If you have a multi-CPU system or if your CPU has multiple cores, -j can work when building FreeBSD. A reasonable number of builds to start is one more than the number of CPUs you have. For example, if you have a quad-core processor, you can reasonably use five build processes by running make -j5 buildworld && make -j5 kernel.

The FreeBSD Project doesn't officially support -j for upgrades, even though many developers use it. If your build fails when using -j, try without -j before complaining.

Prepare to Install the New World

Beware, grasshopper! This is the point of no return. You can easily back out a bad kernel—just boot the older, known good one—but once you install a freshly built world, you cannot revert it out without using your backups. Confirm that you have a good backup before proceeding, or at least recognize that the first irrevocable step is happening right now.

If your new kernel works, you can proceed to install your freshly built userland. First, confirm that your system can install the new binaries. Each new version of FreeBSD expects that the old system supports all the necessary users, groups, and privileges that the new version requires. If a program must be owned by a particular user and that user does not exist on the system, the upgrade will fail. That's where mergemaster(8) comes in.

mergemaster compares the existing configuration files under */etc* to the new files in */usr/src/etc*, highlights the differences between them, and either installs them for you, sets them aside for evaluation, or even lets you merge two different configuration files into one. This is extremely useful during upgrades. You run mergemaster once before installing the new world, to ensure that your system can install the new binaries, and once after installing the new world, to synchronize the rest of */etc* with your new world.

Start with mergemaster(8)'s prebuildworld mode, using the -p flag. This specifically compares */etc/master.passwd* and */etc/group* and highlights any accounts or groups that must exist for an installworld to succeed.

```
# mergemaster -p
❶ *** Unable to find mtree database. Skipping auto-upgrade.

❷ *** Creating the temporary root environment in /var/tmp/temproot
*** /var/tmp/temproot ready for use
*** Creating and populating directory structure in /var/tmp/temproot
```

These initial messages, all preceded by three asterisks, are merge-master explaining what it's doing. The first message announces that mergemaster can't find the autoupgrade database ❶.

mergemaster can perform many updates automatically, as we'll see later in this chapter. mergemaster installs a temporary /etc under /var/tmp/temproot ❷, giving it a pristine set of configuration files to compare with the installed files. After that, we have our first comparison.

```
*** Displaying differences between ❶./etc/master.passwd and installed
version:
❷ --- /etc/master.passwd  Fri Nov  3 11:52:21 2006
❸ +++ ./etc/master.passwd Mon Jun  6 16:19:56 2005
  @@ -1,6 +1,6 @@
❹ -# $FreeBSD: src/etc/master.passwd,v 1.39 2005/06/06 20:19:56 brooks Exp $
❺ +# $FreeBSD: src/etc/master.passwd,v 1.40 2005/06/06 20:19:56 brooks Exp $
  #
❻ -root:$1$GtDsdFlU$F5mTAagzalt7dHImUsNSL1:0:0::0:0:Laptop Admin:/root:/bin/csh
❼ +root::0:0::0:0:Charlie &:/root:/bin/csh
```

One vital piece of information is the file being compared, and merge-master displays the filename ❶ up front. We then see the two different versions of the file being compared, the installed file first ❷ and the upgraded version of the file second ❸. The astute among you will notice that the dates don't seem to make sense; if you're running an older version of FreeBSD, why is your password file newer? The dates given are the dates that the file versions have changed. My password file was last updated on November 3, 2006, while the version of the file in /usr/src hasn't changed since June 6, 2005. A user on my system updated his password recently, that's all.[3] Notice the minus and plus signs at the beginning of these lines. A minus sign indicates that a line is from the currently installed file, while a plus sign shows that a line is from the version in /usr/src.

This is nicely illustrated by the next two lines mergemaster shows. The first password entry, marked by a minus sign, is for the current root user ❻. The second line is the password entry ❼ for the out-of-the-box upgrade. Presumably we want to keep the current password for our root account—we don't want to "upgrade" it to an empty password!

A little further on, we'll see a slightly different entry:

```
 _pflogd:*:64:64::0:0:pflogd privsep user:/var/empty:/usr/sbin/nologin
❶ +_dhcp:*:65:65::0:0:dhcp programs:/var/empty:/usr/sbin/nologin
 uucp:*:66:66::0:0:UUCP pseudo-user
```

The line for the user _dhcp ❶ is preceded by a plus sign, and there is no corresponding _dhcp entry with a minus sign. The user _dhcp does not exist on our current system. If a new user appears in the default FreeBSD config-uration, it's because a program or files in the new system expect to be owned by that user. If you don't add this user to your system, the install will fail.

---

[3] So, I haven't updated this system in a long time? No, I deliberately hacked my /etc/master.passwd to provide an example for this book. Stop looking that deeply at these examples; you'll just distress yourself.

A little later, we see a couple of items:

```
 nobody:*:65534:65534::0:0:Unprivileged user:/nonexistent:/usr/sbin/nologin
❶ -mwlucas:$1$zxU7ddkN$9GUEEVJHOr.owyAwUONFX1:1001:1001::0:0:Michael W Lucas:/
 home/mwlucas:/bin/tcsh
```

The entry with a leading minus sign ❶ is my account. Of course it doesn't exist in the base FreeBSD distribution. I need my account to survive the upgrade, of course.

```
Use 'd' to delete the temporary ./etc/master.passwd
Use 'i' to install the temporary ./etc/master.passwd
Use 'm' to merge the temporary and installed versions
Use 'v' to view the diff results again

Default is to leave the temporary file to deal with by hand

How should I deal with this? [Leave it for later] m
```

Decisions, decisions. We can delete the temporary (new) *master.passwd* file—except, we need the _dhcp user to install our new build of FreeBSD. We could install the new *master.passwd* file, but that would wipe out the accounts that already exist. If you have any doubts, you can view the differences again. The only way to move forward without breaking the new config or your old functionality is to merge the two files together. Enter **m.**

mergemaster splits your command window in half with sdiff(1). The left side displays the beginning of the currently installed file, while the right side shows the new version. Only the sections that differ are shown. Pick the side you want in your new *master.passwd* file.

```
# $FreeBSD: src/etc/master.passwd,v 1.39 2005 | # $FreeBSD: src/etc/master.passwd,v 1.40 2005
```

On the left, we have version 1.39 of the file, and on the right, version 1.40. mergemaster uses these version numbers (among other tools) to determine if a file needs updating, so our new version needs the current version number. Enter **r** to use the entry on the right, and mergemaster displays the next difference.

```
root:$1$GtDsdFlU$F5mTAagzalt7dHImUsNSL1:0:0::  |    root::0:0::0:0:Charlie &:/root:/bin/csh
```

On the left is the beginning of our customized root password entry, and on the right is the default root password. We want the version from our current password file, so enter **l.**

```
                    >    _dhcp:*:65:65::0:0:dhcp programs:/var/empty:/
```

Here's a new entry with no corresponding old entry. We need the user _dhcp to complete the installworld, so enter **r**.

```
mwlucas:$1$zxU7ddkN$9GUEEVJHOr.owyAwUONFX1:10 <
```

And here's my account. If I want to log on as myself after the upgrade, I better enter **l**.

Once we walk through every difference in the file, mergemaster presents our next choices:

```
Use 'i' to install merged file
Use 'r' to re-do the merge
Use 'v' to view the merged file
Default is to leave the temporary file to deal with by hand

 *** How should I deal with the merged file? [Leave it for later]
```

Viewing the merged file is always a good idea, unless you already know you screwed up and want to do it over. Review your merged file with **v**, and if it looks correct to you, install it with **i**.

```
*** Merged version of ./etc/master.passwd installed successfully
 *** Temp ./etc/group and installed have the same CVS Id, deleting
*** Comparison complete
Do you wish to delete what is left of /var/tmp/temproot? [no] y
```

When this minimal check finishes, mergemaster displays its closing messages and offers to clean up after itself. At this point you're done with the temporary root partition installed in */var/tmp/temproot*, so you might as well delete it. mergemaster also offers to handle certain housekeeping chores that result from the changes you made. For example, after creating a new password file, you must update the password database; mergemaster can handle that if you let it.

Finally, mergemaster compares the contents of */etc/make.conf* with the example *make.conf* under */usr/src*. Variables that have been changed or removed are displayed for your attention.

Installing the World

Still in single-user mode, you can install your brand-new FreeBSD with make installworld. You'll see numerous messages scroll down the screen, mostly including the word *install*.

```
# cd /usr/src
# make installworld
```

Some programs and files are no longer in the base system. To see what's obsoleted, run make check-old.

```
# make check-old
>>> Checking for old files
/usr/sbin/pccardc
/usr/share/man/man8/pccardc.8.gz
...
```

This lists every part of the system that was once installed on your system but is no longer required. Confirm that you're no longer using these programs; if you are, either preserve the existing unsupported program or find an alternative. A little later in the output, you'll see the shared libraries that are now obsolete:

```
>>> Checking for old libraries
/lib/libcrypto.so.4
/usr/lib/libssl.so.4
/usr/lib/libroken.so.8
/lib/libatm.so.3
/lib/libc.so.6
...
```

Finally, you'll see a list of directories that are no longer required. Removing a directory is fairly rare—I could only find seven examples of removed directories since make check-old was implemented.

If you're not specifically using any of the old programs or directories, delete them with make delete-old. make(1) prompts you with the name of each file and asks you to confirm that you want to delete the file.

Obsolete Shared Libraries

Obsolete shared libraries require more care. Many third-party programs link against shared libraries. If you delete the shared library, the program will not run. This can be really, really annoying if you, say, delete the library required by your mission-critical application. The only way to restore service is to recompile the program or replace the shared library. We discuss shared libraries in Chapter 12. If none of your programs require the library, you can delete it. Identifying every program that requires a library is a royal pain, however.

For example, check the list of obsolete shared libraries above. One of the entries is libc.so.6. Looking in */lib*, I see that we now have libc.so.7. Perhaps I shouldn't need both libc.so.6 and libc.so.7. However, just about everything depends on libc—it's like the main road through town. If I remove libc, chances are my programs from ports just won't work at all. The presence of these obsolete library versions doesn't hurt anything in the short term; you can bring your system back on line with the old libraries in addition to the new ones and reinstall your add-on software in a more leisurely manner. We'll see how to update your ports later in this chapter.

If you believe that none of the libraries listed as old are important and you can delete them anyway, I highly recommend backing each library up before removing them. By just copying the library to an *old-libs* directory somewhere, you'll make recovery much simpler when you find out that your mission-critical software doesn't work anymore. You can also store old libraries in */usr/lib/compat*, so that your programs will continue to run but the old libraries will be safely out of the way. Another option is to use libchk (*/usr/ports/sysutils/libchk*) to identify programs linked against old libraries.

mergemaster Revisited

We're almost there! While we already updated the passwords and group information in */etc*, we must update the rest of the files. mergemaster has many special functions, all documented in its man page. I'm going to specifically recommend the two that I find notably useful.

When a file is added to the base FreeBSD install, there's no need to compare it to anything. The -i option makes mergemaster automatically install new files in */etc*. I'll get a list of automatically installed files at the end of the mergemaster run.

Another set of files that I don't really care about are files that I have not edited. For example, FreeBSD has dozens of startup scripts in */etc/rc.d*. If I haven't edited a startup script, I just want to install the newest version of the script. The -U flag tells mergemaster to automatically update any base system file that I have not edited.

```
# mergemaster -iU
```

mergemaster walks through every file in */etc*, comparing it to that in the base distribution of FreeBSD. This works exactly the same way as in your pre-installation mergemaster run, so we're not going to walk through it here. Reboot, and your base system is fully upgraded! Now we just have to worry about upgrading your ports.

Finally, the -P option preserves the files that you replace. You need to set a save directory in */etc/mergemaster.rc*. While I prefer to back up the entire system beforehand, using -P to save replaced files locally might be faster than recovering from backup.

Set your preferred mergemaster options in a *.mergemasterrc* file in your home directory or in the file */etc/mergemaster.rc*. Some options in the config file are not available on the command line but are quite handy—for example, I always edit */etc/motd*, so IGNORE_MOTD=yes is very nice.

Upgrades and Single-User Mode

According to the instructions, several parts of the upgrade must be done in single-user mode. Many users consider this an annoyance, or even a handicap. FreeBSD programs are just files on disk, aren't they? Common sense says that you can just copy them to the disk, reboot, and be done with it.

Here is yet another instance where your common sense is trying to ruin your month. On rare occasions, the FreeBSD team needs to make some low-level changes in the system that require running the install in single-user mode. You can have conflicts where vital programs will not run when installed in multi-user mode. This is rare, but if it happens with */bin/sh*, you're in a world of hurt. You have a very straightforward recovery route if that happens: Remove the hard drive from the server, mount it in another machine, boot the other machine, and copy your data off the destroyed system before formatting and reinstalling. Or, you can boot from the recovery CD and pray that your skills are sufficient for the task.[4]

Running in multi-user mode can cause other upgrade problems, such as subtle races, symbol issues, and innumerable other headaches. You can choose to upgrade in multi-user mode, but don't complain if your system has a problem.

It is perfectly safe to build your new world in multi-user mode. You can even build and install your new kernel in multi-user mode. Once you start installing the userland, however, you *must* be in single-user mode and running on your upgraded kernel.

NFS AND UPGRADES

Have a lot of machines to update? Look at NFS, which we discussed in Chapter 8. Build world and all your kernels on a central, fast machine, then export */usr/src* and */usr/obj* from that system to your other clients. Running make installkernel and make installworld from those NFS exports saves build time on all your other machines and guarantees that you have the same binaries on all your FreeBSD boxes.

Shrinking FreeBSD

What's the point of having all this source code if you can't customize your operating system? FreeBSD not only gives you the source code, it provides ready-to-turn knobs to easily customize your FreeBSD build.

These options can be set in either */etc/make.conf* (see Chapter 10) or */etc/src.conf*. Settings in *src.conf* only apply to building the FreeBSD source, while *make.conf*'s settings apply to all source code building. While the full list of *src.conf* options are documented in src.conf(5), Table 13-2 shows options that I find useful on occasion. We make heavy use of these options in Chapter 20.

The build system checks to see if any of these variables are defined. Setting WITHOUT_TOOLCHAIN=NO undefines the variable, but using anything else will define it. (Yes, setting WITHOUT_SENDMAIL=postfix works.)

If you're interested in the exact effect that these options have on your system, I highly recommend Poul-Henning Kamp's build options survey at *http://phk.freebsd.dk/misc/build_options*. You can see what files are removed,

---

[4] This is the voice of experience. Don't do it. Really.

what files change, and which files are no longer installed on the system. I also recommend trying these on a test system before moving to production, as wholesale component removal can have unanticipated effects.

In most cases, adding these WITHOUT_ options includes the removed systems in the make delete-old checks. If you decide that your system does not need Sendmail, for example, the upgrade not only doesn't build a new Sendmail but offers to remove the existing one from the installed system. If you're not building a piece of software, you're better off removing it entirely.

Table 13-2: System Build Options

Option	Effect
WITHOUT_BIND	The system doesn't build any part of BIND, including named, dig, nslookup, or related libraries.
WITHOUT_CVS	The system doesn't build CVS.
WITHOUT_CXX	Do not build the C++ compiler.
WITHOUT_DICT	Do not build the dictionary.
WITHOUT_EXAMPLES	Do not install the examples.
WITHOUT_GAMES	No fun for you on this system!
WITHOUT_GDB	Do not build the debugger.
WITHOUT_HTML	Don't build HTML documentation.
WITHOUT_INET6	Drop IPv6 support.
WITHOUT_INFO	Do not build or install info(5) documentation.
WITHOUT_IPFILTER	Do not build IP Filter.
WITHOUT_IPX	Don't support IPX in any programs.
WITHOUT_KERBEROS	Do not build, install, or support Kerberos.
WITHOUT_LIBPTHREAD	Do not build libpthread (see Chapter 12).
WITHOUT_LIBTHR	Do not build libthr (see Chapter 12).
WITHOUT_LPR	Do not build the printing system.
WITHOUT_MAN	Do not build or install man pages.
WITHOUT_NIS	Do not build or support NIS(8).
WITHOUT_OBJC	Do not support Objective C.
WITHOUT_RCMDS	Do not build or install rlogin, rcp, rcp, rwho, or other r- programs.
WITHOUT_SENDMAIL	Do not build Sendmail.
WITHOUT_SHAREDOCS	Do not install the old BSD documentation.
WITHOUT_TCSH	Let me guess, you're one of those /bin/bash wackos?
WITHOUT_TOOLCHAIN	Do not install compilers, debuggers, and so on. Useful for embedded systems. If you want to use this option, you must specify it on the command line at the make installworld stage. make buildworld fails with this option.

Updating with csup and make

One popular update method glosses over csup with an additional make(1) target. I don't use this myself, but many people prefer it. Instead of using the csup command and your own supfile, you can use the example supfiles and make(1). First, define several variables in */etc/src.conf* or */etc/make.conf*:

```
SUP_UPDATE=yes
```

This tells make(1) that it will be performing software updates.

```
SUP=/usr/bin/csup
```

The SUP setting is the full path to csup (or CVSup, if you're still using that).

```
SUPHOST=cvsup9.us.freebsd.org
```

List a reasonably close FreeBSD CVSup mirror as the SUPHOST.

```
SUPFILE=/usr/share/examples/cvsup/stable-supfile
```

The SUPFILE value tells csup which configuration file to use.

```
PORTSSUPFILE=/usr/share/examples/cvsup/ports-supfile
```

PORTSSUPFILE specifies which supfile to use to upgrade ports. Don't define this if you don't want to update your Ports Collection or if you're using portsnap(8) as discussed later in this chapter.

```
DOCSUPFILE=/usr/share/examples/cvsup/doc-supfile
```

You might guess that this specifies the supfile to use for system documentation. Your guess would be wrong. DOCSUPFILE specifies a supfile to use for the documentation source code, meaning the raw SGML that makes up the Handbook, the FAQ, and all the other books and articles. If you don't have the documentation-building tools, this is nearly useless.

Once you set all these values, you can start your upgrade with:

```
# make update && make buildworld && make buildkernel
```

Is this easier than typing csup /etc/supfile && make buildworld && make buildkernel? Some people think so. It does save you the effort of writing your own supfile, but you must understand the contents of that supfile anyway. Use it if you like.

Cross-Building FreeBSD

No, cross-building isn't putting your server in a dress. FreeBSD runs on several architectures, such as the classic i386, amd64, sparc64, and so on. You can build a version of FreeBSD for any of those machines on any machine you have. For example, I have an antediluvian Sparc workstation (courtesy of David O'Brien) that dates from the 1990s. It's perfectly usable, but build-world on that system would take days. I can build a new FreeBSD for sparc64 on my fast amd64 system, export */usr/obj* and */usr/src* from my amd64 via NFS (see Chapter 8), mount those partitions on my Sparc, and install them normally.

To cross-build FreeBSD for a different architecture, specify the TARGET variable on the command line.

```
# make TARGET=sparc64 buildworld && make TARGET=sparc64 buildkernel
```

The valid targets are listed deep within */usr/src/Makefile.inc1*, but Table 13-3 shows the current usable values.

Table 13-3: Valid TARGET Values

Value	Hardware
amd64	64-bit AMD and Intel hardware
arm	ARM platforms (embedded systems)
i386	Classic x86 architectures
ia64	Intel's Itanium platform
powerpc	PowerPC hardware (early 2000s Mac)
sparc64	Classic Sparc 64-bit hardware

We'll make use of this feature in Chapter 20.

Building a Local CVSup Server

When you upgrade from source, every server must connect to a FreeBSD CVSup server and download the latest code. If you have a lot of servers, that's a lot of connections and a lot of annoyance. Getting firewall holes for all these systems can be a pain in a large company; you can probably get the firewall administrator to open TCP port 5999 for one machine, but not all of them. Every mirror is maintained by a volunteer who is donating the servers and the bandwidth, not to mention the support time. Why download the same bits over and over again?

Also, suppose you log into each of your servers one after the other and upgrade the system source on that machine. In the few minutes between starting each upgrade, the code on the mirror site might change slightly. The mirrors aren't going to stop their updates just because you're in the midst of upgrading four machines, and if you're running several production machines, you'd be best served if all the systems are absolutely identical. Even if they're running a version of -stable somewhere between 7.1-release and 7.2-release, being able to eliminate the different versions of the software as a potential problem can help troubleshooting immensely. You don't want to think, "Gee, server 86 keeps dying; could it be a bug in the slightly different version of FreeBSD I have on that system?" That's the door to madness. One way to address this problem is by running a central CVSup server (also known as a cvsupd server), which is your own local mirror of the FreeBSD source.

Running a cvsupd server isn't particularly easy, but it's less difficult than running a secure web server. The port */usr/ports/net/cvsup-mirror* handles all the tricky bits of configuring a mirror. The port is actually just a script to configure other programs for you. The script offers default suggestions to configure a sensible cvsupd server, but that's all.

One dependency of cvsup-mirror is the full CVSup program; while csup has replaced CVSup as a client, the cvsupd server program is still part of CVSup. By default, CVSup tries to install an X-based GUI. Before setting up your mirror, I strongly recommend installing CVSup without the GUI. You don't need a heavy GUI and all the associated X software to run a server. (If you already have X installed, don't fret about the X GUI; there's just no point in installing the full X suite for this one program.)

```
# cd /usr/ports/net/cvsup-without-gui
# make all install clean
# cd /usr/ports/net/cvsup-mirror
# make all install clean
```

After downloading the script, the install process pauses and prompts you for information. The default answer appears in brackets. Pressing ENTER takes the default.

```
Master site for your updates [cvsup-master.freebsd.org]?
❶cvsup5.us.freebsd.org
How many hours between updates of your files [1]? ❷1
```

First, pick the mirror you want to update from ❶. Do not take the default; instead, enter a reasonably close public mirror. Lowly end users do not rate access to the global master CVSup server reserved for official public mirrors. (As an average committer, I don't rate access to cvsup-master except in truly extraordinary circumstances, and then by request only.) Then, decide how often your mirror will update ❷. The mirrors you download from only update from the master server every hour, so don't update more often than that. I usually enter 168, which updates the repository once a week. If I'm doing server upgrades more than once a week, I'm doing something wrong!

The update process runs from cron (see Chapter 15). In many cases, I remove the scheduled repository update job and only run the update by hand. To update a group of machines to the same version of -stable, all I do is update the cvsupd server once and upgrade all the machines from the server. I frequently upgrade my test machine, put it through several rounds of extensive testing, and upgrade the rest from the same batch of source code, which guarantees good code and identical systems. There is no requirement for you to be more up to date than you wish; the source code is yours to do with as you see fit, after all!

```
Do you wish to mirror the main source repository [y]? y
Where would you like to put it [/home/ncvs]?
```

The main source repository contains the FreeBSD source code. Maintaining a local mirror of it is generally the point of this exercise. */home/ncvs* is the default location for a CVS repository; use it unless you have really good reason not to. Taking the defaults for both of these is a good idea.

```
Do you wish to mirror the installed World Wide Web data [y]? n
Do you wish to mirror the GNATS bug tracking database [y]? n
Do you wish to mirror the mailing list archive [y]? n
```

These three questions offer you the opportunity to really utilize that big hard drive you've been saving for a rainy day. The installed World Wide Web data includes the installed version of the Handbook, the FAQ, and the rest of the FreeBSD website. The GNATS bug tracking database holds all of the FreeBSD Problem Reports (PRs) filed since the Project began in the last century. And the mailing list archive contains a copy of every mailing list ever sent to any FreeBSD mailing list. I don't have time to keep up on all the existing FreeBSD mailing lists, let alone read the archive!

```
Unique unprivileged user ID for running the client [cvsupin]?
Unique unprivileged group ID for running the client [cvsupin]?
Unique unprivileged user ID for running the server [cvsup]?
Unique unprivileged group ID for running the server [cvsup]?
```

The mirror server needs two unique user IDs and the associated groups. Do not use nobody, nonroot, or nogroup—these users share other files on the system, and using them for your cvsupd mirror would aggravate any existing security problems. The default users are generally perfectly fine for this, unless you've already issued the cvsup account to Carl van Stromkern Utley-Peterson or something.

```
Syslog facility for the server log [daemon]?
```

We'll talk about syslog at length in Chapter 19. For now, take the default.

```
Maximum simultaneous client connections [8]?
```

You can easily change the maximum number of connections allowed later, but the default is fine to start with. How many machines will you be updating simultaneously, anyway?

The port offers to install the users and groups you selected earlier, as well as configure syslogd. Let it do so.

```
Would you like me to set up your crontab for hourly updates [y]? y
```

You might not want to have cvsupd update regularly; if not, choose **n** here.

To update your mirror, either use cron(8) (see Chapter 15) or run /usr/local/etc/cvsup/update.sh. You must specify the full path to this command. The first time you update, it will take a long time to download the whole source repository, but subsequent updates are brief. To run the CVSup server that allows clients to connect and update their source code, put cvsupd_enable="YES" in /etc/rc.conf.

Controlling Access

Just because you want to be a good system administrator and have a private repository doesn't mean that you want every Carl van Stromkern Utley-Peterson in the world to be able to download from your mirror. The cvsupd server allows you to control which computers have access to the mirror.

The file /usr/local/etc/cvsup/cvsupd.access controls which hosts may connect to your mirror. Lines beginning with a hash mark (#) denote comments; a plus sign (+) means that the client may connect, and a minus sign (-) means that it cannot. An asterisk (*) means that the client must authenticate, as discussed later in this section.

Each rule in cvsupd.access can refer to either a hostname or an IP address, but IP addresses are preferred. You can use netmasks with IP addresses as well. For example, to allow access from the network 192.168.0.0/16 and explicitly reject clients accessing from elsewhere, use these lines:

```
+192.168.0.0/16
-0.0.0.0/0
```

Controlling access by IP addresses is good for a static network. You might need a more flexible system, however, if you're connecting from random IP addresses. That's where password authentication comes in handy. Unfortunately, the csup client does not support authentication. If you require authentication, install /usr/ports/net/cvsup and read cvsupd(8). Most people, however, find that IP-based access lists meet their needs.

CVS MIRRORS AND DEVELOPMENT

If you want to do FreeBSD development, a CVS mirror is also usable as a local CVS repository. Add your user account to the cvsup group, and you'll have privileges to perform CVS operations on the local repository. If you're not a developer, don't worry about this.

Upgrading the Ports Collection

Just like FreeBSD itself, the Ports Collection is continually updated with new versions of software. Part of upgrading your system includes updating installed ports. Remember that add-on software can have security problems just as the main system software can, and the best defense against intrusion is to keep your software up to date. Upgrading installed software has two steps: first, updating the Ports Collection to the latest version, and then updating the installed software to the version supported in the latest Ports Collection.

If you update your system with csup(1), adding the statement ports tag=. to your supfile seamlessly updates your Ports Collection. If you're tracking an errata branch, however, you probably upgrade your system with FreeBSD Update. Or perhaps you don't want to update your entire system, just the Ports Collection. That's where portsnap(8) comes in handy.

portsnap(8) downloads and installs compressed snapshots and updates of the Ports Collection, helping system administrators keep their installed software up to date. Every hour or so, the central FreeBSD portsnap server gathers together all the changes that have occurred in the Ports Collection since the last time it checked. These changes are collected into a patch set. When you run portsnap(8), you get all of the updates that have accumulated since the last time you updated your ports tree. portsnap(8) applies those changes to your local Ports Collection, giving you the very latest ports.

PORTSNAP VS. CSUP

Use either portsnap(8) or csup(1) to update the Ports Collection, but not both. The two tools are incompatible. csup is most useful if you are tracking -stable or -current, while portsnap is best for production systems where you use binary updates. You can make either portsnap(8) or csup(1) work in either situation, but you must pick one and stick with it!

Configuring portsnap

The file */etc/portsnap.conf* tells portsnap(8) how to handle its updates. While very few people must reconfigure portsnap(8), here are the options you'll most likely want to touch. You might notice that the configuration for portsnap(8) looks much like the configuration for freebsd-update(8). The same person wrote both tools, and they use similar underlying technologies to perform similar tasks. The */etc/portsnap.conf* file contains keywords with values assigned to them.

SERVERNAME=portsnap.freebsd.org

This is the name of your desired portsnap server. The machine *portsnap .freebsd.org* is actually a pool of machines. It's possible that the FreeBSD Project will establish regional or national portsnap servers to distribute the load more sensibly, but for now this is the only available portsnap server.

KEYPRINT=9b5...

> The keyprint is the cryptographic key for the portsnap server. portsnap(8) cryptographically signs updates to guarantee authenticity and integrity. Do not change this.

REFUSE arabic korean

> The REFUSE variable lets you tell portsnap(8) to not update certain categories of software. This example prevents updates to the arabic or korean categories, much as a csup(1) refuse file does. Just as with csup(1), be careful with what you refuse; the Ports Collection is an integrated whole, and you can wind up with an inconsistent system if you arbitrarily refuse large parts of the tree.

Using portsnap(8)

The first time you run portsnap(8), use the fetch extract command:

```
# portsnap fetch extract
```

This tells portsnap to download the portsnap server's latest snapshot of the Ports Collection and extracts it under */usr/ports*. Only use fetch extract once, to initialize portsnap(8) into a known state.

For subsequent updates, use the fetch update command:

```
# portsnap fetch update
```

This downloads all the changes since the last time you ran portsnap(8) and installs those updates in the Ports Collection.

If you wish to schedule a regular portsnap run via cron(1), it's best to use the cron update command instead of fetch update. This helps distribute the load on the FreeBSD portsnap server. Schedule a 5 AM portsnap run in root's crontab with an entry like this:

```
0   5   *   *   *   /usr/sbin/portsnap cron update
```

This kicks off the actual update at a random time between 5 AM and 6 AM, which is *much* more effective than every portsnap(8) user hitting the download server simultaneously at 5 AM.

That's really everything you need to know to use portsnap(8) which is an excellent way to get the latest FreeBSD applications without using csup(1) or updating your entire source tree. The only thing you must do now is get your installed software updated to the version in the Ports Collection.

Updating Installed Ports

If you use csup to update your ports tree, anything you install from now on will be the latest version. But what about your previously installed applications? FreeBSD tracks all sorts of dependency information between add-on packages, and often updating one program will impact dozens of others. This is a royal pain to manage. Wouldn't it be nice to just say, "Update my Apache install," and have FreeBSD manage the dependencies for you? FreeBSD provides two different tools for handling this issue, portupgrade(8) and portmaster(8).

portupgrade is the original updating tool for FreeBSD ports. Written in Ruby, portupgrade maintains databases from the information in the ports tree.

portmaster is a shell script that handles the most common software maintenance tasks without invoking any extra software or databases, but does not cover all possible edge cases. We cover portmaster; while it's not as all-encompassing as portupgrade, it's far simpler, so there's less that can go wrong with it.

Initial portmaster Setup

Look for portmaster in */usr/ports/ports-mgmt/portmaster*. The usual make install clean shuffle installs it. After your install, run portmaster -L to see what it has to say about your installed ports. This can take a few minutes to run, so I suggest capturing the output in a file for leisurely analysis. (You could also use portmaster -l instead; this runs faster and provides the dependency information, but does not note obsolete ports.)

```
# portmaster -L > portmaster.out
```

portmaster categorizes ports by their relationships to one another, taking into account which other software each package requires to work properly. For example, I'm writing this book in OpenOffice.org. To work correctly, OOo requires the X Window System, assorted graphics programs, security libraries, miscellaneous fonts, and a kitchen sink with a garbage disposal of 5.5 horsepower or greater. None of these programs are part of the FreeBSD base system, and if they're not installed, OOo will not run. OOo therefore lists all of these programs as dependencies. In return, all those programs list OOo as a dependent program. These relationships allow portmaster to build a relationship tree between the ports, and portmaster uses tree terminology when referring to ports.

portmaster starts with *root ports*, which do not have dependencies and are not depended on by any other program. For example, portmaster itself requires no software other than itself, and no other program on my system requires portmaster. A few other programs, such as bash, sudo, and zip, are commonly installed root ports.

The *trunk ports* have no dependencies, but are required by other programs. Many shared libraries for graphics, encryption, and mathematics fall into this category, as do a variety of scripting and programming languages. If you use Perl, for example, the base Perl install would almost certainly be a trunk port.

Further up the tree we have *branch ports*, which both require other ports and are required by other ports. Common branch ports include Java, the X Window System, and web browser rendering engines.

Leaf ports are the tips of the tree; they have dependencies, but no programs depend on them. Typical leaf ports include text editors, oversized office suites, web browsers, chat clients, and so on.

When updating ports, it's entirely possible that a change to a trunk or branch port will affect leaf ports. If you upgrade a graphics library to a new version that is incompatible with the old version, don't be surprised if all the graphics programs using that library will no longer function.

Identifying Unneeded Software

Many of us have systems where we install software ad-hoc, play with it for a while, and then forget to remove it when we decide to not use it. When upgrade time comes, it makes sense to remove these software packages rather than spend the time to upgrade them. That's where portmaster's list of root and leaf ports is especially valuable.

portmaster(8) starts its printout with the root ports. Go through the list and identify any programs you no longer want or require. If you're not sure where a package came from, run whereis *packagename* to see where the port lives. Check the package description in the port to jog your memory and, if you still don't recognize the program, or remember it and don't want it, feel free to uninstall it. If it turns out to be something vital, you can always reinstall it later. Do the same with the leaf ports at the end of the list. Why upgrade what you don't need?

portmaster's -e flag uninstalls a port and its dependencies, if those dependencies are not required by other ports. For example, were I to uninstall OpenOffice.org, I would have many ports I no longer need. Running portmaster -e openoffice.org-2.2.0 would remove OOo and all ports required by nothing else but OOo.

Identifying and Upgrading Software

Upgrade candidates appear in portmaster(8) output like this:

```
===>>> linux_base-fc-4_8
        ===>>> New version available: linux_base-fc-4_9
```

My laptop currently has linux_base version 4_8 installed, and 4_9 is available. Is it worth going through an upgrade for a minor point release like that? Maybe, maybe not. You can always check the FreeBSD CVSWeb history for the port to see what changes took place. If it's a critical security issue, you almost certainly want to update, but if not there's no real rush. It is up to you.

If you want to update, just give portmaster the name of the port you want to upgrade. You can use the port name, the full path to the package database for the port, or use a few other methods shown in portmaster(8).

```
# portmaster linux_base-fc-4_8
```

portmaster first searches for any dependencies that need to be upgraded as part of this upgrade and kicks off jobs to upgrade those ports. It also starts fetching distfiles for the upgrade target and the dependencies. portmaster also front-loads the parts of the port build process that require user interaction. It tries to get all of the information it requires from you right up front, so that you can walk away and be assured that your upgrade won't be hung up waiting for you to press ENTER halfway through.

There's always a risk that the upgrade will fail. As uninstalling the old version is a necessary prerequisite to installing the upgrade, there's a window where a failure might leave you without either the old or the new versions of the software. portmaster doesn't just uninstall the port, however; it also creates a backup package of the old version of the software. This backup is deleted once the upgrade succeeds, but you can retain it with the -b flag. The backups are kept in /usr/ports/packages/All. What's more, if you're upgrading a whole chain of packages, portmaster retains the backups of all dependent packages until the entire upgrade is complete. If I try to upgrade OpenOffice.org with portmaster and the build fails, I'll need the older versions of my OpenOffice.org dependencies to use the older version of the software. portmaster tries hard to not leave you with an unusable mix of old and new software.

I like to keep backup packages around until I know that the new version works exactly the way I like, but some of you readers are much smarter than I am and don't require such a safety belt.

Forcing a Rebuild

portmaster can't identify every reason why a port would need an upgrade or reinstall. For example, my test server has the latest version of sudo(8) on it. If we check the shared libraries that program requires, we'll see something interesting:

```
# ldd `which sudo`
/usr/local/bin/sudo:
❶        libutil.so.5=> /lib/libutil.so.5 (0x28093000)
         libpam.so.3 => /usr/lib/libpam.so.3 (0x2809f000)
         libopie.so.4 => /usr/lib/libopie.so.4 (0x280a6000)
❷        libc.so.6=> /lib/libc.so.6 (0x280af000)
         libmd.so.3 => /lib/libmd.so.3 (0x28193000)
```

Remember earlier in this chapter, when libutil.so.5 ❶ and libc.so.6 ❷ showed up as obsolete? Well, if I had blindly erased them, my sudo would no longer work. Instead, I'm now hunting for all the programs that require those libraries. portmaster doesn't see that sudo requires an upgrade, but I see that it requires a reinstall. I could go into the port directory and do a make deinstall && make reinstall, or I could just do:

```
# portmaster sudo
```

This forces portmaster to rebuild sudo(8). The process of building sudo automatically links it against the most recent library, removing one dependency on that obsolete file. If I need to do this with a leaf port, I can use -f to tell portmaster(8) to rebuild all dependencies whether needed or not.

Rebuilding Upward Dependencies

portmaster automatically updates programs *required* by a program you want to update, but it can also be told to upgrade everything that *depends* on the program you're updating. This can quickly cover large numbers of ports if you're updating a critical library. Use the -r flag to tell portmaster to check all the upward as well as downward dependencies.

CAUTION IS FOR THE WEAK! FULL SPEED AHEAD!

If you use the -a flag, portmaster tries to update everything it thinks needs an update. Use -af, and portmaster will rebuild all of your ports.

Changing Dependencies

One important but less frequently needed change is replacing one port with another. For example, suppose I wanted to replace my Emacs 20 install with Emacs 21. portmaster can handle that for us easily with the -o argument. You'll need to specify the new port and the old installed port, in that order:

```
# portmaster -o editors/emacs20 editors/emacs21
```

This isn't common, mind you, but after surviving several major changes in software over the years I'm very grateful the capability exists!

Ignoring Ports

Occasionally, you really don't want to update a port even if you specify recursion. For example, when I build a new OpenOffice.org, my laptop is tied up for a day. I really don't want to update OpenOffice.org as part of another update; I want to choose exactly when that update happens.

portmaster checks each package database directory for a file called *+IGNOREME*. If that file exists, portmaster will not update that package as part of an update of other dependencies.

```
# cd /var/db/pkg/openoffice.org-2.0.20060818
# touch +IGNOREME
```

Even if I update a library that OpenOffice.org depends on and tell portmaster to update every program that depends on that library, portmaster will not update OOo itself. OOo might break as a result of that dependency update, but that's a risk I take when choosing this path.

Other portmaster Features

I highly recommend reading portmaster(8) to see what functions it includes that will help solve your problems. You can resume failed builds, see what portmaster would do if you let it upgrade the system, save packages in your package repository, and so on. If you have a port upgrade problem, portmaster(8) probably has your solution.

Reducing the Size of the Ports Tree

The ports tree grows over time. Part of this growth is good, as new ports are added to the tree. Part of this growth is a necessary evil, such as temporary retention of older versions of software you've just upgraded. The rest of this growth is an unnecessary evil, as files that were once important but are now obsolete are never removed from the system. For example, now that I've updated my Linux package to Fedora Core 4, those distfiles for Fedora Core 3 are no longer useful. Finding and removing old files can save gigabytes of disk space, and that space is not (yet) infinite. While portmaster offers to delete unused distfiles for you, it's still worthwhile to perform global checks for unnecessary distfiles.

portmaster can check for stale distfiles. If you run `portmaster --clean-distfiles`, portmaster(8) will identify each unnecessary distfile and ask if you want to delete it. If you run `portmaster --clean-distfiles-all`, portmaster deletes the old distfiles without asking.

Another common problem is not running `make clean` after installing a port. Often, I want source code easily at hand while first learning a program, so I don't clean my own ports. Eventually I forget about them, and they lounge around filling up disk space. While writing this section, I found that I had neglected to clean up after building OpenOffice.org the last time; no wonder my disk looked bloated! FreeBSD ports are easy enough to clean en masse; just go to */usr/ports* and type `make clean NOCLEANDEPENDS=yes`. This recourses through the ports tree and does a `make clean` for every port, methodically removing every work directory.

With these tools, you can keep your system as up to date as you like. Now let's switch from the basics of FreeBSD administration to some of the things you can do with FreeBSD.

14

THE INTERNET ROAD MAP: DNS

The *Domain Name System (DNS)* is one of those quiet, behind-the-scenes services that doesn't get half the attention it deserves. Although most users have never heard of it, DNS is what makes the Internet as we know it work. DNS, also called *name service*, provides a map between hostnames and IP addresses. Without DNS, your web browsers and email programs wouldn't be able to use the nice and convenient hostnames such as *www.cnn.com*; instead, you'd have to type in a numeric IP address for each server you access. This would greatly reduce the Internet's popularity. To most end users, a DNS failure is an Internet failure, end of story.

Any Internet service you implement requires DNS. We'll discuss how DNS works, how to check DNS, how to configure your FreeBSD system to use DNS, and how to build your own DNS service.

How DNS Works

DNS maps IP addresses to hostnames and hostnames to IP addresses. For example, a user doesn't care that *www.absolutefreebsd.com* is actually 198.22.63.8; he just types the URL into his web browser and DNS handles the translation. As a system administrator, you must be able to install, inspect, and verify DNS information—and you must understand how your system performs these operations.

DNS information can be available in any number of places: on the local system, on a local DNS server, or on a remote nameserver. Unix systems use a *resolver* (a program that knows about all these information sources and can interface with them) to gather DNS answers from all these sources. When a program wants to know the IP address of a host or the hostname for an IP address, it asks the resolver, which consults the appropriate information sources and returns the answer to the program. We'll look at how to configure the resolver later in this chapter.

Most commonly, a resolver directs DNS queries to a *nameserver*—a computer running a program designed to gather DNS information from other computers on the Internet. Once a DNS request hits a nameserver, the nameserver checks its local cache to see if it has looked up that information recently. If it is in the cache, the nameserver returns the same answer as it gave the last user. Nameservers receive many identical DNS requests; for example, the nameserver at one ISP I worked at received several hundred requests per hour for the IP address of *www.cnn.com*. Multiply this by all the Yahoo!, eBay, and MSN requests out there, and you can see why caching answers locally is so important.

Suppose you're looking for information that's a little more obscure, such as the IP address for *www.absolutefreebsd.com*, and the local nameserver doesn't have that answer handy because nobody's gone there lately. Your local nameserver then asks a *root server*, which is a special server that keeps a list of all the nameservers responsible for every top-level domain on the Internet. In a *recursive query*, the root server tells the nameserver to go ask the appropriate nameservers, which may in turn refer the query to still other nameservers. Eventually, your query reaches an *authoritative nameserver* for that domain—the one true source of information about that domain—and your local nameserver gets its actual answer.

Every client on the Internet expects to be able to get information for every domain from that domain's authoritative nameservers. Every domain needs at least two nameservers. If one nameserver fails, the other picks up the load, but if all the nameservers for a domain fail, the domain vanishes from the Internet: Web browsers report that the domain does not exist, email bounces, everyone is at a loss. Even big companies, like Microsoft, have had this happen. Your manager or customers *will* notice you, but not in a good way. Pay attention to your name service!

Basic DNS Tools

FreeBSD includes several tools for inspecting DNS information. Since most DNS runs over UDP (User Datagram Protocol, see Chapter 6), you cannot use telnet to manually query a server as we will do with email and web services later. Your only access to live DNS information is through host(1) and dig(1).

The host(1) Command

Use host(1) for a quick forward DNS check (finding the IP address of a known hostname). For example, to check my publisher's web page, I do the following:

```
# host www.nostarch.com
www.nostarch.com has address 72.32.92.4
```

This is perhaps the simplest DNS query you can have: "Here's a hostname, what's its IP address?" Other seemingly simple queries generate more complicated results.

```
# host www.cnn.com
❶ www.cnn.com is an alias for cnn.com.
❷ cnn.com has address 64.236.24.20
  cnn.com has address 64.236.24.28
  ...
❸ cnn.com mail is handled by 10 atlmail5.turner.com.
  cnn.com mail is handled by 20 nycmail2.turner.com.
  ...
```

This illustrates that one hostname can actually refer to an entirely different hostname—in this case, *www.cnn.com* is actually an alias for a host called *cnn.com* ❶.

The host *cnn.com* actually has eight independent IP addresses ❷ (trimmed in the example). We also see the mail servers that handle all the email for *cnn.com* ❸.

When you type *http://www.nostarch.com* into your web browser, you're actually directing the web browser to go to the machine called *www.nostarch.com* and ask it for its default web page. The browser goes to the single IP address listed for that machine. When you ask for *http://www.cnn.com*, the resolver picks one of the IP addresses listed for that host and gives it to the browser. Similarly, email servers transfer email to one of the hosts identified as a mail handler for the domain. While application programs require more than an IP address to function, the IP is vital. You can't download a web page if you can't find the computer that hosts it!

Digging for Detail

While host(1) is helpful for quick answers, it's certainly not very detailed. Also, you don't know where this information came from—is it from the local machine's cache, or did the nameserver ask the master nameserver for that domain? The standard program for finding detailed DNS information is dig(1). (Another tool, nslookup(1), was popular for a long time but has fallen out of favor and has actually lost functionality in recent years.) dig has a variety of options that allow you to debug a wide range of name service problems; here, I'll cover only the most basic options.

In its most basic form, dig is called with nothing but a hostname. For example, to dig my publisher's web server I enter:

```
# dig www.nostarch.com
❶ ; <<>> DiG 9.3.2-P1 <<>> www.nostarch.com
❷ ;; global options:  printcmd
❸ ;; Got answer:
  ;; ->>HEADER<<- opcode: QUERY, ❹status: NOERROR, id: 33643
  ;; flags: qr rd ra; QUERY: 1, ANSWER: 1, AUTHORITY: 2, ADDITIONAL: 2
❺ ;; QUESTION SECTION:
  ;www.nostarch.com.               IN      A

❻ ;; ANSWER SECTION:
  www.nostarch.com.       2550    IN      A       72.32.92.4
❼ ;; AUTHORITY SECTION:
  nostarch.com.           2550    IN      NS      ns2.laughingsquid.net.
  nostarch.com.           2550    IN      NS      ns1.laughingsquid.net.
❽ ;; ADDITIONAL SECTION:
  ns1.laughingsquid.net.  171750  IN      A       72.3.155.219
  ns2.laughingsquid.net.  171750  IN      A       72.32.93.189
  ;; Query time: 58 msec
  ;; SERVER: 198.22.63.8#53(198.22.63.8)
  ;; WHEN: Mon Nov 20 18:43:22 2006
  ;; MSG SIZE  rcvd: 135
```

Yes, this is a lot of information! When using dig(1), however, you're probably trying to debug something, and when debugging, you want more information rather than less. Let's dissect this.

First, each line that begins with a semicolon is a comment that isn't directly relevant to the answer, but might be important. For example, the first line displays the version of dig you're using ❶.

The second line shows the options dig is set to use ❷. We didn't specify any options, so dig uses its defaults.

Next, we have our first bit of real meat: dig got an answer ❸ from somewhere. The status entry ❹ contains an important word, NOERROR, which tells us that the query was performed without getting an error. If you don't get NOERROR, you have a problem. Common errors include NXDOMAIN, which means that the host or domain you asked about doesn't exist, or SERVFAIL, meaning that the nameserver you're talking to is supposed to know about that domain but doesn't actually have any information on it.

Query Section

In the query section ❺, we see dig's actual query. Our sample includes the following tidbit:

```
;www.nostarch.com.               IN      A
```

This line begins with a semicolon, telling us it's a comment. This is our DNS query in more formal syntax. First, dig confirms that we asked for *www.nostarch.com*, but what's the IN A? DNS can manage many different naming systems, not just Internet-style IP addresses and hostnames. IN indicates that this is an Internet query; all domains on the Internet use the class IN. Last on that line, we have the type of query—here, we're asking for an A, or address, record. We have a hostname, and we want its address. A PTR (pointer) would mean that this is a reverse DNS query (in which we have an IP address and want the associated name). As you work more with dig, you'll see other query types as well.

Answer Section

Next, we have the answer section ❻, which is the meat of our reply.

```
www.nostarch.com.        2550    IN      A       72.32.92.4
```

We asked for *www.nostarch.com*, so that's printed first. The next number, 2250, is the *TTL*, or *time-to-live*, for this information. Our local nameserver may cache this answer for another 2,250 seconds, or roughly 42 minutes. When that time lapses, the local DNS server removes this answer from the cache. If someone asks for that information again, the local DNS server will have to go fetch a fresh answer. The IN, again, indicates that this is Internet-style data, and the A shows that this is an address. Finally, we have the actual IP address of the host *www.nostarch.com*, 72.32.92.4.

Authority Section

To get the IP address of *www.nostarch.com*, we follow the chain of authoritative nameservers. The authority section ❼ lists the nameservers responsible for the domain—in this case, *ns1.laughingsquid.net* and *ns2.laughingsquid.net*. The information about authoritative nameservers may be cached for 2,550 seconds, and these are (once again) Internet addresses.

Additional Section

Finally, in the additional section ❽, dig lists the IP addresses of hosts related to the hosts we queried. dig identified the authoritative nameservers for *nostarch.com*, but you'll need the IP addresses for those servers to make further DNS queries about the *nostarch.com* domain. You get the authoritative DNS server information, but note that the TTL for these answers is much longer than the TTL for the original answer. These answers are good for another 171,750 seconds, or roughly 48 hours. Once this time passes, your nameserver will discard these cached results and go ask the root servers once more for the authoritative DNS servers for *nostarch.com*.

Do a dig on a couple of domains and become familiar with how the output looks.

Finding Hostnames with dig

Suppose you have an IP address and want to identify the associated hostname, much as you might want to find out who owns a phone number. This is a common problem on the Internet—you might see an IP address hitting your website every five seconds and wonder who they are and what they're up to. To look up a name from an IP address, use *reverse lookup* with dig's -x option. Much of the result is identical to the forward lookup; we'll only discuss the notable differences.

```
# dig -x 72.32.92.4
...
;; QUESTION SECTION:
;❶4.92.32.72.in-addr.arpa.        IN       ❷PTR

;; ANSWER SECTION:
4.92.32.72.in-addr.arpa. 3600     IN       PTR     ❸squid14.laughingsquid.net.
```

One of the most obvious differences is that our question ❶ looks really funky. What's this *4.92.32.72.in-addr.arpa* stuff? When you're doing a reverse lookup, the components of your IP address are reversed and placed under the domain *in-addr.arpa*.

We're also looking for a PTR ❷ record, rather than an A record. A PTR query means that you have an IP address and want to know what hostname lives there.

Although we know that *www.nostarch.com* lives at the IP address 72.32.92.4, a reverse lookup reveals that the most correct name for this host is *squid14.laughingsquid.net* ❸. This is much like a phone system; while a whole family can share a single phone, the number is registered to a single person.

Forward and reverse DNS are generally expected to match, but since many hosts can share one IP address, an A record does not necessarily need a matching PTR record. The hostname *www.nostarch.com* maps to 72.32.92.4, but 72.32.92.4 maps to *squid14.laughingsquid.net*. You can, however, expect to find an A record for *squid14.laughingsquid.net* pointing to 72.32.92.4. If the hostname given by a reverse lookup does not have a matching forward record, DNS is incorrectly configured. Tools that rely upon DNS checks, such as certain configurations of TCP wrappers, will reject connections from such systems. You'll also see this on home broadband connections, where you might have a person's domain pointed at an IP with a reverse DNS name from a cable modem host. Automatic tools exist to check forward and reverse DNS matches, as we'll see later in this chapter.

More dig Options

Check dig(1) for a full list of options; below, a few basic ones are covered. The options I most commonly use are querying a particular server and disabling recursion.

Querying a Specific Nameserver

By default, dig queries the first nameserver configured in the resolver. If you're trying to debug a problem, however, you frequently want to query a particular nameserver. The @ option lets you choose a particular nameserver. For example, to ask my local ISP's DNS server *dns1.wideopenwest.com* what it knows about *nostarch.com*, I enter:

```
# dig nostarch.com @dns1.wideopenwest.com
```

The output from this command resembles the sample output shown earlier, except that you'll see references to the nameserver at *dns1.wideopenwest.com*. If you're debugging a problem, review answers from different nameservers carefully; minor differences may show where your problem lies.

Disabling Recursion

By default, a nameserver provides an answer by recursing through its resources. Sometimes you don't want the nameserver to recurse on a query; instead, you want it to tell you only what it has in cache or where it would go to look for an answer. It's frequently helpful to perform the recursion yourself when trying to solve a problem. Specify +norecurse on the command line to trigger this behavior. Try this now with a domain that you're pretty certain your local nameserver has never looked for. If your nameserver has this information cached, the result will be much like our previous example. If it doesn't, however, you'll get this:

```
# dig absolutefreebsd.com +norecurse
...
❶ ;; QUESTION SECTION:
;AbsoluteFreeBSD.com.    IN    A
❷ ;; AUTHORITY SECTION:
❸ com.            33195    IN    NS    A.GTLD-SERVERS.NET.
  com.            33195    IN    NS    B.GTLD-SERVERS.NET.
  com.            33195    IN    NS    C.GTLD-SERVERS.NET.
...
;; ADDITIONAL SECTION:
```

```
  A.GTLD-SERVERS.NET.    98529    IN    A       192.5.6.30
❹ A.GTLD-SERVERS.NET.    129969   IN    AAAA    2001:503:a83e::2:30
  B.GTLD-SERVERS.NET.    98529    IN    A       192.33.14.30
  B.GTLD-SERVERS.NET.    129969   IN    AAAA    2001:503:231d::2:30
  C.GTLD-SERVERS.NET.    98529    IN    A       192.26.92.30
  ...
```

Note that the reply jumps from the question section ❶ right into the authority section ❷. There is no answer, because this nameserver doesn't *have* an answer. Instead, it refers you to the authoritative nameservers for *.com*, the lettered servers ❸ under *gtld-servers.net*. The additional information section gives the IP addresses for those servers as well. Note that some of those servers have IPv6 addresses ❹ as well as the standard IPv4 addresses. If your system does not support IPv6, it will not use the IPv6 addresses.

By referring you to the nameservers for the *.com* domain, this nameserver is saying, "I don't know, I suggest you go ask these guys." You told your nameserver not to recurse, so it's not going out to ask.

To query one of these *.com* nameservers, set a server name and use the norecurse option again.

```
# dig www.absolutefreebsd.com @a.gtld-servers.net +norecurse
```

This refers you to another set of nameservers. Follow the chain down to see exactly how your nameserver resolves queries.

in-addr.arpa

There's one major annoyance with PTR records; they're listed backwards. You see, DNS checks hostname components from right to left. When you look for the host *www.absolutefreebsd.com*, the nameserver first finds the nameserver for *.com*. It then checks under *.com* for *absolutefreebsd.com*, then under *absolutefreebsd.com* for *www.absolutefreebsd.com*. The biggest units are on the right. The *.com* domain was delegated to a master authority, who then delegated the subdivision *absolutefreebsd* to me, and I, in turn, delegated the subdivision *www* to a particular machine.

In IP addresses, the largest units are on the left. Take an IP address 72.32.92.4, for example. The first number is comparable to the whole *.com* domain. The global IP address authority assigned the block 72 to ARIN (the American Registry for Internet Numbers). ARIN, in turn, delegated 72.32 to a particular ISP. The ISP turned around and delegated 72.32.92 to a customer, who assigned 72.32.92.4 to a particular machine. The delegations are very similar in concept, but run from left to right—opposite to the way the hostname delegations work.

It's very easy to confuse a forward IP address with a reversed IP address, so DNS uses a special domain to indicate that an IP address is reversed. Reversed IP addresses have the string *in-addr.arpa* attached at the end. (The reasons for this date back decades and are rather tedious, so we won't go into them.) The bottom line is that our 72.32.92.4 becomes 4.92.32.72.in-addr.arpa.

So, why not just leave the IP address forward and use in-addr.arpa to indicate that it's a reverse DNS check? Glad you asked! The preceding address is a simple one, and digging it searches a very limited space. If you own the 72.32.92.0/24[1] block, however, you might need to query the entire address space assigned you by the ISP, or 92.32.72.in-addr.arpa. You might have to query the whole block of 72.32/16, or 32.72.in-addr.arpa, or perhaps even 72.in-addr.arpa. Each is a check of an increasingly large space, much like doing dig .com. You will probably never need to dig the whole *.com* space, but Internet backbone engineers do, and backbone engineers are the ones who write programs of this sort. One of the problems with using professional tools is that they're geared towards professionals.

QUICK AND DIRTY LOOKUPS

host(1) does the reversal for you transparently. dig also does the reversal for you if you use -x. Don't let the *in-addr.arpa* confuse you, however.

Configuring the Resolver

The resolver is responsible for relaying DNS information to client programs. Configuring your resolver is a vital part of system administration. Even a DNS server needs a configured resolver, because the computer won't know it's a nameserver unless you tell it. Just about anything you do on a network requires a working name service client. Configuring a resolver involves answering a few questions:

- Where does the server look for DNS information?
- What are the local domain names?
- Which nameservers should be queried?

The answers to these questions are configured in */etc/nsswitch.conf* and */etc/resolv.conf*.

Host/IP Information Sources

This should be easy; a server gets its host information from a nameserver, right? I mean, that's what this whole chapter is about, isn't it?

The real world isn't that simple, however. Perhaps you have a small home network with only three machines, and you consider running a DNS server to be unacceptable overhead. Or, you might be on a large corporate network where completing DNS changes takes weeks. FreeBSD (as all Unix-like operating systems) supports both DNS and a hosts file, */etc/hosts*, and you can decide which to query first.

When FreeBSD needs to know the address of a host (or the reverse), by default the query goes first to the hosts file and then the configured

---

[1] We talked about /24s back in Chapter 6; go look again if you're confused.

nameservers. This means that you can have a local override of nameserver results, which is very useful for hosts behind a NAT or on a large corporate network with odd[2] network requirements. Under some bizarre circumstances, you might need to reverse this order to query DNS first and the hosts file second. In modern versions of FreeBSD, this order is set in */etc/nsswitch.conf.* (Older versions used */etc/host.conf* instead, and you'll still find references to */etc/host.conf* here and there in the documentation.)

NAME SERVICE SWITCHING

The file */etc/nsswitch.conf* is used not only by the hostname/IP resolver; it is a configuration file for the general name service switching services. Many different name services exist in a networked operating system. For example, in Chapter 6 we discussed the network service names and port numbers in */etc/services*, as well as the protocol names and numbers. Looking up a protocol name is a name service lookup and can be handled internally by the system in a variety of ways. Determining the UID and GID of a user (see Chapter 7) requires a different sort of name lookup. */etc/nsswitch.conf* determines ordering for all of these queries and more. We're only discussing the hostname service lookups here.

Here's the hostname service lookup configuration from */etc/nsswitch.conf*:

```
hosts: files dns
```

The resolver queries the information sources in the order listed. If you have an additional information source, such as cached (see Chapter 15), add it here. To make the hostname service query the global DNS before the local hosts file, reverse the order.

The second information source is checked only if the first information source cannot find a record. If a host has conflicting information in */etc/hosts* and in DNS, the first one to be checked wins.

Setting Local Domain Names

When you're working on machines on your own network, you don't want to have to type the whole hostname all the time. If you have 30 web servers, typing ssh www19.mycompany.com gets old! You can give the resolver a default local domain, or a list of domains, on the first line of */etc/resolv.conf.*

Specifying the Local Domain

The domain keyword tells the resolver which local domain name to check, by default, for all hostnames. For example, to specify *absolutefreebsd.com* as the local domain, the first line of */etc/resolv.conf* should look like this:

```
domain        absolutefreebsd.com
```

---

[2] Sadly, when it comes to corporate network design, odd is normal.

Once a local domain is specified, any command that ordinarily requires a domain name will assume it to be under *absolutefreebsd.com*. If I type `ping www`, the resolver would append the name *absolutefreebsd.com* to that and give ping the IP of *www.absolutefreebsd.com*.

Specifying a List of Domains

Alternately, use the `search` keyword to specify a list of domains to try. Perhaps my company uses several domain names, and I want to search them all in order. List the domains you want the resolver to query, in order, on the first line of */etc/resolv.conf*:

```
search absolutefreebsd.com blackhelicopters.org stenchmaster.org
```

In this case, the resolver queries these three domains in order until it finds a match (or not). For example, if I type `ping petulance`, the resolver would check for a host named *petulance.absolutefreebsd.com*. If it can't find that, it checks for *petulance.blackhelicopters.org*, and then *petulance.stenchmaster.org*. If no such host exists in any of the three domains, the command fails.

> **DEFAULT DOMAIN**
>
> If you have neither domain nor search entries in */etc/resolv.conf*, the resolver uses the local machine's domain name.

The Nameserver List

Now that your resolver knows which domains to try, tell it which nameservers to use. List each nameserver in */etc/resolv.conf* on a line of its own, in order of preference. The resolver queries the listed nameservers in order. Your complete */etc/resolv.conf* might look something like this:

```
domain absolutefreebsd.com
nameserver 127.0.0.1
nameserver 192.168.8.3
nameserver 172.18.33.4
```

Note that the first IP in this nameserver list is the loopback IP 127.0.0.1. This entry tells the resolver to ask the local machine for DNS information, which means that the resolver expects to find a DNS server running on the local host. While in some rare instances you might not want to use the local nameserver, in most cases, if you are running a nameserver, the local machine should ask the local nameserver for answers.

With nameserver entries and either `domain` or `search` keywords, your resolver is fully configured. Next, you need to configure those information sources that you've told the resolver to use.

Local DNS Overrides with /etc/hosts

The */etc/hosts* file matches Internet addresses to hostnames. While the hosts file is very effective, it only works on a single machine and must be maintained by hand. Dynamic nameservers have largely superseded */etc/hosts*, but the hosts file may still be useful on small networks or behind a Network Address Translation (NAT) device. For example, using the hosts file is just fine if you have one or two servers at home, or if someone else manages your public nameservers. If you have multiple machines that need to be maintained separately, consider building a full-fledged nameserver.

Once upon a time, the Internet had a single text hosts file that provided the hostnames and IP addresses of every node on the Internet. System administrators submitted their host changes to a central maintainer, who issued an updated hosts file every few months. This worked fine when the whole Internet had four hosts on it, and was even acceptable when there were hundreds of hosts. As soon as the Internet began its exponential growth, however, this scheme quickly became unmaintainable.

Each line in */etc/hosts* represents one host. The first entry on each line is an IP address, and the second is the fully qualified domain name of the host, such as *mail.absolutefreebsd.com*. Following these two entries, you can list an arbitrary number of aliases for that host.

For example, a small company might have a single server handling email, serving FTP, web pages, and DNS, as well as performing a variety of other functions. A desktop on that network might have a hosts file that looks like this:

```
192.168.1.2    mail.mycompany.com          mail ftp www dns
```

With this */etc/hosts* entry, the desktop could find the server with either the full domain name or any of the brief aliases listed.

If you find that you need more than two or three host entries, or that maintaining hosts files is becoming a problem, you need a nameserver. A nameserver is far more scalable than a hosts file across multiple machines. While it requires an initial time investment, it's much less labor to maintain a nameserver once it is running.

Building a Nameserver

The most popular DNS server software is *Berkeley Internet Name Daemon (BIND)*. BIND is actually a suite of tools including programs such as host(1), dig(1), and the DNS server program itself, named(8). BIND is maintained by the Internet Software Consortium (*http://www.isc.org*) and is released under a BSD-style license. While BIND has competitors, such as djbdns (*/usr/ports/net/djbdns*), BIND is considered the DNS service reference implementation. Most of BIND's competitors were written years ago, when BIND had a poor security record. BIND has since been rewritten from the ground up. Recent versions are much more secure than older versions, so there's little reason to look at these competitors. No matter which DNS daemon you decide to use, the concepts used in BIND are generally applicable to any nameserver program. One of the most important concepts is the relationship between masters and slaves.

Masters and Slaves

Every domain needs at least two nameservers. One of these is the master for the domain. The *master* holds the authoritative records for that domain. Make any changes to the domain on the master nameserver. *Slaves* replicate their records from the master. Both the master and its slaves are expected to be authoritative—that is, the world assumes that the answers they provide for their domain are 100 percent correct.

One DNS server can be a master for some domains and a slave for others. For example, *absolutefreebsd.com* has two DNS servers: *bewilderbeast .blackhelicopters.org*[3] and *tribble.lodden.com. Bewilderbeast.blackhelicopters.org* is the master nameserver for the domain, while *tribble.lodden.com* is the slave. Whenever I update the DNS record for this domain, bewilderbeast notifies tribble that a newer record is available and the slave's record is updated. If bewilderbeast is assaulted by badgers and disappears from the Internet, tribble will continue to offer DNS information for the domain. Tribble is a master nameserver for *lodden.com*, however, just as bewilderbeast is a slave for other domains. Sysadmins share and swap DNS slave services amongst themselves.

Widely separate your nameservers. If you can swap slave DNS services with someone on a different Internet backbone in another country, preferably on another continent, do so. Many social networking websites offer DNS swap meets. It's best to swap slave DNS services with someone about your size—you don't want to slave several hundred domains in exchange for slaving your company's one domain! If nothing else, any number of companies offer geographically diverse slave DNS for modest fees.

BIND Configuration Files

Both masters and slaves use the same configuration files for the name service daemon, named(8). FreeBSD's default configuration includes the defaults needed to make a simple nameserver, but you'll have to understand the configuration to provide service for your own domain. The main configuration directory is */etc/namedb*, and you'll find several vital files there.

named.root

One file that must be present—but will work out of the box—is *named.root*, which lists the root nameservers. When a nameserver receives a query for a site it doesn't have in its cache, it sends the query to the root nameservers. Root nameservers are identified by their IP addresses, and the

---

[3] A bewilderbeast is like a wildebeest, but far more confused.

global Internet community goes to great lengths to ensure that these addresses change as rarely as possible. This file, therefore, also changes rarely—as of this writing in late 2007, *named.root* changed last in 2004.

localhost-forward.db, localhost-reverse.db

These are the correct forward and reverse zone files for the host localhost on your computer. You don't know what a zone file is? You will, if you keep reading.

named.conf

The core of your DNS configuration is the named configuration file, *named.conf.* If your *named.conf* is broken, your nameserver is hosed. This is where the real meat of DNS configuration takes place.

Configuring BIND with named.conf

At first glance, *named.conf* looks like C code. Don't worry if you don't know C, however, because the rules are very simple and the examples illustrate everything you must know. Any line beginning with two slashes (//) is a comment. Similarly, any text enclosed within the old-fashioned C comment marks, /* and */, is a (possibly multiline) comment. Everything else in *named.conf* is either an option or a zone. A *zone* is a fancy name for a domain—while, strictly speaking, they aren't identical, they're close enough for our purposes. An *option* controls how BIND operates.

Options

If you ignore the comments in the default *named.conf*, the file opens with a list of options, most of which are obscure and commented out. Use options by putting them in the options section of the file, which contains the word *options* and a pair of curly brackets ({ and }). List options within the brackets, separated by semicolons. Here's a very simple options section from a *named.conf* file:

```
options {
        directory       "/etc/namedb";
        pid-file        "/var/run/named/pid";
        dump-file       "/var/dump/named_dump.db";
        statistics-file "/var/stats/named.stats";
        listen-on       { 127.0.0.1; 192.168.0.5; };
};
```

In this example, most of the options have a value of a directory or a file, but the listen-on option lists two IP addresses.

The directory option specifies where named looks for stored DNS files. The default is perfectly fine, especially given that /etc/namedb isn't really /etc/namedb. (Don't freak out yet, keep reading, all will become clear.)

The pid-file is the process ID file, where named stores a text file containing the process ID of the main named process. Assorted named management utilities use the contents of this file.

A `dump-file` contains named's cache of answers it has already retrieved. named dumps its cache to disk upon request. A cache file is mostly used for debugging DNS issues.

If you request named to keep stats and other information about queries, it will use the `statistics-file` to store that information.

The `listen-on` option controls on which IP addresses named accepts connections. If you have dozens of IP addresses on a single server, you might want to confine named to only one of those. This is particularly valuable when you have jails on your system, as it helps prevent misconfigured clients.

BIND supports many, many more options, but these are perhaps the most popular ones. Consult the BIND documentation at *http://www.isc.org* for the complete list of options and their proper uses.

Zones in named.conf

The default *named.conf* defines three zones, or domains, that every nameserver manages by default: the *root zone*, the *IPv4 localhost*, and the *IPv6 localhost*. You shouldn't need to edit these default zones in any way—in fact, if you're thinking of changing them, you're almost certainly doing something wrong. We'll discuss what these zones are for and what they do.

The Root Zone

named uses the root zone when it has no information on a requested domain or host. These queries are recursed through a root nameserver. Here's the *named.conf* entry for the root zone:

```
❶ zone "." {
❷       type hint;
❸       file "named.root";
  };
```

The first entry ❶ identifies the domain this query represents. The single dot in quotes indicates that this is for the entire Internet.

The type ❷ indicates what sort of record this is. The root zone is special, and it is the only zone with the type of `hint`. All other records are either of type `master` or of type `slave`.

Finally, the `file` ❸ keyword tells named which file contains the information for this domain. named looks in the directory specified in the `directory` option for a file of this name and assigns its contents to this zone. We'll look at those detailed zone files later.

Localhost Zones

Remember from Chapter 6 that every computer uses the loopback IP address of 127.0.0.1 to identify itself? The nameserver must provide records for this IP address, or every system call that tries to look up the hostname of the local host will have to wait and time out before continuing. This would really annoy users.

Here's the configuration for the IPv4 localhost zone. You'll find it in *named.conf* just under the root zone:

```
❶ zone "0.0.127.IN-ADDR.ARPA" {
❷       type master;
❸       file "master/localhost.rev";
  };
```

Looks pretty similar to the options statement and the root zone in the previous section, doesn't it?

The zone name ❶ appears in quotes after the word zone. Since this zone is for reverse DNS, we see the domain ends with IN-ADDR.ARPA. If you reverse the IP address, you'll see that it's actually for the 127.0.0 group of IP addresses.

The type ❷ indicates whether this nameserver is a master or a slave for this domain. Every nameserver is a master for the localhost zone.

Finally, the file keyword ❸ tells the nameserver where to get the information for this zone. For this domain, the file is actually in a subdirectory of the named's configuration directory, */etc/namedb/master/localhost.rev*.

The IPv6 version of the localhost entry is very similar. If, like most of the world, you're not yet using IPv6, you can comment it out safely.

Configuring a Slave Domain

Perhaps the easiest DNS task is setting up your nameserver to slave a domain. The entry looks much like the entries for the root zone and the localhost zone. Before configuring your slave, you must know the name of the domain and the IP address of the master nameserver. Here's a sample slave domain, which closely resembles the root and localhost zones:

```
❶ zone "absolutefreebsd.com" {
❷       type slave;
❸       file "slave/AbsoluteFreeBSD.com.db";
❹       masters {
❺               198.63.22.8;
          };
  };
```

Much of this looks very familiar. We have the domain name ❶, the type of domain ❷, and the file ❸ in which the domain information is kept. It's a good idea to keep slave records separate from master records. Not only do the masters get snooty about sharing quarters with the slaves, but it's important to know which records you are truly responsible for and which can be easily reproduced from the master server. Also, the nameserver must have permission to write the slave files but not the master files. It's traditional to name slave files after the domain, with a *.db* extension. Despite what the extension might imply, these files are not binary database files. named(8) creates these files when it downloads the current zone data from the master server.

We then have a label for the master server for the domain ❹ and a list of the IP addresses for the master server ❺. The slave requests the domain's DNS information from the master at regular intervals. The master nameservers must be listed by their IP addresses, not hostnames; after all, a DNS server must be able to bootstrap its own records before it can answer anyone else's queries!

Configuring a Master Domain

The *named.conf* configuration for a master domain is even simpler than for a slave zone:

```
❶ zone "absolutefreebsd.com" {
❷        type master;
❸        file "master/absolutefreebsd.com.db";
  };
```

Once more, there's the domain name ❶, a label for the type ❷ of the zone, and a filename ❸. Unlike the slave domain, you must create this file; we'll look at creating zone files later in this chapter.

Master and Slave File Storage

If you're managing high-end nameservers, you might be responsible for thousands of domains and millions of users. If you screw up, you will have many people very angry at you. Therefore, before you set up hundreds of zones, think about how you're going to arrange them.

Always divide a server's files between those for which your server is a master and those for which your server is only a slave. The default named configuration includes those two directories, but many new DNS admins dump everything into */etc/namedb* and regret it later. Files in the master directory are sacred and must be preserved, and preferably should be under RCS control as well (see Chapter 4). Files under the slave directory aren't exactly garbage, but they don't require careful protection or backups.

If you expect to serve thousands of domains, you might want to divide your master zone files still further. In the past, I've used a set of 36 directories under the master directory, one for each letter and number.

Of course, you can create any arrangement of directories to fit your needs; just remember that you must either live with this arrangement or do some tedious work to change it. Having a too deep or complicated directory structure can be just as annoying as a too shallow or simple one.

Zone Files

We have a configuration file that tells named(8) what domains it is responsible for and where the files with domain information can be found. But we still need those files—we have no real information yet!

Zone files have a rather obscure syntax because BIND was originally written by programmers who were more interested in efficiency and correctness than ease of use. Unlike some other programs from that era (such as Sendmail), zone file configuration is not blatantly user-hostile, even though some parts of the zone files leave new users scratching their heads until they wear long furrows in their skulls.

To learn how to work with zone files, follow the provided examples and you should be all right. Any time you find yourself fingering new grooves in your head, just remember that you're digging through the primordial ooze of the Internet. If DNS was invented today, zone files would probably look very different.[4]

Here's an authoritative reverse DNS zone file for the host localhost at the IP address 127.0.0.1. Let's dissect this file. First, anything beginning with a semicolon is a comment. Our sample begins with comments that I won't bother to reproduce. Comment your zone files liberally; later, it'll help you figure out what the heck you were doing.

```
❶$TTL     3600
❷@ ❸IN ❹SOA ❺test.blackhelicopters.org.
❻root.test.blackhelicopters.org. (
                ❼20061203      ; Serial
                3600           ; Refresh
                900            ; Retry
                3600000        ; Expire
                3600 )         ; Minimum
        IN    NS     test.blackhelicopters.org.
1       IN    PTR    localhost.blackhelicopters.org.
```

The $TTL ❶ statement is the zone's default TTL in seconds. It dictates how long other servers cache information from this zone. You can give your zone data any TTL you like. 3,600 seconds, or 1 hour, is actually a short time. A good average is 10,800, or 3 hours. Choosing a TTL is something of a black art; stick with the default, and you'll be fine in most normal circumstances.

The next section is the *Start of Authority (SOA)* record. This is a brief description of the zone and of how its servers and users should treat it. Every zone has exactly one SOA record. The SOA does not include information about what is in the domain, merely information about how long this information lasts and who is responsible for the domain.

---

[4] If zone files were created today they'd be in XML, for one thing. And they would require two different layers of editing and verification to make a simple change and three layers of parsing and postprocessing to view the output.

The @ symbol ❷ that begins the SOA record is a special character that's shorthand for "whatever zone *named.conf* says this file is for." In this case, *named.conf* says that this file holds data for the zone 0.0.127.in-addr.arpa. When named(8) reads *named.conf* and loads this file into memory, it makes this substitution. Using the actual domain name would be less confusing for new users, but would prevent reusing the same file for multiple domains. Almost nobody spells out the full domain in a zone file.

The IN ❸ represents the type of data. As we've seen before when using dig, IN represents Internet data. SOA ❹ means that this is a Start of Authority record. Both elements appear in every zone file.

Next, we have the name of the machine ❺ where the master file came from. This zone file was created on the machine *test.blackhelicopters.org*.

Then, we have the email address ❻ of the person responsible for this zone. The make-localhost script assumes that the root account on the local machine is the email address. The email address lacks the @ sign, however, because we already used the @ sign as a macro for the domain name.[5] Were we to put the @ in, the email address would become *root0.0.127.IN-ADDR.ARPAtest.blackhelicopters.org*, which is not merely worse to look at but has the added flaw of being wrong. The first dot in the email address is assumed to be an @ sign.

Today, most nameservers don't run a mail server. Best current practice is to use a hostmaster account at your domain name, such as *hostmaster@ absolutefreebsd.com*. Every domain is expected to have a hostmaster email address to respond to DNS issues.

Note the parenthesis at the end of the start of the SOA record. Technically, the SOA record should be on a single line, but that would make it difficult to read. Instead, you can use the parenthesis to break up the SOA into several lines. Each of the next five lines is part of the SOA record, with the closing parenthesis ending the record. Traditionally, the parentheses include a set of timers and the serial number ❼.

The first number is the *serial number*, which is the zone file's version. Every time you edit the file, increase the serial number. While the serial number could be any number you choose, it's most convenient to use the date. You'll usually see the date in *YYYYMMDD* format with two extra digits at the end. This serial number, 20061203, represents December 3, 2006. Use the two extra digits to represent the number of times the file has changed in a day. At times, I've left a domain alone for months only to update it twelve times in a single day.

For example, suppose I create the zone file on May 9, 2008, with a first serial number of 2008050901. If I change the zone file on June 8 of that year, the serial number becomes 2008060801. If I then change the file a second time on that same day, it becomes 2008060802. This system allows up to 100 changes in a day, or roughly one change every 15 minutes. If this isn't enough for you, you're doing something wrong.

---

[5] DNS predates the @ sign as part of email addresses. This overlap is email's fault, not DNS's.

Slave servers use the serial number to determine if they must update their zones from the master. If the zone record on the master server has a higher serial number than the record on the slave, the slave server knows that the zone file has been updated and downloads the latest version from the master.

SERIAL GRIEF

If your secondary nameservers haven't updated their zone files from the master nameserver, it's probably a serial number problem. Even if you are utterly, completely certain that you've incremented the serial number, increment it again and try once more. It'll probably work.

The next number is the *refresh* time, in seconds. This dictates how frequently the slave servers contact the master and check for updates. In this *localhost.rev* sample, a slave server updates every 3,600 seconds, or 60 minutes.

If the slave cannot check its data against the master, it keeps giving answers with its current record—after all, one function of a slave DNS server is to provide service when the master is unreachable. We'll see exactly how this works in "Refresh, Retry, and Expire in Practice" on page 431.

The *retry* value tells the slave how often to try to contact an unreachable master server. Our sample file has a 900-second (15-minute) retry value. If the secondary nameserver cannot update at the 1 hour mark, it tries again every 15 minutes until the master nameserver answers.

The *expire* value, also in seconds, tells the slave when to discard its cached records. It's set to the system administrator's estimate of when giving out bad information becomes worse than giving no information at all. In this example, the expire time is set to 3.6 million seconds, or a little over 41 days.

The last number is the *minimum time-to-live*. In older versions of BIND, this was used as the TTL for every timeout you can think of. Today it's only used as the TTL for negative answers. For example, if you look up the host *givememymoneyback.absolutefreebsd.com*, your nameserver will learn that it doesn't exist. The nameserver caches the fact that the host does not exist for the number of seconds equal to the minimum TTL. Be certain to close the parentheses after the minimum TTL, or named will assume that the remainder of the file is part of the SOA record and will become not only perplexed but downright belligerent.

Now that you have a complete SOA record, you can list actual information for the domain. In our example, these two lines contain the zone's actual host information:

```
      IN    ❷NS     test.blackhelicopters.org.
❶1    IN    ❸PTR    localhost.blackhelicopters.org.
```

Each line has four parts: a hostname or number, the data type, the record type, and the actual data. The first field is either blank or contains a hostname (such as *www*) or a number (such as 12). The name of the zone is automatically attached to this entry, either at the beginning (for reverse DNS) or end (for forward DNS). Since our example is for reverse DNS, we add the domain 127.0.0 onto the 1 ❶ and get the IP address 127.0.0.1.

If the first field is blank, named(8) appends the zone name anyway to give us a sensible default. For example, our first line has no first entry, so named assumes that this line is for 0.0.127.in-addr.arpa, or the network beginning with 127.0.0, the zone specified in *named.conf*.

With DNS, the data type is always IN.

The third field, the type of record we have, is actually useful. An NS ❷ record represents a nameserver. In this example, the only nameserver for this domain is *test.blackhelicopters.org*. If you're distributing *localhost.rev* among several nameservers, add more NS lines for them. On the other hand, a PTR ❸ entry represents a mapping of an IP address to hostname. This zone is for the 127.0.0 network, and the .1 host within this network is the hostname *localhost.blackhelicopters.org*.

Refresh, Retry, and Expire in Practice

While I've mentioned what the refresh, retry, and expire times mean, that's not the same as making you understand how they work. Here's an example.

Suppose you have a domain with a refresh time of 4 hours, a retry time of 1 hour, and an expire time of 48 hours. This means that the slave nameserver contacts the master every four hours to check for updates. If you update the records on the master nameserver, they require up to four hours to propagate to the slave nameservers. So far, so good. Now assume that the master nameserver explodes, scattering its hard drive across three counties. What happens to the slave server and the clients looking for information on the domain?

The clients are the easy part. As the master nameserver is not reachable, remote nameservers query the slave servers. The clients get their answers.

The next time the slave server checks for an updated record, it cannot reach the master. At that point, the slave server changes its check interval. Instead of using the refresh interval of four hours, it uses the retry time of one hour. The slave begins checking every hour for updates, and checks every hour until you restore service at the master nameserver.

If the slave cannot confirm its data for a length of time equal to the expire time, the slave server considers the data too old to be useful. The slave discards the domain information and returns an error to any queries about the domain. The domain disappears from the Internet.

DEFINITIVE DNS DISASTERS

If your master nameserver fails irreparably, you have a length of time equal to the expire time plus the retry time to reconfigure your slave server as your master nameserver.

A Real Sample Zone

The localhost zone file is limited; it only represents one machine and has only one IP address in it. But it's found on every nameserver and includes all the data types required in a zone file, making it a useful real-world example. Now let's consider a zone file that's more representative of the domains you'll be serving—the zone file for *absolutefreebsd.com.*

```
$TTL ❶1h
@ IN ❷SOA blackhelicopters.org. hostmaster.blackhelicopters.org.  (
                              2006121002      ; Serial
                              1d        ; Refresh
                              2h        ; Retry
                              1000h     ; Expire
                              2d )      ; Minimum
          IN    NS      ❸bewilderbeast.blackhelicopters.org.
          IN    NS      tribble.lodden.com.
          IN    ❹MX 20  mail.nobletechnology.net.
          IN    MX 10   bewilderbeast.blackhelicopters.org.
          IN    ❺A      198.22.63.8
www       IN    ❻CNAME  absolutefreebsd.com.
```

This zone resembles the *localhost.rev* zone we discussed earlier, but it's an actual zone file for a real live Internet domain. First, we have the TTL of one hour ❶. A remote nameserver caches information on this domain for one hour. The SOA ❷ record lists the contact information and a variety of timeouts for refresh, retry, and expire, as well as the serial number.

The zone file lists two nameservers, *bewilderbeast.blackhelicopters.org* and *tribble.lodden.com* ❸. According to the times in the SOA, *tribble.lodden.com* compares its records to those of *bewilderbeast.blackhelicopters.org* every day. If the secondary cannot compare records at that time, it tries again every 2 hours. If *tribble.lodden.com* cannot compare its records against the master nameserver for a full 1,000 hours, it stops giving any answer for *absolutefreebsd.com.* Finally, remote nameservers will cache "no such host" responses for two days.

Note that older DNS servers only accepted seconds for these time values. Instead of using 1d to mean "one day," you had to type 86400 for the number of seconds in one day. You'll still see this in old zone files, but there's no need to make yourself do the math for new files.

Mail Exchanger

We then have a new record type, MX ❹, for mail exchanger. While a domain has only one primary mail host, it can have multiple backup mail servers. Nevertheless, incoming email must ultimately reach the appropriate mail server. Here's where you indicate which is the preferred mail server and which are backups. We'll discuss this in some detail in Chapter 16.

The one additional entry in the MX records—a number such as 10 or 20—is the preference. Servers with lower preference numbers are more preferred. In this case, the server *bewilderbeast.blackhelicopters.org* of preference 10 is the preferred mail server for *absolutefreebsd.com.* If the primary server cannot be reached, the backup is *mail.nobletechnology.net.*

Since some day you might want to add another mail exchanger between the two preferences, or change to a completely different set of servers, leave some space between your preference numbers. If you number them 1, 2, 3, and so on, you won't have much flexibility later.

Host Records

Finally, we have actual records for each host in the domain. The most common types of host records are CNAME and A. As we saw in the dig(1) example, a CNAME is an *alias* (or, if you want to be pedantic, a reference to a *canonical name*). An A record ❺ gives the IP address for a hostname. For example, dig(1) will show that the host *absolutefreebsd.com* is an alias for *www.absolutefreebsd.com*. (Remember, when an entry has no name explicitly stated, it defaults to the domain the zone file represents!) The host *www.absolutefreebsd.com* has an Internet address ❻ of 198.22.63.8.

Mail exchangers and nameservers cannot be CNAMEs; they must be actual hostnames.

Dots and Termination in Zone Files

named(8) assumes that all hostnames in a zone file are part of the zone. In the zone file for *absolutefreebsd.com* you don't need to write out www .absolutefreebsd.com; named knows that you're talking about *absolutefreebsd.com*, so you can just list www. named(8) appends the zone name to every host in the zone, unless you say otherwise. This is convenient, except when the host isn't part of the domain. For example, neither of the nameservers for *absolutefreebsd .com* are in the *absolutefreebsd.com* domain. I don't want the master nameserver showing up as *bewilderbeast.blackhelicopters.org.absolutefreebsd.com*, do I?

You've seen that dots can be substituted for the @ sign in email addresses in the zone file's SOA record. Dots are further overloaded, however, into hostname termination symbols. If you put a dot after a hostname, named(8) understands that you've listed the complete hostname including the domain name. As you can see in the preceding examples, every complete hostname after the SOA record has a dot after it. Even the CNAME entry pointing to *www .absolutefreebsd.com* has a dot at the end of it. Without the dot, this alias would point to *www.absolutefreebsd.com.absolutefreebsd.com*. That's certainly not what I want you to type into your browser to find the web page for this book! (Mind you, having that as an actual hostname is something that DNS geeks find funny. Remember that before becoming a DNS geek.)

Reverse DNS Zones

Each block of IP addresses you manage needs a reverse DNS file, listing all the hosts assigned to your various IP addresses. Each A record needs a corresponding PTR record. This amounts to double-entry bookkeeping, which is a great thing in accounting but a tedious annoyance in system administration.

I highly recommend the mkrdns script to automate maintenance of your reverse DNS. This saves you time and reduces the number of DNS errors. mkrdns is a Perl script, so simple that it doesn't even require a port. Search for mkrdns on your favorite search engine, download the script, and place it in */usr/local/bin*.

You must have an existing zone file for your reverse zones for mkrdns to update your records. This zone must have a valid SOA record, but doesn't need any hosts. mkrdns uses your SOA as a template for the zone file it creates. Just run the script like this:

```
# mkrdns /etc/namedb/named.conf
```

You'll see that your reverse DNS files are automatically updated. Just reload your nameserver to make the updates take effect. Oh, we haven't talked about reloading nameservers yet? Let's take care of that right now.

Managing named

On a nameserver, start named(8) automatically at boot time with an *rc.conf* option:

```
named_enable="YES"
```

This enables the startup script */etc/rc.d/named*. You can start and stop named(8) using this script, as we discussed in Chapter 3. Always use `/etc/rc.d/named stop` and `/etc/rc.d/named start` to turn named on and off.

Once named is running, however, you'll need to reload named(8) or have a master nameserver check its zone files for updates. BIND includes the Remote Name Daemon Control, rndc(8), for these tasks.

Configuring rndc

rndc communicates with named(8) via a secure TCP connection, even from the local host. This means that you can manage nameservers on remote systems without logging in. Creating the secure channel requires a shared cryptographic secret, however. BIND includes rndc-confgen(8), a script to generate this shared secret and take all the tedious work out of configuring rndc. Just run `rndc-confgen` to generate your rndc configuration file:

```
# rndc-confgen > /etc/namedb/rndc.conf
```

This file includes both the configuration for rndc(8) itself and a configuration to add to *named.conf*. The *named.conf* section is commented out with hash marks and looks something like this:

```
# Use with the following in named.conf, adjusting the allow list as needed:
# key "rndc-key" {
```

```
#      algorithm hmac-md5;
#    ❶secret "VO5IU1GnxQTlfTxALgciCw==";
# };
#
# controls {
#    ❷inet 127.0.0.1 port 953
#        ❸allow { 127.0.0.1; } keys { "rndc-key"; };
# };
# End of named.conf
```

The interesting bit here is the cryptographic secret ❶ needed to control your nameserver. The secrets in *rndc.conf* and *named.conf* must match, or rndc requests will fail. You'll also see the IP address and TCP port on which named listens for control connections ❷, and the hosts and keys permitted to manage this nameserver ❸. You can allow multiple clients to manage your DNS server, and you could assign each client a separate cryptographic key; read rndc(8) and rndc.conf(5) for details.

Copy the commented out lines of *rndc.conf* into *named.conf*, remove the hash marks, and restart named with /etc/rc.d/named restart. You can now manage your nameserver with rndc.

Using rndc

So, after going to all the trouble to set up rndc, what's so great about it? For a complete list of everything rndc can do, read rndc(8). The most common administrative tasks are: reloading a nameserver, reloading a zone, refreshing a zone, reconfiguring named, and checking named's status.

Reloading a nameserver with rndc reload makes named(8) reread and reprocess its configuration, load all master domains from their text files, and check for updates on all slave domains. This is the most commonly used way to make a nameserver recognize changes in its zones or configuration.

In between reloading a nameserver and completely restarting the nameserver, you can have named check for new zones with rndc reconfig.

To *reload a zone* without reloading the entire nameserver, specify a domain name after the rndc reload command. You might do this if your nameserver is heavily loaded and reloading the entire configuration takes too long or puts too much strain on the network.

Refreshing a zone tells a slave server to immediately check the master server for updates on that zone. For example, if I want the slave server for *absolutefreebsd.com* to check for an update on the master server, I run rndc refresh absolutefreebsd.com on the slave server.

rndc does not let you restart named. To completely restart named, use /etc/rc.d/named restart.

With rndc status, you can see various information about your running nameserver including how many domains you serve, how many clients are querying the server, and so on.

Checking DNS

DNS configuration errors appear in */var/log/messages* whenever you start, restart, or reload named. Look here for errors. The log messages are generally fairly explicit and indicate exactly where named thinks the error is located.

Once you've created your first zone, ask for a complete list of domains to check your work. dig's axfr keyword requests a list of all hosts in the domain:

```
# dig domainname @primarynameserver axfr
```

Read the results. Are all the names as you expected? Do you have hosts with double domain names, such as *www.absolutefreebsd.com .absolutefreebsd.com*? If so, you forgot a dot. Are all of your mail servers and nameservers showing up? If not, fix them.

You can also use dnswalk(1) (*/usr/ports/dns/dnswalk*) to double-check your work. This tool catches a wide variety of standard configuration problems, although it won't catch conceptual problems. If you have a host using a CNAME but the canonical name is an alias back to the first name, creating a loop, dnswalk points it out. If you set your preferred mail exchanger to *mail.whitehouse.gov*, it'll let that pass, however. Use dnswalk like this:

```
# dnswalk absolutefreebsd.com.
```

Note the trailing dot.

Nameserver Security

BIND is a popular target for attackers because it provides a lot of information about your network. Even if an intruder could not get control of your machine, he could pillage DNS for interesting hostnames—for example, "accounting" or "finance." Additionally, named(8) defaulted to running as root for many years. If someone broke into named, he owned your machine. We'll address both of these problems separately.

Controlling Zone Transfers

The dig example I gave for listing an entire domain is called a *zone transfer*. This is the query used by a slave DNS server to update its records of a domain. A prospective intruder would be very interested in the full hostname list. Since the purpose of a nameserver is to serve names, we can't entirely cut out the bad guy's access. We can, however, make sure that named only answers specific queries instead of spilling its guts upon request. With this setup, named answers requests for particular hostnames but denies requests for the entire list from arbitrary clients.

To restrict zone transfers to specific hosts, use the *named.conf* allow-transfer option:

```
options {
    allow-transfer {
        127.0.0.1; 192.168.8.3;
    };
};
```

In this example, the hosts 127.0.0.1 (the local host) and 192.168.8.3 are the only systems permitted to request a zone transfer. Replace those IP addresses with those of your slave nameservers and your primary debugging workstation, and you've concealed a lot of information about your network. You might also add the network staff's desktop machines to this list so that they can perform zone transfers to debug DNS issues.

If needed, named(8) supports much more restrictive access lists on a zone-by-zone basis. See the BIND's documentation in */usr/src/contrib/bind/doc* for more details.

Securing named(8)

How about hackers attacking named(8) itself, trying to get a command prompt on your system? We could run named in a jail (see Chapter 9) to ensure that a successful intruder cannot access anything else on your network. BIND defaults to running in a chroot environment, however. In this case, the BIND chroot environment is a better choice; it only includes those system resources necessary for named to run and nothing more. The chroot is effectively an unprivileged, stripped-down jail. While this is the default configuration, you need to know how it works.

named(8) runs in a root directory of */var/named*. If you look there, you'll see subdirectories of *dev, etc,* and *var*. Running chrooted, named(8) believes that */var/named* is actually */* and that those directories are */dev, /etc,* and */var*. The program can only access these limited subdirectories. Note the absence of, say, */bin* or */sbin*. An intruder can't get a shell or access any programs, because there are no programs to be found!

But, wait a minute. . . . If named(8) is stuck in */var/named*, how can it read the configuration file in */etc/namedb*? Take a closer look at */etc/namedb*; it's actually a symlink to */var/named/etc/namedb*. This is because */etc/namedb* has been the named configuration directory for so long and on so many operating systems that nobody dares remove that link now.

More on BIND

As your network grows, you'll need more information on BIND. Some of its advanced features, such as views, will be very useful for an expanding network. One good source of documentation is */usr/src/contrib/bind9/*, especially the *doc* subdirectory. The standard book on BIND is *DNS and BIND* by Paul Albitz and Cricket Liu (O'Reilly Media, 5th edition, 2006), and I recommend it highly for advanced DNS information.

15

SMALL SYSTEM SERVICES

Even a server with a very narrowly defined role, such as a dedicated web server, needs a variety of small "helper" services to handle basic administrative issues. In this chapter we'll discuss some of those services, such as time synchronization, DHCP services, scheduling tasks, and so on. We'll start by securing your remote connections to your FreeBSD server with SSH.

SSH

One of Unix's great strengths is its ease of remote administration. Whether the server is in front of you or in a remote, barricaded laboratory in a subterranean, maximum-security installation surrounded by vicious guard dogs mentored by a megalomaniacal weasel named Ivan, if you have network access to the machine you can control it just as if you were sitting in front of it.

For many years, telnet(1) was the standard way to access a remote server. telnet is nifty. You can use it to connect to an arbitrary TCP port on a system and manually talk to that server across the network, as this book recommends elsewhere. As a remote administration protocol, however, telnet has one crushing problem: Everything sent over most versions of telnet is unencrypted. Anyone with a packet sniffer, attached anywhere along your connection, can steal your username, your password, and any information you view in your telnet session. When you use telnet, the best password-selection scheme in the world cannot protect your username and password. Intruders place illicit packet sniffers anywhere they can; I've seen them on small local networks, in law firms handling sensitive government work, on home PCs, and on Internet backbones. The only defense against a packet sniffer is to handle your authentication credentials and data in such a way that a packet sniffer cannot capture them. That's where SSH, or secure shell, comes in.

SSH behaves much like telnet in that it provides a highly configurable terminal window on a remote host. But unlike telnet, SSH encrypts everything you send across the network. SSH ensures not only that your passwords can't be sniffed, but also that the commands you enter and their output are encrypted as well. While telnet does have a few minor advantages over SSH in that it requires less CPU time and is simpler to configure, SSH's security advantages heavily outweigh them. SSH also has many features that telnet does not have, such as the ability to tunnel arbitrary protocols through the encrypted session. Like telnet, SSH runs on every modern variant of Unix and even on Microsoft Windows.

SSH encrypts and authenticates remote connections via public key cryptography, as we discussed in Chapter 9. The SSH daemon offers the server's public key to clients and keeps the private key to itself. The client and server use the cryptographic key to negotiate a cryptographically secure channel between them. Since both public and private keys are necessary to complete this transaction, your data is secure; even if someone captures your SSH traffic, they can only see encrypted garbage.

To use SSH, you must run an SSH server on your FreeBSD machine and an SSH client on your workstation.

The SSH Server: sshd(8)

The sshd(8) daemon listens for SSH requests coming in from the network on TCP port 22. To enable sshd at boot, add the following line to */etc/rc.conf*:

```
sshd_enable="YES"
```

Once this is set, you can use the */etc/rc.d/sshd* script to start and stop SSH. Stopping the SSH daemon doesn't terminate SSH sessions that are already in use; it only prevents the daemon from accepting new connections.

Unlike some of the other protocols we look at, sshd is difficult to test by hand. One thing you can do is confirm that sshd is running by using telnet to connect to the SSH TCP port.

```
# telnet localhost 22
```
❶ Trying ::1...
❷ Trying 127.0.0.1...
❸ Connected to localhost.
Escape character is '^]'.
❹ SSH-2.0-OpenSSH_4.4p1 FreeBSD-20060930

Telnet tries the IPv6 address ❶ for localhost, then the IPv4 address ❷, and succeeds ❸. The connection attempt succeeds, and we see that the daemon listening on this port calls itself SSH version 2, implemented in OpenSSH 4.4p1, on FreeBSD, version 20060930 ❹. (The SSH protocol has two versions, 1 and 2. *Always* use version 2.) You can get all this information from a simple telnet command, but it's the last free information sshd offers. Unless you're capable of encrypting packets by hand, on the fly, this is about as far as you can go. Press CTRL-] to close the connection and CTRL-C to leave telnet and return to the command prompt.

SSH Keys and Fingerprints

The first time you start sshd(8), the program realizes that it has no encryption keys and automatically creates them. If the system is just booting, you will be offered a chance to pound on the keyboard for a while to help enhance system randomness. The initializing sshd process will create three pairs of keys.

SSH version 1 uses */etc/ssh/ssh_host_key*, */etc/ssh/ssh_host_key.pub*, */etc/ssh/ssh_host_rsa_key*, and */etc/ssh/ssh_host_rsa_key.pub*. SSH version 1, while not really secure, is much less appallingly insecure than telnet. SSH version 2 uses the RSA key files as well as the DSA key files */etc/ssh/ssh_host_dsa_key* and */etc/ssh/ssh_host_dsa_key.pub*.

The key files ending in *.pub* contain the public keys for each type of key. These are the keys that sshd hands to connecting clients. This gives the connecting user the ability to confirm that the server he is connecting to is really the server he thinks it is. (In the past, intruders have tricked users into logging into bogus machines in order to capture their usernames and passwords.) Take a look at one of these public key files; it's pretty long. Even when a user is offered the chance to confirm that the server is offering the correct key, it's so long that even the most paranoid users won't bother to verify every single character.

Fortunately, SSH allows you to generate a *key fingerprint*, which is a much shorter representation of a key. You cannot encrypt traffic or negotiate connections with the fingerprint, but the chances of two unrelated keys having the same fingerprint are negligible. To generate a fingerprint for a public key, enter the command ssh-keygen -lf *keyfile.pub*.

```
# ssh-keygen -lf /etc/ssh/ssh_host_dsa_key.pub
1024 31:28:4b:6e:aa:23:63:2e:9a:6b:44:00:9f:fd:28:21
/etc/ssh/ssh_host_dsa_key.pub
```

The first number, 1024, shows the number of bits in the key. 1,024 is standard in 2007, but I expect this to increase to 2,048 in the next few years as computing power increases. The hexadecimal string starting with 31 and ending with 21 is the fingerprint of the public key. While it's long, it's much shorter and much more readable than the actual key. Copy this key fingerprint from the original server to a place where you can access it from your client machines, either on a web page or on a paper list. Use this key to confirm your server's identity the first time you connect.

Configuring the SSH Daemon

While sshd comes with a perfectly usable configuration, you might want to tweak the settings once you learn all the features sshd(8) offers. The configuration file */etc/ssh/sshd_config* lists all the default settings, commented out with a hash mark (#). If you want to change the value for a setting, uncomment the entry and change its value.

We won't discuss all the available sshd options; that would take a rather large book of its own. Moreover, OpenSSH advances quickly enough to make that book obsolete before it hits the shelves. Instead, we'll focus on some of the more common desirable configuration changes people make.

After changing the SSH daemon's configuration, restart the daemon with /etc/rc.d/sshd restart.

VersionAddendum FreeBSD-20061110

The VersionAddendum appears in the server name when you connect to sshd's TCP port. Some people recommend changing this to disguise the operating system version. Identifying a computer's operating system is simple enough, however, by using fingerprinting techniques on packets exchanged with the host, so this isn't generally worth the time. (On the other hand, changing the VersionAddendum to DrunkenBadgerSoftware because it amuses you might be worthwhile.)

Port 22

sshd(8) defaults to listening to TCP port 22. If you want, you can change this to a nonstandard port. If you want sshd to listen to multiple ports (e.g., port 443 in addition to port 22, to bypass a badly configured firewall), you can include multiple Port entries on separate lines:

```
Port 22
Port 443
```

Protocol 2

Any modern SSH install only supports version 2 of the SSH protocol by default. SSH version 1 has security problems, and SSH version 2 clients are now free for all widely deployed systems. sshd(8) still supports version 1, however, and you can enable its support here even though it has poor security. List your permitted protocol versions in order of preference, separated by commas.

ListenAddress 0.0.0.0

sshd defaults to listening for incoming requests on all IP addresses on the machine. If you need to restrict the range of addresses to listen on (for example, on a jail server), you can specify it here:

```
ListenAddress 192.168.33.8
```

If you want sshd to listen on multiple addresses, use multiple `ListenAddress` lines.

SyslogFacility AUTH and LogLevel INFO

These two settings control how sshd(8) logs connection information. See Chapter 19 for more information on logging.

LoginGraceTime 2m

This controls how long a user has to log in after getting connected. If an incoming user connects but does not successfully log in within this time window, sshd drops the connection.

PermitRootLogin no

Do not let people log into your server as root. Instead, they should SSH in as a regular user and become root with su(1). Allowing direct root logins eliminates any hope you have of identifying who misconfigured your system and allows intruders to cover their tracks much more easily.

MaxAuthTries 6

This is the number of times a user may attempt to enter a password during a single connection. After this number of unsuccessful attempts to log in, the user is disconnected.

AllowTcpForwarding yes

SSH allows users to forward arbitrary TCP/IP ports to a remote system. If your users have shell access, they can install their own port forwarders, so there's little reason to disable this.

X11Forwarding yes

Unix-like operating systems use the X11 (or X) protocol to display graphical programs. In X, the display is separated from the physical machine. You can run, say, a web browser on one machine and display the results on another.

As X has had a checkered security history, many admins reflexively disable X forwarding. Denying X forwarding over SSH doesn't disable X forwarding in general, however. Most users, if denied SSH-based X forwarding, just forward X over unencrypted TCP/IP using either X's built-in network aware-ness or a third-party forwarder, which in most circumstances is far worse than allowing X over SSH. If your sshd server has the X libraries and client pro-grams installed, a user can forward X one way or another; it's best to let SSH handle the forwarding for you. If you don't have the X software installed, then X11Forwarding has no effect.

MaxStartups 10

This is the number of connection attempts that can occur at the same time. If more users than specified by MaxStartups attempt to SSH to the server simul-taneously, sshd(8) refuses some of the connection attempts until other users log in, timeout, or fail to log on enough times to be disconnected.

Banner /some/path

The banner is a message that is displayed before authentication occurs. The most common use for this option is to display legal warnings. The default is to not use a banner.

Subsystem sftp /usr/libexec/sftp-server

SSH allows you to securely copy files from one system to another with scp(1). While scp works well, it's not very user-friendly. The sftp server provides an FTP-like interface to file transfer, reducing the amount of time you must spend on user education but still maintaining solid security.

Managing SSH User Access

By default, anyone with a legitimate shell can log into the server. Using the configuration variables AllowGroups, DenyGroups, AllowUsers, and DenyUsers, sshd(8) lets you define particular users and groups that may or may not access your machine.

When you explicitly list users who may SSH into a machine, any user who is not listed cannot SSH in.

For example, the AllowGroups option lets you restrict SSH access to users in specified groups defined in */etc/group* (see Chapter 7). If this option is set and a user is not in any of the allowed groups, he cannot log in. Separate multiple groups with spaces:

```
AllowGroups wheel webmaster dnsadmin
```

If you don't want to give a whole group SSH access, you can list individual users with AllowUsers. By using AllowUsers, you disallow SSH access for everyone except the listed users.

The DenyGroups list is the opposite of AllowGroups. Users in the specified system groups cannot log in. The listed group must be their primary group, meaning it must be listed in */etc/master.passwd* and not just */etc/group*. This limitation makes DenyGroups less useful than it seems at first; you cannot define a general group called nossh and just add users to it, unless you make it their primary group as well. Explicitly listing allowed groups is a much more useful policy.

Finally, the DenyUsers variable lists users who may not log in. You can use this to explicitly forbid certain users who are in a group that is otherwise allowed.

These four different settings make it possible for a user to be in multiple groups simultaneously. For example, one user might be in a group listed in AllowGroups and a group listed in DenyGroups. What then? The SSH daemon checks these values in the order: DenyUsers, AllowUsers, DenyGroups, and AllowGroups. The first rule that matches wins. For example, suppose I'm a member of the wheel group. Here's a snippet of *sshd_config*:

```
DenyUsers: mwlucas
AllowGroups: wheel
```

I cannot SSH into this machine, because DenyUsers is checked before AllowGroups.

SSH Clients

Of course, FreeBSD comes with the SSH client, as do most Unix-like operating systems. If possible, use the included SSH client—it's part of OpenSSH, developed by a subset of the OpenBSD team, and is not only the most popular implementation but also the best. If you've been sentenced to run a Microsoft operating system, I recommend PuTTY, which is free for commercial or noncommercial purposes and has excellent terminal emulation.

This is a FreeBSD book, so we'll focus on FreeBSD's OpenSSH client. You can configure the client in a variety of ways, but the most common configuration choices available simply disable the functions offered by the server. If you're really interested in tweaking your client's behavior, read ssh_config(5).

To connect to another host with SSH, type ssh *hostname*. In response, you'll see something like this:

```
# ssh sardines.blackhelicopters.org
The authenticity of host 'sardines.blackhelicopters.org (192.168.1.1)' can't
be established.
DSA key fingerprint is a4:df:7c:7e:0e:27:e5:21:b4:f4:0e:2b:c9:10:5f:ea.
Are you sure you want to continue connecting (yes/no)? yes
```

Your client immediately retrieves the public key from the host you're connecting to, and checks its own internal list of SSH keys for a matching key for that host. If the key offered by the server matches the key the client has in its list, the client assumes you're talking to the correct host. If the client does not have the host key in its list of known hosts, it presents the key fingerprint for your approval.

The fingerprint presented by the SSH client should be identical to the fingerprint you generated on your server. If the fingerprint is not identical, you're connecting to the wrong host and you need to immediately disconnect. If it matches, accept the key and continue. Once you accept the fingerprint, the key is saved under your home directory in *.ssh/known_hosts*.

If you're building a new server on your local network for your private use, perhaps you don't have to manually compare the key fingerprints. You should still copy the key fingerprint, however, since you'll eventually want to connect from a remote location and will need to verify the key. If many people will connect to a server, it's generally okay to put the fingerprint on a web page. You must decide how much security you need. I strongly encourage you to error on the side of caution.

Accept the host key, and you'll be allowed to log into the server. While using a private key with a passphrase is preferable to using passwords, a password with SSH is still better than telnet.

Copying Files over SSH

The SSH client is fine for command-line access, but what about moving files from one system to another? SSH includes two tools for moving files across the network, scp(1) and sftp(1).

scp(1) is "secure copy" and is ideal for moving individual files. scp takes two arguments: first, the file's current location, then the desired location. The desired location is specified as *<username>@<hostname>:<filename>*. Suppose I want to copy the file *bookbackup.tgz* from my local system to the remote server *bewilderbeast.blackhelicopters.org*, giving the remote copy a different name. I would run:

```
# scp bookbackup.tgz mwlucas@bewilderbeast.blackhelicopters.org:bookbackup-
january.tgz
```

If you want to give the new copy the same name, you can leave off the filename in the second argument:

```
# scp bookbackup.tgz mwlucas@bewilderbeast.blackhelicopters.org:
```

scp(1) also lets you copy files from a remote system to your local system:

```
# scp mwlucas@bewilderbeast.blackhelicopters.org:bookbackup-january.tgz
bookbackup.tgz
```

If you don't want to change the filename on the local system, you can use a single dot as the destination name:

```
# scp mwlucas@bewilderbeast.blackhelicopters.org:bookbackup.tgz .
```

Finally, if your username on the remote system is the same as your local username, you can delete the username and the @ sign. For example, to back up my work I just use:

```
# scp bookbackup.tgz bewilderbeast.blackhelicopters.org:
```

While this looks complicated, it's quite useful for quickly moving individual files around the network.

If you like interactive systems or if you don't know the precise name of the file you want to grab from a remote server, sftp(1) is your friend. sftp(1) takes a single argument, the username and server name, using scp's syntax for a remote server:

```
# sftp mwlucas@bewilderbeast,blackhelicopters.org
Connecting to bewilderbeast...
Password:
sftp> ls
```

sftp(1) looks much like a standard command-line FTP client; it supports the usual FTP commands such as ls (list), cd (change directory), get (download a file), and put (upload a file). One important difference is that sftp(1) does not require a choice between ASCII and binary transfers; it just transfers the file as is.

With SSH, scp, and sftp, you can completely eliminate cleartext passwords from your network.

> ### OPENSSH SECURES EVERYTHING
>
> Many network programs include support for communicating over SSH. Additionally, OpenSSH can create arbitrary tunnels between TCP ports on different machines. Thanks to OpenSSH, you can avoid sending any data unencrypted over your network.

Network Time

If a database starts entering dates three hours behind, or if emails arrive with dates from tomorrow, you'll hear about it pretty quickly. Time is *important*.[1] You have three tools to manage system time: tzsetup(8) controlling the time zone, the network time correction tool ntpdate(8), and the continuous time-adjustment program ntpd(8). Start by setting your time zone manually, then use Network Time Protocol.

Setting the Time Zone

Time zone is easy to manage with tzsetup(8), a menu-driven program that makes the appropriate changes on your system for each time zone. Global organizations might use on their systems the default of UTC (Universal Time Clock), while others use their own local time. Enter tzsetup, follow the geographic prompts, and choose the appropriate time zone for your location.

---

[1] The most important time of all, of course, is the "time to go home."

Network Time Protocol

Network Time Protocol (NTP), is a method to synchronize time across a network. You can make your local computer's clock match the atomic clock at your government's research lab or the time on your main server. Computers that offer time synchronization are called time servers and are roughly lumped into two groups, Tier 1 and Tier 2.

Tier 1 NTP servers are directly connected to a highly accurate time-keeping device. If you really need this sort of accuracy, then what you really need is your own atomic clock. If the time lag caused by the speed of light is acceptable, a USB radio clock such as that found on an inexpensive GPS is very nice.

Tier 2 NTP servers feed off the Tier 1 NTP servers, providing time service as a public service. Their service is accurate to within a fraction of a second and is sufficient for almost all non–life sustaining applications. Some digging will even lead you to Tier 3 time servers, which feed off of Tier 2 servers.

The best source of time servers is the list at *http://www.pool.ntp.org*. This group has collected public NTP servers into round-robin DNS pools, allowing easy NTP configuration. These NTP servers are arranged first in a global list, then by continent, and then by country. For example, if you're in Canada, a brief search on that site leads you to *0.ca.pool.ntp.org*, *1.ca.pool.ntp.org*, and *2.ca.pool.ntp.org*. We'll use these servers in the examples below, but look up the proper servers for your country and use those instead when setting up your own time service.

Configuring ntpd(8)

ntpd(8) checks the system clock against a list of time servers. It takes a reasonable average of the times provided by the time servers, discarding any servers too far away from the consensus, and gradually adjusts the system time to match the average. This gives the most accurate system time possible, without demanding too much from any one server, and helps keep errant hardware in check. Configure ntp in */etc/ntpd.conf*. Here's a sample:

```
server 1.ca.pool.ntp.org
server 2.ca.pool.ntp.org
server 3.ca.pool.ntp.org
```

This system checks three time servers for updates. If you list only one server, ntpd(8) slaves its clock to that one server and shares any time problems that server experiences. Using two time servers guarantees that your system will not know what time it is; remember, NTP takes an average of its time servers but throws out any values too far out of range of the others. How can NTP decide if one server is wrong when it only has two values to choose from? Using three time servers is optimal; if one server runs amok, ntpd recognizes that the time offered by that server does not make sense against the time offered by the other two servers. (Think of this as a "tyranny of the majority"; the one guy whose opinion differs from the rest doesn't get any voice at all.)

Instant Time Correction

ntpd(8) is great at keeping the system clock accurate over time, but it only adjusts the local clock gradually. If your time is off by hours or days (which is not unlikely at install time or after a long power outage), you probably want to set your clock correctly before letting any time-sensitive applications start. ntpd(8) includes that functionality as well, with ntpd -q.

To perform a single brute-force correction of your clock, use ntpd -q. This connects to your NTP servers, gets the correct time, sets your system clock, and exits.

```
# ntpd -q
ntpd: time set -76.976809s
```

This system's time was off by about 77 seconds, but is now synchronized with the NTP servers.

Do not change the clock arbitrarily on a production system. Time-sensitive software, such as many database-driven applications, has problems if time suddenly moves forwards or backwards.

If you have really good hardware with an excellent clock, using ntpd -q at boot handles all of your time problems. Very few people have that sort of hardware, however. Most of us have to make do with commodity hardware with notoriously poor clocks. The best way to ensure you have accurate time is to run ntpd(8) to gently adjust your clock on an ongoing basis.

ntpd(8) at Boot Time

To have ntpd perform a one-time clock synchronization at boot and then continually adjust the clock afterwards, set the following in */etc/rc.conf*:

```
ntpd_enable="YES"
ntpd_sync_on_start="YES"
```

Redistributing Time

While ntpd does not use a large amount of network bandwidth, having every server on your network query the public NTP servers is a waste of network resources—both yours and the time server donors'. It can also lead to very slight (subsecond) variances in time on your own network.

I recommend setting up a single authoritative time server for your network. Have this server synchronize its clock with the global NTP pool. Configure each server on your network to point to this server for its NTP updates. That way, every clock on your network will be perfectly synchronized. Any clock errors will occur either everywhere on your network (which tells you that the time server has an issue) or only on one server (which will indicate a problem on that particular machine). You will not have to trawl through NTP logs to try to determine if a particular server in the global time server pool has somehow messed up your system clock. It is best to enforce this policy via firewall rules at your network border; allowing only your time server to communicate with outside NTP servers eliminates one common source of temporal chaos.

Name Service Switching and Caching

Any Unix-like system performs innumerable checks of many different name services. We've already talked about the Domain Name System that maps hostnames to IP addresses (see Chapter 14), but there's also a password entry lookup service, a TCP/IP port number and name lookup service, an IP protocol name and number lookup service, and so on. You can configure how your FreeBSD system makes these queries and what information sources it uses through nsswitch (name service switching). FreeBSD also has a name service caching daemon, nscd(8), that stores the results of name service queries you've already made, reducing both network traffic and the time needed to make these queries.

/etc/nsswitch.conf

The name service switching system, which manages how FreeBSD looks up network information, is configured in */etc/nsswitch.conf*. Each name service has an entry including the type of the service and the information sources it uses. We previously saw an example of name service switching in Chapter 14. Remember this entry for host lookups?

```
hosts: files dns
```

This means, "Look for IP addresses in the local files first, and then query DNS." The other information sources work similarly. FreeBSD, like most other Unix-like operating systems, supports name service switching for the information sources listed in Table 15-1.

Table 15-1: Lookups Supporting Name Service Switching

Lookup	Function
groups	Group membership checks (*/etc/group*)
hosts	Hostname and IP checks (DNS)
networks	Network entries (*/etc/networks*)
passwd	Password entries (*/etc/passwd*)
shells	Checks for valid shells (*/etc/shells*)
services	TCP and UDP services (*/etc/services*)
rpc	Remote procedure calls (*/etc/rpc*)
proto	TCP/IP network protocols (*/etc/protocols*)

Most of these you don't want to muck with, unless you like breaking system functionality. If you have a Kerberos or an NIS domain, for example, you might want to have your FreeBSD box attach to them for user and group information—but if you don't, reconfiguring the password lookups would just make your system work harder or stop working at all!

For each name service, you must specify one or more sources of information. Many of these name services are very simple and default to having a single authoritative source of information—a file. Others, such as the hosts name service, are more complicated and have multiple sources. A few are very complicated simply because of the vast array of information available and the many possible ways to get that information. As this book does not cover Kerberos, NIS, or any other enterprise-level user management systems, we won't cover changing password, group, and shell information sources. If you're in such an environment, read nsswitch.conf(5) for details.

The services we'll cover have three valid information sources: files, dns, and cache. *Files* are the standard text files containing information for the service. For example, network protocols are traditionally stored in */etc/protocols*, network services in */etc/services*, and passwords in */etc/passwd* and friends. A source of *dns* means that the information is available on a DNS server, as is typical for the hosts service. Finally, *cache* means that the information must be requested from the local name service caching daemon.

List each desired information source in the order you want them to be tried. Our hosts entry tells the name service lookup to try the local file first, and then query the DNS server. If you want your system to try the local cache first, use instead:

```
hosts: cache files dns
```

Now that you can point your name service queries anywhere you want, let's look at enabling the caching daemon.

Name Query Caching with nscd(8)

Analyzing my DNS server logs, it quickly became apparent that the two systems that make the most queries on my network are the proxy server and the network management server. This makes sense—after all, the proxy calls up dozens of web pages a second for users, and the management system hits every vital system on my network every few minutes. While these clients do not place an unbearable load on the system, there's no reason for them to keep performing the same checks on data that rarely changes. For example, the management workstation looks up the IP address of each router and switch every sixty seconds. That data is almost static, so those checks are not only inelegant but actively annoying when I'm reading my DNS query logs. Similarly, if your server is integrated into a large network, you might have to authenticate against a Kerberos domain or an LDAP directory, so your system would make thousands of network-traversing password checks a minute. Even the */etc/services* file can contain thousands of entries, and parsing the file for each and every lookup takes time.

The caching daemon, nscd(8), handles every information source managed by *nsswitch.conf*. Each type of lookup requires a line in the nscd configuration file, */etc/nscd.conf*. By default, nscd(8) caches all six services. Each entry has a keyword and either a cache name and a value, or just a value. For example, the default entry for host lookups is:

```
enable-cache hosts yes
```

The keyword is enable-cache, the cache name is hosts, and the value is yes. With this, nscd(8) stores hostname queries. If you edit */etc/nsswitch.conf* to have the hosts name service first try nscd, the results of all name service queries will be nscd locally. Between *nsswitch.conf* and nscd(8), my proxy servers and network management station make only a fraction of the queries to my DNS server.

nscd(8) and Timing

While nscd has a whole slew of options that might be useful in certain rare circumstances, the two that I find most generally helpful are timing options. Control the length of time nscd(8) stores an answer with the options negative-time-to-live and positive-time-to-live.

positive-time-to-live tells nscd(8) how long to retain cached answers. For example, suppose you're using nscd(8) for host name lookups. By setting the positive-time-to-live, you tell nscd to retain each answer for that number of seconds before discarding it and looking for a fresh answer. The following entry tells nscd(8) to retain host information for 600 seconds, or 10 minutes:

```
positive-time-to-live hosts 600
```

After 10 minutes, nscd(8) discards the old answer and lets the name service switcher look further for a fresh answer. When that fresh answer arrives, nscd(8) stores it for another 10 minutes. The default positive-time-to-live is 3,600 seconds, or 1 hour.

In addition to storing positive responses, nscd(8) also stores negative responses. If you ask for the host *nonexistent.absolutefreebsd.com*, you'll learn that there is no such host. nscd(8) stores that negative answer as well. You can control how long that negative answer remains in the cache with negative-time-to-live, with the same syntax as positive-time-to-live. By default, the negative-time-to-live for all information is 60 seconds.

Zeroing the Cache

Now and then you can get bad information in your cache. For example, my network management system checks every vital network device every few minutes. If I have to change the IP address on a router, I don't want the management station to start bleating about the disappearing router; I want it to go fetch the new answer immediately, without waiting for an hour. A user can erase his own part of the cache by using nscd's -i option, while root can erase the whole cache with -I.

For example, I erase my own hosts cache with:

```
# nscd -i hosts
```

If I do not erase the cache, my system will update with the new information according to nscd's time-to-live settings.

nscd(8) at Boot

Start nscd(8) automatically at boot by setting:

```
nscd_enable="YES"
```

in */etc/rc.conf.*

inetd

The inetd(8) daemon handles incoming network connections for less frequently used network services. Most systems don't have a steady stream of incoming FTP requests, so why have the FTP daemon running all the time? Instead, inetd listens to the network for incoming FTP requests. When an FTP request arrives, inetd(8) starts the FTP server and hands off the request. Other common programs that rely on inetd are telnet, tftp, and POP3.

inetd also handles functions so small and rarely used that they're easier to implement within inetd, rather than route them through a separate program. This includes discard (which dumps any data received into the black hole of */dev/null*), chargen (which pours out a stream of characters), and other functions. These days, most of these services are not required and are disabled by default, but you can enable them if necessary.

> **INETD(8) SECURITY**
>
> Some sysadmins think of inetd(8) as a single service with a monolithic security profile. Others say that inetd(8) has a bad security history. Neither is true. inetd(8) in itself is secure, but it absorbs a certain amount of blame for the programs it forwards requests to. Some services provided by inetd (such as telnet and ftp) are inherently insecure, while others have had a troubled childhood and act out as a result (i.e., qpopper). Use inetd(8) just as you would any other network server program: Do not run inetd unless you need it, and then confirm that it offers only trusted and secure programs!

/etc/inetd.conf

Take a look at */etc/inetd.conf.* Most daemons have separate IPv4 and IPv6 configurations, but if you're not running IPv6 you can ignore the IPv6 entries. Let's look at one entry, the FTP server configuration.

---

❶ftp   ❷stream   ❸tcp   ❹nowait   ❺root   ❻/usr/libexec/ftpd   ❼ftpd -l

The first field ❶ is the service name, which must match a name in */etc/services*. inetd performs a service name lookup to identify which TCP port it should listen to. If you want to change the TCP/IP port your FTP server runs on, change the port for FTP in */etc/services*. (You could also change the first field to match the service that runs on the desired port, but I find that this makes the entry slightly confusing.)

The socket type ❷ dictates what sort of connection this is. All TCP connections are of type `stream`, while UDP connections are of type `dgram`. While you might find other possible values, if you're considering using them, either you're reading the documentation for a piece of software that tells you what to use, or you're just wrong.

The protocol ❸ is the layer 4 network protocol, either `tcp` (IPv4 TCP), `udp` (IPv4 UDP), `tcp6` (IPv6 TCP), or `udp6` (IPv6 UDP). If your server accepts both IPv4 and IPv6 connections, use the entries `tcp46` or `udp46`.

The next field ❹ indicates whether inetd should wait for the server program to close the connection, or just start the program and go away. As a general rule, TCP daemons use `nowait` while UDP daemons need `wait`. (There are exceptions to this, but they're rare.) inetd(8) starts a new instance of the network daemon for each incoming request. If a service uses `nowait`, you can control the maximum number of connections inetd accepts per second by adding a slash and a number directly after `nowait`, like this: `nowait/5`. One way intruders (usually script kiddies) try to knock servers off the Internet is by opening more requests for a service than the server can handle, and by rate-limiting incoming connections you can stop this. On the other hand, this means that your intruder can stop other people from using the service at all. Choose your poison carefully!

We then have the user ❺ that the server daemon runs as. The FTP server ftpd(8) runs as root, as it must service requests for many system users, but other servers run as dedicated users.

The sixth field ❻ is the full path to the server program inetd runs when a connection request arrives. Services integrated with inetd(8) appear as internal.

The last field ❼ gives the command to start the external program including any desired command-line arguments.

Configuring inetd Servers

While */etc/inetd.conf* seems to use a lot of information, adding a program is actually pretty simple. The easiest way to learn about inetd(8) is to implement a simple service with it. For example, let's implement a Quote of the Day (qotd) service. When you connect to the qotd port, the server sends back a random quote and disconnects. FreeBSD includes a random quote generator in its games collection, fortune(1). This random quote generator is all we need to implement an inetd-based network program. We must specify a port number, a network protocol, a user, a path, and a command line.

port number

The *etc/services* file lists qotd on port 17.

network protocol

The qotd service requires that you connect to a network port and get something back, so it needs to run over TCP. Remember, UDP is connectionless—a reply is not required. We must specify `tcp` in our inetd configuration, which means that we must specify `nowait` in the fourth field.

user

Best practice says to create an unprivileged user to run the qotd service, modeled after users such as pop or proxy. For this example, we'll just use the general unprivileged user nobody, but if you were implementing this in production you'd want to create an unprivileged user qotd.

path

Find fortune at *usr/games/fortune*.

Running the Command

fortune(6) does not require any command-line arguments, but you can add them if you like. Believers in Murphy's Law can use `fortune murphy`, while Star Trek fans can get quotes with `fortune startrek`. (The latter correctly includes only the One True Star Trek, not any of the wannabe followups.) I use `fortune -o`, as anyone who connects to my server deserves what they get.

Sample inetd.conf Configuration

Putting this all together, the entry for qotd in */etc/inetd.conf* looks like this:

```
qotd    stream    tcp    nowait    nobody    /usr/games/fortune    fortune
```

You might think this example trivial, but providing other services out of inetd(8) is no more difficult.

Starting inetd(8)

First, enable inetd(8) at boot by adding the following entry to */etc/rc.conf*:

```
inetd_enable=YES
```

With this set, start inetd by hand with `/etc/rc.d/inetd start`.

Now that inetd is running, telnet to port 17 and test our new service:

```
# telnet localhost 17
❶ Trying 127.0.0.1...
Connected to localhost.
Escape character is '^]'.
❷ It is difficult to produce a television documentary that is both
incisive and probing when every twelve minutes one is interrupted by
```

```
twelve dancing rabbits singing about toilet paper.
                    -- Rod Serling
Connection closed by foreign host.
```

It works! We have the usual TCP/IP connection information ❶ and our random fortune ❷. (As an added bonus, you also know why I don't write for television.)

Changing inetd's Behavior

inetd behaves differently depending on the flags you set for it. The default flags turn on TCP wrappers, as configured in */etc/hosts.allow* (see Chapter 9). Table 15-2 lists some of the useful flags.

Table 15-2: inetd(8) Flags

Flag	Description
-l	Log every successful connection.
-c	Set the maximum number of connections per second that can be made to any service. By default, there is no limit. Note that "unlimited" is not the same as "infinite"—your hardware only handles so many connections.
-C	Set the number of times one IP address can connect to a single service in one minute. This connection rate is unlimited by default, but using this can be useful against people trying to monopolize your bandwidth or resources.
-R	Set the maximum number of times any one service can be started in one minute. The default is 256. If you use -R 0, you allow an unlimited number of connections to any one service.
-a	Set the IP address inetd(8) attaches to. By default, inetd listens on all IP addresses attached to the system.
-w	Use TCP wrappers for programs started by inetd(8), as per *hosts.allow* (see Chapter 9).
-W	Use TCP wrappers for services integrated with inetd(8), as per *hosts.allow* (see Chapter 9).

As an extreme example, if you want to use TCP wrappers, allow only two connections per second from any single host, allow an unlimited number of service invocations per minute, and only listen on the IP address 192.168.1.2, you would set the following in */etc/rc.conf*:

```
inetd_flags="-Ww -c 2 -R 0 -a 192.168.1.2"
```

With inetd(8), almost anything can be a network service.

DHCP

Dynamic Host Configuration Protocol (DHCP) is the standard method for handing out IP addresses to client computers. While DHCP services are not integrated with FreeBSD out of the box, they are commonly required to implement such services as diskless workstations and PXE installs. We'll cover the basics of DHCP configuration here, without delving into DHCP's advanced features, to give you just enough information to set up your basic office, diskless clients, or global network of interconnected offices.

The FreeBSD Ports Collection includes ISC dhcpd, from the same folks who brought us BIND (see Chapter 14), in */usr/ports/net/isc-dhcp3-server*. Install that port per the instructions in Chapter 11. You'll be offered a screen of initial options that highlight many of ISC dhcpd's features and capabilities, such as LDAP integration. The default options are suitable for almost any environment and include many desirable security features. The tools installed include dhcpd(8), the configuration file */usr/local/etc/dhcpd.conf*, and extensive manual pages.

How DHCP Works

DHCP can be terribly complicated in a complex network, but is rather simple in an office Ethernet environment. Each DHCP client sends a broadcast across the local Ethernet asking for someone, anyone, to provide network configuration information. If your DHCP server is on that local Ethernet, it answers directly. If your DHCP server is on another network segment, the router for that network segment needs to know which IP address to forward the DHCP request to. The DHCP server then loans configuration information to the client and tracks which clients have been assigned which IP addresses. A configuration issued to a client is called a *lease*. Like the lease you pay on a home or auto, DHCP leases expire and must be renewed occasionally.

The client can request certain features—for example, Microsoft clients ask for the IP address of the WINS server, while diskless systems ask where to find a kernel. You can manage all these options as necessary.

Each client is uniquely identified by the MAC address of the network card used to connect to the network. ISC dhcpd tracks MAC and IP addresses, as well as leases, in the file */var/db/dhcpd/dhcpd.leases*. In this file, you can identify which hosts have which IP addresses. If a host disappears from the network for a time and returns, dhcpd(8) reissues the same IP to that client if that IP is still available.

Managing dhcpd(8)

Enable dhcpd(8) in */etc/rc.conf* with:

```
dhcpd_enable="YES"
```

With this set, you can use the script */usr/local/etc/rc.d/isc-dhcpd* to start and stop the daemon.

Configuring dhcpd(8)

The file */usr/local/etc/dhcpd.conf* contains all the configuration for dhcpd. While ISC dhcpd(8) can fill a book on its own, we'll focus on the functions needed for a basic small office as well as those used in the examples later in this book. The default *dhcpd.conf* is well commented and includes still more examples, while the online manual is painfully exhaustive. We're going to assume that you're running a single DHCP server on your network, and that your server should answer all requests for DHCP services. (It is entirely possible to cluster ISC dhcpd for fault tolerance, but that's beyond our scope here.) Start your *dhcpd.conf* with a few general rules for client configuration:

```
❶ option domain-name "absolutefreebsd.com";
❷ option domain-name-servers 192.168.1.11, 192.168.1.12;
❸ default-lease-time 3600;
❹ max-lease-time 14400;
❺ authoritative;
❻ ddns-update-style none;
❼ log-facility local7;
```

Each DHCP client registers its hostname with the DHCP server, but it must learn the local domain name. (It's also possible for the DHCP server to set the client's hostname.) Set this with the domain-name option ❶. You can give your DHCP clients any domain name you like; they do not need to share the domain name of the server. You can include multiple domains if you separate them with spaces, but not all operating systems will recognize additional domain names.

Every TCP/IP client needs a DNS server or two. Specify them with the option domain-name-servers ❷. Separate multiple DNS servers with commas.

The normal duration of a lease is given (in seconds) by the default-lease-time option ❸. After the lease time runs out, the client requests a new DHCP lease from the DHCP server. If the client cannot reach the DHCP server, it continues to use the old lease for a number of minutes equal to the maximum life of the lease, specified with max-lease-time ❹.

If this is the only DHCP server for your network, be sure to inform dhcpd(8) that it is the last word on client configuration with the authoritative keyword ❺.

DHCP integrates with dynamic DNS, which is a topic we don't cover in this book. The most common user of dynamic DNS is Microsoft Active Directory. If you're using AD, chances are that you're using the Microsoft DHCP Server and not ISC dhcpd. Without AD, you really don't need dynamic DNS. Tell the server to not bother updating the global DNS with ddns-update-style none ❻.

Finally, you can tell dhcpd(8) where to send its log messages ❼. See Chapter 19 for more information on logging.

Each subnet on your network needs a subnet statement to identify configuration information for DHCP clients on that subnet. For example, here's a network statement for a single small office network:

```
❶ subnet 192.168.1.0 netmask 255.255.255.0 {
❷   range 192.168.1.50 192.168.1.100;
❸   option routers 192.168.1.1;
❹   option netbios-name-servers 192.168.1.3, 192.168.1.5;
  }
```

Each subnet declaration starts by identifying the network number and netmask ❶ of the subnet. Here, we have a subnet using the IP network number 192.168.1.0 with the netmask 255.255.255.0, or the IP addresses 192.168.1.1 through 192.168.1.255. The information that follows in brackets all pertains to hosts on that particular subnet.

The range keyword ❷ identifies the IP addresses that dhcpd(8) may issue to clients. In this example, we have 51 IP addresses available for clients. If 52 DHCP clients connect at once, the last host won't get an address.

Define a default route with the routers option ❸. Note that you cannot define additional routes with dhcpd(8); instead, your local network router needs to have the proper routes to reach the destination. If you have multiple gateways on your local network, your gateway transmits an ICMP redirect to the DHCP client to give it an updated route. (If you have no idea what this means, that's all right. When you need it, you'll abruptly comprehend what I'm talking about, and if you never need it, you've just wasted the two seconds it took to read this aside.)

You can take pity on your Microsoft clients and identify the WINS servers ❹. It is very common for each network segment to have a WINS server. If you have only one network, or only one set of WINS servers, you can put the netbios-name-servers option outside of the subnet declaration.

If you have multiple subnets, create multiple subnet statements.

That's it! Edit your *dhcpd.conf*, start dhcpd(8), and watch your logs to see clients getting addresses.

Printing and Print Servers

Printing on Unix-like operating systems is a topic that makes new sysadmins cry and seasoned sysadmins ramble on about the good old days when printers were TTY devices and about the younger generation not knowing how good they have it.[2] The most common printing situations are printers directly attached to a computer via a parallel or USB port, and printers attached to a network print server.

If you have a printer attached directly to your FreeBSD machine, I suggest that you install CUPS (*/usr/ports/print/cups*), the Common Unix Printing System. This suite of software manages many popular consumer-grade and commercial printers, from lowly inkjets to big laser printers. I'm not going into any detail about CUPS, as it varies by printer model. Learn more about CUPS at *http://www.cups.org*.

You can also use CUPS to access remote printers, but in many cases that's overkill. I recommend CUPS for remote printers when you have multiple remote printers and you might want to switch between them. On the other hand, I want all of my servers to use the printer that's near my desk. A simple lpd(8) configuration makes this work easily.

Accessing a remote printer that's managed by another host is very simple, however. You must run a local printer daemon and tell that printer daemon

---

[2] We're right; you don't know how good you have it.

where to find its printer. The remote print server must speak the lpd protocol on TCP port 515. Test for its presence by telnetting to that port; if you get a response, the server speaks lpd. Most Unix-like printer servers speak that protocol, and if you're in a Microsoft environment, you need to ask your Windows administrator to install Print Services for Unix.

To enable lpd(8) on your system, add:

```
lpd_enable="YES"
```

to */etc/rc.conf* so lpd starts at boot. Start and stop lpd(8) by hand with /etc/rc.d/lpd start and stop.

/etc/printcap

The */etc/printcap* file controls printer setup with lpd(8). Printers have dozens and dozens of options, from the cost per page to manually setting a string to feed a new sheet of paper.

Every printer your system knows about needs an entry in */etc/printcap*, the printer capability database. This file is, by modern standards, in a rather obtuse format and will look very unfamiliar to anyone who hasn't previously worked with termcap(5). Fortunately, to access a print server you don't need to understand printcap(5), you just need to follow the template below.

To connect to a printer on a print server, you must have the print server's hostname or IP address and its name for the printer you want to access. Make an entry in */etc/printcap* following the template below. Pay special attention to the colons and backslashes, they are absolutely vital.

```
❶ lp|printername:\
❷        :sh=:\
❸        :rm=printservername:\
❹        :sd=/var/spool/output/lpd/printername:\
❺        :lf=/var/log/lpd-errs:\
❻        :rp=printername:
```

Our first line ❶ shows the printer's names. Each printer can have any number of names, separated by the pipe symbol (|). The default printer on any Unix-like system is called lp, so list that as one of the names for your preferred printer. One other name should be the name used by the print server for your printer (i.e., "3rdFloorPrinter"). Be warned, Microsoft print servers frequently share one printer under several different names, and use different names to handle printing differently. If you find this to be the case on your network, be sure to choose the PostScript name.

By default, the system will precede each print job with a page giving the job name, number, host, and other information. Unless you're in an environment with a single massive shared printer, this is probably a waste of paper. The :sh:\ entry ❷ suppresses this page.

The rm (remote machine) variable ❸ provides the hostname of the print server. You must be able to ping this server by the name you give here.

Each printer requires a unique spool directory ❹, where the local print daemon can store documents in transit to the print server. This directory must be owned by user root and group daemon.

Unlike spool directories which must be different, printers can share a common log file ❺.

Finally, specify the remote printer name ❻. Be sure you end */etc/printcap* with a newline; don't just terminate the file immediately after the printer name. Also, note that unlike every other entry in this template, the last line does not require a trailing backslash.

After editing */etc/printcap*, you must restart lpd(8), but once that's done you can view your print queue with lpq(1) and watch for any problems in */var/log/lpd-errs*.

TFTP

Let's end our discussion of small network services with perhaps the smallest network service still used, the Trivial File Transfer Protocol, or TFTP. *TFTP* lets you transfer files from machine to machine without any authentication whatsoever. It's also much less flexible than file copy protocols such as SCP or FTP. TFTP is still used by makers of embedded devices (such as Cisco) to load system configurations and operating system updates. We only cover it here because diskless clients use TFTP to download their operating system kernel and get their initial configuration information. tftpd(8) runs out of inetd(8) on TCP port 69.

> **TFTP SECURITY**
>
> TFTP is not suitable for use on the public Internet. Anyone can read or write files on a TFTP server! Only use TFTP behind a firewall or at least protect it tightly with TCP wrappers (see Chapter 9).

Setting up a tftpd(8) server involves four steps: choosing a root directory for your server, creating files for the server, choosing an owner for your files, and running the server process.

Root Directory

tftpd(8) defaults to using the directory */tftpboot*. This might be suitable if you have only a couple files that you rarely access, but the root partition is best reserved for files that don't change often. You don't want a TFTP upload to crash your system by filling the root partition! I usually put my tftpd(8) root directory in */var/tftpboot* and add a symlink to */tftpboot*:

```
# mkdir /var/tftpboot
# ln -s /var/tftpboot /tftpboot
```

Now you can create files for access via TFTP.

tftpd and Files

Users can both read and write files via TFTP. If you want tftpd(8) users to be able to read a file, the file must be world-readable:

```
# chmod +r /var/tftproot/filename
```

Similarly, tftpd(8) will not allow anyone to upload a file unless a file of that name already exists and is world-writable. Remember, programs and regular files have different permissions. A program must have execute permissions in addition to read and write permissions, so you must set permissions differently for programs and files. You can use touch(1) to pre-create files that you'll want to upload via TFTP.

```
# chmod 666 /var/tftproot/filename
# chmod 777 /var/tftproot/programname
```

Yes, this means that anyone who knows a file's name can overwrite the contents of that file. Make vital files read-only.[3] This also means you don't have to worry about someone uploading a big file and filling your hard drive.

File Ownership

Files in a TFTP server should be owned by a user with the least possible privilege. If you only run a TFTP server intermittently, you can use the nobody user. For example, if you only need the TFTP server to perform the occasional embedded device upgrade, let the nobody user own your files and just turn tftpd(8) off when it's not needed. If you run a permanent TFTP server, however, it's best to have a dedicated tftp unprivileged user to own the files. The tftp user does not need to own the *tftproot* directory and, in fact, should have an entirely different home directory. He only needs ownership of the files available to users.

tftpd(8) Configuration

tftpd(8) is configured entirely through command-line arguments, and there aren't many of them. For a full list, read tftpd(8), but here are the most commonly used ones.

If you create a user just to run tftpd(8), specify that user with the -u argument. If you do not specify a user, tftpd runs as nobody.

I recommend logging all requests to your TFTP daemon. The -l argument turns on logging. tftpd(8) uses the LOG_FTP facility, which you must enable in *syslog.conf* (see Chapter 19).

tftpd supports chrooting (see Chapter 9) with the -s flag. This lets you confine tftpd(8) to your selected directory. You don't want users to tftp

---

[3] Unless, of course, you'd like to try installing someone else's server configuration file as the new IOS on your Cisco router. Be sure to tell the Cisco support tech to activate the phone recorder before you describe your problem; he'll want to share this one with his co-workers.

world-readable files such as */boot/kernel/kernel*, just on general principle! Always chroot your tftpd(8) installation.

You can chroot TFTP clients by IP address with the -c argument. In this case, you must create a directory for every client permitted to connect. For example, suppose the only host you want to give TFTP access to is your router, with the IP address of 192.168.1.1. You could create a directory */var/tftproot/192.168.1.1* and use -c. You must also use -s to define the base directory of */var/tftproot*. This is a good compromise when you must offer TFTP to only one or two hosts, but you don't want the world to have access to your TFTP server.

You can choose to allow a client to write new files to your TFTP server. This is a bad idea, because it lets remote users fill up your hard disks with arbitrary files. If you must have this functionality, use the -w flag.

For example, suppose you want to log all requests to tftpd, chroot to */var/tftpboot*, run the server as the user tftpd, and chroot clients by IP address. The command to run tftpd would look like this:

```
tftpd -l -u tftpd -c -s /var/tftpboot
```

Enter this into *inetd.conf* as described earlier, restart inetd(8), and you're in business!

Scheduling Tasks

The FreeBSD job scheduler, cron(8), allows the administrator to have the system run any command on a regular basis. If you need to back up your database nightly or reload the nameserver four times a day, cron is your friend. cron(8) configuration files are called *crontabs* and are managed with crontab(1). Every user has a separate crontab stored in */var/cron/tabs*, and the global crontab file is */etc/crontab*.

User Crontabs vs. /etc/crontab

The purpose of */etc/crontab* is different from that of individual users' crontabs. With */etc/crontab*, root may specify which user will run a particular command. For example, in */etc/crontab* the sysadmin can say, "Run this job at 10 PM Tuesdays as root, and run this other job at 7 AM as www." Other users can only run jobs as themselves. Of course, root can also edit a user's crontab.

Also, any system user can view */etc/crontab*. If you have a scheduled job that you don't want users to know about, place it in a user crontab. For example, if you have an unprivileged user for your database, use that unprivileged user's crontab to run database maintenance jobs.

/etc/crontab is considered a FreeBSD system file. Don't overwrite it when you upgrade! One way to simplify upgrading */etc/crontab* is to set your custom entries at the end of the file, marked off with a few lines of hash marks (#).

Finally, while you edit */etc/crontab* with a text editor, edit a user crontab with crontab -e.

cron and Environment

crontabs run in a shell, and programs might require environment variables to run correctly. You can also specify environment variables on the command line for each command you run from cron. cron does not inherit any environment variables from anywhere; any environment programs need must be specified. For example, here's the environment from */etc/crontab* on a FreeBSD 7 system:

```
SHELL=/bin/sh
PATH=/etc:/bin:/sbin:/usr/bin:/usr/sbin
HOME=/var/log
```

Yes, this is extremely minimal! Feel free to add environment variables as needed to user crontabs, but be conservative when changing */etc/crontab*. If you need a custom environment variable, it's safest to use a user crontab rather than */etc/crontab*, because many of the commands in */etc/crontab* are for core system maintenance.

Crontab Format

Beneath the environment statements, a user crontab is divided into six columns. The first five columns represent the time the command should run, as minute, hour, day of the month, month of the year, and day of the week, in that order. An asterisk (*) in any column means *every one*, while a number means *at this exact time*. Minutes, hours, and days of the week begin with 0, and days of the month and months begin with 1. Also, thanks to an ancient disagreement between AT&T and BSD, Sunday can be represented by either 7 or 0. After the time, list the command to be run at that time.

/etc/crontab has one extra column: the user under which to run the command. It goes between the time specification and the command itself. Check out the many examples in */etc/crontab* if you like.

Sample Crontabs

Assume that we're editing the crontab of an unprivileged user to schedule maintenance of a program. As */etc/crontab* has column headings at the top, we'll demonstrate user crontabs here. (To use these examples in */etc/crontab*, just add the user before the command.) Here, we want to run the program */usr/local/bin/maintenance.sh* at 55 minutes after each hour, every single hour:

```
55    *    *    *    *    /usr/local/bin/maintenance.sh
```

Asterisks tell cron to run this job every hour, on every day of the month, every month, and on every weekday. The 55 tells cron to only run this job at minute 55.

To run the same job at 1:55 PM every day, use the following:

```
55    13    *    *    *    /usr/local/bin/maintenance.sh
```

Here, 13 represents 1:00 PM on the 24-hour clock, and 55 is the number of minutes past that hour.

One common mistake people make when using cron is specifying a large unit of time but missing the small one. For example, suppose you want to run the job every day at 8 AM:

```
*    8    *    *    *    /usr/local/bin/maintenance.sh
```

This is wrong. Yes, the job will run at 8:00 AM. It will also run at 8:01, 8:02, 8:03, and so on, until 9 AM. If your job takes more than one minute to run, you'll quickly bring your system to its knees. The correct way to specify 8:00 AM, and only 8:00 AM, is this:

```
0    8    *    *    *    /usr/local/bin/maintenance.sh
```

To specify ranges of time, such as running the program once an hour, every hour, between 8 AM and 6 PM, Monday through Friday, use something like this:

```
55   8-18   *    *    1-5    /usr/local/bin/maintenance.sh
```

To specify multiple exact times, separate them with commas:

```
55   8,10,12,14,16    *    *    *    /usr/local/bin/maintenance.sh
```

More interestingly, you can specify fractions of time, or *steps*. For example, to run a program every five minutes, use:

```
*/5   *    *    *    *    /usr/local/bin/maintenance.sh
```

You can combine ranges with steps. To run the program every five minutes, but one minute after the previous example, use this:

```
1-56/5   *    *    *    *    /usr/local/bin/maintenance.sh
```

Control the day a job runs with two fields: the day of the month and the day of the week. If you specify both, the job will run whenever *either* condition is met. For example, tell cron to run a job on the 1st and the 15th of every month, plus every Monday, as follows:

```
55   13   *    1,15   1    /usr/local/bin/maintenance.sh
```

If your job has a nonstandard environment, set the environment on the command line just as you would in the shell. For example, if your program requires a LD_LIBRARY_PATH environment variable, you can set it thus:

```
55    *    *    *    *    LD_LIBRARY_PATH=/usr/local/mylibs ;
/usr/local/bin/maintenance.sh
```

cron also supports special scheduling, such as "annually" or "daily," with the @ symbol. Most of these terms are best not used, as they can be ambiguous. While the machine knows exactly what they mean, humans tend to misunderstand! One useful crontab entry is for "whenever the system boots," which is @reboot. This lets an unprivileged user run jobs when the system boots. Use the @reboot label instead of the time fields:

```
@reboot    /usr/local/bin/maintenance.sh
```

cron(8) lets you schedule your work any way you like, eliminating the human being from many routine maintenance tasks.

Now that you have a decent understanding of the common small services provided by FreeBSD, let's go on to heavier services such as email.

16

SPAM, WORMS, AND VIRUSES (PLUS EMAIL, IF YOU INSIST)

The Internet's killer application is email, no matter what you hear from the marketing office down the hall. Email is so ubiquitous that it has become the preferred delivery mechanism for unsolicited advertising, viruses, worms, and other malicious communication, simply because everybody on the Internet has it. This chapter discusses how to handle email flow in the server-to-server case, the client-to-server case, and the server-to-client case. On today's Internet, each of these situations uses a slightly different protocol.

FreeBSD excels as a mail server and handles millions of emails every day. The FreeBSD Project itself runs some of the busiest email servers in the world for its mailing lists. FreeBSD on decent hardware can receive and transmit over 40,000 pieces of email an hour. That's an average of 11 messages a second, complete with any rambling text, inflated graphics, and overblown HTML the messages might include. To get this kind of performance, however, you must understand how email works.

Email Overview

Most legitimate email originates with a user at a desktop computer. This is most often a Windows or Mac workstation with Outlook, Eudora, Thunderbird, or one of their cousins—although you can send email with almost any operating system.

The client sends the email to an email server. Almost every company or ISP has at least one dedicated email system. The server performs some basic sanity checking on the email to ensure that it complies with Internet standards, and then searches for a server that claims responsibility for the destination. When your email server finds a destination server, it transmits the email to that server. When the recipient checks his email, his mail client software goes to the mail server and downloads the new messages to his desktop. If the recipient replies, the whole process is reversed.

Finding Mail Servers for a Domain

Mail servers exchange email with each other, but how do they find each other? For example, my personal email comes from the domain name *blackhelicopters.org*. If I write an email to a user at *freebsd.org*, how does my mail server find the mail servers for *freebsd.org*?

Each domain publishes mail exchanger (MX) records through DNS. We briefly touched on MX records in Chapter 14. (In the absence of MX records, email falls back on A records, which are much less flexible.) The DNS record for a domain that receives email includes one or more MX records, each with a number indicating preference. Here we find the mail exchangers for *freebsd.org* with an MX query:

```
# dig freebsd.org mx
...
;; QUESTION SECTION:
;freebsd.org.                IN      MX

;; ANSWER SECTION:
freebsd.org.        381     IN      MX      10 mx1.freebsd.org.
```

freebsd.org has only one MX server, with a preference of 10. Any incoming email for *freebsd.org* goes through *mx1.freebsd.org*. Compare this to a large business, such as *cnn.com*:

```
# dig cnn.com mx
...
;; QUESTION SECTION:
;cnn.com.                    IN      MX
```

```
;; ANSWER SECTION:
❺ cnn.com.                3600      IN      MX      30 lonmail1.turner.com.
❻ cnn.com.                3600      IN      MX      40 hkgmail1.turner.com.
❶ cnn.com.                3600      IN      MX      10 atlmail3.turner.com.
❷ cnn.com.                3600      IN      MX      10 atlmail5.turner.com.
❸ cnn.com.                3600      IN      MX      20 nycmail1.turner.com.
❹ cnn.com.                3600      IN      MX      20 nycmail2.turner.com.
```

CNN has six mail exchangers! Two servers have priority 10, the lowest number, so any machine sending email to *cnn.com* tries either *atlmail3.turner.com* ❶ or *atlmail5.turner.com* ❷ first. If the chosen server is down, the sending server tries the other one. If both priority 10 servers are down, the priority 20 servers, *nycmail1.turner.com* ❸ and *nycmail2.turner.com* ❹, are tried next, in random order. If all of the priority 10 and priority 20 servers are down, the sending server tries the priority 30 ❺ and then the priority 40 ❻ server. At least one of these should be up and accepting email.

Having a single MX record is becoming an increasingly popular antispam measure. If your domain has a valid DNS, the sender queues the email for several days. Frequently, a backup mail exchanger doesn't know what email recipients are valid at a domain, making it a prime candidate for spam acceptance. Many spamming tools use backup MXs as routes into the domain. While I've previously said that every domain should have multiple MX hosts, it's becoming increasingly difficult to have them without multiplying the time you spend fighting spam.

Undeliverable Email

When the mail server can find the mail exchangers for a domain but none of the exchangers are accepting email, the mail server places the message in a queue. Every fifteen minutes or so, the server attempts to deliver the message again. Internet standards allow five days to deliver an email message.[1] If the message cannot be delivered in five days, a bounce message is returned to the sender.

If the mail server cannot find any MX records for a domain, nor any record for a host with the same name as the domain, the message immediately bounces back to the sender. The user will then ask you why his perfectly valid email message bounced, which is when you get to point out that *yahoo.com* is not spelled with a *Q*.

The two errors are very different, and the mail sender will have a very different experience with them. This is one reason why it is best to have your secondary nameserver distant from your master nameserver, so that when your primary nameserver and mail exchanger go away, email will still reach you when service is restored.

---

[1] Be sure to tell the sales people in your office that email can legitimately take up to five days to be delivered. They turn this fascinating color.

The SMTP Protocol

Server-to-server email runs over the Simple Mail Transfer Protocol (SMTP), on TCP port 25. By default, email is not encrypted and has no integrity verification system. It's a very old protocol, from the days before security was such a great concern. It's actually pretty easy to send email by hand, without using a client. Mail transmission by hand is yet another useful trick for debugging difficult problems or impressing your friends. (Just don't try to impress girls with it; it doesn't work, trust me.)

You can determine if a host can receive email by using telnet to connect to the SMTP port:

```
# telnet hostname 25
```

If you get an answer, a mail server is running on the system. If the connection is rejected, that server does not accept email. Let's connect to a FreeBSD system and see if it accepts email:

```
# telnet bewilderbeast.blackhelicopters.org 25
Trying 198.22.63.8...
Connected to bewilderbeast.blackhelicopters.org.
Escape character is '^]'.
220 bewilderbeast.blackhelicopters.org ESMTP Sendmail 8.13.8/8.13.8; Thu, 7
Jun 2008 22:06:25 -0400 (EDT)
```

Not only does this answer prove that a mail server is running on the host, we can see the exact version of the server software (Sendmail 8.13.8) and the local date, time, and time zone. The only mysterious part of this response is the first term, the 220. Every response from an email server includes a response code and a human-readable response. The sending program only has to read the leading number; the rest of the response is there for the convenience of your feeble brain. Several sites on the Internet list and describe all the possible SMTP response codes.

Now let's start a conversation with the email server. Open negotiations with the helo command and the hostname you're connecting from:

```
helo pesty.blackhelicopters.org
```

The server answers with something like this:

```
250 bewilderbeast.blackhelicopters.org Hello d149-67-12-
190.col.wideopenwest.com [67.149.190.12], pleased to meet you
```

The response includes the response code (250) and the hostname you're talking to (bewilderbeast.blackhelicopters.org). The Hello means that the server is willing to talk to you and it identifies the machine you're connecting from. While my laptop is named *pesty.blackhelicopters.org*, the reverse DNS on my source IP indicates that I'm actually connected through a Wide Open West cable modem. *Pesty* is a legitimate hostname only behind my home NAT device.

Now tell the mail server who sent the message with the mail from: command and the author's email address:

```
mail from: <mwlucas@AbsoluteFreeBSD.com>
250 2.1.0 mwlucas@AbsoluteFreeBSD.com... Sender ok
```

If the server is still willing to speak with you, it returns a 250 code and tells you that you may proceed. If the server is not willing to speak with you, it rejects your connection now. Now name the recipient with the rcpt to: command.

```
rcpt to: <mwlucas@blackhelicopters.org>
250 2.1.5 mwlucas@blackhelicopters.org... Recipient ok
```

If you're really testing this, be sure to use another email address and not mine.

The mail server now knows both the sender and the recipient. This is the most common place where email transmission is rejected, as discussed in "Relay Control" on page 472. Now you're ready to send your email. Issue the data command:

```
data
354 Enter mail, end with "." on a line by itself
```

Type whatever message you like here. Just like the instructions after the code 354 say, when you've finished your message, enter a single dot on a line by itself. The following example sends an email with the words Test message to your recipient:

```
Test message
.
```

After you type the lone dot, the mail server should return a 250 to indicate acceptance of the message and give you a message ID for the email.

```
250 2.0.0 l5827nBE004533 Message accepted for delivery
```

Type quit to exit.

This technique can be used for both good and evil. As an administrator, you can test your email configuration without mucking with a client that might obscure test results. It's also trivial to forge email simply by creating your own mail from: statement. In some circles, forging email to a friend is a rite of passage. There are very few legitimate reasons for forging email, however.[2]

Relay Control

Generally speaking, a mail server accepts either email destined for its local domains or email being sent from local domains. If the mail server for *absolutefreebsd.com* receives an email for a legitimate user at *absolutefreebsd.com*, it should accept the message. If the server receives an email from a user with an *absolutefreebsd.com* address, and if other access controls are met, the server should accept the message and pass it on to the recipient. If, however, someone completely unrelated to *absolutefreebsd.com* attempts to use that mail server as a relay for email to a third party, the server should reject it.

People who send junk email (aka *spam*) search constantly for email servers that allow anyone to transmit email through them. If your server allows open relaying, you are a potential source of junk email. If you allow unrestricted relay through your servers, various antispam groups will blacklist you. You will lose email connectivity to 30 to 40 percent of the Internet until you fix your relay access.

So, what are these "other access controls" I mentioned? One of the most common is restricting the IP addresses that can relay email through your server. By only allowing hosts on your corporate network to send email through your servers, you instantly eliminate outsiders' ability to use your servers to transmit junk email.

If you provide email service to roaming users, however, the situation becomes more complicated. You must allow those roaming users to send and receive email without reconfiguring their laptops, and you must prevent unauthorized users from illicitly stealing your bandwidth to send junk email.

Stopping Bad Email

Just as you want good email to arrive quickly, you do not want junk email to reach your users. Junk email includes spam, viruses, worms, and anything else you throw away unopened. While it's possible for a legitimate user of your service to start sending junk email, best practice is to have terms of service that not only forbid this behavior, but also include high punitive damages to compensate you for the complaints you will receive and for the time you'll spend getting yourself off of blacklists. The two common methods used against junk email are *blacklists* and *greylisting*.

---

[2] I legitimately forge email to teach junior sysadmins that email is untrustworthy. Want to transform your junior Windows tech into a properly paranoid admin? Forge an email from the domain controller with the subject "Daily Status Haiku" and a body of "These things are certain: death, taxes, and data loss. Guess which has occurred." They will never forget a) that email can be forged, and b) your face.

Junk email blacklists contain lists of hosts that send junk email. As a public service, blacklist maintainers allow mail administrators to check each incoming message against the blacklist. When email arrives from a blacklisted IP address, the server rejects the email. When you use a blacklist, you are trusting the blacklist administrator to have sensible policies on adding and removing spammers, as well as to apply those policies uniformly no matter how infuriating someone behaves towards them. The former is easy, while the latter is not so simple.

Greylisting is perhaps the most effective antispam technique developed in the last few years that doesn't involve actual violence. Spam, worms, and viruses are not usually sent in strict accordance with the SMTP protocol; mail servers adhere to the standard more closely. Email is not a real-time communication medium; mail servers are supposed to try several times to deliver a message before returning it to the sender. The botnets that send junk email do not follow that protocol; instead, they try each recipient address only once and go on to the next recipient. By having your mail server accept messages from new servers only on the second delivery attempt, you weed out the real mail servers from the botnets.

FreeBSD's integrated mail server, sendmail(8), supports both junk email blacklists and greylisting quite well.

Sendmail

For many years now, Unix-like operating systems have included the traditional Sendmail Mail Transfer Agent (MTA), or mail server. This program is huge, obtuse, and downright intimidating to new administrators. Many experienced system administrators also find it huge, obtuse, and downright intimidating. Sendmail even breaks one of the cardinal rules of Unix-like systems: Instead of many small tools that each do a single job well, Sendmail is a huge program that performs many jobs. When Sendmail was written, the very idea of a program that could be configured by a file, without having to recompile the program, was revolutionary. The fact that the Sendmail configuration looked like the result of placing an excited gerbil on a keyboard really wasn't relevant. Take a look in */etc/mail/sendmail.cf* for a very basic sendmail(8) configuration file.

Today, editing *sendmail.cf* by hand is no longer necessary nor desirable. Sendmail configuration has become much simpler and more manageable, and FreeBSD has integrated sendmail(8) into the system in such a way as to make email setup as simple and painless as possible.

During the years that Sendmail management wasn't so easy, however, people who didn't like Sendmail's configuration developed competitors that were simpler, easier to use, and had better security. The most popular are Postfix (*/usr/ports/mail/postfix*) and Qmail (*http://cr.yp.to/qmail.html*). Both are good tools. The FreeBSD Project uses Postfix to handle its massive email lists, some of the biggest in the world. FreeBSD lets you seamlessly replace its integrated Sendmail installation with one of these other packages or with any other mailer you like.

mailwrapper(8)

For many years, Sendmail was the only mail server available for Unix-like systems. As such, a lot of add-on software expects to find */usr/sbin/sendmail* and expects it to behave just like Sendmail. What makes matters worse, Sendmail actually behaves differently when called by different names. The program mailq(1) is actually the same file as the program sendmail(8), but since it has a different name, it behaves differently. As so many other programs must emulate Sendmail exactly, down to this multiname behavior, it's not as easy as just erasing your Sendmail binary and replacing it with something else.

As a result, an administrator on an unfamiliar Unix-like system might have no idea what */usr/sbin/sendmail* really is! If someone previously installed several different mail servers just to experiment, you'll have to resort to detective work and a bit of luck just to identify your so-called Sendmail.

FreeBSD does an end-run around all this by using a separate mailwrapper(8) program. This mail wrapper directs email requests to the desired mail server program. You'll find a file */usr/bin/sendmail*, but that is actually mailwrapper(8) disguising itself as Sendmail. This mail wrapper redirects Sendmail requests to the preferred mail programs installed elsewhere.

The */etc/mail/mailer.conf* file contains a list of program names, along with the paths to the actual programs to be called. For example, here's the default *mailer.conf* redirecting everything to sendmail(8):

```
sendmail      /usr/libexec/sendmail/sendmail
send-mail     /usr/libexec/sendmail/sendmail
mailq         /usr/libexec/sendmail/sendmail
newaliases    /usr/libexec/sendmail/sendmail
hoststat      /usr/libexec/sendmail/sendmail
purgestat     /usr/libexec/sendmail/sendmail
```

Each of these six "programs" in the left column is actually a name that other programs might use for Sendmail. Alternative mailers such as Postfix and Qmail actually have separate programs with these names. If you use an alternative mailer, you must edit *mailer.conf* to give the proper path to the mailer programs. When you use the Ports Collection to install an alternative mailer, the port prints instructions on exactly how to update *mailer.conf* for your installation. Follow those instructions for your new MTA to work. If you install an alternative mailer without using the Ports Collection, you must edit *mailer.conf* on your own.

Submission vs. Reception

FreeBSD (as well as all Unix-like systems) uses Sendmail in multiple ways. Some FreeBSD machines accept email from the Internet and either relay it on to other machines or deliver it to local users. Other FreeBSD machines do not receive email, but only generate it. Sendmail handles each of these jobs slightly differently.

The Sendmail submit daemon handles the email sent (or submitted) from the local machine. In most cases, this email is simply forwarded to a mail exchanger. For example, all of the servers on my network forward their daily status email to the actual mail server so I receive them. A server trusts email originating locally far more than email arriving from the Internet, so the Sendmail process that handles these messages uses a much less restrictive configuration and performs far fewer checks. This Sendmail process only listens to the network on the localhost IP address 127.0.0.1, and therefore other hosts on the network cannot use it.

The Sendmail inbound daemon accepts email from other hosts on the network. This Sendmail process requires extensive care and feeding. This is the Sendmail process that an intruder will try to compromise, and is the potential conduit of junk email. We will spend the most energy on configuring the inbound daemon.

The two configurations are mutually exclusive. When you have a full-fledged Internet mail server on your system, you do not need to have a weaker instance of Sendmail handling local email much in the same way most people don't leave the house to sleep in the tool shed. FreeBSD automatically disables the submission Sendmail daemon and its queue handlers when inbound Sendmail is activated.

Enable the submit and inbound mail daemons separately in */etc/rc.conf*. For a full description of all Sendmail configuration options read rc.sendmail(8), but here are the basic four:

```
sendmail_enable="NO"
sendmail_submit_enable="YES"
sendmail_outbound_enable="YES"
sendmail_msp_queue_enable="YES"
```

The plain `sendmail_enable` turns on the inbound Sendmail daemon. If you only want to send email from the local host and not receive email, turn on `sendmail_submit_enable`. The `sendmail_outbound_enable` and `sendmail_msp_queue_enable` settings handle transmission and retransmission of email sent from the local host.

The vast majority of Sendmail configuration here applies to the inbound Sendmail daemon. The submit Sendmail process requires very little configuration. When we're talking about a piece of configuration useful for the submit Sendmail, we'll specifically mention that. Otherwise, everything is for the inbound Sendmail instance. It's not that these features won't work with the submit Sendmail; rather, they just don't make sense. For example, why have hostname or IP-based access controls or antispam protection on a daemon that can only be reached from the local host?

Sendmail Logging

sendmail(8) logs all transactions, errors, and restarts to */var/log/maillog*. Check it out to see your email activity, especially after making any configuration changes. When I'm working on the mail system, I prefer to open the log in a separate terminal window and display new entries as they appear, using tail -F:

```
# tail -F /var/log/maillog
```

Whenever Sendmail sends, receives, or rejects a piece of email, it logs a message. tail -F shows this log in real time. Hit CTRL-C to stop showing the log and get your command prompt back.

Configuring Sendmail

The directory */etc/mail* contains all the human-friendly Sendmail configuration files, plus a couple human-hostile ones. For most common tasks on a server that accepts incoming email, you only need to worry about four files: */etc/mail/access*, */etc/mail/aliases*, */etc/mail/mailertable*, and */etc/mail/relay-domains*.

The *access* file lets you set per-host and per-domain access controls for your mail server.

The *aliases* file contains a map of email redirections for the local host.

The *mailertable* allows you to override MX records for this mail server. The *mailertable* is notably useful when you're using your FreeBSD system to provide an additional layer of security for a proprietary system with a poor security record, such as Microsoft Exchange.

The *relay-domains* file lists domain names and addresses that your server will relay email for. Most of the systems here will be desktop clients that use your machine as a mail server, but the list might also include other domains that you provide backup MX services for.

Each of these files (except *relay-domains*) has a corresponding database file ending in *.db*. Like */etc/passwd.db* and */etc/spwd.db*, these database files are built from the text files to let a program access data quickly. When you change the text file, you must also update the corresponding database file, as we'll see when we discuss each file.

The access File

The */etc/mail/access* file lets you dictate who may send email through your system. This is most commonly used for rejecting email from undesirable correspondents. By default, Sendmail rejects all email not destined for the local system. This file lets you override other Sendmail rules, in particular junk email blacklists. The access database is best used for occasional exceptions to other Sendmail configuration settings, although there are a few tasks that can only be accomplished in the access database.

The file *etc/mail/access* has two columns. The left column is either a domain name, a hostname, an IP address, or a block of IP addresses where a piece of email originates. The right side is a statement of how email from those hosts is to be handled; it is one of RELAY, OK, REJECT, or DISCARD. You can also specify a custom ERROR message for certain hosts or domains. Skilled Sendmail administrators can also provide custom error codes, but those require that you know far more about SMTP than we cover in this book.

For example, here we specifically allow all email from the local host, 127.0.0.1. This is always a good rule, just in case someone in one of your junk email blacklists makes a mistake and lists the local host in the spammer database. A RELAY rule tells Sendmail to relay email for any matching host. This tells your Sendmail daemon that it should relay email originating locally to any destination. Listing the legitimate IP ranges of your network here also helps in case your company is ever listed in a blacklist that you're using. While you'd certainly stop using a blacklist that lists you, this avoids the headaches that occur between the time your site is blacklisted and the time you figure it out. Like *etc/login.access*, *etc/mail/access* does not understand modern subnets but instead matches the portion of the address range you list. Here, I want to include the address range 192.168.0.0/23 but must list two separate blocks of 192.168.0 and 192.168.1 instead:

```
127.0.0.1     RELAY
192.168.0     RELAY
192.168.1     RELAY
```

A more restrictive rule is OK, meaning that the Sendmail daemon should accept but not relay email from the matching hosts. Suppose you have a partner company that is continually being listed on a junk email blacklist because they share an ISP with a notorious junk mailer. You can specifically receive email from them with an OK rule:

```
theircompany.com    OK
```

Even more restrictive is the REJECT rule, which tells Sendmail to categorically refuse any email from the matching source. Suppose that someone with the IP address 192.168.8.83 is sending you huge amounts of email in an attempt to fill up your mail server's hard drive. You can specifically reject email from them with a REJECT rule:

```
192.168.8.83     REJECT
```

You can reject email with a custom ERROR message by specifying it in the right hand side of the rule. Normal Sendmail rejections use the message code 550. Your custom error message will be visible to end users, so exercise some tact in creating it. Quote your custom message so that Sendmail won't eliminate the spaces or scramble it some other way.

```
suckycompany.com     ERROR: 550 "Your momma dresses you funny"
```

Finally, some hosts treat you so bad that you don't want to see email from them, ever. You don't even want to reject messages from them, you just want to throw them away unread. Use a DISCARD rule for this:

```
absolutefreebsd.com    DISCARD
```

The aliases File

The */etc/mail/aliases* file contains redirections for email sent to specific accounts or usernames. Each line starts with an alias name, followed by a colon and a list of real users on the system to forward the email to. Email aliases work on systems using either the inbound or the submit Sendmail configuration.

Forwarding Email from One User to Another

Many people prefer to have email sent to root to be redirected to a real user's account. The following example forwards all email sent to root to another user:

```
root:    mwlucas@AbsoluteFreeBSD.com
```

Many email addresses actually don't have accounts associated with them. For example, the required postmaster address doesn't usually have an actual account. You can use an alias to forward this to a real account.

```
postmaster:    root
```

So, postmaster forwards to root, and root forwards to me. I get all the email for both *root@* and *postmaster@* on this machine.

The *aliases* file already contains a variety of standard addresses for Internet services, as well as aliases for all of the default FreeBSD service accounts. They all go to root by default. By defining a real email address as a destination for your root email, you will automatically get all system administration email.

Aliased Mailing Lists

You can also list multiple users to create small local mailing lists. This doesn't scale for dynamic lists where users subscribe and unsubscribe frequently, but it's sufficient for quick and simple lists:

```
sales:   mwlucas, bpollock, sales@nostarch.com
```

Forwarding Email to Files

Among the *aliases* file's more interesting features is the ability to redirect email to something other than an email account. If you list a filename,

Sendmail appends the message to that file. You can maintain a permanent log of the user mwlucas's email with something like this:

```
mwlucas:    /var/log/mwlucas-mail, mwlucas
```

Forwarding Email to Programs

You can also send email to a program for automated handling. Just put a pipe symbol (|) followed by the full path to the program. For example, if you have a script that processes incoming email to a certain address, you can use this line to redirect the email:

```
orders:    |/usr/local/bin/process-orders.pl
```

Inclusions

Finally, you can include other files in the *aliases* file. This allows a highly trusted user to modify an alias on her own. The file must be a list of email addresses, one per line.

```
clientlist:    include:/usr/home/salesdude/clientlist.txt
```

The mailertable File

The *mailertable* file allows you to selectively override MX records. While this was important when networks used to have connections to non-Internet email systems such as UUCP, today this allows you to turn FreeBSD into a firewall or bastion host of some sort. In more than one instance, I've had a Microsoft Exchange system that I couldn't expose directly to the Internet. By using a FreeBSD machine as my public MX host and a *mailertable* on the FreeBSD machine, I could protect the Exchange system without investing in an expensive email firewall.

While I don't have an Exchange system at *absolutefreebsd.com*, let's pretend for a moment that I do. My hosts are named *freebsd.absolutefreebsd.com* and *exchange.absolutefreebsd.com*. My DNS record would read:

```
absolutefreebsd.com    IN    MX    10    freebsd.absolutefreebsd.com
```

The public would then send all email to the FreeBSD machine.
On the FreeBSD machine, I would use a *mailertable* entry like this:

```
.absolutefreebsd.com    smtp:[exchange.absolutefreebsd.com]
```

This would make the FreeBSD machine ignore the MX record for the domain on the left side of the column and instead forward the email for that domain to the host *exchange.absolutefreebsd.com*.

The relay-domains File

Sendmail simplifies providing backup MX services for other domains. As with secondary DNS, one of the best ways to handle backup MX services is to find an entity of similar size to swap that service with. You certainly don't want to invest a lot of time in a backup MX service, especially for an organization other than your own, and using a similar-sized organization with a similar level of technical skill helps assure that your partner won't cause you many more problems than you already have.

The file */etc/mail/relay-domains* lists all of the domains and/or IP addresses you relay email for. List each domain or address here, one per line. For example, here's an entry to provide backup MX services for *absolutefreebsd.com*:

```
absolutefreebsd.com
```

Hard, isn't it? Note that you must also list the server in the domain's DNS record for backup MX services to work.

Making Changes Take Effect

The *access, aliases,* and *mailertable* files all have corresponding database (*.db*) files. Much like the password file, these database files are provided for fast and easy reference to the contents by Sendmail and other programs. When you edit one of these files, you must update the corresponding database file. Modern Sendmail manages these databases with make(1). To update the *access* and *mailertable* files, go to the */etc/mail* directory and type make maps:

```
# cd /etc/mail
# make maps
```

make(1) compares the age of each text file with that of the database files and will rebuild the database if the text file is newer.

To rebuild the *aliases* database, either run newaliases(8) or make aliases:

```
# cd /etc/mail
# make aliases
```

Why does the *aliases* database have its own special rebuild command? The *aliases* database was the first database in Sendmail, so a special command was written for it. As these databases proliferated, however, a more generic method appeared.

Database changes take effect immediately upon rebuilding the database. Other changes are more intrusive, however, and require restarting the entire mail system. Changing the *mailertable* is one of those changes. While you can restart the email system in a variety of ways, I recommend using the FreeBSD startup system so that your mail server behaves consistently after reboots:

```
# /etc/rc.d/sendmail restart
```

This will make all changes take effect, including those in text files.

Purists might note that */etc/rc.d/sendmail* is actually a front end for the shell script */etc/rc.sendmail*. The */etc/rc.sendmail* file predates the rc.d startup system and remains in place for historical compatibility.

Virtual Domains

By default, Sendmail rejects all email not destined for the local host. This works if your local host has the same name as your domain—that is, if the mail server for *absolutefreebsd.com* is a machine actually named *absolutefreebsd.com*. Frequently, that's not the case. For example, the mail server for *absolutefreebsd.com* is a machine named *bewilderbeast.blackhelicopters.org*. With email systems, a *virtual domain* allows a server to receive email for a different domain. One FreeBSD machine can handle hundreds or thousands of virtual domains.

Configuring a virtual domain has three steps. First, tell the mail server that it is responsible for a domain's email. Then, redirect email for users in that domain to the appropriate accounts. Finally, publish an MX record for that domain pointing to your mail server.

The /etc/mail/local-host-names File

The */etc/mail/local-host-names* file specifies the hosts and domains that this machine accepts email for. By adding a host or domain name to this file, you tell Sendmail that the local machine is the final destination for email bound for that host or domain. This file contains a list of domains and hosts, one per line, like this:

```
blackhelicopters.org
absolutefreebsd.com
absoluteopenbsd.com
pgpandgpg.com
ciscoroutersforthedesperate.com
...
```

Do not list domains from which you do not accept email! Sendmail believes it is the final word for any domain listed here, and if the email cannot be delivered locally, it returns an error message to the sender. You won't annoy anyone but your own users by listing remote domain names here.

User Mapping

Now that Sendmail will accept email for the domain, tell the system where to deliver email for that domain. By default, Sendmail looks for an account with the same name as in the email address. My machine receives email for both *blackhelicopters.org* and *absolutefreebsd.com*. By default, Sendmail delivers email for *mwlucas@absolutefreebsd.com* to the local user mwlucas, and email for *mwlucas@blackhelicopters.org* to the local user mwlucas as well. Perhaps these are two different people; in theory, the user *mwlucas@blackhelicopters.org* could be Mark W. Lucas, no relation to yours truly.[3] I don't want his email, and he couldn't stomach mine. You cannot forbid overlapping user email names in different domains. The solution is to provide Sendmail with a map of accounts in the virtual usertable, */etc/mail/virtusertable*. Here are some sample entries:

```
stenchmaster@blackhelicopters.org     chris
postmaster@blackhelicopters.org       mwlucas
mwlucas@blackhelicopters.org          mwlucas
silence@blackhelicopters.org          error:nouser spambait address
@blackhelicopters.org                 error:nouser no such user
```

The first entry maps a particular email address on the left-hand side to a particular user account on the right-hand side. Email to *stenchmaster @blackhelicopters.org* is delivered to the local account chris. The next two entries route particular email addresses in the domain to a user account on the local system. The fourth entry is slightly more interesting, as it returns an error to the sender. I want the system to return a "no such user" error to anyone sending email to the address *silence@blackhelicopters.org*. I use this address when I must fill out an online form for someone who I just *know* is going to spam me. I'll activate it for a few minutes to get the silly little registration email, activate the account, and then block the address again. Finally, the last entry is a generic rule for the domain as a whole. By specifying *@blackhelicopters.org* without a username, I'm telling Sendmail to apply this rule to all email addresses without a more specific rule. Messages to email addresses not on this list get an error of "no such user."

Once upon a time, many system administrators used such a catch-all email address for their own domains and created email addresses on the fly. "You want to talk to me? Here's your personal email address at my domain." Now that spammers perform dictionary attacks, however, having such a catch-all rule directing to a real person's account is a great way to catch huge amounts of spam.

DICTIONARY ATTACKS

A dictionary attack is where the intruder tries every possible username, one after the other. A spammer would perform a dictionary attack by trying every possible email address at a domain. By emailing in quick succession *aardvark@yourdomain.com*, *aardwolf@yourdomain.com*, *aaron@yourdomain.com*, and so on, right down the dictionary, the spammer hopes that some pieces of junk email will reach real human beings before he gets shut off. The word list in */usr/share/dict/words* includes 235,882 words; if your mail server accepts every one of those words as a valid email address at your domain and redirects it all to your personal account, you will have no choice but to erase all your email and hope that nobody sent you anything important during the attack.

---

[3] Of course, in real life they do go to the same person. But you get the idea.

Make similar entries for your other virtual domains. If you want *mwlucas@absolutefreebsd.com* and *mwlucas@blackhelicopters.org* to go to different accounts, just create separate maps in the *virtusertable*:

```
mwlucas@absolutefreebsd.com      michael
mwlucas@blackhelicopters.org     mwlucas
```

I suggest listing your virtual domains in alphabetical order, to reduce confusion when you have thousands of domains on one machine.

Like other large Sendmail configuration files, sendmail(8) accesses the *virtusertable* through a database file that you must keep up to date. Changes to the *virtusertable* do not take effect until you update the database by going into */etc/mail* and running make maps, just as you would update other Sendmail databases.

Now just publish an MX record for the domain pointing to your mail server, and your email virtual domain is ready for action.

Changing sendmail.cf

Remember that horrible configuration file, */etc/mail/sendmail.cf*? Yes, you do need to change it. Do not edit *sendmail.cf* directly, however. Sendmail actually includes tools to build this configuration file out of other configuration files. Yes, this is strange by today's standards, but when Sendmail was created it was cutting edge. (I am assured that this is what young, hip people call, "Kickin' It Old Skool.")

FreeBSD includes two *.cf* files, *sendmail.cf* and *submit.cf*. The *sendmail.cf* file configures Sendmail to transmit email to other systems and to the inbound Sendmail process, if running. Sendmail uses the *submit.cf* file only if in the submit configuration, and then only for processing the local unsent email queue. The *submit.cf* file is actually much simpler, if you have the inclination and stamina to read it. These files are built automatically by applying the rules in two separate files, *freebsd.mc* and *freebsd.submit.mc*.

The *.mc* files are configuration files for the m4 macro language processor. The m4(1) command reads the instructions from those files and the definitions stored in */usr/share/sendmail/cf* to actually build the *.cf* files. You define Sendmail's desired behavior in the *.mc* files, and use m4 to build appropriate Sendmail configuration files from them. For example, let's look at *freebsd.mc*.

While the file begins with hash marks as comments, once the actual configuration starts, the hash mark is no longer used; instead, the string dnl serves to comment out anything you want m4(1) to ignore. Some of the lines in that file might be fairly obvious:

```
...
FEATURE(access_db, ❶`hash -o -T<TMPF> /etc/mail/access❷')
...
FEATURE(mailertable, `hash -o /etc/mail/mailertable')
FEATURE(virtusertable, `hash -o /etc/mail/virtusertable')
...
```

Hey, we just talked about the *access* file, the *mailertable*, and the *virtusertable*! These statements tell m4(1) to include these features, using the databases (hashes) made from the specified filenames. This might not be so scary after all.

Take a careful look at those statements, however. We define a feature and then specify a configuration for that feature in quotes. The first quote mark is actually a backtick ❶, however, while the second is a straight, up-and-down single quote mark ❷. These quotes must appear exactly like this, with exactly these characters, or m4(1) will not properly parse the file.

You'll also see some configuration options commented out with the characters dnl:

```
dnl Dialup users should uncomment and define this appropriately
dnl define(`SMART_HOST', `your.isp.mail.server')
```

If you want to use a smart host, you would remove the leading dnl from the second line and fill in the hostname of your mail server. We'll learn about smart hosts later in this chapter.

By changing entries in the *.mc* file and rebuilding the configuration file, you control how Sendmail operates. We'll use this functionality to customize your system. I'll provide two simple examples here, and then we'll build on this in later sections.

Custom .mc Files

The Sendmail *Makefile* looks for default *.mc* files named after the full hostname of the system. For example, my laptop *pesty.blackhelicopters.org* has two *.mc* files: */etc/mail/pesty.blackhelicopters.org.mc* and */etc/mail/pesty.blackhelicopters.org.submit.mc*. If those files do not already exist, make(1) copies *sendmail.mc* and *submit.mc* to create them.

I have never encountered a situation where it made sense to edit the *submit.mc* file; while it's possible that such situations exist, I would suggest that if you're thinking of editing it, you're solving the wrong problem. Almost always, you need to edit the *<hostname>.mc* file.

Start by copying *freebsd.mc* to *<hostname>.mc*, and then make all your changes to that file. Let's start by configuring a smart host.

Smart Hosts

A *smart host* is a local mail server that knows how to send email outside the local network. I don't want my laptop to contact remote mail servers directly; I want it to hand the email to my dedicated mail server, which does all the hard work of looking up MX records, identifying servers, and transmitting and retransmitting until the remote server condescends to accept my email. My laptop needs to be free for more important work, like playing MP3s and writing this drivel.

You can configure a smart host in your *<hostname>.mc* file. Remember the sample of a smart host in the last section? Just edit that to provide the name of your smart host and rebuild *sendmail.cf*. The smart host for my network is the overworked *bewilderbeast.blackhelicopters.org*, so I edit */etc/mail/pesty.blackhelicopters.org.mc* as follows:

```
dnl Dialup users should uncomment and define this appropriately
define(`SMART_HOST', `bewilderbeast.blackhelicopters.org')
```

I've deleted the `dnl` from the beginning of the second line. This uncomments the `SMART_HOST` setting and lets m4(1) notice this line. I've carefully left the special quote marks intact, in their original places, surrounding the hostname of my local mail exchanger. Now I rebuild the *sendmail.cf* with `make all` and install it with `make install`:

```
# cd /etc/mail
# make all
/usr/bin/m4 -D_CF_DIR_=/usr/share/sendmail/cf/   /usr/share/sendmail/cf/m4/cf.m4
pesty.blackhelicopters.org.mc > pesty.blackhelicopters.org.cf
# make install
install -m 444 pesty.blackhelicopters.org.cf /etc/mail/sendmail.cf
install -m 444 pesty.blackhelicopters.org.submit.cf /etc/mail/submit.cf
```

You can watch make(1) using the *<hostname>.mc* file to build a *<hostname>.cf* file and then installing it as *sendmail.cf*. Once I restart sendmail(8), my changes take effect. My laptop will send all email to *bewilderbeast.blackhelicopters.org* for delivery to remote sites.

If you use a different file for your *<hostname>.mc* file, set the */etc/make.conf* variable `SENDMAIL_MC` to the full path of your preferred *.mc* file.

Rejecting Spam Sources

Perhaps the simplest way to reduce incoming junk email is to use a *blacklist*. A blacklist is a list of IP addresses known to send junk email. A variety of different people maintain blacklists, with differing criteria, granularity, and severity. Think about your requirements before choosing a blacklist. You can find a list of antispam blacklists using any search engine.

Before using a blacklist, consider the size of the organization maintaining it. "Fred's Anti-Spam Blacklist" might be maintained by a single person, whose energy for maintaining that list ebbs and surges. A small blacklisting organization might have very strong prejudices for or against different types of email activity, and you must carefully evaluate the organization's standards before implementing their blacklist. Also, investigate how the organization adds and removes entries in its blacklist. Do they take submissions from the public? If so, how do they verify those submissions? How do people get off the blacklist? Will the organization blacklist large chunks of IP space because of the behavior of one or two small networks within that block? If so, using that blacklist would prevent you from receiving email from those IP blocks. That might not be a problem for you personally, but you need to consider all these factors before choosing a blacklist for other people's email.

As of this writing, my preferred antispam blacklist is Spamhaus (*http://www.spamhaus.org*). Created in 1999, Spamhaus provides free service to low-traffic mail servers and inexpensive service to high-volume sites. Their ZEN blacklist includes IP addresses known to be controlled by junk emailers, addresses assigned to end users (dial-up, DSL, cable, and so on) who should never send email directly, and addresses in botnets. Any of these could be a source of spam, viruses, and worse, and by rejecting all email from these addresses you can cut your junk email load considerably. If you provide smart host services to clients using SASL for relay access (as discussed in the next section), ZEN might block those users from sending email. Use SBL instead of ZEN. We will use the Spamhaus ZEN service as our example blacklist in this section, but you can use any blacklists you prefer.

The default *sendmail.mc* includes a sample blacklist entry:

```
dnl Unc
```

The default blacklist at *http://www.mail-abuse.org* is a for-pay service for all users, even the low-volume ones, but it provides a template for blacklist configuration. Check your blacklist for the necessary host information and then add a rule similar to the following, all on a single line:

```
FEATURE(❶`dnsbl', ❷`zen.spamhaus.org', ❸`"550 Mail from "
❹$`'&{client_addr} " refused - see ❺http://www.spamhaus.org/zen/"')
```

We tell Sendmail to use the DNS-based blacklist feature ❶ and check for entries at the domain *zen.spamhaus.org* ❷. We also provide a custom rejection message ❸, including the IP address of the client ❹ and a pointer ❺ to more information.

Rebuild your *sendmail.cf*, restart Sendmail for the blacklist to take effect, and watch your email log for incoming messages. Messages blocked by the blacklist appear in */var/log/maillog* like this:

```
Jun 16 12:10:13 bewilderbeast sm-mta[40174]: ruleset=check_relay, arg1=82-
46-225-100.cable.ubr04.dund.blueyonder.co.uk, arg2=127.0.0.4, relay=82-46-
225-100.cable.ubr04.dund.blueyonder.co.uk [82.46.225.100], reject=550 5.7.1
Mail from 82.46.225.100 refused - see http://www.spamhaus.org/zen/
```

That's one piece of junk email you don't have to waste any more time on. While blacklists are far from perfect, they can cut your junk email load considerably. Another powerful tool is greylisting, as we'll see next.

Greylisting

Blacklists provide unilateral protection against known spam sources. Whitelists document known good email sources. The key word in both of these statements is "known." Stopping unknown threats is much harder than stopping the known ones. *Greylisting* provides a decent middle ground that lets you reject known bad email and accept known good email, while helping you sort everyone else into one of these categories.

Most junk email sources try to deliver as much email as possible to as many recipients as possible. To do this, they use a stripped-down version of the SMTP protocol. In particular, most botnets don't try multiple times to deliver email. Real mail servers will try for up to five days to deliver a legitimate message, while botnets try once and give up when they're told to try again later. Greylisting takes advantage of this difference between real email servers and spam botnets to accept the former and reject the latter.

The first time a greylisting mail server receives a connection from a previously unknown mail server, it returns an error code that means, "Temporary failure, please try again later." The greylisting server records the IP address, sender, and recipient of the attempted email. If the remote mail server attempts to deliver the same email again after a configurable timeout period, the local mail server accepts the message. The greylisting server adds the sender, recipient, and IP address to a list of good email transactions and accepts all email matching that description for a certain number of days without challenge. The average spam source tries once, or possibly twice within a brief time, and gives up.

It's very true that spammers adapt, and some botnets have taken to retransmitting email after a few hours. The good news is, that time gives blacklist maintainers a chance to identify the new spam source and add the source IP to their blacklist. Greylisting gives you a chance to take advantage of their work.

One of the big objections to greylisting is that it slows legitimate email. That's true, up to a point. The email administrator can add known good IP addresses and domains to a *whitelist*, a list of email sources that are never greylisted. That way, email from your big clients and important business partners will always pass through immediately.

You can find many different greylisting implementations for many different MTAs. In my opinion, the most powerful and useful is Bob Beck's spamd(8) from OpenBSD. This greylist system uses the PF packet filter and can do many things[4] to reduce junk email overhead, but is comparatively complicated to configure. If you are using PF on your mail server, you should investigate spamd(8). Here, we use milter-greylist (*/usr/port/mail/milter-greylist*), which is simpler but provides nearly as good (but much less amusing) results as spamd.

---

[4] My favorite PF/spamd trick is packet shaping on incoming spam, so that incoming spammers are suddenly reduced to having the equivalent of a 900-baud modem. One PF/spamd machine can keep botnet hosts busy for days while using almost none of your system resources. Best of all, while the spambot is trying to transmit email to you, it isn't sending thousands of other junk emails. This is one of the very few computer features that still makes me smile years after I've learned of it.

Configuring milter-greylist

After installing milter-greylist, look at the configuration file */usr/local/etc/mail/greylist.conf*. This is a standard Unix-style configuration file containing variable assignments, with hash marks indicating comments. Use the configuration file to specify timeouts, peer email exchangers, whitelist addresses and recipients, and many other features. We'll discuss only the features necessary for average systems here. Be sure to read greylist.conf(5) for the full details of greylisting. milter-greylist is quite mature, and it probably supports your odd situation.

Base Program Settings

At the top of *greylist.conf*, you'll find a set of basic program settings. You should not need to change these.

```
pidfile "/var/run/milter-greylist.pid"
socket "/var/milter-greylist/milter-greylist.sock"
dumpfile "/var/milter-greylist/greylist.db"
user "mailnull"
```

The pidfile records the process ID of the running milter-sendmail(8) daemon. The socket is a Unix socket where a running Sendmail daemon can communicate with the milter-greylist daemon. The dumpfile is the database of identified good email. When milter-greylist identifies a new good email source, it is added to this database. Finally, the user specifies the unprivileged user to run the milter-greylist daemon.

MX Peers

When a network has multiple mail exchangers, legitimate email can try one server after another in order to get through. This is the behavior of legitimate mail exchangers, so greylisting must support it. The peer option lets you define other mail exchangers running milter-greylist that should synchronize greylist databases with one another. For example, if my main mail server has three backup MX servers at 192.168.1.1, 172.16.18.3, and 10.19.84.3, I would list them all as peers:

```
peer 192.168.1.1
peer 172.16.18.3
peer 10.19.84.3
```

Once I make corresponding entries for the other mail exchangers, they automatically exchange greylist data amongst themselves.

Lists of Addresses

You can define lists of IP addresses separately, using the keyword list, a name, and the keyword addr. Enclose the addresses in the list within curly brackets and separate them by spaces. For example, you might create a list called my network that defines the IP addresses in your organization:

```
list "my network" addr {198.22.63.0/24 192.168.0.0/16}
```

Like many other files with potentially long lines, a backslash (\) indicates that the entry continues on the next line. Here's the start of a list of major mail servers that break with greylisting:

```
list "broken mta" addr {    \
        12.5.136.141/32      \ # Southwest Airlines (unique sender)
        12.5.136.142/32      \ # Southwest Airlines
        12.5.136.143/32      \ # Southwest Airlines
...
```

Each is commented after the backslash for easy identification, and the list can run as long as needed and still be legible.

Lists of Domains

Lists of domains are similar to lists of addresses. Each domain needs to be the actual domain name of the mail server making the incoming connection, not the domain name of the end user's email address. For example, I want to give my publisher's email special handling, so I create a list that includes his domains. Email from my publisher might come from a *nostarch.com* server or from one of the publisher's ISP's machines in the *laughingsquid.net* domain. Use the domain keyword to specify a list of domains:

```
list "good domains" domain { nostarch.com laughingsquid.net}
```

Lists of Users

You can create lists of your users that need special greylisting rules with the rcpt option:

```
list "spam lovers" rcpt { sales@absolutefreebsd.com cstrzelc@stenchmaster.com }
```

Access Controls

milter-greylist applies rules to incoming connections as defined by *access control lists (ACLs)*. Access lists allow you to apply greylisting as broadly or as finely as you like. milter-greylist checks incoming messages against the access control lists in order and applies the first matching rule to the email. Use the special acl default for your last rule to define the mail server's behavior for all email that doesn't match an earlier rule, much like default accept and default deny in packet filtering. For example, the following ACLs allow email from your local network, the known broken mail servers, and my publisher. Some of my users who do not want greylisting are specifically whitelisted, but all other email is greylisted:

```
acl whitelist list "my network"
acl whitelist list "good domains"
acl whitelist list "broken mta"
acl whitelist list "spam lovers"
acl greylist default
```

The first entry automatically allows all email from the IP addresses defined in the list my network. The second allows all email from the domains listed in the list good domains. The third permits all email from the IP addresses defined in the list broken mta. The fourth entry specifies users who do not experience greylisting—that is, they get all email immediately. The last one greylists all other email as a default, requiring all senders to prove that they're proper mail servers before accepting their offered email.

Greylist Timing

By default, milter-greylist has a thirty minute retry requirement. While some spambots try to retransmit junk email within a few minutes, very few of them will wait 30 minutes. Spambot behavior will change as computers become more powerful, and I would not be shocked to see later generations retransmit after longer and longer windows. You will need to adjust the duration of the temporary failure. Use the delay keyword in the greylist ACL to set this. You can use the abbreviations d, h, and m for days, hours, and minutes. Here I set the challenge duration to two hours, an absurdly long time as of 2007 but, sadly, probably quite sensible for a year or two from now:

```
acl greylist default delay 2h
```

Once a mail sender has passed the greylist challenge, milter-greylist caches the sender's authenticity for three days before challenging the sender again. Incoming email from this sender is not delayed during this time. You might want to change this timeout as well, depending on your environment. Use the autowhite keyword to set this. Here, we tell milter-greylist to allow successful senders to send email without further challenge for 30 days:

```
acl greylist default autowhite 30d
```

As a rule, the timing of greylist challenges depends highly upon your environment. You might find that a five-minute delay suffices to meet your antispam needs without unduly delaying email, while other people might need several hours of delay to cut their junk email acceptably.

Attaching milter-sendmail to Sendmail

milter-greylist runs outside of Sendmail. How can you tell Sendmail to talk to milter-greylist? The key is Sendmail's milter interface, allowing outside programs to attach to Sendmail and provide additional functionality.

When you install milter-greylist from ports, you'll see instructions on how to attach Sendmail to milter-greylist. As a rule, you add lines to the end of *<hostname>.mc* and rebuild *sendmail.cf*. For example, as of this writing the milter-greylist port told me to add the following to my mail server's *.mc* file:

```
dnl j,{if_addr},{cert_subject},i,{auth_authen} are already enabled by default
define(`confMILTER_MACROS_HELO', confMILTER_MACROS_HELO``, {verify}'')
define(`confMILTER_MACROS_ENVRCPT', confMILTER_MACROS_ENVRCPT``, {greylist}'')
INPUT_MAIL_FILTER(`greylist', `S=local:/var/milter-greylist/milter-
greylist.sock, F=T, T=R:30s')
```

The `define` entries assign values to macros within Sendmail, while the `INPUT_MAIL_FILTER` statement tells Sendmail to run incoming email through a filter available at the specified Unix domain socket.

I added these lines to *sendmail.mc* and ran `make all restart`. Sendmail abruptly started talking to my running milter-greylist process, and 15 minutes later my steady stream of junk email became a trickle of pure, clean, legitimate email.[5]

Sendmail Authentication with SASL

Your most problematic users are those who want to use your email facilities from anywhere in the world. The mail server will accept email from anywhere, so long as it's destined for a user at the machine. When your company president flies to the big customer meeting in Antarctica, however, he will expect the mail server to accept messages from his client despite all your fancy relay controls intended to exclude spammers. You can provide this with the *Simple Authentication and Security Layer (SASL)*. SASL requires users to authenticate to the mail server before the server will relay email for that client. This means that legitimate users can use the mail exchanger from anywhere in the world, while users who cannot authenticate can only use it from known good IP addresses.

Supporting SASL in Sendmail requires rebuilding Sendmail from source. To avoid mucking with the Sendmail install in the base system, FreeBSD includes a port of Sendmail in */usr/ports/mail/sendmail*. There, you can build Sendmail with custom options and use it instead of the base system Sendmail. Using a port means that you can rebuild Sendmail to your specifications more easily, without having to apply patches to the base system Sendmail (and having your next upgrade overwrite them). If you look at the port's *Makefile* you'll see that Sendmail supports many options, from database backends to LDAP integration. Go into the port directory and type:

```
# make SENDMAIL_WITH_SASL2=YES all install clean
```

This will build SASL version 2 and a SASL-aware Sendmail and install them under */usr/local*, like any other port.

---

[5] Receiving only non-spam email doesn't mean I actually answer any of that email, mind you. I seem to have reached that point in life where my main goal is to *stop* receiving information.

saslauthd(8)

The saslauthd(8) daemon processes authentication requests from other software. In this case, we want Sendmail to request users to authenticate against the FreeBSD password database. Authenticated users can relay email, unauthenticated users cannot. You must enable saslauthd(8) in */etc/rc.conf* to handle Sendmail's authentication requests:

```
saslauthd_enable="YES"
```

Either reboot your system or run `/usr/local/etc/rc.d/saslauthd start` to activate saslauthd(8).

mailer.conf and Your New Sendmail

At this point, you have a new Sendmail installed as an add-on package. Activate it in *mailer.conf* just as you would Postfix or Qmail. Since the port installs the Sendmail binary as */usr/local/sbin/sendmail*, your new *mailer.conf* will look like this:

```
sendmail        /usr/local/sbin/sendmail
send-mail       /usr/local/sbin/sendmail
mailq           /usr/local/sbin/sendmail
newaliases      /usr/local/sbin/sendmail
hoststat        /usr/local/sbin/sendmail
purgestat       /usr/local/sbin/sendmail
```

Building sendmail.cf

While your custom Sendmail binary supports SASL, you must still configure sendmail(8) to accept SASL authentication. We also want to use SSL for our authentication information, to avoid transmitting usernames and passwords in clear text. Add the following entries to */etc/mail/<hostname>.mc* :

```
TRUST_AUTH_MECH(`GSSAPI DIGEST-MD5 CRAM-MD5 LOGIN')dnl
define(`confAUTH_MECHANISMS', `GSSAPI DIGEST-MD5 CRAM-MD5 LOGIN')dnl
define(`CERT_DIR', ❶`/usr/local/etc/certs')dnl
define(`confCACERT_PATH', `CERT_DIR')dnl
define(`confCACERT', `CERT_DIR/hostname.pem')dnl
define(`confSERVER_CERT', `CERT_DIR/hostname.pem')dnl
define(`confSERVER_KEY', `CERT_DIR/hostname-key.pem')dnl
define(`confCLIENT_CERT', `CERT_DIR/hostname.pem')dnl
define(`confCLIENT_KEY', `CERT_DIR/hostname-key.pem')dnl
define(`confAUTH_OPTIONS', `A p y')dnl
DAEMON_OPTIONS(`Port=smtp, Name=MTA')dnl
DAEMON_OPTIONS(`Port=smtps, Name=TLSMTA, M=s')dnl
```

With this configuration you tell Sendmail that users must log in to authorize email relaying.

We also provide a SSL certificate location ❶, which you might wish to change to fit with the rest of your system. For example, if you use Dovecot as we suggest in the next section, you might find configuration simpler if you put your certificates in */etc/ssl/certs*. You can use one SSL certificate for multiple services on the same host, after all.

Once you have these entries, run `make all install` in */etc/mail* to build and install the new *sendmail.cf*.

Testing SASL

Restart Sendmail with `/etc/rc.d/sendmail restart`, and your Sendmail install should be ready to perform SASL-authenticated email relaying. The simplest way to verify this is by configuring an email client to use SASL and trying to send email to a host not on your network. I keep a Yahoo! email account just for this sort of testing; if I can deliver email to Yahoo! I can probably deliver it almost anywhere else.

Most consumer email clients show SASL as a checkbox saying something like, "My outgoing email server requires authentication." Have it use the same credentials as used for downloading email. Your client should now be able to send email without trouble, while clients who do not authenticate will be rejected.

Oh, wait; you don't have credentials to get mail, do you? Now that we're done with Sendmail's ability to send and receive email, let's get email from the server to the client.

IMAP and POP3

While you can log directly into your FreeBSD system and read your email, your customers and end users probably want to use pretty graphical email clients such as Thunderbird or Eudora. FreeBSD supports these clients through a variety of ports and packages. The two standard protocols for transferring email to clients are IMAP and POP3.

The *Internet Message Access Protocol*, or *IMAP*, allows desktop clients to synchronize their email with a centralized server. Multiple client machines can synchronize their mailboxes with an IMAP server, so if you have both a laptop and a desktop system, they can both get all of the email sent to your account. IMAP is popular in corporate environments, where you allow clients to retain email on the server. I do not recommend using IMAP in an ISP environment, however. ISP customers with IMAP begin to expect that you will keep all their email forever and are vastly disappointed, even hurt, when a hardware failure demonstrates the flaws in this thinking. Make your customers responsible for their own email storage. Still, IMAP is very nice for an office environment, and we'll cover IMAP over SSL later in this chapter.

The *Post Office Protocol* (*POP*, now in version 3) is a simpler protocol that lets users download email to a desktop. POP3 is popular with Internet service providers and many small businesses precisely because of its simplicity. Most

IMAP servers can provide POP3 services as well as IMAP, so a single daemon meets all of our needs. We'll cover POP3 over SSL, which provides protection of usernames and passwords as well as concealing message contents.

Simple IMAP servers, such as imap-wu, only let you synchronize your clients with the standard Unix mail spool in */var/mail*. Others, such as Cyrus IMAP, support tens of thousands of users. The Dovecot IMAP server hits a nice medium ground, being full-featured enough to support most environments but simple enough to not require dedicated staff. Additionally, Dovecot's author has put up one thousand euros of his own money as a reward for the first person to "demonstrate a remotely exploitable security hole in Dovecot." Many people have spent a good amount of time trying to claim that reward, and nobody's managed yet.

Installing Dovecot

You'll find Dovecot in */usr/ports/mail/dovecot*. Dovecot can interoperate with LDAP servers, different types of databases, and different authentication systems; it also supports many other configuration options. For our basic mail server, however, we only need a standard Dovecot install serving the users on our FreeBSD system. Go to the port directory and run `make all install clean`.

Dovecot installs a whole bunch of documentation in */usr/local/share/doc /dovecot* and example configuration files in */usr/local/etc*. Like Apache, Dovecot has plenty of configuration settings that are best left alone unless you specifically need the feature. We're going to focus on providing both POP3 and IMAP services over SSL. While you can also provide email services without SSL or other cryptographic protections, this is a very bad idea on today's Internet.

Configuring Dovecot

Copy the sample Dovecot configuration file */usr/local/etc/dovecot-example.conf* to */usr/local/etc/dovecot.conf*, then open it in a text editor. Believe it or not, there are very few changes you must make to have Dovecot working securely on FreeBSD.

By default, Dovecot offers unencrypted IMAP and POP3 services. That's a common standard on the Internet today, but all modern email clients support transferring authentication credentials and messages over a secure SSL connection. The protocols entry defines the protocols Dovecot offers. Change both the IMAP and POP3 entries to the SSL version by adding s to the end of their names:

```
protocols = imaps pop3s
```

Now define where Dovecot keeps its SSL certificates using the ssl_cert_file and ssl_key_file variables. Dovecot includes a script to create a proper self-signed certificate, or you can use a commercial certificate as discussed in Chapter 9.

```
ssl_cert_file = /etc/ssl/certs/dovecot.pem
ssl_key_file = /etc/ssl/private/dovecot.pem
```

If you change the default paths provided, you must edit the self-signed certificate generation script to reflect the correct paths. A FreeBSD purist would certainly tell you to edit the script and put the certificates in */usr/local /etc/ssl*, but then every time you upgrade Dovecot you'd need to modify the script again. The location of the SSL files isn't too important so long as you document how your system is configured.

Creating a Dovecot SSL Certificate

While you could create a self-signed certificate as described in Chapter 9, Dovecot includes a shell script to create this certificate for you and arrange it exactly as Dovecot wishes. The directory */usr/local/share/dovecot* contains the shell script and a configuration file. Open the configuration file, *dovecot-openssl .cnf*, in a text editor. The settings should look very familiar from Chapter 9, but since that was almost half a book ago, we'll look at them quickly.

The top of the file contains settings such as the certificate type and strength. Leave all of this alone. You can set the values further down to reflect your environment, however.

The C variable is your two-letter country code. I'm in the United States, so I would put C=US.

ST is your state or province, and L is your locality or city. I'm from Detroit, Michigan, so I would put:

```
ST=Michigan
L=Detroit
```

O is the organization. If you have a company, list it here. If not, list your own name.

OU is the organizational unit, or the section of your organization responsible for this system. I generally just put Email Team here.

The common name is the reverse DNS name of the server where clients connect to get their email, which is almost certainly the same as the hostname of your mail server. For example, the common name of my mail server is *bewilderbeast.blackhelicopters.org.*

emailAddress is the address of the person responsible for this server. This might be a group or role account, such as *helpdesk@mycompany.com.*

This is all the configuration necessary for Dovecot to generate its own self-signed certificate. Now just run the *mkcert.sh* script:

```
# /usr/local/share/dovecot/mkcert.sh
```

Poof! Your self-signed certificate is ready.

Running Dovecot

Enable Dovecot in */etc/rc.conf* with dovecot_enable="YES", then run /usr/local /etc/rc.d/dovecot start. */var/log/maillog* will show Dovecot starting and tell you that it's initializing SSL.

You now should have a running Dovecot server! Configure your client to communicate with the server and try it out. Be certain to tell the client that an SSL connection is required! Any errors will appear in */var/log/maillog*.

The hard part now is separating a server error from a client error. All email clients have their own problems, glitches, and features. Separating a client error from a server problem, especially when unfamiliar software is involved, can be quite annoying. A vital skill in email client troubleshooting is the ability to test email accounts without using the client at all.

Testing POP3S

We configured POP3 to use SSL, which means we cannot just telnet to the POP3 port (110) and speak directly to the server. In Chapter 9, however, we saw how to use openssl(1) to connect to remote ports with a telnet-like interface. We can use that to access the mail server's SSL POP3 interface. POP3S runs on port 995. Here, we talk to the POP3S interface on my email system:

```
# openssl s_client -connect bewilderbeast.blackhelicopters.org:995
CONNECTED(00000003)
...
+OK Dovecot ready.
```

Now that you're connected and Dovecot is ready for you, identify yourself with the user command.

```
user mwlucas
+OK
```

Now use the pass command to give your password. It will be displayed on the screen in clear text. Be certain nobody's looking over your shoulder while you do this!

```
pass n0tmyr3alpassw0rd!
+OK Logged in.
```

I'm connected! What kind of email do I have?

```
list
+OK 2 messages:
1 1391
2 4258
```

Message 1 is 1,391 bytes, while message 2 is 4,258 bytes. To view a message, use retr and the message number.

If you can run these commands, you can be certain that basic POP3S functions correctly. Getting a random email client to work with POP3S is beyond the scope of this book as well as, probably, of most users.

Testing IMAPS

You can test IMAPS much the same as you tested POP3S, and for similar reasons. Testing IMAPS by hand removes any client problems from troubleshooting. IMAPS is a much more complicated protocol than POP3, and some of the commands you'll have to run are uglier. (In fact, my tech editor says that I am a braver man than he is for even attempting to run IMAP by hand. Bah!) IMAPS runs on port 993, but the openssl(1) command is otherwise identical to that used for testing POP3S:

```
# openssl s_client -connect bewilderbeast.blackhelicopters.org:993
CONNECTED(00000003)
...
* OK Dovecot ready.
```

Note that IMAPS uses an asterisk (*) instead of the plus sign (+) used by POP3S. Every IMAP command begins with a number. For example, use 01 LOGIN followed by your username and password to identify and authenticate to the server:

```
01 LOGIN mwlucas n0tmyr3alpassw0rd!
01 OK Logged in.
```

We're connected to our IMAP server. Now use the 02 LIST command to see what directories IMAP knows about in our account:

```
02 LIST "" *
* LIST (\NoInferiors \UnMarked) "/" "Junk E-mail"
* LIST (\NoInferiors \UnMarked) "/" "mwlucas"
* LIST (\NoInferiors \UnMarked) "/" "INBOX"
02 OK List completed.
```

So far, so good. Let's see what's in the INBOX with 03 SELECT:

```
03 SELECT INBOX
* FLAGS (\Answered \Flagged \Deleted \Seen \Draft)
* OK [PERMANENTFLAGS (\Answered \Flagged \Deleted \Seen \Draft \*)] Flags
permitted.
❶ * 2 EXISTS
* 0 RECENT
* OK [UIDVALIDITY 1185130816] UIDs valid
* OK [UIDNEXT 3] Predicted next UID
```

My default mail folder has 2 messages ❶. We see that the next message is number 3, so the messages are numbers 1 and 2. Let's see if we can get the first message out by entering the following command:

```
06 UID fetch 1:1 (UID RFC822.SIZE FLAGS BODY.PEEK[])
```

You should see the first email message in the user's default email folder spilled out to the screen. (If you've already been running IMAP for a while, your email server will probably have a message higher than 1.) Finally, use 07 LOGOUT to disconnect from IMAP.

If you can do all of this, you have basic IMAP over SSL functionality. Check your client configuration.

While you can go much, much further with Sendmail and Dovecot, you can now provide basic email services to both corporate users and customers. Let's learn about providing web services on FreeBSD.

17

WEB AND FTP SERVICES

The Internet started back in the 1970s, but didn't become a household name until the advent of the Web in the 1990s. The Netscape Corporation took the Mosaic web browser and transformed it into a commercial product, sparking an information and communication revolution that's still rolling on. Although many dot-com companies crashed and burned, the age of global person-to-person communication began with the Netscape web browser. Technologies such as peer-to-peer file sharing have expanded the Internet even further, but what still comes to most people's minds when someone says "Internet" is the Web.

FreeBSD's web server performance is legendary. For many years some Microsoft subsidiaries used FreeBSD in preference to their own Windows platforms, and Microsoft even released a shared source ".NET for FreeBSD" toolkit. Yahoo! runs FreeBSD, as do a variety of other high-demand web server farms. Netcraft surveys of the most reliable web hosting services in the world consistently show that about a third of them run FreeBSD.

You can build your own highly reliable web and FTP services on FreeBSD.

How a Web Server Works

A basic web server is fairly straightforward: A web browser opens a TCP connection to the server and requests a page; the web server spits out the page and closes the connection. That's the easy part. Things become considerably more complicated when you use server modules, dynamic pages, and so on.

The Web uses HyperText Transfer Protocol (HTTP), which is a very simple protocol similar to POP3. Over the last few years, functions have been added to HTTP to make it more complicated, but basic HTTP operations are simple enough to be performed by hand. Try it yourself—telnet to port 80 on a server and type GET /:

```
# telnet www.blackhelicopters.org 80
Trying 198.22.63.8...
Connected to www.blackhelicopters.org.
Escape character is '^]'.
GET http://www.blackhelicopters.org/
<HTML>
<body bgcolor="black">

<center><font color="white">Nothing to see here.<br>This is not the
site you're looking for.</br>

</html>
Connection closed by foreign host.
```

If you've ever looked at any HTML, the output should look familiar. If not, try the View Source option in your web browser next time you view a web page. You'll see that this is the actual HTML that generates the pretty picture in your browser. If you can't get this much from your web server, it probably isn't working.

The Apache Web Server

If you look under */usr/ports/www*, you'll see several different web servers. You'll find dhttpd, thttpd, bozohttpd, XS-HTTPD, and more, each with its own special features. For example, tclhttpd is a web server implemented entirely in Tcl. If you need a special-purpose web server, chances are it's available. We'll concentrate on the most popular web server, Apache.

FreeBSD includes ports of several versions of Apache, but most of these are legacy versions. If you have an application that specifically requires Apache version 1.3 with particular modules, FreeBSD will support you. For most new installs, however, you want the latest version. As of this writing, that's Apache 2.2. While Apache supports many different features, such as LDAP and SQL backends, for the moment we're just going to concentrate on basic Apache configuration. Apache 2.2 installs fine either from the port (*/usr/ports/www/apache22*) or from the package.

Apache Configuration Files

You'll find Apache 2.2's configuration files in */usr/local/etc/apache22*. While Apache configuration has changed a lot over the years, the current configuration layout strikes a good compromise between complexity and modularity. The key files are *httpd.conf*, *mime.types*, and *magic*.

mime.types

The *mime.types* file contains a list of all standard file types and their identifying characteristics. When a web server is transmitting a file to a client, it must identify the type of file so the client can handle it appropriately. You don't want your web browser to interpret a video stream as HTML! The mappings in *mime.types* provide Apache with the necessary information to correctly specify these types. The Apache's *mime.types* file is largely comprehensive. Even if a program's documentation tells you to add some information to *mime.types*, confirm that that information isn't already there before making any changes. You should almost never edit this file.

magic

The *mime.types* file cannot deal with every file type in the world. Apache's built-in *mime_magic* module uses the information in the *magic* file to try to identify the otherwise unknown file types. Throughout my many years of system administration, whenever I thought that I needed to change anything in the *magic* file, I was wrong.

httpd.conf

The *httpd.conf* file is where the interesting things happen. The file is well commented and is several hundred lines long, so I won't exhaustively analyze it. If you really want to know everything about Apache, you can find several big books on the topic. We'll cover those particular settings that you must configure, as well as some popular options. Whatever you do, don't change anything you don't understand.

The subdirectories *Includes*, *extra*, and *envvars.d* all add particular functions to Apache, separating the core server functionality from frequently changed add-ons. For example, each of the functions in the *extra* directory can be enabled by uncommenting a single line in *httpd.conf*. We'll see how this works and how you can use this design to enforce your security policy.

Core Apache Configuration

While Apache supports many different features in its complicated configuration, getting a basic web server up and running is quite simple. First, set `apache_22_enable="YES"` in */etc/rc.conf*. After that, setting up your first website is just a matter of making a few minor changes to *httpd.conf*.

Server Root Path

The ServerRoot setting specifies the directory containing all the website files and server programs. When you reference another file in *httpd.conf*, Apache prepends the ServerRoot to it unless you begin the filename with a slash (/).

```
ServerRoot "/usr/local"
```

With the default ServerRoot, a configuration entry of *libexec/apache22* indicates the real directory of */usr/local/libexec/apache22*. An entry of */var/log/httpd .log* remains unchanged, however. I don't recommend changing this, simply because so much of the default Apache configuration relies on ServerRoot being */usr/local.*

Listen

The Listen option controls which TCP ports or IP addresses Apache binds to. The default is port 80 (the standard port for HTTP) on every IP address on the local machine:

```
Listen 80
```

You can also specify individual IP addresses by listing them on a line:

```
Listen 192.168.8.44
```

By combining these, you can listen on a single IP address on an unusual port:

```
Listen 192.168.8.44:8080
```

Use multiple Listen statements to make Apache available on any number of ports or IP addresses on your system.

User and Group

These options specify an unprivileged user under which Apache will run. FreeBSD ships with the user and group www specifically for web server use. While occasionally you'll hear someone suggest running Apache as root, don't do it no matter what; if an intruder breaks into an insecure application on your web server, he'll get root access as a side benefit!

```
User www
Group www
```

Administrator's Email Address

The web server needs to know the email address of the system administrator. Apache automatically inserts this information into various output and error pages.

```
ServerAdmin webmaster@blackhelicopters.org
```

Address harvesters can get this address pretty easily, so be sure to have basic antispam protections on this address.

Server Name

This is the name of your website. It must be a real hostname with a DNS entry, or Apache won't start. For testing purposes, however, you can use an entry in */etc/hosts* instead of an actual DNS entry. You can also list an IP address.

```
ServerName www.absolutefreebsd.com
```

Document Root Path

The document root directory is where you place the HTML files that make up the actual website. Apache's default site contains a simple message indicating the web server works, which is nice but won't draw many visitors. If you place your own HTML documents here, the Ports Collection will notice the change and complain when you try to upgrade. It's best to choose your own directory for your own documents. I prefer to place my websites in */var/www*, as I try to keep the contents of */usr* as static and unchanging as possible.

```
DocumentRoot "/var/www/mywebsitename"
```

Apache Logs

Apache has fairly sophisticated logging facilities and allows you to choose your desired level of detail in your logs. You can also design your own log formats, but I highly recommend using one of the default log formats. Many third-party tools can process and analyze Apache logs, but if you redesign your logs, these tools will fail.

Basic Logs

The easiest log is the error log. If you have multiple websites running on a single server, I recommend renaming the default error log to include the site name:

```
ErrorLog /var/log/httpd-mysite-error.log
```

The log that interests most web administrators is the list of requests for files. To log site access, define a log format and then declare where to place the logs in that format. Apache 2.2 includes three log formats:

- The *common* log format includes the IP address of the client, the time of the request, and the file requested.

- The *combined* log format includes everything from the common log format, as well as the site that referred the client to this site and the user agent used by the client.
- The *combinedio* log format includes everything from the combined log format, as well as the actual number of bytes transferred over the network. This data size information includes the headers and other metainformation transferred with the actual documents.

Once you choose or define a log format, implement it with a `CustomLog` statement:

```
CustomLog /var/log/httpd-mysite-access.log combinedio
```

You can have several `CustomLog` statements for each site and use each log for a different purpose. For example, you may be using an Apache module that provides special functionality that you want to log, but you don't want to break the web log analysis software used by your clients. Use multiple `CustomLog` statements to write multiple logs for the same site.

Rotating Logs

A good rule of thumb is that each 10,000 requests generate about 1MB of log files. This might not seem like much on a small site, but even a small website can get that many requests over months. My (extraordinarily lame) personal website gets approximately 60,000 hits a year.[1] A busy site can generate this many hits in minutes. If you don't rotate your logs, finding information in them becomes nearly impossible.

Apache doesn't handle logging as gracefully as most other server programs, mainly because Apache is designed to handle thousands and thousands of simultaneous users. If you simply use newsyslog(8) to rotate your logs as you do for other programs, Apache will corrupt its own logs. Apache supports logging to programs, however. I recommend handling your logs via rotatelogs(8), included with Apache. Use a piped call to rotatelogs(8) instead of a filename in your log statements. Here's an example:

```
ErrorLog "|/usr/local/sbin/rotatelogs /var/log/httpd-mysite-error-log 86400"
```

Instead of a filename, we have a call to rotatelogs(8) and then a base filename. The trailing number is the number of seconds between log file rotations, 86,400 seconds being equal to one day.

Similarly, use rotatelogs(8) for the access log by specifying the log type at the end of the entry. You can also make use of the `ServerRoot` path to avoid typing the entire path to rotatelogs(8).

```
CustomLog "|sbin/rotatelogs /var/log/httpd-mysite-access-log 86400" combined
```

---

[1] This is not a plea for more web traffic to my home page. Really. Should you feel the urge to visit my website, I suggest you get some fresh air and exercise instead.

The following examples use `ErrorLog` only because those entries are slightly shorter and therefore easier for your lazy author to type. They all apply equally well to access logs.

You can rotate logs based on their size, which will be completely irrelevant to time but might make your life easier. Here, we split the error log every 5 megabytes:

```
ErrorLog "|sbin/rotatelogs /var/log/httpd-mysite-error-log 5M"
```

By default, rotatelogs names each log file by the time the log starts, in seconds since the epoch. While you can translate epochal time to human-friendly time easily enough with date(1), you can also make rotatelogs use a human-friendly date for the filename. Here, the error log's filename includes the time the file was created:

```
ErrorLog "|sbin/rotatelogs /var/log/httpd-mysite-error-log.%Y-%m-%d-%H_%M_%S 86400"
```

If you have a special logging situation that rotatelogs(8) cannot solve, investigate cronolog (*/usr/ports/sysutils/cronolog*) or httplog (*/usr/ports/sysutils/httplog*) instead. I've never been in such a situation, however.

Apache Modules

Apache is a modular program, much like the FreeBSD kernel. Apache can handle such diverse things as Microsoft Front Page extensions, scripting languages (including PHP), and embedded Perl. Apache 2.2's core functions are contained in modules. You could choose to disable some of these, but doing so would change the standard web server behavior and cause you grief. You can find Apache modules to compress pages before transmission, vastly decreasing bandwidth. FreeBSD has many modules in the Ports Collection under */usr/ports/www*. Module port names begin with *mod_*, such as mod_gzip.

APACHE MODULES VS. KERNEL MODULES

While kernel modules are not Apache modules, FreeBSD includes a kernel module just to optimize web servers. If a client sends a long HTTP request, that request might take a long time (in computer terms) to completely arrive. The *HTTP accept filter* buffers incoming HTTP traffic in the kernel until a complete request arrives. With this buffering, the web server doesn't waste time waiting for a request to arrive; it receives the whole request at once and can act on it. Enable the HTTP accept filter by setting `apache22_http_accept_enable="YES"` in */etc/rc.conf*.

Load and unload Apache modules via the configuration file. The entries look like this:

```
LoadModule authn_file_module libexec/apache22/mod_authn_file.so
LoadModule authn_dbm_module libexec/apache22/mod_authn_dbm.so
LoadModule authn_anon_module libexec/apache22/mod_authn_anon.so
...
```

Each entry consists of a LoadModule statement, the name of the module, and the file where that module can be found. The filenames respect ServerRoot, so these files are are actually in */usr/local/libexec/apache22*.

Here are some of the popular Apache modules available in the Ports Collection. Other people's definition of popular will probably differ from mine, but that's their prerogative.[2] Most of these can be found in */usr/ports/www*.

mod_bandwidth Allows controlling the amount of bandwidth used by a site. Very useful for virtual servers where clients have a certain amount of bandwidth per month.

mod_dtcl Embeds a Tcl interpreter in Apache, for faster Tcl-based applications.

mod_fastcgi Accelerates CGI scripts.

mod_gzip Accelerates websites and decreases bandwidth usage by compressing content. Highly recommended.

mod_mp3 Turns Apache into a streaming MP3 server.

mod_perl2 Embeds a Perl interpreter in Apache, for faster Perl applications.

mod_python Embeds a Python interpreter in Apache, for faster Python applications.

mod_ruby Embeds a Ruby interpreter in Apache, for faster Ruby applications.

mod_webapp-apache2 Connects Apache to Tomcat for Java application servers.

php5 Provides the popular PHP web scripting language. (This module is in */usr/ports/lang/php5*.) When you install PHP, it gives you the choice to pull in MySQL, another popular tool.

You'll find many other Apache modules scattered throughout the Ports Collection. When you have an Apache problem, I suggest searching the Web; chances are the software you need is already there.

Many of these ports configure themselves in *httpd.conf* upon installation. If you're using revision control on *httpd.conf* (as you should!), this means that you'll need to check out *httpd.conf* before you install the port. If a port doesn't configure itself upon installation, read the module documentation; chances are there's a good reason why. You might have to make some decisions about how you want the software to behave before configuring Apache.

---

[2] Yes, I do allow people to disagree with me. Even though they're wrong.

Directories and Permissions

Apache has many interesting features, but it's not a good idea to enable everything everywhere—a bit of sloppy programming can result in you broadcasting extra information from your website or even allowing an intruder to break in. Apache permissions are set on a directory-by-directory basis. The configuration looks a little like XML: You have a `Directory` label in angle brackets, a list of permissions and settings, and then a closing `Directory` with a backslash. Any options or settings between the opening and closing `Directory` statements affect that directory:

```
<Directory /path/to/files>
    ...options and settings...
</Directory>
```

By default, Apache uses very restrictive permissions and settings. For example, you'll see the following entry right at the top of the directory listings in *httpd.conf*:

```
<Directory />
    AllowOverride None
    Order deny,allow
    Deny from all
</Directory>
```

Apache has features to allow users to override the default server configuration and change server options, password protection, MIME types, and so on. The `AllowOverride None` line means that users cannot use these features unless we explicitly permit them. The `Order` and `Deny` statements mean that no directory on the system may be accessed from the Web. This is a *default deny* security stance. Unless you specify otherwise, every directory on your system has these permissions.

Now that you've disallowed everything, you can explicitly enable the features you want. Here are some settings you might find of interest.

Controlling Access by IP Address

The `Allow` and `Deny` options list the IP addresses and hostnames that Apache permits to access content in a directory. Apache compares client IP addresses against the `Allow` and `Deny` lists in the order given in the `Order` statement, and then permits or rejects access requests based on the results. When `Order` is `deny,allow`, Apache permits access unless prohibited by a `Deny` statement. When `Order` is `allow,deny`, Apache denies access unless explicitly permitted by an `Allow` statement. The last matching rule applies.

```
    Order allow,deny
    Allow from all
```

This example, the default for the *DocumentRoot* directory, specifically sets a default deny policy and then allows all hosts to access the site with the `Allow` statement. As with TCP wrappers, you can use the special all host to indicate every host. You can block some sites by adding a `Deny` statement to this default:

```
Order allow,deny
    Deny from 192.168.0.0/16
    Allow from all
```

Here, you've blocked certain IP addresses from reaching your site. You could also use hostnames, if you're willing to rely on reverse DNS for your web server security:

```
Order allow,deny
    Deny from *.absolutefreebsd.com
    Allow from all
```

In this case, all I must do to access your site is walk over to a machine that has reverse DNS not in the *absolutefreebsd.com* domain. Changing my reverse DNS is easier than changing my IP address.

Inversely, you can easily restrict access to your internal website to your company's IP addresses only by doing something like this:

```
Order deny,allow
    Allow from 192.168.0.0/16
    Deny from all
```

You'll see similar examples throughout the Apache configuration files.

Directory Options

Options are general server features enabled and disabled on a directory-by-directory basis. They allow a web server to do all sorts of nifty things, such as execute CGI scripts, password protect directories, and change language handling. These options give web developers a lot of power but can also generate a lot of support calls. Enabling only the necessary options reduces the amount of time you spend troubleshooting problems later.

Inside a directory entry, specify options with the `Options` keyword. For example, to enable the `ExecCGI` and `MultiViews` options in the directory */var/www/mysite/cgi-bin*, use the following configuration:

```
<Directory /var/www/mysite/cgi-bin>
    Options ExecCGI, MultiViews
</Directory>
```

Now let's see what options Apache supports.

None

The `None` option disables all options. The sample *httpd.conf* ships with `Options` set to `None`. If you're building your *httpd.conf* on top of the default configuration, you must explicitly enable any options you want to use.

All

The `All` option is Apache's built-in default. If you don't specify any options, almost any Apache option works on the website. If the user uploads a password-protection script to control directory access, it will work. If a user uploads a CGI script that exploits a system flaw to start a root shell on a high-numbered port, granting everyone in the world a backdoor onto your system, that will work too. The `All` option allows every Apache option *except* `MultiViews` (as shown on the next page).

ExecCGI

Apache can run any CGI scripts in this directory.

FollowSymLinks

You can use *symlinks—symbolic links*, or file aliases, as discussed in ln(1)—to point to other files or directories on the server. A user could symlink to just about any file on the server, and that file will be visible if the file permissions allow.

SymLinksIfOwnerMatch

The server follows symlinks if the owner of the symlink is the owner of the file that the symlink points to. In English, this means that a user can employ symlinks only to point to her own documents.

Includes

Server-side includes (shell commands inside HTML files, also known as *SSI*) and CGI scripts work in this directory. SSI can be a serious security risk unless securely programmed. After all, you're allowing anyone who can see your website to run the command you use in your HTML page. Conniving visitors can make a command do things the web designer never intended. Search the Web for discussions on the security of SSI, and you'll find enough to keep you busy for a long, long time. If you don't know how to use SSI safely, don't enable this!

IncludesNOEXEC

This allows server-side includes, but disables the #exec feature and the include function of server-side includes. Without the #exec feature, SSI commands must be written within carefully restricted parameters. Basically, this permits simple server-side includes and CGI scripts but eliminates many common security holes. Just because the most common security holes are eliminated doesn't mean that this is safe; you're just making the intruder's work a little harder.

Indexes

If a directory doesn't contain an index document (*index.html*), the `Indexes` option lets the server return a prettily formatted list of the directory contents. You might consider this a security problem, depending on the contents of your directory. For example, if someone browses the directory of my personal web page I don't really care, but if they browse a directory containing my private code, I care a great deal. (In my case it's because my private code is embarrassing, but other people have code that's actually worth money.)

MultiViews

This option permits the server to handle HTML documents written in multiple languages. For example, a web developer can write a single page that contains text in English, Chinese, and Spanish. `MultiViews` allows the server to negotiate the desired language with the client's web browser.

Configuration by Users

One of the interesting things about Apache is that users may upload their own configuration files, and the server will read and use them. The `AllowOverride` keyword lets the Apache administrator dictate what configuration settings users may or may not adjust in a given directory. This allows web developers to handle much routine configuration themselves, as well as to install insecure CGI scripts in random locations.

Users place configuration overrides in a file called *.htaccess* in the affected directory. If you're running a corporate web server and your web developer basically gets what he wants, there's no reason not to allow whatever override he desires. If you're running an ISP web server and you don't allow a certain group of clients to use CGI scripts, don't enable the `ExecCGI` option and disable the override that permits CGI use.

`AllowOverride` appears on a single line within a `Directory` statement, followed by the allowed overrides. Here is a reasonable set of defaults for most websites:

```
AllowOverride FileInfo AuthConfig Limit Indexes
```

These are some valid `AllowOverride` statements that you might allow users to adjust via a *.htaccess* file.

AuthConfig

`AuthConfig` allows the user to password protect directories. This is a safe option; it is generally expected on server farms where any idiot with a credit card can get an account.

FileInfo

`FileInfo` permits users to insert their own MIME information for files in a directory. While it's generally better to add MIME information to the server's *mime.types* file, some users think they need this.

Indexes

The `Indexes` override lets the user control how directory indexing is handled, including setting a new default document, controlling how icons appear in server-generated indexes, and so on.

Limit

Users who can override `Limit` configuration can use the `Allow`, `Deny`, and `Order` keywords to build their own hostname and IP address controls on their directories. This option is also quite safe.

None

> The None override means that the user may not override any server configuration. This is a good default, but it is a little too restrictive for most environments.

Options

> Finally, you could allow your users to set their own directory options as discussed in the previous section. This is useful if you trust your web developers or if you don't care that someone might upload an insecure program and get your server compromised.

Other Directory Settings

While Apache lets you tweak all kinds of settings in each directory, we're only going to cover the most essential settings here. You can find many, many more settings in the Apache documentation.

Index Documents

The DirectoryIndex statement defines the names of default documents in directories. When a client requests a directory rather than a filename, Apache checks for files with these names, in order. Change this if you're using a tool such as PHP (whose filenames end in *.php*) or those Windows web page editors that use *.htm* or, worse, insist on naming the index page *default.htm*.

```
DirectoryIndex index.php index.htm index.html
```

Aliases

Use the Alias statement to provide shortcuts to directories on your website, much like a symlink. You can use an Alias statement to join disparate directories into a single coherent site without using FollowSymlinks like a maniac. This is especially useful with third-party programs and web applications.

```
Alias /icons/ "/usr/local/www/icons"
```

This example means that if someone calls up *http://www.absolutefreebsd.com/icons*, they would actually be viewing the directory */usr/local/www/icons*, even though the DocumentRoot of my site is nowhere near that directory.

You probably still need a Directory statement to grant permissions to the aliased directory.

Custom Error Pages

In addition to serving web pages, web servers can also display errors to the client. While Apache includes standard error pages, you can create your own custom error pages and direct clients to them. Specify the ErrorDocument keyword, the error number, and the name of the file to be served:

```
ErrorDocument 404  /missing.html
```

404 is the code for the classic "Page not found" error. When a user requests a page that doesn't exist, he gets the file *missing.html* instead.

Password Protection and Apache

Restricting a website to users with a username and password is a common requirement. Apache can authenticate via all sorts of username and password schemes, from integration with LDAP and Kerberos domains to databases to plaintext files. We're going to examine two standard methods of authentication: Apache password files and Radius authentication.

Password Files

Password files are very common in environments where you have only a few users accessing a password-protected directory. They're also popular in virtual host environments, where users want to control access to their own sites. Do not put the password file in a directory in the website itself, or users could download it and try to crack the passwords. Put the password file in a directory completely outside any website. If you have user accounts on your system, and a user manages the website, you can put the password file in the user's home directory.

Create an empty password file with touch(1), then use htpasswd(1) to add usernames and change user passwords. The syntax is very simple:

```
# htpasswd passwordfile username
```

For example, to add a user named mwlucas to the password file *webpasswords*, I would run htpasswd webpasswords mwlucas. To change that user's password, I would use the exact same command. The password contains a single line for each user, listing the username and a password hash:

```
mwlucas:iJf2e7KIgS5i6
```

To remove a user from the database, just remove the corresponding entry from the password file. You can also use htpasswd(1)'s -D flag, but I find that removing users with vi(1) is easier than trying to remember this.

Now tell Apache to apply password protection to the directory. While you can configure password protection directly in *httpd.conf*, it's most common to configure authentication in a *.htaccess* file. That way, changes to your authentication system don't necessitate reloading the entire web server. End users commonly want to reconfigure their own authentication systems, and using password files is an easy way to accomplish this. Define AllowOverride AuthConfig for the password-protected directory (or the entire site), then create a *.htaccess* file in the protected directory that looks something like this:

```
AuthName "Employees Only"
AuthType basic
AuthUserFile /home/mwlucas/sitepasswords
require valid-user
```

`AuthName` is the text that appears in the password prompt box. You can place any text you like between the quotes, and it will be shown by the web browser.

`AuthType` tells Apache how to configure authentication with the client. For standard usernames and passwords, use an `AuthType` of `basic`.

The `AuthUserFile` directive tells Apache where the user database is kept and what kind of database it is. In this case, we're pointing Apache to a htpasswd(1) user file.

The `require valid-user` statement tells Apache that it should prompt for a username and password, and only grant access to users who have valid credentials.

Radius User Authentication

Radius is a decent way to authenticate against third-party directory services, such as Active Directory and LDAP. You can find a whole variety of Radius servers, from freely available OpenRADIUS to the Internet Authentication Service bundled with Windows servers. The nice thing about Radius integration is that you don't need to muck about with LDAP or Kerberos, because enterprise directory management teams can be reluctant to allow nonstandard systems to talk to the directory. In most cases, you can just build a Radius server and let it authenticate against your enterprise directory without involving anyone else. While an Internet search shows several Radius authenticators for Apache, I prefer mod_auth_xradius (*/usr/ports/www/mod_auth_xradius*). It works well with modern Apache and is fairly easy to configure.

First, configure your Radius server. If you're in an enterprise or service provider setting, chances are you already have a Radius server. Many different vendors provide Radius servers, each with its own pluses and minuses. FreeBSD includes several in the Ports Collection. The good news is that Apache doesn't need any fancy Radius features; any Radius server suffices. If you are in a Microsoft Active Directory environment, check out Internet Authentication Services. It's very small, and chances are you can get your AD administrator to install it for you. Your fellow employees will be happy that your web app provides a logon integrated with their desktop accounts, when so many don't.

Now tell Apache to load the module. Go to the end of the `LoadModule` list and add it:

```
LoadModule auth_xradius_module libexec/apache22/mod_auth_xradius.so
```

Then, configure the Radius cache. Apache uses the cache to store the list of users who have successfully authenticated. Without a cache, Apache makes a Radius request for every object on every web page. This might be dozens of requests for a single click of the mouse, which is obviously undesirable.

```
AuthXRadiusCacheTimeout 300
AuthXRadiusCache dbm "/tmp/auth_xradius_cache"
```

The `AuthXRadiusCacheTimeout` tells Apache how long to cache objects, in seconds. The `AuthXRadiusCache` line tells Apache where to store the cache. In this case, I'm using a `dbm` (hash database) file in *tmp*. If you have untrusted users logging into your web server on the command line, place your cache in a directory that users cannot access, but on a dedicated server *tmp* is adequately secure.

Now, tell your protected directory to require Radius authentication. You could do this in a *.htaccess* file just as you do for usernames and passwords, but I recommend placing the configuration directly into *httpd.conf*. Sites using Radius authentication are generally managed by a system administrator, not by users. Place your configuration directly into a `Directory` statement. For example, I run Nagios on FreeBSD. Here's a configuration for password-protecting the *nagios* directory with Radius:

```
<Directory /usr/local/www/nagios>
        AllowOverride None
        ...
        AuthName "Nagios"
        AuthBasicProvider "xradius"
        AuthType basic
        AuthXRadiusAddServer "radius.absolutefreebsd.com" "RadiusSecret"
        AuthXRadiusTimeout 2
        AuthXRadiusRetries 2
        require valid-user
</Directory>
```

While this looks confusing at first glance, it's not that bad if you go through it slowly. The `AllowOverride` statement specifically disallows configuration of the directory via a *.htaccess* file. As we're configuring the directory within the web server itself, that's perfectly fine.

The `AuthName` entry gives the text displayed in the user-visible password prompt.

`AuthBasicProvider` tells Apache where to get its source of authentication information. While the password file has been built into Apache for many years, so Apache knows about it by default, when you use add-on authentication systems you must tell Apache.

The `AuthType` of basic indicates that you're using HTTP basic authentication.

To tell Apache where to find your Radius server and the shared secret, use the `AuthXRadiusAddServer` value. Put both the server name and the shared secret in quotes.

A Radius server should respond in less than a second. To tell Apache how many seconds to wait for an answer before trying again, use `AuthXRadiusTimeout`. To tell Apache how many times to retry, use `AuthXRadiusRetries`.

Finally, tell Apache that the user must provide a valid username and password to get access.

While this example is specific to Radius, in particular the XRadius module, you can apply the same principles to any other authentication module. Read the module documentation and configure Apache as required. While it won't look exactly like the Radius setup, chances are it will be very similar.

Groups and .htaccess

One useful feature of usernames and passwords is the ability to restrict access by group. Perhaps you have a large website, where authenticated users get access to the majority of the site content but only a few of those authenticated users should have access to the administrative area. You can use groups to accomplish this. Apache group files look much like */etc/group*: a group name, followed by a colon, followed by a comma-delimited list of users:

```
administrators: mwlucas, gedonner
```

Then, tell Apache about the group file and add a `require-group` statement to the *.htaccess* file or directly to *httpd.conf*:

```
authgroupfile /usr/local/etc/apache22/users/webgroup
require-group administrators
```

This way, your administrators have a single password for both the semi-public and administrative areas of your site, but only the administrators can access the administrative area. You can use this function to divide your website in any way by creating more groups.

Including Other Configuration Files

One feature that makes Apache configuration easier to manage is the ability to include other configuration files. Older *httpd.conf* files were over a thousand lines long and included large amounts of text irrelevant to most users. These features are now segmented off into separate configuration files. Near the end of *httpd.conf* you'll see entries like this:

```
...
# Fancy directory listings
❶ #Include etc/apache22/extra/httpd-autoindex.conf
# Language settings
#Include etc/apache22/extra/httpd-languages.conf
# User home directories
#Include etc/apache22/extra/httpd-userdir.conf
...
```

By uncommenting the configuration entry, you enable the functionality in the included file. For example, to enable fancy directory listings you would uncomment the line pointing to that configuration file ❶. Of course, you must review the file to confirm that the functionality is configured as you wish.

The default Apache configuration file has two directories set aside for included configurations: *extra* and *Includes*. The *Includes* directory is for your use. Any file in the *Includes* directory with a name ending in *.conf* is sucked into the global Apache configuration. We'll use this feature when we create virtual hosts later in this chapter. The files in *extra* come with Apache and cover special Apache functions that are not required in every setting, but are sufficiently popular to be integrated with Apache itself. These functions are:

MPM   The multiprocessing module tells Apache how to handle worker processes. All the settings in this file are defaults.

Multi-Language Error Messages   Apache defaults to providing error messages in English. If you need to support multiple languages, enable this module. The browser and the server will negotiate a language for the error messages.

Fancy Directory Listings   The default Apache autoindex function looks rather drab. The fancy directory module tells Apache to generate prettier directory indexes.

Language Settings   You can give Apache a different native language and tell it about different character sets.

User Home Directories   Traditionally, a user's home directory on a web server was available as a web page via *http://<servername>/~<username>*. This module enables this functionality. You can see this in play at my home page, *http://www.blackhelicopters.org/~mwlucas*.

Status   Apache can generate a web page that tells you about Apache's status, configuration, and other real-time information.

Virtual hosts   You can run multiple websites on a single web server through virtual hosts. We'll cover virtual hosts later in this chapter.

Manual   Apache ships with the manual for the version you installed. Enabling this makes the manual available on the website for easy reference.

WebDAV   DAV lets you create a shared file area where users can upload and download documents. You must consider the security of your site and read the WebDAV documentation before enabling this.

Defaults   Apache includes many default settings set in the code itself. If you must override these settings, load this default configuration and make your changes here.

SSL   SSL is important enough that we dedicate a section later in this chapter specifically to HTTPS sites.

Each of these functions has a configuration file in *extra*. Take a look there for more details.

Virtual Hosting

Virtual hosting occurs when one web server handles multiple websites. The server is configured to handle web requests for each of the hosted domains. Many companies need a very small website, with just a few pages of information and perhaps a CGI script or two. This is an excellent application for virtual hosting. I've run thousands of virtual domains on one FreeBSD system without putting the system load up over 0.2. When each site pays $19.95 a month to handle a couple dozen hits a day, you're quickly looking at real money on inexpensive hardware.

One common stumbling block to understanding virtual hosts is the belief that the *www* in a URL is a magic incantation that points to a website. This is incorrect. When you type a URL such as *http://www.freebsd.org,* you're telling your browser to go to a machine named *www.freebsd.org* and check its website. The *www* started off as system administrators' shorthand for "the server with our *w*orld *w*ide *w*ebsite on it" and has spread into popular usage. If you pay attention, you'll see websites on machines with many different names. With virtual hosts, many hostnames point to one machine. The server needs to differentiate between the requests for different domains and then answer each request with the appropriate file. To enable virtual hosts, uncomment the Include line for virtual hosts in *httpd.conf* and restart Apache.

Configuring Virtual Hosts

As one Apache server can handle thousands of virtual hosts, I suggest placing the configuration for each server in its own file in the *Includes* directory. If you end the filename in *.conf,* Apache will automatically include the configuration on the next reload. Further, I recommend naming the file after the domain it serves. You'll end up with files like *www.customer1.com.conf, www.customer2.com.conf,* and so on. Compared to sorting through a single monolithic configuration file, this makes site troubleshooting much easier.

Apache supports two different styles of virtual hosts: name-based and IP-based. *Name-based* virtual hosts assume that the client asks for the name of the website. All browsers since Netscape 3 and IE 4 support this behavior. Name-based virtual hosts are almost always the proper choice. An *IP-based* virtual host is attached to a single individual IP address; this is only necessary when a virtual host needs a SSL certificate. You can use both on a single server.

Here's a name-based virtual server configuration for *absolutefreebsd.com.* It's installed as */usr/local/etc/apache22/Includes/absolutefreebsd.com.conf.*

```
<VirtualHost *:80>
❶      ServerAdmin webmaster@absolutefreebsd.com
❷      DocumentRoot /var/www/absolutefreebsd.com
❸      ServerName absolutefreebsd.com
❹      ServerAlias www.absolutefreebsd.com
❺      ErrorLog /var/log/http/absolutefreebsd.com-error_log
❻      CustomLog /var/log/http/absolutefreebsd.com-access_log combined
</VirtualHost>
```

The first thing to note is the `<VirtualHost>` and `</VirtualHost>` tags. Everything between these tags defines a single virtual host. The `*:80` entry tells Apache that a request for this website can come to port 80 on any IP address on this host.

Just like our main server, a virtual host needs a `ServerAdmin` ❶ and `DocumentRoot` ❷, where Apache will find the documents that make up the website. The web server also needs `ErrorLog` ❺ and `CustomLog` ❻ directives. (You can have all of your virtual websites log to a single file, but then you'll have to sort them out later.)

Perhaps the most interesting thing here is the `ServerName` and `ServerAlias` directives. The server name ❸ is *absolutefreebsd.com*. The `ServerAlias` ❹ directive gives this site a second name, *www.absolutefreebsd.com*. Apache serves up the same site for either name. If someone doesn't type the *www* part of the site name, you still want them to reach the page.

The IP-based virtual host is almost identical to the name-based host, with the exception of the content of the `<VirtualHost>` tags. Instead of using `*:80` to indicate that you're listening for requests for this host on all addresses on the machine, you use a single IP address:

```
<VirtualHost 192.168.1.5:80>
    ServerAdmin webmaster@AbsoluteFreeBSD.com
    ...
```

This virtual host attaches to the IP address 192.168.1.5. This is only useful for a site using HTTPS, which must have its own unique IP address. See "HTTPS Websites" on page 520.

This virtual host entry should contain everything needed for this website. For example, the Nagios server for which I configured Radius authentication earlier in this chapter is actually a virtual host. The Radius configuration should go into the virtual host configuration file rather than *httpd.conf* itself.

THE DEFAULT HOST

If you're using virtual hosts, the first host you set up will be the default website. Make sure that the DocumentRoot and error logs are the same as you set for the default site in *httpd.conf*. I also recommend removing the sample name-based virtual host from the virtual host configuration in *extra/httpd-vhosts.conf*.

Tuning Virtual Hosts

Once you have your minimal virtual host working, you can add some more touches. Here we'll discuss various options that work with both IP-based and name-based virtual hosts.

Port Numbers

You can serve different sites on different TCP/IP ports. You've probably seen this before—a hostname in a URL may end in a colon followed by a number. If Apache is listening on ports 80 and 8080, for example, you could have a different virtual host on each port, as long as you add the port number after the IP address in the `VirtualHost` directive.

Here's an example configuration that creates two different sites on two different ports. If I was to use these in production, I'd fill them out with logging statements and administrator information, but this example is intentionally simple:

```
<VirtualHost *:80>
    DocumentRoot /var/www/www.absolutefreebsd.com
    ServerName www.absolutefreebsd.com
</VirtualHost>
<VirtualHost *:8080>
    DocumentRoot /var/www/data.absolutefreebsd.com
    ServerName data.absolutefreebsd.com
</VirtualHost>
```

Of course, you could point both of these sites to the same directory to serve the same content, or you could have them both listening on port 80. It doesn't really matter, so long as it solves your problem.

Options and AllowOverride

By default, virtual hosts inherit the `Options` and `AllowOverride` settings of the Apache root directory. The default permissions are very restrictive, allowing no access from anywhere. You can use the `Options` and `AllowOverride` statements with a virtual host. Any option that is valid in *httpd.conf* is valid on a virtual host. This lets you set server configuration on a site-by-site basis; for example, you could allow server-side includes on one virtual host but not on others. The following virtual host has `Options` settings that override the server's defaults and special privileges for the `DocumentRoot` directory:

```
<VirtualHost *:80>
    DocumentRoot /var/www/absolutefreebsd.com
    ServerName absolutefreebsd.com
    Options IncludesNOEXEC
</VirtualHost>
<Directory /var/www/absolutefreebsd.com>
    AllowOverride AuthConfig
</Directory>
```

This makes your virtual host almost as flexible as a dedicated server—until your customers want their own custom Apache modules installed, of course. That's when you sell them a jailed server and let them install their own modules.

HTTPS Websites

Many online shopping malls and password-protected areas use what they call *secure websites*. What they mean by this is that they use SSL to encrypt traffic between the server and the client. While these sites aren't as secure as the name implies, SSL provides a vital layer of protection. SSL functionality is integrated with Apache via the *extra/httpd-ssl.conf* file. Uncomment the entry for this file in *httpd.conf* to enable SSL.

All SSL web servers need a secure certificate. We discussed generating a certificate request and creating a self-signed certificate in Chapter 9. For your private use, a self-signed certificate is sufficient, but anything that faces the public really needs a certificate from an accredited CA. If you attempt to use a self-signed certificate on a customer-facing application, the client's web browser will spew scary looking warnings about your lack of security.

The completed certificate has two parts: a certificate file (*hostname.crt*) and a host key (*hostname.key*). Place these files in a directory outside of the web content, so that nobody can download them from the web server itself. Be sure to make these files readable only by the web server unprivileged user and not by regular users:

```
# chmod 600 hostname.crt
# chmod 600 hostname.key
# chown www:www hostname.crt
# chown www:www hostname.key
```

Now that you have the certificate on the system, tell Apache about it. In the past, SSL configuration used to bring tears to the eyes of experienced system administrators; today, it only requires four lines within your virtual host configuration:

```
<VirtualHost 192.168.1.5:443>
    ServerName secure.absolutefreebsd.com
    SSLEngine on
    SSLCertificateFile etc/apache22/ssl.crt/hostname.crt
    SSLCertificateKeyFile etc/apache22/ssl.key/hostname.key
    ...
```

First, note that the we're using an IP-based virtual host that's listening on port 443. Standard HTTPS sites run on TCP port 443.

The ServerName is extremely important for HTTPS websites. The ServerName should exactly match the reverse DNS of this IP address and the name on the SSL certificate. If the three names do not exactly match, the user might see security warnings. ServerAlias is not useful for HTTPS websites.

We then turn the SSL engine on for the site and list the full path to the certificate and the host key. Use the full hostname for the files containing the certificate and key.

SECURE WEB SERVERS AND SSL

I recommend avoiding the term "secure website" when you mean SSL. Encrypting the network traffic between the client and the server only defends against one particular type of network attack. Intruders can still penetrate either the server or the client. A secure web server requires regular maintenance, good web design, and an educated system administrator who is left alone long enough to do his job. While that last one looks like a significant barrier, it pales compared to one of the requirements for a secure web client: an educated user!

Controlling Apache

Apache is a complicated program that you can manage in several different ways. While apachectl(8) works quite well, I recommend using FreeBSD's integrated Apache startup script. This script runs apachectl(8) with any special settings needed for your environment and ensures that the next time your system boots, your Apache server works as it did before shutting down. Apache is a little different from most other programs, however, so you have several different arguments you can use other than the plain old start and stop. The common options are start, stop, restart, graceful, gracefulstop, and configtest.

/usr/local/etc/rc.d/apache22 start activates Apache with all modules as configured. There is no longer any special command for starting SSL web servers. If the server configuration is invalid, it prints out the problem with the config and does not start the service.

/usr/local/etc/rc.d/apache22 stop shuts off Apache immediately, terminating all open connections without completing the requests.

/usr/local/etc/rc.d/apache22 restart checks the server configuration. If it finds a configuration problem, the script prints out the problem and does nothing. If the configuration is valid, it stops and immediately starts Apache.

/usr/local/etc/rc.d/apache22 graceful performs a graceful restart. Open connections are allowed to complete before being shut down. While this might seem unnecessary, it's quite important when you serve large files or have a group of web servers behind a load balancer. Like restart, this command checks the configuration before shutting down the service and takes no action if there is a configuration problem.

/usr/local/etc/rc.d/apache22 gracefulstop shuts Apache down without abruptly terminating open connections. Open connections are permitted to remain open and complete their requests before the process shuts down.

/usr/local/etc/rc.d/apache22 configtest checks the Apache configuration and prints out any problems it sees. This is the function used by the restart and graceful commands to validate the configuration before shutting down the current process.

Now that you can manage Apache, let's see how you can get files to and from the server itself.

File Transfer

A web server isn't any good without web content. While I design my websites on FreeBSD, my websites are hideous.[3] Web design professionals usually design their sites on a workstation and upload them to the server. The standard methods for file transfer are FTP and sftp/scp.

FTP, the File Transfer Protocol, is the classic method of moving files from one computer to another over the Internet. Most of your users will prefer to use FTP. Like many other protocols, FTP has not aged well. FTP has problems in many modern environments. Over the years, fixes for these issues have been bolted onto the specification, creating a Frankensteinian horror of a protocol that lurches after network administrators when they turn away even for a moment. While FreeBSD makes handling FTP as easy as possible, you'll still need to do some work to keep it chugging along.

FTP Security

FTP transmits passwords and usernames in clear text, which means anyone with a packet sniffer can capture this information. Nobody except the network administrator should have a packet sniffer on your local network, but if your users are on remote networks or behind cable modems, their passwords are vulnerable.

As the system administrator, however, you should never, *never*, ***never*** transmit your password over the network in clear text! Instead, use scp(1) and sftp(1) to move files between machines.

The FTP Client

FTP is a fairly complex protocol which, unlike POP3 or SMTP, cannot be easily tested via telnet(1). You must use an FTP client. To connect to a host, just type ftp and the hostname:

```
# ftp sardines
Connected to sardines.blackhelicopters.org.
220 sardines.blackhelicopters.org FTP server (Version 6.00LS) ready.
Name (sardines:mwlucas):
```

The client sends your local username as a default, but you can enter a different username if necessary. You'll then be asked for your password:

```
331 Password required for mwlucas.
Password:
230 User mwlucas logged in.
Remote system type is UNIX.
Using binary mode to transfer files.
ftp>
```

---

[3] Mind you, my websites are not hideous because I design them on FreeBSD. They are hideous because my personal strengths of cynicism, sarcasm, and bitterness are completely inapplicable to making web pages look nice.

If everything goes as planned, you're now logged into the remote server with a shell almost like a command shell. You cannot execute commands, but you can move around and view files using standard Unix commands such as ls and cd.

To download a file with FTP, use the get command and the filename:

```
ftp> get .cshrc
local: .cshrc remote: .cshrc
229 Entering Extended Passive Mode (|||50451|)
150 Opening BINARY mode data connection for '.cshrc' (614 bytes).
100% |*********************************| 614     272.17 KB/s     00:00 ETA
226 Transfer complete.
614 bytes received in 00:00 (193.48 KB/s)
ftp>
```

As you watch, your FTP client opens a connection to transfer the file. A line of asterisks crawls across the screen as the file moves, and an ETA line updates with the length of time remaining in the download. When the file transfer finishes, you'll see a notification, the size of the file you transferred, and an FTP prompt.

Similarly, use the put command to copy files from your local system to the FTP server. The output looks almost the same as that for get, so I won't repeat it here.

Use the mget and mput commands to move multiple files at once. For example, if you want to download all the files that end in *.html*, enter mget *.html. Annoyingly, the server will prompt you to confirm every single file. You can toggle the verification on and off with the prompt command.

Finally, you can view text files over FTP. The less command displays the contents of a remote file, one page at a time, exactly like less(1). While it's rude to view a file and then download it, using less to view *README* and index documents is fine.

Binary and ASCII Transfers

The difference between binary and ASCII transfers is a big source of user confusion, caused by the different handling of the return and newline characters. DOS and Unix systems have long disagreed on how to mark the end of a line, as you might have noticed when moving files between the two systems. An Internet search will uncover many documents describing the issue in painful detail and many more articles denouncing one side or the other for being Just Plain Wrong. All you need to know is how to live with the problem and get on with your life.

While you can transfer both binary and text files in binary mode, you cannot transfer binary files in ASCII mode. Unix-like systems default to using binary transfers, while Windows-based systems default to using ASCII. You can tell an FTP server to use binary transfers with the bin command and ASCII with the a command. Binary works for everything, so use binary mode for all FTP transfers and you'll never have this problem.

The FTP Server

Now that you know how to use the FreeBSD FTP client, let's look at how to provide FTP services. Your first task is to decide if you're going to run your FTP daemon, ftpd(8), from inetd(8) or in standalone mode.

FreeBSD defaults to running the FTP daemon from inetd(8). Most systems don't get that many FTP requests, and inetd can easily handle the few requests that do arrive. If you won't be supporting more than a couple hundred of simultaneous FTP sessions, inetd(8) works well. Just uncomment the FTP line in */etc/inetd.conf* (see Chapter 15) and restart inetd. Any changes to the ftpd(8) command line can be made in *inetd.conf.*

However, if your FTP server handles hundreds or thousands of simulta-neous connections, running FTP from inetd just adds to the system overhead. You'll want to set up FTP in standalone mode, where it is permanently listening to the network and handling requests itself. Confirm that ftpd(8) is not running out of inetd and then set ftpd_enable="YES" in */etc/rc.conf.* You can either start ftpd(8) with */etc/rc.d/ftpd* or reboot.

You can adjust ftpd(8) in many different ways through command-line flags. Add these flags to the ftpd(8) line in */etc/inetd.conf* or to ftpd_flags in */etc/rc.conf.* Now, let's look at the features that FreeBSD's ftpd(8) offers.

Logging ftpd(8) Usage

ftpd(8) has two levels of logging. If you specify -l once (this is the default in */etc/inetd.conf*), ftpd(8) will log all successful and unsuccessful login attempts. If you specify it twice, ftpd(8) logs all FTP activities: downloads, uploads, directory creation and destruction, and so on.

Read-Only Mode

You might want to prevent FTP users from uploading files, replacing files, or changing the server's filesystem in any way. This is good for a server that only provides downloads, such as a mirror site. Use the -r flag to set this behavior.

Write-Only Mode

Perhaps you want a server where users can only upload files, not download them. In this case, use the -o flag.

Timeout

By default, if a user leaves an FTP session idle for 15 minutes (900 seconds), it is disconnected. You can set a new idle timeout with the -t flag, specifying the number of seconds of permitted idle time.

FTP User Control

Two common concerns with running an FTP server are that it can allow users to download arbitrary system files and that FTP passwords can be sniffed. You don't want your server compromised because some dingbat user used his password at the local cybercafe, his login was stolen, and the intruder down-loaded key system files! The best way to control users is by choosing who may log in and which directories those legitimate users may access.

Chrooting Users

You can lock FTP users into their own home directories with chroot(8). To the user, their home directory will look like the top of the filesystem. They won't be able to leave their home directory or access arbitrary system files. This is much like a small jail. Chrooting is useful for web servers that have multiple clients on one machine—that is, web servers with many virtual hosts. After all, customers only need to see their own directories, not anyone else's.

To chroot a user, add her username to the file */etc/ftpchroot*. Put each user on a new line. Every time a user logs in via FTP, the user's account is checked against */etc/ftpchroot*. If the username appears there, the user is locked into her home directory. A chrooted user has complete control of her home directory (unless you set the permissions otherwise) and can create as many subdirectories and store as many files as the disk space allows; the user just can't leave her home directory and explore the system.

You can also list groups in */etc/ftpchroot*, chrooting all users who are in that group. Preface group names with an @ sign (for example, @customers).

Suppose we have a system with two web designers, Gordon and Chris. These admins should only upload files into their home directories. Similarly, we have a group of users who maintain their own websites. These clients are all in the group webclients. To chroot all of these users, set up */etc/ftpchroot* like this:

```
gordon
chris
@webclients
```

All of these users are now restricted to their home directories.

Disallowing Users' FTP Access

The file */etc/ftpusers* is deceptively named. Instead of a list of users permitted to use FTP, it contains a list of users who are *not* allowed to use FTP. FreeBSD's default */etc/ftpusers* contains a variety of system accounts, such as root and nobody. No system administrator should log in as root!

You can list groups in this file by prefacing them with the @ symbol. I habitually ban members of the wheel group from using FTP. People who have access to the root password should never transmit their own password in clear text. Anyone whom I would trust with root access knows how to use SSH, scp(1), and sftp(1)!

FTP Server Messages

The FTP server provides two different connection messages: */etc/ftpwelcome* and */etc/ftpmotd*.

When a client first makes an FTP connection, ftpd(8) displays the contents of */etc/ftpwelcome*. You can put here the terms of use, legal warnings, capacity statements, obscenities and threats, or whatever else you like. Users see this message before they even get a login prompt. This is an excellent place to put an "Unauthorized use not permitted" message. While not as much fun as an "Unauthorized users will be prosecuted to the full extent of an unfriendly Rottwieler and my 12-gauge shotgun" message, the former is actually admissible in court if an intruder hijacks your server.

Once the user has logged in, ftpd(8) displays the contents of */etc/ftpmotd*. This is a good place to remind your users of the system terms of service.

Setting Up Anonymous FTP Servers

Anonymous FTP sites are a popular way to provide files and documents to the Internet at large. Anonymous FTP sites are frequently broken into, however. While FreeBSD's ftpd(8) is quite robust and secure, you should still take basic precautions and configure your server properly to avoid problems. Here are a few recommendations:

- Do *not* share anonymous and non-anonymous FTP services on a single server.

- Set ftpd to run read-only by starting it with the -r flag.

- Use ftpd's -S flag to log all anonymous FTP activity to the file */var/log/ftpd*. This file must exist before ftpd(8) starts using it, so run touch /var/log/ftpd first.

- Create a nonprivileged user ftp for ftpd(8). This user's home directory will be the root of the anonymous FTP directory, and all files you want the world to see must be placed in this directory.

- Create the directory */home/ftp/pub* for the traditional *pub* folder in an FTP server and change the permissions on the ftp user's home directory to prevent that user from changing the home directory. This will force all uploaded files (if permitted) to go into *pub*.

Anonymous FTP Pitfalls

Allowing just anyone to upload to your server might seem friendly. You might have bandwidth and disk to spare, and you might desire to provide a public service. In an ideal world (such as the Internet of the '80s and early '90s), this would be lovely.

If you allow anyone to store data on your system, however, people can use your FTP server to store illegal software, child porn, or terrorist data. To make it harder for you to find, they can create hidden directories or disguise the data. Even if you go looking through all the crud people upload, you'll probably ignore files that look innocuous. It's not your fault that the file labeled *CookieRecipies.txt* is actually a MPEG of the Gerbil Liberation Front training for its secret mission to cram the President of the United States into a giant wheel and make him run for his life. But you'll have a hard time explaining that to Homeland Security.

Chrooting sftp(1) and scp(1)

Finally, a quick word on sftp(1) and scp(1). These are file transfer services that run over SSH (see Chapter 15), providing authentication, integrity, and nonrepudiation for data transfers. sftp is a secure replacement for FTP, while scp replaces rcp(1). Users who transfer files to a server can use these protocols instead of FTP.

One problem that system administrators face is that of chrooting users of these services. While it's nice that you can provide a secure encrypted connection for users to transfer their data, you still don't want them to download random files from all over your server! For these users, I recommend scponly (*/usr/ports/shells/scponly*). A user whose shell is set to */usr/local/bin/scponly* will only have sftp and scp access to your server.

Now that you can serve websites and FTP data, let's spend some time with FreeBSD's disk layer. Say hello to GEOM!

18

DISK TRICKS WITH GEOM

FreeBSD has an incredibly flexible disk management system called GEOM. *GEOM* is an infrastructure system that allows kernel developers to easily program modules, called *GEOM classes*, for different types of disk functionality. FreeBSD uses GEOM to support disk encryption, journaling, several different types of software RAID, and exporting disk devices across the network. The GEOM tools provide flexibility, redundancy, and ease of implementation for both developers and system administrators. We'll take you through FreeBSD's disk partitioning tools and then cover several of the popular GEOM classes.

Throughout this chapter, we'll experiment with disk devices. Any time you touch a disk's layout or format, you risk the data on that disk. While it's entirely possible to manipulate unused disk space without affecting data on the rest of the disk, learning how to do that is still risky. *Back up your data.* Better still, find an unused disk and learn on it! (On the other hand, learning on the disk that contains your most precious data will nicely focus your mind.)

We specifically discuss the disk formats used with i386 and amd64 systems. Other platforms have slightly different disk management systems. Sparc uses a disklabel at the front of the disk, but no slice table. The ia64 platform uses slices based on GPT, while partitioning an ARM disk is by far the easiest part of making FreeBSD run on that hardware.

GEOM Essentials

GEOM is a generic framework that allows almost arbitrary layering of storage devices. Different GEOM modules transform storage media in various ways. Additionally, these modules are stackable; the output of one can be used as the input for another. You want your hard drives mirrored? Sure. How about mirroring across the network? No problem. What if you want the drive encrypted, as it's mirrored, across the network, in stripes? Wake me up when you want something difficult, buddy. Mind you, FreeBSD doesn't promise massive performance through too many GEOM layers, but it can be done.

GEOM separates storage devices into consumers and providers. A *consumer* lies beneath the module, while a *provider* offers services to the next layer up. For example, suppose you're using a GEOM class to mirror the hard drives */dev/da0* and */dev/da1* into one virtual disk, */dev/mirror/mirror0*. The disk devices are consumed by the mirrored disk, while the combined device node */dev/mirror/mirror0* is a provider that offers services to the next layer.

FreeBSD sees all providers identically. A physical hard disk is just another provider. Maybe you're putting a filesystem right on the provider, or perhaps */dev/mirror/mirror0* is a consumer of the GEOM disk encryption module. In any case, to use any of FreeBSD's advanced disk features, you must know a little more about hard disk management.

Disk Drives 102

Historically, data on disk could be mapped to a location on the hard drive. This location could be expressed in terms of cylinders, tracks, and sectors. Remember, each hard disk is made of a stack of disk platters. Each disk platter has a series of circular rings, or *tracks*, arranged much like the growth rings in a tree. These tracks hold data as a string of zeroes and ones. A *head* moves over a particular track at a certain distance from the center of the disk and reads this data as the platter spins beneath it. When you request data from a particular track, the head shifts its position and lets that track rotate past beneath it, catching the data much as a parent might snatch a child off a spinning merry-go-round.

If you stack the tracks on top of one another from all the platters, you have a *cylinder*. The innermost track of each platter forms cylinder 0. The next-innermost is cylinder 1. The 1,603rd track of each platter is cylinder 1,602. Many operating systems expect to find that disk slices encompass complete cylinders and get quite irate if they don't.

Each track is broken up into segments called *sectors,* or *blocks,* which can each hold a certain amount of data (512 bytes for many years now). Each sector within a track has a unique number, starting with 1.

So, sectors combine into tracks, which are stacked into cylinders, which combine to describe the disk's *geometry.* This all seems straightforward enough, and would be if you could rely on it.

Over the years, both hard drive manufacturers and operating systems have set and broken limits. This applies to all aspects of machine design— some of you probably remember when 640KB was the maximum RAM that could be put in a PC. A few of you even remember when 640KB was an unimaginably vast amount of RAM and you had no idea what to do with it.[1] Hard drive manufacturers avoided these limits by tricking the system BIOS and/or the operating system. If you're a hard drive manufacturer making a hard drive with 126 sectors per track, and the most popular operating system can only accept 63 sectors per track, you have a problem. The easy solution is to teach your hard drive to lie. If you claim you have half as many sectors per track but twice as many platters, the numbers still add up, and all operating systems can still identify unique blocks. A lie makes the problem go away. You'll encounter several different types of these translations if you read about disk management history. A leading FreeBSD developer summed this all up nicely with, "It's all just lame *x*86 BIOS crap, though."

By the time hard drive information reaches the user, it has quite possibly been through one or more such translations. If you have hardware RAID, either on a local RAID card or from a SAN, geometry information is obviously bogus. Today, the important thing to understand is how this fits together in a logical sense, not necessarily in a physical sense. Accept the lies your hard drive tells you, even when they're obvious.

Many operating systems try to optimize performance based on cylinder information. Geometry translations make these optimization schemes not work as intended.

Slicing Disks

Remember from Chapter 8 that FreeBSD divides disks in two distinct ways: *slices* and *partitions.* A slice is a BIOS partition, the only sort of partition recognized by older Microsoft Windows systems. A FreeBSD partition is a subdivision of a slice. FreeBSD lets you configure slices and partitions separately. A single disk (on i386 and amd64) can have up to four slices, and each slice can have up to eight partitions. FreeBSD filesystems are on partitions inside slices.

Before the first slice, you'll find the *Master Boot Record (MBR)* at cylinder 0, head 0, sector 1. The MBR contains the slice table as well as the system's initial bootstrapping code. The MBR is strictly limited to 512 bytes, which seemed like a lot of space at the time it was defined. A booting computer

---

[1] And yes, I know, I know, some of you weren't even born then! Please review the footnote on page 4.

reads the MBR of the boot drive to identify disk slices, finds the slice with the operating system on it, and activates the bootstrap code on that slice. You can use any portion of the disk after the MBR for FreeBSD.

Viewing the Slice Table with fdisk(8)

To read and edit the slice table in the MBR, use fdisk(8). fdisk always needs one argument, the name of the disk you want to examine. Here I run fdisk on one of my test hard drives:

```
# fdisk /dev/da2
******* Working on device /dev/da2 *******
parameters extracted from in-core disklabel are:
❶ cylinders=1116 heads=255 sectors/track=63 (16065 blks/cyl)

❷ Figures below won't work with BIOS for partitions not in cyl 1
parameters to be used for BIOS calculations are:
cylinders=1116 heads=255 sectors/track=63 (16065 blks/cyl)

❸ Media sector size is 512
Warning: BIOS sector numbering starts with sector 1
Information from DOS bootblock is:
❹ The data for partition 1 is:
sysid 165 (0xa5),(FreeBSD/NetBSD/386BSD)
❺     start 63, size 17928477 (8754 Meg), flag 80 (active)
❻         beg: cyl 0/ head 1/ sector 1;
          end: cyl 1023/ head 254/ sector 63
❼ The data for partition 2 is:
<UNUSED>
The data for partition 3 is:
<UNUSED>
The data for partition 4 is:
<UNUSED>
```

This particular SCSI disk claims to have 1,116 cylinders, 255 heads, and 63 sectors per track ❶. Remember, a *head* is a mechanical device that sits above the platter. 255 heads would be an awful lot to cram within a single hard drive! While I prefer that systems that lie to me pay me the courtesy of making the lies believable, we have no choice but to accept the hard drive's answers and treat them as fact. No matter how many heads, cylinders, and sectors this hard drive really has, I'm confident it has 17,928,540 sectors (1,116 × 255 × 63 = 17,928,540).

Back when hard drives first implemented translations, you might gather conflicting drive geometry information from different sources. fdisk(8) provides all the information it can gather about the drive ❷ in the hope that the system administrator can sort out enough truth to use the drive. This is rarely necessary on modern drives; these days, the information in these first two sections should always be identical.

While all hard drives should have a sector size of 512 bytes ❸, fdisk(8) is kind enough to verify this.

We then see the information for each of the four possible slices on the disk. Our first partition ❹ is labeled as a FreeBSD partition. Each operating system has a unique slice identifier, and the 165 marks this as a FreeBSD slice.

We also see which of the millions of sectors are assigned ❺ to this slice. Slice 1 begins at sector 63—remember, the MBR takes up the first head on the first cylinder, or sectors 1 through 62. Slice 1 fills 17,928,477 sectors, so it ends at sector number 17,928,539 (17,928,477 + 62 = 17,928,539). The disk has 17,928,540 sectors, but don't forget the MBR. This disk is full.

One annoying thing is that the MBR only has enough bits in its slice table to indicate up to 1,024 cylinders per disk. (This limitation created the 504MB limit on hard drives.) This disk has far more cylinders than that! That means you cannot use the cylinder counts ❻ in each individual partition to measure the disk. The only meaningful number is the number of sectors.

Finally, slices 2, 3, and 4 are unused ❼.

Backing Up the Slice Table

Before changing the slice table on a disk, back up the old slice table. This lets you restore the disk to its previous configuration, should you make an error. To back up the slice table, use fdisk(8)'s -p flag:

```
# fdisk -p /dev/da0 > da0.slice.backup
```

To restore a disk's slice table from the backup, use the -f flag and the name of the backup file:

```
# fdisk -f da0.slice.backup /dev/da0
```

If you haven't touched the hard drive since reslicing it, you might even get your data back. Most of the time, however, restoring the slice table won't restore the data in those slices, merely the disk configuration. You must restore the data from backup.

Changing the Slice Table

fdisk(8) not only lets you view the table, you can edit it both interactively and via scripts as well. The simplest way to initialize a new FreeBSD disk is to tell fdisk(8) to mark it with a single large slice dedicated to FreeBSD. It's common enough that fdisk's -I flag is dedicated to doing exactly that. The -B flag tells FreeBSD to completely reinitialize the MBR, which is always a good idea when starting over. Here, we reinitialize the SCSI disk /dev/da17 to have a single FreeBSD partition:

```
# fdisk -BI /dev/da17
```

You could also write your custom slice table in the same format that fdisk(8) uses to back up the slice table, and write that slice table to the disk just like restoring a backup. This is generally inadvisable for most users.

If you use a backup file, fdisk(8) assumes that you know what you're doing—even when you clearly don't. fdisk(8) includes an interactive mode that automatically detects a large number of subtle error conditions and offers alternatives that won't mess up your hard drive. I suggest always using interactive mode to edit slice tables. The -u flag enters fdisk(8)'s interactive mode.

Remember, we covered using sysinstall in Chapter 8 to reslice, repartition, and reformat hard drives. Use fdisk(8) if sysinstall won't work for some reason or if you want more detailed control over the process.

DISKS AND MATH

When working with fdisk(8) and disklabel(8), do as much math as possible beforehand on a piece of scratch paper. If you have to do more math partway through the process, do that on scratch paper as well. Disk management uses large numbers, and you should spend your valuable brain power on ensuring you entered them correctly rather than on manipulating them. While simple addition, subtraction, and division might seem easy, most disk configuration errors are caused by errors in third grade math. By writing out all the numbers beforehand, you will save yourself the embarrassment of learning that you can't do third-grade math.

Let's use fdisk(8) to split our sample hard drive into two roughly equal slices. We know that this hard drive has 17,928,477 sectors. This means we want each slice to be about 8,964,238 sectors.

```
# fdisk -u /dev/da17
******* Working on device /dev/da17 *******
```

fdisk prints the drive geometry information, then asks if you want to change the disk geometry. Changing the geometry is almost always a bad idea unless you have a thorough, almost intimate understanding of your particular disk, so leave it alone:

```
Do you want to change our idea of what BIOS thinks ? [n] n
```

You'll then get a printout of the first slice's configuration and will be asked if you want to change it:

```
The data for partition 1 is:
sysid 165 (0xa5),(FreeBSD/NetBSD/386BSD)
    start 63, size 17928477 (8754 Meg), flag 80 (active)
        beg: cyl 0/ head 1/ sector 1;
        end: cyl 1023/ head 254/ sector 63
Do you want to change it? [n] y
```

Today, slice 1 uses up all of the sectors on the disk. We want to reduce the number of sectors in slice 1 and assign the remainder to slice 2. Slice 1 begins in sector 63 and uses about 8,964,238 sectors. We just have to tell fdisk(8) that. Hit ENTER to take the defaults:

```
Supply a decimal value for "sysid (165=FreeBSD)" [165]
Supply a decimal value for "start" [63]
❶ Supply a decimal value for "size" [17928477] 8964301
❷ fdisk: WARNING: partition does not end on a cylinder boundary
  fdisk: WARNING: this may confuse the BIOS or some operating systems
  Correct this automatically? [n] y
❸ fdisk: WARNING: adjusting size of partition to 8964207
  Explicitly specify beg/end address ? [n]
  sysid 165 (0xa5),(FreeBSD/NetBSD/386BSD)
❹     start 63, size 8964207 (4377 Meg), flag 80 (active)
        beg: cyl 0/ head 1/ sector 1;
        end: cyl 557/ head 254/ sector 63
  Are we happy with this entry? [n] y
```

We let the slice begin right where FreeBSD thinks it should, but change the number of sectors in the slice ❶. fdisk(8) does a bit of calculation and points out that this slice doesn't end evenly on a cylinder ❷. The odds that your calculated slice size would end on a cylinder boundary are close to negligible. Slices ending mid-cylinder can be a problem, especially if you have a multiboot machine. Always let fdisk(8) correct this problem. fdisk(8) shows the size in sectors ❸ of your new slice and displays the new slice entry ❹ before asking you to confirm the change and proceeding to the next slice:

```
The data for partition 2 is:
<UNUSED>
Do you want to change it? [n] y
Supply a decimal value for "sysid (165=FreeBSD)" [0] 165
Supply a decimal value for "start" [0] 8964270
Supply a decimal value for "size" [0] 8964207
```

This slice has never been used before, so it has no defaults. We must enter the slice type, as well as the starting sector. Slice 1 used 8,964,207 sectors, and the MBR used 62, so we've used up 8,964,269 sectors (8,964,207 + 62 = 8,964,269). Our slice can start at sector 8,964,270. The disk has 17,928,477 sectors in total, leaving us 8,964,207 sectors for this slice (17,928,477 − 8,964,269 = 8,964,207). Let's see what fdisk(8) thinks of these numbers:

```
fdisk: WARNING: partition does not start on a head boundary
fdisk: WARNING: partition does not end on a cylinder boundary
fdisk: WARNING: this may confuse the BIOS or some operating systems
Correct this automatically? [n] y
```

fdisk(8) doesn't think much of these numbers at all, but it knows what to do. Let fdisk(8) make its corrections.

```
fdisk: WARNING: adjusting start offset of partition to 8964333
Explicitly specify beg/end address ? [n]
sysid 165 (0xa5),(FreeBSD/NetBSD/386BSD)
    start 8964333, size 8964207 (4377 Meg), flag 0
        beg: cyl 558/ head 1/ sector 1;
        end: cyl 91/ head 254/ sector 63
Are we happy with this entry? [n] y
```

Again, don't explicitly specify the beginning or end address. fdisk(8) has already done the hard work for you, so let it stand.

You'll then be prompted to change the other two slices, if you desire. You have no space left on the disk, so you really can't use those slices right now:

```
Partition 1 is marked active
Do you want to change the active partition? [n]
```

Remember, the active partition is the slice with the root filesystem on it. The boot loader hands control of the booting system to the slice you indicate. If this is not a boot drive, the active partition is irrelevant.

```
We haven't changed the partition table yet. This is your last chance.
...
Information from DOS bootblock is:
1: sysid 165 (0xa5),(FreeBSD/NetBSD/386BSD)
    start 63, size 8964207 (4377 Meg), flag 80 (active)
        beg: cyl 0/ head 1/ sector 1;
        end: cyl 557/ head 254/ sector 63
2: sysid 165 (0xa5),(FreeBSD/NetBSD/386BSD)
    start 8964333, size 8964207 (4377 Meg), flag 0
        beg: cyl 558/ head 1/ sector 1;
        end: cyl 91/ head 254/ sector 63
3: <UNUSED>
4: <UNUSED>
Should we write new partition table? [n] y
```

This really is your last chance to salvage any data on that disk. Review the slice table and, if the numbers look sensible, enter Y to write your new slice table to the hard drive.

That's everything you need to do to get a slice table on a disk. Now let's make some partitions in those slices.

Partitioning Slices

The i386-style slice table is not sufficient to meet FreeBSD's partitioning needs. A slice table only supports four disk divisions, while FreeBSD needs a root partition, swap space, /usr, /var, and /tmp. The system administrator might need his own collection of partitions as well. A *disklabel* is a special data block at the beginning of a slice that indicates partitions' positions within a slice. Different platforms have different disklabel formats and requirements—i386 and amd64 use *bsdlabels*, sparc64 uses *sunlabels*, and so on. On all platforms, disklabel(8) provides native disklabel management. If you're working on an unfamiliar hardware architecture, be absolutely certain to read disklabel(8) before trying to edit the disk!

Reading Disklabels

To view a slice's disklabel, run disklabel(8) with the device name of a slice as an argument. For example, slice 1 on disk ad0 is */dev/ad0s1*:

```
# disklabel /dev/ad0s1
# /dev/ad0s1:
❶8 partitions:
#        ❷size ❸offset ❹fstype [❺fsize ❻bsize ❼bps/cpg]
  a:  1048576         0    4.2BSD     2048    16384        8
  b:  2097152   1048576      swap
  c: 39179889         0    unused        0        0              # "raw" part, don't edit
  d: 10485760   3145728    4.2BSD     2048    16384    28552
  e:  2097152  13631488    4.2BSD     2048    16384    28552
  f: 23451249  15728640    4.2BSD     2048    16384    28552
```

The disklabel shows that the disk supports up to eight partitions ❶, although only six are configured. Partitions are named by letters a through h. While the disk supports "up to eight" partitions, that doesn't mean that you'll actually get eight usable partitions from your new disk. Partition a is traditionally the root partition. While you could use this for normal data, I prefer not to risk confusing myself. The b partition is traditionally swap space. While FreeBSD only swaps on partitions labeled as swap in */etc/fstab*, you can bet having a b partition used for data would confuse me when I'm troubleshooting at 3 AM. Finally, the c partition is the label for the whole slice. While FreeBSD no longer needs the c partition, that doesn't mean that all of the add-on tools I might use would understand a c partition with data on it! It's been around so long that I would not dream of using it for data. This means that you can have up to six data partitions on your root disk (d to h, plus possibly a).

Each partition has a size ❷ in sectors and an offset ❸ from the beginning of the slice. The offset is how far into the slice the partition begins, in sectors. Remember, sector counts start at 0. Partition c covers the entire disk, with a size of 39,179,889 sectors and an offset of 0. In this example, partition a has a size of 1,048,576 and an offset of 0. The root partition is the first on the slice. Partition b begins 1,048,576 sectors into the slice, or right after the end of slice a, and has a size of 2,097,152. If partition a takes up 1,048,576 sectors, and partition b takes up 2,097,152 sectors, then the next partition must begin at sector 3,145,728 (1,048,576 + 2,097,152 = 3,145,728). Check out the offset for partition d. This is all just basic addition.

Each partition needs a filesystem type ❹. The only types of filesystems normally used within a FreeBSD disklabel are 4.2BSD (any FreeBSD filesystem such as UFS or UFS2), swap (for swap space), or unused (for the c partition or empty space). FreeBSD supports other filesystem types, but it's very rare to plop a FAT or a CD filesystem in the middle of your FreeBSD hard disk, and odds are you'll never see a disk with a Sixth Edition Unix partition in the middle of it.

The next two columns give the size of fragments ❺ and blocks ❻ for UFS and UFS2 filesystems. FreeBSD defaults to using 16KB blocks and 2KB fragments. We talked about UFS2 design back in Chapter 8. The defaults are a good average on most modern systems. If you have a special-purpose filesystem that will only hold files of an unusual size, you might want to change the block size. For example, if your application uses millions of files that are only 6KB each, it makes sense to change the block size to 8KB. The minimum size is 4KB. If your application will use only a few files, but they're monstrously huge, you might want to use 32KB or even 64KB blocks. One word of warning, however: FreeBSD expects the fragment size to be exactly one-eighth of the block size. Using another ratio for block:fragment size reduces performance.

The final column ❼ gives the number of cylinders in a cylinder group in this filesystem. Always, *always* let FreeBSD calculate this. Given the number of lies—er, sorry, I mean "translations"—that hard drives and operating systems perform on hard disk geometry, and the fact that you can't do anything useful by changing cylinder group information, leave it alone.

Now that you understand disklabels, let's make our own.

Backing Up and Restoring Disklabels

Before doing anything, back up the current disklabel to a file:

```
# disklabel /dev/da0s1 > da0s1.label.backup
```

With this file, you can restore the disklabel to its previous state with disklabel's -R flag:

```
# disklabel -R /dev/da0s1 da0s1.label.backup
```

Abracadabra! Your old disklabel has been restored!

Editing Disklabels

To create or rearrange partitions on a slice, change the disklabel. Changing the disklabel destroys the partitions on the disk. This means that any data on that disk is lost. (It really isn't "destroyed until you write new data on the drive"; it's just lost.) I recommend editing the disklabels only on new disks without any data, or on disks with excellent backups. You cannot edit the disklabel on slices with mounted partitions.

For example, here's the disklabel on one of my test disks:

```
# disklabel /dev/da0s1
# /dev/da0s1:
8 partitions:
#        size   offset   fstype   [fsize bsize bps/cpg]
  c: 17767827        0   unused       0     0           # "raw" part, don't edit
  d: 17767827        0   4.2BSD    2048 16384 28552
```

Decide how you want to partition this disk. According to fdisk(8), this slice has 8,675MB of free space. I want 1GB of swap space, two 2GB partitions, and a fourth partition with all the remaining space (3.5GB, more or less). All of these partitions use the standard block size and fragment size. Now, edit the disklabel using the -e flag, and you'll get a copy of the disklabel in a text editor. To create the four desired partitions, I edit the label to look like this:

```
# /dev/da0s1:
8 partitions:
#        size   offset    fstype   [fsize bsize bps/cpg]
  b: 1G             *     swap
  c: 17767827      0      unused      0      0          # "raw" part, don't edit
  d: 2G             *     4.2BSD    2048 16384 28552
  e: 2G             *     4.2BSD
  f: *              *     4.2BSD
```

Where are all the sector and offset counts? disklabel(8) recognizes the abbreviations K (kilobytes), M (megabytes), and G (gigabytes), and can do the multiplication necessary to get a proper number of sectors in a partition of that size. We just have to specify the size of each partition in the desired units. Note the size of partition f, however. Here, the asterisk (*) tells disklabel to use all of the remaining space. You can also use percentages in a disklabel to say, for example, "Give this partition 50 percent of the remaining free space."

disklabel(8) can also calculate the proper offset for each partition. The asterisk (*) tells disklabel(8) to calculate the offset for you.[2]

Finally, note the fragment and block sizes. The fragment and block sizes of partition d are explicitly stated, but only because the original label had a partition d that listed these values and I didn't bother to erase them. disklabel(8) assumes the default unless you specifically tell it otherwise.

Save your work and exit the text editor, then look at your new disklabel:

```
#        size    offset    fstype   [fsize bsize bps/cpg]
  b: 2097152        16      swap
  c: 17767827        0      unused      0      0          # "raw" part, don't edit
  d: 4194304   2097168     4.2BSD    2048 16384 28552
  e: 4194304   6291472     4.2BSD      0     0     0
  f: 7282051  10485776     4.2BSD      0     0     0
```

You can see that the sectors and offsets have been calculated, but what about the block and fragment sizes on partitions e and f? When you create filesystems on these partitions, newfs(8) will fill these in with the default values.

Replicating Drive Slicing and Partitioning

So, you can both back up and restore slice tables and disklabels from files. Shouldn't you be able to use these to duplicate slicing and partitioning on identical disks? Why yes, you can! First, confirm that your disks are truly

---

[2] Remember, BSD grew features because the program authors needed them. Apparently the authors of disklabel(8) knew that they couldn't do third grade math either, so don't feel bad.

identical. Not all 80 gig disks have the same number of sectors. If your disks are slightly different, you can replicate the smallest disk on all of the other disks.

First, edit your first disk's slice and partition tables exactly the way you want all of your disks to be subdivided. Back up that disk's disklabels and slice table to files, then "restore" those configurations to the other disks. For example, here the disk */dev/da0* has a single slice. We copy the slice table of that disk and the disklabel of that slice, and restore them to the drive */dev/da2*:

```
# fdisk -p /dev/da0 > da0.slice.table
# disklabel /dev/da0s1 > da0s1.disklabel
# fdisk -f da0.slice.table /dev/da2
# disklabel -R /dev/da2s1 da0s1.disklabel
```

Use fdisk(8) and disklabel(8) to verify the new configuration of the disk */dev/da2*. You can use this to mass-produce identically partitioned disks when you want to, say, use GEOM classes to build a storage array.

Missing Disklabels

Occasionally you might come across a slice with no disklabel at all. I find this most commonly on test disks, when I have been repartitioning and reslicing the disk to test some goofball idea. If a slice has no disklabel, create one with -w:

```
# disklabel -w /dev/da0
```

You new disklabel now has a single a partition covering the entire slice. Editing this to fit your needs is much easier than writing a disklabel from scratch.

Building Filesystems

Now that you have slices and partitions, you're almost ready to use the disk. All that remains is creating a filesystem. Use newfs(8) to create a UFS filesystem on a newly allocated partition. Use the -U flag to enable soft updates. We'll talk about some other newfs(8) options as we proceed through this chapter, but for the moment we just want to create standard UFS2 filesystems:

```
# newfs -U /dev/da2s1d
/dev/da2s1d: 2048.0MB (4194304 sectors) block size 16384, fragment size 2048
        using 12 cylinder groups of 183.77MB, 11761 blks, 23552 inodes.
        with soft updates
super-block backups (for fsck -b #) at:
 160, 376512, 752864, 1129216, 1505568, 1881920, 2258272, 2634624, 3010976,
 3387328, 3763680, 4140032
```

newfs(8) starts by printing out basic information about the new filesystem, such as its size, the number of sectors and blocks, and the size of blocks and fragments. You'll then see the number of inodes. newfs(8) prints out the location of each superblock as it proceeds, just so you know it's doing something. (This used to be much more important when computers were much slower than they are today; newfs(8) could take minutes to run on a large filesystem, and it was nice to see that it was working and didn't just lock up.)

You can specify the block and fragment sizes with the -b and -f flags, respectively. If you do not specify the block and fragment sizes on the command line, newfs(8) checks the disklabel for this information. If you do not specify these, newfs(8) uses the defaults. I prefer to specify these in the disklabel, simply because that gives me a better opportunity to double-check my work. In any case, newfs(8) updates the disklabel with the block and fragment sizes for later reference.

Now that you can slice, partition, and format disks at will, let's look at some more advanced topics in disk management. One such topic is RAID.

RAID

One of the big requirements in any serious data storage system is *RAID*, or a *Redundant Array of Independent Disks*. The *I* in the definition once meant *Inexpensive*, but that's relative. A one-petabyte RAID array costs far less than a single one-petabyte disk, but it is still rather expensive. A RAID system splits data between the drives to improve performance or reliability. RAID can work in either hardware or software.

Hardware vs. Software RAID

FreeBSD supports both hardware and software RAID. Hardware RAID is managed by the SCSI controller, and host adapters that provide RAID are called *RAID controllers*. When you run RAID in hardware, the controller handles all the computations of how to arrange data on the hard drives. Most hardware RAID systems are very stable, and a hardware controller is usually the most efficient way to handle RAID.

One problem with hardware RAID is that different controllers store data on the disks in different formats. If your RAID controller goes bad, you cannot replace it with a RAID controller of a different brand; it probably won't recognize the data on your disks. If you store critical data on a hardware RAID array, you must have either a support agreement that provides you with an identical controller in case of failure, a spare controller of the same make and model, or excellent backups.

Software RAID is managed by the operating system, and the OS figures out how to arrange the data on the disks. Compared to hardware RAID, this method slightly increases system load but uses less expensive equipment. You also don't run the risk of losing your data when you cannot find a replacement RAID controller of the exact same type.

Using hardware RAID is typically much simpler than software because all you have to do is follow the manual. RAID controllers usually have a simple menu-driven BIOS that lets you set virtual disk sizes, restore damaged disks, and configure your virtual disks. Software RAID, on the other hand, demands that the system administrator actually knows what he's doing. If you want to know about hardware RAID, read your RAID controller's manual—we're discussing software RAID. Many of the types of RAID supported by FreeBSD also appear in hardware.

Many RAID manufacturers provide software tools to manage their controllers from the operating system. You can manage and configure amr(4) arrays with megarc (*/usr/ports/sysutils/megarc*), mfi(4) arrays with MegaCli (*/usr/ports/sysutils/linux-megacli*), and aac(4) arrays with aaccli (*/usr/ports/sysutils/aaccli*). 3Ware provides management software for twe(4) and twa(4) controllers, and Areca provides a management program for arcmsr(4) controllers.

GEOM RAID and Disk Size

For any RAID system, all of your hard drives must be the same size—or, at least, you must use the same amount of space on each hard drive. If you have a set of 10 500GB drives in a RAID array, but one of the drives fails and you must replace it with a 700GB drive, you can only use 500GB of that drive. You cannot use the remaining 200GB on that oversized drive without hampering the performance of the entire array.

We're going to assume that the disks or slices you use for software RAID are all the same size. If you have several drives, check fdisk(8) for each to confirm they are all the same size. If some of the drives are of slightly different size, even by just a couple hundred sectors, GEOM uses the smallest drive size as a limit.

Technically, you don't have to have a slice table on data storage volumes. You can run a mirror or a stripe on top of the raw disk—it's all the same to GEOM. Our examples do not use slice tables on the disks.

Parity and Stripe Size

Many RAID types use parity for error detection. *Parity* is just a very, very simple checksum to ensure that data is copied correctly. A RAID system uses parity for error detection, so that it can determine the proper state of a section of disk. This gives the disk array the ability to provide redundancy. RAID systems that use parity generally need to dedicate some disk space to parity, but most of these systems configure a parity area transparently.

Similarly, RAID levels that distribute data amongst multiple drives can use different stripe sizes. The *stripe size* is the size of the chunk of file written on a single drive. For example, if you have a 512KB file and a stripe size of 128KB, this file is written in four stripes scattered amongst your disks. You'll see papers and references claiming that such-and-such stripe size is better for this or that reason. These arguments might even be true—*for particular workloads.* If you really want to experiment with stripe sizes, do so with your own real operations on your own hardware. You might get a performance boost, but chances are it won't be very much. In our examples, we'll default to using 128KB stripes unless specified otherwise. 128KB is a nice middle-of-the-road value that works well for most workloads.

RAID Types

RAID comes in several varieties. Most hardware supports RAID-0, RAID-1, and RAID-5. There are other types, however. FreeBSD notably supports RAID-3, which is useful for certain applications. You'll also see RAID 0+1 and RAID 10, with occasional appearances from RAID 50 and RAID 6.

RAID-0, or *striping*, is not really redundant and technically isn't RAID at all. It requires at least two disks, and data is shared between the disks in a way that increases throughput and disk size. You can use RAID-0 to combine several 500GB hard drives into a multiterabyte virtual disk, but a hard drive failure on any one drive destroys all of the data on all drives. You must restore from backup to access any data on that drive. RAID-0 is useful if you need a single really big filesystem, but it provides no reliability benefits and is actually more vulnerable than a single disk. The size of the RAID-0 array is the size of all the hard drives combined.

RAID-1, or *mirroring*, is where the content of one disk is duplicated on another. This is a great way to achieve low-cost reliability. I use mirroring on all of my servers. Mirroring can give even a cheap desktop-chassis server some measure of data protection. The size of the RAID-1 array is the size of the smallest hard drive in the array.

In RAID-3, or *striping with a dedicated parity disk*, a spare hard drive is used to maintain parity and integrity data for the data striped across the remaining hard drives. This means that a failure in any one hard drive won't cause loss of data. You must have an odd number of disks—at least three—to use RAID-3. For certain applications, the dedicated parity drive provides higher throughput. RAID-3 can only satisfy one I/O request at a time, however. If you're loading large files one at a time, you might consider RAID-3. The size of the RAID-3 array is the size of all but one of your hard drives combined.

RAID-5, or *striping with parity shared across all drives*, is the current industry standard for redundancy. Much like RAID-3, it uses parity to provide data redundancy; loss of a single drive doesn't destroy any data. Unlike RAID-3, the parity space is divided amongst all of the drives. Throughput is unexceptional, but a RAID-5 array can serve multiple I/O requests simultaneously. The size of your RAID-5 array is the combined size of all but one of your hard drives. Unfortunately, FreeBSD 7 does not have a stable software implementation of RAID-5. You'll find references to gvinum(8), a GEOM-based port of the Vinum volume manager that supports RAID-5, but this software is not yet fully reliable. Other implementations are in development, but not available at this time.

RAID 0+1 is a *mirror of striped disks.* You require disks in multiples of 2, with a minimum of 4. Set up an array of disks in RAID 0, so that you have a single large disk area. Then, mirror the entire array onto an identical set of hard drives. The size of the RAID 0+1 array is the total size of half of your hard drives, much like RAID-1. RAID 0+1 is not as fault-tolerant as RAID 10, so it is rarely used. We will not discuss it.

RAID-10 is a *stripe of mirrored disks.* You need disks in multiples of 2, with a minimum of 4, and (for full redundancy) two separate disk controllers. Disks are paired into mirrors, and data is then striped across the mirrors. As the system does not have to calculate parity, this is the fastest-performing high-availability disk system you can find. The size of the array is the total of half of your hard drives.

GEOM can provide all of these RAID types, and more, in software.

Generic GEOM Commands

Most GEOM-related commands (such as gstripe(8), graid3(8), and friends) support a set of common subcommands to assess and control various GEOM operations. While you can use these commands through geom(8), I find it less confusing to use the command for a specific module such as gstripe(8). For example, the status subcommand shows the condition of a particular GEOM subsystem. I can ask GEOM about the status of all of my RAID-3 devices by running geom raid3 status. I find it easier to use graid3(8) and type graid3 status. We'll use the latter form throughout the examples in this chapter. Almost every GEOM module has the four commands load, unload, list, and status.

The load command activates the kernel module for that class. For example, gstripe load loads the *geom_stripe.ko* module into the kernel. Similarly, the unload command removes that module from the kernel.

The status command prints the condition of the devices of that type. For example, here we see the condition of the GEOM-mirrored disk set on my mail server:[3]

```
# gmirror status
      Name     Status  Components
mirror/gm0  COMPLETE  ad1
                      ad2
```

The format of this output varies between GEOM modules, as appropriate for the device.

Finally, the list command lists all the module's *consumers,* or the devices underlying the module. The list command is frequently a synonym for "other interesting stuff about this module that doesn't quite fit in the other three

---

[3] "What, after all this griping about using SCSI disks in servers you're using IDE?" Yes, but it's my personal mail server. I get more email than I want, so having my hard disks catch on fire really wouldn't upset me. I doubt your boss would say the same thing.

commands," such as debugging output. For example, here's a snippet of the list output from a graid3 device:

```
# graid3 list
❶ Geom name: MyRaid3
  State: COMPLETE
  Components: 3
❷ Flags: ROUND-ROBIN
  GenID: 0
  ...
❸ Providers:
❹ 1. Name: raid3/MyRaid3
     Mediasize: 18210036736 (17G)
     Sectorsize: 1024
     Mode: r1w1e1
  Consumers:
❺ 1. Name: da0
  ...
```

This particular server has a graid3 device called MyRaid3 ❶. We see some generic information applicable to most GEOM-based devices: The device is complete (meaning that all the disks in the device are present, working, and up to date) and has three consumers. We then get into graid3-specific debugging information ❷.

Under the Providers heading ❸, we see the list of devices provided by this GEOM class. This server offers a RAID-3 device under */dev/raid3/MyRaid3* ❹. We can see the size of the device, block size, and other useful disk information.

We also have the Consumers section ❺, which lists all of the underlying disks in the GEOM device. Here you'll find information not only about the disks themselves, but also about the interaction of those disks with the GEOM module.

These commands constitute the interface of the various GEOM modules providing software-based disk virtualization.

Striping Disks

FreeBSD uses gstripe(8) to configure and manage disk striping. This lets you create a single virtual disk out of two or more smaller disks. Striping has the advantage of sharing transactions between the hard drives, theoretically multiplying throughput by the number of drives in the array. (Reality rarely mimics theory, of course!)

For this example, I'm using three hard drives, */dev/da0*, */dev/da1*, and */dev/da2*. Each has a single slice, with only one partition (d) on that slice. While you can use a manual method to configure the striped drive each time you need it, I assume that you want the striped drive to be automatically available at boot.

First, load the geom_stripe kernel module with gstripe load. You can also specify geom_stripe_load="YES" in */boot/loader.conf* to load striping at boot.

Creating a Striped Provider

Now tell the drives that they're in a striped provider. Below, we create a stripe named MyStripe. This stripe includes the three drives. Use the -s flag to give the stripe size of 131,072 bytes, or 128KB. The -v flag tells gstripe(8) to be more verbose:

```
# gstripe label -v -s 131072 MyStripe /dev/da0 /dev/da1 /dev/da2
Metadata value stored on /dev/da0.
Metadata value stored on /dev/da1.
warning: /dev/da2: only 9105018368 bytes from 9186602496 bytes used.
Metadata value stored on /dev/da2.
Done.
```

Here we see that gstripe(8) stores information about the striped provider on the disks. The man page tells us that stripe information is stored in the last sector of the disk. We can also see that the disk */dev/da2* is slightly larger than the others, but gstripe(8) is smart enough to not use the excess space on that disk.

Now that you've created your striped provider, look in */dev/stripe*:

```
# ls /dev/stripe/
MyStripe
```

We have the disk device */dev/stripe/MyStripe*. This virtual disk doesn't require a disklabel or a slice table, although you can use them if you like. Mind you, aggregating several disks into a single large partition only to divide them up again might seem odd. You just need a filesystem and a mount point for the new drive. Don't forget newfs(8)'s -U for soft updates.

```
# newfs -U /dev/stripe/MyStripe
/dev/stripe/MyStripe: 26042.8MB (53335720 sectors) block size 16384, fragment size 2048
        using 142 cylinder groups of 183.77MB, 11761 blks, 23552 inodes.
        with soft updates
super-block backups (for fsck -b #) at:
 160, 376512, 752864, 1129216, 1505568, 1881920, 2258272, 2634624, 3010976, 3387328,
...
```

Take a close look at the output of newfs(8) above. Somehow, newfs(8) found cylinder groups in this virtual disk. fdisk(8) reports finding cylinders, heads, and sectors. This should really drive home that cylinder, head, and sector information doesn't mean much; sectors are the only thing that matters.

Now you can mount and use your striped disk, listing devices under */dev/stripe* in */etc/fstab* just as you would any other disk device.

gstripe Destruction

If you want to stop striping (say, because you want to upgrade to something with redundancy), be sure to tell your disks that they're no longer part of a stripe. Unmount the striped device and run `gstripe clear /dev/da0 /dev/da1 /dev/da2` to erase the stripe configuration from the disks. You can then unload the kernel module.

Daily Status Check

If you'd like FreeBSD to perform a status check on your gstripe(8) devices every day and include the results in your daily periodic(8) message, just add `daily_status_gstripe_enable="YES"` to *etc/periodic.conf*.

Mirroring Disks

FreeBSD configures and manages mirrored disks with gmirror(8). While mirrors are traditionally pairs of disks, you can have a mirror with any number of disks. Mirrored disks are one of the simplest forms of fault tolerance; if a single drive fails, the data remains on the mirror. When choosing drives to mirror, it's best to make them physically separate: on different controllers, different cables, even different servers if possible. For this example, I'm using two SCSI hard drives, *dev/da0* and *dev/da1*.

Mirroring a disk writes metadata at the very end of each partition, overwriting any data already there. I recommend only mirroring drives and partitions that are newly created, as any data on these partitions tends to be written at the front end of the partition. Older partitions frequently have files scattered throughout the entire space.

Load the geom_mirror kernel module, or run `gmirror load`. To load mirroring support at boot, add `geom_mirror_load="YES"` to *boot/loader.conf*.

Creating a Mirror

gmirror(8) works much like gstripe(8): Identify the disks that you want to mirror and use gmirror(8) to label the disks as participants. Unlike gstripe(8), however, you usually create a mirror of a disk that already has data on it. In this example, I'm already using disk *dev/da7* for *usr/ports*. (Technically, I'm using *dev/da7s1d* as the partition, but that's the only partition on the disk.) You can only configure mirroring on unmounted disks, so I have to unmount this partition before attempting the mirror. Labeling the disk as part of a mirror is very fast, however.

```
# umount /usr/ports/
# gmirror label -v MyMirror /dev/da7
Metadata value stored on /dev/da7.
Done.
# mount /dev/da7s1d /usr/ports/
mount: /dev/da7s1d : No such file or directory
```

Ack! What happened to our partition? Don't panic. Your disk is now part of a mirrored device called MyMirror in */dev/mirror*:

```
# ls /dev/mirror/
MyMirror        MyMirrors1      MyMirrors1c     MyMirrors1d
# mount /dev/mirror/MyMirrors1d /usr/ports/
```

A check of */usr/ports* shows that your data is once again available.

View the status of disks in your mirror with gmirror's status command:

```
# gmirror status
          Name    Status   Components
mirror/MyMirror   COMPLETE  da7
```

All of the disks in your mirror are completely up to date. As there's only one disk, that's what you would expect! Add disks to the mirror set with the insert command. You must provide two arguments, the name of the mirror and the drive you want to use:

```
# gmirror insert MyMirror /dev/da2
```

Once you have added the disk, check the mirror's status:

```
# gmirror status
          Name    Status    Components
mirror/MyMirror   DEGRADED  da7
                            da2 (11%)
```

The mirror set is not fully up to date yet—it takes a few minutes to copy data from the "good" disk to the new mirroring disk. Depending on the disk size and the speed of your disk system, this might take from a few minutes to several hours. You can always check mirror status to see how your update is progressing.

Repairing Mirrors

The main purpose of a mirror is redundancy; when one hard drive dies, you want to be able to recover data and/or maintain operations. Your hardware dictates your ability to continue operations and/or recover. If you have a system with hot-swappable SCSI or SATA drives, you can repair mirrors on the fly, but if you're using an ATA system you'll probably have to shut down to replace the bad hard drive.

First, remove the broken drive from the mirror set with gstripe(8)'s forget command. Despite the scary-sounding name, this instructs gmirror(8) to remove all drives that are not currently available from the mirror configuration. The forget command does not erase the whole mirror! Then just use the same insert command you used to add a drive to the configuration in the first place:

```
# gmirror forget MyMirror
# gmirror insert MyMirror /dev/da8
```

Mirrored Boot Disks

Mirroring your boot disk isn't as hard as you might think. While it's even possible to mirror your drives during installation using the emergency shell, we'll take a slightly easier route and do it after installation.

First, make sure that your */boot/loader.conf* loads the geom_mirror kernel module. Without this, FreeBSD won't be able to find the boot disk; it'll be on a disk device that the kernel cannot recognize. I suggest rebooting once just to be absolutely certain that geom_mirror loads at boot.

Your next problem is helping FreeBSD find the boot drive. In a default FreeBSD install, your root partition is on a disk device such as */dev/ad0s1a*. When you have your root drive on a mirrored disk, however, your root partition will be on a device like */dev/mirror/MyBootDrives1a*. Your other partitions and slices will be on similar devices. You must have the correct devices in */etc/fstab* for FreeBSD to boot correctly. People suggest all sorts of tricks to change */etc/fstab* in single-user mode, without even vi(1) available. You can use sed(1) or ed(1), or you can mount */usr* to get vi(1). But why not make the change in multi-user mode, saved in a separate file?

Copy */etc/fstab* to */etc/fstab-mirror*. Edit that file to give the new device names for your partitions. For example, suppose you intend to create a drive RootMirror0 for your boot drive. Here's a small */etc/fstab*:

```
/dev/ad0s1a            /       ufs     rw      1       1
/dev/ad0s1e            /usr    ufs     rw      2       2
/dev/ad0s1d            /var    ufs     rw      2       2
```

Once you have your mirror created, FreeBSD will expect an */etc/fstab* like this instead:

```
/dev/mirror/RootMirror0s1a    /       ufs     rw      1       1
/dev/mirror/RootMirror0s1e    /usr    ufs     rw      2       2
/dev/mirror/RootMirror0s1d    /var    ufs     rw      2       2
```

As you know what the necessary */etc/fstab* looks like, create it ahead of time while you have your friendly text editor handy. Triple-check your work, however; it's much easier to make certain your filesystem table is correct than muck around with the boot loader or the fixit CD!

Now reboot into single-user mode. In single-user mode, FreeBSD mounts only the root partition in read-only mode. While you can't normally configure any GEOM module on a mounted disk, setting the sysctl kern.geom.debugflags to 16 lets you do exactly that. This won't help you if you want to get your root partition on almost any other sort of RAID, but in the case of mirrored disks it works nicely. In single-user mode, put your new */etc/fstab* in place, enable GEOM debugging, and then create your root mirror:

```
# cp /etc/fstab /etc/fstab-nomirror
# cp /etc/fstab-mirror /etc/fstab
# sysctl kern.geom.debugflags=16
# gmirror label -v RootMirror0 /dev/ad0
```

After you reboot, FreeBSD should find your root partition on the new mirrored GEOM disk. Your mirror has only one disk in it, mind you, which makes it a pretty wimpy mirror. Once you're in multi-user mode again, however, just run the appropriate insert command to add the backup disk:

```
# gmirror insert RootMirror0 /dev/ad6
```

Congratulations! You have boot disk redundancy.[4] If you lose your main hard drive, you'll need to tell the BIOS to boot the other hard drive—but that's fairly minor compared to losing all your data.

MULTI-WAY MIRRORS

While mirrors are traditionally two disks, using three-way mirrors can dramatically decrease the time necessary for database backups without affecting redundancy. Put your database data on a three-way mirror. When you want to run a cold backup, shut down the database, remove a hard drive from the mirror, and start the database again. Back up the hard drive removed from the mirror at your leisure; when the backup is done, throw the third drive back into the mirror and let it recover normally.

Destroying Mirrored Disks

If you no longer want to mirror your disks, use the gmirror stop command on the mirror name. You can then run gmirror clear to erase gmirror's metadata from the disks previously involved in the mirror:

```
# gmirror stop MyMirror
# gmirror clear /dev/da7 /dev/da2
```

This frees these disks for use in other GEOM modules.

Daily Status Check

FreeBSD can include a status check of your mirrored disks in its daily periodic(8) run. Just add the line daily_status_gmirror_enable="YES" to /etc/periodic.conf.

RAID-3

While RAID-3 doesn't have a great deal of mindshare in the IT community, it is very fast in applications such as CAD systems, which tend to work with single large files. To use RAID-3, you need at least 3 disks, or an odd number

---

[4] One question people ask is, "Why call this drive RootMirror0 and not just RootMirror?" When you stick the slice name on the end of the device name, it comes out as RootMirror0s1, and that confuses me more than RootMirror0s1. Name the devices anything you like, so long as you don't confuse yourself or your co-workers.

of disks above 3, such as 5, 7, 9, 11, and so on. Manage RAID-3 arrays with graid3(8). As with the other RAID schemes, it's best to make these disks as physically separate as possible.

First, load the RAID-3 kernel module with graid3 load. You can also use kldload(8) or put geom_raid3_load="YES" into /boot/loader.conf.

Creating a RAID-3

You should start to recognize a trend here: Identify the disks you want to include in the RAID-3 and use graid3(8) to label these disks as participants. Unlike gmirror(8), creating a RAID-3 destroys any data on these disks. In this example, I'll use /dev/da0, /dev/da1, and /dev/da2 to create a RAID-3 device called MyRaid3. The last disk device you specify will be your parity device.

```
# graid3 label -v -r MyRaid3 /dev/da0 /dev/da1 /dev/da2
Metadata value stored on /dev/da0.
Metadata value stored on /dev/da1.
warning: /dev/da2: only 9105018368 bytes from 9186602496 bytes used.
Metadata value stored on /dev/da2.
Done.
```

This looks much like creating a mirror or stripe, with the exception of the -r flag. Using -r with labeling makes graid3(8) use the parity disk when reading, which accelerates random I/O requests but slows down sequential I/O. As most disk activity is random, I've chosen to use it.

The disk devices are in /dev/raid3. Create a filesystem with newfs -U /dev /raid3/MyRaid3, mount it as you like, and start loading it with data!

Repairing a RAID-3

RAID-3 offers a certain level of redundancy and fault tolerance. For example, if one of our drives fails, you will see it in the status report:

```
# graid3 status
          Name      Status   Components
raid3/MyRaid3  DEGRADED  da2
                            da0
```

That doesn't look good. What happened to /dev/da1? We'll figure that out later,[5] but for now the important thing is to restore service. I have several warm spares in the SCSI array, so let's put one in place to restore our redundancy.

---

[5] An investigation would show that someone ripped the drive out of the array to generate a failure so he'd have something to write about. Fortunately, my boss doesn't read my books.

First, let's remove any reference to the old drive from our RAID-3. List the devices and get the number of each drive:

```
# graid3 list
...
1. Name: da2
   Mediasize: 9186603008 (8.6G)
...
```
❶   Number: 2
❷   Type: PARITY
```
2. Name: da0
   Mediasize: 9105018880 (8.5G)
...
```
❸   Number: 0
❹   Type: DATA
```
...
```

We're looking for the type and number of each disk that's left in the RAID-3. Disk */dev/da2* is disk number 2 ❶ in the array; it is the parity ❷ disk. Disk */dev/da0* is disk number 0 ❸ and contains data ❹. So, we've lost one of the data disks, but it's backed up courtesy of the parity disk. Had we lost the parity disk, our RAID-3 would be working roughly as a striped disk until we replaced the parity disk.

We have disks 0 and 2 of our three disks, so the disk that failed was number 1. Start by removing drive number 1 from the RAID-3 device, making room for a replacement device. (Remember, a RAID-3 device can only have an odd number of members, so you can't just add another drive.) Then add in a new drive number 1, device */dev/da3*:

```
# graid3 remove -n 1 MyRaid3
# graid3 insert -n 1 MyRaid3 da3
graid3: warning: da3: only 9105018368 bytes from 9186602496 bytes used.
```

Well, that seemed painless, although we wasted a little bit of disk space because our new disk was larger than the old one. But did it work? Check the status.

```
# graid3 status
          Name     Status   Components
raid3/MyRaid3  DEGRADED   da2
                          da0
                          da3 (1%)
```

It certainly seemed to work. Wait a little to see if the array rebuilds successfully.

Destroying a RAID-3

If you no longer want to use the RAID-3 device, unmount the partition and use the `graid3 stop` command on the mirror. You can then erase graid3's metadata from the disks involved:

```
# graid3 stop MyRaid3
# graid3 clear /dev/da3 /dev/da2 /dev/da0
```

You can then use these disks elsewhere—say, in a RAID-10.

RAID-10

The stripe of mirrored disks, or RAID-10, is perhaps the fastest way to get large amounts of high-performance storage. Disks are grouped into mirrors, and then data is striped across the pairs. There is no parity disk; instead, mirroring provides redundancy, and striping provides performance. While it uses a whole lot of disks, RAID-10 is the only real choice for high-throughput performance.

Technically, RAID-10 is a *nested RAID*. It's a RAID 0 running on top of RAID 1. Start by creating your mirrors (RAID 1) and then stripe (RAID 0) the data across those mirrors. GEOM lets you build layers like this easily.

RAID-10 is normally used in high-performance, high-availability environments. It's too expensive to use for customer web pages when a regular mirror would suffice, but, oddly, the finance department seems willing to spend that kind of money when their own data is at risk. It is very important for the mirrored disks, if at all possible, to be on different controllers and in different SCSI shelves in different racks.

RAID-10 Setup

Write down your disk arrangement before you begin, so you don't get confused. We'll use four hard drives: */dev/da0*, */dev/da2*, */dev/da3*, and */dev/da4*.[6] Drives da0 and da2 are paired as mirror1, da3 and da4 make up our mirror2. If possible, da0 and da3 should not be on the same SCSI controller as da2 and da4.

Configure your mirrors with the gmirror(8) command:

```
# gmirror label -v mirror0 /dev/da0 /dev/da2
# gmirror label -v mirror1 /dev/da3 /dev/da4
```

Check `gmirror status` to verify that all the mirrors were created as specified and that each mirror is complete.

---

[6] Not only did I unceremoniously rip */dev/da1* out of the SCSI cage, but I'm far, far too lazy to get out of my chair to plug it in back in.

Now create a gstripe(8) volume that includes both mirror devices. We'll use the standard stripe size and call the device raid10:

```
# gstripe label -v -s 131072 raid10 /dev/mirror/mirror0 /dev/mirror/mirror1
Metadata value stored on /dev/mirror/mirror0.
warning: /dev/mirror/mirror1: only 9105017856 bytes from 9186601984 bytes
used.
Metadata value stored on /dev/mirror/mirror1.
Done.
```

You're done.

No, really. That's everything. There's a raid10 device in */dev/stripe*. Run newfs -U /dev/stripe/raid10 to put a filesystem on the device, mount it, and you're ready to go!

RAID-10 Status

To verify the condition of a RAID-10 array, you must check the status of both the mirrors and the stripe device:

```
# gmirror status
          Name     Status   Components
mirror/mirror0  COMPLETE   da0
                           da2
mirror/mirror1  COMPLETE   da3
                           da4
# gstripe status
         Name  Status  Components
stripe/raid10    UP   mirror/mirror0
                      mirror/mirror1
```

The important things you learn here is that the mirrors are working. If one of the mirrors is degraded, replace the drive and rebuild the mirror. The stripe device needs no maintenance; as with a regular gstripe(8) partition, entirely losing one of the mirrors would destroy data. Remember to separate your mirrored disks as widely as possible.

Destroying a RAID-10

To stop using the RAID-10, you must destroy the stripe and then destroy the mirrored disks just as you would for any other RAID-0 and RAID-1 array.

Journaling Filesystems with gjournal(8)

Traditional wisdom says that the best way to ensure filesystem integrity is by using a *journaling* filesystem. A journaling filesystem writes all disk changes to a small file, or *journal*, before writing them to the actual filesystem. This means that changes are safely and quickly cached on disk, so that in case of a power outage there is less chance of data loss. The system then goes back and reads the journal, writing the changes to the filesystem proper in a leisurely fashion. On boot, the system checks the journal file for any changes that were not yet written to disk and makes those changes, ensuring up-to-date data.

For years, FreeBSD relied on soft updates to provide many journaling-like features without implementing a full journaling filesystem. As disks grew larger and larger, however, they increasingly challenged soft updates. UFS and UFS2 are well known as stable and reliable filesystems. Implementing journaling requires digging around in the guts of UFS2—which, even if done by a programmer with a rare combination of sunny optimism and rampaging paranoia, would still risk FreeBSD's hard-earned reputation.

This remained a tough nut to crack until the introduction of GEOM's stackable filesystem modules. If adding journaling to UFS2 is a difficult problem, why not create a disk layer beneath UFS2 to do the journaling for us? That's where gjournal(8) fits in. gjournal(8) only needs minor hooks in the filesystem layer to teach the filesystem where to write its changes, and then gjournal actually writes the changes to the disk. This eliminates fsck(8) at boot after a crashed system.

gjournal(8) is a new feature in FreeBSD 7 and is actually a rather radical approach to filesystem journaling. While many people use gjournal(8) with great success, it should still be considered an experimental feature as of this time. I use it on a multiterabyte filesystem with millions of Netflow files. Compared to the mature UFS, however, gjournal(8) is an untested child. While bugs get fixed when found, you might be the lucky one to find a new bug that puts data at risk. Consider yourself warned.

The journal file uses one gigabyte of disk by default. This makes it unsuitable for small filesystems. I usually use soft updates on filesystems of 20GB or smaller, and configure journaling on anything larger. Journaling and soft updates are mutually exclusive; you may use both on the same server, but not on the same filesystem.

Implementing gjournal(8) on a filesystem destroys any data on that filesystem. (In rare circumstances this can be avoided, but this is a safe assumption most of the time.) If you want to convert an existing filesystem to use gjournal, be sure to back it up first and be prepared to restore it from backup. Given the size of modern disks, I find it fairly simple to back up the 400MB or so of an out-of-the-box FreeBSD /usr partition to another partition on the disk, configure journaling on /usr in single-user mode, and restore /usr. Other partitions start with much less data and are hence easier to convert. Once gjournal(8) loses its experimental status, I expect support for it will be integrated into the installer.

Configuring gjournal(8)

gjournal(8) requires a journal file. This can be a standalone disk device, or it can actually be included in the partition containing the journaled filesystem. If both the journal and the filesystem are on the same disk device, there's no performance reason to separate the two. If you can place your journal on a separate disk device, however, you might see better performance. (Again, two old-fashioned ATA drives on the same controller don't count!) For our initial examples, we're going to assume that you have the journal file on the same disk partition as the filesystem to be journaled.

Load the kernel module with gjournal load or manually load the *geom_journal.ko* kernel module. You can also load the module at boot time in */boot/loader.conf*.

Now label the partition as a gjournal(8) user. Here we convert */dev/da0s1d*, the single partition on this disk, to use journaling:

```
# gjournal label /dev/da0s1d
gjournal: File system exists on /dev/da0s1d and this operation would destroy it.
Use -f if you really want to do it.
```

All right, *convert* isn't the word I want. We eradicate the existing filesystem and plop a journal file at the end of the partition.

```
# gjournal label -f /dev/da0s1d
```

gjournal prepares a journaling device for this partition. Instead of creating a separate directory in */dev* for journal devices, it appends *.journal* to the end of the partition's device name. All further filesystem operations are done on the journaling device.

Jounalling and newfs(8)

Now create a filesystem on the journal device. Instead of the -U that enables soft updates, use -J to enable journaling.

```
# newfs -J /dev/da0s1d.journal
/dev/da0s1d.journal: 7651.7MB (15670656 sectors) block size 16384, fragment size 2048
...
```

One thing to note here is the size of the journaling device. This is an 8.5GB disk, but the journaling device is 7,651MB. Where's my remaining gigabyte? The journal file ate it. This is normal and expected.

Mounting Journaled Filesystems

Most UFS2 partitions are mounted noasync, but any journaled filesystems must be mounted async. As we discussed in Chapter 8, async mounts just dump data right to the disk and don't wait to confirm that the data is safely written to the disk. Journaling handles verification and integrity checking. Specify async as a mount option in */etc/fstab*:

```
/dev/da0s1d.journal      /usr          ufs      rw,async        2       2
```

Using a Separate Journal Device

The main advantage of using a separate journal device is that you might—*might*—be able to preserve the existing filesystem. gjournal(8) stores its metadata in the last sector of the partition. If that sector is used by the filesystem, then the filesystem cannot be converted and must be newfs'ed. Use the journal device as the second argument when you label the device. Here we label */dev/da0s1d* as a journaling filesystem using */dev/da1s1e* as the journaling device. If you are using the last sector of the to-be-journaled filesystem, gjournal(8) will warn you.

```
# gjournal label /dev/da0s1d da1s1e
```

Instead of using newfs(8) to build a journaled filesystem on */dev/da0s1d*, use tunefs(8) to enable journaling and disable soft updates on an existing filesystem:

```
# tunefs -J enable -n disable /dev/ad0s1d
```

Now mount the new journaled filesystem async using the *.journal* device node.

De-Journaling Partitions

Just as with the RAID-based GEOM modules, use gjournal stop to shut down the journal and gjournal clear on the device node to remove gjournal metadata from the partition:

```
# gjournal stop da0s1d.journal
# gjournal clear /dev/da0s1d
```

Then unload the kernel module to completely shut down journaling on your system.

Filesystem Encryption

FreeBSD supports two different disk encryption methods, GBDE and GELI. Both tools work very differently, support different cryptographic algorithms, and are designed for different threat models. People talk about encrypting disks all the time, but you rarely hear discussions of what disk encryption is supposed to protect the disk from.

GBDE, or *Geom-Based Disk Encryption*, has specific features for high-security environments where protecting the user is just as important as concealing the data. In addition to a cryptographic key provided by the user, GBDE uses keys stored in particular sectors on the hard drive. If either key is unavailable, the partition cannot be decrypted. Why is this important? If a secure data center (say, in an embassy) comes under attack, the operator might have a moment or two to destroy the keys on the hard drive and render the data unrecoverable. If the bad guys have a gun to my head and tell me to "Enter the passphrase or else," I want the disk system to say The passphrase is correct, but the keys have been destroyed. I don't want a generic error saying Cannot decrypt disk. In the first situation, I still have value as a blubbering hostage; in the latter, either I'm dead or the attackers get unpleasantly creative.[7]

GELI is much more flexible, but won't protect me from bodily harm the way GBDE might. If someone might steal my laptop for the confidential documents on it, or if an untrusted system user might snoop my swap space to steal secrets, GELI suffices. GELI doesn't try to protect my person, just my data. As I won't take any job that poses a higher than average risk of exposure to firearms (keeping in mind that I live in Detroit), that's perfectly fine with me. GELI also uses FreeBSD's cryptographic device driver, which means that if your server has a hardware cryptographic accelerator, GELI takes advantage of it transparently.

I should mention that in most cases, filesystem encryption is not only pretentious but actively increases the risk of data loss. More data is lost to encryption misconfiguration or lost keys than to theft. When I hear someone say, "I've encrypted my whole hard drive!" I have a nearly psychic vision of the future where that same person is saying, "I've lost access to everything on my hard drive!" More often than not I'm correct. Consider carefully if you really, truly *need* disk encryption.

In this example, we'll use GELI to encrypt a disk partition on */dev/da0*, storing the cryptographic keys on the USB storage device mounted on */media*. You might find it more sensible to use a filesystem in a file (see Chapter 8) as an encrypted partition. Very few people actually need to encrypt their entire hard drive, and in certain circumstances, doing so might raise suspicions. I have enough trouble explaining to airport security why my computer "looks so weird." In their minds, a boot prompt that says Insert cryptographic key and enter cryptographic passphrase is only one step away from This man is a

---

[7] Just for the record: If you have a sharp stick and the proper attitude, you can have my passphrases.

dangerous lunatic who requires a very thorough body cavity search. If you really do need to encrypt certain documents, chances are they only total a few megabytes. That's a perfect application for a filesystem in a file.

Kernel Configuration

GELI requires the kernel module *geom_eli.ko*, which in turn requires *crypto.ko*. You can load these at boot in */boot/loader.conf* or add the appropriate devices to your kernel configuration:

```
options GEOM_ELI
device crypto
```

Generating and Using a Cryptographic Key

GELI lets you use a key file and/or a passphrase as cryptographic keys for an encrypted device. We'll use both. To generate your cryptographic key file, use dd(1) to grab a suitable amount of data from */dev/random* and write it to a file. Remember, */media* is where our USB device is mounted. If you really want to protect your data, create your key directly on the USB device and don't leave it on your filesystem where a hypothetical intruder could recover it. (Even deleting the file still leaves remnants that a skilled attacker could conceivably use.)

```
# dd if=/dev/random of=/media/da0.key bs=64 count=1
1+0 records in
1+0 records out
64 bytes transferred in 0.000149 secs (429497 bytes/sec)
```

The 64 bytes of data constitute a 512-bit key. You can increase the size of the key if you like, at the cost of extra processor overhead when accessing the encrypted filesystem. Don't forget that your passphrase also increases key complexity.

To assign a passphrase to the key, use geli init. The -s flag tells geli(8) the desired sector size on the encrypted filesystem; 4,096, or 4KB, is usually a decent sector size for this application. The -K indicates the key file. You must also specify the device to be encrypted.

```
# geli init -s 4096 -K /media/da0.key /dev/da0
Enter new passphrase:
Reenter new passphrase:
```

A passphrase is much like a password except that it can contain spaces and be of any length. If you really want to protect your data, I recommend using a passphrase that is several words long, contains non-alphanumeric characters, and is not a phrase in your native language.

Now that you have a key, attach it to the device to be encrypted.

```
# geli attach -k /media/da0.key /dev/da0
Enter passphrase:
```

geli(8) now knows that */dev/da0* is an encrypted disk and that the file */media/da0.key* contains the key file. Once you enter the passphrase, you can access the decrypted contents of the encrypted disk at the new device node */dev/da0.eli*. Of course, you need a filesystem to put any data on that disk.

Filesystems on Encrypted Devices

Before you build a filesystem on your encrypted device, purge the disk of any lingering data. newfs(8) doesn't actually overwrite most of the bits in a new partition; it simply adds superblocks that indicate the location of inodes. If you've used this disk before, an intruder would be able to see chunks of old files on the disk. Worse, he'd see chunks of encrypted data placed there by GELI. Before you put a filesystem on the disk, it's best to cover the disk with a deceptive film of randomness to make it much more difficult for an intruder to identify which blocks contain data and which do not. Use dd(1) again:

```
# dd if=/dev/random of=/dev/da0.eli bs=1m
8684+0 records in
8683+1 records out
9105014784 bytes transferred in 1575.226434 secs (5780131 bytes/sec)
```

As you can see, this elderly system needed over 25 minutes to cover the whole 8.5GB disk with high-quality randomness. The amount of time necessary varies with system speed and the amount of randomness available. A cryptographic accelerator increases the amount of available randomness nicely.

Now that your disk is full of garbage, put a filesystem on it and attach it to your system. Do not use soft updates on your encrypted disk. Encrypting a disk device decreases system performance anyway.

```
# newfs /dev/da0.eli
# mount /dev/da0.eli /mnt
```

Your encrypted disk device is now available on */mnt*. Store your confidential files there.

Deactivating Encrypted Disks

When you have finished with your encrypted partition, shut down GELI and return the partition to its inaccessible, encrypted state. First unmount the partition, then use geli detach to disconnect the encrypted disk from the key.

While other GEOM modules usually place metadata in the last sector of a partition, GELI does no such thing. You don't have to clear any metadata from a GELI partition before using it elsewhere. You must remember which partitions are encrypted and which are just empty, especially if you have many free disks in your system. A completely encrypted disk doesn't even have a disklabel on it, so it's easy to confuse an encrypted disk with a blank one!

Encrypting Swap Space with geli(8)

If you allow untrusted users to log onto your system, you might find it sensible to encrypt your swap space. I find this useful on servers where multiple users log in to use a particular application. Instead of generating a key that requires protection, FreeBSD randomly generates a passphrase-free key on every boot and encrypts the swap space with it. This scrambles the data in the swap partition sufficiently so that no intruder can capture sensitive information from swap space. While both GBDE and GELI support swap encryption in this manner, we're going to stick with GELI.

In addition to loading the geom_eli kernel module at boot, you have to make a minor change to */etc/fstab*. By adding the *.eli* extension to your swap device name, you tell FreeBSD to automatically use a GELI-encrypted swap partition. So, for example, the swap space on my machine would change from:

/dev/ad0s1b	none	swap	sw	0	0

to:

/dev/ad0s1b❶.eli	none	swap	sw	0	0

This minor change ❶ is all you need to encrypt your swap. Personally, I find it most useful to simply add more memory to a secure server so it does not have to swap to disk, but that might not be an option for you.

Disk Device Network Exports

You need a CD burner in machine A, but it's installed in machine B? Or maybe it's a hard drive partition you need to access, or even a filesystem on disk? Not a problem! Just export the device across the network through geom_gate and mount it on the other machine.

Why bother to export the device, when you could just log into the other machine? Perhaps you want to use a piece of software that expects to access a device rather than a file. Maybe you want to take an image of an unmounted partition, and the machine with that partition doesn't have enough space to hold that image. Perhaps you'd like to use gmirror(8) across the network, so if one machine dies you have an up-to-date copy of the disk. Or maybe just because it's kind of nifty and will make other system administrators look at you cross-eyed. geom_gate is a client-server application; the system with the device to be exported is the server and the system that mounts the remote device is the client. Both client and server require the *geom_gate.ko* kernel module loaded.

geom_gate Security

The geom_gate client-server connection is not encrypted, so anyone who could intercept the traffic can see the transactions. Mind you, they'll probably have a great deal of difficulty recognizing the contents of that traffic! If you're using geom_gate across an untrusted network, a VPN or at least an SSH tunnel is advisable. geom_gate traffic uses TCP port 3080 by default. (If you want to have some real fun, you can stack geom_gate on top of GELI!)

The server has access control in the form of an exports file, much like NFS. The server only exports the devices specified in the *exports* file, and only to the identified clients.

geom_gate Server Setup

You can only export CDs, disk images, and partitions with geom_gate. You cannot export tape drives, devices such as */dev/random* or */dev/io*, or terminal devices. If you can't mount(8) it, you cannot export it. A device cannot be mounted while exported, however; it must be mountable but unmounted.

To export a device, list it in the geom_gate exports file, */etc/gg.exports*. Each entry in the *exports* file has this format:

```
host      permissions     device
```

The host can be either an IP address (e.g., 192.168.1.2), a network (e.g., 192.168.1.0/24), or a hostname (such as *pesty.blackhelicopters.org*).

Assign each exported device read-write (RW), read-only (RO), or write-only (WO) privileges.

Finally, list the exact device node you want to export. For example, here we permit read-only access to the server's CD drive from every host on my private network and then assign read-write access to the disk device */dev/da0* from my laptop's IP address:

```
192.168.1.0/24    RO    /dev/acd0
192.168.1.202     RW    /dev/da0
```

Now start ggated(8). As of this writing, ggated(8) is not integrated into the rc.d startup system. Fortunately, you've all read Chapter 12 so you know exactly how to write a rc.d script that integrates perfectly with FreeBSD. ggated(8) should work without any arguments:

```
# ggated
```

geom_gate is now listening for client requests on TCP port 3080.

geom_gate Client Setup

Now that we have something exporting devices, let's fire up a client. The client doesn't need a configuration file, just the ggatec(8) command. Use this syntax to create a local device node for a device node exported from a remote server:

```
# ggatec create -o permissions servername devicename
```

For example, suppose we want read-only access to the server's CD drive. The server is named *sardines.blackhelicopters.org*, and the CD is */dev/acd0*. This device is listed in */etc/gg.exports* on the server.

```
# ggatec create -o ro sardines /dev/acd0
ggate0
```

ggatec(8) replies with the local device node (*/dev/ggate0*) that corresponds to the remote device node (*/dev/acd0*). If this is really an exported CD device, I should be able to see the CD in that drive.

```
# mount -t cd9660 /dev/ggate0 /cdrom/
```

A simple `ls /cdrom` shows that the server's CD is now mounted on the client. Pretty cool, huh?

The next question is, how far can you take this? Let's export an actual hard drive and see what sort of abuses we can inflict upon it.

```
# ggatec create -o ro sardines /dev/da0
ggate1
```

The obvious thing to try is to use this as a regular hard drive. Can we fdisk(8), disklabel(8), and newfs(8) it? The short answer is, no, we can't. fdisk(8) can't write the first sector of the drive. We can't use disklabel(8) because disklabels belong on slices, not on whole disks, and we didn't export */dev/da0s1*, only */dev/da0*. If we export */dev/da0s1*, we won't get the various partitions beneath it, only the whole slice. You must be very specific about what you export, and even then you cannot perform low-level operations on it. Once you have partitions and a filesystem on the server disk, however, you can mount those filesystems as you desire and access data on them transparently.

```
# ggatec create -o ro sardines /dev/da0s1a
ggate3
# mount /dev/ggate3 /mnt
```

The remote disk */dev/da0s1a* is now mounted locally at */mnt*.

Identifying geom_gate Devices

After you've been using geom_gate for a while, it's easy to forget exactly which devices you have mounted from which machines. The device name */dev/ggate* isn't a too helpful mnemonic for the actual device. ggatec(8) has a list command that gives details on locally mounted geom_gate devices. Use the -v flag to get detailed information on the remote devices:

```
# ggatec list -v
        NAME: ggate0
        info: sardines:3080 /dev/acd0
      access: read-only
     timeout: 0
 queue_count: 0
...
```

While ggatec(1) lists a great deal of information about each device, the important bits for most of us are the remote device server, the remote device name, and the type of access we have to that device.

Shutting Down geom_gate

When you're finished with the exported devices, remove them from the client. Unmount the device on the client locally and then use ggatec(8)'s destroy function. For example, if we have */dev/ggate0* mounted as */cdrom*:

```
# umount /cdrom
# ggatec destroy -u 0
```

The -u flag supplies the number of the ggate device we are eliminating. We use -u 0 because we are shutting down device ggate0.

On the server side, just stop ggated(8) with pkill(1):

```
# pkill ggated
```

Poof! Your network devices are no longer exported.

Oops! Rescuing geom_gate

Suppose you weren't quite done with geom_gate when you killed it. For example, I unmounted */cdrom* before destroying */dev/ggate0*, but I still had */dev/ggate3* mounted at */mnt*. I cannot access that partition now, I cannot unmount it, and if I try to copy data to it, the command hangs. What to do? ggatec(8) has a rescue command for exactly this sort of situation. Restart ggated(8) on the server and then start a new ggatec(8) process on the client.

The syntax for rescue is much like that for create, except that you can specify a ggate device node number. Here we reactivate */dev/ggate3* for our */mnt* mount point:

```
# ggatedc rescue -o rw -u 3 sardines /dev/da0s1a
```

There. Now, nobody needs to know that you goofed!

Mirroring Disks Across the Network

Two servers can share a single disk image. When data is written to one disk, it is transparently copied to the other. You can use this to achieve a certain degree of high availability with commodity hardware. Use ggated(8) to provide disk exporting and gmirror(8) to handle the replication.

Remember that network speed is much lower than disk speed, and that mirroring disks across the network is a bad choice for I/O-intensive applications. For example, as you read this, I expect 3Gbps SATA-II disks to be common. That's three gigabits a second, or three times the speed of a gigabit network! When combined with the fact that not all gigabit network hardware actually runs at gigabit speeds, if you're actually using those 3Gbps of disk I/O, a networked backup will sadly disappoint you. For low-I/O applications, however, a network-mirrored disk of vital data might be useful.

In the example below, we mirror a 100MB file-backed filesystem across the network. This is large enough to be useful for, say, a small database, but small enough to run on my modest network.

Backup Server Setup

Create a 100MB file on one server and then copy it to the other server. This way, you start with the same data file on both sides, hopefully reducing the initial synchronization time. The simplest way to create a file of a given size is with truncate(1):[8]

```
# truncate -s100m /var/db/dbmirrorbackup.img
```

truncate(1)'s -s flag dictates the size of the file to create. You can use k for KB, m for MB, or G for GB. (You can also use t for TB, but we don't quite have disks of that size. Yet.)

Now, configure */etc/gg.exports* to allow our primary server to access this disk image. The primary server (in this example, at 192.168.1.2) needs read/write privileges on this device:

```
192.168.1.2  RW      /var/db/dbmirrorbackup.img
```

Now start ggated(8). Your backup server is ready.

---

[8] If truncate(1) is the easiest way to make a file, why did I make you use dd(1) back in Chapter 8? Because you need to know dd(1). It was for your own good.

Primary Server Setup

The primary server is slightly more complicated—but not by much. First, attach a ggate device to the remote file:

```
# ggatec create backupserver /var/db/dbmirror.img
ggate0
```

Our remote filesystem file is available locally as */dev/ggate0*. Now, load gmirror(8) and label the ggate device as a mirror. Here, our mirror device is called remotemirror0:

```
# gmirror load
# gmirror label remotemirror0 /dev/ggate0
```

We now have a mirror device. We need a local filesystem file, created just like the backup filesystem:

```
# truncate -s100m /var/db/dbmirrorprimary.img
```

Attach the local file to a memory device, so it gets a device node, and then insert that device node into the mirror:

```
# mdconfig -a -t vnode -f /var/db/dbmirrorprimary.img
md0
# gmirror insert remotemirror0 /dev/md0
```

You'll see that the mirror quickly becomes up to date. There's no data in it, after all!

```
# gmirror status
                   Name     Status   Components
mirror/remotemirror0   DEGRADED   ggate0
                                   md0 (33%)
```

When the mirror is up to date, which should not take more than a couple of minutes for a filesystem of this size, use newfs(8) and mount it:

```
# newfs -U /dev/mirror/remotemirror0
# mount /dev/mirror/remotemirror0 /database
```

You now have a distributed mirror mounted on */database*.

Depending on your system load and the throughput on this network-mirrored disk, you might find it useful to mount the disk noatime to minimize disk writes.

Mirror Failover and Recovery

The purpose of a mirrored disk is to allow you to recover data after a disk failure, and the purpose of mirroring a disk across the network is to allow you to recover after a server failure. You can use heartbeat (*/usr/ports/sysutils/heartbeat*) in combination with mirrored disks to create a low-cost, high-availability solution, automatically making one system take over when the other fails. With heartbeat, one system watches another and can take over operations when the master system disappears.

Your client machine would be the primary server and would handle system activity most of the time. In the event of a system failure, however, the backup machine takes on the role of the master machine. The backup machine can activate its copy of the mirror with mdconfig(8) and mount(8):

```
# mdconfig -a -t vnode -f dbmirrorbackup.img
md0
# fsck -B /dev/md0
# mount /dev/md0 /database
```

You can then activate your database server program and start using the data on the mirrored partition.

When the master system recovers, it reattaches the backup file as a ggate device, relabels the mirror, inserts the local partition into the mirror, and lets the mirror rebuild from the backup. Once the mirror is completely rebuilt, heartbeat can switch services back to the master machine. Scripting and automating failover are not terribly difficult but highly implementation- and environment-dependent, so we'll have to leave that for you.

High availability like this works best if you use a transactional database, such as PostgreSQL as opposed to MySQL. It's also best if you can keep the amount of "live" data on your mirrored partition to a minimum, relying on periodically archiving data to the other server's remote disk. High availability requires careful application design and should not be taken lightly.

This concludes our tour of the most popular GEOM modules. While you'll find several other modules of interest in FreeBSD, with the background you've gained from this chapter deploying any of them will be fairly straightforward and pain free. Let's move on into a topic near every system administrator's heart: performance.

19

SYSTEM PERFORMANCE AND MONITORING

Even if "It's slow!" is not the most dreaded phrase a system administrator will ever hear, it's pretty far up on that list. The user doesn't know why the system is slow and probably can't even quantify or qualify the problem any further than that. It just *feels* slow. Usually there's no test case, no set of reproducible steps, and nothing particularly wrong. A slowness complaint can cause hours of work as you dig through the system trying to find problems that might or might not even exist. One phrase is more dreadful still, especially after you've invested those hours of work: "It's still slow."

An inexperienced system administrator accelerates slow systems by buying faster hardware. This exchanges "speed problems" for costly parts and even more expensive time. Upgrades just let you conceal problems without actually using the hardware you already own, and sometimes they don't even solve the problem at all.

FreeBSD includes many tools designed to help you examine system performance and provide the information necessary to learn what's actually slowing things down. Once you understand where a problem is, identifying the solution to the problem becomes much simpler. You might actually need faster hardware, but sometimes shifting system load or reconfiguring software might solve the problem at much less expense. In either case, the first step is understanding the problem.

Computer Resources

Performance problems are usually caused by running more tasks than the computer can handle. That seems obvious, but think about it a moment. What does that really mean?

A computer has four basic resources: input/output, network bandwidth, memory, and CPU. If any one of them is filled to capacity, the others cannot be used to their maximum. For example, your CPU might very well be waiting for a disk to deliver data or for a network packet to arrive. If you upgrade your CPU to make your system faster, you will be disappointed. Buying a whole new server might fix the problem, but only by expanding the existing bottleneck. The new system probably has more memory, faster disks, a better network card, and faster processors than the old one. You have deferred the problem until the performance reaches some new limit. However, by identifying where your system falls short and addressing that particular need, you can stretch your existing hardware much further. After all, why purchase a whole new system when a few gigabytes of relatively inexpensive memory would fix the problem? (Of course, if your goal is to retire this "slow" system to make it your new desktop, that's another matter.)

Input/output is a common bottleneck. A PCI bus has a maximum throughput, and while you might not be pushing your disk or your network to their limits, you might be saturating the PCI bus by heavily using them both simultaneously.

One common cause of system slowdowns is running multiple large programs simultaneously. For example, I once thoughtlessly scheduled a massive database log rotation that moved and compressed gigabytes of data at the same time as the daily periodic(8) run. Since the job required shutting down the main database and caused application downtime, speed was crucial. Both the database job and the periodic(8) run slowed unbearably. Rescheduling one of them made both jobs go more quickly.

We're going to look at several FreeBSD tools for examining system performance. Armed with that information, we'll consider how to fix performance issues. Each potential bottleneck can be evaluated with the proper tools. FreeBSD changes continually, so later systems might have new tuning options and performance features. Read tuning(7) on your system for current performance tips.

Checking the Network

If your system's slowness stems from network problems, you need more bandwidth or you must make better use of the bandwidth you have. This can be summarized as, "You can't fit ten pounds of bandwidth in a five-pound circuit." If your T1 is full, making everything else slow, stop filling it!

To check for bandwidth problems, begin by monitoring how much bandwidth your system is using. Consult netstat -m and netstat -s, and look for errors or places where you're out of memory or buffers. Use a packet sniffer or Netflow to catch your big traffic generators, and use MRTG or Cricket to track utilization on a long-term basis.

Other system conditions are much more complicated. Start by checking where the problem lies with vmstat(8).

General Bottleneck Analysis with vmstat(8)

FreeBSD includes several programs for examining system performance. Among these are vmstat(8), iostat(8), and systat(1). We'll discuss vmstat because I find it most helpful; iostat(8) is similar to vmstat(8), and systat(1) provides the same information in an ASCII graphical format.

vmstat(8) shows the current virtual memory statistics. While its output takes getting used to, vmstat(8) is very good at showing large amounts of data in a small space. Type **vmstat** at the command prompt and follow along.

```
# vmstat
procs      memory      page                    disks  faults      cpu
r b w    avm     fre   flt  re  pi  po    fr  sr ad0   in    sy    cs us sy id
3 0 0  580416 1388912  234  11   7   0   209   0   0  171  5796  3816  3 10 87
```

vmstat divides its display into six sections: process (procs), memory, paging (page), disks, faults, and cpu. We'll look at all of them quickly and then discuss in detail those parts that are the most important for investigating performance issues.

Processes

vmstat(8) has three columns under the procs heading.

r The number of processes that are blocked waiting for CPU time. These processes are ready to run but cannot get access to the CPU. If this number is high, your CPU is the bottleneck.

b The number of processes that are blocked waiting for system input or output—generally, waiting for disk access. These processes will run as soon as they get their data. If this number is high, your disk is the bottleneck.

w The number of processes that are runnable but are entirely swapped out. If you regularly have processes swapped out, your memory is inadequate for the work you are doing on the system.

Memory

FreeBSD breaks memory up into chunks called *pages*. These pages, allocated to processes, are all of uniform size. The size of a page is hardware- and OS-dependent. The system treats each page as a whole—if FreeBSD must shift memory into swap, for example, it does that on a page-by-page basis. The memory section has two columns.

avm The average number of pages of virtual memory that are in use. If this value is abnormally high or increasing, your system is actively consuming swap space.

fre The number of memory pages available for use. If this value is abnormally low, you have a memory shortage.

Paging

The page section shows how hard the virtual memory system is working. The inner workings of the virtual memory system are an arcane science that I won't describe in detail here.

flt The number of page faults, where information needed was not in real memory and had to be fetched from swap space or disk.

re The number of pages that have been reclaimed or reused from cache.

pi Short for *pages in;* this is the number of pages being moved from real memory to swap.

po Short for *pages out;* this is the number of pages being moved from swap to real memory.

fr How many pages are freed per second.

sr How many pages are scanned per second.

Moving memory into swap is not bad, but consistently recovering paged-out memory indicates a memory shortage. Having high fr and flt values can indicate lots of short-lived processes—for example, a CGI script that starts many other processes or a cron job scheduled too frequently.

Disks

The disks section shows each of your disks by device name. The number shown is the number of disk operations per second, a valuable clue to determining how well your disks are handling their load. You should divide your disk operations between different disks whenever possible and arrange them on different buses when you can. If one disk is obviously busier than the others, and the system has operations waiting for disk access, consider moving some frequently accessed files from one disk to another. One common cause of high disk load is a coredumping program that can restart itself. For example, a faulty CGI script that dumps core every time someone clicks on a link will greatly increase your disk load.

If you have a lot of disks, you might notice that they don't all appear on the vmstat display. vmstat(8) is designed for 80-column display and therefore cannot list every disk on a large system. If, however, you have a wider display and don't mind exceeding the 80-column limit, use the -n flag to set the number of drives you want to display.

Faults

Faults are not bad; they're just received system traps and interrupts. An abnormally large number of faults is bad, of course—but before you tackle this problem, you need to know what's normal for your system.

in   The number of system interrupts (IRQ requests) received in the last five seconds.

sy   The number of system calls in the last five seconds.

cs   The number of context switches in the last second, or a per-second average since the last update. (For example, if you have vmstat update its display every five seconds, this column displays the average number of context switches per second over the last five seconds.)

CPU

Finally, the cpu section shows how much time the system spent doing user tasks (us), system tasks (sy), and how much time it spent idle (id). top(1) presents this same information in a friendlier format, but only for the current time, whereas vmstat lets you view system utilization over time.

Using vmstat

So, how do you use all this information? Start by checking the first three columns to see what the system is waiting for. If you're waiting for CPU access (the r column), then you're short on CPU horsepower. If you're waiting for disk access (the b column), then your disks are the bottleneck. If you're swapping (the w column), you're short on memory. Use the other columns to explore these three types of shortages in more detail.

Continuous vmstat

You're probably more interested in what's happening over time, rather than in a brief snapshot of system performance. Use vmstat's -w flag and a number to run it as an ongoing display updating every so many seconds. FreeBSD recalculates its virtual memory paging counters every five seconds, but other counters are updated continuously:

```
# vmstat -w 5
 procs      memory      page                    disks     faults         cpu
 r b w     avm    fre   flt  re  pi  po    fr   sr ad0 ad4   in   sy   cs us sy id
 1 1 0  184180  12876     8   0   0   0    30   11   0   0 1143  122  517  0  1 99
 0 1 0  184180   8360     1   0   0   0   260    0 373   0 1513  419 2287  0  5 95
 0 1 0  184180   7984     0   0   0   0   224    0 387   1 1528  428 2318  0  5 95
 0 1 0  184180  14892     0   0   0   0    62  346 188   1 1328  221 1322  0  3 96
...
```

Every five seconds, an updated line appears at the end. You can sit there and watch how your system's performance changes when scheduled jobs kick off or when you start particular programs. Hit CTRL-C when you're done. In this example, processes are sometimes waiting for CPU time (as shown by the occasional 1 in the r column), but we have something waiting for disk access all the time.

An occasional wait for a system resource doesn't mean you must upgrade your hardware; if performance is acceptable, don't worry about it. Otherwise, however, you must look further. In this case, I'm looking at vmstat(8) because someone reported a performance problem. vmstat(8) shows that something is waiting for disk all of the time. Let's see just how busy our disks are.

Disk I/O

We looked at disk management in Chapter 8, and again in Chapter 18. When it comes to performance, disk speed is a common bottleneck. If programs repeatedly wait for disk activity to complete before proceeding, they run more slowly. This is commonly called *blocking on disk*, meaning that the disk is preventing program activity. The only real solution for this is to use faster disks, install more disks, or reschedule the load.

While FreeBSD provides several tools to check disk activity, my favorite is gstat(8), so we'll use that. Just enter gstat without arguments for a display that updates every second or so:

```
 L(q)  ops/s    r/s   kBps   ms/r    w/s   kBps   ms/w   %busy Name
    0      0      0      0    0.0      0      0    0.0     0.0| ❶ad0s1b.eli
```

1	213	211	1066	4.6	2	4	9.2	97.9|	❷ad0
0	0	0	0	0.0	0	0	0.0	0.0|	acd0
1	213	211	1066	4.7	2	4	9.2	98.0|	❸ad0s1
0	0	0	0	0.0	0	0	0.0	0.0|	ad0s1a
0	0	0	0	0.0	0	0	0.0	0.0|	ad0s1b
0	0	0	0	0.0	0	0	0.0	0.0|	ad0s1c
0	0	0	0	0.0	0	0	0.0	0.0|	ad0s1d
0	2	0	0	0.0	2	4	9.2	0.9|	ad0s1e
1	211	211	1066	4.7	0	0	0.0	98.2|	❹ad0s1f

We see a line for each disk device, slice, and partition, and various information for each. gstat(8) shows all sorts of good stuff, such as the number of reads per second (r/s), writes per second (w/s), the kilobytes per second of reading and writing, as well as the number of milliseconds each read or write takes. The first thing to look for is the %busy column, second from the right.

The swap space partition ❶, our first entry, is idle. Disk ad0 ❷ is running at 97 percent of capacity, however. No wonder our system feels slow! Slightly further down, we see that the big disk activity on disk ad0 is actually concentrated on slice ad0s1 ❸. Most of the slices are idle, and there's just a smidge of activity on ad0s1e. Partition ad0s1f ❹, however, is *very* busy, at 98.2 percent utilization and hundreds of reads per second. Checking */etc/fstab* or mount(8) shows that ad0s1f is */usr* on this server. Something is reading lots and lots of data from this disk . . . but what? To find out, we need other tools.

CPU, Memory, and I/O with top(1)

The top(1) tool provides a good overview of system status, displaying information about CPU, memory, and disk usage. Just type top to get a full-screen display of system performance data. The display updates every two seconds, so you have a fairly accurate, close to real-time system view.

```
❶last pid:    977;  ❷load averages:  1.14,  0.80,  0.18    ❸up 0+00:18:03  18:30:34
❹41 processes:  2 running, 39 sleeping
❺CPU states:  0.0% user,  0.0% nice,  2.1% system,  0.0% interrupt, 97.9% idle
❻Mem: 106M Active, 139M Inact, 130M Wired, 8164K Cache, 68M Buf, 1607M Free
❼Swap: 4096M Total, 4096M Free

PID USERNAME    THR PRI NICE    SIZE    RES STATE  C   TIME  WCPU COMMAND
840 mwlucas       1  96    0    278M 24740K select 1   0:33  1.76% Xorg
873 mwlucas       1  96    0    113M 81916K CPU0   0   0:51  0.59% acroread
903 mwlucas       6  20    0    169M   103M kserel 0   0:31  0.00% soffice.bin
853 mwlucas       1  96    0   7924K  6608K select 1   0:04  0.00% wmaker
762 root          1  96    0   3208K   964K select 1   0:02  0.00% moused
859 mwlucas       1   4    0  18496K 10544K select 0   0:00  0.00% yank
...
```

Very tightly packed, isn't it? top(1) crams as much data as possible into a standard 80 × 25 terminal window or X terminal. Let's take this apart and learn how to read it.

PID Values

Every process on a Unix machine has a unique *process ID*, or *PID*. Whenever a new process starts, the kernel assigns it a PID one greater than the previous process. The last PID value is the last process ID assigned by the system. In the previous example, our last PID is 977 ❶. The next process created will be 978, then 979, and so on. Watch this number to see how fast the system changes. If the system is running through PIDs more quickly than usual, it might indicate a process forking beyond control[1] or something crashing and restarting.

Load Average

The *load average* ❷ is a somewhat vague number that offers a rough impression of the amount of CPU load on the system. The load average is the average number of threads waiting for CPU time. (Other operating systems have different load average calculation methods.) An acceptable load average depends on your system. If the numbers are abnormally high, you need to investigate. Many Pentiums feel bogged down at a load average of 3, while some modern systems are still snappy with a load average of 10.

top(1) lists three load averages. The first (1.14 in our example) is the load average over the last minute, the second (0.80) is for the last five minutes, and the last (0.18) is for the last 15 minutes. If your 15-minute load average is high, but the 1-minute average is low, you had a major activity spike that has since subsided. On the other hand, if the 15-minute value is low but the 1-minute average is high, something happened within the last 60 seconds and might still be going on now. If all of the load averages are high, the condition has persisted for at least 15 minutes.

Uptime

The last entry on the first line is the *uptime* ❸, or how long the system has been running. This system has been running for 18 minutes, and the current time is 18:30:34. I'll leave it up to you to calculate when I booted this system.

Process Counts

On the second line, you'll find information about the processes currently running on the system ❹. Running processes are actually doing work—they're answering user requests, processing mail, or doing whatever your system does. Sleeping processes are waiting for input from one source or another; they are just fine. You should expect a fairly large number of sleeping processes at any time. Processes in other states are usually waiting for a resource to become available or are hung in some way. Large numbers of non-sleeping, non-running processes hint at trouble. The ps(1) command shows the state of all processes.

---

[1] Some users actually try to consume system resources by starting too many programs. This is called *forkbombing*. These users are like script kiddies, but not as educated and without the sense of self-preservation.

Process Types

The CPU states line ❷ indicates what percentage of available CPU time the system spends handling different types of processes. It shows five different process types: user, nice, system, interrupt, and idle.

The user processes are average everyday programs—perhaps daemons run by root, or commands run by regular users, or whatever. If it shows up in ps -ax, it's a user process.

The nice processes are user processes whose priority has been deliberately manipulated. We'll look at this in detail in "Reprioritizing with Niceness" on page 584.

The system value gives the total percentage of CPU time spent by FreeBSD running kernel processes and the userland processes in the kernel. These include things such as virtual memory handling, networking, writing to disk, debugging with INVARIANTS and WITNESS, and so on.

The interrupt value shows how much time the system spends handling interrupt requests (IRQs).

Last, the idle entry shows how much time the system spends doing nothing. If your CPU regularly has a very low idle time, you might want to think about rescheduling jobs or getting a faster processor.

TOP AND SMP

On an SMP system, top(1) displays the average use among all the processors. You might have one processor completely tied up compiling something, but if the other processor is idle, top(1) shows the CPU usage of only 50 percent.

Memory

The Mem line ❻ represents the usage of physical RAM. FreeBSD breaks memory usage into several different categories.

Active memory is the total amount of memory in use by user processes. When a program ends, the memory it had used is placed into *inactive memory* and the data pulled from the disk is put into *cache memory*. If the system has to run this program again, it can retrieve the software from memory instead of disk.

Similarly, the Buf entry shows the size of the memory buffer. This buffer contains most of the data recently read from the disk. The memory in Buf is actually a subset of the active, inactive, and cache entries, not an entirely separate category.

Free memory is totally unused. It might be memory that has never been accessed, or it might be memory released by a process. This system has 1,607MB of free RAM. If you have a server that's been up for months, and it still has free memory, you might consider putting some of that RAM in a machine that's hurting for memory. This top(1) snapshot comes from my laptop, which needs every bit of RAM it can get just on general principles.

FreeBSD will shuffle memory between the inactive, cache, and free categories as needed to maintain a pool of available memory. Memory in the cache is most easily transferred to the free pool. When cache memory gets low and FreeBSD needs still more free memory, it picks pages from the inactive pool, verifies that it can use them as free memory, and moves them to the free pool. FreeBSD tries to keep the total number of free and cache pages above the sysctl vm.v_free_target. (Remember, the page size is given by the sysctl hw.pagesize which is 4,096 on i386 and amd64 systems.)

This means that having free memory does not mean that your system has enough memory. If vmstat(8) shows that you are swapping at all, you are out of memory. You might have a program that releases memory on a regular basis. Also, FreeBSD will move some pages from cache to free in an effort to maintain a certain level of free memory.

FreeBSD uses *wired* memory for in-kernel data structures, as well as for system calls that must have a particular piece of memory immediately available. Wired memory is never swapped or paged.

Swap

The Swap line ❼ gives the total swap available on the system and how much is in use. Swapping is using the disk drive as additional memory. We'll look at swap in more detail later in the chapter.

Process List

Finally, top(1) lists the processes on the system and their basic characteristics. The table format is designed to present as much information as possible in as little space as possible. Every process has its own line.

PID   First, we have the process ID number, or PID. Every running process has its own unique PID. When you use kill(1), specify the process by its PID. (If you don't know the PID of a process, you can use pkill(1) to kill the process by its name.)

Username   Next is the username of the user running the process. If multiple processes consume large amounts of CPU or memory, and they are all owned by the same user, you know who to talk to.

Priority and niceness   The PRI (priority) and NICE columns are interrelated and indicate how much precedence the system gives each process. We'll talk about priority and niceness a little later in this chapter.

Size   Size gives the amount of memory that the system has set aside for this process.

Resident memory   The RES column shows how much of a program is actually in memory at the moment. A program might reserve a huge amount of memory, but only use a small fraction of that reservation at any time. For example, as I type this, my OpenOffice.org program has allocated 169MB but is only using 103MB. (As an interesting side note, X.org's memory usage includes the memory on your video card, which is separate from your main system memory.)

State   The STATE column shows what a process is doing at the moment. A process can be in a variety of states—waiting for input, sleeping until something wakes it, actively running, and so on. You can see the name of the system call a process is waiting on, such as select, pause, or ttyin. On an SMP system, when a process runs you'll see the CPU it's running on. In our example output, acroread is running on CPU0.

Time   The TIME column shows the total amount of CPU time the process has consumed.

WCPU   The weighted CPU usage shows the percentage of CPU time that the process uses, adjusted for the process's priority and niceness.

Command   Finally, we have the name of the program that's running.

Looking at top(1)'s output gives you an idea of where the system is spending its time.

top(1) and I/O

In addition to the standard CPU display, top(1) has an I/O mode that displays which processes are using the disk most actively. While top(1) is running, hit M to enter the I/O mode. The upper portion of the display still shows memory, swap, and CPU status, but the lower portion changes considerably.

PID	USERNAME	VCSW	IVCSW	READ	WRITE	FAULT	TOTAL	PERCENT	COMMAND
3064	root	89	0	89	0	0	89	100.00%	tcsh
767	root	0	0	0	0	0	0	0.00%	nfsd
1082	mwlucas	2	1	0	0	0	0	0.00%	sshd
1092	root	0	0	0	0	0	0	0.00%	tcsh
904	root	0	0	0	0	0	0	0.00%	sendmail
...									

The PID is the process ID, of course, and the USERNAME column shows who is running the process.

VCSW stands for *voluntary context switches*; this is the number of times this process has surrendered the system to other processes. IVCSW means *involuntary context switches* and shows how often the kernel has told the process, "You're done now, it's time to let someone else run for a while."

Similarly, READ and WRITE show how many times the system has read from disk and written to disk. The FAULT column shows how often this process has had to pull memory pages from swap, which makes for another sort of disk read. These last three columns are aggregated in the TOTAL column.

The PERCENT column shows what percent of disk activity this process is using. Unlike gstat(8), top(1) displays each process's utilization as a percentage of the actual disk activity, rather than the possible disk activity. If you have only one process accessing the disk, top(1) displays that process as using 100 percent of disk activity, even if it's only sending a trickle of data. gstat(8) tells you how busy the disk is, but top(1) tells you what's generating that disk activity and where to place the blame. Here we see that process ID 3064 is generating all of our disk activity. It's a tcsh(1) process, also known as "some user's shell." Let's track down the miscreant.

Following Processes

On any Unix-like system, every userland process has a parent-child relationship with other processes. When FreeBSD boots, it creates a single process by starting init(8) and assigning it PID 1. This process starts other processes, such as the */etc/rc* startup script and the getty(8) program that handles your login request. These processes are children of process ID 1. When you log in, getty(8) starts a new shell for you, making your shell a child of the getty process. Commands you run are either children of your shell process or part of your shell. You can view these parent-child relationships with ps(1) using the -ajx flags (among others).

```
# ps -ajx
USER       PID  PPID  PGID   SID JOBC STAT  TT       TIME COMMAND
root         0     0     0     0    0 WLs   ??    0:00.01 [swapper]
root         1     0     1     1    0 ILs   ??    0:00.01 /sbin/init --
root         2     0     0     0    0 DL    ??    0:00.79 [g_event]
...
haldaemon  826     1   826   826    0 Ss    ??    0:02.80 /usr/local/sbin/hald
root       827   826   826   826    0 I     ??    0:00.06 hald-runner
...
```

At the far left we have the username of the process owner, then the PID and parent PID (PPID) of the process. This is the most useful thing we see here, but we'll briefly cover the other fields.

The PGID is the process group ID number, which is normally inherited from its parent process. A program can start a new process group, and that new process group will have a PGID equal to the process ID. Process groups are used for signal processing and job control. A session ID, or SID, is a grouping of PGIDs, usually started by a single user or daemon. Processes may not migrate from one SID to another. JOBC gives the job control count, indicating if the process is running under job control (i.e., in the background).

STAT shows the process state—exactly what the process is doing at the moment you run ps(1). Process state is very useful as it tells you if a process is idle, what it's waiting for, and so on. I highly recommend reading the section on process state from ps(1).

TT lists the process's controlling terminal. This column shows only the end of the terminal name, such as v0 for ttyv0 or p0 for ttyp0. The example shows only processes without a controlling terminal, indicated by ??, but we'll see another example with terminals shortly.

The TIME column shows how much processor time the process has used, both in userland and in the kernel.

Finally, we see the COMMAND name, as it was called by the parent process. Processes in square brackets are actually kernel threads, not real processes.

So, how can this help us track a questionable process? In our top(1) I/O example, we saw that process 3064 was generating almost all of our disk activity. Run **ps -ajx** and look for this process:

```
...
  root     3035 3034 3035 2969  1 S+   p0  0:00.03 _su -m (tcsh)
❶ chris    2981 2980 2981 2981  0 Is   p1  0:00.03 -tcsh (tcsh)
❷ root     2989 2981 2989 2981  1 I    p1  0:00.01 su -m
❸ root     2990 2989 2990 2981  1 D    p1  0:00.05 _su -m (tcsh)
❹ root     3064 2990 3064 2981  1 DV+  p1  0:00.15 _su -m (tcsh)
  mwlucas  2996 2995 2996 2996  0 Is   p2  0:00.02 -tcsh (tcsh)
...
```

Our process of interest ❹ is owned by root and is a tcsh(1) instance, just as top's I/O mode said. It's actually running under su(1), however, which means that there's a real person behind this performance problem. Process 3064 is a child of process 2990 ❸, which is a child of process 2989 ❷, both of which are owned by root. Process 2989 is a child of 2981 ❶, however, which is a shell run by a real user. You might also note that these processes are all parts of session 2981, showing that they're probably all run in the same login session. The TT column shows p1, which means that the user is logged in on /dev/ttyp1, the second virtual terminal on this machine.

It's normal for a system to experience brief periods of total utilization. If nobody else is using the system and nobody's complaining about performance, why not let this user run his job? If this process is causing problems for other users, however, we can either deprioritize it, use our root privileges to kill the job, or show up at the user's cubicle with a baseball bat.

Paging and Swapping

Using swap space isn't bad in and of itself, as FreeBSD uses swap as virtual memory. Swap space is much slower than chip memory, but it does work, and many programs don't need to have everything in RAM in order to run. A typical program spends 80 percent of its time running 20 percent of its code. Much of the rest of its code covers startup and shutdown, error handling, and so on. You can safely let those bits go to swap space with minimal performance impact.

Swap caches data that it has handled. Once a process uses swap, that swap remains in use until the process either exits or calls the memory back from swap.

Swap usage occurs through *paging* and *swapping*. Paging is all right; swapping is not so good, but it's better than crashing.

Paging

Paging occurs when FreeBSD moves a portion of a running program into swap space. Paging can actually improve performance on a heavily loaded system because unused bits can be stored on disk until they're needed—if ever. FreeBSD can then use the real memory for actual running code. Does it really matter if your system puts your database startup code to swap once the database is up and running?

Swapping

If the computer doesn't have enough physical memory to store a process that isn't being run at that particular microsecond, the system can move the entire process to swap. When the scheduler starts that process again, FreeBSD fetches the entire process from swap and runs it, probably consigning some other process to swap.

The problem with swapping is that disk usage goes through the roof and performance drops dramatically. Since requests take longer to handle, there are more requests on the system at any one time. Logging in to check the problem only makes the situation worse, because your login is just one more process. Some systems can handle certain amounts of swapping, while on others the situation can quickly degenerate into a death spiral.

When your CPU is overloaded, the system is slow. When your disks are a bottleneck, the system is slow. Memory shortages can actually crash your computer. If you're swapping, you *must* buy more memory or resign yourself to appalling performance.

vmstat(8) specifically shows the number of processes swapped out at any one time.

Performance Tuning

FreeBSD caches recently accessed data in memory because a surprising amount of information is read from the disk time and time again. If this information is cached in physical memory, it can be accessed very quickly. If the system needs more memory, it dumps the oldest cached chunks in favor of new data.

For example, the top(1) output we're discussing is from my laptop. On it, I had started Firefox so I could check my comics.[2] The disk had to work for a moment or two to read in the program. I then shut the browser off so I could focus on my work, but FreeBSD leaves Firefox in the system buffer cache. If I start Firefox again, FreeBSD will just pull it from memory instead of troubling the disk, which dramatically reduces its startup time. Had I started another large process, FreeBSD would have dumped the web browser from the cache to read in the new program.

---

[2] Sluggy Freelance (*http://www.sluggy.com*), Help Desk (*http://www.ubersoft.net*), and User Friendly (*http://www.userfriendly.org*), if anyone cares. Fear the bunny.

If your system is operating well, you will have at least a few megabytes of free memory. The sysctls `vm.v_free_target` and `hw.pagesize` tell you how much free memory FreeBSD thinks it needs on your system. If you consistently have more memory than these two sysctls multiplied, your system is not being used to its full potential. For example, on my laptop I have:

```
# sysctl vm.v_free_target
vm.v_free_target: 13745
# sysctl hw.pagesize
hw.pagesize: 4096
```

My system wants to have at least $13,745 \times 4,096 = 56,299,520$ bytes, or about 54MB, of free memory. I could lose a gigabyte of RAM from my laptop without flinching, if it wasn't for the fact that I suffer deep-seated emotional trauma about insufficient RAM.

Memory Usage

If you have a lot of memory in cache or buffer, you don't have a memory shortage. You might make good use of more memory, but it isn't strictly necessary. If you have low free memory, but a lot of active and wired memory, your system is devouring RAM. Adding memory would let you take advantage of the buffer cache.

When you're out of free space and have little or no memory in cache or buffer, investigate your memory use further. You might well have a memory shortage. Once you start to use swap, this memory shortage is no longer hypothetical.

Swap Space Usage

Swap space helps briefly cover RAM shortages. For example, if you're untarring a huge file you might easily consume all of your physical memory and start using virtual memory. It's not worth buying more RAM for such occasional tasks when swap suffices.

In short, swap space is like wine. A glass or two now and then won't hurt you and might even be a good choice. Hitting the bottle constantly is a problem, however.

CPU Usage

A processor can only do so many things a second. If you run more tasks than your CPU can handle, requests will start to back up, you'll develop a processor backlog, and the system will slow down. That's CPU usage in a nutshell.

If performance is unacceptable and top(1) shows your CPU hovering around 100 percent all the time, CPU utilization is probably your problem. While new hardware is certainly an option, you do have other choices. For example, investigate the processes running on your system to see if they're all necessary. Did some junior sysadmin install a SETI@Home client

(*/usr/ports/astro/setiathome*) to hunt for aliens with your spare CPU cycles? Is anything running that was important at one time, but not any longer? Find and shut down those unnecessary processes, and make sure that they won't start the next time the system boots.

Once that's done, evaluate your system performance again. If you still have problems, try rescheduling or reprioritizing.

Rescheduling

Rescheduling is easier than reprioritizing; it is a relatively simple way to balance system processes so that they don't monopolize system resources. As discussed in Chapter 15, you and your users can schedule programs to run at specific times with cron(1). If you have users who are running massive jobs at particular times, you might consider using cron(1) to run them in off hours. Frequently, jobs such as the monthly billing database search can run between 6 PM and 6 AM and nobody will care—finance just wants the data on hand at 8 AM on the first day of the month, so they can close out last month's accounting. Similarly, you can schedule your make buildworld && make buildkernel at 1 AM.

Reprioritizing with Niceness

If rescheduling won't work, you're left with reprioritizing, which can be a little trickier. When reprioritizing, you tell FreeBSD to change the importance of a given process. For example, you can have a program run during busy hours, but only when nothing else wants to run. You've just told that program to be *nice* and step aside for other programs.

The nicer a process is, the less CPU time it demands. The default niceness is 0, but niceness runs from 20 (very nice) to -20 (not nice at all). This might seem backwards; you could argue that a higher number should mean a higher priority. That would lead to a language problem, however; calling this factor "selfishness" or "crankiness" instead of "niceness" didn't seem like a good idea at the time.[3]

top(1) displays a PRI column for process priority. FreeBSD calculates a process's priority from a variety of factors, including niceness, and runs high-priority processes first whenever possible. Niceness affects priority, but you cannot directly edit priority.

If you know that your system is running at or near capacity, you can choose to run a command with nice(1) to assign the process a niceness. Specify niceness with nice -n and the nice value in front of the command. For example, to start a very selfish make buildworld at nice 15, you would run:

```
# nice -n 15 make buildworld
```

---

[3] Besides, "selfish" and "cranky" are already taken by the system administrators themselves.

Only root can assign a negative niceness to a program, as in `nice -n -5`. For example, if you have a critical kernel patch that must be applied urgently and you want the compile to finish as quickly as possible, use a negative niceness:

```
# cd /usr/src
# nice -n -20 make kernel
```

NICE VS. TCSH

The tcsh(1) shell has a nice command built in. That built-in nice uses the renice(8) syntax, which is different from nice(1). I'm sure there's a reason for that other than annoying tcsh users, but that rationale escapes me at the moment. If you specifically want to use nice(1), use the full path */usr/bin/nice*.

Usually, you don't have the luxury of telling a command to be nice when you start it, but instead have to change its niceness when you learn that it's absorbing all of your system capacity. renice(8) reprioritizes running processes by their process IDs or owners. To change the niceness of a process, run renice with the new niceness and the PID as arguments.

For example, one of my systems is a logging host that also runs several instances of softflowd(8), flow-capture, Nagios, and other critical network awareness systems. I also have other assorted pieces of software running on this system, such as a CVSup server for my internal hosts. If I find that intermittent load on the CVSup server is interfering with my Nagios-based network monitoring or my syslogd(8) server, I must take action. Renicing the cvsupd(8) server will make the clients run more slowly, but that's better than slowing down monitoring. Use pgrep(1) to find cvsupd(8)'s PID:

```
# pgrep cvsupd
993
# renice 10 993
993: old priority 0, new priority 10
```

Boom! FreeBSD now schedules the cvsupd process less often than other processes. This greatly annoys the users of that service, but since I'm the main user and I'm already annoyed that's all right.

To renice every process owned by a user, use the -u flag. For example, to make my processes more important than anyone else's, I could do this:

```
# renice -5 -u mwlucas
1001: old priority 0, new priority -5
```

The 1001 is my user ID on this system. Again, presumably I have a very good reason for doing this, beyond my need for personal power.[4] Similarly, if that user who gobbled up all my disk I/O insists on being difficult, I could make his processes very, very nice, which would probably solve other users' complaints.

Investigating Software

We've spent a lot of time discussing tuning FreeBSD to solve performance problems. That's only logical, as this is a FreeBSD book. Don't forget about your software, however! You can frequently solve performance problems by tweaking the software that's causing the problems. For example, I have a set of Perl CGI scripts that thrash disks and choke CPUs. A Google search showed that these scripts behave much better running under mod_perl2. I changed the web server configuration, and the problem went away. This is far, far easier than changing the operating system configuration.

THE BOTTLENECK SHUFFLE

Every system has bottlenecks. If you eliminate one bottleneck, performance will increase until another bottleneck is hit. The system's performance is bound by the slowest component in the computer. For example, a web server is frequently network-bound because the slowest part of the system is the Internet connection. If you upgrade your 1.5Mb/s T1 to a 2.4Gb/s OC-48, the system will hand out its sites as fast as its other components allow. The hypothetical "eliminating bottlenecks" that management often demands is really a case of "eliminating bottlenecks that interfere with your usual workload."

Now that you can look at system problems, let's learn how to hear what the system is trying to tell you.

Status Mail

If you look in */etc/crontab*, you'll see that FreeBSD runs maintenance jobs every day, week, and month through periodic(8). These jobs perform basic system checks and notify the administrators of changes, items requiring attention, and potential security issues. The output of each scheduled job is mailed daily to the root account on the local system. The simplest way to find out what your system is doing is to read this mail; many very busy system administrators just like you have collaborated to make these messages useful. While you might get a lot of these messages, with a little experience you'll learn how to skim the reports looking for critical or unusual changes only.

The configuration of the daily, weekly, and monthly reports is controlled in *periodic.conf*, as discussed in Chapter 10.

---

[4] Being selfish doesn't count as a good reason to renice -20 your processes. Or so I've been told.

You probably don't want to log in as root on all of your servers every day just to read email, so forward root's mail from every server to a centralized mailbox. Make this change in */etc/aliases*, as discussed in Chapter 16.

The only place where I recommend disabling these jobs is on embedded systems, which should be managed and monitored through some other means, such as your network monitoring system. On such a system, disable the periodic(8) checks in */etc/crontab*.

While these daily reports are useful, they don't tell the whole story. Logs give a much more complete picture.

Logging with syslogd

The FreeBSD logging system is terribly useful. Any Unix-like operating system allows you to log almost anything at almost any level of detail. While you'll find default system logging hooks for the most common system resources, you can choose a logging configuration that meets your needs. Almost all programs integrate with the logging daemon, syslogd(8).

The syslog protocol works through messages. Programs send individual messages, which the syslog daemon syslogd(8) catches and processes. syslogd(8) handles each message according to its facility and priority level, both of which client programs assign to messages. You must understand both facilities and levels to manage system logs.

Facilities

A *facility* is a tag indicating the source of a log entry. This is an arbitrary label, just a text string used to sort one program from another. In most cases, each program that needs a unique log uses a unique facility. Many programs or protocols have facilities dedicated to them—for example, FTP is such a common protocol than syslogd(8) has a special facility just for it. syslogd also supports a variety of generic facilities that you can assign to any program.

Here are the standard facilities and the types of information they're used for.

auth   Public information about user authorization, such as when people logged in or used su(1).

authpriv   Private information about user authorization, accessible only to root.

console   Messages normally printed to the system console.

cron   Messages from the system process scheduler.

daemon   A catch-all for all system daemons without other explicit handlers.

ftp   Messages from FTP and TFTP servers.

kern   Messages from the kernel.

lpr   Messages from the printing system.

mail   Mail system messages.

mark   This facility puts an entry into the log every 20 minutes. This is useful when combined with another log.

news   Messages from the Usenet News daemons.

ntp   Network Time Protocol messages.

security   Messages from security programs such as pfctl(8).

syslog   Messages from the log system about the log system itself. Don't log when you log, however, as that just makes you dizzy.

user   The catch-all message facility. If a userland program doesn't specify a logging facility, it uses this.

uucp   Messages from the Unix-to-Unix Copy Protocol. This is a piece of pre-Internet Unix history that you'll probably never encounter.

local0 through local7   These are provided for the system administrator. Many programs have an option to set a logging facility; choose one of these if at all possible. For example, you might tell your customer service system to log to local0.

While most programs have sensible defaults, it's your job as the system administrator to manage which programs log to which facility.

Levels

A log message's *level* represents its relative importance. While programs send all of their logging data to syslogd, most systems only record the important stuff that syslogd receives and discard the rest. Of course, one person's trivia is another's vital data, and that's where levels come in.

The syslog protocol offers eight levels. Use these levels to tell syslogd what to record and what to discard. The levels are, in order from most to least important:

emerg   System panic. Messages flash on every terminal. The computer is basically hosed. You don't even have to reboot—the system is doing it for you.[5]

alert   This is bad, but not an emergency. The system can continue to function, but this error should be attended to immediately.

crit   Critical errors include things such as bad blocks on a hard drive or serious software issues. You can continue to run as is, if you're brave.

err   These are errors that require attention at some point, but they won't destroy the system.

warning   These are miscellaneous warnings that probably won't stop the program that issued them from working just as it always has.

notice   This includes general information that probably doesn't require action on your part, such as daemon startup and shutdown.

---

[5] You might think this is funny now, but just wait until it happens to you.

info This includes program information, such as individual transactions in a mail server.

debug This level is usually only of use to programmers and occasionally to sysadmins who are trying to figure out why a program behaves as it does. Debugging logs can contain whatever information the programmer considered necessary to debug the code, which might include information that violates user privacy.

none This means, "Don't log anything from this facility." It's most commonly used to exclude information from wildcard entries, as we'll see shortly.

By combining level with priority, you can categorize messages quite narrowly and treat each one according to your needs.

Processing Messages with syslogd(8)

The syslogd(8) daemon catches messages from the network and compares them to entries in */etc/syslog.conf.* That file has two columns; the first describes the log message, either by facility and level, or by program name. The second tells syslogd(8) what to do when a log message matches the description. For example, look at this entry from the default *syslog.conf*:

```
mail.info                               /var/log/maillog
```

This tells syslogd(8) that when it receives a message from the `mail` facility with a level of `info` or higher, the message should be appended to */var/log/maillog.*

Wildcards

You can also use wildcards as an information source. For example, this line logs every message from the `mail` facility:

```
mail.*                                  /var/log/maillog
```

To log everything from everywhere, uncomment the `all.log` entry and create the file */var/log/all.log*:

```
*.*                                     /var/log/all.log
```

This works, but I find it too informative to be of any real use. You'll find yourself using complex grep(1) statements daisy-chained together to find even the simplest information. Also, this would include all sorts of private data.

Excluding Information

Use the none level to exclude information from a log. For example, here we exclude authpriv information from our all-inclusive log. The semicolon allows you to combine entries on a single line:

```
*.*; authpriv.none        /var/log/most.log
```

Comparison

You can also use the comparison operators < (less than), = (equals), and > (greater than) in *syslog.conf* rules. While syslogd defaults to recording all messages at the specified level or above, you might want to include only a range of levels. For example, you could log everything of info level and above to the main log file while logging the rest to the debug file:

```
mail.info                 /var/log/maillog
mail.=debug               /var/log/maillog.debug
```

The mail.info entry matches all log messages sent to the mail facility at info level and above. The second line only matches the messages that have a level of precisely debug. You can't use a simple mail.debug, because the debugging log will then duplicate the content of the previous log. This way, you don't have to sort through debugging information for basic mail logs, and you don't have to sort through mail transmission information to get your debugging output.

Local Facilities

Many programs offer to log via syslog. Most of these can be set to a facility of your choice. The various local facilities are reserved for these programs. For example, by default dhcpd(8) (see Chapter 15) logs to the facility local7. Here, we catch these messages and send them to their own file:

```
local7.*                  /var/log/dhcpd
```

If you run out of local facilities, you can use other facilities that the system is not using. For example, I've once used the uucp facility on a busy log server on a network that had no uucp services.

Logging by Program Name

If you're out of facilities, you can use the program's name as a matching term. An entry for a name requires two lines: the first line contains the program name with a leading exclamation mark and the second line sets up logging. For example, FreeBSD uses this to log ppp(8) information:

```
!ppp
*.*                       /var/log/ppp.log
```

The first line specifies the program name and the second one uses wildcards to tell syslogd(8) to append absolutely everything to a file.

The !*programname* syntax affects all lines after it, so you must put it last in *syslogd.conf.*

Logging to User Sessions

When you log to a user, any messages that arrive appear on that user's screen. To log to a user session, list usernames separated by commas as the destination. To write a message to all users' terminals, use an asterisk (*). For example, the default *syslog.conf* includes this line:

```
*.emerg                  *
```

This says that any message of emergency level will appear on all users' terminals. Since these messages usually say "Goodbye" in one way or another, that's appropriate.

Sending Log Messages to Programs

To direct log messages to a program, use a pipe symbol (|):

```
mail.*                   |/usr/local/bin/mailstats.pl
```

Logging to a Logging Host

My networks habitually have a single logging host that handles not only the FreeBSD boxes but also Cisco routers and switches, other Unix boxes, and any syslog-speaking appliances. This greatly reduces system maintenance and saves disk space. Each log message includes the hostname, so you can easily sort them out later.

Use the at symbol (@) to send messages to another host. For example, the following line dumps everything your local syslog receives to the logging host on my network:

```
*.*                      @loghost.blackhelicopters.org
```

The *syslog.conf* on the destination host determines the final destination for those messages.

On the logging host, you can separate logs by the host where the log message originated. Use the plus (+) symbol and the hostname to indicate that the rules that follow apply to this host:

```
+dhcpserver
local7.*         /var/log/dhcpd
+ns1
local7.*         /var/log/named
```

If you're using this configuration, I recommend placing your generic rules at the top of *syslog.conf* and per-host rules near the bottom.

Logging Overlap

syslog doesn't log on a first-match or last-match basis; instead, it logs according to every matching rule. This means you can easily have one log message in several different logs. Consider the following snippet of log configuration. (The first line is taken from the default FreeBSD *syslog.conf* but is trimmed to fit legibly on paper.)

```
*.notice;authpriv.none          /var/log/messages
local7.*                        /var/log/dhcp
```

Every message of level notice or more is logged to */var/log/messages*. We have our DHCP server logging to */var/log/dhcp*. This means that any DHCP messages of notice level or above will be logged to both */var/log/messages* and */var/log/dhcpd*. I don't like this; I want my DHCP messages only in */var/log/dhcpd*. I can deliberately exclude DHCP messages from */var/log/messages* by using the none facility:

```
*.notice;authpriv.none;local7.none      /var/log/messages
```

My */var/log/messages* syslog configuration frequently grows quite long as I exclude every local facility from it, but that's all right.

SPACES AND TABS

Traditional Unix-like operating systems require tabs between the columns in *syslog.conf*, but FreeBSD permits you to use spaces. Be sure to use only tabs if you share the same *syslog.conf* between different operating systems.

---

syslogd Customization

FreeBSD runs syslogd by default, and out of the box it can be used as a logging host. You can customize how it works through the use of command-line flags. You can specify flags either on the command line or in *rc.conf* as syslogd_flags.

Allowed Log Senders

You can specify exactly which hosts syslogd(8) accepts log messages from. This can be useful so you don't wind up accepting logs from random people on the Internet. While sending you lots of logs could be used to fill your hard drive as a preparation for an attack, it's more likely to be the result of a misconfiguration. Your log server should be protected by a firewall in any case. Use the -a flag to specify either the IP addresses or the network of hosts that can send you log messages, as these two (mutually exclusive) examples show:

```
syslogd_flags="-a 192.168.1.9"
syslogd_flags="-a 192.168.1.0/24"
```

While syslogd(8) would also accept DNS hostnames and domain names for this restriction, DNS is really an unsuitable access control device.

You can entirely disable accepting messages from remote hosts by specifying the -s flag, FreeBSD's default. If you use -ss instead, syslogd(8) also disables sending log messages to remote hosts. Using -ss removes syslogd(8) from the list of network-aware processes that show up in sockstat(1) and netstat(1). While this half-open UDP socket is harmless, some people feel better if syslogd(8) doesn't appear attached to the network at all.

Attach to a Single Address

syslogd(8) defaults to attaching to UDP port 514 on every IP address the system has. Your jail server needs syslogd, but a jail machine can only run daemons that bind to a single address. Use the -b flag to force syslogd(8) to attach to a single IP:

```
syslogd_flags="-b 192.168.1.1"
```

Additional Log Sockets

syslogd(8) can accept log messages via Unix domain sockets as well as over the network. The standard location for this is */var/run/log*. No chrooted processes on your system can access this location, however. If you want those chrooted processes to run, you must either configure them to log over the network or provide an additional logging socket for them. Use the -l flag for this and specify the full path to the additional logging socket:

```
syslogd_flags="-l /var/named/var/run/log"
```

The named(8) and ntpd(8) programs come with FreeBSD and are commonly chrooted. The */etc/rc.d/syslogd* is smart enough to add the appropriate syslogd sockets if you chroot these programs through *rc.conf*.

Verbose Logging

Logging with verbose mode (-v) prints the numeric facility and level of each message written in the local log. Using doubly verbose logging prints the name of the facility and level instead of the number:

```
syslogd_flags="-vv"
```

These are the flags I use most commonly. Read syslogd(8) for the complete list of options.

Log File Management

Log files grow, and you must decide how large they can grow before you trim them. The standard way to do this is through *log rotation*. When logs are rotated, the oldest log is deleted, the current log file is closed up and given a new name, and a new log file is created for new data. FreeBSD includes a basic log file processor, newsyslog(8), which also compresses files, restarts daemons, and in general handles all the routine tasks of log file shuffling. cron(1) runs newsyslog(8) once per hour.

When newsyslog(8) runs, it reads */etc/newsyslog.conf* and examines each log file listed therein. If the conditions for rotating the log are met, the log is rotated and other actions are taken as appropriate. */etc/newsyslog.conf* uses one line per log file; each line has seven fields, like this:

```
/var/log/ppp.log        root:network    640   3     100  *     JC
```

Let's examine each field in turn.

Log File Path

The first entry on each line (/var/log/ppp.log in the example) is the full path to the log file to be processed.

Owner and Group

The second field (root:network in our example) lists the rotated file's owner and group, separated by a colon. This field is optional and is not present in many of the standard entries.

newsyslog(8) can change the owner and group of old log files. By default, log files are owned by the root user and the wheel group. While it's not common to change the owner, you might need this ability on multi-user machines.

You can also choose to change only the owner, or only the group. In these cases, you use a colon with a name on only one side of it. For example, :www changes the group to www, while mwlucas: gives me ownership of the file.

Permissions

The third field (640 in our example) gives the permissions mode in standard Unix three-digit notation.

Count

This field specifies the oldest rotated log file that newsyslog(8) should keep. newsyslog(8) numbers archived logs from newest to oldest, starting with the newest as log 0. For example, with the default count of 5 for */var/log/messages*, you'll find the following message logs:

```
messages
messages.0.bz
messages.1.bz
messages.2.bz
messages.3.bz
messages.4.bz
messages.5.bz
```

Those of you who can count will recognize that this makes six archives, not five, plus the current log file, for a week of logs. As a rule, it's better to have too many logs than too few; however, if you're tight on disk space, deleting an extra log or two might buy you time.

Size

The fifth field (100 in our example) is the file size in kilobytes. When newsyslog(8) runs, it compares the size listed here with the size of the file. If the file is larger than the size given here, newsyslog(8) rotates the file. If you don't want the file size to affect when the file is rotated, put an asterisk here.

Time

So far this seems easy, right? The sixth field, rotation time, changes that. The time field has four different legitimate types of value: an asterisk, a number, and two different date formats.

If you rotate based on log size rather than age, put an asterisk here.

If you put a plain naked number in this field, newsyslog(8) rotates the log after that many hours have passed. For example, if you want the log to rotate every 24 hours but don't care about the exact time when that happens, put 24 here.

The date formats are a little more complicated.

ISO 8601 Time Format

Any entry beginning with an @ symbol is in the restricted ISO 8601 time format. This is a standard used by newsyslog(8) on most Unix-like systems; it was the time format used in MIT's primordial newsyslog(8). Restricted ISO 8601 is a bit obtuse, but every Unix-like operating system supports it.

A full date in the restricted ISO 8601 format is 14 digits with a T in the middle. The first four digits are the year, the next two the month, the next two the day of the month. The T is inserted in the middle as a sort of decimal point, separating whole days from fractions of a day. The next two digits are hours, the next two minutes, the last two seconds. For example, the date of March 2, 2008, 9:15 and 8 seconds PM is expressed in restricted ISO 8601 as 20080302T211508.

While complete dates in restricted ISO 8601 are fairly straightforward, confusion arises when you don't list the entire date. You can choose to specify only fields near the T, leaving fields further away as blank. Blank fields are wildcards. For example, 1T matches the first day of every month. 4T00 matches midnight of the fourth day of every month. T23 matches the twenty-third hour, or 11 PM, of every day. With a *newsyslog.conf* time of @T23, the log rotates every day at 11 PM.

As with cron(1), you must specify time units in detail. For example, @7T, the seventh day of the month, rotates the log once an hour, every hour, on the seventh day of the month. After all, it matches all day long! A time of

@7T01 would rotate the log at 1 AM on the seventh day of the month, which is probably more desirable. You don't need more detail than an hour, however, as newsyslog(8) only runs once an hour.

FreeBSD-Specific Time

The restricted ISO 8601 time system doesn't allow you to easily designate weekly jobs, and it's impossible to specify the last day of the month. That's why FreeBSD includes a time format that lets you easily perform these common tasks. Any entry with a leading cash sign ($) is written in the FreeBSD-specific *month week day* format.

    This format uses three identifiers: M (day of month), W (day of week), and H (hour of day). Each identifier is followed by a number indicating a particular time. Hours range from 0 to 23, while days run from 0 (Sunday) to 6 (Saturday). Days of the month start at 1 and go up, with L representing the last day of the month. For example, to rotate a log on the fifth of each month at noon I could use $M5H12. To start the month-end log accounting at 10 PM on the last day of the month, use $MLH22.

ROTATING ON SIZE AND TIME

You can rotate logs at a given time, when they reach a certain size, or both. If you specify both size and time, the log rotates whenever either condition is met.

Flags

The flags field dictates any special actions to be taken when the log is rotated. This most commonly tells newsyslog(8) how to compress the log file, but you can also signal processes when their log is rotated out from under them.

Log File Format and Compression

Logs can be either text or binary files.

    Binary files can only be written to in a very specific manner. newsyslog(8) starts each new log with a "logfile turned over" message, but adding this text to a binary file would damage it. The B flag tells newsyslog(8) that this is a binary file and that it doesn't need this header.

    Other log files are written in plain old ASCII text, and newsyslog(8) can and should add a timestamped message to the top of the file indicating when the log was rotated. Additionally, compressing old log files can save considerable space. The J flag tells newsyslog(8) to compress archives with bzip(1), while the Z flag specifies gzip compression.

Special Log File Handling

newsyslog(8) can perform a few special tasks when it creates and rotates log files. Here are the most common; you can read about the others in newsyslog.conf(5).

If you don't want to back up certain logs, use the D flag to set the NODUMP flag on newly created log files.

Perhaps you have many similar log files that you want to treat identically. The G flag tells newsyslog that the log file name at the beginning of the line is actually a shell glob, and that all log files that match the expression are to be rotated in this manner. To learn about regular expressions, read regexp(3). Bring aspirin.

You might want newsyslog to create a file if it doesn't exist. Use the C flag for this. The syslogd program will not log to a nonexistent file.

The N flag explicitly tells newsyslog to not send a signal when rotating this log.

Finally, use a hyphen (-) as a placeholder when you don't need any of these flags. However, you will need one of the *newsyslog.conf* flags further down the line, such as when specifying the path to a pidfile.

Pidfile

The next field is a pidfile path (not shown in our example, but look at */etc/newsyslog.conf* for a couple of samples). A pidfile records a program's process ID so that other programs can easily view it. If you list the full path to a pidfile, newsyslog(8) sends a kill -HUP to that program when it rotates the log. This signals the process to close its logfiles and restart itself. Not all processes have pidfiles, and not all programs need this sort of special care when rotating their logs.

Signal

Most programs perform logfile rotation on a SIGHUP, but some programs need a specific signal when their logs are rotated. You can list the exact signal necessary in the last field, after the pidfile.

Sample newsyslog.conf Entry

Let's slap all this together into a worst-case, you-have-*got*-to-be-kidding example. A database log file needs rotation at 11 PM on the last day of the month. The database documentation says that you must send the server an interrupt signal (SIGINT, or signal number 2) on rotation. You want the archived logs to be owned by the user dbadmin and only viewable by that user. You need six months of logs. What's more, the logs are binary files. Your *newsyslog.conf* line would look like this:

```
/var/log/database   dbadmin:  600   6   *   $MLH23   B   /var/run/db.pid   2
```

This is a deliberately ugly example; in most cases you just slap in the filename and the rotation condition and you're done.

FreeBSD and SNMP

Emailed reports are nice but general, and logs are difficult to analyze for long-term trends. The industry standard for network, server, and service management is *Simple Network Management Protocol*, or *SNMP*. Many different vendors support SNMP as a protocol for gathering information from many different devices across the network. FreeBSD includes an SNMP agent, bsnmpd(8), that not only provides standard SNMP functions but also gives visibility to FreeBSD-specific features.

bsnmpd (short for *Begemot SNMPD*) is a minimalist SNMP agent specifically designed to be extensible. All actual functionality is provided via external modules. FreeBSD includes the bsnmpd modules for standard network SNMP functions and modules for specific FreeBSD features, such as PF and netgraph(4). bsnmpd does not try to be all things to all people, but rather offers a foundation where everyone can build an SNMP implementation that does only what they need, no more and no less.

SNMP 101

SNMP works on a classic client-server model. The SNMP client, or *agent*, sends a request across the network to an SNMP server. The SNMP server, bsnmpd, gathers information from the local system and returns it to the client.

An SNMP agent can also send a request to make changes to the SNMP server. If the system is properly (or improperly, depending on your point of view) configured, you can issue commands via SNMP. This "write" configuration is most commonly used in routers, switches, and other embedded network devices. Most Unix-like operating systems have a command-line management system and don't usually accept instruction via SNMP. Writing system configuration or issuing commands via SNMP requires careful setup and raises all sorts of security issues; it's an excellent topic for an entire book. No system administrator I know is comfortable managing their system via SNMP. With all of this in mind, we're going to focus specifically on read-only SNMP.

In addition to having an SNMP server answer requests from an SNMP client, the client can transmit SNMP *traps* to a trap receiver elsewhere on the network. An SNMP agent generates these traps in response to particular events on the server. SNMP traps are much like syslogd(8) messages, except that they follow the very specific format required by SNMP. FreeBSD does not include an SNMP trap receiver at this time; if you need one, check out snmptrapd(8) from net-snmp (*/usr/ports/net-mgmt/net-snmp*).

SNMP MIBs

SNMP manages information via a *Management Information Base*, or *MIB*, a tree-like structure containing hierarchical information in ASN.1 format. We've seen an example of a MIB tree before: the sysctl(8) interface discussed in Chapter 5.

Each SNMP server has a list of information it can extract from the local computer. The server arranges these bits of information into a hierarchical tree. Each SNMP MIB tree has very general main categories: network, physical, programs, and so on, with more specific subdivisions in each. Think of the tree as a well-organized filing cabinet, where individual drawers hold specific information and files within drawers hold particular facts. Similarly, the uppermost MIB contains a list of MIBs beneath it.

MIBs can be referred to by name or by number. For example, here's a MIB pulled off a sample system:

```
interfaces.ifTable.ifEntry.ifDescr.1 = STRING: "fxp0"
```

The first term in this MIB, `interfaces`, shows us that we're looking at this machine's network interfaces. If this machine had no interfaces, this first category would not even exist. The `ifTable` is the interface table, or a list of all the interfaces on the system. `ifEntry` shows one particular interface, and `ifDescr` means that we're looking at a description of this interface. This MIB can be summarized as, "Interface number 1 on this machine is called fxp0."

MIBs can be expressed as numbers, and most SNMP tools do their work natively in numerical MIBs. Most people prefer words, but your poor brain must be capable of working with either. A MIB browser can translate between the numerical and word forms of an SNMP MIB for you, or you could install */usr/ports/net-mgmt/net-snmp* and use snmptranslate(1), but for now just trust me. The preceding example can be translated to:

```
.1.3.6.1.2.1.2.2.1.2.1
```

Expressed in words, this MIB has 5 terms separated by dots. Expressed in numbers, the MIB has 11 parts. That doesn't look quite right if they're supposed to be the same thing. What gives?

The numerical MIB is longer because it includes the default `.1.3.6.1.2.1`, which means *.iso.org.dod.internet.mgmt.mib-2*. This is the standard subset of MIBs used on the Internet. The vast majority of SNMP MIBs (but not all) have this leading string in front of them, so nobody bothers writing it down any more.

If you're in one of those difficult moods, you can even mix words and numbers:

```
.1.org.6.1.mgmt.1.interfaces.ifTable.1.2.1
```

At this point, international treaties permit your co-workers to drive you from the building with pitchforks and flaming torches. Pick one method of expressing MIBs and stick to it.

MIB Definitions and MIB Browsers

MIBs are defined according to a very strict syntax and are documented in *MIB files*. Every SNMP agent has its own MIB files; bsnmpd's are in */usr/share/snmp*. These files are very formal plaintext. While you can read and interpret them with nothing more than your brain, I highly recommend copying them to a workstation and installing a MIB browser so that you can comprehend them more easily.

MIB browsers interpret MIB files and present them in their full tree-like glory, complete with definitions of each part of the tree and descriptions of each individual MIB. Generally speaking, a MIB browser lets you enter a particular MIB and displays both the numerical and word definitions of that MIB, along with querying an SNMP agent for the status of that MIB.

If you have a FreeBSD (or lesser Unix-like) workstation, use mbrowse (*/usr/ports/net-mgmt/mbrowse*) for MIB browsing. Windows systems have many options, but Getif (*http://www.wtcs.org*) is a decent no-cost choice. If you don't want to use a graphical interface for SNMP work, check out net-snmp (*/usr/ports/net-mgmt/net-snmp*) for a full assortment of command-line SNMP client tools.

SNMP Security

Many security experts state that SNMP really stands for "Security: Not My Problem!" This is rather unkind but very true. SNMP needs to be used only behind firewalls on trusted networks. If you must use SNMP on the naked Internet, use packet filtering to keep the public from querying your SNMP service. SNMP agents run on UDP port 161.

SNMP provides basic security through *communities*. If you go looking around you'll find all sorts of explanations why a community is not the same thing as a password, but a community *is* a password. Most SNMP agents have two communities by default: public (read-only access) and private (read-write access). Yes, there's a default that provides read-write access. Your first task whenever you provision an SNMP agent on any host, on any OS, is to disable those default community names and replace them with ones that haven't been widely documented for decades.

SNMP comes in different versions. Version 1 was the first attempt, and version 2c is the modern standard. You'll see references to SNMP version 3, which uses advanced encryption to protect data on the wire. Very few vendors actually implement SNMPv3, however. FreeBSD's bsnmpd(8) uses SNMPv2c. This means that anyone with a packet sniffer can capture your SNMP community name, so be absolutely certain you're only using SNMP on a private network. Making SNMP queries over an untrusted network is a great way to have strangers poking at your system management.

Configuring bsnmpd

Before you can use SNMP to monitor your system, you must configure the SNMP daemon. Configure bsnmpd(8) in */etc/snmpd.config*. In addition to including the default communities of public and private, the default configuration does not enable any of the FreeBSD-specific features that make bsnmpd(8) desirable.

bsnmpd Variables

bsnmpd uses variables to assign values to configuration statements. Most high-visibility variables are set at the top of the configuration file, as you'll see here:

```
location := "Room 200"
contact := "sysmeister@example.com"
system := 1      # FreeBSD
traphost := localhost
trapport := 162
```

These top variables define values for MIBs that should be set on every SNMP agent. The location describes the physical location of the machine. Every system needs a legitimate email contact. bsnmpd(8) runs on operating systems other than FreeBSD, so you have the option of setting a particular operating system here. Lastly, if you have a trap host, you can set the server name and port here.

Further down the file, you can set the SNMP community names:

```
# Change this!
read := "public"
# Uncomment begemotSnmpdCommunityString.0.2 below that sets the community
# string to enable write access.
write := "geheim"
trap := "mytrap"
```

The read string defines the read-only community of this SNMP agent. The default configuration file advises you to change it. Take that advice. The write string is the read-write community name, which is disabled by default further down in the configuration file. You can also set the community name for SNMP traps sent by this agent.

With only this configuration, bsnmpd(8) will start, run, and provide basic SNMP data for your network management system. Just set bsnmpd_enable="YES" in /etc/rc.conf to start bsnmpd at boot. You won't get any special FreeBSD functionality, however. Let's go on and see how to manage this.

Detailed bsnmpd Configuration

bsnmpd(8) uses the variables you set at the top of the configuration file to assign values to different MIBs later in the configuration. For example, at the top of the file you set the variable read to public. Later in the configuration file, you'll find this statement:

```
begemotSnmpdCommunityString.0.1 = $(read)
```

This sets the MIB begemotSnmpdCommunityString.0.1 equal to the value of the read variable.

Why not just set these values directly? bsnmpd(8) is specifically designed to be extensible and configurable. Setting a few variables at the top of the file is much easier than directly editing the rules further down the file.

Let's go back to this begemotSnmpdCommunityString MIB set here. Why are we setting this? Search for the string in your MIB browser, and you'll see that this is the MIB that defines an SNMP community name. You probably could have guessed that from the assignment of the read variable, but it's nice to confirm that.

Similarly, you'll find an entry like this:

```
begemotSnmpdPortStatus.0.0.0.0.161 = 1
```

Checking the MIB browser shows that this dictates the IP address and the UDP port that bsnmpd(8) binds to (in this case, all available addresses, on port 161). All MIB configuration is done in this manner.

Loading bsnmpd Modules

Most of bsnmpd's interesting features are configured through modules. Enable modules in the configuration file by giving the begemotSnmpdModulePath MIB a class that the module handles and the full path to the shared library that implements support for that feature. For example, in the default configuration you'll see a commented-out entry for the PF bsnmpd(8) module:

```
begemotSnmpdModulePath."pf"     = "/usr/lib/snmp_pf.so"
```

This enables support for PF MIBs. Your network management software will be able to see directly into PF when you enable this, letting you track everything from dropped packets to the size of the state table.

As of this writing, FreeBSD's bsnmpd(8) ships with the following FreeBSD-specific modules. All of these modules are disabled by default, but you can enable them by just uncommenting their configuration file entries.

Netgraph   Provides visibility into all Netgraph-based network features, documented in snmp_netgraph(3).

PF   Provides visibility into the PF packet filter.

Hostres   Implements the Host Resources SNMP MIB, snmp_hostres(3).

bridge   Provides visibility into bridging functions, documented in snmp_bridge(3).

Restart bsnmpd(8) after enabling any of these in the configuration file. If the program won't start, check */var/log/messages* for errors.

With bsnmpd(8), syslogd(8), status emails, and a wide variety of performance analysis tools, you can make your FreeBSD system the best-monitored device on the network. Now that you can see everything your system offers, grab a flashlight as we explore a few of FreeBSD's darker corners.

20

THE FRINGE OF FREEBSD

If you hang around the FreeBSD community for any length of time, you'll hear mention of all sorts of things that can be done if you know how. People build embedded FreeBSD devices and ship them to customers all over the world, who don't even know that they have a Unix-like server inside the little box running their air conditioner or radio relay station. People run FreeBSD on machines without hard drives, supporting hundreds or thousands of diskless workstations from a single server. You'll find bootable CDs and USB devices that contain complete FreeBSD systems, including all the installed software you could ever want. These things aren't difficult to do, once you know the tricks.

In this chapter, we're headed into the fringes of FreeBSD—the really cool things that are done by FreeBSD users, but aren't necessarily supported by the mainstream FreeBSD Project. While you can find support and assistance through the usual channels, you must be prepared to debug and troubleshoot everything in this chapter even more than usual.

/etc/ttys

The file *etc/ttys* controls how and where users may log into your FreeBSD system. While you can set per-user restrictions on account logins elsewhere, the *etc/ttys* file controls which devices are available for logins and how they can be used. While most people use only the console and SSH connections that FreeBSD ships with, you can configure other devices to allow logins.

Remember, *tty* is short for *teletype*. Once upon a time, the main output interface for a Unix-like system was a teletype. Anything you can log in on is considered a tty. FreeBSD supports many different types of terminal devices, from old-fashioned serial terminals to the usual keyboard/video/mouse console to SSH and telnet sessions. FreeBSD systems offer four standard login devices, or *terminals*: the console, virtual terminals, dial-up terminals, and pseudoterminals.

The *console* is the only device available in single-user mode. On most FreeBSD systems, this is either a video console that includes the monitor and keyboard, or a serial console accessed from another system. Once the system hits multi-user mode, the console is usually attached to a virtual terminal instead. The console device is */dev/console*.

A *virtual terminal* is attached to the physical monitor and keyboard. If you're not using X, you can have multiple terminals on your one physical terminal. Switch between them with ALT and the function keys. For example, the next time you're at a console, hit ALT-F2. You'll see a fresh login screen, with ttyv1 after the host name. This is the second virtual terminal. Hitting ALT-F1 takes you back to the main virtual terminal. By default, FreeBSD has eight virtual terminals and reserves a ninth for X Windows. You can use the eight virtual text terminals even when you're in X, and some X desktops provide multiple X virtual terminals. The virtual terminals are the */dev/ttyv* devices.

A *dial-up terminal* is connected via serial line. You can attach modems directly to your serial ports and let users dial into your server. This is not so common these days, but the same functionality supports logging in over a serial console. Dial-up terminals are the */dev/ttyd* devices.

Finally, a *pseudoterminal* is implemented entirely in software. When you SSH into your server, you don't need any actual hardware, but the software still needs a device node for your login session. Pseudoterminals are the */dev/ttyp* devices.

Configure access to terminal devices in */etc/ttys*. Most terminal devices don't require configuration—after all, if you can get a pseudoterminal it's because you've been authenticated and authorized to connect through SSH, telnet, or some other network protocol. The useful things you can do here are setting the console to require a password and enabling logins over a serial console.

/etc/ttys Format

A typical entry in */etc/ttys* looks like this:

```
ttyv0    "/usr/libexec/getty Pc"        cons25  on  secure
```

The first entry is the console device. In this case, ttyv0 is the first virtual terminal on the system.

The second field is the program that is spawned to process login requests on this terminal. FreeBSD uses getty(8) for this on everything except pseudo-terminals. Pseudoterminals process their login requests through whatever daemon the user logs in through.

The third entry is the terminal type. You've probably heard of the vt100 terminal, or even the Sun terminal. On FreeBSD, the monitor uses a type of cons25, which is a 25-character by 80-character screen. Pseudoterminals use the terminal type of network; their features are determined by the server daemon and the client software.

The fourth entry determines if the terminal is available for logins or not. This is either on for accepting logins or off for not allowing them. Pseudo-terminals are activated upon demand.

This example also includes the keyword secure, which tells getty(8) that root may log in to this console.

Offering terminals is a low-level system task handled directly by init(8). Changes to */etc/ttys* do not take effect until you restart init(8). init is always PID 1.

```
# kill -1 1
```

Insecure Console

When you boot FreeBSD in single-user mode, you get a root command prompt. This is fine for your laptop and works nicely for servers in your corporate datacenter, but what about machines in untrusted facilities? If you have a server in a co-location center, for example, you probably don't want just anyone to be able to get root-level access to a machine. You can tell FreeBSD that the physical console is insecure and make it require the root password to enter single-user mode. The system will then boot from power-on to multi-user mode without requiring a password, but will require the password when you explicitly boot in single-user mode.

Requiring a password in single-user mode does not completely protect your data, but it does raise the bar considerably. A lone tech working late, when nobody's looking, could boot your system into single-user mode and add an account for himself in only fifteen minutes or so. Dismantling your machine, removing the hard drives, mounting them into another machine, making changes, and bringing your server back online requires much more time, is far more intrusive, and is much more likely to be noticed by co-location management.

Find the console entry in */etc/ttys*:

```
console none                            unknown off secure
```

You'll see that the console terminal isn't as full-featured as other terminals; it doesn't run getty(8) and uses the generic unknown terminal type. The console is intended for use only in single-user mode or when attached to another terminal, however, so that's fine.

To make the console require a root login when booted into single-user mode, change the secure to insecure.

Serial Logins

We talked about serial consoles back in Chapter 3. In addition to providing console access, FreeBSD lets you log in through a serial port. In many Unix-like systems in the 1970s and 1980s, this was the only way to get a login prompt. While it's fallen into disfavor today thanks to the ubiquitous network, a serial login is very useful on a system where you already have a serial console or where the system does not support a video console. Systems without the standard video monitor and keyboard are called *headless systems.*

To enable logging in on a serial line, find the */etc/ttys* entry for your serial port. The default configuration lists four dial-up terminals, ttyd0 through ttyd3. These correspond to serial ports sio0 through sio3, or COM1 through COM4. Let's assume you have a serial console attached to the first serial port.

```
ttyd0    "/usr/libexec/getty std.9600"   dialup  ❶off secure
```

This is pretty easy to configure. The port is off ❶. Change it to on.

Serial logins are slower than network logins. They're limited by the speed of the serial port. This can be a problem when you have a serial console and a serial login. The console prints debugging messages to your serial login session, which takes up bandwidth on the serial port. If you have a lot of log messages arriving quickly, they can prevent you from using the serial console. Even so, a serial login is invaluable for headless servers and embedded devices, as we'll see later in this chapter.

Diskless FreeBSD

While FreeBSD isn't difficult to manage, dozens or hundreds of nearly identical systems can become quite a burden. One way to reduce your maintenance overhead is to use *diskless* systems. Diskless systems are not forbidden to have hard drives; rather, they load their kernel and operating system from an NFS server elsewhere on the network.

Why use a diskless system for your server farm? Multiple systems can boot off of a single NFS server, centralizing all patch and package management. This is excellent for collections of terminals, computation clusters, and other environments where you have large numbers of identical systems. Rolling out an operating system update becomes a simple matter of replacing files on the NFS server. Similarly, when you discover that an update has problems, reverting it is as simple as restoring files on the NFS server. In either case, the only thing you have to do at the client side is reboot. As the clients have read-only access to the server, untrusted users cannot make any changes to their local systems that couldn't be undone by rebooting. If you have only a couple of systems, running diskless might be too much work for you, but any more than that and diskless is a clear winner.

Before you can run diskless systems, you must have an NFS server, a DHCP server, a TFTP server, and hardware that supports diskless booting. Let's go through each and see how to set it up.

TEST, TEST, TEST!

Your first diskless setup will be much like your first firewall setup: error-prone, troublesome, and infuriating. I strongly suggest that you test each step of the preparation so that you can find and fix problems more easily. Test instructions are provided for each required service.

Diskless Clients

Machines that run diskless must have enough smarts to find their boot loader and operating system over the network. There are two standard ways of doing this: BOOTP and PXE. *BOOTP*, the Internet Bootstrap Protocol, is an older standard that fell out of favor long ago. *PXE*, Intel's Preboot Execution Environment, has been supported on almost every new machine for years now, so we'll concentrate on that.

Boot your diskless client machine and go into the BIOS setup. Somewhere in the BIOS you will find an option to set the boot device order. If the machine supports PXE, one of those options will be the network. Enable that option and have the machine try it first.

Your diskless client is ready. Now let's get the server ready.

DHCP Server Setup

While most people think of DHCP as a way to assign IP addresses to clients, it can provide much more than that. You can configure your DHCP server to provide the locations of a TFTP server, an NFS server, and other network resources. Diskless systems make extensive use of DHCP, and you'll find that we use DHCP options you never tried before. Configuring the ISC DHCP server to handle diskless systems is pretty straightforward, once you have the MAC address of your diskless workstation.

MAC Address

To assign configuration information to a DHCP client, you need the MAC address of that client's network card. Some BIOS implementations provide the MAC addresses of integrated network cards, and some server-grade hardware has labels with the MAC address printed on them. Those options, however, are too easy, so we'll try the hard way.

When a machine tries to boot off the network, it makes a DHCP request for its configuration information. While you don't have a diskless configuration yet, any DHCP server logs the MAC address of clients. For example, when I boot my diskless client, my DHCP log shows:

```
Jul 27 10:15:49 sardines dhcpd: DHCPDISCOVER from 00:00:24:c1:cb:a4 via fxp0
Jul 27 10:15:49 sardines dhcpd: DHCPOFFER on 192.168.1.78 to 00:00:24:c1:cb:a4 via fxp0
```

This client has a MAC address of 00:00:24:c1:cb:a4 and has been offered IP address 192.168.1.78. Given this information, we can create a DHCP configuration to assign this host a static IP address and provide its boot information.

DHCP Configuration: Specific Diskless Hosts

We configured basic DHCP services in Chapter 15. Here's a sample dhcpd(8) configuration for a diskless client. This does not go inside a subnet statement, but is a top-level statement on its own.

```
❶ group diskless {
❷         next-server 192.168.1.1;
❸         filename "pxeboot";
❹         option root-path "192.168.1.1:/var/diskless/1/";
❺         host diskless1.blackhelicopters.org {
❻                 hardware ethernet 00:00:24:c1:cb:a4 ;
❼                 fixed-address 192.168.1.99 ;
          }
  }
```

We define a group called diskless ❶. The group will allow us to assign certain parameters to the group and then just add hosts to the group. Every host in the group gets those same parameters.

The next-server setting ❷ tells the DHCP clients the IP address of a TFTP server, and the filename option ❸ tells clients the name of the boot loader file to request from that TFTP server. Remember from Chapter 3 that the boot loader is the software that finds and loads the kernel. Finally, option root-path ❹ tells the boot loader where to find the root directory for this machine. All of these options and settings are given to all clients in the diskless group.

We then assign our diskless client to the diskless group using the host statement and the hostname of this system ❺. Our first client is called diskless1. This client is identified by its MAC address ❻ and is assigned a static IP ❼. It also receives the standard configuration for this group.

Create additional host entries just like this for every diskless host on your network.

Restart dhcpd(8) to make this configuration take effect. Now reboot your diskless client. The DHCP log should show that you have offered this client its static address. However, the DHCP client cannot boot any further without a boot loader, which means you need a TFTP server.

DHCP Configuration: Diskless Farms

Perhaps you have a large number of identical diskless hosts, such as thin clients in a terminal room. It's perfectly sensible to not want to make a static DHCP entry for each thin client. Let these hosts get their boot information from the DHCP server, but without specifying a host address. They'll just take an address out of the DHCP pool.

You can also specifically identify hosts that are requesting DHCP information from PXE and assign those hosts to a specific group of addresses. A host booting with PXE identifies itself to the DHCP server as a client of type PXEclient. You can write specific rules to match clients of that type and configure them appropriately. Look in the DHCP manual for information on how to match on vendor-class-identifier and dhcp-client-identifier.

tftpd and the Boot Loader

We covered configuring a TFTP server in Chapter 15. The TFTP server must provide the *pxeboot* file for your diskless clients. FreeBSD installs *pxeboot* in the */boot* directory.

```
# cp /boot/pxeboot /tftpboot
# chmod +r /tftpboot/pxeboot
```

Try to download *pxeboot* via TFTP from your workstation. If that works, reboot your diskless client and watch it try to boot. The console should show a message like this:

```
Building the boot loader arguments
Relocating the loader and the BTX
Starting the BTX loader
```

You've seen this message before, when a regular FreeBSD boots off its hard drive. Your diskless client will stop here, because it can't mount the userland that doesn't yet exist. That's a job for your NFS server.

The NFS Server and the Diskless Client Userland

Many tutorials on diskless operation suggest using the server's userland and root partition for diskless clients. That might be easy to do, but it's not even vaguely secure. Your diskless server probably has programs on it that you don't want the clients to have access to, and it certainly has sensitive security information that you don't want to hand out to a whole bunch of workstations. Providing a separate userland is a much wiser option.

While you can provide a separate userland in many ways, I find that the simplest is to slightly modify the jail(8) construction process from Chapter 9. First, make a directory for our diskless clients, and then install a userland and kernel in that directory. Here we install our new userland in */var/diskless/1*:

```
# mkdir -p /var/diskless/1
# cd /usr/src
# make installworld DESTDIR=/var/diskless/1
# make installkernel DESTDIR=/var/diskless/1
# make distribution DESTDIR=/var/diskless/1
```

This installs a vanilla FreeBSD userland in */var/diskless/1*.

Now tell your NFS server about this directory. I intend to install several diskless systems on this network, so I offer this directory via NFS to my entire subnet. The clients do not need write access to the NFS root, so I export it read-only. The following */etc/exports* line does this:

```
/var/diskless/1 -ro -maproot=0 -alldirs -network 192.168.1.0 -mask 255.255.255.0
```

Restart mountd(8) via */etc/rc.d/mountd* to make this share available and try to mount it from a workstation. Confirm that the directory contains a basic userland visible from the client and that you cannot write to the filesystem. After that, reboot your diskless client and see what happens. It should find the kernel and boot into an unconfigured multi-user mode. Depending on the server, client, and network speed, this might take a while to complete. My main laptop netboots nearly as quickly as it boots from the hard drive, while my 266 MHz Soekris net4801 takes several minutes to boot.

IMPROVING DISKLESS NFS SECURITY

Once your diskless farm is running, you could go back and assign a different user for the NFS root account. Running find /var/diskless/1 -user 0 -exec chown nfsroot changes the owner of all files owned by root to be owned by the user nfsroot. You can then edit the *exports* file to map root to the nfsroot user. When you're first learning, however, don't try to get fancy.

At this point, you could configure your userland to specifically match your single diskless client. You could make changes in */etc*, such as creating */etc/fstab* that reflects your needs, and copy password files into place. That would suffice for one client, but FreeBSD has infrastructure designed specifically to support dozens or hundreds of clients off the same filesystem. Let's look into how this is done.

Diskless Farm Configuration

One of the benefits of diskless systems is that multiple machines can share the same filesystem. However, even on machines that are mostly identical, you'll probably find that you must make certain configuration files slightly different. FreeBSD includes a mechanism for offering personalized configuration files on top of a uniform userland by remounting directories on memory filesystem (MFS) partitions and copying custom files to these partitions.

FreeBSD's default diskless setup lets you set up diskless workstations across multiple networks and subnets—an invaluable feature when you have a large network. If you only have a few diskless systems, however, you might find it slightly cumbersome at first. Over time, however, you'll find that you make more and more use of it. Diskless systems are a convenient solution to many problems.

On boot, FreeBSD checks to see if it's running diskless by looking at the vfs.nfs.diskless_valid sysctl. If the sysctl equals 0, you're running off a hard drive; otherwise you're running diskless. On diskless systems, FreeBSD runs the */etc/rc.initdiskless* script.

Diskless configuration is kept in the */conf* directory on the NFS client, which is the *conf* directory under the NFS root. While we refer to this directory as */conf*, in our example this directory could be found on the server in */var/diskless/1/conf*.

You must create a few subdirectories: at least */conf/base* and */conf/default*, as well as, possibly, separate directories for subnets and/or individual IP addresses. The contents of these directories are used to build memory filesystems on top of the mounted root partition, so you can make changes for individual hosts.

The easiest way to explain this is by example. We'll make a common change and configure */etc* as a memory filesystem on our diskless hosts.

The /conf/base Directory

The */conf/base* directory contains basic information about the partitions we're going to remount. Anything in this directory affects all of our diskless clients. Every directory that gets remounted on a memory filesystem needs a further subdirectory under */conf/base*. As we want to remount our */etc* filesystem, we create */conf/base/etc*.

Activating Diskless Remounting

In our */conf/base/etc* directory, we must tell FreeBSD to remount */etc* on our clients. Create a file named *diskless_remount* containing the name of the directory to remount. This sounds complicated, but it just means that the file */conf/base/etc/diskless_remount* contains the single word:

/etc

This tells FreeBSD to build an MFS */etc* and mount it appropriately on our diskless client.

Populating and Trimming Remounted Filesystems

By default, *rc.initdiskless* copies the server directory to populate the memory filesystem. That is, our MFS */etc* is a copy of what's in */etc* on the read-only NFS filesystem. Some files are not necessary on your MFS filesystem, however. For example, diskless systems shouldn't keep logs locally so they don't need *newsyslog* or */etc/newsyslog.conf.* You don't back up diskless clients, so */etc/dumpdates* is also unnecessary. Browsing */etc* will reveal quite a few files that you don't need on your MFS */etc.* Keeping your diskless */etc* small saves memory, which can be very useful on small systems. If you remove too much, however, your system will not boot, and the list of necessary files is not intuitive. For example, if your remove */etc/mtree*, the machine will hang in single-user mode because it cannot repopulate the MFS */var* partition.

Put the full paths to your unwanted files and directories in the file */conf/base/etc.remove.* For example, the following entries remove the */etc/gss* and */etc/bluetooth* directories as well as the file */etc/rc.firewall*:

```
/etc/gss
/etc/bluetooth
/etc/rc.firewall
```

Not so hard, is it? Now let's put some things back into our configuration.

The /conf/default Directory

The *default* directory contains files issued to all diskless clients. Many files are the same on all clients, such as */etc/fstab.* You put those files in an *etc* directory under */conf/default.* For example, to distribute */etc/fstab* to all of your clients, you would store it as */conf/default/etc/fstab.*

Anything you put in the *default* directory overrides the same files provided by remounting the base system.

Per-Subnet and Per-Client Directories

Very few files are unique to certain diskless hosts. You might have a diskless DNS server that needs a particular *named.conf* file, or a diskless NTP server that needs a unique *ntp.conf.* If nothing else, every diskless host should have unique SSH keys.

The diskless system provides the ability to override the base configuration on a per-subnet and a per-IP basis. The per-subnet override requires a directory named after the broadcast address of the subnet. For example, our diskless box has an IP of 192.168.1.99 and a netmask of 255.255.255.0. The broadcast address on its network is 192.168.1.255. Any files that need copying to every diskless client on this network should be placed in */conf/192.168.1.255/etc.*

Similarly, you can specify overrides on a per-IP basis by using a directory with the same name as the IP address. To place a custom *rc.conf* on our test diskless system and only that system, save it as */conf/192.168.1.99/etc/rc.conf.*

Anything in the per-IP directories overrides the same files in the per-subnet directory. Similarly, anything in the per-subnet directory overrides the same files in the default directory, which override the files in the base directory.

DISTRIBUTING RC.CONF TO DISKLESS HOSTS

While most FreeBSD administrators use */etc/rc.conf* as the sole configuration point for the system, remember that you can also use */etc/rc.conf.local*. This is especially useful for diskless systems. If you want to have a diskless farm where all of the machines run identical services, you can distribute a single *rc.conf* to all the hosts. Place anything that is truly local to an individual machine in */etc/rc.conf.local* and distribute it only to that diskless client. This is the easiest way to keep a large number of systems synchronized.

Diskless Packages and Files

Naked systems without software aren't very useful. Inevitably, you'll want to install packages on your diskless systems. You also must install configuration files on diskless clients.

Installing Packages

The key to installing software on the diskless clients is to install it in the directory the diskless clients will use as their filesystem. You can install packages in nonstandard directories with pkg_add(8)'s chroot function. You must copy the software to the diskless client directory before starting.

```
# cp /usr/ports/packages/All/jdk-1.5.0.11p5,1.tbz /var/diskless/1
# pkg_add -C /var/diskless/1 /jdk-1.5.0.11p5,1.tbz
```

Remember, chroot changes the root directory of a process. Before pkg_add(8) does anything, it changes its root to */var/diskless/1*. As far as pkg_add(8) is concerned, the package is now in the root directory.

You can also use ports on your diskless clients, but it's slightly more complicated. If you need a customized port, I recommend building it into a package and then installing with pkg_add -C to cleanly chroot it.

Diskless Configuration Files

You must decide if you want identical configuration files distributed amongst all of your diskless clients or on a client-by-client basis. Are your configuration files unique to each diskless client, or do you manage them separately? Here's how you can configure the most common configuration files for diskless operation.

/etc/rc.conf

Every host needs a basic *rc.conf*. While the hostname and IP address are already set by DHCP, you must tell the system to create a writable */var* and */tmp* filesystem if nothing else.

/etc/fstab

Every FreeBSD machine needs a filesystem table. Even diskless machines have filesystems, after all! Here's the */etc/fstab* from our sample diskless machine:

192.168.1.1:/var/diskless/1	/	nfs	ro	0 0	
md	/tmp	mfs	-s=30m,rw	0 0	
md	/var	mfs	-s=30m,rw	0 0	
md	/etc	mfs	-s=2m,rw	0 0	

If you provide other partitions (such as home directories), you'll want to list them here as well. You might also choose to use local hard disks to provide swap and scratch space. If you use local disk on a public or semi-public machine, however, I recommend using newfs(8) on those partitions at each boot so that any data left behind by previous users does not pose a security risk to the next user.

SSH Keys

If your diskless hosts provide SSH services, they need unique SSH keys. Now and then you will hear of someone who uses the same SSH keys across his entire diskless farm. While the traffic is encrypted and hence cannot be read in transit, shared keys make it impossible to tell one remote machine from another.

Left to its own devices, FreeBSD automatically creates new SSH keys for a host at boot. As these keys are written to a memory filesystem, they are lost at every shutdown. Remember that the SSH client software caches the key for each remote host it connects to and refuses to connect if the key changes. If the SSH keys on your diskless hosts keep changing, you will quickly become annoyed. The simplest thing to do is go into each client's configuration directory on the server and create the keys there:

```
# cd /var/diskless/1/conf/192.168.1.99/etc
# mkdirs ssh
# cd ssh
# touch ssh_host_key
# ssh-keygen -t dsa -f ssh_host_dsa_key -N ''
# ssh-keygen -t rsa -f ssh_host_rsa_key -N ''
```

If you have many diskless clients, write a script for this.

As the permanent filesystem is mounted read-only, root can actually do very little damage to a diskless workstation. Considering this, you might decide that you want to SSH to your diskless workstations as root instead of creating passwords for each of your administrators. Copy */etc/ssh/shhd_config* to your */conf/default/etc/ssh* directory and set PermitRootLogin to yes to enable this. (While doing this on a server with a read-write filesystem is a terrible security risk, the fact that a diskless system is ephemeral changes the rules.)

Password Files

Presumably you'll want a password file on your diskless system. FreeBSD does not have a good method for creating password files independent of the main system. It's best to create the password files on a test machine or in a jail, then copy the four key password files (*master.passwd*, *passwd*, *pwd.db*, and *spwd.db*) from */etc* into the appropriate *conf* directory. (You can use pwd_mkdb(8)'s -d option to create and install the database files, but you still have to perform some drudgery to create a suitable password file in the first place.) You could also run chroot(8) to lock yourself into your diskless root directory on the server and run adduser(8) there.

syslogd.conf

Remember, you have no hard drive. If you want your diskless system to use syslog, you must provide a logging host.

You'll certainly find other files you need, but this should get you started in diskless networking.

> **DISKLESS INSTALLATION**
>
> One common headache these days is that small servers don't always come with CD drives. While the machine doesn't need a CD during operation, its absence complicates installation. Diskless booting makes that problem go away. NFS can export a FreeBSD installation CD image and have the installation target boot with the CD image as its root directory. You'll boot directly into sysinstall!

NanoBSD: Building Your Own Appliances

News flash: Computers are expensive.

Many people dedicate a computer to a single purpose, such as a firewall/NAT device. It's quite true that a high-end 486 running FreeBSD is perfectly capable of handling network connectivity in a small office, but computers have costs beyond the base hardware. These systems are bulky, use a lot of power for the job they do, and frequently, their ancient hard drives are staggering on the verge of death. If you're in a business environment, your manager does not want to hear, "You know that old desktop that was so slow you wouldn't let the receptionist endure it any longer? I put it back into service as the web server." FreeBSD lets you cluster fairly easily, but there's a reason industry publications never mention a RAIC (Redundant Array of Inexpensive Crap).[1] Of course, you can always use your

---

[1] That's because the industry would rather sell you a Redundant Array of *Expensive* Crap, but that's another story.

hard-earned IT budget to purchase a new machine with full warranty, but we all have other things we'd rather buy than a computer that will sit 99 percent idle. All this adds up to "expensive." It's enough to make even the most rabid open source advocate consider purchasing an inexpensive firewall appliance, exchanging flexibility and certainty for low-power, cheap-to-replace silence.

You can get the best of both worlds by building your own appliance on low-power, inexpensive hardware. FreeBSD is used heavily in the embedded market. Companies such as NetApp and Juniper build high-performance devices on top of FreeBSD. Tools for building FreeBSD images for embedded devices are integrated with the core FreeBSD source tree. You'll come across many methods of doing this, but the most widely used method is NanoBSD (*/usr/src/tools/tools/nanobsd*).

Many companies manufacture small, inexpensive, low-end computers, but my favorite is Soekris (*http://www.soekris.com*). Soekris boxes are roughly the size of a paperback book. They have no fan, no video card, very low power requirements, and are designed specifically to work with open source operating systems. The CPU, memory, serial and USB ports, and network interfaces are soldered directly onto the motherboard. You can buy them as a plain motherboard or with a case. You can use a hard drive or mini-PCI card with them, or use a flash card as a drive. Best of all, they're only a couple hundred dollars—cheap enough to slide through most accounting departments without you having to fill out a mass of paperwork. You don't get a warranty with them, but for the price of one small rackmount server you can buy ten Soekris boxes. If one dies, throw it away and plug the next one in. Mind you, these systems are so simple that I've never had one die in production.[2]

We'll use one of these systems with a flash card instead of a hard drive. All the examples in this section were implemented on a Soekris net4801, with a 266 MHz processor, 128MB RAM, and an AC/DC power supply. For average use, I recommend either a 128MB or 256MB flash card. Anything more than 256MB is a waste, unless you have really really big programs on your embedded system. As I write this, however, even 128MB cards are getting difficult to find; you will probably have to use the smallest flash drive you can find. Other vendors offer similar hardware, but you'll have to modify these instructions slightly. (We're on the fringe of FreeBSD, remember?)

For my example here, I'm building the smallest possible DNS server, with only those programs that are strictly necessary for supporting DNS.

What Is NanoBSD?

NanoBSD is a shell script that builds a stripped-down version of FreeBSD suitable for simple devices. A *simple device* means that the system is built to perform a very particular task or tasks. A NanoBSD system can make an excellent nameserver, or an excellent firewall, or an excellent router. It makes a lousy desktop, however, as desktop systems are expected to support

---

[2] The one in my test lab that I spilled the Slurpee on doesn't count. The sparks were really nifty, though.

many complicated functions and add functions over time. Similarly, most multipurpose servers are poor NanoBSD candidates. If you want to convert your NanoBSD firewall into a NanoBSD DNS server, you'll need to build a new NanoBSD image and reinstall from scratch. That's not very difficult, but you would never expect to do that on a server.

NanoBSD can be complicated, and you'll probably need several attempts to make your first working NanoBSD disk. What's worse, the configuration process isn't easy to break apart for step-by-step explanation. You will probably want to read this section twice.

Building a NanoBSD image has two main steps: building the operating system and disk image, and then customizing that disk image for your environment. We're going to learn about NanoBSD the same way, by first focusing on getting a NanoBSD image that boots on your hardware, and then looking at customizing that image.

Your Hardware and Your Flash Drive

NanoBSD builds a version of FreeBSD tuned to your specifications and then installs it to a disk image suitable for copying directly to a flash drive. Before you can build the disk image, you must know your hardware's idea of your flash card's geometry. Flash drives don't have cylinders or heads, but they tell the computer that they do. Worse, different computers might see the geometry differently. While tools such as diskinfo(8) might work, they might provide incorrect answers depending on the exact hardware. The only way to authoritatively identify your flash card's geometry is by mounting it in the target system, powering it on, and checking what the flash card reports.

A Soekris uses the serial port as a default console. Unlike many other embedded systems, however, a Soekris uses a default port speed of 19,200bps instead of 9,600bps. Attach a null modem cable to the Soekris serial port, plug the other end into your computer's serial port, and open up a tip(1) session at 19,200bps.

```
# tip -19200 sio0
```

Now power up your Soekris. After the POST messages, you'll see a screen much like this:

```
comBIOS ver. 1.28  20050529  Copyright (C) 2000-2005 Soekris Engineering.

net4801

0128 Mbyte Memory                        CPU Geode 266 Mhz

❶Pri Sla  KODAK ATA_FLASH               ❷LBA 984-4-32  63 Mbyte

Slot   Vend Dev  ClassRev Cmd  Stat CL LT HT  Base1     Base2    Int
-----------------------------------------------------------------
0:00:0 1078 0001 06000000 0107 0280 00 00 00  00000000  00000000
...
```

This informative screen tells you interesting things about the hardware, but what we're most concerned with is the disk information. This flash drive shows up as the primary slave device ❶. Also, the machine sees this 63MB flash card as having 984 cylinders, 4 heads, and 32 sectors ❷. We can prepare a NanoBSD image to fit this geometry. Shut down your Soekris box and remove the flash drive. The next time you power it on, the flash drive will boot it into FreeBSD.

NANOBSD AND DISKLESS SYSTEMS

If you have a diskless infrastructure available, netboot your NanoBSD system diskless one time. This will give you the *dmesg.boot* for the system, which will help you make a good kernel configuration. It will also tell you what device name your system uses for the flash drive, saving you a round of customization later on.

The NanoBSD Toolkit

You'll find NanoBSD in */usr/src/tools/tools/nanobsd*. The base toolkit includes a directory called *Files*, the shell script *nanobsd.sh*, and the file *FlashDevice.sub*.

The *Files* directory contains files that will be copied to your NanoBSD image. NanoBSD comes with a few scripts to make managing NanoBSD systems a little easier, and you can add your own later.

The file *FlashDevice.sub* contains geometry descriptions of various flash storage devices. This file is woefully incomplete due to the innumerable flash drive vendors, but very easy to expand.

The real brains of NanoBSD are in the shell script *nanobsd.sh*. This is actually a driver for the build-from-source process discussed in Chapter 13.

In addition to these files, you'll need a NanoBSD configuration file and possibly a *packages* directory.

Expanding FlashDevice.sub

Chances are, your flash card is not already listed in *FlashDevice.sub*. Adding it is very straightforward and only takes a few moments. All you do is copy an existing entry and modify it to match your card. You must know the disk brand and size, as well as the disk geometry as seen by the target device. You can get the brand and size off the flash card label. The Soekris displays the geometry in its BIOS screen, as do most hardware vendors. An entry for a new card will look like this:

```
❶      samsung)
           #Source: mwlucas@freebsd.org
           case $a2 in
❷      128|128mb)
❸          NANO_MEDIASIZE=`expr 130154496 / 512`
❹          NANO_HEADS=8
❺          NANO_SECTS=32
```

```
            ;;
❻      *)
            echo "Unknown Samsung Corp Flash Capacity"
            exit 2
            ;;
       esac
       ;;
```

First, we list the card manufacturer ❶, in alphabetical order within the file.

We know one size of flash drive, the one in our hand. This is a 128MB ❷ device. We want the script to accept either 128 or 128mb as an argument, so we specify both of them.

NANO_MEDIASIZE ❸ equals the number of cylinders, times the number of heads, times the number of sectors per track, times by 512. Calculate this number and make the substitution in the expr(1) statement. (Yes, NanoBSD immediately divides this value by 512 again.)

The NANO_HEADS ❹ and NANO_SECTS ❺ statements are taken directly from the heads and sectors seen by the target device.

We also have a default statement ❻, so that if you try to use a Samsung 256MB flash card without configuring it, NanoBSD will abort early on instead of building a bogus image.

Add an entry like this to *FlashDevice.sub*, and you can proceed to configuring your NanoBSD build.

NanoBSD Configuration Options

Customize a NanoBSD build with a configuration file. FreeBSD doesn't include a NanoBSD configuration file by default, for a good reason: Every NanoBSD install is slightly different. You can find many sample files on the Internet, and I'll include my own sample file here. As FreeBSD changes, however, you must tweak your configuration. A NanoBSD configuration that works with FreeBSD 7.0 won't be quite right for FreeBSD 7.5 and will quite probably fail on FreeBSD 8.0. You can have multiple configuration files for different types of NanoBSD builds.

Here are some of the useful configuration settings and how they can be used.

NANO_NAME=full

This is the name you assign to this particular build of NanoBSD. NanoBSD uses this to assign the names to work directories and to the disk image file.

NANO_SRC=/usr/src

This is the location of the source tree NanoBSD uses to build its disk images. If you want to use a different location, change this variable. You can build NanoBSD on any version of FreeBSD reasonably close to the version you're running on.

NANO_TOOLS=tools/tools/nanobsd

The NanoBSD scripts and files are considered to be part of the FreeBSD source code. This means that when you run csup, the files that came with

NanoBSD can be updated. If you make changes to any of the NanoBSD files, csup(1) will undo those changes and return the files to their default state. If you change the NanoBSD core components, you'll want to copy the NanoBSD directory somewhere else under the source tree (such as */usr/src/tools/tools/local-nanobsd*). Tracking the changes between your custom NanoBSD tools and the system base NanoBSD tools is your problem.

NANO_PACKAGE_DIR=${NANO_SRC}/${NANO_TOOLS}/Pkg

NanoBSD looks in this directory for any packages to install on the completed disk image. By default, this is */usr/src/tools/tools/nanobsd/Pkg*.

NANO_PMAKE="make -j 3"

This defines the -j flag NanoBSD gives to make(1) during the buildworld and buildkernel processes. If you have trouble building NanoBSD during either buildworld or buildkernel, try setting this to make -j 1.

CONF_BUILD=' '

NanoBSD uses any options defined here at the make buildworld stage. You can find a complete list of options that work on your version of FreeBSD in src.conf(5).

CONF_INSTALL=' '

NanoBSD uses any options defined here at the make installworld stage. Again, see src.conf(5) for the supported options.

CONF_WORLD=' '

NanoBSD uses anything in this variable as flags during the whole build process.

NANO_KERNEL=GENERIC

You'll almost certainly want a custom kernel for your NanoBSD image. Specify it here. This should be the name of a file under */usr/src/sys/i386/conf*.

NANO_CUSTOMIZE=""

By default, NanoBSD does not apply any customization scripts to the disk image building process. We'll talk about customizing disk images later in this chapter. Specify any customization scripts that you want to use in this variable.

NANO_NEWFS="-b 4096 -f 512 -i 8192 -O1 -U"

NanoBSD builds disk image filesystems with newfs(8). Specify any options you want here. Remember that NanoBSD runs its disk mounted read-only, so you should not need any custom options here.

NANO_DRIVE=ad0

You must identify how your device sees its flash drive. The easiest way to do this is to boot the target device and see what it thinks the hard drive is.

NANO_MEDIASIZE=1000000

This gives the size of your flash drive in 512-byte sectors.

NANO_IMAGES=2

NanoBSD lets you put multiple operating system images on a single flash drive. This can make upgrades very easy, but uses twice as much space. As flash drives are now more than large enough to hold almost any FreeBSD image you can build, there's rarely any reason to change this.

NANO_CODESIZE=0

You can define how much of your flash drive you want to allocate for your NanoBSD operating system slices. If you set this to 0, the disk image building script makes the operating system slices as large as possible.

NANO_CONFSIZE=2048

NanoBSD also creates a slice for configuration data, as we'll see later. This specifies the size of this slice, in 512-byte sectors. 2,048 sectors equals 1 megabyte.

NANO_DATASIZE=0

NanoBSD can optionally create a fourth slice for data storage. It is conceivable, though not common, to build a NanoBSD device that stores data on a long-term basis. If set to 0, *nanobsd.sh* doesn't create a data partition. If set to a negative number, NanoBSD makes the data slice as large as possible.

NANO_RAM_ETCSIZE=10240

This is the size of the memory disk used for */etc*, in 512-byte sectors. 10240 is 5MB.

NANO_RAM_TMPVARSIZE=10240

This is the size of the memory disk shared between */var* and */tmp*. 5MB is large enough so long as you don't try to write to your logs.

NANO_SECTS=63 and NANO_HEADS=16

These define the geometry of the flash drive you're using. Do not set these in your configuration file! Configure your flash card correctly in *FlashDevice.sub* instead.

FlashDevicesamsung128

This tells NanoBSD to take the disk device geometry from the *FlashDevice.sub* file, instead of using the NANO_SECTS and NANO_HEADS values. This sample entry means to use a 128MB flash device made by Samsung.

A Sample NanoBSD Configuration

All this looks impressive, but how do we use it? Let's create a configuration file and walk through it. Remember, I'm building a DNS server on a Soekris device. Any variable I don't set gets the default value.

```
#configuration for building a Soekris DNS server
❶ NANO_NAME=SoekrisDNS
  NANO_IMAGES=2
❷ NANO_KERNEL=SOEKRIS
❸ NANO_DRIVE=ad1
```

```
           NANO_PMAKE="make -j 3"
           FlashDevice samsung 128
           customize_cmd cust_comconsole
           customize_cmd cust_allow_ssh_root
           customize_cmd cust_install_files
❹  CONF_INSTALL='
           WITHOUT_TOOLCHAIN=YES
           '

           CONF_WORLD='
           COMCONSOLE_SPEED=19200
           NO_MODULES=YES
           WITHOUT_ACPI=YES
           WITHOUT_ASSERT_DEBUG=YES
           WITHOUT_ATM=YES
           WITHOUT_AUDIT=YES
           WITHOUT_AUTHPF=YES
❺  #WITHOUT_BIND=YES
           WITHOUT_BLUETOOTH=YES
           WITHOUT_CALENDAR=YES
           WITHOUT_CPP=YES
           WITHOUT_CVS=YES
           WITHOUT_CXX=YES
           WITHOUT_DICT=YES
           WITHOUT_DYNAMICROOT=YES
           WITHOUT_EXAMPLES=YES
           WITHOUT_FORTH=YES
           WITHOUT_FORTRAN=YES
           WITHOUT_GAMES=YES
           WITHOUT_GCOV=YES
           WITHOUT_GDB=YES
           WITHOUT_GPIB=YES
           WITHOUT_GROFF=YES
           WITHOUT_HTML=YES
           WITHOUT_I4B=YES
           WITHOUT_INET6=YES
           WITHOUT_INFO=YES
           WITHOUT_IPFILTER=YES
           WITHOUT_IPX=YES
           WITHOUT_KERBEROS=YES
           WITHOUT_LIBPTHREAD=YES
           WITHOUT_LIBTHR=YES
           WITHOUT_LPR=YES
           WITHOUT_MAILWRAPPER=YES
           WITHOUT_MAN=YES
           WITHOUT_NCP=YES
           WITHOUT_NETCAT=YES
           WITHOUT_NIS=YES
           WITHOUT_NLS=YES
           WITHOUT_NLS_CATALOGS=YES
           WITHOUT_NS_CACHING=YES
           WITHOUT_OBJC=YES
           WITHOUT_PAM_SUPPORT=YES
           WITHOUT_PF=YES
           WITHOUT_PROFILE=YES
           WITHOUT_RCMDS=YES
```

```
WITHOUT_RCS=YES
WITHOUT_RESCUE=YES
WITHOUT_SENDMAIL=YES
WITHOUT_SHAREDOCS=YES
WITHOUT_SPP=YES
WITHOUT_SYSCONS=YES
WITHOUT_USB=YES
#WITHOUT_WPA_SUPPLICANT_EAPOL=YES
WITHOUT_ZFS=YES
'
```

I start by giving this disk image a unique name with the NANO_NAME variable ❶. I have a custom kernel configuration ❷ for this device. Where did I get this kernel configuration? I booted the Soekris diskless to capture */var/run/dmesg.boot* off of a GENERIC kernel, and then I searched the Internet for other net4801 kernels to identify the potentially useful options other people used. The only annoying thing about booting this device diskless is that you must disable ACPI in the boot loader.

Thanks to the diskless boot, I know that the net4801 sees the flash slot as drive */dev/ad1* ❸. If I don't set this in my configuration file, on my first NanoBSD I would get complaints that the kernel could not find the root partition on */dev/ad0*.

I then list the various customize_ scripts I want to use on this image. We'll talk about customizations later in this chapter. All of these scripts are in the default NanoBSD toolkit, and I recommend using them for your first image.

We then have special options for make(1) to use during the install process. We'll look at the options a little later, but for now you just need to know that WITHOUT_TOOLCHAIN tells make(1) to not install the compiler, libraries, or other tools needed to build software. We won't be building ports on an embedded system!

Take careful note of how the CONF_INSTALL ❹ variable is set. We have a single tick mark (') after the equal sign, our variable on a line of its own, and then a single tick mark (') afterwards. This helps keep multiple options separate and makes the file readable. We do something similar for CONF_WORLD, in the next section. NanoBSD expects that each variable will be listed on its own line, as it builds a private *make.conf* out of them.

Each of the options in CONF_WORLD tells NanoBSD to not build a particular section of FreeBSD. Most are self-explanatory; for example, WITHOUT_ACPI says to not build ACPI. NO_MODULES means to not build kernel modules. I am deliberately not building systems that I don't want to put on my finished disk image, such as Sendmail, games, and packet filters.

These options are all buried within FreeBSD's build structure. Some of them have been around for years; others are new. Some of them will disappear—there's no guarantee than any of them will work a few releases down the road. Your src.conf man page has the current list of build variables for the installed version of FreeBSD. I include the whole list just so you can see how aggressive you can be in cutting. Yes, FreeBSD is so much smaller than many Linux versions; but this doesn't mean it can't be made smaller still! Some of the build options listed in src.conf(5) should not be used for

NanoBSD, however. For example, `WITHOUT_SETUID_LOGIN` has bad effects on your login. `WITHOUT_SYMVER` removes symbol versioning, which makes it impossible to use binaries compiled on other FreeBSD machines on your NanoBSD image. Be certain you understand what a build option really does before enabling it.

Also, note that you might have to disable some of these build options for particular NanoBSD images. I'm building a DNS server, so I need BIND. I commented out the `WITHOUT_BIND` ❺ entry in my configuration file for this particular build.

In the `CONF_INSTALL` option, I list the only option that is used not with builds but with installations of FreeBSD 7.0. The `WITHOUT_TOOLCHAIN` tells make `installworld` to not install the compiler, headers, or related tools on the disk image. We need to build a new compiler to build the new FreeBSD, but we don't need it installed on our final image. The installation process won't try to install anything that we stripped out of the build, but running make `buildworld` requires an up-to-date compiler.

This is a complete NanoBSD configuration file. Now, let's use it to build our custom disk image.

Building NanoBSD

Run *nanobsd.sh* as a shell script, specifying the configuration file with -c:

```
# /bin/sh nanobsd.sh -c mynanoconfig.txt
```

A NanoBSD build prints fairly generic log messages as it proceeds:

```
## Clean and create object directory (/usr/obj/nanobsd.SoekrisDNS/)
## Construct build make.conf (/usr/obj/nanobsd.SoekrisDNS//make.conf)
## run buildworld
### log: /usr/obj/nanobsd.SoekrisDNS//_.bw
## build kernel (SOEKRIS)
...
## build diskimage
### log: /usr/obj/nanobsd.SoekrisDNS//_.di
# NanoBSD image completed
```

If you get the `NanoBSD image completed` message, the build succeeded. If not, the build failed at the last stage you see in the log. It's not uncommon to perform multiple rounds of troubleshooting to get a configuration file that works properly, especially when aggressively using `WITHOUT_` options to reduce FreeBSD's size.

NanoBSD Build Directory

NanoBSD uses a build directory under */usr/obj* named after `NANO_NAME`. Our configuration file specifies that we're building a NanoBSD called SoekrisDNS, so our build directory is */usr/obj/nanobsd.SoekrisDNS*. Go to that directory and look at the files. You'll find several oddly named files, some large directories, and disk images.

NanoBSD uses files beginning with _. as markers, logs, and temporary directories. Despite the terseness of the messages you saw during the build process, NanoBSD doesn't actually discard the output of the commands it runs to build your disk image; it just redirects it to other files.

Table 20-1: NanoBSD Build Files

File	Purpose
_.bk	make buildkernel log
_.bw	make buildworld log
_.cust.<X>	Installing customization X
_.di	fdisk disk image
_.dl	Disklabel disk image
_.env	The environment used while building NanoBSD
_.etc	make distribution log
_.fdisk	fdisk(8) configuration
_.ik	make installkernel log
_.iw	make installworld log
_.w	Newly built world
disk.image	Disk image of a single slice
disk.full	Disk image of complete device

Use the log files to help solve build and configuration problems.

NanoBSD Build Troubleshooting

NanoBSD's error messages when a build fails aren't terribly helpful. For example, here's a complete output of a failed NanoBSD build:

```
# /bin/sh nanobsd.sh -c soekris-dns.conf
## Clean and create object directory (/usr/obj/nanobsd.SoekrisDNS/)
## Construct build make.conf (/usr/obj/nanobsd.SoekrisDNS//make.conf)
## run buildworld
### log: ❶/usr/obj/nanobsd.SoekrisDNS//_.bw
```

You can see that the build process failed, but not why.

To get the actual error, look at the log file specified in the message. In this case, the log is the file */usr/obj/nanobsd.SoekrisDNS/_.bw* ❶. The end of that log file shows the last output from the failed build process. You'll see the usual sort of error for that part of the upgrade process.

One thing to remember is that NanoBSD uses make -j3 by default. This can obscure error messages in the log, as the error that caused the crash might be several lines before the apparent end of the build.

Why would a NanoBSD install fail when a regular upgrade from source works fine from the same source code? The leading cause of build failures is a choice of incompatible build options for the source tree. My NanoBSD configuration file includes many different WITHOUT_ options. You might notice that some of them are commented out. At the time I built this disk image, those options broke the build. While my embedded DNS server doesn't really need the software provided by the options I commented out, not including these options broke my NanoBSD build. (WITHOUT_BIND, of course, is commented out because I actually want BIND on this image.)

Another problem you can have when you're building a NanoBSD image is when the build completes, but the disk image construction dies with:

```
/usr/obj/nanobsd.SoekrisDNS/_.mnt: write failed, filesystem is full
```

Your files take up more space than is available on the drive. By default, the */conf* slice takes up 1 megabyte. NanoBSD splits the remaining space in half. If you have a 128MB flash card, each of the two NanoBSD images should get 63.5MB of disk space. If your FreeBSD build, including any additional files and the installed packages, is larger than that, image construction will fail. Don't forget that flash card vendors measure disk space the same way disk drive manufacturers do, in base 10 rather than base 2. Your 128MB flash card is actually a bit smaller than that. You need to put only one NanoBSD image on the disk, reduce the amount of stuff you include, or get a larger flash card.

The Completed Build

So, your build finished! Take a look at the disk image and see what's in it:

```
# mdconfig -af _.disk.full
md0
```

If you run fdisk(8) against the disk image, you'll see that it has three slices in use, two large ones and a very small third one. The two large slices are our NanoBSD images. Mount one and look around in it.

```
# mount /dev/md0s1a /mnt
```

Some poking around reveals that your NanoBSD system is complete but doesn't really do anything. It's an unconfigured FreeBSD install. Nevertheless, I recommend copying it to a flash disk and test-booting it on your target hardware to make sure it runs. Install NanoBSD on the flash disk */dev/da0* by running:

```
# dd if=disk.full of=/dev/da0
```

Now remove the flash drive, install it in your Soekris or other device, fire up your serial console, and turn on the power.

Serial Console Speeds

If you boot a vanilla FreeBSD install on a Soekris box, you'll have problems. Soekris hardware uses a default serial console speed of 19,200bps, while FreeBSD uses a more common 9,600bps. This means that if you connect your terminal at 19,200, you'll see all of the Soekris boot messages, but when FreeBSD starts, you'll see garbage. If you connect your terminal at 9,600, you'll see the FreeBSD messages but nothing but garbage from the Soekris.

Changing the FreeBSD console speed will be one of the first customizations we perform on our FreeBSD system. For an initial test of your FreeBSD image, however, boot your Soekris and console in at 9,600bps.

Customizing NanoBSD

Now that you have a vanilla FreeBSD install that boots on your hardware, let's customize it to meet our needs. Theoretically, you can customize NanoBSD in two ways: by editing the finished disk image or by changing the build to create the desired disk image. The first method is easy, but undesirable. If you're actually using NanoBSD in a production environment, one day you'll have to build a new disk image. Perhaps you must apply a security patch, or you'll find an application where a second NanoBSD box would be ideal. By modifying the build, you greatly ease producing a correct and usable updated image. You have three tools to modify the build: customization scripts, copying files, and adding packages.

Customization Scripts

Customization scripts are shell script functions inside *nanobsd.sh* or within your configuration file. Use a customization script to change a file that's likely to change as FreeBSD grows. For example, FreeBSD updates the included version of SSH every few releases. You don't want to write a custom sshd(8) configuration file and load it unilaterally, as that would quite possibly be incompatible with newer versions of OpenSSH. The sensible thing to do is use a configuration script to make changes to the *sshd_config* included with the system, no matter what version it might be. NanoBSD includes a customization script just for that.

```
cust_allow_ssh_root () (
        sed -i "" -e '/PermitRootLogin/s/.*/PermitRootLogin yes/' \
          ${NANO_WORLDDIR}/etc/ssh/sshd_config
)
```

This simple sed(1)[3] script changes one line in */etc/ssh/sshd_config* to allow the root user to SSH into the NanoBSD system. This script would break if the PermitRootLogin option was renamed or removed, but that will happen rarely if ever. You can include anything you like in a customization script, even spawning a complicated Perl script that takes NANO_NAME as an argument and writes a custom *rc.conf* for your image.

---

[3] sed(1) and awk(1) expertise is another thing that separates the Real Sysadmins from the young punks. Reading shell scripts is an excellent way to pick up enough about these tools to fool people into thinking you're an expert.

NanoBSD includes four customization scripts:

cust_comconsole
> Enables serial console and serial login.

cust_allow_ssh_root
> Allows root to SSH into the system.

cust_install_files
> Copies files under the *Files* directory into completed image.

cust_pkg
> Installs packages from the *Pkg* directory into completed image.

As you've probably gathered, customization scripts drive the other two methods of tweaking your image.

Adding Packages

Create a *Pkg* directory in the NanoBSD directory. The customization script *cust_pkg* installs any packages you place in this directory on your image. That's really it.

If you're short on space, however, you don't need to install the entire package. Find the binary for the program you want to run, use ldd(1) to identify the necessary libraries, and just copy those files to your image.

Adding Files

The *cust_install_files* customization script copies files from the tree under the *Files* directory into your completed image. By default, the *Files* directory contains a single subdirectory called *root*. The contents of this directory are copied into */root* on the image.

If you regularly build NanoBSD images, I recommend changing the *cust_install_files* script. NanoBSD includes several files in the *Files* directory, and those are considered system files. When you update your source tree, csup(1) wipes out any changes you made to any files under the *Files* directory. Copy *cust_install_files* into your configuration file, give it a name like *cust_install_dns_files*, and point it to a directory other than *Files*.

I'm building a DNS server, so I need a custom *named.conf* and *rndc.conf*. These files go in */var/named/etc/namedb*, so I must create the directory */usr/src/tools/tools/nanobsd/Files/var/named/etc/namedb* (ick!) and put my custom files in there.

Similarly, I need an *rc.conf*. I'll create *Files/etc/rc.conf* for my configuration. I need SSH keys, which I create exactly as I would for a diskless workstation. Similarly, I want a *syslog.conf* that writes to my networked log server.

One last annoyance when working with Soekris hardware is the serial console speed. We set the serial console speed in our configuration file with the COMCONSOLE_SPEED variable, telling FreeBSD to use a default console speed of 19,200. If you didn't do that, the simplest way to accommodate the difference in port speed is to set FreeBSD to use the higher console speed.

You can do this with the proper entries in *boot/loader.conf*. Just create the following entries in *Files/boot/loader.conf*:

```
comconsole_speed="19200"
console="comconsole,vidconsole"
```

This gives your NanoBSD install a serial console with a default speed of 19,200bps. It won't take effect until the boot loader starts, however. You're really better off building your whole NanoBSD world with a console speed of 19,200 through a CONF_WORLD variable.

Perfecting Customizations

One of the headaches in building a NanoBSD image is getting the right set of customizations for your purpose. You'll add every file and every setting you think you need in your image, copy the completed image to a flash drive, and boot it on your device only to realize you forgot something and must add a file to the image.

While building a NanoBSD image takes a while, the longest part of the process is building the world and kernel. You can add a file to the customization image and rerun the image-building process without building a whole new world and kernel by adding the -b flag to *nanobsd.sh*:

```
# /bin/sh nanobsd.sh -b -c myconfig.txt
```

This skips the buildworld and buildkernel stages, and assembles a fresh disk image with your updated files.

Using NanoBSD

So you have a NanoBSD image that boots and includes all the software you need. You've copied it to a flash drive and are running it without trouble. What happens when you must make a minor change or install an upgrade?

Not to worry. NanoBSD has special provisions for both these cases.

Minor Updates

NanoBSD uses the cfg slice to handle minor changes. Any files on */cfg* are copied to the running NanoBSD's */etc* partition during boot. This means that you can make changes to, say, */etc/rc.conf* without building a whole new image. For a good example of how this is used, take a look at the *change_password* script in *Files/root*. This script runs passwd(1) to let you change root's password, mounts */cfg* read-write, copies the vital password files to */cfg*, and unmounts */cfg*. The next time the system boots, NanoBSD copies those vital password files to */etc*.

Whenever you make changes to your running NanoBSD system, I recommend making corresponding changes to your NanoBSD build system. This way, when you have to roll a new disk image, your changes will be all captured and up to date.

Updating Disk Images

So, you've built a NanoBSD image and are running it on a Soekris box nailed to the top of a windmill so you can use custom SNMP scripts to manage power output. One day you have to do an upgrade. Do you break out a ladder and a crowbar so you can climb to the top of the windmill and install a new flash card? No, most FreeBSD developers are far too sedentary to tolerate any such thing.[4]

Remember, a NanoBSD system has two disk images. Only one of them runs at any moment. The included upgrade scripts allow you to upgrade the disk image that is not in use at the moment. You then reboot onto the new image. If the new image doesn't work, you can boot the original image, restoring service while you work out what went wrong.

Upgrade a NanoBSD installation remotely over SSH with the scripts *updatep1* and *updatep2*. If your system is running slice 1, use the script *updatep2*. If you're on slice 2, run *updatep1*. In addition to providing a command prompt, SSH lets you transfer files or even run commands on remote systems. Here, we are logged into our NanoBSD system and want to update slice 2 with a disk image on the server 192.168.1.5:

```
# ssh 192.168.1.5 ❶cat _.disk.image | sh /root/updatep2
```

We connect to the remote system and feed it the output of cat(1) ❶—in this case, the image of a single partition. On the remote system, we run the *updatep2* script, which runs some basic sanity checking to confirm we aren't trying anything too daft and then copies the disk image to the unused slice. It also sets the new boot default to the freshly upgraded slice. If the upgrade doesn't work correctly—that is, if the system boots but the application doesn't run correctly—use the serial console to boot on the other slice, or use boot0cfg(8) on the running system to tell NanoBSD to boot the other slice next time.

Once you start to experiment with NanoBSD, you can find any number of uses for it. In addition to custom-built appliances, I use NanoBSD to provide a userland for jails and diskless workstations. If you want more full-featured bootable FreeBSD media, though, take a look at FreeSBIE.

Live Media with FreeSBIE

Compared to NanoBSD, FreeSBIE takes a different approach to creating purpose-built FreeBSD installs and has a different target. While NanoBSD is trying to satisfy users of small media, FreeSBIE targets live read-only media such as CDs, DVDs, and big flash devices. Having much more disk space gives FreeSBIE a certain amount of flexibility lacking in NanoBSD. While I prefer using NanoBSD for appliance functions, many people use FreeSBIE to build bootable CDs that turn any old workstation into an appliance-style server.

---

[4] Put a good drink at the top of that windmill, however, and you'll get three out of four developers up the ladder before you can blink. It's all a question of alinging your needs with their priorities.

Using a live CD is as simple as booting off of the CD. The operating system on the CD should identify your hardware, configure the installed software, and in general boot into a fresh and usable operating system. If you want detailed information about using a running FreeSBIE install, check out the FreeSBIE website at *http://www.freesbie.org*. We're going to focus on building your own customized FreeSBIE disk.

FreeSBIE builds a fresh world and kernel from the source code in */usr/src*, but then takes its packages from the system you're building on. This means that your build system must have a fairly coherent and clean set of packages. If you've abused your system and your package records are inaccurate, you can't use them to build a FreeSBIE live CD.

While we refer to a FreeSBIE live CD throughout this section, all of this applies to building DVDs and flash devices as well.

FREESBIE AND FREEBSD

FreeSBIE is not an integrated part of FreeBSD. While the FreeSBIE developers work very hard to support newer versions of FreeBSD, their work still lags slightly behind mainstream FreeBSD development. This chapter was written using FreeSBIE 2, which is designed for FreeBSD 6. I expect FreeBSD 7 support shortly after FreeBSD 7 is released. When you start working with FreeSBIE, be prepared to do your own investigation and troubleshooting.

Installing the FreeSBIE Toolkit

You can get the very latest FreeSBIE tools from the FreeSBIE CVS repository available through *http://www.freesbie.org*, or, if you have an up-to-date Ports Collection, you can install it from */usr/ports/sysutils/freesbie*. Everything in the FreeSBIE toolkit installs under */usr/local/share/freesbie*.

The FreeSBIE toolkit includes very few instructions. Most of the documentation is available only on the FreeSBIE website, *http://www.freesbie.org*.

Configuring FreeSBIE

Under */usr/local/share/freesbie/conf* you'll find the default FreeSBIE configuration file *freesbie.defaults.conf*. Do not edit this file directly; instead, create a *freesbie.conf* file in the same directory. Anything in *freesbie.conf* overrides the same setting in *freesbie.defaults.conf*.

As of FreeSBIE 2.0, here are some commonly changed configuration options. The example configuration below shows as you would configure it in your customized *freesbie.conf* file, not as it appears in *freesbie.defaults.conf*. (The default configuration file has special syntax to allow your custom configuration to override those values.)

For your first FreeSBIE build, I recommend changing as little as possible. While many options might be tempting to change, sticking as close to the defaults as possible gives the best initial results. Overly ambitious initial customization causes build failures. As with so many other things, I recommend you learn about FreeSBIE's hidden catches one at a time.

BASEDIR="/usr/local/freesbie-fs"

This is the directory where FreeSBIE installs its freshly built world, packages, and custom files.

CLONEDIR="/usr/local/freesbie-clone"

FreeSBIE uses this directory as a temporary staging area when building images.

SRCDIR="/usr/src"

This is the source tree that FreeSBIE uses to build its world and kernel.

ISOPATH="/usr/obj/FreeSBIE.iso"

FreeSBIE puts the completed ISO at this location.

IMGPATH="/usr/obj/FreeSBIE.img"

This is the full path to a completed UFS FreeSBIE image for flash media.

MAKEJ_WORLD="-j3"

This determines the -j argument for make(1) to use when building world. Set this to -j1 if you have a build failure and want to determine if it's an actual problem or just a parallelization issue.

MAKEJ_KERNEL="-j1"

This sets the parallelization of make(1) when building the kernel.

MAKEOPT="-DNO_CLEAN"

If you want to use any make(1) options for the world and kernel builds, specify them here.

KERNELCONF="/usr/src/sys/i386/conf/CUSTOMFREESBIE"

This is the full path to the FreeSBIE kernel configuration file. I find that the kernel configuration provided with FreeSBIE only works well with the same version of FreeBSD that the FreeSBIE developers are using. As of FreeBSD 7.0, a FreeSBIE build takes advantage of the following non-GENERIC options:

```
options      GEOM_UZIP
options      GEOM_LABEL
options      VESA
options      SC_PIXEL_MODE
```

I additionally remove all SCSI and RAID controllers, as I really don't need access to those disks. If I don't want to touch the hard drive I'll also remove the atadisk device so that my disk image cannot find any IDE disks. If you want firewall features, add the PF kernel options.

MAKE_CONF="/etc/make.conf"

This defines the custom *make.conf* you want to use for your FreeSBIE build. Note that as the packages are copied from the installed system, any special *make.conf* settings will not apply to the packages. You might as well use *src.conf* instead.

SRC_CONF="/etc/src.conf"

You can customize the source build with *src.conf*, just as you can with the primary FreeBSD build. Specify the full path to your FreeSBIE-specific *src.conf* here.

FILE_LIST="/home/mwlucas/freesbie-files.txt"

You can specify exactly which files you want to install on your FreeSBIE disc. If you specify a file list, FreeSBIE installs only the files on that list into the image. (Effectively, this means that only files on this list are copied from the FreeSBIE base dir to the FreeSBIE clone dir.) This means you must make a 100 percent complete list of all the files on the live CD. This is most useful for NanoBSD-like small systems, in my opinion.

PRUNE_LIST="/home/mwlucas/freesbie-prune.txt"

This file contains a list of files and directories that are included in the build, but must be removed before building the live CD image. Any files listed in the prune list file are removed from the cloned directory before the image is built from that directory. This can be very useful to reduce the size of a live CD.

PKGFILE="/home/mwlucas/freesbie-packages"

This file contains a list of packages, one package per line, without version information. FreeSBIE installs all of the packages on this list onto your live image. If you do not set this, FreeSBIE's make packageselect command creates a package list in the file */usr/local/share/freesbie/conf/packages*.

EXTRA="customroot rootmfs etcmfs sound xautostart"

FreeSBIE provides a variety of plug-ins to enable different functions on the live CD. We'll cover the standard plug-ins later.

MINIMAL=YES

If you define MINIMAL, FreeSBIE builds the smallest FreeBSD it can. This creates a result similar to NanoBSD. A MINIMAL build only works reliably with whatever version of FreeBSD the FreeSBIE developers are using.

NO_BUILDWORLD=YES

By defining this, you tell FreeSBIE to not build a new userland. You must have a freshly compiled userland available in */usr/obj*.

NO_BUILDKERNEL=YES

This tells FreeSBIE to not build a new kernel and use the previously compiled kernel in */usr/obj* instead.

```
MAKEOBJDIRPREFIX="/usr/freesbie/obj"
```
While you can set this to provide a separate FreeSBIE build area, doing so is not recommended. Many shell scripts assume that the recently built userland and kernel are under */usr/obj*.

```
NO_COMPRESSEDFS=YES
```
This tells FreeSBIE to use an uncompressed filesystem on the ISO image.

FreeSBIE Plug-ins

FreeSBIE provides *plug-ins* to more thoroughly customize disk images. While a default FreeSBIE build is perfectly serviceable, plug-ins let you turn on and off different features on your live CD. Plug-ins install extra configuration scripts or enable different automated functions on your bootable image. All of the plug-in scripts are in */usr/local/share/freesbie/extra*. The *README* file describes all of the default plug-ins.

List all of the plug-ins you want to use in the EXTRA value in *freesbie.conf*. Here are some of the plug-ins I find most interesting or useful.

adduser

The adduser plug-in adds the user freesbie to the live CD. You can specify a username of your own choosing with the FREESBIE_ADDUSER variable in *freesbie.conf*.

autologin

When you enable the autologin plug-in, the user freesbie is automatically logged in at boot.

comconsole

Enabling the comconsole plug-in in the build adds the serial console as a second console. Setting the configuration option SERIAL_ONLY=YES in *freesbie.conf* builds an image that only uses the serial console. You could also do this by adding a custom *loader.conf* into the image through the customroot plug-in.

customroot

The customroot plug-in lets you add arbitrary files to your live CD. Any files in the directory */usr/local/share/freesbie/extra/customroot* are copied to your new image. Use subdirectories as necessary to put the files in the proper place. For example, if you want a custom */etc/rc.conf*, put it in */usr/local/share/freesbie/extra/customroot/etc/rc.conf*. By adding a custom */usr/local/share/freesbie/extra/customroot/var/named/etc/namedb/named.conf*, you can have an easily replaceable secondary nameserver that boots off of read-only media. Any files added by this plug-in override any other file source in FreeSBIE.

customscripts

The FreeSBIE build process runs any scripts found in */usr/local/freesbie/ extra/customscripts* immediately before creating the ISO image. You can add users or edit files automatically with this plug-in.

etcmfs

This tells the system to use a memory filesystem for */etc*.

l10n.sh

This plug-in lets the live CD user choose an international character set. This is useful for non-English speakers.

mountdisks

With this plug-in enabled, FreeSBIE mounts any UFS, FAT, or NTFS slices found on the system the live CD runs on.

pf

This plug-in creates and activates a simple "block all incoming, allow all outgoing" PF ruleset upon boot.

rootmfs

This plug-in makes the live CD use a memory filesystem for root. While the user can make changes to the root directory, they disappear upon a reboot.

sound

Upon boot, the live CD autodetects the sound card and installs the correct sound driver.

swapfind

If the system running the live CD has any swap partitions, FreeSBIE finds and uses them. This requires writing to the disk, of course, which might be undesirable.

varmfs

The live CD uses a memory filesystem for */var*. This makes local logging possible, but the logs won't survive a reboot.

xautostart

The live CD starts X at boot.

xconfig

The live CD automatically configures X at boot. This is desirable when using xautostart.

xconfigure-probe

FreeSBIE uses an alternate method to automatically configure X at boot. (As X offers multiple methods to configure a display, this dichotomy isn't anything the FreeSBIE team can solve.)

Choosing Packages

You can create a text file containing all the packages you want to install on your live CD, or you can use `make packageselect` in */usr/local/share/freesbie*. This command creates a menu of all the packages installed on your build system and lets you select which ones you want to install on your live CD. When you select a package, all dependencies are pulled in automatically.

Building a FreeSBIE Image

To build a FreeSBIE CD from your configuration, just do:

```
# cd /usr/local/share/freesbie
# make iso
```

FreeSBIE builds a complete FreeBSD, trims and expands it as desired, installs packages, runs the customization scripts, and compresses the whole thing into a customized live CD image.

If you want to create a flash image instead of an ISO, use `make flash`. FreeSBIE asks which flash device you want to use, initializes it, builds a FreeSBIE userland, and installs it on the specified flash device.

Rebuilding FreeSBIE

FreeSBIE uses dotfiles much like ports to indicate when it's finished with a step. By default, these files are in */usr/obj/usr/local/share/freesbie*.

If you want to rebuild FreeSBIE without rebuilding world, delete the files for the stages that you've completed already.

This is the last stop in our exploration of FreeBSD's darker corners. Now let's see what to do when things go really, really, *really* wrong.

21

SYSTEM (AND SYSADMIN) PANICS AND CRASHES

One of the nicest things about FreeBSD is its stability; the only Blue Screen of Death you can find is a screensaver. In fact, I ran FreeBSD for almost a year before seeing a machine crash for reasons other than bad hardware. FreeBSD can crash, or *panic*, but it allows you to recover from a panic fairly easily—so don't, er, panic. You can even connect to the remote console during a panic and force a reboot. FreeBSD provides the tools you need to discover exactly what happened as well as extensive debugging information about the panic. Even if you don't know what to do with this information, you can submit a problem report and discuss the matter with the FreeBSD development team.

What Causes Panics?

When does a system panic? Panicking is a choice made by the kernel when it faces an unresolvable conflict. If the system achieves a condition that it doesn't know how to handle, or if it fails its own internal consistency checks, it panics. Production versions of FreeBSD are increasingly difficult to panic, but it can still happen. The easiest way to panic a system is to do something daft, like pull out a non–hot swappable hard drive while it's in use. Panics are not uncommon when running -current; they're not frequent, mind you, but they're not rarities.

FreeBSD is very complex, and neither its royal blood lineage nor the open source development process can protect it from all bugs. Fortunately, that heritage and the development process do give you the tools you need to provide the information for other people to debug your problem. You might begin with a cryptic error code, but you'll quickly learn that your string of garbage characters means something to someone.

I recommend that every system be prepared to capture a crash dump before it is allowed to enter production. FreeBSD captures crash dumps by default, but if you reconfigure your server or have special disk partitioning you'll want to confirm that crash dumps will still work. This precaution will be wasted on most of your servers, but the preparation really takes very little time. When one of your several servers panics, you'll be glad that you have all of the crash information on hand.

Recognizing Panics

When a system panics, it stops running all programs and stops listening to the network. On a released version of FreeBSD, or when tracking -stable, a system that panics automatically reboots. Not all unexplained reboots are panics—if you have a bad power supply or bad memory, for example, the hardware failure can cause a reboot without any sort of log or console message. You might have messages in your error log if you panic, depending on the type of panic. If you have your system configured to display panics rather that reboot, you'll see a console message much like this:

```
panic: _mtx_lock_sleep: recursed on non-recursive mutex ahc_lock @ /usr/src/
sys/dev/aic7xxx/aic7xxx_osm.h:203

cpuid = 0
KDB: enter: panic
[thread pid 12 tid 100002 ]
Stopped at        kdb_enter+0x32: leave
db>
```

The only part of this message that seems even vaguely sensible to me is the first line. I know that a mutex is a kind of kernel lock (see Chapter 12), and my SCSI card uses the ahc driver. This makes sense, actually; I triggered this panic on a -current machine by running fdisk(8) on a SCSI hard drive.[1]

---

[1] Also known as, "I guess I'm not writing Chapter 18 today, as it is FreeBSD's will that I write Chapter 21." And here I was, wondering how I was going to get a good panic for this chapter.

The db> at the bottom is a debugger command prompt. Hit ENTER a couple of times and you'll see that you can enter commands. They aren't useful Unix commands, but they will help you get more information out of the system.

Responding to a Panic

If you get a panic, the first thing to do is get a copy of the panic message. Since FreeBSD is no longer running, the standard methods for copying data from your machine won't work—you cannot SSH in, and script(1) is no longer viable. The console might even be completely locked up and unresponsive instead of being in the debugger. In any event, you must have that error message.

FreeBSD didn't always automatically reboot after a panic; originally it just sat there displaying the panic message. The first time I saw a panic, I scrambled for paper and pen. Eventually I found an old envelope and a broken stub of pencil that made marks if you held it at just the right angle, and crawled between the server rack and the rough brick wall. I balanced the six-inch black-and-white monitor in one hand, and with my other hand I held the envelope against the wall. Apparently I grow a third hand under duress, because I got the panic message onto the envelope somehow. Finally, scraped and cramped, I slithered back out of the rack and victoriously typed the whole mess into an email. Surely the FreeBSD Project's Panic Emergency Response Team would be able to look at this garbage and tell me exactly what had happened.

I quickly learned that FreeBSD has no elite group standing by to take my problem report. Instead, I got a lonesome email: "Can you send a backtrace?" When I asked how, I was directed to a man page. (See Chapter 1.) Fortunately, the panic was easily reproducible—the only thing that had to happen to recreate the issue was for a customer to log in to the system. I spent the rest of the day struggling to master serial logins and core dumps.

The problem with the panic message on my envelope was that it only gave a tiny scrap of the story. It was so vague, in fact, that it was like describing a stolen car as "red, with a scratch on the fender." If you don't give the car's make, model, VIN, and license plate number, you cannot expect the police to make much headway. Similarly, without much more information from your crashing kernel, the FreeBSD developers cannot catch the criminal code.

There's a really simple way around this problem, however: Configure all of your machines to handle a panic before the panic happens. Set them up when you install the server. I now configure all my machines for proper panic processing prior to permitting them in production. That way, you'll be ready for disaster and you'll know exactly what to do if a machine ever panics. This might seem like a novel idea, and it certainly isn't emphasized in the FreeBSD documentation, but it makes sense. If none of your systems ever panics, you don't have anything to complain about. If you get a panic, you're ready and you'll be able to present the FreeBSD folks with complete debugging information without any trouble.

Preparations

While you can manage a panic in several ways, I prefer to dump the memory to disk for leisurely processing. You need a swap partition slightly larger than your kernel's memory usage. While it's possible that you might need to dump the entire contents of your physical RAM, it seems FreeBSD 7.0 kernel dumps are less than half a gigabyte in most cases. If you are using something that requires a great deal of kernel memory, such as the experimental ZFS support, your kernel dumps will be much larger. If you do not have a sufficiently large swap partition, you must either reinstall or add another hard drive with an adequate swap partition. (Remember I brought this up back in Chapter 2? Don't you wish you'd listened to me then?) While having a */var* partition sufficiently large to hold the kernel dump is helpful, it isn't mandatory.

The Crash Dump in Action

The kernel crash-capturing process works somewhat like this: If a properly configured system crashes, it saves a copy of the kernel memory. The copy is called a *dump*. The system cannot save the dump straight to a file. The crashed kernel doesn't know anything about filesystems, for one thing, and the filesystem might be corrupt or a write could corrupt it. The kernel understands partitions, however, so it can write the dump to a partition. The best partition available is the swap partition, which is memory scratch space. FreeBSD defaults to dumping on the first swap partition on the system, placing the dump as close to the end of the partition as possible. After the dump, the computer reboots.

FreeBSD enables swap during the reboot and then checks its filesystems for cleanliness. The partitions will almost certainly be dirty after a panic. Perhaps they're journaled or use background fsck(8), but the system cannot guarantee that. FreeBSD must enable swap before running fsck(8), because fsck(8) might need swap space. Hopefully, you have enough memory for fsck(8) to not require swapping, and if swapping is necessary, hopefully you have enough swap space to avoid overwriting the dump file lurking at the end of the swap partition.

Once FreeBSD has a filesystem where it can save a core dump, it checks the swap partition for a dump. If it finds a core dump, FreeBSD runs savecore(8) to copy the dump out of swap and into a proper filesystem file, clears the dump from swap space, and continues rebooting. You now have a kernel core file usable for debugging.

Configuring Crash Dumps

FreeBSD defaults to saving core dumps on the first available swap partition and, on every reboot, checks that partition for a dump. You can change this behavior as necessary to fit your system.

The obvious change you might need is to place your dump in a different swap partition, especially if you had to add a hard drive to get enough swap to hold your dump. Set the dump device with the dumpdev variable in */etc/rc.conf*:

```
dumpdev="/dev/ad4s1b"
```

Remember, */etc/fstab* lists all the swap partitions.

savecore(8) automatically places kernel dumps in */var/crash*. If your */var* partition is not large enough to contain the dump, however, set a different directory with the dumpdir variable in *rc.conf*:

```
dumpdir="/usr/crash"
```

While savecore also supports a few other options, such as compression, they aren't usually necessary on modern systems.

SERIAL CONSOLES AND PANICS

While a serial console is not strictly necessary for panic debugging, it can be invaluable when dealing with a stuck machine. The ability to capture everything with script(1), if nothing else, makes a serial console worthwhile. On a remote machine, a serial console is a necessity. If you really want to be prepared for a panic, make sure all of your machines have serial consoles or at least dual consoles. If possible, log the output of your serial consoles; this way, you'll get the panic message even if the system is not configured for crash dumps.

With a debugging kernel and a dump device, you're as ready for a panic as you can be.

Debugging Kernels

The FreeBSD kernel build process makes large amounts of debugging information available in the kernel. You'll find the primary debugging information in the *symbols* files, which provide a map between the machine code and the source code. This map also includes a complete list of source code line numbers so that developers can learn exactly where a problem occurred. Without this information, the developer is stuck trying to map a kernel core to the source code by hand, which is somewhat like solving a million-piece jigsaw puzzle without a picture or even a guarantee that you have all the pieces. This would be an ugly job regardless, but it becomes even uglier when you consider that the developer doing the work is an unpaid volunteer. Symbols are important.

Including the debugger in the kernel eases the debugging process if you have console access or if you have a serial console on a remote machine. While you can use entirely off-line debugging, at times having the debugger handy during a crash simplifies troubleshooting.

To retain debugging information and include the kernel debugger, ensure your kernel configuration includes these lines:

```
makeoptions    DEBUG=-g
options        KDB
options        KDB_TRACE
options        DDB
```

When you add the DDB option to your kernel, FreeBSD will no longer automatically reboot after a panic. Do you want your system to reboot itself after a panic, or do you want it to wait for you to intervene? If the system is at a remote location, you'll almost certainly want to trigger a dump and reboot automatically after a panic, but if you're at the console, you might want it to wait for you to tell it to reboot.

To reboot automatically, use the kernel option KDB_UNATTENDED:

```
options        KDB_UNATTENDED
```

This option tells FreeBSD to reboot after a panic even if DDB is in the kernel. When the system panics, you'll see a message telling you to hit the spacebar to enter the debugger; if you don't do it, the system will reboot in 15 seconds.

When Panic Strikes: Manual Crash Dumps

Suppose you have a debugging kernel installed, your swap partition can contain your dump, and your machine is not configured to reboot automatically after a panic. One day, one of your machines disappears from the network. You look at the console only to find a cryptic message followed by a db> prompt. Or, perhaps you hit ENTER on the serial console only to see the db> prompt appear. FreeBSD is waiting for you to tell it to reboot after a panic.

While you have the machine in the debugger, take a moment to capture some of the debugging output. If the panic message is there, copy it. If not, tell the debugger to reprint it:

```
db> panic
panic: from debugger
cpuid = 0
Uptime: 2m38s
panic: _mtx_lock_sleep: recursed on non-recursive mutex ahc_lock @ /usr/src/
sys/cam/cam_periph.h:182
...
```

The debugger repeats the panic message for your convenience.
You could also ask the debugger for more information about the panic:

```
db> trace
Tracing pid 12 tid 100002 td 0xc2117c00
kdb_enter(c0a908ed,0,3e9,c0b9fe2c,0,...) at kdb_enter+0x32
```

```
panic(c0a8f7ce,c0a54565,c0a4ba56,b6,c228ca30,...) at panic+0x124
_mtx_lock_sleep(c228ca30,c2117c00,0,c0a4ba56,b6,...) at _mtx_lock_sleep+0x47
_mtx_lock_flags(c228ca30,0,c0a4ba56,b6,780,...) at _mtx_lock_flags+0xef
...
```

This might go on for several pages. If you have a serial console, be certain to capture it all.

Before you reboot the machine, dump the kernel.

```
db> continue
Physical memory: 243 MB
Dumping 62 MB: 47 31 15
Dump complete
= 0xf
```

FreeBSD counts down how much memory remains to be dumped and reboots the system when finished.

If you don't want to dump, you can just reboot the machine:

```
db> reset
```

Your server will reboot and return to service.

If you have set KDB_UNATTENDED, the machine will reboot without any of this, just as if you had entered continue.

Using the Dump

If you're a kernel developer, this is where you stop listening to me and rely upon your own debugging experience. If you're a system administrator, however, you probably don't know enough about C and kernel internals to have any real hope of debugging a complicated kernel issue. Therefore, we'll focus on extracting enough information to give a developer a good shot at identifying the problem.

After a dumped panic, you'll find the files *vmcore.0* and *info.0* in */var/crash*. (Each subsequent crash gets a consecutively higher number.) The *info.0* file contains basic information about the dump, such as the partition the dump came from, the date, and if the dump succeeded. The *vmcore.0* file is the memory image of the kernel at the time of the crash. You have a complete record of what the kernel was thinking at the time it panicked.

If your system crashes frequently, crash dumps can grow to fill your */var* partition. If you have multiple instances of a certain type of crash, you only need one dump of that type. Crash dumps from older versions of FreeBSD are probably useless and can be deleted.

Getting a Backtrace

Go to the directory containing the kernel that panicked. This might be your currently running kernel, or perhaps a test kernel. The kernel directory has two files for every module, one named after the kernel module and the other with the word *.symbols* appended. The *.symbols* files are the debugging images. Once you're in the kernel directory, run kgdb(1) giving it the *kernel.symbols* filename and the full path to the *vmcore* for your crash:

```
# cd /boot/kernel.panicked/
# kgdb kernel.symbols /var/crash/vmcore.0
```

kgdb(1) prints a synopsis of gdb(1)'s copyright and license (kgdb(1) is actually a modified gdb(1) specifically tweaked for debugging kernels). Then you'll see a copy of the original panic message and finally get a kgdb prompt. Here, at long last, you can get the requested backtrace.

```
(kgdb) backtrace
#0  doadump () at pcpu.h:195
#1  0xc048c629 in db_fncall (dummy1=-875263368, dummy2=0, dummy3=524358,
    dummy4=0xcbd489e4 "ÐèHÀ") at /usr/src/sys/ddb/db_command.c:486
#2  0xc048cb95 in db_command_loop () at /usr/src/sys/ddb/db_command.c:401
#3  0xc048e305 in db_trap (type=3, code=0) at /usr/src/sys/ddb/db_main.c:222
#4  0xc0772426 in kdb_trap (type=3, code=0, tf=0xcbd48b88)
    at /usr/src/sys/kern/subr_kdb.c:502
#5  0xc09faa2b in trap (frame=0xcbd48b88) at /usr/src/sys/i386/i386/trap.c:620
#6  0xc09e053b in calltrap () at /usr/src/sys/i386/i386/exception.s:139
#7  0xc07725a2 in kdb_enter (msg=0xc0a908ed "panic") at cpufunc.h:60
#8  0xc074b954 in panic (
    fmt=0xc0a8f7ce "_mtx_lock_sleep: recursed on non-recursive mutex %s @
%s:%d\n") at /usr/src/sys/kern/kern_shutdown.c:547
#9  0xc07400b7 in _mtx_lock_sleep (m=0xc228ca30, tid=3255925760, opts=0,
    file=0xc0a51887 "/usr/src/sys/dev/aic7xxx/aic7xxx_osm.h", line=203)
    at /usr/src/sys/kern/kern_mutex.c:311
#10 0xc07402df in _mtx_lock_flags (m=0xc228ca30, opts=0,
    file=0xc0a51887 "/usr/src/sys/dev/aic7xxx/aic7xxx_osm.h", line=203)
    at /usr/src/sys/kern/kern_mutex.c:187
...
```

This is a complete list of everything the kernel did, in reverse order. Line 0 shows that the debugger called the doadump function, which performs the crash dump to disk. Immediately below that we see assorted debugging calls. Line 8 includes our panic message and the word panic itself; this is where our server started turning belly-up.

A panicking kernel will call a function called panic and sometimes trap. You'll see variants on these two words, such as db_trap, kdb_trap, calltrap, and so on, but we're only interested in the plain unadorned trap or panic call. Search through your kgdb(1) output for either of these functions. In our previous example, line 8 includes a call to panic. Lines 3, 4, and 5 contain functions that the panic helper calls when attempting to figure out exactly what happened and what to do about it.

Line 9 shows what happened immediately before the system decided to panic in line 8. Line 9 reads:

```
#9  0xc07400b7 in _mtx_lock_sleep (m=0xc228ca30, tid=3255925760, opts=0,
    file=0xc0a51887 "/usr/src/sys/dev/aic7xxx/aic7xxx_osm.h", line=203)
    at /usr/src/sys/kern/kern_mutex.c:311
```

The hex numbers don't mean much to me, but this sure looks a lot like our panic message. FreeBSD got confused while executing code from line 203 of */usr/src/sys/dev/aic7xxx/aic7xxx_osm.h*. This gives the developer a pretty good idea of where to start looking for the problem. We can look a little closer, however. Enter the up command and the line you're interested in:

```
(kgdb) up 9
#9  0xc07400b7 in _mtx_lock_sleep (m=0xc228ca30, tid=3255925760, opts=0,
    file=0xc0a51887 "/usr/src/sys/dev/aic7xxx/aic7xxx_osm.h", line=203)
    at /usr/src/sys/kern/kern_mutex.c:311
311                    KASSERT((m->lock_object.lo_flags & LO_RECURSABLE) != 0,
```

Here we see the actual line of code that was compiled into the panicking code. At this point, I must surrender you to a kernel developer's tender mercies. Including this in a problem report will save a round of email, however, and it's quite possible that a developer will just say "Oops!" and send you a fix with no further troubleshooting. Use the quit command to leave kgdb(1):

```
(kgdb) quit
```

If you build another kernel, be certain to save the panicked kernel for further debugging. You can only debug a kernel dump with the kernel that panicked.

The above is a pretty good start on a problem report. You can see exactly where the system broke and what line of code it broke on. Interested developers would quite probably write you back and tell you other things to type at the kgdb prompt, but you are well on your way to getting the problem solved and helping the FreeBSD folks squash a bug.

vmcore and Security

The *vmcore* file contains everything in your kernel memory at the time of the panic, which might include sensitive security information. Someone could conceivably use this information to break into your system. A FreeBSD developer might request a copy of the *vmcore* file and the bad kernel for many legitimate reasons; it makes debugging easier and can save countless rounds of email. Still, carefully consider the potential consequences of someone having this information. If you don't recognize the person who asks or if you don't trust him, don't send the file!

If the panic is reproducible, however, you can cold-boot the system to single-user mode and trigger the panic immediately. If the system never starts any programs containing confidential information and nobody types any passwords into the system, the dump cannot contain that information. Reproducing a panic in single-user mode generates a security-information-free, sanitized dump. Boot into single-user mode and then run:

```
# mount -ar
# /etc/rc.d/dumpon start
# command_that_panics_the_system
```

The first command mounts the filesystems as read-only, so that you won't have to fsck(8) yet again after a panic. The second command tells FreeBSD where to put a dump. Finally, run the command that triggers the panic. Triggering the panic might require more than one command, but this should get a clean dump for you in most cases. If your panic requires that you load confidential information into memory, that information will be present in the dump.

Submitting Problem Reports

You might argue that I should have included this in Chapter 1 on "Getting More Help." *Problem Report (PR)* sounds impressive, doesn't it? A problem report is not where you say that you have a problem, however, it's where you prove that *FreeBSD* has a problem. Yes, I said *prove*. It's not that FreeBSD is innocent until proven guilty, but for you to submit a proper problem report, you must substantiate your claim. Problem reports filed without evidence will be closed with a terse response such as "not a bug" or "useless PR." The proper forum to cry for help is a search engine, or perhaps even *FreeBSD-questions@FreeBSD.org*.

You can also file a PR to submit an improvement to the FreeBSD Project. The key word here is *improvement*, not *wish*. This sort of PR needs actual code attached along with a history of its testing and any other necessary information.

WHAT IS NOT A PROBLEM REPORT?

Any variation on "I don't know what I'm doing" doesn't belong in a problem report. This includes "FreeBSD doesn't work the way I think it should" or "Something bad happens when I do something dumb." If you break your arm, the hospital has to take you no matter what sort of foolish thing you did, but the FreeBSD team is much more choosy. Similarly, any variation on "The software included in FreeBSD isn't at the version I would like" is not a problem report. FreeBSD doesn't update to the latest and greatest compiler the second it becomes available, for example, and might *never* update to that particular compiler. There's always a reason for these decisions, and opening a PR to whine about them will get you nothing but a comment like "Install it from ports" and an immediately closed PR.

Finally, problem reports are collaborative. By filing a PR, you are indicating a willingness to work with the FreeBSD developers to resolve your issue. This might mean applying a patch, or trying a different command, or running debugging commands and sending the output to the developers. Filing a PR and expecting an answer like, "Fixed, go do this" is unrealistic. If you are not willing to work with the development team, don't open a PR. Of course, including the proper information in a PR helps resolve the issue much more quickly. If you can include everything the developer needs to know in your initial report, you'll get a much more prompt answer.

Repeat after me: "Free software. Donated support time." Remember this when your RAID card device driver makes your hard drives spin to a conga beat.

Finally, it's best if you're running a recent version of FreeBSD when filing a PR. Someone will look at a problem report based on a version of FreeBSD a release or two back, but nobody's going to look at a PR for FreeBSD 2.2-stable.

Before Filing a PR

Ideally, you won't ever have to file a problem report. Not only is a proper problem report a lot of work for you, it's a lot of work for the developers. The FreeBSD Project has a mailing list dedicated to assessing the PR database and guiding problem reports to the likely owners. While sending an email to a FreeBSD mailing list announces your woes to thousands of people, opening a PR announces your woes to thousands of people *and* demands that they handle virtual paperwork for you. Before filing a PR, be absolutely certain that both you and the FreeBSD Project need it.

First, treat your issue as a general problem and look through the usual FreeBSD resources. Review the FAQ and the Handbook. Search mailing list archives and the Internet for other people who have had this problem. Check the problem report system for an already open PR on this. Then ask on *FreeBSD-questions@FreeBSD.org* if anyone else has seen this behavior. Is this expected, or should you open a PR? The questions people ask about your problem will be invaluable in troubleshooting your problem and in creating your problem report.

Before starting your PR, gather every bit of information that might possibly be helpful. This includes:

- Verbose boot output
- System version
- Custom kernel configuration (if any)
- Debugging output from the problem

Can you reproduce this problem? For a developer to actually investigate the problem, you need a reproducible test case. If your server starts singing show tunes at 3 AM, that is a problem. If it only happened once and you can't reproduce it, you're best served by keeping your mouth shut so people don't think you're a loony. If it happens whenever you run a particular combination of commands on certain hardware, however, the matter can be verified and investigated, so that either the problem is resolved or someone offers your server a recording contract.

FreeBSD tracks problem reports with GNATS, a long-standing bug tracking system. While newer and flashier systems exist, none of them meets the FreeBSD Project's requirements. Before you submit a problem report, take a look at the existing PR database to see what's included in existing problem reports. You can search the PR database at *http://www.freebsd.org/support.html*. Does your problem resemble any problems in the PR database? Are there any comments on those PRs? How about any debugging output?

Can you reference another PR in yours, saying that it might be related? Or, does another PR exactly match your issue, and can you use any information in there?

Assuming you get this far, you might actually need to file a problem report. Let's see what not to put in it.

Bad PRs

The easiest way to understand a good PR is by reading some bad ones and identifying what qualifies them as such. While bad PRs are easy to find, I picked one and rewrote it so as to not embarrass anyone (with my luck, the original author is reading this right now!). I came across this problem report a few days ago:

> When I boot the FreeBSD 6.2-REL ISO image, I can't get past the "Welcome to FreeBSD!" options screen. The boot menu is stuck, and each time the screen refreshes it stays at 10. It doesn't matter what I press, the system never boots. If I press a whole bunch of buttons, I eventually get a kernel panic. The same ISO image launches in VMWare, the countdown appears, and I can install it to a partition on the disk. I've also tried enabling/disabling USB keyboard legacy support in BIOS without success.

The PR includes the model number of the motherboard, keyboard, and mouse. The instructions on repeating the problem suggest booting the ISO image with a similar configuration of hardware.

First off, the reader obviously has a problem with FreeBSD. It might even be that FreeBSD has a problem. I have no doubt that the system fails at boot exactly as advertised. But there's no evidence and no diagnostic information. The reproduction process is not very useful; if every 6.2 installation CD caused this behavior on common hardware such as this, the development team would never have signed off on the release.

Including the hardware make and model is not as useful as you might think. Vendors occasionally change chipsets in a piece of hardware without changing the model number. The verbose boot information identifies the actual hardware in the machine in a way that the model number never can.

If I experienced this behavior, I would first try burning a second CD. Perhaps the first write of the disk was bad. If the behavior persisted, I would download a FreeBSD 6.1 ISO. If the 6.1 ISO also failed, I would ask on the -questions@ mailing list for "further advice before I file a PR." If I could install FreeBSD 6.1, but not 6.2, I would include the kernel and verbose boot information from the 6.1 install in my problem report. I would also include a link to the mailing list archive of any discussion on my problem.

As you might guess, nobody has followed up on this problem report. Your goal is to file a problem report that is so complete and compelling that the developers will want to work on it. Show that you are easy for a volunteer to work with.

The FreeBSD FAQ includes a joke by Dag-Erling Smørgrav: "How many -current users does it take to change a light bulb?" The answer is one thousand, one hundred, and sixty nine, and includes "three to submit PRs about it, one of which is misfiled under doc and consists only of 'it's dark.'" If your PR amounts to "it's dark," it's a bad problem report.

Good PRs

You can enter PRs using the web interface, but I find that rather clunky. If you like graphic interfaces, you might try gtk-send-pr (*/usr/ports/sysutils/gtk-send-pr*). I always use send-pr(1) for problem reports. I find that send-pr(1) lets me consider my problem report carefully, even coming back to it a day later after I've had a chance to think about it. Begin by printing a blank PR form with -P and placing it in a file:

```
# send-pr -P > problemreport.txt
```

Now open the problem report in a text editor. Here's a sample of the template:

```
To: FreeBSD-gnats-submit@freebsd.org
From: Michael W Lucas <mwlucas>
Reply-To: Michael W Lucas <mwlucas>
Cc:
X-send-pr-version: 3.113
X-GNATS-Notify:
>Submitter-Id:     current-users
>Originator:       Michael W Lucas
>Organization:     <organization of PR author (multiple lines)>
>Confidential:     no <FreeBSD PRs are public data>
>Synopsis:         <synopsis of the problem (one line)>
>Severity:         <[ non-critical | serious | critical ] (one line)>
>Priority:         <[ low | medium | high ] (one line)>
>Category:         <choose from the list of categories above (one line)>
>Class:            <[ sw-bug | doc-bug | change-request | update | maintainer-
update ] (one line)>
>Release:      FreeBSD 7.0-CURRENT i386
>Environment:
System: FreeBSD pesty.blackhelicopters.org 7.0-CURRENT FreeBSD 7.0-CURRENT #0:
Wed May 21 13:29:50 EDT 2008 mwlucas@pesty.blackhelicopters.org:/usr/obj/usr/
src/sys/GENERIC i386
      <machine, os, target, libraries (multiple lines)>
>Description:
      <precise description of the problem (multiple lines)>
>How-To-Repeat:
      <code/input/activities to reproduce the problem (multiple lines)>
>Fix:
      <how to correct or work around the problem, if known (multiple lines)>
```

Both the web interface and the text form have the same fields; the difficulty lies in filling out the form correctly. The blank template also includes several lines beginning with SEND-PR, which send-pr(1) deletes from the form upon submission. Similarly, any text in angle brackets (< and >) is a comment, and send-pr(1) deletes it. The template lists legitimate choices inside the angle brackets. Let's go over it, one chunk at a time.

The discussion below applies mostly for system panics, the most frustrating type of problem report. FreeBSD also uses the PR database for submission of new ports and new features, however. Fill out these sorts of submissions appropriately for the submission, as per the documentation at the FreeBSD website.

To:
> This field is the email address of the FreeBSD PR database. Leave that alone.

From, Reply-To:
> Make sure these lines contain valid email addresses. GNATS will reply to your email address with your PR number, and interested developers will try to contact you here.

cc:
> You might want to copy someone else on your PR. My boss feels better when he is copied on support requests for issues that he thinks are critical, for example.

X-send-pr-version, X-GNATS-Notify, Submitter-Id:
> Leave these fields unchanged.

Originator:
> This is your name, generally pulled from the system environment. While some folks use handles on the Internet, I recommend using your real name. It's difficult to treat a serious problem with the attention it deserves if it comes from "Mr. Ticklebottoms."

Organization:
> This field is not used, so you can put here whatever you like.

Confidential:
> FreeBSD's GNATS is a public database, and you should never enter confidential information in a problem report. Changing this will result in send-pr refusing to submit the PR. If you believe that you have discovered a bug with security implications, contact *security-officer@FreeBSD.org*. Don't contact the security officer just because you want to list your root password in the PR, however.

Synopsis:
> This is the most critical single line field in the problem report. Give a brief, one-line description of the problem. Developers use this field to decide if they are interested in a PR. A synopsis like, "FreeBSD sucks and blows at the same time!" will get closed or ignored, while a subject like, "Panic under heavy I/O load, backtrace attached" has a good chance of attracting skilled attention. If you have a patch to fix the problem, put the word PATCH at the beginning of the synopsis and someone will look at that very quickly. (They might not accept the patch, mind you, but they'll look at it.)

Severity:

This field can be either non-critical, serious, or critical. Pick a reasonable one. Critical issues affect every user of FreeBSD. Serious problems affect users of a particular device driver or in a common environment. Everything else is non-critical. If you get a reputation listing trivial reports as critical, you'll find yourself being ignored fairly quickly. The FreeBSD Project works on the honor system, and reputation counts for more than you might think.

Priority:

You can enter either low, medium, or high. The priority field has been so badly abused that it is now meaningless and ignored. I recommend either low or medium.

Category:

You must enter one of the options listed in the comments area at the top of the PR form. The categories include things such as ports, www, docs, bin, kern, and misc. Pick a category where your problem fits in. I normally use kern for kernel problems, bin for userland problems, ports for issues with the Ports Collection, or doc for doc problems.

Class:

This is a type of problem. If you can crash a program or the system, it's a sw-bug.

Release:

send-pr(1) automatically puts your system type here. If you're filling out a PR on a system other than the one you're reporting on, put the FreeBSD release you're reporting on here.

Environment:

Put the output of uname -a here. You can add additional information to this field to describe other relevant parts of your machine. For example, if the machine is a heavily loaded web server, mention that. If you have a snippet of a configuration file that reproduces the panic, put it here. The Environment section should be very brief. You might wish to obscure the hostname for security reasons.

Description:

The Description field is a free-form, plaintext section for you to go into detail about the issue. Don't rant or rave; just describe what happens. Include all your error messages. If it's possible to get a crash dump, do so and include the debugger output. Also, include your kernel configuration and the boot messages from a verbose boot.

How-To-Repeat:

Give brief instructions on how to replicate this error. For some PRs, this can be very short: "Read FreeBSD-questions for a week and see how often this is asked" is a perfectly legitimate How-To-Repeat for doc changes. More technical problems require detailed information.

Fix:

> The most important part of the PR goes under `Fix`. If you have a patch that fixes the problem, put it here. If you have a way to work around the problem, put it here. Anything you've discovered about how to solve the problem goes here. Sometimes, the most unusual fix or condition provides the vital clue for the solution. If you have no idea of how to solve or work around this issue, leave `Fix` blank. Putting random thoughts or speculation into the `Fix` field does not improve the quality of the PR.

A Sample PR

Given the above, let's fill out a sample problem report about the crash I debugged in the first half of this chapter. It's a real crash that I encountered while attempting to write Chapter 18, so I actually did need a solution. Immediately after updating my system to FreeBSD-current as of July 4, 2007, I started getting crashes when accessing my external SCSI array. I had planned to use this cage to demonstrate GEOM modules, and I needed it working right away. The panic message seems to indicate a problem with the ahc0 driver. I fill out my name and email address in the spaces at the top and then go to the more interesting parts of the form:

```
>Submitter-Id:    current-users
>Originator:      Michael W Lucas
>Organization:    none
>Confidential:    no
>Synopsis:        panic: _mtx_lock_sleep: in aic7xxx_osm.h (with backtrace)
>Severity:        serious
>Priority:        medium
>Category:        kern
>Class:           sw-bug
>Release:         FreeBSD 7.0-CURRENT i386
```

The `Submitter-Id` remains unchanged. I am the originator, and anyone who mentions the word *organization* in reference to me gets laughed at. This PR is not confidential.

The `Synopsis` is difficult. I put in the first part of the panic string and the location of the panic, and mention that I have a backtrace. That's about all that will fit on a single line.

As this error affects a single device, but causes a panic, it's serious. I assign it `medium` priority, just because I can't bring myself to call it `low` and yet the developers won't think it's critical.

This is a kernel panic, so its category is `kern`. I can crash the kernel, so it is in the class of `sw-bug`.

The `Environment` gives me a little more flexibility. I start with the output of `uname -a` and then talk about what makes my environment special:

```
This is a standard i386 system with an external SCSI array attached.
Verbose dmesg is attached.
```

The Description is my opportunity to tell the FreeBSD team what the problem is:

```
This system performs fine on an April 22 2007 kernel. I updated to -current on
July 4, 2007, and immediately started seeing these panics. Upon further
testing, I found that I could read data just fine from the SCSI drives, but
that attempting to write to the drives resulted in this panic. The panic
message and backtrace are attached.
```

How-To-Repeat is where I give step-by-step instructions on how to trigger this bug:

```
/dev/da7 is my test drive. I can run:
# fdisk /dev/da7
and read the slice table as often as I wish without trouble. A simple write
operation such as
# fdisk -BI /dev/da7
panics the system. This does not happen every time, but if I run this command
a few times in a row, it regularly and reliably panics. My record is five
successful "fdisk -BI /dev/da7" runs, one after the other in quick succession,
before the sixth panics the system.
```

This succinctly describes my problem, without screaming that I have a deadline and really need to get Chapter 18 written before my legion of devoted fans[2] arrive at my door with pitchforks and torches demanding their book. I have clear instructions on how to reproduce the problem. I also must include the verbose boot messages and the kernel backtrace in this section.

Submitting the PR

Your system must have a working outbound email system to send a PR. If you cannot send email from a machine, do not use send-pr(1) on it. Save your problem report and related files on a machine that can send email and use send-pr(1) there. Use send-pr(1)'s -f flag to specify a completed PR template:

```
# send-pr -f prreport.txt
```

Your PR is now submitted. Nothing to it, once you have all the information!

After Submitting the PR

A few hours after submitting the problem report, I received an email stating that I was now the proud submitter of PR kern/114489. No matter how you submit the PR, you'll receive a confirmation email with a PR number within several hours. Any response you make to that email will automatically attach to that PR, so long as you don't change the subject. You can submit patches and responses from any computer with a working email system.

---

[2] Three fans might not qualify as a legion, and Amanda is more of a sarcastic fan than a devoted one, but I take what I can get.

Similarly, GNATS includes any response a developer makes to your PR in its history of the problem report. Now that your PR is in the FreeBSD database, it'll be tracked forever. That is not a guarantee that anyone will act on your issue or that your problem will be solved; it'll simply be recorded, publicly, forever.

If it seems that your PR has been forgotten for several weeks, drop a friendly note to the appropriate mailing list with your PR number and a brief explanation of the issue and why it's important. Since FreeBSD is a volunteer effort, it's quite possible that something happened to the person who would normally handle that sort of PR. While many FreeBSD developers are professional programmers, for many of them this is still a hobby that must take a backseat to sick kids or the big work deadline. If nothing else, you can contact one of the commercial support firms listed on the FreeBSD website.

Within a couple of days, I had responses from developers offering patches to fix the problem. The first round of patches exposed bugs elsewhere, but patches to resolve those followed quickly. As you can see by the presence of Chapter 18, I was able to get a solution to my problem.

A surprising number of difficult PRs are closed quickly when they include the proper information. Just remember that the FreeBSD folks do this out of love for their work, not because they must. They want to produce quality code, which is stronger motivation than a paycheck. If you can help them produce a quality product, they will happily work with you.

As of late 2007, I've submitted several dozen problem reports. Most have been solved and/or committed, and then closed. The odd ones out were mostly trivial goofs on documentation that lives under */usr/src/contrib*, an area where the FreeBSD Project specifically disavows responsibility for minor fixes. If a doofus like me can get over 90 percent of his problem reports successfully closed, anyone can. Be warned, however; if you submit enough correct patches, you'll find that the committers you work with will start to talk about you behind your back. Eventually they will grow tired of acting as the secretary for your high-quality work and will offer you commit access. If you refuse, they will offer more insistently. Don't worry, becoming a committer is not that painful. The rumors that the FreeBSD Project initiation ritual involves a group of Danes with axes behind a bikeshed are completely untrue. Mostly.

Keep filing good problem reports anyway; that's the only way FreeBSD improves!

AFTERWORD

If you've made it this far, you now know how to manage and use FreeBSD as a platform for just about any server task. You might have to learn how new programs work, but you know enough about the operating system to make FreeBSD support just about anything. Congratulations! FreeBSD is a wonderful, flexible platform, capable of assuming just about any role in your network. To wrap things up, I'd like to talk briefly about some other aspects of FreeBSD.

We've talked about the obvious parts of FreeBSD throughout this book: the programs, the kernel, the features, and so on. One thing we haven't talked about much is the community that creates all of this.

The Community

The FreeBSD community includes computer scientists, experienced programmers, users, system administrators, documentation writers, and just about anyone who is interested in the system. They come from all walks of life, from all over the world, and have education levels ranging from high school to post-doctoral. I personally have had dealings with FreeBSD users from every continent and most large islands on the planet.[1] Nationality simply isn't important, nor is race, color, or creed.

Some are computer scientists. Some work at ISPs or manufacturing firms. Some are physicians, and some work as clerks in video rental shops. At one point I worked closely with a brilliant developer who turned out to be too young to drive. Oddly enough, time zone *is* important, but only because it impacts the ability of developers to communicate with one another. Since most of the community's interaction is online, the only things that represent you are your words and your work. These are the people who improve FreeBSD and drive it forward, making it more than a collection of ones and zeroes and more than just a way to serve websites.

One of the interesting things about the FreeBSD community is that it has developed methods for coping with changes in its leadership. Many open source projects have a single leader or a small static leadership team. When those people decide to move on, their project is probably over. Someone else might branch or fork that project, but the original community usually fragments. The people who created the FreeBSD Project have mostly moved on to other things, but the community has grown other leaders. After three generations of leadership, FreeBSD as a project has demonstrated a resilience to leadership changes that is almost unique in the open source world. Today's FreeBSD leaders take a very active interest in their own replacements, mentoring and coaching those junior members of the community who seem most likely to become the leaders of the 2010s. What's more, we always welcome those who came before us, both in the CVS repository and at the bar.

Why Do We Do It?

Each person works on FreeBSD for his own reasons. A tiny portion of people are paid to improve the code, either by corporations dependent on FreeBSD or government agencies such as DARPA. Many developers work on FreeBSD as a hobby, so they can program things more correctly than they are allowed to at their day job. How many of you have had work projects completed less successfully than you would like because of a deadline? FreeBSD's deadlines are announced months or years in advance, and developers set their own work habits and their own levels of contribution.

Many of us are not software developers, but work on some other part of FreeBSD instead. Some write documentation, some design the websites, some just hang out on mailing lists and answer user questions. People spend hours and hours working on FreeBSD-related matters. Why? I can assure you that the royalties on this book will not come close to compensating me for the

---

[1] Yes, this includes a man who took his FreeBSD laptop on a cruise to Antarctica. With his wife. On their 20th anniversary. He did not mention whether his wife threw the laptop overboard or not. If she did, I imagine he just bought a better one when they got back.

evenings I could have spent with my family. I'm writing this Afterword on a porch on a cliff in Ontario, Canada, overlooking Lake Erie. Everybody else has gone out to walk the trails and chase butterflies, hopefully not over that same cliff. Why would I choose to do this instead?

We do it for the satisfaction of creating something useful to the rest of mankind and to return some of what we've been given.

You're free to simply take what FreeBSD offers and do whatever you wish with it. After a while of doing this, I found that I wanted to return something to the community. This is how the community grows, and a growing community means that FreeBSD will prosper.

If you want some of that satisfaction yourself, there's a place for you too.

What Can You Do?

If you're interested in supporting the FreeBSD Project, for whatever reason, there's a space for you in every part of the Project. Ever since I started using FreeBSD back in 1996, every so often someone posts on a mailing list, "I'd like to help, but I can't code." (In fact, I think I've sent that message myself!) The standard response to these messages is silence. If you've already decided that you can't help, you're right; you can't. Once you decide that you can help, however, you can.

Nobody denies that some high-visibility programmers are the celebrities of FreeBSD. Many of these people have impressive skills, and most of us could never dream of being the next Robert Watson or Jordan Hubbard. However, even if you can't program your way out of a paper bag, you can still help. Turn it around and ask a different question.

Don't ask what FreeBSD needs. You can't provide that, unless you have a large bank balance begging for a charitable cause to belong to. (If you have piles of cash, however, the FreeBSD Foundation would be happy to help you out.) Don't say, "Wouldn't it be cool if FreeBSD did such-and-such" if you can't create that yourself. What do you do? Any large organization needs many different people, and whatever skills you have today are useful to the FreeBSD Project.

I know people who run FreeBSD-related websites and provide valuable resources such as *http://bsdforums.com* and *http://www.freshports.org*. These people are respected contributors.

I know FreeBSD users who are web designers and documentation writers. They contribute content to the website. Do enough of that, and you'll be a committer.

I know FreeBSD users who contribute to user mailing lists, answering questions. Do enough of that and you'll want to update the FAQ. Submit enough FAQ updates, and you'll become a committer.

I write copiously, and passably well. I wrote some updates for the FAQ, and now this book. The FAQ updates made me a committer, although I would say that this book is the greater contribution. The mere sight of code I've written makes small children cry and old ladies make the sign to ward off the evil eye, but the FreeBSD folks welcome me and treat me as a partner simply because I do the work.

What is it that *you* do? What do you enjoy doing? Leverage that skill. It will be appreciated.

If Nothing Else . . .

If you truly have no useful skills, and you have no other ideas, reread this book. Read the documentation on the FreeBSD website. Subscribe to *FreeBSD-questions@FreeBSD.org* and help other users. Many people started this way.

I encourage you to direct people to existing information resources whenever possible. When someone asks a question in the FAQ, guide them there. If the question has been asked before, suggest that they search the mailing list archives. Teaching people to help themselves is the most effective use of your time—not just in FreeBSD, but out in the world as well. As the old saying goes, teach a man to fish and you can sell him fishhooks. After answering questions for a while, you'll see the shape of the Project's needs. One of those needs will almost certainly match your skills.

Getting Things Done

Here's the big secret of success in FreeBSD: Everything that it contains is there because somebody saw a need that he could fill and did something about it. NetBSD and FreeBSD started when a bunch of 386BSD patchkit users got sick of waiting for the next patchkit release. I didn't ask for permission to write this book before starting. The fine folks over on *bugbusters@FreeBSD.org* don't wade through the PR database for fun; they do it because they think it's important enough to spend their time on. (Actually, if you're a programmer, going through the PR database and looking for problems you can solve is one of the best contributions you can make.)

Once you have an idea, search the mailing list for discussions about it. Many projects are suggested but never implemented. If someone's previously brought up your idea, read the archived discussion. If the idea met with general approval, you can assume that you'll get the same reaction. If nobody's working on the project any more, get to work! The FreeBSD team will be perfectly happy if the first time they hear from you is an email message saying, "Hi, my patches for implementing such-and-such feature in the installer are available at this URL."

Whatever you do, don't post a question to the mailing list that says, "Why doesn't someone else do the work for X?" Most of these suggestions fall into three categories: obvious ("Hey, wouldn't it be cool if FreeBSD ran on mainframes?"), foolish ("Why isn't there a kernel option BRINGMEACOLDBEER?"), or both ("Why not support my Sinclair ZX80?"). In any of these cases, the person asking is both unqualified to perform the work himself and claims to be helpless to support others who *could* do the work. All these suggestions do is annoy people and waste bandwidth.

In short: Shut up and work. Do what you can do, and do it well, and people will appreciate it. Programmers can help by picking an idea off the FreeBSD Project Ideas List or jumping into the *bugbusters@FreeBSD.org* mailing list and wading through the PR slurry. Nonprogrammers can help by picking a hole and filling it in. You might become a leader in the Project, or you might be known as "That dude who hangs out on *-questions@* and helps people with ACPI." All are absolutely vital. Your help makes FreeBSD prosper and grow. Stick around long enough, and you just might find yourself one of FreeBSD's new leaders.

I look forward to seeing you on the mailing lists.

SOME INTERESTING
SYSCTL MIBS

This appendix is a dictionary of some useful sysctl MIBs, as well as some sysctl MIBs that are no longer useful but have long been discussed in FreeBSD forums. Chapter 5 discusses tools for manipulating sysctl MIBs. When a MIB is discussed in detail elsewhere in the book, a reference is made to the appropriate chapter. Your system certainly has many more sysctls than these, but described here are those that I've tripped over repeatedly.

Remember, thoughtless use of sysctls can easily damage or destroy a working system. For example, if you set a limit on resource usage below the value needed at that moment, you can crash a process or a system. Be sure you understand the implications of what you're doing before setting a sysctl. If you don't understand it, that's what test systems are for.

For each sysctl, I list a sample value from my test system so you can see what the value should look like.

Each sysctl description indicates when the sysctl can be changed. Some sysctls can be changed at any time, others can be changed only at boot. A few are read-only.

For each sysctl, I also mention if it is a variable, toggle, or tunable. *Variables* have a wide variety of ranges. *Toggles* have only two legitimate values, 1 (the described service is on) and 0 (the service is off). *Tunables* are set in the boot loader. (Strictly speaking, a boot tunable is different from a sysctl, but you set the sysctl by setting the tunable.)

kern.osrelease: 7.0-RELEASE

> Read-only. This displays the running version of FreeBSD, such as 7.2-release, 8.0-current, and so on.

kern.maxvnodes: 100000

> Run-time variable. The maximum number of vnodes (virtual filesystem nodes) the system can have open simultaneously.

kern.maxproc: 6164

> Boot-time tunable. The maximum number of processes the system can run at any one time.

kern.maxfiles: 12328

> Run-time variable and boot-time tunable. The maximum number of files that the system can have open for reading or writing at any one time.

kern.argmax: 262144

> Read-only. The maximum number of characters you can use in a single command line. You might run up against this in some unusual circumstances. If you do, please see xargs(1).

kern.securelevel: -1

> Run-time variable. The current kernel security level. See Chapter 9.

kern.hostname: bewilderbeast.blackhelicopters.org

> Run-time tunable. The hostname, as set in */etc/rc.conf.*

kern.posix1version: 200112

> Read-only. This gives the version of POSIX the kernel complies with. If you need to change this, please feel free to contribute code to support other POSIX versions.

kern.ngroups: 16

> Read-only. The maximum number of groups any one user may belong to.

kern.boottime: { sec = 1187744126, usec = 946476 } Tue Aug 21 20:55:26 2007

> Read-only. This gives the time the system booted, in both epochal time and as a human-friendly date.

kern.domainname:

> Run-time variable. This offers the YP/NIS domain name, not the TCP/IP domain name. If you are not using YP/NIS, it will be blank.

kern.osreldate: 700052

Read-only. This is the FreeBSD version, not an actual date. Various ports configure themselves with this sysctl value.

kern.bootfile: /boot/kernel/kernel

Read-only. This is the kernel file that the system booted. While you could technically change this, don't. Reboot on a new kernel instead. The only time this changes on a running system is when you tell FreeBSD to install a new kernel and move the old kernel to */boot/kernel.old*, but that's a very special case.

kern.maxfilesperproc: 11095

Run-time variable. This is the maximum number of files a single process can open.

kern.maxprocperuid: 5547

Run-time variable. The maximum number of processes one user ID can run simultaneously.

kern.ipc.somaxconn: 128

Run-time variable. The maximum number of new connections the system will accept at any one time. If you're running a heavily loaded server, you might need to increase this to 256 or even 512.

kern.ipc.maxpipekva: 16777216

Boot-time tunable. This is the maximum amount of kernel memory that can be used by pipes.

kern.ipc.pipekva: 212992

Read-only. This is the current amount of memory used by pipes.

kern.ipc.shmmax: 33554432

Run-time variable. This is the maximum size of a System V shared memory segment. You might have to tune this for programs that use large amounts of shared memory, notably databases.

kern.ipc.shmseg: 128

Boot-time tunable. This is the maximum number of System V shared memory segments any one process can open.

kern.ipc.shmall: 8192

Run-time variable. This is the maximum number of pages available for System V shared memory.

kern.ipc.shm_use_phys: 0

Run-time toggle, boot-time tunable. Enabling this tells FreeBSD it can never swap out shared memory segments. This can improve performance if you are using large amounts of System V shared memory, but by making shared memory unpageable you can hurt the performance of every other program on your system.

kern.ipc.numopensockets: 70

Read-only. This is the number of open sockets of all sorts, including network and local domain sockets.

kern.ipc.maxsockets: 12328

Run-time variable, boot-time tunable. This is the total number of sockets available on the system. This includes Unix domain sockets as well as network sockets.

kern.logsigexit: 1

Run-time toggle. A program that exits abnormally usually sends a signal. When this toggle is set, the name of the program and the exiting signal are logged to */var/log/messages*.

kern.init_path: /sbin/init:/sbin/oinit:/sbin/init.bak:/rescue/init:/stand/ sysinstall

Read-only. init(8) is the program that actually starts running the userland. This sysctl lists the paths where the kernel looks for init(8). If you've damaged your system (say, during an upgrade gone bad), this provides a series of backup paths the system checks for a copy of init(8). This sysctl is also available in the boot loader as init_path.

kern.init_shutdown_timeout: 120

Run-time variable. This is the number of seconds that userland processes have to shut themselves off during the shutdown process. After this many seconds, the kernel shuts itself off no matter what might be running.

kern.randompid: 0

Run-time variable. If set to 0, each newly assigned process ID is one greater than the previous. If set to a larger number, the next PID is random. As the value of this sysctl increases, the randomness of the next PID increases.

kern.openfiles: 246

Read-only. This is the number of files currently open on the system.

kern.module_path: /boot/kernel;/boot/modules

Run-time variable. This lists the directories where kldload(8) checks for kernel modules.

kern.maxusers: 384

Boot-time tunable. For many years, kern.maxusers was a general-purpose hint the system administrator could set to tell BSD and FreeBSD how much memory to allocate for certain types of system tasks. Modern FreeBSD systems auto-tune kern.maxusers. Any documentation that suggests changing kern.maxusers is almost certainly obsolete.

kern.sync_on_panic: 0

Run-time toggle. When FreeBSD panics (see Chapter 21), it unmounts all disks without synchronizing them first. This results in *dirty disks*, as discussed in Chapter 8. If you set this sysctl, FreeBSD will attempt to sync the disks before shutting down. This is extremely dangerous, as you have no way to know the condition of a panicked system. You might actually damage data or the underlying filesystem by attempting to sync your disks after a panic, resulting in a sysadmin panic as well as a system panic.

kern.coredump: 1

Run-time toggle. By default, when a program crashes, FreeBSD writes a core dump. Setting this to 0 disables core dumps. It is most useful on embedded and diskless systems.

kern.nodump_coredump: 0

Run-time toggle. Enabling this tells FreeBSD to set the nodump flag on core files. See Chapter 4.

kern.timecounter.choice: TSC(-100) i8254(0) dummy(-1000000)

Read-only. This lists the hardware clocks available on your system. Most modern hardware has four common options, in order from best to worst: ACPI, i8254, TSC, and dummy. The numbers give relative accuracy of the various clocks.

kern.timecounter.hardware: i8254

Run-time variable. You can change this to use a different hardware clock. Your choices are provided in the kern.timecounter.choice sysctl. By default, FreeBSD uses the best available clock.

kern.timecounter.smp_tsc: 0

Boot-time tunable. If this equals 0, do not use the TSC hardware clock on this hardware. TSC does not work correctly on most SMP systems.

kern.sched.name: 4BSD

Read-only. This is the name of the scheduler in the running kernel.

kern.sched.quantum: 100000

Run-time variable. This gives the maximum number of microseconds a process can run if other processes are waiting for CPU time when using the 4BSD scheduler. If you're considering changing this, you are almost certainly doing something wrong. The ULE scheduler does not offer this sysctl.

kern.sched.preemption: 1

Read-only. This shows if preemption is enabled in the kernel. Preemption allows a more urgent kernel thread to interrupt a less urgent kernel thread.

kern.log_console_output: 1

Run-time toggle, boot-time tunable. By default, FreeBSD sends console messages to syslogd. (Console messages do not include responses to commands typed on the console, just messages that the system logs to the console whether someone is logged in or not.) Changing this to 0 disables this feature.

kern.smp.disabled: 0

Boot-time toggle. Disable SMP in */boot/loader.conf* by setting kern.smp .disabled to 1.

kern.smp.cpus: 2

Read-only. This is the number of CPUs running on the system.

kern.filedelay: 30

Run-time variable. This dictates how often FreeBSD synchronizes file data between the vnode buffer cache and the disk. More frequent synchronization causes increased disk load, while decreasing the synchronization frequency increases risk. Only system administrators who thoroughly understand the buffer cache should even consider touching this.

kern.dirdelay: 29

Run-time variable. This controls how often the system synchronizes directory data between the buffer cache and the disk. It should be set to slightly less than the kern.filedelay sysctl. Again, only highly experienced system administrators should consider changing this.

kern.metadelay: 28

Run-time variable. This controls how often FreeBSD synchronizes filesystem metadata between the buffer cache and the disk. It should be set to slightly less than the kern.dirdelay sysctl. Again, for highly experienced system administrators only! Mucking with synchronization is a great way to get a deep education in data loss.

vm.v_free_min: 3258

Run-time variable. The minimum number of pages of cache and free memory that must be available before a process waiting on memory will be awakened and told to run.

vm.v_free_target: 13745

Run-time variable. The minimum number of pages of combined free and cache memory that the virtual memory manager tries to maintain or exceed.

vm.v_free_reserved: 713

Run-time variable. If the number of pages of free memory falls below this value, the virtual memory manager will start swapping out processes.

vm.v_inactive_target: 20617

Run-time variable. FreeBSD tries to keep at least this much memory inactive, by making active pages inactive.

vm.v_cache_min: 13745

vm.v_cache_max: 27490

Run-time variable. The minimum and maximum desired size of the virtual memory cache queue.

vm.swap_enabled: 1

Run-time toggle. This controls the use of swap space. If set to 0, your system will not swap. This is most useful for diskless systems.

vm.swap_idle_enabled: 0

Run-time toggle.

vm.swap_idle_threshold1: 2

Run-time variable.

vm.swap_idle_threshold2: 10

Run-time variable. Setting the swap_idle_enabled sysctl tells the virtual memory manager to pull idle processes into swap more quickly than other processes. The threshold sysctls tell the system how many seconds to wait before considering different sorts of processes idle. The defaults are fine for most people; just enabling vm.swap_idle_enabled should do the trick. This can help some systems stay afloat when they're desperately short on memory and are swapping out entire processes.

vm.exec_map_entries: 16

Boot-time toggle. This is the maximum number of processes that can be started simultaneously.

vfs.nfs.diskless_valid: 0

Read-only. If 0, this system is not running diskless. If non-zero, the system is running diskless.

vfs.nfs.diskless_rootpath:

Read-only. This gives the path to the root filesystem of a diskless machine.

vfs.nfs.diskless_rootaddr:

Read-only. This gives the IP address of the root filesystem of a diskless machine.

vfs.vmiodirenable: 1

Run-time toggle. Allows UFS to use the virtual memory system to cache directory lookups, increasing disk performance.

vfs.usermount: 0

Run-time toggle. If enabled, users may mount filesystems on mount points that they own. This allows unprivileged users to mount floppy disks and CDs. See Chapter 8.

vfs.ffs.doasyncfree: 1

Run-time variable. This tells the UFS filesystem to asynchronously update inodes and indirect blocks after reorganizing disk space. See the sysctl vfs.ffs.doreallocblks.

vfs.ffs.doreallocblks: 1

Run-time variable. By default, FreeBSD reorganizes its disks so that files are contiguous at all times. In effect, UFS continuously defragments itself. Set this to 0 to disable this behavior.

net.inet.ip.portrange.lowfirst: 1023
net.inet.ip.portrange.lowlast: 600

Run-time variables. Some programs or protocols require connections to be made from low-numbered ports, indicating that they are started by privileged processes. Remember, an outgoing TCP/IP connection uses a port on the local system. Also remember that ports from 0 through 1023 can only be opened by root. This means that if a connection comes from a low-numbered port, it's theoretically running as root. (This involves trusting that the machine initiating the connection has not been broken in to.) FreeBSD uses ports between those given by `net.inet.ip.portrange.lowfirst` (default of 1023) and `net.inet.ip.portrange.lowlast` (default of 600). I only know of one instance where changing this makes sense. The IPMI firmware on some Intel NICs always intercepts UDP packets bound for ports 623 and 664. If you don't have one of those cards, leave this alone.

net.inet.ip.portrange.first: 49152
net.inet.ip.portrange.last: 65535

Run-time variable. When FreeBSD allocates a random port for an outgoing connection from unprivileged processes, it uses ports between those given by `net.inet.ip.portrange.first` (default of 49152) and `net.inet.ip.portrange.last` (default of 65535).

net.inet.ip.portrange.hifirst: 49152
net.inet.ip.portrange.hilast: 65535

Run-time variable. Some programs specifically request a high-numbered port for an outgoing connection. By default, this range of ports overlaps with the ports specified by `net.inet.ip.portrange.first` to `net.inet.ip.portrange.last`, but you can separate these ranges by using the `hifirst` and `hilast` sysctls.

net.inet.ip.portrange.reservedhigh: 1023
net.inet.ip.portrange.reservedlow: 0

Run-time variable. This specifies the range of ports that can only be opened by root.

net.inet.ip.portrange.randomized: 1

Run-time variable. By default, FreeBSD will allocate random ports within the ranges allocated for that type of connections.

net.inet.ip.portrange.randomcps: 10

Run-time variable. This is the maximum number of random port allocations within a single second. If more than this many ports are needed, FreeBSD switches to sequential port allocation to avoid consuming all system randomness.

net.inet.ip.portrange.randomtime: 45

Run-time variable. This is the number of seconds FreeBSD will use sequential TCP/UDP port allocations before reverting to random port allocation.

net.inet.ip.forwarding: 0

Run-time toggle. You might want FreeBSD to act as a router, gateway, or firewall. With this set, the system forwards packets between interfaces.

`net.inet.ip.redirect:` 1

Run-time toggle. With this set, a FreeBSD system acting as a router or gateway will send ICMP redirect packets to other systems on the network. It has no effect if the system is not routing.

`net.inet.ip.ttl:` 64

Run-time variable. This is the maximum number of hops any non-ICMP protocol may take across the network.

`net.inet.ip.sourceroute:` 0

Run-time toggle. This enables forwarding of source-routed packets. Source routing is generally considered a bad idea on the public Internet.

`net.inet.ip.accept_sourceroute:` 0

Run-time toggle. This enables acceptance of source-routed packets. If you don't know what source routing is, just accept my word that this is a really bad idea in almost all cases.

`net.inet.ip.fastforwarding:` 0

Run-time toggle. This sysctl greatly accelerates packet throughput on routers and gateways. It does so by eliminating most of the sanity and integrity checks performed on packets and by completely eliminating any packet-filtering rules.

`net.inet.ip.check_interface:` 0

Run-time toggle. This provides basic antispoofing protection for your server. It's only useful on a router, gateway, or firewall. Most of the time, this is better done at the firewall level.

`net.inet.icmp.icmplim:` 200

Run-time variable. This is the maximum number of ICMP requests the system will answer per second. Systems that have a huge amount of ICMP requests (mostly those running security and network tools such as Nessus, nmap, and Nagios) will need to increase this. Set this to 0 to disable ICMP throttling altogether.

`net.inet.icmp.drop_redirect:` 0

Run-time toggle. This tells FreeBSD to ignore ICMP redirect packets. Most of the time redirects improve performance, but I have had edge cases where ignoring redirects was the proper course of action.

`net.inet.icmp.log_redirect:` 0

Run-time toggle. If set, FreeBSD will log all ICMP redirects to the console. (You didn't really need that console for anything useful, did you?)

`net.inet.icmp.bmcastecho:` 0

Run-time toggle. This enables responses to requests to the broadcast address of a network. While this facilitated troubleshooting and was originally required for standards compliance, responding to broadcast pings was such a security problem that it's now disabled by default on all modern operating systems.

```
net.inet.tcp.rfc1323:  1
net.inet.tcp.rfc3042:  1
net.inet.tcp.rfc3390:  1
```
Run-time toggles. These enable various TCP methods described in the corresponding RFCs and should be perfectly safe. Some very, very old systems might have slow or problematic throughput when communicating with your FreeBSD system with these enabled.

```
net.inet.tcp.sendspace:  32768
net.inet.tcp.recvspace:  65536
```
Run-time variable. These give the default initial buffer size for a new TCP/IP connection. While FreeBSD allocates these buffers dynamically as the throughput to the remote host requires, these values provide a good starting point. While you will find advice about changing these values in much old documentation, today they should be left alone.

```
net.inet.tcp.log_in_vain:  0
```
Run-time toggle. This enables logging any attempt to connect to a TCP port when no program is listening on that port. On the public Internet, this can generate a huge amount of output. I suggest enabling this on a test system just so you can see what sort of crap flies around the Internet these days, and then turning it off so that you can use your console again.

```
net.inet.tcp.blackhole:  0
```
Run-time toggle. By default, TCP/IP returns an error code when you attempt to connect to a closed port. This shows up as a "Connection reset by peer" error. If you set this to 1, attempts to connect to closed TCP ports are dropped without sending an error. This slows down port scans and can add some semblance of security to your system. It is not a replacement for packet filtering, however!

```
net.inet.tcp.delayed_ack:  1
```
Run-time toggle. This tells FreeBSD to attempt to include TCP ACK information on a data packet instead of sending additional packets to signal the end of a connection.

```
net.inet.tcp.recvbuf_auto:  1
```
Run-time toggle. This enables automatic resizing of receive buffers.

```
net.inet.tcp.recvbuf_inc:  16384
```
Run-time variable. This is the size of the increment by which receive buffers are changed by automatic sizing.

```
net.inet.tcp.recvbuf_max:  262144
```
Run-time variable. This is the maximum size of any one receive buffer on the system.

```
net.inet.tcp.slowstart_flightsize:  1
```
Run-time variable. This specifies the number of packets FreeBSD will send during the slow-start portion of a TCP transaction across a wide area network.

net.inet.tcp.local_slowstart_flightsize: 4

Run-time variable. This specifies the number of packets FreeBSD will send during the slow-start portion of a TCP transaction across the local network.

net.inet.tcp.newreno: 1

Run-time toggles. This toggles RFC2582 connection recovery, also known as the TCP NewReno Algorithm.

net.inet.tcp.tso: 1

Run-time toggle. Some network hardware can handle breaking network requests into packets with proper sizes for the medium. For example, with certain network cards, FreeBSD can just hand a lump of data to the card and ask it to break that lump up into packets. This allows for more optimized communication with the network card and less work for the CPU. This tells FreeBSD to use the hardware to perform segmentation when supported.

net.inet.tcp.sendbuf_auto: 1

Run-time toggle. This enables automatic sizing of TCP connection send buffers.

net.inet.tcp.sendbuf_inc: 8192

Run-time variable. This gives the amount to increase or decrease the TCP send buffer each time a change is needed.

net.inet.tcp.sendbuf_max: 262144

Run-time variable. This is the maximum size of a single TCP send buffer.

net.inet.tcp.sack.enable: 1

Run-time toggle. FreeBSD uses selective ACK by default, but occasionally very old hosts have trouble with this feature.

net.inet.tcp.do_tcpdrain: 1

Run-time toggle. This tells FreeBSD to flush packets from the reassembly queue when it is low on mbufs. Now that FreeBSD automatically allocates mbufs from kernel memory, this is much less useful than it once was.

net.inet.tcp.always_keepalive: 1

Run-time toggle. By default, FreeBSD checks all TCP connections to see if they're still alive. Normally, if a connection between two hosts drops, these keepalives tell the systems to close down the connection. If you disable this behavior, FreeBSD will not check if the connection between the hosts is up or down; rather, it will assume that the connection is up until it cannot pass data.

net.inet.udp.log_in_vain: 0

Run-time toggle. This logs attempts to connect to any UDP port where no program is listening.

`net.inet.udp.blackhole: 0`

Run-time toggle. Like TCP, UDP sends an error message when someone attempts to connect to a port that doesn't have anything listening on it. If you set this to 1, attempts to connect to closed UDP ports are dropped without sending an error. This slows down port scans.

`net.link.log_link_state_change: 1`

Run-time toggle. If enabled, FreeBSD will log every time a network interface goes up or down.

`debug.debugger_on_panic: 1`

Run-time toggle. If set, FreeBSD will enter the debugger on a panic.

`debug.trace_on_panic: 0`

Run-time toggle. If set, FreeBSD automatically prints a stack trace when it enters the debugger after panicking.

`debug.witness.watch: 1`

Run-time variable, boot-time tunable. With WITNESS compiled into the kernel, FreeBSD performs additional sanity checking of all kernel locks. Setting this to 0 disables these checks. Once you turn WITNESS off, you cannot turn it back on without rebooting. Note that you will not get the benefits of WITNESS when you disable it; specifically, if your system panics due to locking while under heavy load, you won't get the lock message that would have told a FreeBSD developer where to find the problem.

`debug.witness.skipspin: 1`

Boot-time toggle. This tells WITNESS to not perform any checks on spin locks. Checking spin locks with WITNESS makes almost any machine unbearably slow. Skipping spin locks, but using WITNESS in all other cases, makes WITNESS only slow instead of unbearably slow. This is the same as the kernel option `WITNESS_SKIPSPIN`.

`debug.minidump: 1`

Run-time toggle, boot-time tunable. By default, FreeBSD only dumps kernel memory on a panic. Set this to 0 to dump the entire contents of physical memory on panic.

`hw.ata.ata_dma: 1`

Boot-time toggle. This enables DMA in IDE devices. Set this to 0 if your hardware uses PIO instead of DMA. If your hardware is old enough to require PIO, you probably know about it.

`hw.ata.atapi_dma: 1`

Boot-time toggle. This enables DMA in ATAPI devices. Set this to 0 if your hardware uses PIO instead of DMA or if your hardware has a buggy DMA implementation. Again, if your hardware is old enough to require PIO, you probably know about it.

hw.ata.wc: 1

Boot-time toggle. This enables IDE write caching, as supported by some hard drives. Write caching uses a small buffer on the hard drive to cache writes en route to the disk, improving performance at a cost in reliability. Set this to 0 to disable write caching and enhance data safety. See Chapter 8.

hw.syscons.kbd_reboot: 1

Run-time toggle. With this enabled, the old-fashioned CTRL-ALT-DELETE sequence reboots the system. Set this to 0 to disable this behavior.

compat.linux.osrelease: 2.4.2

Run-time variable. This defines the version of Linux supported by Linux mode. Some Linux programs behave differently when this is changed. While you can change it on the fly, if any Linux programs are in use, the system will panic. It's best to let the Linux mode software do this for you.

security.jail.set_hostname_allowed: 1

Run-time variable. This dictates whether jail administrators can change the hostname of their jail. See Chapter 9.

security.jail.socket_unixiproute_only: 1

Run-time variable. This controls whether jail owners can use protocols other than TCP/IP. See Chapter 9.

security.jail.sysvipc_allowed: 0

Run-time variable. This determines whether jail owners can use System V IPC calls. See Chapter 9.

security.jail.enforce_statfs: 2

Run-time variable. When set to 0, jailed users can see all mount points and partitions on the system, both inside and outside the jail. When set to 1, only mount points below the jail's root are visible. When set to 2, only the jail's root mount point is visible.

security.jail.allow_raw_sockets: 0

Run-time variable. When set, root in a jail can create raw sockets. See Chapter 9.

security.jail.chflags_allowed: 0

Run-time toggle. The jail administrator can use chflags(1). See Chapter 9.

security.jail.list:

Read-only. This lists all the active jails on the system. FreeBSD changes this as you start and stop jails, but you cannot change this sysctl with sysctl(8) to activate new jails. See Chapter 9.

security.jail.jailed: 0

Read-only. If set to 1, the program that queried the sysctl is running inside a jail. See Chapter 9.

security.bsd.see_other_uids: 1

Run-time toggle. By default, users can see processes belonging to other users through ps(1) and related tools. Setting this to 0 disables this visibility.

security.bsd.see_other_gids: 1

Run-time toggle. By default, users can see processes belonging to other groups through ps(1) and related tools. Setting this to 0 disables this visibility.

security.bsd.unprivileged_read_msgbuf: 1

Run-time toggle. By default, unprivileged users can read the system message buffer through dmesg(8). This includes users inside jails. Setting this to 0 disables that visibility, which is usually desirable in a jail server.

security.bsd.hardlink_check_uid: 0

Run-time toggle. By default, users can create hard links—see ln(1)—to any file. If you set this to 1, users cannot create hard links to files owned by other users.

security.bsd.hardlink_check_gid: 0

Run-time toggle. By default, users can create hard links to files owned by any group. If you set this to 1, users can only create hard links to files that are owned by a group they belong to.

security.bsd.overworked_admin: 3.1415925

Read-only. If you've actually read this whole appendix, you've obviously been working too hard. Put this book down. Go outside. Get some fresh air for an hour or two. You'll feel better. If you thought this was a real sysctl MIB, however, stay outside and offline for at least two days.

INDEX

C

CA (Certificate Authorities), 282
cache memory, 577, 578
caching
  and name service switching, 450–453
  zeroing, 452–453
cash symbol ($), for user name in environment fields, 200
CAT5 cable, 159
  console connections over, 73
Category field, in problem report, 651
CD images, viewing contents, 235
CD packages, 322–323
CD9660 option, for kernel, 133
cdrtools, 226
CDs
  booting from, 45, 46
  as fixit disk, 115
  installing FreeBSD from, 46–47
  ISO 9660 filesystem for, 230
  preparing boot, 47–48
  purchasing with FreeBSD, 43
central processing unit (CPU)
  FreeBSD support for, 131
  information display, in startup messages, 76–77
  load on system, 576
  multiple, 143, 344–349
  requirements, 36
  and SMP, 347–348
  usage and performance, 583–584
  vmstat information on, 573
certification as Unix, 9
CERT directory, 44
Certificate Authorities (CA), 282
certificates, 282–285
  creating request, 283–284
  obtaining signed, 284–285
  self-signed, 285
  for SSL web servers, 520
CFLAGS option, in /etc/make.conf, 307
challenge password, for certificate, 284
CHANGES file, for ports infrastructure, 318
check-ins, multiple, 112–113
checksum, 333
chflags command, 203
chmod command, 65
chown command, 193
chpass() command, for changing accounts, 185–186
chroot command, 286, 525, 613
  for tftpd server, 463
chroot environment, for BIND, 437
ci command, 107

CIFS (Common Internet File Sharing).
  See Common Internet File Sharing (CIFS)
ciphertext, 280
Cisco, Fast EtherChannel (FEC), 175
Class A network, 153
Class B network, 153
Class C network, 153
class environment, for users, 199
Class field, in problem report, 651
cleaning ports, 338–339
cleartext, 280
clients
  FTP, 522–523
  for geom_gate, 563
  for NFS, restricting, 247
  for SSH, 445–447
cloned interfaces statement, 176
CLONEDIR option, for FreeSBIE, 632
CNAME host records, 433
co command, 107
  for old versions of file, 111
coaxial cable, 159
code freeze, 374
cold backup, 96
collections, for csup, 384
collision domain, 159
combined log format, for Apache, 504
combinedio log format, for Apache, 504
comconsole plug-in, for FreeSBIE, 634
COMCONSOLE_SPEED variable, 628
command line, 14, 15
command prompt
  as intruder's goal, 262
  root, in single-user mode, 605
  shell for, 188–189
  in single-user mode, 63
  SNMP tools, 600
commands
  displaying for loader, 66
  man pages for documenting, 21–24
comments
  hash marks (#) for, 130
  to remove entry from kernel configuration, 131
  slashes (//) for, 424
commercial operating system, 12
committers, 5–6, 654
  becoming, 657, 658
Common Internet File Sharing (CIFS), 243, 248–252
  configuring, 249
  file ownership, 252
  kernel support for, 249
  mounting share, 251

I

paging, 581–582
  vmstat information on, 572–573
PAM (Pluggable Authentication
    Modules), 310
panic function, 644–645
panics
  causes, 637–638
  configuring computer to process, 639
  manual crash dumps, 642–643
  recognizing, 638–639
  responding to, 639–642
  and serial consoles, 641
  triggering in single-user mode, 645–646
parallel builds, optimization with, 390
PARANOID keyword, in TCP wrappers,
    267, 269
parent-child relationship, of processes, 580
parity, 542–543
partitions, 211–212, 531. *See also* root
    partition
  block size for, 41
  creating, 241
    during install process, 52–53
    slices, 536–537
  de-journaling, 557
  encrypted, 80
  /etc/fstab file entry for, 241
  GELI to encrypt, 558–560
  for jails, 290–291
  mounting onto filesystem, 214–215
  replication of, 539–540
  restoring filesystem on empty, 103
  space remaining, 215–217
  for swap space, 537
  tar for backups, 95
  unmounting, 215
pass command, 496
passphrase, 284, 559, 560
passwd command, 65, 184–185
passwd_format option, 201
passwdtype setting, in *adduser.conf* file, 183
password expiration field, in
    /etc/master.passwd file, 187
password keyword, in */etc/nsmb.conf* file, 250
passwords
  for Apache, 512–515
  files on diskless system, 615
  for FTP, 522
  for groups, 191
  for single-user mode, 605
  for user accounts, 182
    changing, 184–185
    expiration dates, 186
    file for, 184

patch of source code files, 318
patching system, 180
path, to loaded kernel, 67
path variable, in *login.conf*, 200
PC Weasel, 71
pc98, 34, 36
pciconf command, 127
per-client directory, for diskless hosts,
    612–613
performance
  computer resources and, 570
  disk input/output, 574–575
  following processes, 580–581
  of network, 571
  optimization, partitioning and, 38
  problem solving, 570
  of software, 586
  status mail, 586–587
  swap and paging, 581–582
  system status information, 575–579
  tuning, 582–586
    CPU usage, 583–584
    memory usage, 583
    swap space, 583
periodic command, 586
Perl, 323
PermiRootLogin, for SSH, 443
permissions
  for Apache, 507–515
  of device node, 254
  and foreign filesystems, 228
  for log file, 594
  NFS and, 246
  restoring for extracted files, 97
  Revision Control System and, 108
  viewing with ls, 193
personal data field, in */etc/master.passwd*
    file, 187
per-subnet directory, for diskless hosts,
    612–613
PF (packet filter), 273
  activating rules, 279–280
  configuring, 275–277
  enabling, 273
  rule sample, 278–279
PF module for bsnmpd, 602
pf plug-in, for FreeSBIE, 635
pfctl program, 279–280
pf_enable variable, 83
_pflogd group, 194
PGID (process group ID), 580
pgrep command, 585
phpt Apache module, 506
Physical Address Extensions (PAE), 139,
    142–143

security, *continued*
  packet filtering, 272–280
    activating rules, 279–280
    configuring, 275–277
    default accept and default deny, 273–274
    rule sample, 278–279
    and stateful inspection, 274–275
  for ports and packages, 340–341
  potential attackers, 178–180
  public key encryption, 280–286
    certificates, 282–285
    connecting to SSL-protected ports, 285–286
    OpenSSL configuration, 281–282
  response to hacking, 300
  restricting login ability, 195–197
  restricting system usage, 197–201
  risks, 177–178
  root password, 189–190
  securelevels, 204–207
    definitions, 204–205
    limitations, 206
  shells, 188–189
  for SNMP, 600
  system monitoring, 299–300
  TCP wrappers, 265–272
    configuring, 265–271
    example, 271–272
  unprivileged users, 261–263
  user accounts, 181–188
    creating, 181–183
    deleting, 188
    editing, 183–188
  and *vmcore* file, 645–646
  workstation vs. server, 207
security facility, 588
security.bsd.hardlink_check_gid sysctl, 674
security.bsd.overworked_admin sysctl, 674
security.bsd.see_other_gids sysctl, 674
security.bsd.see_other_uids sysctl, 674
security.bsd.unprivileged_read_msgbuf sysctl, 674
security.jail.allow_raw_sockets sysctl, 673
security.jail.allow_raw_sockets sysctl value, 290
security.jail.chflags_allowed sysctl, 673
security.jail.chflags_allowed sysctl value, 290
security.jail.enforce_statfs sysctl, 673
security.jail.enforce_statfs sysctl value, 290
security.jail.jailed sysctl, 673
security.jail.jailed sysctl value, 290
security.jail.list sysctl, 673
security.jail.list sysctl value, 290

security.jail.set_hostname_allowed sysctl, 673
security.jail.set_hostname_allowed sysctl value, 289
security.jail.socket_unixiproute_only sysctl, 673
security.jail.socket_unixiproute_only sysctl value, 289
security.jail.sysvipc_allowed sysctl, 673
security.jail.sysvipc_allowed sysctl value, 289–290
SELECT command, for IMAP, 497
selecting options from sysinstall menus, spacebar for, 50
Sendmail Mail Transfer Agent, 86, 473–476
  attaching milter-greylist to, 490–491
  authentication with SASL, 491–493
  configuration options, 475, 476–481
  Makefile for, 484–485
  submission vs. reception, 474–475
sendmail.cf file, 483
  building, 492–493
sendmail_enable variable, 86
sendmail_outbound_enable variable, 86
send-pr, 649
serial consoles, 70–75
  disconnection, 75
  hardware, 71
  and panics, 641
  physical setup, 73
  software, 71–72
  speeds for Soekris, 626–627, 628
  use, 73–75
Serial Line Internet Protocol (SLIP), 135
serial number, of zone file, 429–430
serial port
  logging in through, 606
  on Soekris, as default console, 617
server farm, diskless system for, 606
Server Message Block (SMB), 248
ServerName, for Apache, 503
ServerRoot setting, for Apache, 502
servers
  device node management on, 253
  security, vs. workstation, 207
SERVERS provider, for rc scripts, 352
server-side includes, 509
set command, to change variables, 67
setenv command, 92
setenv variable, in *login.conf*, 200
setuid programs, preventing running, 220
Severity field, in problem report, 651
sftp program, 447, 527
shared libraries, 87, 354–358
  attaching to programs, 355–357

There's more to keeping FreeBSD free than meets the eye.

They work hard behind the scenes and you hardly ever see them. They're The FreeBSD Foundation and they quietly fund and manage projects, sponsor FreeBSD events, Developer Summits and provide travel grants to FreeBSD developers. The FreeBSD Foundation represents the Project in executing contracts, license agreements, copyrights, trademarks, and other legal arrangements that require a recognized legal entity. The Foundation's funding and management expertise is essential to keep FreeBSD free. And keeping it free is getting more costly every year.

That's why they need your help. The work of The FreeBSD Foundation is entirely supported by your generous donations.

**To make a donation
visit our web site at:**

www.freebsdfoundation.org

Please, help us today. Help keep FreeBSD free.

The FreeBSD Foundation P.O. Box 20247, Boulder, CO 80308, USA
Phone: +1-720-207-5142 Fax: +720-222-2350 Web: www.freebsdfoundation.org

Electronic Frontier Foundation
Defending Freedom in the Digital World

Free Speech. Privacy. Innovation. Fair Use. Reverse Engineering. If you care about these rights in the digital world, then you should join the Electronic Frontier Foundation (EFF). EFF was founded in 1990 to protect the rights of users and developers of technology. EFF is the first to identify threats to basic rights online and to advocate on behalf of free expression in the digital age.

The Electronic Frontier Foundation Defends Your Rights!
Become a Member Today!
http://www.eff.org/support/

Current EFF projects include:

Protecting your fundamental right to vote. Widely publicized security flaws in computerized voting machines show that, though filled with potential, this technology is far from perfect. EFF is defending the open discussion of e-voting problems and is coordinating a national litigation strategy addressing issues arising from use of poorly developed and tested computerized voting machines.

Ensuring that you are not traceable through your things. Libraries, schools, the government and private sector businesses are adopting radio frequency identification tags, or RFIDs – a technology capable of pinpointing the physical location of whatever item the tags are embedded in. While this may seem like a convenient way to track items, it's also a convenient way to do something less benign: track people and their activities through their belongings. EFF is working to ensure that embrace of this technology does not erode your right to privacy.

Stopping the FBI from creating surveillance backdoors on the Internet. EFF is part of a coalition opposing the FBI's expansion of the Communications Assistance for Law Enforcement Act (CALEA), which would require that the wiretap capabilities built into the phone system be extended to the Internet, forcing ISPs to build backdoors for law enforcement.

Providing you with a means by which you can contact key decision-makers on cyber-liberties issues. EFF maintains an action center that provides alerts on technology, civil liberties issues and pending legislation to more than 50,000 subscribers. EFF also generates a weekly online newsletter, EFFector, and a blog that provides up-to-the minute information and commentary.

Defending your right to listen to and copy digital music and movies. The entertainment industry has been overzealous in trying to protect its copyrights, often decimating fair use rights in the process. EFF is standing up to the movie and music industries on several fronts.

Check out all of the things we're working on at http://www.eff.org and join today or make a donation to support the fight to defend freedom online.

ELECTRONIC FRONTIER FOUNDATION · 454 SHOTWELL STREET · SAN FRANCISCO, CA 94110 · 415.436.9333

HACKING, 2ND EDITION
The Art of Exploitation

by JON ERICKSON

While many security books merely show how to run existing exploits, *Hacking: The Art of Exploitation* was the first book to explain how exploits actually work— and how readers can develop and implement their own. In this all-new second edition, author Jon Erickson uses practical examples to illustrate the fundamentals of serious hacking. You'll learn about key concepts underlying common exploits, such as programming errors, assembly language, networking, shellcode, cryptography, and more. And the bundled Linux LiveCD provides an easy-to-use, hands-on learning environment. This edition has been extensively updated and expanded, including a new introduction to the complex, low-level workings of computers.

DECEMBER 2007, 480 PP. W/CD, $49.95 ($54.95 CDN)
ISBN 978-1-59327-144-2

THE TCP/IP GUIDE
A Comprehensive, Illustrated Internet Protocols Reference

by CHARLES M. KOZIEROK

From Charles M. Kozierok, the creator of the highly regarded PC Guide (www.pcguide.com), comes *The TCP/IP Guide*. This completely up-to-date, encyclopedic reference on the TCP/IP protocol suite will appeal to the newcomer and the seasoned professional alike. Kozierok details the core protocols that make TCP/IP internetworks function and discusses the most important classic TCP/IP applications, integrating IPv6 coverage throughout. Over 350 illustrations and hundreds of tables help to explain the finer points of this complex topic. The book's personal, user-friendly writing style enables readers of all levels to understand the dozens of protocols and technologies that run the Internet, with full coverage of PPP, ARP, IP, IPv6, IP NAT, IPSec, Mobile IP, ICMP, RIP, BGP, TCP, UDP, DNS, DHCP, SNMP, FTP, SMTP, NNTP, HTTP, Telnet, and much more.

OCTOBER 2005, 1616 PP. *hardcover*, $89.95 ($111.95 CDN)
ISBN 978-1-59327-047-6

PHONE:
800.420.7240 OR
415.863.9900
MONDAY THROUGH FRIDAY,
9 A.M. TO 5 P.M. (PST)

FAX:
415.863.9950
24 HOURS A DAY,
7 DAYS A WEEK

EMAIL:
SALES@NOSTARCH.COM

WEB:
WWW.NOSTARCH.COM

MAIL:
NO STARCH PRESS
555 DE HARO ST, SUITE 250
SAN FRANCISCO, CA 94107
USA

UPDATES

Visit *http://www.nostarch.com/abs_bsd2.htm* for updates, errata, and other information.

COLOPHON

Absolute FreeBSD, 2nd Edition was laid out in Adobe FrameMaker. The font families used are New Baskerville for body text, Futura for headings and tables, and Dogma for titles.

The book was printed and bound at Malloy Incorporated in Ann Arbor, Michigan. The paper is Glatfelter Thor 50# Smooth, which is made from 15 percent postconsumer content. The book uses a RepKover binding, which allows it to lay flat when open.